ARAB POLITICS BEYOND THE UPRISINGS

ARAB POLITICS BEYOND THE UPRISINGS

EXPERIMENTS IN AN ERA OF RESURGENT AUTHORITARIANISM

Thanassis Cambanis & Michael Wahid Hanna, EDITORS

A CENTURY FOUNDATION BOOK

The Century Foundation Press • New York

About The Century Foundation

The Century Foundation is a progressive, nonpartisan think tank that seeks to foster opportunity, reduce inequality, and promote security at home and abroad. Founded in 1919 by the progressive business leader Edward A. Filene, The Century Foundation is one of the oldest public policy research institutes in the country. Through our evidence-based research and policy analysis, we seek to inform citizens, guide policymakers, and reshape what government does for the better.

Library of Congress Cataloguing-in-Publication Data
Available from the publisher upon request.

Manufactured in the United States of America
Cover design by Torge Peters
Text design by Cynthia Stock

Contents

PART III: Culture and Media

Part IV: Governance

Acknowledgments

This project would not have been possible without the generous support of the Carnegie Corporation of New York, as well as that of the Board of Trustees and our colleagues at The Century Foundation, led by Chairman Bradley Abelow and President Mark Zuckerman, who afforded us the time and space to continue Century's commitment to international policy research.

Several colleagues provided invaluable advice in shaping the research and execution of this inquiry into Arab politics. Emile Hokayem provided crucial guidance about coordinating multiple research projects and producing an edited volume. Many others helped refine ideas, suggest contributors, or otherwise inform the thinking in this project. Those to whom we owe a debt of gratitude include but are not limited to: Waleed Hazbun, Yezid Sayigh, Issandr El Amrani, Seteney Shami, Omar S. Dahi, Jihad Yazigi, Sarah El Deeb, Lina Attalah, Heba Morayef, Fateh Azzam, Hafsa Halawa, Sharif Abdel Kouddous, Sami Ben Gharbia, and Annia Ciezadlo.

The Century Foundation's editorial team devoted copious energy and care to the preparation of this work. We are particularly indebted to Jason Renker, Molly Bangs, Abby Grimshaw, Lucy Muirhead, and our foreign policy associates Lily Hindy and Sima Ghaddar. Editor Eamon Kircher-Allen brought consistency, a critical eye, and hawkish attention to detail to the entire volume.

It goes without saying that any mistakes and errors are ours alone.

— Thanassis Cambanis and Michael Wahid Hanna

1

Introduction

A Broader Approach to Arab Politics

THANASSIS CAMBANIS

The Arab world continues its intense, long reckoning with new political forces even as authoritarian systems reassert control and as some states have devolved into violence. The Middle East and North Africa are in the middle of an era of epochal contestation. Tectonic processes burst to the surface with the popular uprisings of 2010–11, and continue today, albeit often in less visible forms. The region's political energies run the gamut from radical and revolutionary to reactionary and repressive, and are engaged in serious efforts to rearrange the map of hard power and governance. At stake is control, legitimacy, and competition between established and emerging ideologies. Political thought and organization persist whether the times are quiescent or violent. The regional restoration of authoritarianism has not resolved the pivotal struggle underway, although for the time being it has shifted the balance in favor of reactionaries.

Arab Politics beyond the Uprisings: Experiments in an Era of Resurgent Authoritarianism—the result of a multi-year effort at The Century Foundation, supported by the Carnegie Corporation of New York—studies some of the considerable political energy shaping the Arab world. Momentum cuts in all directions—for repression as well as for change—but hard power and political ideology are being profoundly contested. Just as important as the subject matter of this collection's case studies are the methods that they deploy: detail-rich narrative and ethnography that offer grist for analysis and the development of theory, rather than the other way around.

Keeping an Eye on Political Ferment

The research in this volume seeks to identify the ideas and mechanics at play in a region where governance, state control, and legitimacy are being contested—by established forces as well as new constituencies empowered since the peak of the uprisings. No longer is Arab politics a slow-moving competition dominated by dictators, monarchs, and organized Islamist parties. A host of actors are now vying for political space, including empowered bureaucracies and institutional players, wealthy individuals, militants, populist political movements, civil society organizations, journalists, artists, and protesters. Generations of repression failed to erase political life, which has sprouted in marginal and at times unexpected places. From some of these quarters, new thinkers and activists have proceeded to challenge the power of the state, lay their own claims to hard power, and articulate different visions of political life and governance. These energies and movements are by no means always benign or idealistic. Their ideology and goals vary, and they include many actors whose primary focus is the construction of a more resilient authoritarian order.

Quite clearly, political energy and aspiration have survived the political uprisings and their short-term defeat. It is less clear in what direction that energy will push the Arab states and whether the reversal of the popular revolts will become permanent.

At the time of this writing, more than six years have passed since much of the Arab world erupted in revolt against decades of corrupt authoritarian misrule. Today, the region's story is largely one of authoritarianism restored, or fiercely defending itself in civil wars that are reducing some states to ruin. The optimism of 2011 can feel like a historical artifact, an idealistic, perhaps naïve aspiration built on hope without any firm analytical foundations.

However, the underlying causes of the uprisings for the most part remain unresolved. And political life throughout the region has changed irreversibly, even in places like Syria or Egypt that have suffered pronounced backlash and repression since the peak revolutionary moments of 2011. These changes are not always for the better, and in some cases have quite clearly been for the worse. Yet there are considerable forces at play in the Middle East and North Africa today, engaged directly in the political sphere as never before. Existing communities and institutions, such as the independent media, have taken part in political discourse and idea creation with renewed vigor. Plutocrats and wealthy individuals, always a key adjunct to ruling regimes in weak states, have expanded their political agency. As resurgent authoritarians increase pressure on civil society, political efforts have continued in the human rights and reform communities. In some cases, authoritarian pressure has spawned new, sometimes radical political challenges from political organizers determined to throw off old ideological and sectarian labels. As authoritarians have silenced political discussions in traditional venues, such as labor unions and talk shows, the breach has been filled by spaces that are relatively new to overt politics, such as the fine arts. In states weakened by civil war, experiments at self-rule and new politics have emerged in the ungoverned interstices. Some are malignant, like the Islamic State group, some carry on the inclusive reform rhetoric of the early uprisings, and some fall in between. All of them represent profound and ongoing disruptions of the political order that existed before the uprisings. However the wars evolve, the effects of these experiments on politics and society will be enduring.

There is no evidence-based reason to believe that progress is inevitable in the Arab world, any more than there is evidence that it is doomed to an eternity of sclerotic despotism. The region is still rife with extensive and abiding aspirations for a new order: there are efforts at creation, and a backlash against them; the erosion of state institutions and local initiatives to replace them; and fragmented challenges to fragmenting ideologies of legitimacy. These efforts and trends are too frequently glossed over in simplistic judgments of the uprisings' failures and successes. The Arab world remains in dramatic flux, and contains a multitude of possibilities.

Better Techniques for Understanding Arab Politics

The Century Foundation conceived this project with two primary aims. First, to document with clarity and precision the forces at play in the region, with special attention to under-studied regional interactions, ideological shifts, and political spaces not traditionally associated with the pursuit of hard power or political change. Second, to showcase an approach steeped in granular detail and historical context, so as to record some of the region's contemporary political history before it fades from living memory. This approach, we hope, will enrich the understanding of policy makers, analysts, and scholars who are rooted outside the region, bring them in closer contact with those from and based in the Arab world, and foster a spirit of communal inquiry and cooperation.

During the last wave of popular uprisings, many close observers of Arab political life, including some of its central participants, were shocked by the widespread popular anger that coalesced in 2010–11, and by the unexpected potential of people power to bring recalcitrant governments to heel. In fact, much of the thinking and organizing that bubbled into public view during the revolts had long been coalescing, and in plain sight—at least plain enough for a few activists and researchers who were interested and receptive.

Many factors contributed to the failure to fully appreciate Arab political dynamics prior to 2010, especially the growing energy and courage of the constituencies willing to oppose government policies. Before the uprisings, many observers of Arab politics tracked popular movements and smaller activist efforts, but few expected them to play an important or influential role. Analysts looking for drivers of political instability often discounted activity in marginal or secondary spaces such as the arts, among students and the wealthy, and in civil society. Soft politics and culture were often considered separate and unrelated to the pursuit of hard power, which supposedly only took place in spaces such as political parties, labor unions, the military, and the ruler's inner circle.

Of course, it is easy in hindsight to pinpoint crises or movements that later proved important. Still, there are lessons to be learned from analysts' oversights in the lead-up to the upheaval. For one, it pays for researchers and policy analysts to invest attention in a wide array of political and social actors. Traditional power centers and institutions remained important throughout the peak period of popular revolt, but were also joined by a crowd of suddenly important new entrants to the political arena. Effective research and analysis required quickly adapting to an expanded range of actors. Looking ahead to the coming period of political ferment and contestation in the Arab world, observers, analysts, and policymakers should position themselves to best understand the forces at play and the drivers of instability, transition, and restoration.

This project doesn't claim to predict which social phenomena will play future roles as drivers of instability or change—to do so is plainly impossible. Instead, these studies should encourage a broad and agnostic analysis of a wide range of political spaces. These contemporary histories and ethnographic reports improve the analytical tools at our disposal and contribute important qualitative data. This is not to suggest that a deeper and more nuanced understanding of political, social, and cultural dynamics will allow for more accurate predictions of coming instability. Rather, our hope is that this research can place analysts in a better position to understand the next unexpected political events that occur in the Arab world.

Historical Perspective

The popular uprisings that began in December 2010 in Tunisia sparked a wave of engagement across the Middle East and North Africa, whose reverberations continue to this day. Throughout 2011, the region was enthralled by bold ambitions for a new dawn of accountable governance, transparency, and rights. It was considered inevitable that an old generation of dictators would be swept away, and it was widely believed that massive change, driven by the inchoate power of the people, would manage to implement revolutionary change without violence or civil strife.

Tunisia alone seems to have charted a relatively favorable course. Elsewhere, the best scenarios are where the status quo survived without widespread violence, as in Jordan, Lebanon, Morocco, or Saudi Arabia. In other countries, uprisings were quashed, as in Bahrain; dictatorships returned, as in Egypt; or war decimated the state, as in Iraq, Libya, Syria, and Yemen.

Human rights monitoring, advocacy, direct action, and documentary journalism all have critical roles to play in holding state power accountable. But none function by design as a pathway to power, or even to reform or change. They are adjuncts, not levers—and certainly not direct sources of hard power. One of the distortions of authoritarianism is that it neuters representative and mobilizing hard-power institutions—labor unions, political parties, and so on—that normally act to check and balance the government. As a result, ill-equipped soft spaces often take up the role of balancing and challenging the state. In authoritarian states, journalists, human rights monitors, and other entities conceived as referees or watchdogs end up substituting for the opposition, since the state has eliminated all formal rivals. For decades, this set-up neutralized challenges to the state. But the endemic, generational failures of states to deliver on promises of services, security, and citizenship actually transformed these soft-power incubators into viable contenders for hard power.

This project emphasizes the basic tools of qualitative research, with detailed descriptions, interviews, and contemporary histories that enable comparative analysis. A firmly grounded understanding of what has happened and what is happening today makes the best starting point for any policy analysis about what is to be done and what might happen next. The project's approach carries, we believe, great potential for use in researching other spaces as incubators of political ideation, including but not limited to the economy, burgeoning institutions like the civil defense corps in rebel Syria (known as the White Helmets), initiatives to document history and culture across the region, sports fan clubs, informal groupings of the wealthy, militias, and prisons. This project puts forward data that should be useful even without the analyses that accompany it, and the case studies should be of enduring use to those who study and observe the Arab region.

Research across Sectors and National Boundaries

We cannot, in this volume, tackle every overlooked or under-researched case that came to mind, so we begin with a selection of studies that shed light on emerging political dynamics and illustrate the approach we want to promote. We would have liked to include studies on Egyptian prisons as incubators of political thought; wealthy individuals, such as Egyptian billionaire Naguib Sawiris, as influential political vectors; pan-Arabism among online media activists and journalists around the region; nongovernmental organizations' coping strategies adapted to post-uprising crackdowns; and other ideas. But the inquiries in this volume make a sound start, both in charting new territory and in embodying an analytical approach based on observation and ethnography. (Versions of the research in this book have also been released as Century Foundation reports.[1]) We have organized the research into four loose categories: ideas and practice, civil society, culture and media, and governance.

The first section, focusing on ideas and practice, examines regional factors and trends that illustrate the cross-border interactions and learning that played an integral role in the revolts and the reaction to them. We chose just a few fundamental concepts that have been central during the recent period to underscore the importance of ideology, regional modeling and emulation, and the overt borrowing that takes place among governments and movements within the Arab world. Michael Wahid Hanna charts the role of liberalism—notable, like secularism, more for its absence than its presence. He focuses on Egypt, as part of a larger inquiry into the intellectual history and future prospects of liberalism as an organizing idea in Arab politics. Nathan J. Brown and Benjamin Helfand tackle the broad yet shallow adoption of a legal reform paradigm by revolutionary movements. Their close look at judicial reform constituencies in revolutionary Egypt, and the stalled truth and reconciliation effort in Tunisia, tells a cautionary tale for movements that substitute ready-made rule of law rhetoric for an articulated political agenda of their own. Monica Marks draws authoritatively on the details of Tunisia's transition, the lone clear-cut success story from the uprisings, to question how extensively Arab countries should set expectations based on the trajectory of their neighbors. Shared political idioms and forces shape the wider Arab region, but specific factors make Tunisia's transition away from dictatorship of only limited use as a blueprint for other Arab states. Michael Stephens tells the story of the battle for influence between the wealthy monarchies of the Arabian Peninsula, whose regional ambitions have been an underestimated driver of Arab politics. Stephens's account persuasively illustrates the significance of Gulf foreign policy. Despite a mismatch between financial resource and policymaking capacity, the monarchies have driven many of the region's political pathologies, including entrenched disputes between competing Islamist factions and between Islamist and secular authoritarians. The chapters in this section apply interdisciplinary methods to a regional canvas, and assume a coherent if limited affinity within the Arab region. Usually such analysis is reserved for factors like religion, jihadi mobilization, the resource curse, the regional impact of the Palestinian-Israeli conflict, or American or Russian influence. The studies in this project apply the same broad palette to other forces and ideologies that spring from the region.

The second section focuses on civil society, the wellspring for much of the activism during the uprisings and a continuing source of opposition to unfettered state power. The Arab world's vibrant civil society has long disproved arguments that the region lacks initiative. In the period since the uprisings, however, critical sectors of civil society have been saddled with outsized expectations as they try to fill voids left by indifferent governments or ineffectual political parties. I examine the efforts of a fledgling Lebanese political movement, Beirut Madinati, which challenged the existing political order and self-consciously tried to learn from the previous popular reform and dissident movements in the region. Beirut Madinati's wide appeal but limited successes raise important questions about the potential for popular protest movements on their own to pressure ossified political systems. Sima Ghaddar looks at another Lebanese movement, a grassroots coalition that tried without success to alter the country's citizenship laws so that women would be able to pass nationality to their spouses and children. She argues that citizens can benefit from improved services and political representation even in the aftermath of failed efforts to change laws. Khaled Mansour chronicles the unprecedented levels of repression deployed against Egypt's vibrant human rights community as part of a wider crackdown on civil society by the authoritarian regime. He argues that a critical and free civil society is not only a moral imperative, but a necessary precursor for economic and political health. Karim Medhat Ennarah demythologizes Egypt's organized "Ultras," or extreme soccer fans. He documents the history of the Ultras and the struggle for accountability and justice after seventy-two fans were killed in a stadium stampede in Port Said in 2012. The inconclusive saga challenges neat preconceptions about class, justice, and agency in Egypt's popular uprising.

The third section looks at culture and media. These chapters analyze political spaces that are often relegated to the margins as vectors of "soft power," or as cultural artifacts that reflect social currents without playing a meaningful role in political life. Especially in authoritarian states that close traditional avenues of political expression and contestation, other public spaces assume outsize importance. As a result, arts, cultural activities, journalism, and online communities often become some of the sole or most important forums for political organizing, argument, and expression. Are artists and journalists political forces in their own right, or do they reflect hard politics and activism that have been banished from the public sphere by security states? The answer, it seems, is both. Ursula Lindsey profiles art activists in Morocco who have self-consciously taken up a banner that they believe political activists have dropped—and who fashion themselves, through their arts work, as a bulwark against Islamists. All power politics is local, social and cultural, Lindsey's research suggests. Political cartoonists in Egypt have pushed the red lines of free expression, argues Jonathan Guyer in a rich and nuanced chronicle of one of the few public spaces that has preserved a measure of critical autonomy during Egypt's authoritarian relapse. Far from serving as a mere safety valve, Guyer writes, cartoonists manage to criticize authorities and nurture oppositional ideas at a time when such activity is rarer and more dangerous than ever. Sultan Sooud Al Qassemi affords us a longer view of a similar phenomenon, showing the dual role of fine arts painters as simultaneously darlings and critics of the ruling elite. Egypt's painters have acted as a sort of social conscience, opportunistically flitting between the roles of political gadfly and activist. The political relevance of fine arts cannot be denied, he writes, but nor should it be overstated, as painters, like many other displaced political exponents, navigate the narrow lanes of permissible discourse in an authoritarian state. Also in Egypt, the online publication *Mada Masr* emerged as one of the more dynamic, and long-lasting revolutionary institutions founded in the spirit of the 2011 uprising. Like many of its peer collectives, *Mada* has tried to embody revolutionary ideals while building an institution it hopes can challenge state power. Laura C. Dean's oral history of *Mada* tells an important story about Egypt, and simultaneously embodies a style of case study research we believe is vital to documenting and understanding Arab politics in opaque times. Expanding on some of the dynamics that drive *Mada*, Marc Lynch investigates the wider context of the thought communities built on new media platforms. He finds that many of the same forces that drove the 2010–11 wave of revolts persist, and that despite authoritarian pressure, so do the tools and spaces where critical dissident communities organized and sharpened their ideas. Social media, Lynch argues, will play a major role in future waves of change in the Arab world.

The fourth and final section examines governance. Arab authoritarians, like their peers around the world, often justify their abuses with the paternalistic claim that their subjects simply aren't ready for democracy or any other form of self-governance. And yet the Arab region is hosting more experiments than ever before in self-rule and autonomous local governance. What can we learn from some of the pivotal cases of governance since the uprisings? This project's governance studies explore the mechanics of rule in areas of Syria and Egypt where traditional power arrangements have come under strain or have collapsed entirely. (There is much related work to be undertaken across the region, but especially in zones of conflict or absentee state rule, including Lebanon, Libya, Yemen, and Syria.) Starting in Syria, Samer Abboud expands our view of the conflict to include a mostly underestimated factor: the new elite created by the wartime economy. Syria's new conflict class, Abboud argues, perpetuates the strife and will play an important role in any postwar order. Yasser Munif delves into the early revolutionary period in the city of Manbij, where leftist and nationalist rebels briefly created alternative power structures that radically challenged not only Syria's regime but also dominant Western, neoliberal norms. In a pathbreaking study of the intersection of Islamist ideology, warlordism and the wartime smuggling economy, Aron Lund tells the story of the rise and fall of a Syrian rebel enclave on the edge of Damascus. His rich account forces us to understand the local and mercenary motives of many of the Syrian conflict's most pivotal actors. It also provides a template for analyzing conflict, ideology, and self-rule on a bedrock of unsparing, holistic observations that take into account a sometimes bewildering sweep of actors and motivations. Sam Heller employs a similar approach to examine the record of rebel self-rule in the province of Idlib through the competition between two dominant Islamist militias for control and the loyalty of residents. An empirical account of the local government and service networks built by the Islamist militias drives a broader inquiry into the problems of establishing alternative substates in the shadow of even a weak authoritarian central authority like Bashar al-Assad's. Related efforts have gathered momentum in communities in Egypt and Syria where noncombatants have carved out elements of local rule or local initiative through various guises of civilian local or popular committees. Cilja Harders and Dina Wahba draw on extensive fieldwork over a long period of time to assess the potential of the popular committees that have brought new, if flawed, forms of representation to marginalized neighborhoods in Cairo. Asya El-Meehy asks critical questions about whether these organic local committees and councils in Syria and Egypt fulfil their stated promises of inclusion, representation, and transparency. Her original empirical research suggests that experiments in local self-rule often fall short of their aims and ideals.

Root Causes and Future Change

We hope that the chapters in this volume encourage detail-rich studies that are overtly engaged in policy analysis and addressing the needs of policymakers. We have carefully chosen these case studies not only for the topics they focus on, but for the methods they employ. If the community of analysts, academics, policy makers, journalists and others concerned with the political condition of the Arab states is to better understand it, there needs to be an accurate map of the political landscape and the forces at play. Traditional power centers remain pivotal and are often the only elements of the political equation subjected to thorough study and analysis. But as the last few decades have shown, Arab political efforts are underway beyond known spaces such as the military, the ruling party, official opposition, and labor unions.

We are concerned with the past: the root causes, the structural factors, the details of social displacement, repression, and political aspiration. Equally, we are concerned with the future: where change might come from, where the forces of the status quo or of authoritarianism are likely to flourish, and how these competing forces might fare. A complete picture of the present political moment requires detailed ethnographic data along with a contextualizing theoretical framework. Citizens and rulers in the Arab world will continue to litigate their governing compacts in the coming years against a backdrop of increasing turbulence not just in the Middle East and North Africa but worldwide. Many of the pathologies studied in isolation as phenomena of the Arab world will more and more obviously be understood as universal political phenomena. Specific context and history will be all the more crucial to differentiate the outcomes and effects of street protests, popular movements, authoritarian executives, balkanized institutions, entrenched networks of patronage, and corruption. The nineteen studies collected here will provide an invaluable guide to the next phase of political struggle in the Arab world. We also believe they provide a template for analyzing popular politics in authoritarian contexts.

Note

1. Report versions from the project "Arab Politics Beyond the Uprisings" can be accessed online at The Century Foundation's website, https://tcf.org/topics/world/arab-politics/.

PART I

Ideas and Practice

2

Explaining Absence
The Failure of Egypt's Liberals

MICHAEL WAHID HANNA

Explanations for the absence of liberalism in contemporary Egypt continue to rely on simplistic analyses that present the Arab world as doomed by age-old traditions and rigid texts. With a detailed discussion of Egypt's dynamic history, this chapter presents a more thorough and nuanced view of liberalism's failures in Egypt. By extension, the chapter also lays the foundation for analyzing the absence of liberalism in the broader Arab world, as well as its near-term prospects. Egypt is a quintessential encapsulation of regional trends toward authoritarianism and Islamist militancy. Its political life remains static, polarized, and trapped between limited and unsatisfactory modes of governance. The country's predicament has thus telegraphed a wider failing: it now functions as something of a negative indicator for a region that has often relied on it for intellectual, political, and cultural regeneration. This chapter is also intended as the start of a broader regional exploration of the weak performance of liberal political platforms in the Arab world.

As the initial promise of the Arab uprisings has collapsed and curdled, many have revisited nagging questions posed by political dysfunction in the Arab world. The trajectory of events moved rapidly from openness and ambition to reaction and survival, and recurrent themes of modern Arab political life have reasserted themselves. As Fouad Ajami noted in 1981, "It has been hard for the Arabs to escape from a deep historical dilemma: prison or anarchy."[1] That dilemma endures.

Amid this current resurgence of Arab authoritarianism and Islamist militancy, both liberalism and secularism have had little traction. Neither force has had a perceptible impact on recent Arab and Egyptian history; in fact, liberalism and secularism have fallen further into obscurity. The notion of open and pluralistic societies in the Arab world is more distant than ever. Egypt is a quintessential encapsulation of these many trends and now functions as something of a negative indicator for a region that has often relied on it for intellectual, political, and cultural regeneration. Egypt is, in a sense, an incubator of troublesome pathologies and a proving ground for the failure of liberalism.

The region's dysfunction remains a topic of sharp debate that has taken on increasing political salience as the ferocious autocratic response to the uprisings has coalesced alongside the rise of the Islamic State and the refugee crisis. Cumulatively, these trends have reinforced notions of the Arab world as the epicenter of global instability and conflict. The region continues to be distinct, and its seeming imperviousness to political progress has hardened Western opinions about Arab and Muslim politics and culture, with an outsized focus on how religion is shaping the region's politics and culture.

But many of these narratives are simplistic. The peculiar pathologies of the Arab world and the current failures of liberalism and secularism have emerged from the complex modern history of the region, the decisions of political and intellectual leaders, and the contingencies that shaped its political culture. Certainly, Egypt has its own unique history and sociocultural traditions, including religion, which have shaped that political culture. But a fatalistic view of those precursors as rigid and permanent is thoroughly misguided. It is not historical destiny that is shaping Arab politics, driving the rise of religion, or producing the failure of secular and liberal forces.

In an effort to explicate this state of affairs many intellectuals and political leaders have lapsed into ahistorical readings of religion, politics, law, and culture. In this telling, liberalism's inability to take hold in Egypt and the rest of the Arab world is framed as something intrinsic and inherent, bound up in tradition and text.

Even as military-led governance and Islamist rule perform poorly, liberalism still fails to make major inroads into the Egyptian public sphere. What remain striking about Egypt's political culture are the poverty and limited boundaries of discourse. Not a single party in the era after the fall of Hosni Mubarak (president 1981–2011) could be described as putting forward, defending, and maintaining a liberal vision and approach to governance.[2] In current political discourse, the basic aspirations of liberal democracy, including individual liberty, equality of citizenship, and a tolerance for diversity, and the mechanisms by which such aspirations may be secured, such as constitutional government, separation of powers, competitive elections, a free press, and transparency, are notable by their absence. One can only assume from those choices that such a political posture was nearly universally understood to be unviable, even among the minority of political actors who themselves held liberal views in private.

To understand the contemporary predicament of liberal thought in Egypt we must examine the modern historical variables that have pushed Egypt to this bleak present. This chapter will offer a brief survey of the most salient of those variables while offering an assessment of liberalism's future prospects. The centrality of Egypt to modern Arab political life amplifies the importance of these developments; Egypt remains a regional model and indicator despite its diminished status and stunted political culture. Egypt's failures have telegraphed a wider regional failing and absence, despite the particularities of each country. Exploring the basis of those failures helps to explain why political life remains static, polarized, and trapped between limited and unsatisfactory modes of governance. This chapter is also intended as the start of a broader regional exploration of the weak performance of liberal political platforms in the Arab world.

Arab Failure and Religious Revival

The religious revival of the Arab world has clouded perceptions of recent history and obscured the incremental and concerted manner in which Islamism has cemented itself in contemporary political culture. "Given the prominence of Islam in public life across much of the Arab world today, it is easy to forget just how secular the Middle East was in 1981," argues Eugene Rogan.[3] Similarly, Carrie Rosefsky Wickham notes: "that there is nothing 'natural' about the success of Islamist outreach in a Muslim country is indicated by the dominance of leftist movements in the Arab world as recently as the 1960s and early 1970s."[4]

The ubiquity of Islamism is a thoroughly modern phenomenon and represents a major shift in the political landscape of the Arab world. R. Stephen Humphreys wrote, before the Arab uprisings, that "religious language and action have permeated Middle Eastern politics. . . . Since the late 1970s all the most visible protest and revolutionary movements have marched under the banner of Islam."[5] Further, even in many places, such as Egypt, where Islamists have failed in formal terms, they have achieved a practical victory. Ardent opponents of Islamism, such as Egypt's Abdel Fattah el-Sisi, have essentially adopted and championed key strands of Islamist thought, albeit in the service of the state.

Significantly, this rising Islamic religiosity also occurred alongside the withering of liberal political thought in Egypt, a process that began in the era of Arab nationalism, and accelerated in the wake of its demise. Tellingly, while the post-1967 moment helped to produce a new radicalism that sought to outflank the Arab nationalist regimes, this inflection point did little to rekindle broader interest in liberalism.

A discussion of the religious revivalist current in the Arab world is of course essential to any accounting of modern Arab and Egyptian political life.[6] That revival, however, should not be understood as an authentic and inevitable expression of immutable traits. Instead, it should be seen as a highly contingent series of developments. The seminal historian Albert Hourani believed that there was merit in examining the ways in which the history and evolution of societies in the region were informed by Islam, but warned against "seeing history in terms of an endless repetition of certain patterns of behavior, derived from an unchanging system of beliefs."[7]

Egypt's catastrophic defeat by Israel in June 1967 also plays a critical role in this history, but the seeds of revivalism clearly predate it. Israel Gershoni and James P. Jankowski point to the 1930s as the beginnings of "a more profound cultural reorientation developing in Egypt. . . .the return of Islam to a primary position in Egyptian intellectual discourse and public life."[8] In their description, Islam "provided the basis for the new common national culture uniting elite and mass."[9] Reflecting on these profound changes, the Egyptian intellectual Salama Musa lamented the eclipse of the ideas of Egyptian nationalists who had understood Egypt to be "the homeland of all Egyptians, Muslims, Christians, and Jews, nonbelievers and atheists, and there is no place for religion in patriotism."[10]

The grim realities of modern Arab political life have at times produced an overly romantic and nostalgic view of interwar Egypt and what has often been described as Egypt's liberal era. An exaggerated reading of that history and the liberal trends of that era have also contributed to the air of resignation and disappointment surrounding Egyptian politics.

Notwithstanding such anachronistic exaggerations, the interwar period did produce an intellectual elite that valued and championed liberal thought and, most importantly, helped to shape the trajectory of political life and social change. Bruce Rutherford has written that "Egypt's liberal tradition incorporates the core principles of classical liberalism: a clear and unbiased legal code, the division of state power into separate branches, checks and balances among these branches, and respect for basic civil and political rights."[11] Egypt's truncated, flawed, and corrupt liberal era was marred by the machinations of the British, who continued to exert significant influence over Egyptian political life, and King Farouk, who retained significant power during his reign (1936–52) and sought to expand it. Despite these challenges, liberal thought continued to function as a significant force in public life.

The peculiar circumstances of the interwar years undermined the political possibilities of the time. The government in Egypt owed its existence to a colonial power and was tightly controlled by it, even as it sought to channel the fundamentally incompatible demands of the populace it represented, which was adamantly seeking the permanent and total expulsion of Great Britain.[12] In the face of these contradictory demands, Egypt's political order was "inevitably perceived—both by European powers and by [its] own citizens—as weak, ineffectual, and even clownish."[13] The animating intellectual currents of that era would also be tarnished by these glaring shortcomings.

Those shortcomings helped to usher in the period of military domination that has so profoundly shaped Egypt's modern history.

This process was unfolding in parallel with the reorientation of Egyptian identity away from the territorial and tightly focused nationalism that marked Egypt's struggle against colonialism. As Hourani describes the currents that produced Egyptian nationalism in the late nineteenth and early twentieth century, he notes that "the relationship between Islam and Egyptian nationalism was not so simple: the idea of an Egyptian nation, entitled to a separate political existence, involved not only the denial of a single Islamic political community, but also the assertion that there could be a virtuous community based on something other than a common religion and revealed law."[14]

Transnational currents of both Arab nationalism and religious revivalism eclipsed Egypt's early twentieth-century nationalism. That process was aided by the dramatic demographic and social shifts that occurred during the presidency of Gamal Abdel Nasser (1956–70), as increased access to education and rural-to-urban migration created a new middle class, often in opposition to the old elites. That new middle class would come to represent the backbone of support for both movements, and would push liberal thought further to the edge of mainstream discourse.

Despite Nasser's crushing repression of the Muslim Brotherhood, the group continued to sustain itself both in prison and in exile. That doggedness would provide the platform for the Brotherhood's resurgence as Egypt's politics again shifted following the 1967 war and Nasser's death in 1970. That resurgence was aided by the specific shifts away from Nasser that his successor Anwar Sadat (president 1970–81) pursued, but it was also given support by the introspection and frustration of that juncture in Egyptian history. The most far-reaching political and intellectual responses to the crushing defeat of 1967 saw the failures of secular Arab nationalism as evidence of "the bankruptcy of the entire framework of secular politics."[15] That bankruptcy could be seen by "its utter futility and impotence in the face of [Egypt's] enemies."[16] Mohamed Abul Ghar, the former head of the Egyptian Social Democratic Party and a supporter of the July 2013 coup, summarized this Islamist critique: "According to the narrative of the Islamists, Egypt's military defeat by Israel in the 1967 war was an inevitable result of the country's alienation from Islam under Nasser. The same narrative suggests that the 1973 military victory under Sadat was the result of the country's re-embrace of Islam."[17]

Revivalism could be seen in the number of Arab nationalists, Marxists, and radicals who abandoned their previous creeds and adopted Islamism as the language and thought of opposition, and in the process created a newfound vernacular for reformism.[18] It was also given further purchase by the process of instrumentalization and co-option of Islam that would come to dominate Egyptian public life. Facing an upswing in both belief and fervor, autocratic rulers throughout the Arab world sought to turn faith into an instrument for their own purposes.

For Egypt, this took the initial form of Sadat's encouragement of religious forces as a counterweight to the leftist and Nasserist actors whom he saw as a threat to his ability to consolidate and rule effectively. Most notably, Sadat's cultivation of religious sources of legitimacy resulted in the adoption of Article 2 of the constitution, which made "the principles of the Islamic Sharia" a chief source of legislation. Article 2 was subsequently tightened further, making sharia "the chief source of legislation." These constitutional and legal shifts were not simply window-dressing—they reflected the ways in which the Egyptian public sphere was becoming increasingly Islamized. Cumulatively, these attempts to neuter the political challenge represented by Islamism may have helped to insulate successive Egyptian regimes from the most threatening mode of political opposition, but it came at the cost of establishing Islamist thought as the baseline for much political activity, even among non-Islamists.

The regional oil boom of the 1970s also had major implications on the trajectory of religious and political thought in the region. This massive influx of oil wealth shifted both power dynamics in the region and patterns of migration. The effect of this massive influx of private oil wealth in Egypt could be seen in the increased funding that went into the establishment and development of private mosques, either through Gulf Arab patrons or through the remittances of Egyptian workers in the Gulf.[19]

Events outside the Arab world, such as the Iranian Revolution of 1979 and the anti-Soviet jihadist resistance, injected further energy into Islamist opposition movements and fueled their mainstreaming and their radicalization, but in both cases, helped establish their relevance.

Militarized Society

The rise of military-led governance in Egypt is far from unique and occurred elsewhere in the developing world. For Egypt, the early military domination of the state under Nasser was not the sole cause of the destruction of organized liberalism or liberal intellectual trends, but clearly played a key role, particularly when judged in conjunction with the other notable developments of the latter half of the twentieth century.

Among the first major institutional steps of the Free Officers (the small group of junior Egyptian officers who ousted King Farouk and seized power in July 1952) was the disbanding of Egypt's parliament and the abolishing of political parties in 1953. Political power was concentrated in the hands of military leaders, who saw themselves as the country's only effective vanguard in the effort to modernize and develop the country. The Egyptian historian Anouar Abdel-Malek aptly described this state of affairs: "The fact was that the officers denied to every other social class, to any national group other than the army, the right and duty to lead the rebirth of Egypt. They alone possessed the tool of power essential to a country still under the military subjugation of imperialism."[20]

As the military regime institutionalized its social and political changes, the Egyptian military became less concerned with governance and reform and more occupied with the sustainability of a military-led political order from which it derived significant privileges and prerogatives.[21] Under Nasser, the military was visible and involved in many facets of governance. In 1966, half of the cabinet of Prime Minister Sid'qi Suleiman was composed of active-duty military officers. Despite the harsh setback of 1967 and the reorganization of the military, the ongoing conflict with Israel and its occupation of the Sinai Peninsula provided a continuing justification for the military's outsized role in public life.

The nature of that role would evolve over time and the supremacy of the armed forces would be eroded as Egypt's authoritarianism became much more focused on the president himself. This process had its roots in Nasser's rule but accelerated under both Sadat and Mubarak. On the eve of Egypt's uprising in January 2011, it was an authoritarian state but had long ago ceased to be a military regime. Instead, Egypt was an autocratic system in which competing centers of authority had emerged, albeit one in which the military continued to be the silent guarantor of regime stability. The military was further removed from governance and civilian politics and more concentrated on the economic interests of the institution. The uprising represented a major political opening for the Egyptian military, and the aftermath of Egypt's failed political transition resulted in the military's direct intervention in and usurpation of civilian politics.

Nonetheless, the military's initial domination of post-revolutionary Egypt stunted the growth of all avenues for political expression and dissent. However, as incremental space for controlled politics emerged, the political and intellectual landscape had similarly shifted, favoring the vitality of Islamist thought, which came to be seen as the main vehicle for expressing oppositional politics in Egypt.

The Work of Repression

Among the most notable legacies of the Arab authoritarian order has been the impoverishment of political culture. The constricting of space for regional politics boosted the fortunes of political Islam in light of the lack of credible alternatives.[22] Latching on to this feature of modern Arab political life, Arab liberals themselves have adopted simplistic rationalizations for the preeminence of Islamism as the primary mode for oppositional politics. Reflecting on his life and experiences, the Syrian dissident Yassin al-Haj Saleh has, using a familiar narrative, explained the rise of Islamism as a function of authoritarianism and repression: "Islam, in our society, is the limit of political poverty. When you don't have any political life, people will mobilize according to the lowest stratum of an imaginary community. This deeper identity is religion. . . . But when you crush politics, when there is no political life, religious identity will prosper."[23] While this analysis at least seeks to grapple with modern history, it does little to illuminate the actual distinctiveness of the Arab world. Repression is by no means the exclusive province of the Arabs, and yet the pathologies of the Arab world remain distinct from other countries and regions that have suffered similar repression, including other Muslim-majority countries.

Still, authoritarianism and repression are certainly a part of the explanation for the rise of Islamism, particularly when assessed in conjunction with the host of other trends that have helped to produce the region's present-day political culture. Because of those trends, repression of independent political life in Egypt has been more successful in degrading non-Islamist political currents, particularly liberal thought.

One obvious level in which these asymmetries are manifested is organizational. Tarek Masoud argues that Islamist success is primarily a function of "the different political opportunities facing Islamists and their rivals."[24] He describes these institutional advantages by arguing that Egypt is "replete with religious institutions, from mosques to religious societies to charitable associations that, though forced to be apolitical during Mubarak's reign, embed both ordinary citizens and Islamist political activists in common networks of social action, making it easy for the latter to build trust with the former when an opening in the political system finally presented itself."[25] This materialist argument largely rejects approaches to this issue that offer ideological explanations of Islamist success, and by extension, liberal weakness.

Of course, repression has not simply focused on squelching secular organizations and pathways to political expression.[26] In fact, Egypt and other regimes have also sought to suppress religiously-motivated political action, and it is their continued resilience and traction in the face of such state efforts that is distinctive. As Masoud writes, "If mosques became focal points of dissent under authoritarianism, they did this *despite* the presence of heavy regulation by the regime."[27]

But this inherent sympathy for Islamists and Islamist politics among significant strands of the populace is not simply a function of superior organization. This sympathetic posture crucially relies on a fundamental openness to Islamist politics and a trust in those who deliver that message. Masoud himself puts forward a materialist theory of Islamist prominence that understands Islamists' electoral supremacy as an outgrowth of "their ability to meet preexisting, exogenous, and largely nonreligious policy demands."[28] It is also worth noting that the electoral fortunes of Islamists in Egypt have varied over time and that non-Islamists have been competitive in specific settings. In the first round of Egypt's 2012 presidential elections, for instance, the three avowedly non-Islamist candidates, Ahmed Shafik, Hamdeen Sabahi, and Amr Moussa, received more than 55 percent of the vote and finished second, third, and fifth respectively. The fourth place finisher, Abdel Moneim Aboul Fotouh, was a former member of the Brotherhood who ran as a crossover candidate and highlighted his support from both Islamists and non-Islamists. Further, following Mohamed Morsi's turbulent and truncated presidency (2012–13), popular support for the Brotherhood clearly ebbed.

Nonetheless, the initial trust placed in Islamists in the early post-Mubarak period was itself reflective of the broader social changes that have convulsed Egypt and the region and created ideological affinities with Islamist thought and receptiveness to Islamist parties. That receptiveness was also the product of concerted efforts and the cultivation of "a new, activist conception of Islam" in which it was incumbent on Muslims to "participate in the Islamic reform of society and state."[29]

Notably, despite these developments, redistributive economic policy continues to hold broad sway among the Egyptian populace. In assessing leftist underperformance in the Mubarak era, Masoud suggests that voter incentives in an era of patronage politics were skewed and that poor voters who might have been receptive to the left's economic ideas chose the immediate material rewards that patronage offered.[30] This line of argument assumes that economic policies, particularly with respect to redistributive policies, are the logical terrain upon which Egyptian politics takes place. Masoud further argues that the left was never discredited in Egypt, even after 1967, and that "Egyptians continue to identify themselves as leftists, Nasserists, or socialists in significant number."[31]

What remained of those leftist currents, however, was a flimsy vestige of an earlier era and a testament to the shallow ideological project of Nasserism. In the post-Nasser era, and up until the present, what Egypt inherited from Nasserism is a malleable and inchoate support for redistributive economic policies with little attachment to coherent ideology. These affinities were partly an outgrowth of Nasser's reforms, which created a new class that was largely dependent on the state for education and employment.[32] This remains the principle legacy of the Nasserist era, despite the shift in economic policies under Sadat and then Mubarak. In explaining the founding of the April 6 Youth Movement, Walid Shawky argues that the "political scene had few ideological stances for outreach or mobilization aside from the Muslim Brotherhood. Most organizations or movements are built around the coalescing of members around a founding concept, giving them a reason for joining and sustained involvement, and forming a bond between members. April 6 was different: We bonded over a shared emotional and psychological state, rather than an ideological conviction."[33] In fact, this description could be applied much more broadly, and reflects the overall health of Egyptian public life—and helps to explain the inability of many non-Islamist groups to organize effectively.

Perhaps most importantly for present purposes, in correctly identifying the Egyptian left as a natural competitor to Islamists, Masoud implicitly concedes the near total organizational absence of liberalism as a political force. This points to an important legacy of Nasser and his particular brand of repression and ideology, which cultivated leftist economic impulses and produced fragile constituencies of supporters for such policies. Diminished in that era was any significant or meaningful ideological or political work focusing on liberalism, which had been tarnished by the failures of interwar politics and undermined by the expansion of a new middle class and urban elite that benefited from Nasser's social policies. That legacy has produced a constricted political culture in which Islamists and statists continue to represent the only viable political movements capable of contesting national power. In the face of the Brotherhood's missteps, non-Islamist political currents were emboldened, but this turnaround did little to boost the prospects of liberalism.

A Tunisian Exception?

Egypt's failures have been broadly predictive of the poverty of modern Arab political life, and that broader landscape has shared in many of the same historical processes that produced the illiberalism that defines the region. Nonetheless, those historical processes remain the critical factor in understanding the elaboration and sustainment of political culture, and it is also why the case of Tunisia offers interesting and contradictory outcomes. Within the present-day Arab world, the counterexample of Tunisia exemplifies the ways in which the contingencies of history can alter and shape societies and political cultures. While this brief comparison is only intended as a reference point, deeper comparative study would be useful in elucidating the mechanisms that have produced divergent outcomes despite a degree of shared history.

The decisions of leaders and the variance in historical development in Tunisia have affected the trajectory of politics, culture, and society. Of course, since the fall of Zine El Abidine Ben Ali (president 1987–2011), Islamists have done quite well in electoral terms. But what is distinct about Tunisia is the fact that secularism (as distinct from liberalism) exists as a potent political force with a vibrant and active constituency. This is not to equate secularism with liberal politics, although the two currents of thought are often functional complements. Instead, the example of secularism in Tunisia is reflective of the ways in which specific decisions and approaches have helped to shape a distinctive intellectual history that stands in stark contrast to the evolution of thought in the rest of the region. It is a concrete example of the ways in which political cultures cannot stand apart from history, law, and politics, and are instead a direct product of such contingent and variable processes.

Rory McCarthy argues that "under presidents Bourguiba and Ben Ali, the state sought to subordinate religion and to claim the sole right to interpret Islam for the public in an effort to win the monopoly over religious symbolism."[34] While this approach differs from a classic separation of religion and state, the fact remains that post-independence Tunisia's aggressive approach to modernization has produced a viable set of politics that posits the necessity of a secular state. While not wholly abandoning Islam, Habib Bourguiba (president 1956–87) could confidently state that "what was just a century ago appears today as unjust."[35] Of course, such views did not go unchallenged within Tunisian society and produced various kinds of opposition and backlash. They would also be revisited by Bourguiba himself and later Ben Ali as the social and cultural mores of the Arab world evolved during the wave of religious revivalism. Nonetheless, this approach to religion, politics, and identity was unique in the Arab world, and has produced a unique outcome.

Politics in Tunisia is varied to the extent that "actors on both the Islamist and secular-leftist sides of the political spectrum struggled against purists within their respective camps to forge cross-ideological compromises, both before and after the revolution."[36] Speaking in 2013, Beji Caid Essebsi, the current president of Tunisia and then the head of the political party Nidaa Tounes, could state clearly that "a modern society needs a secular state where religion doesn't intervene."[37] Such a stance is scarcely imaginable for even a fringe politician in Egypt, and yet in the context of Tunisia, this political platform was one that could propel Essebsi to the presidency. Tunisia's historic efforts at controlling religious discourse failed in producing a thoroughly secular and homogenous society, but clearly did result in the creation of a vocal secular component that could compete politically by prioritizing the themes of secularism. The influence of those historical and political currents is such that Rachid al-Ghannouchi, the head of Ennahda, an Islamist party, has explicitly stated that his party "doesn't oppose secularism—it opposes laïcité."[38]

Acknowledging the possibility of establishing and sustaining different kinds of secularist politics in the Arab world should not be understood as an endorsement of Tunisia's approach to modernization and development, which was flawed for a variety of reasons. However, it is an example of the ways in which history, contingency, and agency can produce outcomes that diverge significantly from the conventional script assigned to Arab societies. That particular history has produced in Tunisia "a delicately counter-balanced set of actors that simply does not exist in any other Arab country."[39] In this specific example, one can see broader possibilities for alternatives to the recurrent Arab political dilemma, including liberalism.

Few Liberals to Be Found

In the immediate post-Mubarak political environment, few political currents put forth an avowedly liberal platform. Several parties, such as the Wafd Party, the Free Egyptians, and the Egyptian Social Democratic Party offered elements of liberal thought, but fell far short of active engagement on a liberal agenda.

The animating rationales of the uprising were a frustration with authoritarian excess—whether in the form of police abuse or corruption—inchoate calls for accountability, a vague commitment to redistributive economic policies, and platitudes about freedom. In one sense, these broad and unspecific themes represented a kind of lowest common denominator and a tactical choice by the broad-based constellation of divergent forces that made up and produced the mass mobilization that eventually helped force the ouster of Mubarak. Conspicuously, social and cultural issues were studiously avoided, in large part because these issues would raise inevitable tensions and fears among non-Islamists and would threaten the viability of the anti-Mubarak alliance. For the Islamists, who were keen not to be seen as the guiding power behind the protest movement—both in terms of how the uprising would be perceived by domestic and foreign audiences—setting aside social and cultural matters was a logical choice in light of their own confidence in their prospective political prospects. The time for such matters would come, but not before a transition had been set in motion.

Beyond these tactical considerations, however, the broad sloganeering that characterized this early phase was a reflection of the poverty of Egyptian political life and political culture. As the April 6 member Walid Shawky reflected, "Politics was represented by groups of people with similar ideas and a political project they then persuaded others to support—although, due to oppression and corruption, even this was not the reality at the time, despite the decorative presence of political parties and a parliament."[40] To the extent that there was broad societal consensus on key issues, they were largely defined by the dominant modes of Egyptian political thought, namely Nasserism and Islamism. As such, broad traction could be found in the economic realm and on the fraught issue of the role of Islam in public life.

The resonant message of economic justice through greater redistributive economic policies remains a stubborn legacy of Nasserism, despite the fact that many political currents, including the Muslim Brotherhood, had practically abandoned such an economic vision in their own party platforms. Despite years of efforts at market-based economic reform focused on economic growth, "the evidence suggested that—regardless of whatever tangible improvements those policies had made—they were at odds with the sensibilities of the majority of the people."[41] Tellingly, the public-facing electioneering of the post-Mubarak period was dominated by vague calls for redistributive economic policy.[42]

Similarly, on the issue of Islam and public life, there seemed to exist a great deal of societal consensus, and the political discourse surrounding the role of sharia in the constitution was indicative of a foundational shift. Hamdeen Sabahi, the Nasserist political leader who would later contest the 2012 presidential elections, in 2011 explicitly stated his support for Article 2.[43] Even ostensibly liberal political parties or individuals advocated a status quo approach to the issue, often as a defensive measure to ensure that even more restrictive clauses were not formally adopted. In numerous private conversations with non-Islamist political leaders and activists in the immediate aftermath of the fall of Mubarak, it was assumed that the existing constitutional approach to sharia represented a floor and that any efforts to re-litigate the issue would redound to their detriment.

Of course, the scope of liberal political currents in Egypt is not solely defined by the approach toward redistributive economic policy or the role of sharia, and in the case of the former, not necessarily even in tension. However, in response to these political realities, even ostensibly liberal parties opted not to defend liberalism or even provide a liberal political platform or agenda. In practice, such a worldview lacked serious traction among the intellectual and political elite and also the broader populace.

Re-Militarization of State and Society

Since the coup that unseated Morsi in 2013, the role of the Egyptian military has expanded even further in both political and economic terms. As previously discussed, the period from the fall of Mubarak and the ouster of Morsi had already seen the transformation of the Egyptian military's role away from the quiescence that characterized much of the Mubarak period, particularly after the ascension of Field Marshall Mohamed Hussein Tantawi to minister of defense in 1991.

This outcome was not a certainty following the ouster of Mubarak and was primarily a function of the fragmenting of the broad-based yet weakly-connected opposition. The collapse of that tactical alliance was the key event that shaped the ill-fated transition period. It also opened the door to military control of the political process and placed the armed forces in the role of arbiter of disputes among political parties and currents. That period allowed the military to triangulate among the various political parties and leaders of that time, but also came at some cost to the reputation of the military.[44] Nonetheless, that period transformed how the armed forces related to politics and would provide the foundation upon which the July 2013 coup was launched.

The military has dominated the post-coup period, and the hierarchies within the regime have evolved in a way that prioritizes the military and the security establishment more broadly. With the ascension of Sisi to the presidency, military personnel are ubiquitous in the decision-making organs of the state. The reliance of President Sisi on a close circle of military figures is matched by the regime's continued distrust of civilian politics and civilian politicians. In fact, the attitude of the regime is actively hostile to the very notion of independent political life and it has instead sought to cultivate a civilian political sphere that would serve as an obedient supporter of government policies.

In that vein, Sisi has opted to remain above political party life. Instead, the military-backed regime led an effort to create a pro-Sisi parliament in the 2015 elections. The state and the security establishment were central in putting together the pro-Sisi electoral list For the Love of Egypt (FLE), which won 120 seats in an election with poor voter turnout. Derided as "the security establishment list" by the Wafd Party (which later joined it, as did many other parties that were initially opposed), the FLE effort was led by former general Sameh Seif al-Yazal.[45] In addition, the military helped fund the campaign of the pro-Sisi Nation's Future Party, which won fifty-three seats. Provincial politics reflect a similar influence—Sisi has again favored the appointment of military and former military leaders to provincial governorships. As of September 2016, when Sisi appointed five more former generals as governors, only eight of the twenty-seven provincial governors had civilian backgrounds.

The corollary to the growing influence of the security establishment in all facets of society has been the neutering of civilian political life. To the extent that politics exist as a forum for adjudicating policy disputes, it has essentially become confined to the regime itself and the different institutions of the state. As Amr Adly argues, the Sisi regime "has so far relied on a sociopolitical alliance made up of the military and security forces and groups of public sector employees that was formed in opposition to the January 2011 uprising against Mubarak, to secure its own legitimacy and maintain social stability."[46]

The end result of these developments is a further fragmented and stunted civilian political sphere. It has also meant that the Sisi regime has limited tools to cultivate support for its policies and initiatives and there are very limited "institutionalized channels for mediation and interest representation of the social groups whose support it seeks to maintain."[47] The legacy of this period will further hamper the already damaged prospects for the normalization of Egyptian political life and the re-emergence of civilian leadership. The statist authoritarianism of the regime is a further blow to the prospects of any form of independent politics, let alone liberalism, and, of course, a calamity for the prospect of good governance.

The growth of the military's political role has also been tracked by the change in its economic role, which was sizeable long before it seized power. While anecdotal assessments of the military's share of the economy are often exaggerated and lack credible supporting data,[48] the military's economic role has grown consistently since the 1980s. The initial impulse for increasing military involvement in the economy has often been misunderstood. The expanded economic portfolio of "the military and its affiliates can be traced back to the 1980s, when Egypt set on the path to economic transformation. This military economy has coexisted with the multifaceted expansion of the private sector and the emergence of a major capitalist class in the past two decades."[49] However, the post-2013 period has marked a qualitative and quantitative shift, as the military has become integral to economic policy and planning. The increasing role of the Egyptian military has not solely been a function of venality—although that is a factor. It has also been driven by a lack of trust in nonmilitary alternatives, the administrative/regulatory ease of military-led projects, an immediate focus on job creation, and an affinity for megaprojects that also serve propaganda aims and echo an earlier period of Egyptian history. In this setting, the regime has generally turned to the military and affiliated business entities as the vehicle to push "for public investment and implementing projects in vital sectors such as energy, infrastructure, housing, and transportation."[50]

The scope of those military-led economic projects has ranged from large-scale infrastructure projects like the Suez Canal development (estimated to cost around $8 billion)[51] to fish farming, solar energy, and the importation of infant milk formula.[52] In January 2017, the Egyptian military obtained the license required to form a pharmaceutical company.[53]

Regardless of the specific motivations and the exaggerated reporting on the military's share of the overall economy, it is clear that much of the business community is wary of the regime and is increasingly skeptical of its ability to undertake consistent and coherent economic policies. There are also reasonable fears that the private sector will begin to suffer from the more recent expansion and diversification of military economic activities. However, elements of the business community will likely be cowed by the selective rewarding of specific business constituencies. It is likely that the key economic role of the state and the military will produce its own version of a crony capitalist class that would be dependent on state favoritism. On a political level, the fears of the business community about the sustainment of the current political order will outweigh short-term frustrations with military-led governance and retard the emergence of a politically-minded and independent business community, which could be a future proponent of a liberal political and economic order.

Destruction of Civil Society

In the Mubarak era, a semicontrolled civil society space was permitted to function within the boundaries of acceptable practice. Much like the media of that time, this entailed both intermittent and varying levels of harassment and repression and a cognizance of regime red lines. This semicontrolled space nonetheless allowed for various forms of civil society to test boundaries and to demonstrate different modes of civic engagement. Many of these organizations, particularly the human rights community, played an important role in the Egyptian uprising and its aftermath, serving to both document and amplify regime abuses and advocate for various kinds of rights-based reform.[54]

For the reconfigured regime following the July 2013 coup, the lessons of that earlier era were quite clear, and the security establishment's approach to civil society has been marked by unremitting hostility and unprecedented levels of repression in an effort to squelch even nascent efforts for reform, transparency, and accountability. Even prior to the July 2013 coup, the transitional authorities demonstrated a fundamental suspicion of such efforts, particularly as it pertained to the issue of foreign funding. Their prosecution of foreign and domestic democracy-promotion organizations—including the National Democratic Institute, the International Republican Institute, and Freedom House—was stark evidence of this suspicion.

That attitude has become more pronounced under the Sisi regime's coordinated assault on civil society. The regime's repression has expanded well beyond the human rights community and has also targeted a much broader cross-section of NGOs, including "cultural initiatives, independent media outlets, feminist organizations, Nubian associations, and even co-working spaces or cafes where young people gather."[55]

At present, the civil society community is under relentless pressure and its activities have been severely curtailed. The preexisting limitations of Egyptian civil society suggest that even without the current campaign of repression, it was not a viable vehicle for supporting popularly-grounded democratization and reform efforts. Vincent Durac argues that "a conceptualization of Arab civil society in liberal terms is destined to disappoint since liberal and democratic values have much shallower roots than would be required for successful challenge to authoritarian rule. Indeed, evidence is lacking either for the prodemocratic orientation of civil society in the Arab world or its capacity to drive democratic reform."[56] Without drawing definitive conclusions about this assessment, there are two obvious observations that can be made based on recent history. First, the small and isolated human rights wing of Egypt's civil society community, which has always been dependent on foreign sources of funding, is insufficient as an anchor for pushing forward a rights-based agenda. Second, it is clear that the current steps, largely successful, to eviscerate that human rights community and to hobble civil society will surely be even more of a setback for any potential future process of democratization—and by extension, liberalization—in Egypt.[57]

Existential Fears

The winner-takes-all structure and the particular trajectory of Egypt's failed political transition after the ouster of Mubarak heightened the perception of existential stakes and produced an illiberal politics across the political divide. Subsequently, the instability ushered in by the ouster of Morsi produced a different strain of existential fear both among regime supporters and in a broad cross-section of the populace, focused on the rising threat posed by radicalization, anti-state violence, and terrorism. In both cases, any possible liberal political currents were blunted by the existential fears that gripped and distorted the political calculations of the regime and its supporters, non-Islamist opposition actors, and much of the general public.

This existential crisis was a function of the unexpectedly dominant position of Islamist parties in Egypt's first freely-elected parliament. While most prognostications assumed Muslim Brotherhood electoral ascendancy, the extent to which they dominated the elections shocked Egypt's non-Islamists and reoriented the politics of the period. The Muslim Brotherhood and the other more reactionary Salafi parties captured a supermajority in those elections and were then firmly in control of the constitutional drafting process. For Islamists, who had experienced an unprecedented political opening and astonishing early electoral victories, the moment seemed ripe for reappraising their political ambitions upward. Perhaps as importantly, the Muslim Brotherhood came to see the right-wing Salafi parties as a potential threat to their future electoral fortunes, and sought to foreclose the possibility of challenges from the Islamist right. Accordingly, Islamist ambition dominated the politics of this juncture. Relatedly, Islamists were no longer reliant on consensual transitional politics and were emboldened to embark on a majoritarian path, untethered from non-Islamist concerns and reservations.

For non-Islamists, the stakes at this foundational juncture were heightened and the means for influence seemingly limited. As a result, non-Islamists came to see the military and the institutions of the state as the primary defense against Islamist ambitions to remake the state and redefine Egyptian identity. These tendencies fostered support for military intervention into political life and paved the way for the July 2013 coup. This defensive posture also produced a cautious politics more focused on stymying Islamist consolidation than achieving political and policy goals. Needless to say, this confluence of events was not conducive to producing an open and pluralistic style of politics, particularly as the military-led political order shed its connections to civilian-led politics.

The post-coup political and security environment again presented Egyptian society with a sense of existential struggle. After the coup, popular fears of state collapse and anti-regime violence, often cultivated by the regime, became a key source of regime legitimacy. The radicalization of certain Islamist groups and the threat of violence and terrorism became a first-order priority and emboldened the security establishment. In this setting, those fears have strengthened collectivized notions of the common good and further eroded respect or concern for individual rights and freedoms.[58] This has produced a decidedly authoritarian approach to governance, politics, and dissent.

Regional Instability, Global Reaction

When viewed regionally, the Arab uprisings appeared to represent a moment of cascade. While each individual uprising was a product of country-specific conditions, as the uprisings spread from Tunisia to each successive country, it was clear that they drew upon a common vocabulary and sought motivation, inspiration, and confidence from events elsewhere in the Arab world. While the dreams of Arabism are long dead, the Arab world still shares, to a great extent, a common media space and a linked political consciousness and identity. Much as those initial moments of optimism and openness shaped the region's political climate, the violence, repression, instability, and sectarianism of the current juncture have an outsized impact on political developments.

In many respects, this instability has produced a reactionary sentiment and a reduction in expectations. Regional examples of state collapse and civil war—such as Iraq, Libya, Syria, and Yemen—have created political cautiousness and an aversion to political tumult. For Egypt, recent history and the regional landscape make for a cautionary tale that now inhibits politics and risk-taking. Regional insecurity now limits the possibilities for genuine political openings and inhibits liberal politics, which have been overwhelmed by hypernationalism, statism, economic deprivation, fear, and Islamist militancy.

These regional trends toward reactionary politics are also being strengthened by the global environment, which has witnessed an upsurge in right-wing populist demagoguery, serial setbacks to the liberal international order, and intensified great power competition and friction. This moment of globalized instability has been a major setback to liberalism and has seen a rise in authoritarian currents in previously unimaginable settings. This has been a boon to authoritarian leadership throughout the world, and the Sisi regime has warmly embraced these shifts.

Of course, the preferences of outside parties have never had a determinative impact on Egypt's politics. In fact, in many ways the post-Mubarak era has been notable for the inability of key Western and Arab countries to exercise meaningful leverage on Egyptian decision-making. Nonetheless, outside preferences and pressure can have some impact on the margins, particularly when that support is channeled in directions favored by the Egyptian regime. While negative leverage has proved ineffectual, the shifts in the international environment, particularly in the wake of the 2016 presidential election in the United States, are likely to reinforce and strengthen current political trends in Egypt. These international shifts represent yet another factor that will support regime sustainability and limit the willingness to allow for meaningful forms of political expression and dissent. In short, international politics, while not decisive, will only serve to hinder political reform, and the international political environment will undercut any potential efforts to cultivate liberal politics in Egypt. Egypt has long been an inhospitable environment for liberalism and outside influences will only further reinforce that inhospitableness.

Bleak Path Forward

The future of liberalism in Egypt is tightly bound up with the broader trajectory of the country's political, social, and cultural indicators. As with all other political factions, the prospects of liberal political currents remain reliant on the regime's approach to civilian politics. Any shift in popular attitudes will likely require a softening in the regime's approach to political expression, dissent, and organizing. Even in the case of a political opening, the fate of liberal politics will depend on revitalizing what has now been reduced to a niche and situational set of political attachments. The prospects for such a daunting project are of course heavily linked with the broader health of Egyptian society. In this sense, assessments of Egypt's current and future prospects more generally are an important gauge for understanding the likelihood of political, social, and economic regeneration.

Faced with overwhelming disappointment at the state of Egypt and the region, some analysis now suggests that the current juncture is merely a phase along an inexorable path to progress. "On the surface, the political upheavals look like failed revolts against dictatorships. But dig a bit deeper into the societies of these Arab countries and there are reasons to believe what we see is not a simple revolt, but an epochal revolution," argues Koert Debeuf, using the trajectory of revolutions in eighteenth and nineteenth century Europe as a reference point.[59] Others have sought to portray the positive legacies sustaining the initial impetus for the uprising: "Even after four years of repression and political engineering, the regime has failed to revive the stable authoritarian order that once existed in the country. More importantly, the social struggles that paved the way for the January 25 revolution continue to challenge the new ruling establishment and, at points, have exposed its weakness and kept it on the defensive."[60] Guarded optimism will almost certainly be proven correct if the timeframe for analysis is essentially open-ended, but isn't particularly enlightening about the present and immediate future.

Alaa Abdel Fattah, a prominent Egyptian activist who is currently imprisoned, offers a more realistic and decidedly pessimistic assessment. "The revolution has been defeated and everything is ruined," he wrote from jail. "The clique that is now in power is attempting to control every aspect of public life, this endeavor is doomed to failure but the price is the devastation of people's lives." There are no bold predictions about success or resistance here—just a focus on the inevitable failure of the current authoritarian political project.[61]

The failure of the current regime will not necessarily bring liberalism, or for that matter, anything that represents an improvement. While the current course of the Egyptian regime is doomed to be unsuccessful, this does not assure any kind of political shift or rupture. In fact, the more likely course of failure is incremental. Many of the structural factors previously discussed—such as the fragmented state of political opposition, unmitigated state repression, societal fatigue, fear of both state collapse and broad-based retributive violence, regional instability, and a lack of effective political alternatives—all ensure that the current regime remains sustainable despite its ineffectiveness. Any efforts to regenerate political vitality will necessarily be long-term projects, particularly as politics in Egypt and the Arab world are intimately tied to the broader political and intellectual currents in the region. Those currents are by no means immutable, but they are also not prone to immediate shifts. A viable liberal politics is neither inevitable nor doomed, but will once again depend on the course and contingencies of history.

Notes

1. Fouad Ajami, *The Arab Predicament: Arab Political Thought and Practice Since 1967* (Cambridge: Cambridge University Press, 1981), 27.

2. Michael Wahid Hanna, "Egypt's Non-Islamist Parties," in *Egypt After the Spring: Revolt and Reaction*, ed. Emile Hokayem and Hebatalla Taha (London: International Institute for Strategic Studies, 2016), 107.

3. Eugene Rogan, *The Arabs: A History* (New York: Basic Books, 2009), 399.

4. Carrie Rosefsky Wickham, *Mobilizing Islam: Religion, Activism, and Political Change in Egypt* (New York: Columbia University Press, 2002), 206.

5. R. Stephen Humphreys, *Between Memory and Desire: The Middle East in a Troubled Age* (Berkeley and Los Angeles: University of California Press, 2001), 131.

6. Hussein Ali Agrama, *Questioning Secularism: Islam, Sovereignty, and the Rule of Law in Modern Egypt* (Chicago: The University of Chicago Press, 2012), 9. Agrama argues that it is curious that this trend toward Islamic religiosity is "seen as a problem within social theory." Without delving too deeply into the theoretical basis of this hesitance or the necessity that such religiosity will create illiberal tendencies, the practical ramifications of this increased religiosity for Egyptian society and the types of politics it has inspired or legitimated are indeed problematic for their impact on civil and political rights.

7. Albert Hourani, *Islam in European Thought* (Cambridge: Cambridge University Press, 1991), 100. Hourani went on to argue the dangers of drawing "a sharp distinction between the 'true' Islam and something else, or to give a privileged position to the formal statements of textbooks of law or theology." (Hourani, *Islam in European* Thought, 101.)

8. Israel Gershoni and James P. Jankowski, *Redefining the Egyptian Nation 1930–1945* (Cambridge: Cambridge University Press, 1995), 54.

9. Ibid., 55.

10. Ibid., 77.

11. Bruce K. Rutherford, *Egypt after Mubarak: Liberalism, Islam, and Democracy in the Arab World* (Princeton: Princeton University Press, 2008), 32. Rutherford also notes that these basic notions of liberalism were first codified in Egypt's 1882 "Fundamental Law."

12. Humphreys, *Between Memory and Desire*, 116.

13. Ibid., 116.

14. Hourani, *Islam in European Thought*, 193.

15. Ajami, *The Arab Predicament*, 74.

16. Emmanuel Sivan, "Arab Nationalism in the Age of the Islamic Resurgence," in *Rethinking Nationalism in the Arab Middle East*, ed. Israel Gershoni and James Jankowski (New York: Columbia University Press, 1997), 222.

17. Mohamed Abul Ghar, "Farag Fouda: The Man Who Died for the Love of Egypt," *Ahram Online*, June 23, 2016, http://english.ahram.org.eg/NewsContentP/4/223587/Opinion/Farag-Fouda-The-man-who-died-for-the-love-of-Egypt.aspx.

18. Sivan, "Arab Nationalism in the Age of the Islamic Resurgence," 219.

19. Wickham, *Mobilizing Islam*, 97–98, 122.

20. Anouar Abdel Malek, *Egypt: Military Society: The Army Regime, The Left, and Social Change Under Nasser* (New York: Random House, 1968), 178.

21. Steven A. Cook, *Ruling but Not Governing: The Military and Political Development in Egypt, Algeria, and Turkey* (Baltimore: Johns Hopkins University Press), 2007, 15.

22. Humphreys, *Between Memory and Desire*, 146.

23. Murtaza Hussain and Marwan Hisham, "Syria's 'Voice of Conscience' Has a Message for the West," *The Intercept*, October 26, 2016, https://theintercept.com/2016/10/26/syria-yassin-al-haj-saleh-interview/.

24. Tarek Masoud, *Counting Islam: Religion, Class and Elections in Egypt* (New York: Cambridge University Press, 2014), 31.

25. Ibid., 6.

26. Ibid., 23.

27. Ibid., 23.

28. Ibid., 32.

29. Wickham, *Mobilizing Islam*, 120.

30. Masoud, *Counting Islam*, 47.

31. Ibid., 59.

32. Amr Adly, "Egypt's Regime Faces an Authoritarian Catch-22," Carnegie Middle East Center, July 21, 2016, http://carnegie-mec.org/2016/07/21/egypt-s-regime-faces-authoritarian-catch-22-pub-64135.

33. Walid Shawky, "How the Margins Became the Center: On Protest, Politics and April 6," *Mada Masr*, November 25, 2016, http://www.madamasr.com/en/2016/11/25/opinion/u/how-the-margins-became-the-center-on-protest-politics-and-april-6/.

34. Rory McCarthy, "Re-Thinking Secularism in Post-Independence Tunisia," *The Journal of North African Studies* 19, no. 5 (2014): 3.

35. Ibid., 7.

36. Monica Marks, "Purists vs. Pluralists: Cross-Ideological Coalition Building in Tunisia," in *Tunisia's Democratic Transition in Comparative Perspective*, ed. Alfred Stepan (New York: Columbia University Press, 2017), 3. Marks points out that the most effective opposition to cross-ideological cooperation between Islamists and secularists often came from the most vehement Tunisian secularists, and that intra-secularist debate about the appropriate approach to Islamists was longstanding (pp. 3, 8). In short, secularism is a varied and potent political force in Tunisia.

37. Ibid., 5.

38. Quoted in Marks, "Purists vs. Pluralists," 27. Marks suggests that Ennahda has sought to push forward Anglo-American understandings of secularism in contrast to the much more rigid approach of French laïcité.

39. Monica Marks's chapter in this volume, "Tunisia's Unwritten Story."

40. Shawky, "How the Margins Became the Center: On Protest, Politics and April 6."

41. Masoud, *Counting Islam*, 127.

42. Ibid., 147. Masoud's statistical research has also produced counterintuitive results with respect to voter preferences and perceptions. While many Islamists have adopted market-based economic policies, "Egyptians appear to think that Islamists favor redistribution over growth, and they think that Islamists believe that the government is responsible for the welfare of individuals. More important, respondents appeared to think that Islamists are *more redistributive* and *more welfare-statist* than parties such as the NPUR [Nationalist Progressive Unionist Rally], a party that describes itself as 'the party of workers and farmers.'"

43. Ibid., 140.

44. For further discussion of the role of the armed forces in the political transition, see Michael Wahid Hanna, "Egypt's Non-Islamist Parties," 116–20.

45. Hossam Bahgat, "Anatomy of an Election," *Mada Masr*, March 14, 2016, http://www.madamasr.com/en/2016/03/14/feature/politics/anatomy-of-an-election/.

46. Adly, "Egypt's Regime Faces an Authoritarian Catch-22."

47. Ibid.

48. As Abdel-Fatah Barayez argues, "though limited, hard data shows that [the military] is present in many sectors but does not occupy a commanding position in any, and indeed has no presence in a range of crucial economic sectors." (Abdel-Fatah Barayez, "'This Land Is Their Land': Egypt's Military and the Economy," *Jadaliyya*, January 25, 2016, http://www.jadaliyya. com/pages/index/23671/.) Unfounded suggestions that the military controls up to 40 percent of Egypt's economy are presented without factual basis and are unbelievable on their face when considering that Egypt's 2015 GDP was $330.8 billion. During the Mubarak era, the military did seek to "provide senior officers with post-retirement career tracks and financial security, and the armed forces as a whole with major income streams." (Yezid Sayigh, "Above the State: The Officers' Republic in Egypt," *Carnegie Middle East Center*, August 2012, http://carnegieendowment.org/files/officers_republic1.pdf.) But that growing economic role occurred alongside the expanding private sector, which has grown significantly since the introduction of Sadat's economic reforms in the 1970s. (Barayez, "This Land is Their Land.") This is not to suggest benign or fringe impact with respect to the military's economic activity. As Barayez argues, "the current regulatory and legal framework and its rentier repercussions are negatively impacting the cost of investment, the social cost of housing for middle and poorer classes, and the overall question of the access to assets in Egypt." (Ibid.) It is also possible that the impact of the more recent post-Sisi economic shifts and expansion will have a more significant effect on the private sector in the future.

49. Ibid.

50. Ibid.

51. "Egypt Awards Suez Project to Group Including Army," *Reuters*, August 19, 2014, http://www.voanews.com/a/egypt-awards-suez-project-to-group-including-army/2418369.html.

52. Lina Attalah and Mohamed Hamama, "The Armed Forces and Business: Economic Expansion in the Last Twelve Months," *Mada Masr*, September 9, 2016, http://www.madamasr.com/en/2016/09/09/feature/economy/the-armed-forces-and-business-economic-expansion-in-the-last-12-months/.

53. "Egypt's Military to Enter Pharmaceutical Industry," *Reuters*, January 22, 2017, http://www.reuters.com/article/us-egypt-health-military-idUSKBN1560UL.

54. See Khaled Mansour's chapter in this volume, "Egypt's Human Rights Movement: Repression, Resistance, and Co-optation."

55. Amy Austin Holmes, "The Attack on Civil Society Outside Cairo," *Sada*, January 26, 2017, http://carnegieendowment.org/sada/67810.

56. Vincent Durac, "A Flawed Nexus?: Civil Society and Democratization in the Middle East and North Africa," Middle East Institute, October 15, 2015, http://www.mei.edu/content/map/flawed-nexus-civil-society-and-democratization-middle-east-and-north-africa.

57. Mansour, "Egypt's Human Rights Movement."

58. Michael Wahid Hanna, "Public Order and Egypt's Statist Tradition," *The Review of Faith and International Affairs* 13, no. 1 (2015): 23.

59. Koert Debeuf, "The Arab Spring Is Far From Over," *Politico*, January 22, 2017, http://www.politico.eu/article/arab-spring-not-over-repercussions-for-middle-east-region-unrest/.

60. Jadaliyya Egypt Editors, "January 25 at Six," *Jadaliyya*, January 25, 2017, http://www.jadaliyya.com/pages/index/25939/january-25-at-six?mc_cid=3ced8a2e59&mc_eid=0ca285fd1b.

61. "Arab Spring Revisited—The Battle for Democracy in Egypt," *The Economist*, January 25, 2017, https://www.youtube.com/watch?v=DaUR2w0eETc.

3

Reforming Justice

The Failure of Politics and Rule-of-Law Reform in Egypt and Tunisia

NATHAN J. BROWN AND BENJAMIN HELFAND

Despite high expectations at the onset of the uprisings, the disconnect of judicial and legal institutions from the political process left them unable to push for reform (or sometimes even uninterested or hostile to it). This disconnect and its consequences were especially pronounced in the trajectory of Egypt's judiciary since 2011, and in the politics that engulfed Tunisia's truth commission. As a result, calls for rule of law and legal reform proved broad but shallow, and have largely been pushed aside. For different reasons, Egypt and Tunisia were considered especially promising testing grounds for constitutional and legal reform, so their medium-term failure provides a particularly daunting precedent for the Arab region.

In 2011, uprisings throughout the Arab world garnered attention and admiration not only for what they were against—they called for the fall of the "regime" even though the regime being targeted varied—but also what they were for. There were, of course, many agendas at work in the upheavals, but in all countries there was a diffuse demand for a different kind of politics—one in which the holders of authority were accountable to those whose lives they ruled. Thus there was an early focus by activists leading the uprisings on constitutional reform, transitional justice, and the rule of law. For anybody who had been following political debates in the societies for the previous decade or two, the support for such ideas was no surprise; they had been the focus of growing discussion for years. The only surprise was their transformation from diffuse hopes to mass demands.[1]

Yet more than five years later, few of those demands have been met. And the problem may be precisely in the fact that they were diffuse hopes: diffuse in the sense that they were everybody's wish but nobody's priority; and hopes in the sense that they were aspirations that did not cohere around a specific program or agenda. In the initial enthusiasm of the uprisings, it was not yet clear how widely the various camps diverged or how disparate some demands were. And as post-uprising politics unfolded, various groups were able to pursue their own visions of how the state and regime should be reshaped, often forgetting their earlier commitment to reforming the rule of law, or pursuing only those parts of reform that were consistent with their partisan or short-term objectives.

The diffuse hopes were not extinguished, however. Their ability to attract diverse supporters may have been shattered and their mass appeal lost in the disillusioning political environment in the Arab world today, but pockets of support for reform remain. The inability of those pockets to find political traction will likely mean that issues connected with the rule of law will continue to fester unaddressed, with comprehensive reform proposals the province of perceptive but politically isolated specialists.

Such appears to be the case in Egypt, where demands for justice have given way to renewed forms of repression. And it is even true in Tunisia, where efforts at transitional justice have stalled due to fierce political opposition and a lack of widespread citizen engagement with the transitional justice process. Political opposition has impeded Tunisia's transitional justice efforts at every step of the process, from the design phase to the truth-telling and investigation efforts of the Truth and Dignity Commission.

Prior to 2011, it was possible to develop general ideas about how to build the rule of law that could attract principled support. But after 2011, the various political forces at work did not feel they had the luxury of acting on such a principled consensus. These forces prioritized their own vision of reform, sometimes leading them to postpone any attempts at reform and sometimes leading them to pursue only those aspects that served their partisan or institutional interests. This was not necessarily an indication that verbal support for reform was a cynical ruse. Instead, it was much more a sign that the cause of reform must be pursued through—and not outside of—a political process. That process did lead to some changes in both countries. But in Egypt, it led to a renewed authoritarianism in which the judiciary won some concessions to its vision of reform but only because it was a part of the resurgent authoritarianism; in Tunisia it led to the development of a legal and institutional framework to support transitional justice but one that has since been orphaned and may not have the political support it needs to pursue the task.

Egypt: Judges Win but Reform Loses

Perhaps the most promising ground for a real reform wave was in Egypt, where in the decade prior to the 2011 uprising a group of judges had developed some concrete proposals, and intellectuals and opposition movements had begun to develop parallel ideas. Those ideas were ready-made for the wide array of political parties, intellectuals and leaders active during the period of revolutionary politics that peaked from 2011–12. As Egyptian political forces availed themselves of this legalistic reform agenda, judges, lawyers, and watchdog groups played direct roles in establishing or advising a shifting array of political parties and revolutionary groups. The existence of a broad set of actors advocating rule-of-law reform appeared to give the uprising itself a legalistic voice.

The proposals combined the platitudinous (an end to corruption), the backward-looking (trials of old regime figures), and the highly specific (strengthening of the Supreme Judicial Council), depending on the speaker. But they were all cast in legal language. And they did not lack sincerity. Many showed deep sophistication. But while many of these elements could have been unified into a reform program that was comprehensive, the polarizing politics of the post-uprising period dissolved the apparent consensus into warring factions. As the struggle among factions grew bitterer, Egypt's judiciary emerged as an interest group clearly distinct from the other political constituencies empowered by the fall of Hosni Mubarak. Judges boasted real accomplishments in the tumultuous environment but their victories can hardly be seen as triumphs for accountability and the rule of law.

Seeking Independence Prior to 2011

The Egyptian judiciary had always retained some degree of autonomy; Egyptian regimes anxious for specific legal rulings tended to operate through writing authoritarian laws and setting up special courts rather than completely subduing the regular judiciary. Of course, this autonomy was very much incomplete: there were ways in which the judiciary was kept under a watchful eye, through key appointments (such as the head of the public prosecution or the presidency of the Supreme Constitutional Court). But after a full frontal assault on the judiciary in the waning days of Gamal Abdel Nasser's presidency (1956–70), his successors Anwar Sadat (1970–81) and Mubarak (1981–2011) backed off, allowing the judiciary considerable autonomy over internal affairs. And while court judgments rarely affected core regime interests, in the 1980s and especially the 1990s, they began to touch sensitive terrain, forcing the registration of opposition parties, placing balloting under judicial supervision, revamping the electoral system, and throwing out charges against torture victims. The verdicts were sometimes deeply inconvenient for a security-conscious and authoritarian regime. They were made possible by a growing—if quite incomplete—institutional autonomy of large parts of the judicial apparatus. But the rulings were not more than inconvenient. In all these cases, there was generally an alternative for the executive to implement its preferences (for instance, the regime found new ways to manipulate elections beyond the reach of judicial oversight, and it transferred some cases to military courts to get the verdicts it wanted).[2]

Yet elements within the judiciary resented the limitations on judicial independence, both formal and informal, and chafed at the ways in which the executive branch doled out benefits (such as lucrative non-judicial work) to co-opt individual judges and, it seemed at times, the judiciary as a whole. Some judges spoke out publicly; others worked through the Judges Club, an organization that began as a social club in the 1930s but evolved into something like a professional association, to express their unhappiness and draft reform proposals.

In 2005, a reformist wing within the Judges Club came out on top in internal elections and resolved to take up issues that it regarded as unresolved for decades. It focused its attention on a new law of judicial organization that would remove what it saw as the strong fetters on judicial independence. Many of the demands were not new—some had been developed in the 1980s when the reformist wing also had the upper hand. But whereas that earlier effort took place at a time at which the judges could count on intellectual support from some circles, this new effort took place just as some opposition movements (of various leftist, nationalist, liberal, and Islamist coloration) became bolder. The Kifaya movement, a coalition of opposition forces, was willing to move to street demonstrations and public confrontations. This challenged the Brotherhood to show its own willingness to challenge the regime. The opposition groups, often deeply divided and mutually suspicious, competed to embrace the judicial demands and rallied in support of the judges.

A period of cross-fertilization began in which opposition movements and intellectuals across the spectrum picked up on some of the judicial demands, most of which focused on a new law of judicial organization, one that would place judicial matters even more squarely in the hands of judicial bodies. The way in which this would render the judicial apparatus a virtually self-perpetuating body attracted judicial support and provoked nearly no discussion among regime critics, anxious as they were to support a body of actors pushing for reform within the state. Eager to buttress any tool that could limit the domination of the presidency and the security apparatus and hold them accountable to clear legal standards, the opposition movements embraced the judicial agenda with enthusiasm.

The judges were themselves hardly a unified camp. Some of the reformists had Islamist inclinations; others were more liberal or nationalist. Such differences were submerged for the moment. Indeed, with a strong professional ethos barring partisan affiliation, most judges avoided parading their loyalties. Only much later did the extent of the divisions within the reformist camp become clear. And while the reformists had the upper hand in the middle of the decade, its thrust was soon blunted. Some judges did view the reformist wing of the judiciary as excessively political, and the regime itself stonewalled the demands, with the result that the reform wave generated much attention but was able to show few results.

A Moment of Triumph?

But the alliances forged in the middle of the first decade of the twenty-first century did have lasting impact that was not immediately apparent. When the popular uprising of 2011 quickly snowballed and brought down Mubarak, some of the judicial reformers were prominent. And their ideas informed more general calls for various aspects of the rule of law, including accountability of senior officials, ending executive interference in judicial affairs, and constitutional reform. In the enthusiastic atmosphere of 2011, many of those who participated in overthrowing the regime spoke a recognizably legal language when pressing for political reform.

In that heady atmosphere, reforming judges pressed ahead. The Judicial Council and the Judges Club both dusted off the idea of a comprehensive new law of judicial organization and set to work on their separate but similar drafts. The Supreme Constitutional Court managed to convince the governing military council (the body that succeeded Mubarak on an interim basis while a new constitution was drafted) to modify its own law to allow the court to select one of its own senior members as chief justice, writing the president of the republic out of the process. While Mubarak had been willing to allow many state institutions considerable autonomy, he generally kept top appointments within his reach.

Administrative courts acted quickly to dissolve the ruling party of the old regime, the National Democratic Party, and reverse some unpopular economic measures.

Demands to try Mubarak and former regime officials were accompanied by a judicial insistence that any measures be taken in the regular court system. Egyptian judges were accustomed to seeing special court systems established when rule changed hands. Thus suspicious of what those in other societies (including, as we shall see, Tunisia) term "transitional justice," they viewed existing courts as the best body to deal with offenses committed under the old regime.

While upset at a deteriorating security situation that left courtrooms exposed (and sometimes attacked by relatives of those placed on trial), judges seemed poised to get what they wanted, supported by a diverse coalition of revolutionary and reformist actors.

However, the revolutionary coalition's unity proved to be extremely shallow. As it broke apart within months of Mubarak's fall, it robbed judges of any political support for reform—and the chasms opening up in the Egyptian polity infected the judiciary as well.

The Victory of the Judiciary, but Not of Reform

In the two and a half years after Mubarak's overthrow, Egypt passed through a period of political tumult. A series of referenda and elections delivered an interim constitution, an elected parliament, and an elected president. The country took these steps uncertainly and sometimes haphazardly in an atmosphere of political mobilization, growing polarization between Islamist and non-Islamist forces, deteriorating internal security, and disarray and discontent in state institutions.[3]

In elections, Egyptian politics seemed to be veering in an Islamist direction, with the Muslim Brotherhood winning a plurality of seats in the parliament as well as the presidency. Constitution drafting was assigned to an assembly selected by the Islamist-dominated parliament. Some judges from the earlier reform movement made clear their support for the country's Islamist political direction, with a few accepting leading positions (such as vice president, minister of justice, and chair of the Constituent Assembly, which headed the drafting of a new constitution).

But while some prominent judges sided with the Islamists, important judicial bodies were aligning against them. A judiciary that had seemed divided between reformist and status quo wings soon began fracturing and then coalescing in new ways, with some of the reformists backing the Islamists but others swinging into opposition to the emerging order, sometimes even joining hands with old-regime elements.

In April 2012, the administrative courts dissolved the Constituent Assembly for being insufficiently representative of Egyptian society. The parliament promptly selected a similar body—just in time, it turned out, since the Supreme Constitutional Court dissolved the lower house of the parliament shortly afterwards (on the grounds that the parliamentary election law had unconstitutionally discriminated against independent candidates). The Islamists readied a counterattack by leading demonstrations outside court buildings, increasing presidential powers by decree and pushing the law of judicial organization—but now in a form that would require most senior judges to retire. As Egyptians voted in their country's first genuinely contested presidential election, battle lines had already been drawn between the elected branches of the government, dominated by Islamists, and the unelected judiciary, which styled itself the defender of the Egyptian state against the Islamist intrusion. The anti-Islamist tenor of much judicial politics owed its origin to a number of factors—lingering loyalties to the old regime; fear that the Islamists would be majoritarian in a manner that ran roughshod over legal procedures; resentment that a middle-class movement from outside of the state seemed to be instructing state bodies with their own sense of mission; and some fears of Islamist ideology and agendas.

By 2013, the diffuse consensus of 2011 had completely dissolved. A general support for strengthening the rule of law and judicial independence—and a more specific set of proposals for a new law of judicial organization—had not disappeared but had instead sparked as much disagreement as agreement. The reasons were purely political. As the Egyptian polity fractured, all actors emphasized short-term political maneuvers over more long-term or structural concerns. Thus "judicial reform" became a tool in Islamist hands to subdue recalcitrant courts; their opponents in turn used the issue to claim that Islamists were acting in a dictatorial fashion. Any discussion of institutional change got lost in the crossfire.

Opponents of the Islamists, backed by state actors (including the military and security forces as well as some judges), sponsored massive countrywide demonstrations on June 30, 2013. On July 3 the military moved in to depose the president and suspend the constitution. It installed the chief justice of the Supreme Constitutional Court as interim president while the constitution was revised and new parliamentary and presidential elections were held.

As a result of the coup, judges as individuals and the judiciary as a body emerged in a very powerful position. On an individual level, the interim president was a senior judge; as a new regime slowly formed, judges were assigned to a number of influential positions. Judges had powerful roles in revising the constitution. The speaker of the parliament was a judge. The minister of justice—himself a former judge—emerged as a powerful voice for the new order. On an institutional level, the judiciary received guarantees of independence in the revised constitution, some of which they had sought for a generation (such as authority over the selection of the head of the public prosecution). The agenda judges followed was an Egyptian one; in the xenophobic atmosphere of 2013, few were interested in examining international models of building the rule of law.

But the result was something quite different from what the advocates of judicial reform had long sought. What judges had achieved was not a triumph for general principles related to the rule of law so much as a set of concessions for the judiciary's corporate interests. In the post-coup political environment, a consortium of state institutions—the military, the security services, the judiciary, the religious establishments, and other parts of the bureaucracy—dominated the political environment and recast the state apparatus to vitiate mechanisms of democratic accountability and insulate themselves from external pressures. This explains the odd pattern of clauses in the country's 2014 constitution—while the regular judiciary was given greater independence, the military courts were also given strong autonomy that left them virtually unaccountable to any civilian actor. The military, police, and religious establishments were similarly walled off from any kind of effective oversight. While a parliament was eventually elected, the political environment was so constricted and the electoral law so tilted against political parties that it proved to be a noisy but largely toothless body.

Courts were enthusiastic participants in the new order. Unlike previous episodes of political repression in Egypt, when leaders had to resort to special courts when they needed rapid convictions in large numbers, this time the normal judicial bodies willingly joined in. Terrorism circuits were created by presidential decree but staffed by regular judges and attached to regular courts (a different pattern than the one that emerged under the pre-2011 order in which such cases were divvied up among a group of exceptional courts in order to deliver them to more reliable judges than the ones who staffed the regular courts). There was no clearer sign that, as much as observers spoke of the new regime in personalized terms (as "Sisi's regime," referring to the president, Abdel Fatteh el-Sisi), something much broader was at work. It was the Egyptian state—a set of institutions guided by the presidency and the various parts of the security apparatus to be sure, but also characterized by islands of autonomy, fiefdoms, and stolid structures of authority—that was reasserting itself, not simply a single strongman. The judiciary received clear signals from the presidency but it did not need them to act.

The terrorism courts began delivering a staggering series of mass verdicts against the Brotherhood and its alleged supporters, on occasion even sentencing dead people to execution. And they did so long before Sisi could exercise the presidential tools. Dissidents were hauled in for questioning. Security forces operated with impunity. Courts credulously accepted the flimsy evidence produced by abusive security bodies. And judges who had backed the Islamists were dismissed by other judges.

Egyptian judges generally have a very strong sense of loyalty to the Egyptian state and supporters of the political and social order. As suspicious as they may sometimes be of executive influence, Egyptian judges tend not to behave as freestanding actors mediating between the state and the society or among various social entities, but rather as enforcers of the law and interests of the state, standing above and guiding the society in what they see as a principled fashion. The judiciary as a body shows real willingness to distance itself from the executive, but little interest or willingness to distance itself from the state. And as far as many judges are concerned, that state has just come under severe attack by an alien force. The invaders managed to temporarily seize the presidency; for a while, key institutions of state—including, most shockingly to judges, courts themselves—were quite literally besieged by these outsiders.

Of course, not all judges feel this way, but many do seem to share the sense of crisis that has led perhaps to some of the brutal efficiency displayed when trying some cases. And while judges varied in their enthusiasm for the new order— with senior judges often overturning some of the most egregious judgments and courts continuing to issue occasional verdicts that clearly defied regime wishes— the judiciary as a body made its overall orientation clear. In this respect, it pays to note that it makes far more sense to speak of the partial independence of the Egyptian judiciary than to speak of the independence of an individual judge: Judges are responsible not only to the law and their own consciences but also to each other. While judges may have full authority to reach their own decisions, the frequency of multiple-judge panels, extensive rights of appeal, judicial control over matters of appointments and promotion, and the fact that the judiciary is a lifetime career—and one that is often passed from father to son—combine to give the judiciary a very strong sense of corporate identity.

The movement for judicial reform that had attracted such broad backing revealed itself to be a very weak if broad coalition. Islamists, liberalists, nationalists, leftists, and judges had all called for judicial reform. All agreed that meant an end to executive control over the judiciary. But some sought this independence because the executive was in hands other than their own, while others sought to end torture, abuse, and corruption through stronger legal mechanisms. Some judges in the reformist camp sympathized with these rule-of-law goals but most wished above all to realize corporate autonomy and secure professional goals.

The diversity of the proreform coalition was scarcely visible as long as the Mubarak regime was the main adversary. But it became rapidly clear after Mubarak fell. It was not that the demand for reform was insincere or shallow but that the word reform meant different things to different people. This can be seen most clearly in the matter of judicial personnel. For judges, reform meant that they would be able to staff, police, and patrol their own ranks, without a meddlesome executive branch using its various tools to create a pliant judicial body. In the period before Mubarak, this vision was one that opposition forces were willing to support. But after 2011, Islamists in particular came to feel that reform must also include purging senior judges too close to the old regime or too resistant to the democratic (and Islamist) order they saw emerging. Some non-Islamist revolutionaries saw the judiciary as a bastion of privilege and conservative thinking. Their reform ideas were rarely developed into concrete proposals, but they likely would have included a purge of a different sort.

These various orientations made for a coherent set of demands but a very disparate coalition that politics soon pulled sharply apart. The judges, part of a resurgent state apparatus, got much of what they desired. Their conception of the rule of law was one in which they, as legal professionals and specialists, were allowed to operate without the kibitzing of other institutions and forces, much like a heart surgeon is able to operate without an anxious family gathered around his or her side. Such an analogy would not have resonated with those who wanted state structures to be more accountable to the people rather than to their corporate sense of mission, but for the time being at least, those who voice alternative orientations have been silenced.

Tunisia: Transitional Justice Struggles to Find Supporters

In Tunisia, the ground appeared to offer a more promising basis for genuine legal reform, since there was something approaching a democratic transition and the question of judicial reform was wrested out of the judiciary's hands. Unlike Egypt's transitional leadership, Tunisia's transitional politicians and domestic civil society groups did not reject study of other nations' transitional experience. Instead, the joint efforts of domestic and international civil society groups and the Tunisian legal community drove judicial reform. These groups were responsible for the establishment of Tunisia's transitional justice project and its engine, the Truth and Dignity Commission (TDC), in December 2013.[4] The completion in June 2016 of the TDC's truth-telling collection project (the first of five components), which included the collection of more than sixty-five thousand files related to human rights abuses, marked a major milestone for the commission as it continued to pursue its duties.

Despite this seeming success, however, intense political opposition has plagued the TDC, which compounded by a failure to construct a broad-based constituency in the Tunisian public. Although the commission initially enjoyed the political backing of Tunisia's transitional government, that support was quickly eroded following Tunisia's 2014 parliamentary elections, as political forces expressly opposed to the TDC's work took power. Simultaneously, a series of commissioner resignations rocked the TDC, further damaging the commission's legitimacy, which was already suffering from an inability to meet the high expectations of the Tunisian public. Facing strong political opposition and on the verge of a crisis of legitimacy, the TDC failed to win buy-in from many Tunisians because it did not engage in an effective public outreach campaign. This aggregation of factors has pushed Tunisia's transitional justice process to the verge of collapse in just two short years, as the country's dominant political actors have little interest in pursuing any form of revolutionary accountability.

Many transitional justice processes take decades before the full effect of their work comes to fruition. For example, the aims of Argentina's truth commission, which investigated the abuses of the country's 1976–83 military dictatorship, were only realized more than a decade after the commission published its final report in 1984.[5] Yet even slow-moving processes such as Argentina's tend to creep decidedly forward from their inception. In Tunisia, however, the transitional justice project seems to be crashing against the shoals of politics just two years after it got started, in large part because it has political support from neither the government nor the Tunisian public at large. Such support would be crucial, especially now, for the commission's efforts to pursue any measures aimed at achieving accountability, justice, and rule of law reform.

Transitional Justice in Theory

The phrase "transitional justice" has come to have a particular set of meanings in international parlance about governance and the rule of law: "the array of processes designed to address past human rights violations following periods of political turmoil, state repression, or armed conflict" as well as the advancement of the rule of law.[6] Although lacking any single agreed-upon definition, "rule of law" is generally understood to involve adherence to well-known rules or laws that restrict arbitrary government action.[7] Transitional justice processes are inherently political: they seek to transform how a society understands what constitutes justice, and to present a particular conception of what the state and its institutions should look like. Transitional justice gained currency as a paradigm during Latin America's transitions from dictatorship to democracy in the 1980s, and played a prominent role in South Africa's post-Apartheid transition. Following the fall of the Soviet Union, transitional justice was at the forefront of Eastern Europe's transitions to democracy and has continued to play an important role in the transitional efforts of Burundi, Ivory Coast, Kenya, and Sierra Leone. It is because transitional justice efforts are intended to redefine a society's conception of justice that they are inherently political processes.[8]

Tunisia's transitional justice agenda developed through the joint efforts of international organizations and Tunisian civil society groups including the International Center for Transitional Justice (ICTJ), an organization that specializes in assisting countries in implementing transitional justice measures.[9] This agenda grew out of an international conference convened in Tunis in April 2011 to determine the most suitable transitional justice mechanisms for addressing the past in Tunisia.[10] Many of the Tunisian civil society participants in this conference later contributed to the work of the National Transitional Justice Consultation process in 2012, with several of these organizations sitting on the technical committee that authored the first draft of Tunisia's transitional justice law, the Organic Law on the Organization of Transitional Justice Foundations and Area of Competence.[11] From its conception in late 2011, Tunisia's civil-society-driven transitional justice process was an ambitious project broadly consisting of five components: truth telling, the provision of reparations to victims, criminal accountability for the perpetrators of serious crimes, institutional reform, and reconciliation.[12] Notably, prior to the 2011 revolution, Tunisians had little faith in their legal system and understood the judiciary to function as an instrument of the regime.[13] According to Mohamed Salah Ben Aissa, Tunisian Minister of Justice in both the post-2011 interim government and for a period of eight months in the government of the current president, Beji Caid Essebsi, the Tunisian legal system by the end of the Zine El Abidine Ben Ali's presidency (1987–2011) "did not enjoy the public's trust and the judiciary was in a state of crisis."[14]

At its core the TDC seeks to build the rule of law and restore citizen faith in state institutions, serve as a mechanism to transform how Tunisians conceive the rule of law, and demonstrate that the law can protect rights and freedoms.[15] Mostapha Bazaaoui, president of the TDC's committee on Functional Review and Institutional Reform, described the primary aim of Tunisia's transitional justice project as the establishment of "a culture of forgiveness without forgetting the past . . . by seeking reconciliation and not revenge."[16] Similarly, Salwa El-Gantri, the head of the Tunis office of the ICTJ, described to us Tunisia's transitional justice project as a rule-of-law initiative, at the center of which must be the trials of individuals accused of committing gross violations of human rights before and during the revolution.[17] Yet rather than being the cornerstone of a new order, the TDC supporters and critics have clashed over everything from the appointment of commissioners to the commission's economic corruption component. Centrist and leftist political groups have characterized the TDC as Islamist-dominated, even as other critics say the commission is too motivated by those same parties—including the ruling party, Nidaa Tounes—and civil society groups engaged in transitional justice efforts. Along with the current government's efforts to dismantle the commission's economic corruption component project, this all threatened to derail the transitional process entirely.

The TDC's struggle to fulfill its mandate can be understood as a product of three factors. First, the TDC has failed to generate broad public engagement. Second, the circumstances of the TDC's creation allowed critics to portray it as politically motivated. And third, Nidaa, a political party that draws some of its membership from old-regime figures, views the TDC as a threat, and has used its control of the government to stymie the commission.

A Disconnect between the Tunisian Public and the Truth and Dignity Commission

The TDC was established by a group of Tunisian civil society organizations with the support of the Tunisian legal community, and international nongovernmental organizations including the ICTJ, the Tunisian Center for Transitional Justice, and the Tunisian Network for Transitional Justice. As the creation of several specialized organizations, the TDC initially struggled to present the important nature of its work to the Tunisian public in a convincing manner.

This allowed the Tunisian public and the commission to grow disconnected. The disconnect has been exacerbated by the difficulty the TDC has had in mobilizing the Tunisian public and civil society organizations to support its work and is directly responsible for transitional justice fading from the mainstream view in Tunisia.[18] Initially, many Tunisians expressed high hopes for what the TDC would be able to achieve, expecting the commission to pursue prosecutions of former regime officials responsible for committing rights violations, establishing unrealistic expectations for what the commission would be able to accomplish in its early years. The TDC received three thousand complaints in its first month of operations and twelve thousand complaints between December 2014 and May 2015. But as the TDC became embroiled in turmoil following an opaque commissioner appointment process and the resignation of four commissioners—just a year after its inauguration—its legitimacy came under threat. Tunisians began to lose faith in the TDC because of its sluggish pace and its failure to combat corruption.[19]

Political projects require constituencies if they are to be successful. The TDC's failure to generate such a constituency originated with the opaque nature of the commissioner selection process, which lacked significant public involvement. The commission also did not obtain the formal support of civil society groups during the appointment process, because the Troika—the coalition of two secularist parties and the Islamist Ennahda, which governed from mid-2011 until 2014—had politicized it.[20] All of this created an environment where transitional justice faded from view for many Tunisians.

The TDC's insufficient engagement with the public has created a situation where many Tunisians, especially those living in more remote parts of the country, do not fully understand its purpose. For instance, some Tunisians mistakenly believe that the commission has prosecutorial powers, when its mandate is essentially to document the past, creating unrealistic expectations of what the TDC is capable of achieving.[21] Although the commission did travel throughout Tunisia to gather testimonies from individuals who suffered abuse at the hands of the former regime, it lacked a robust communication and public outreach program, and confusion grew about its function. And even more broadly, the TDC lacks the broad-based constituency, among individuals in government and in the public at large, required for its efforts to expose the truth about past human rights violations, institutionally reform components of Tunisia's governmental structure, and to lay the foundation for the eventual prosecution of serious human rights violators. The TDC also suffers from a severe lack of support amongst the current government. Nidaa's membership is connected to the former regime and has little desire to disturb the economic status quo, or pursue accountability for economic and political crimes committed during the dictatorship.

The Politicization of the TDC

The original legislative design for the TDC was based on a model that sought to be nonpolitical, and included an appointment procedure allowing each political bloc in the Chamber of Deputies to appoint one member to the TDC's commissioner selection panel.[22] However, when the draft transitional justice law was presented to the Ennahda-led government in December 2013, the appointment procedure was altered to allow membership on the selection panel to be determined via proportional representation in the Chamber of Deputies.[23] This was in part a result of the positions of Ennahda's Troika partners, the two secular parties Ettakatol and the Congress for the Republic (CPR), the latter being the most pro-revolutionary party in the National Constituent Assembly (NCA). Ettakatol and CPR fought hard in December 2014 for the inclusion of an electoral lustration provision in the transitional justice law, which would have prohibited politicians affiliated with the old regime from becoming candidates for office. Many Ennahda parliamentarians originally supported the lustration provision, though the party's leaders ultimately prevented its inclusion.[24]

Still, Ennahda supported a proportional appointment procedure for the TDC because, like its Troika partners, it wanted to capture the transitional justice process by appointing individuals with close ties.[25] It is also possible that Ennahda was attempting to improve the likelihood that Islamists targeted under the regime would receive reparations, many of whom were potential constituents.[26] Ennahda's politicization of the TDC appointment procedure was a last attempt by the Troika to influence the transitional justice process before ceding power following the 2014 parliamentary elections, in which Nidaa won a plurality running on an explicitly anti-Islamist platform. In practice this change allowed Ennahda to appoint a plurality of the members on the Commissioner selection panel, reinforcing civil society groups' fear that Ennahda would dominate the transitional justice process and that the TDC would be an Islamist project.[27] Ennahda and its coalition partners in the NCA viewed this revised legislative design as an opportunity to exert greater influence over the commissioner appointment process. Instead, the effect of this legislative change was to alienate a number of civil society groups and deprive the TDC of their support and partnership, precisely because these groups felt the TDC would be an Islamist-dominated venture. To understand Ennahda's posturing during the debate over Tunisia's transitional justice law, it is necessary to know something of Ennahda's history of persecution by the former regime, and its desire to seek revolutionary justice—while simultaneously fending off secularist fears that Ennahda was nothing more than Tunisia's rendition of Egypt's Muslim Brotherhood.

Furthermore, Tunisia's transitional justice law was promulgated following the political assassinations of Chokri Belaid, a prominent lawyer and leftist politician, and Mohamed Brahmi, a member of the NCA. This political violence damaged an already tense relationship between the secular and Islamist members of the NCA. The appointment of a former deputy in the Ben Ali regime to serve as a commissioner on the TDC only further enraged civil society groups, prompting the Tunisian Network of Transitional Justice and two other transitional justice NGOs to challenge the appointment process before Tunisia's administrative court.[28] The court rejected their petition, prompting several civil society groups to express opposition to the construction and establishment of the Truth and Dignity Commission.[29]

Political Opposition

The TDC has faced significant political opposition to its work since Nidaa came to power in Tunisia's 2014 elections. In a campaign that focused on the Ennahda-led government's political shortcomings, Nidaa promoted itself to Tunisian voters as the competent, secular alternative. Despite Ennahda's electoral success in the 2011 elections for the NCA, many Tunisians blamed the party for the country's fragile security and faltering economy. Following the overthrow of the Muslim Brotherhood-led government in Egypt and the assassination of Belaid and Brahmi—both prominent Tunisian leftist politicians—Ennahda willingly moderated its support for revolutionary reforms. But in taking a more conciliatory posture to remain politically viable, Ennahda allowed transitional justice to entirely fade from its political agenda. Things became even more complicated, however, after Nidaa took power and the fragile coalition upon which it was founded began to fragment over ideological differences, particularly Nidaa's decision to form a coalition government with Ennahda.[30] Prior to the 2014 elections, Nidaa united various secular groups on the basis of their joint opposition to the Troika. Following the Troika's collapse, Nidaa itself began to fracture due to ideological differences and internal power dynamics. In January 2016, tensions within the secular Nidaa party culminated with the resignation of more than two-dozen legislators and cost Nidaa its plurality in parliament. This shift in political power, combined with Tunisia's struggling economy, and a slew of terrorist attacks in sum drained the political momentum from the transitional justice agenda.[31]

Furthermore, Essebsi and TDC president Sihem Bensedrine have clashed over the TDC's investigatory powers. In December 2015, Bensedrine attempted to collect the presidential archives from the presidential palace. A contingent of armed police prevented her entry to the palace compound. This failed attempt only amplified the animosity between the TDC and Essebsi, who viewed Bensedrine's efforts as an assault on the presidency. The blocking of the TDC's investigation also caused many Tunisians to feel that there was a wider effort by some figures—including Nidaa and Essebsi—to bury their past involvement in the regimes of Habib Bourguiba (president 1956–1987) and Ben Ali. (Essebsi was once the director of national security and later minister of the interior under Bourguiba.)[32]

And Nidaa's opposition to the TDC was indeed partly an attempt to insulate members of the economic and political elite from legal repercussions for their former connections to the Ben Ali regime. But this is not the whole picture. Nidaa is a coalition of secular groups, many of which were divided before the revolution and continue to be divided as the unifying threat posed by Ennahda has subsided.

In an interview with *The Guardian,* Bensedrine lamented that while "Truth commissions around the world [have] the state on their side. . . . We may be the one case where the state is going against us; it is a paradox."[33] Bensedrine's comments encapsulate the lack of political support that exists for Tunisia's transitional justice project. Nidaa has worked to impede the ability of the TDC to conduct its mission, attempting to quash its budget and stifle the political will required for significant systemic change.[34] In July 2015, the Essebsi government proposed a draft economic reconciliation law that would have directly undermined the TDC's economic corruption component by precluding the TDC from acting as a mediator in cases of economic crimes. The TDC's mediation process authorizes the TDC to draft arbitration agreements between individuals responsible for economic crimes and their victims. In return for reparation payments and publication of the settlement, the perpetrator is granted amnesty for any related criminal charges.[35] The law would supersede the commission's mandate, establishing an opaque process controlled by the presidency to provide amnesty to former public servants and businessmen involved in the embezzlement of state funds.[36] Although this draft economic reconciliation bill has not yet become law (and was shelved as of November 2016), it demonstrates the fierce political resistance the TDC faces from the Essebsi government.

Ennahda, which currently holds a plurality in the Tunisian Parliament, has thus far declined to support the work of the TDC, siding with Nidaa against the commission. Ennahda's leadership perceives the party's place as being within the current coalition government, and has adopted a consensus-seeking agenda aimed at maintaining the status quo. Ennahda has pursued this consensus-oriented strategy on the basis that it is necessary for a successful democratic transition.[37] In line with this stance, Ennahda has supported draconian new anti-terror legislation as well as the Nidaa-backed economic reconciliation law, which is aimed at undermining the TDC. Ennahda's leadership appears to view inclusion in the current coalition government as the best protection against the risk of a return to oppression, and thus far the party has supported policy in line with this vision. Simply put, it appears that the current government has little interest in pursuing accountability for serious human rights violations and economic crimes committed under the Bourguiba and Ben Ali regimes in the immediate future.[38]

On paper, Tunisia has established a robust transitional justice project designed with the intention of bringing about serious political, economic, and institutional reform. Yet in practice this process and the institution central to its success, the TDC, has been hampered by an internal failure to cultivate widespread public support and intense political opposition by the very political forces responsible for its development. Following the revolution, the Troika's transitional government engaged in a sincere effort to pursue rule-of-law reform, as well as revolutionary justice and accountability. They adopted one of the most progressive constitutions in the Arab world and established a robust transitional justice initiative. These two accomplishments, combined with Tunisia's general success at transitioning to a more inclusive and democratic system of government, distinguished the country's experience from that of Egypt. But as the realities of post-revolutionary governance set in and Tunisia's transition came under threat from a series of terror attacks, the quest for accountability was one of the first revolutionary demands jettisoned by Ennahda as it sought to remain politically salient and stave off the potential for a soft coup (as happened in Egypt). The fear of a resurgence in support for authoritarianism further quieted any calls for accountability and transitional justice as Tunisia's political elites sought to protect their already established democratic gains and maintain the status quo. For Ennahda the status quo meant retaining its political relevance, whereas for Nidaa the status quo entailed protecting the perceived legitimacy and economic supremacy of its membership. These distinct agendas fostered a political environment where transitional justice, rule of law, and accountability were shelved in favor of policies intended to induce stability and economic recovery.

However, if Tunisia's nascent democratic order evolves into a stable, full-fledged democracy, the TDC's efforts could have a broader impact than what observers have predicted. And there are some positive indicators of the potential for future reform. In October 2016, Tunisia transformed its Supreme Judicial Council, the country's highest judicial authority, into a body elected by members of the legal profession. The election of the council's members is intended to insulate it from executive control, while preventing the judiciary from exercising exclusive control over its domain, as is the case in Egypt. However, the council's full impact on rule-of-law reform efforts remain to be seen and will likely not be felt until it appoints the members of Tunisia's Constitutional Court.

Although the TDC has faced significant political challenges since its inauguration, it is important to remember that it can take decades for a truth commission's work to bear fruit for transitioning societies. But unless Tunisia's leading political forces make justice, rule-of-law reform, and accountability for past crimes the focal point of their vision for the future—a dubious outcome given the current political climate—the TDC is unlikely to achieve its lofty ambitions of revolutionary justice and accountability.

Conclusion

The Arab uprisings of 2011 were remarkable for their legalistic overtones and their demands for the rule of law and official accountability. Yet the disparity between the initial calls for reform and the eventual outcomes tells an important story of how reform movements can be co-opted and deflected by political actors who pursue their own political ends. It also shows how even widespread demands can be subject to the political winds of the societies in which they operate. Most of all, it shows that "reform" is not a single thing but instead a cause championed by those with disparate agendas. Similarly, "rule of law" is not a readily identifiable way of doing things, but rather an umbrella term for a host of ideas on the role that law and courts should play in society.

To be sure, there is at the core of the "rule of law" an idea that authority must articulate clear and fair standards, that it should do so in terms that are publicly expressed in legal form, that it should not discriminate or serve partisan interests, and that officials exercising authority are themselves accountable to legal standards that they cannot manipulate for their own ends.

Few would quarrel with such an idea, but the various forces at work in Egypt and Tunisia seized on to various parts of it rather than the whole. For Egyptian judges, reform has come to mean a decrease in interference from outside forces (whether from other state institutions or political or social groups). For Egyptian Islamists and some revolutionaries, the rule of law came to mean that state officials (including judges) need to follow the will and interests of the people (or the instructions of God, which for many Islamists are the same). For the leaders of the Egyptian state, it means that law must serve those who provide order for the society. For Tunisian political forces, the rule of law is a desirable long-term goal, but one that has been overtaken by short-term concerns. For their part, Tunisian advocates of transitional justice do understand that the rule of law is a goal that needs to be achieved in full, and that it requires patient long-term work.

The coalition supporting legal reform in Egypt had a well-articulated agenda before 2011, but the opportunity to implement that agenda after Mubarak fell was squandered as the coalition came apart in a suspicious and polarized environment. In Tunisia as in Egypt, efforts at rule-of-law reform have been largely compromised and deflected by political actors seeking to secure their personal, partisan, or institutional interests. However, unlike Egypt, the political space in Tunisia was initially more conducive to at least starting real reform, and resulted in the promulgation of a progressive constitution and a transitional justice project driven by the rule of law. But as that political space evolved and the Islamist-led transitional government lost power, reform initiatives that had appeared to have widespread support were no longer able to maintain political traction, reducing their constituencies to the isolated policy specialists responsible for their development. The frustration of transitional efforts in Tunisia is a prime example of what happens when expert-driven rule-of-law reforms fail to gain the political support of those in power, while also having little pull with recalcitrant officials.

Reform initiatives that focus on the rule of law are inherently political. In both Egypt and Tunisia, the influential forces that emerged following each country's uprising were able to latch on to the idea of rule of law, both out of a real desire to see such reforms implemented but also for their political expediency. Yet once these reforms were no longer politically advantageous to the emerging leadership, attempts to implement them faltered. Both countries illustrate the stark reality that such political support is immensely difficult to cultivate and sustain.

Notes

1. Nathan J. Brown, "Constitutional Revolutions and the Public Sphere," in *The Arab Uprisings Explained: New Contentious Politics in the Middle East*, ed. Marc Lynch (New York: Columbia University Press, 2014), 296–312.

2. For explorations of judicial politics in Egypt, see James Rosberg, "Roads to the Rule of Law: The Emergence of an Independent Judiciary in Contemporary Egypt" (PhD. diss., Mas-

sachusetts Institute of Technology, 1995); Nathan J. Brown, *The Rule of Law in the Arab World: Courts in Egypt and the Gulf* (Cambridge: Cambridge University Press, 1997); Mona El-Ghobashy, "Taming the Leviathan: Constitutionalist Contention in Contemporary Egypt" (PhD. diss., Columbia University, 2006); Tamir Moustafa, *The Struggle for Constitutional Power: Law, Politics, and Economic Development in Egypt* (Cambridge: Cambridge University Press, 2007); Mahmoud Hamad, "When the Gavel Speaks: Judicial Politics in Modern Egypt" (PhD. Diss., University of Utah, 2008); Bruce K. Rutherford, *Egypt after Mubarak* (Princeton: Princeton University Press, 2008); and Nathalie Bernard-Maugiron, ed., *Judges and Political Reform in Egypt* (Cairo: American University in Cairo Press, 2009).

3. See the collection of essays in Emile Hoyakem and Hebatalla Taha, eds., *Egypt After the Spring: Revolt and Reaction* (New York: Routledge, 2016).

4. See Republic of Tunisia, "Organic Law on Establishing and Organizing Transitional Justice," unofficial translation by the International Center for Transitional Justice, accessed November 29, 2016, http://www.ohchr.org/Documents/Countries/TN/TransitionalJustice Tunisia.pdf.

5. See Tricia D. Olsen, Leigh A. Payne, and Andrew G. Reiter, "The Justice Balance: When Transitional Justice Improves Human Rights and Democracy," *Human Rights Quarterly* 32(2010): 980–1007; Ruti Teitel, ed., *Globalizing Transitional Justice* (Oxford: Oxford University Press, 2015); and Brigitte Weiffen, "The Forgotten factor—the Impact of Transitional Justice on the Development of the Rule of Law in Processes of Democratization," *Zeitschrift für Vergleichende Politikwissenschaft* 6.S2 (2012): 125–47.

6. Tricia D. Olsen, Leigh A. Payne, and Andrew G. Reiter. "The Justice Balance: When Transitional Justice Improves Human Rights and Democracy," *Human Rights Quarterly*, 32, no.4, November 2010: 980–1007.

7. For a more detailed discussion of the "rule of law" concept see Ruti Teitel, "Transitional Jurisprudence: The Role of Law in Political Transformation," *Yale Law Journal*, 106(1997): 2009-80. See also, Eva Bellin, "Building Rule of Law in the Arab World: Paths to Realization," in *Building Rule of Law in the Arab World: Tunisia, Egypt, and Beyond*, ed. Eva Bellin and Hedi E. Lane (Colorado: Lynne Reinner Publishers, 2016), 1–8.

8. Teitel, "Transitional Jurisprudence."

9. International and regional organizations involved in the development of Tunisia's transitional justice process included the ICTJ, the UN Office of the High Commissioner for Human Rights (OHCHR), the Arab Institute for Human Rights, and the Al-Kwakibi Democracy Center. Tunisian organizations involved in the process included the Tunisian League for Human Rights, the Tunisian Center for Transitional Justice, and the Tunisian Network for Transitional Justice. (This list is not exhaustive but meant to identify the kinds of organizations involved in the development of Tunisia's transitional justice process.)

10. This conference, convened by the ICTJ in partnership with the Arab Institute for Human Rights, the Tunisian League for Human Rights, and the UN OHCHR, explored transitional justice measures related to five substantive areas that included criminal accountability for past human rights violations, security sector reform, truth-seeking, gender justice, and reparations. See ICTJ, "Addressing the Past, Building the Future: Justice in Times of Transition," April 14–15, 2011, https://www.ictj.org/publication/addressing-past-building-future-justice-time-transition-conference-report.

11. Also translated as "Organic Law on Establishing and Organizing Transitional Justice."

12. Article 1 of Tunisia's law on establishing transitional justice defines the scope of the country's transitional justice process: "In this law, transitional justice shall mean an integrated process of mechanisms and methods used to understand and deal with past human rights violations by revealing their truths, and holding those responsible accountable, providing reparations for victims, and restituting them in order to achieve national reconciliation,

preserve and document that collective memory, guarantee the non-recurrence of such violations, and transition from an authoritarian state to a democratic system which contributes to consolidating the system of human rights."

13. Mohamed Salah Ben Aissa, "What Independence? Judicial Power in Tunisia," in *Building Rule of Law in the Arab World: Tunisia, Egypt, and Beyond*, ed. Eva Bellin and Hedi E. Lane (Colorado: Lynne Reinner Publishers, 2016), 53–66.

14. Ben Aissa, "Judicial Power in Tunisia."

15. See Articles 2–15 of Tunisia's law on establishing transitional justice, http://www.ohchr.org/Documents/Countries/TN/TransitionalJusticeTunisia.pdf.

16. Mostapha Bazaaoui, interview with Benjamin Helfand, Tunis, January 11, 2016.

17. Salwa El Gantri, who was a program officer at the time we interviewed her, believes that trials, specifically fair trials that lead to the truth, are crucial for restoring citizen trust in a judiciary and legal system that lacks the trust of the majority of the Tunisian citizenry. Salwa El Gantri, interview with Benjamin Helfand, Tunis, January 11, 2016. The centrality of prosecution for transitional justice is somewhat controversial in the field.

18. Amine Ghali (program director for the Al-Kawakibi Center for Democratic Transition), interview with Benjamin Helfand, Tunis, January 10, 2016.

19. Judge Ahmed Ouerfelli (Juridical Advisor to President Moncef Marzouki from 2011 to 2013), interview with Benjamin Helfand, Tunis, January 10, 2016.

20. Rim El Gantri, "Tunisia in Transition: One Year after the creation of the Truth and Dignity Commission," ICTJ Briefing, 2015, https://www.ictj.org/sites/default/files/ICTJ-Briefing-Tunisia-TJLaw-2015.pdf.

21. Salwa El Gantri, interview.

22. The original legislative proposal for the establishment of Tunisia's transitional justice project was drafted by a technical committee made up of five civil society organizations: the Tunisian Center for Transitional Justice, the Al-Kawakibi Democracy Transition Center, the Tunisian Network for Transitional Justice, the Tunis Center for Human Rights and Transitional Justice, and the National Coordination on Transitional Justice. Salwa El Gantri, "The Role of Lawyers as Transitional Actors in Tunisia," Lawyer, Conflict, and Transition Project, August 2015, https://lawyersconflictandtransition.org/themainevent/wp-content/uploads/2014/07/THE-ROLE-OF-LAWYERS-AS-TRANSITIONAL-ACTORS-IN-TUNISIA-ENGLISH.pdf.

23. Salwa El Gantri, interview. See Article 23 of Tunisia's law on establishing transitional justice, which outlines the representation of parliamentarian blocs and parliament members who do not belong to a parliamentarian bloc on the special committee to select members of the TDC.

24. Monica Marks, "Tunisia's Ennahda: Rethinking Islamisim in the Context of ISIS and the Egyptian Coup," Rethinking Political Islam series working paper, Brookings Institution, 2015, https://www.brookings.edu/wp-content/uploads/2016/07/Tunisia_Marks-FINALE.pdf.

25. These individuals included Sihem Bensedrine who is currently president of the TDC and closely linked to Ettakatol. Ghali, interview.

26. Ghali, interview.

27. Salwa El Gantri, interview.

28. Rim El Gantri, "Tunisia in Transition: One Year after the creation of the Truth and Dignity Commission," ICTJ Briefing, 2015, https://www.ictj.org/sites/default/files/ICTJ-Briefing-Tunisia-TJLaw-2015.pdf.

29. Although Article 22 of the Transitional Justice law explicitly states that members of the TDC may not have held a position in the Tunisian government in the period from July 1, 1955 nor have held a partisan responsibility in the dissolved Constitutional Democratic Rally (Ben Ali's political party), the administrative court ultimately rejected the petitions. "The Organic

Law on Establishing and Organizing Transitional Justice," Article 22, http://www.ohchr.org/
Documents/Countries/TN/TransitionalJusticeTunisia.pdf

30. See Scott Williamson, "A Silver Lining in the Nidaa Tounes Split," *Sada Journal*, The Carnegie Endowment for International Peace, 2016, http://carnegieendowment.org/sada/?fa=62624.

31. See Rim El Gantri, "Tunisia in Transition."

32. See Christ Stephen, "Attacks by 'Deep State' Leave Tunisia Truth Commission in Crisis," *The Guardian*, September 11, 2015, http://www.theguardian.com/world/2015/sep/11/attacks-state-tunisia-truth-commission-crisis-democracy. Salwa El Gantri, interview. The Tunisian Committee for the Defense of Victims of Torture filed a lawsuit against Essebsi in March 2012 for his involvement in the repression of the followers of a political rival of then President Bourguiba. In an attempt to insulate members of Nidaa Tounes with connections to the regime, on October 22, 2011, one day before Tunisians elected a National Constituent Assembly to form a new government, the interim government left behind by Ben Ali altered the statute of limitations on torture crimes to fifteen years: enough to consign any wrongdoings on Essebsi's part to the history books. See Mischa Benoit-Lavelle, "Former Prime Minister Beji Caid Essebsi Charged with Torture," *Tunisia Live* (March 2012), http://www.tunisia-live.net/2012/03/16/former-prime-minister-beji-caid-essebsi-charged-with-torture/.

33. Stephen, "Attacks by 'Deep State.'"

34. Alex Djerassi (non-resident associate, Middle East Program, Carnegie Endowment for International Peace), interview with Benjamin Helfand, Washington, DC, March 10, 2016.

35. As of July 1, 2016 the TDC had received 685 requests for economic reconciliation related to government corruption. For a more detailed discussion of the TDC's economic corruption component see "Tunisia: Amnesty Bill Would Set Back Transition," Human Rights Watch, July 14, 2016, https://www.hrw.org/news/2016/07/14/tunisia-amnesty-bill-would-set-back-transition.

36. Rim El Gantri, "Tunisia in Transition," 1; and Scott Williamson, "Transitional Justice Falters in Tunisia," *Sada Journal*, Carnegie Endowment for International Peace, September 22, 2015, http://carnegieendowment.org/sada/?fa=61365.

37. Rory McCarthy, "How Tunisia's Ennahda Party Turned From its Islamist Roots," *The Monkey Cage*, May 23, 2016, https://www.washingtonpost.com/news/monkey-cage/wp/2016/05/23/how-tunisias-ennahda-party-turned-from-their-islamist-roots/?wpisrc=nl_cage&wpmm=1.

38. See Rim El Gantri, "Tunisia in Transition."

Tunisia's Unwritten Story

The Complicated Lessons of a Peaceful Transition

MONICA MARKS

Pundits and analysts have celebrated Tunisia's post-revolution transition as a paradigm for peaceful change. Alone among the Arab countries that rose up in 2011, Tunisia successfully adopted a new political system while maintaining relative stability. The popular story of this transition features high-minded secularist heroes who saved the revolution from the hands of bumbling Islamists. But this narrative is deeply flawed. A close look at the 2013 National Dialogue negotiations reveals a more complicated history. In reality, Tunisia averted disaster because powerful players—including the country's trade union, Islamists, and remnants of the old regime—pursued self-interest in a uniquely Tunisian context that ultimately facilitated compromise. The result has been imperfect: old-regime reactionaries fared far better than is commonly understood, and socioeconomic gains remain elusive. Thus, rather than providing an easily exportable model, Tunisia's National Dialogue carries more complex lessons for other transitions, both within the Arab world and beyond.

The crowning global recognition for Tunisia's fraught but still-floating post-revolutionary political transition came on October 9, 2015. On that day, Tunisia's National Dialogue Quartet—a group of four civil society organizations that negotiated the country through a political crisis in 2013—learned they had won the Nobel Peace Prize.

The announcement came as a much-needed breath of fresh air at a time when hope generated by the 2011 Arab uprisings had been all but extinguished. Egypt's revolution had reversed, giving way to a dictatorship more brutal than before. Libya's transition had unraveled, producing two rival governments and a nearly failed state. Islamic State jihadists, who held territory in Syria and Iraq, had recruited from and conducted terrorist attacks in countries across the region, including Tunisia. And Syria's hemorrhaging of civilian casualties and refugees continued unabated in what had become the worst humanitarian crisis since World War II. Tunisia—the country where a fruit seller's suicide had, less than five years earlier, sparked the Arab uprisings—remained the sole success story of those uprisings, managing to avoid the chaos, authoritarian reversal, and state collapse that had befallen its neighbors.

This was thanks in part to its favorable starting conditions. Tunisia was a comparatively well-educated middle-income country with a strong state, no history of military interventionism, and no major sectarian or ethnic divides. Even before the Arab uprisings, Tunisia's favorable conditions for democratization had prompted some scholars to refer to the "Tunisian paradox." It was a country with strong democratizing potential that was nevertheless a brutal police state under the thumb of a kleptocratic strongman, the autocrat Zine El Abidine Ben Ali (president from 1987 until his overthrow in January 2011). With the revolution, the paradox seemed finally to have been resolved: Tunisia had proved it indeed had the qualities necessary for success.

But the survival until now of Tunisia's transition was also a result of political processes that can't be explained away with such deterministic generalizations about economic development and education levels. Its political elites steered the country back from the brink of catastrophe in Summer 2013, when a political crisis largely of their own making threatened to derail the transition. The Quartet, along with prominent Islamist and old-regime-linked politicians, played a vital role in saving Tunisia's transition that year with an experiment in negotiated crisis management known as the National Dialogue. It was the success of the National Dialogue that prompted the Nobel Committee to award the Quartet the Peace Prize.

Bogus Narratives, Fuzzy Lessons

In the Quartet's Nobel victory, supportive Western onlookers saw a chance to congratulate Tunisians on a transition well-done and to hold up their example as an inspiring model for other Arab countries. Tunisia's transition, however, remained rife with challenges, and the Quartet's role poorly understood.[1]

Despite its importance in an especially dangerous chapter of Tunisia's post-revolutionary transition, few regional experts understood the drivers behind the Quartet's formation or the key interests of its members. In Western capitals that took an interest in Tunisia, such as Brussels, Paris, London, and Washington, the Quartet was widely perceived as an apolitical group of secular civil society actors who had tenaciously forced elected but untrustworthy Islamists to step down from power. The group's Nobel Prize therefore represented a triumph not only for Tunisia's democratic transition, but also for the supposedly secular character of its society. In the eyes of many Western analysts who played a key role in shaping these views, these goals were linked, if not inseparable. Many of these observers had not properly field-tested their assumptions, instead relying on infrequent visits to Tunisia or occasional meetings with prominent Tunisians in Western capitals, where self-justifying accounts from leading Quartet activists often supported their assumptions.[2]

In this way, a beguiling and enduring narrative was born. Inchoate and instinctual, based more on analysts' assumptions than on careful rendering of facts on the ground, it became the standard reading of a story not yet written. It cast the Quartet members—especially the Tunisian General Labor Union (UGTT), Tunisia's powerful trade union and the Dialogue's undisputed standard-bearer—as righteous mediators standing midway between Tunisia's seemingly familiar secular actors and its devil-we-know Islamist political elites. Manifestly political, the Quartet nevertheless appeared in English- and French-language press, and in many analysts' accounts, as unblemished civil society saviors. And that was before they won the Nobel Prize.

The story held that a group of civil society "outsiders," in cooperation with allegedly apolitical technocrats, rescued elected government from incompetent Islamists. More informed but still simplistic versions of the story portrayed the Quartet as apolitical mediators equally opposed to both political Islamists and counter-revolutionary old regime elites. In both these narratives, the heroic Quartet peacefully prodded Tunisia's Islamists out of power without eroding the country's nascent democratic institutions. Tunisia thereby avoided collapsing into chaos, like Libya, or crude coup making, like Egypt. Told this way, the lessons of Tunisia's National Dialogue shone in bold, broad brushstrokes: soft power prevailed.

The trouble is, that's not quite what happened. The 2013 National Dialogue, rather than offering an easily exportable model of how to rescue transitions in danger, had complex origins and destinations rooted in Tunisia's history, its revolution, and its political and institutional relationships. Rather than being framed as a transcendent civil society mediation overcoming a secular/Islamist binary, the National Dialogue should be read as having occupied one pivotal moment in a three-way struggle for power between Tunisia's secular left (embodied by the UGTT), its Islamist center-right (embodied by the Ennahda political party), and a range of political figures and economic elites connected to the old regime. This last group was represented to an important degree by the employers' association (the Tunisian Confederation of Industry, Trade, and Handicrafts, known by its French acronym, UTICA) and elements of Tunisia's now-ruling party, Nidaa Tounes.

This three-way struggle—possible only after the reemergence of the long-suppressed Ennahda party following Ben Ali's ouster—produced in post-revolutionary Tunisia a counterbalancing effect capable of checking excesses of power. Any two actors could offset gains or threats posed by the third. But it also produced a pattern of self-interested positioning in which these groups' political goals have subsumed the pursuit of core revolutionary goals, such as institutional reform and transitional justice.

Though the Quartet certainly deserves praise for its role in resolving the 2013 political crisis, Western reactions to its Nobel generally glossed over these details, revealing a troubling lack of knowledge about the dips and twists of Tunisia's transition. Popular narratives captured basic contours of crisis and resolution, but omitted the context that explained those events. As a result, the story of 2013's political crisis, and the National Dialogue that resolved it, was reduced to a simple case of democracy saved.

In stripping reality of its messy complexities, such shorthand retellings continue to replace more granular understandings of the National Dialogue, more than a year after the Quartet's Nobel victory. Ill-informed narratives have prevented a key chapter of Tunisia's transition from being understood historically on its own terms. Responses to the case of the Quartet's Nobel Prize victory have therefore distilled two wider but linked problems: a tendency to rely heavily on minimalistic, often misleading accounts of events in Tunisia's transition, and an impulse to apply fuzzily understood lessons from Tunisia to other places. This necessarily renders it difficult—if not impossible—to suss out the real lessons from Tunisia's experience that might translate to other transitions in the Arab world and beyond.

Ultimately, the Quartet's Nobel Prize victory, rather than bookending a successfully completed transition, underscored the precious fragility of Tunisia's transitional process, which hinged on recalibrations of power between a triangle of competing political nodes. The 2013 National Dialogue process presents an excellent case study for understanding how this locally specific triangle of actors contested their interests. These actors did ultimately resolve the crisis—but it is crucial to understand that it was a crisis of their own making.

Broadening the lessons of Tunisia's experience to other countries, however, requires a bit more delicacy. First, one must understand the events as they unfolded. The following sections home in on Tunisia's 2013 National Dialogue process as an example of a critical but grossly misunderstood juncture in Tunisia's transition. I then discuss how those self-interested motives interlinked to produce the political crisis of summer 2013, and how the Dialogue resolved that crisis. Finally, I examine what lessons, if any, the experience bears for other countries that are struggling to emerge from authoritarian rule and its aftermath.

An Energized Union Seeks a Larger Role

The Dialogue's initiator and leader was Tunisia's general trade union, the UGTT—a group whose secular unionist values represent many Tunisians, especially those on the left. The UGTT sees its role in society differently than most other trade unions. From its founding in 1946, the UGTT's leaders have seen it as responsible for a special, dual mission: defending the rights of workers, but also—and perhaps more importantly—guaranteeing Tunisia stays on a sovereign, "modern" path.

The organization's history informs its self-understanding: the UGTT coordinated resistance against the French during Tunisia's fight for independence. In the early 1950s, when French authorities arrested Tunisia's nationalist leadership—including its future first president, Habib Bourguiba—the young union, led by its now-iconic founder, Farhat Hached, stepped in to steer the revolutionary cause. Because of its leading role in Tunisia's anticolonial struggle, the UGTT is imbued with a huge amount of historical and popular legitimacy. It has also traditionally seen itself as a kind of nationalist lodestar, a popularly legitimate force that can and should keep Tunisia on a sovereign, secular path. Boasting 750,000 members in a population of just under eleven million, it also holds a powerful political bargaining chip: by calling a general strike, the UGTT can grind the economy to a standstill. It is difficult to overstate how unique a role the UGTT has played in Tunisian society and politics. No other trade union in the Middle East and North Africa region has wielded a comparable level of economic or political influence, and no other trade union can lay claim to such a central role in the anticolonial independence struggle.

Despite its legacy and large membership, the UGTT's leadership was heavily co-opted under Tunisia's first two presidents, Bourguiba and Ben Ali. Ben Ali took co-optation to a new level, buying off the UGTT's top brass with free cars, special access to loans and guarantees of legal immunity should they face accusations of wrongdoing. The famous Gafsa mining basin protests of 2008— which scholars argue presaged and potentially jump-started Tunisia's revolution—began as a local union action against the UGTT's corrupt national leadership.[3] The revolutionary protests of late 2010 and early 2011 reflected this split between the UGTT's corrupt national leadership and its respected, relatively independent role at the local level. Revolutionary protests started from local UGTT headquarters, but some protesters carried signs indicting union bosses' corruption with messages like "RCD, UGTT: corrupt traitors"—a reference to Ben Ali's old party, the Constitutional Democratic Rally (RCD).[4]

After Ben Ali's departure, the UGTT was eager to reestablish its credibility and reassert political influence. At its December 2011 conference, the UGTT ousted its corrupt general secretary, Abdessalam Jrad, and other Ben Ali-era leaders. A reenergized union sought to assert itself as an independent force—one that could powerfully oppose, partner with, or even supervise the role of government.

This new mission created tension between the UGTT and the post-revolutionary Troika government. The Troika, a coalition of three parties, came to power through Tunisia's first democratic elections in October 2011 and was led by Ennahda, a center-right Islamist party that had been banned for decades. Though it formed a coalition with two smaller, mostly secular parties (Ettakatol and Congress for the Republic, or CPR) Ennahda's victory stunned many secularists, pro-union leftists, and political and economic elites.

The UGTT's leadership had long viewed Islamists as a broad and blurry group inherently opposed to modern values. Ideological hostilities ran deep. "Since we were young people at university [in the 1970s and 1980s] we've been fighting for different visions of the state," said Mongi Ammami, an adviser to the UGTT's Secretary General. "Our vision is modern, theirs is seventh-century."[5] Like other UGTT leaders I interviewed who had been imprisoned and tortured alongside Ennahda members under the regimes of Bourguiba and Ben Ali, Ammami (who was imprisoned by the former of the two dictators) tended to consider Islamism the main threat to unionism, rather than old regime authoritarianism. "Bourguiba did what he thought he had to do . . . he defended republican values," Ammami told me in 2014. "But Islamists have a totally different project, khilafa [building a caliphate]. It's a fascist discourse."[6]

UGTT leaders also saw Ennahda as a political competitor intent on dismantling unionism. "At the end of the day, Islamists don't believe in syndicalism," said one nationally prominent UGTT leader during an interview in 2012. "They just want solidarity under God."[7] In the years following Tunisia's revolution, UGTT leaders worried that Ennahda—with the support of supposedly Islamist revolutionary militias, Salafi jihadists, and even some members of its Troika coalition partner CPR— intended to weaken the union by infiltrating it from within and attacking it from without. The UGTT twice held large protests against Ennahda in 2012; in February, in response to garbage dumped outside union offices, and in December, after police fired birdshot on union-backed demonstrators.[8] The UGTT's leaders strongly believed Ennahda was behind these abuses.

The UGTT especially decried the role of the Leagues to Protect the Revolution (LPR), a group that UGTT leaders claimed functioned as Ennahda's militia. The LPR were a complex collection of former neighborhood watch committees formed to provide security in the aftermath of Ben Ali's ouster. As police returned to the streets in spring 2011, many committees simply dissolved. Others continued and set up shop in local RCD offices. Some of these acted as grassroots revolutionary pressure groups. Others morphed into thuggish mafia-style units, using RCD archives, which contained a wealth of potentially incriminating information about many Tunisians, as collateral to blackmail townsfolk. With few exceptions, scholars and journalists neglected interviewing the Leagues.[9] Though there was no evidence to support UGTT leaders' assertion that the Leagues had functioned as Ennahda's shock troops, or its militia, the UGTT's narrative stuck. First Tunisian media and later Nidaa Tounes also helped to spread the story. Western analysts, often sympathetic to the UGTT's secular and pro-labor orientations, would frequently repeat rather than interrogate this narrative.

Ennahda's Growing Mistrust of UGTT

For its part, Ennahda claimed the UGTT was intentionally sabotaging Tunisia's economy to topple the Islamist-led Troika. Ennahda leaders I interviewed throughout 2012 and 2013 described UGTT leaders as leftist provocateurs ideologically prejudiced against Islamists. Many suggested that the UGTT's leaders were intentionally taking a hands-off approach to thousands of wildcat strikes happening throughout the country. Some even claimed that the UGTT, possibly with support from the RCD, was stoking these strikes to make governance an especially impossible job.

Research has suggested that such assertions, like some of the UGTT's claims against Ennahda, are untrue.[10] Yet with the economy in post-revolutionary free fall, Ennahda leaders, thoroughly inexperienced in governing, tended to approach the UGTT with fear and frustration, unsure how to transform what they perceived as obstructionism into constructive collaboration. One crucial mistake Ennahda leaders made was encouraging their supporters to counter-protest at UGTT demonstrations during 2012. Instead of cooperating to solve Tunisia's socioeconomic challenges, the UGTT and Ennahda spent much of 2012 locked in a destructive cycle of competing street protests that directly contributed to Tunisia's 2013 political crisis.[11]

Ennahda placed itself in further opposition to the union by allegedly awarding public administration jobs to its own supporters.[12] Ennahda leaders denied wrongdoing, claiming that winning parties in established democracies often exercise their prerogative to make political appointments. Ennahda's spokesperson Zied Ladhari attempted to discredit the source of these accusations,[13] a man named Abdelkader Labbaoui, president of the Tunisian Union of Public Service and Administrative Neutrality (UTSPNA). Ladhari claimed that Labbaoui was a member of Nidaa Tounes's executive board. Labbaoui fiercely denied these claims and on November 26, 2013 Nidaa Tounes released a statement asserting that Labbaoui did not sit, and had never sat, on its executive board.[14] While critics of Ennahda viewed its alleged administrative stacking as an incontrovertible fact, Ennahda members described these accusations as an unfair but predictable backlash against Ennahda from old-regime-linked elites—whom they described as an entitled class that felt shocked and outraged at Ennahda's victory in Tunisia's 2011 elections.

Aside from UTSPNA's general estimates, little data or qualitative research studies exist that support the claim that Ennahda massively stacked administrative posts, placing incompetent loyalists where skilled technocrats should have been. More research is needed to prove or disprove these claims. Yet there are at least three reasons why Ennahda might have perceived the practice of stacking as conferring certain strategic benefits. The party may have intended the granting of public administrative posts as a kind of ad hoc transitional justice, rewarding its followers for their support during years of persecution. It may also have seen stacking as a step toward creating a usable bureaucracy at a post-revolutionary moment when it perceived Tunisia's administrations as hostile toward Islamists, and rigidly authoritarian in their history and mindset. Finally, Ennahda may have understood stacking as providing a kind of insurance policy should Tunisia's political winds blow in more counter-revolutionary or anti-Islamist directions.

Whatever the rationale, the perception that Ennahda stacked administrative posts brought the party into heightened conflict with the UGTT, which condemned it for threatening the public administration's neutrality. Some prominent members of the UGTT, along with anti-Islamist parties like Nidaa Tounes and the Popular Front, went further, claiming Ennahda was covertly seeking to Islamize the Tunisian state.

UGTT Starts the First National Dialogue to Pressure Ennahda

Escalating tensions between Ennahda and the UGTT played a central role in precipitating the 2013 National Dialogue—a project that began fully one year earlier than most observers realize. The UGTT began what they labeled a "National Dialogue" in June 2012 in an explicit attempt to apply pressure on Ennahda, a party UGTT leaders perceived as jeopardizing both the union's national influence and the "civic" (i.e. secular) character of the state. The summer 2012 National Dialogue formed the basis of the 2013 National Dialogue itself, for which the UGTT and its fellow Quartet mediators won the Nobel Peace Prize.

In the months prior to June 2012, Ennahda—freshly installed in the Constituent Assembly—had engaged in protracted debates over whether or not the word "sharia" should appear in Tunisia's new constitution.[15] These conversations generated identity-based controversy and engendered fears among secular and leftist Tunisians that Ennahda would railroad their views, imposing a majoritarian conservatism on the country.[16] The UGTT's first attempt to call a National Dialogue in summer 2012 was therefore motivated in part by a feeling that the union had a historical obligation to intervene in the protection of secular ideals. Its intervention found strong support among well-established secular civil society organizations that shared its suspicions regarding Ennahda. Two of these, the League of Human Rights and the Bar Association, helped the UGTT convene the 2012 Dialogue. UTICA joined the following year, rounding out what became the 2013 National Dialogue Quartet, which won the Nobel in 2015.

But in the summer of 2012, the National Dialogue initiative faced strong pushback from Ennahda and its coalition partner, CPR, a stubbornly revolutionary human rights-oriented party. Together, Ennahda and CPR believed the Dialogue was an attempt by unelected actors to dictate the democratic political process. They were especially disturbed by the Dialogue's inclusion of Nidaa Tounes, an unelected party heavily driven by ex-RCD money and manpower, which included in its executive bureau a number of leading UGTT figures who shared Nidaa's strong anti-Islamist stance. Ennahda and CPR leadership thus felt that the 2012 Dialogue wasn't a neutral, civil society process, but that it was something much worse: a vehicle for the old regime to exert unelected control on Tunisia's freshly elected government and legislature.[17]

Seeds of a Crisis

Ennahda and CPR's position, however, grew less tenable after a series of destabilizing events, including the September 2012 attack on the U.S. Embassy in Tunis and two high-profile political assassinations in 2013.

The first assassination, on February 6, 2013, targeted leftist politician Chokri Belaid, a vocal critic of Ennahda and long-time defender of trade unionists. Though Islamic State militants eventually claimed responsibility, many secular and leftist Tunisians believed Belaid's assassination proved what they had always suspected: that Ennahda's supposedly "moderate" Islamism masked support for violent jihadist extremism. Since Ennahda's re-entry to Tunisian politics in 2011, they had consistently asserted that Ennahda was using democracy as a tool to establish authoritarian theocracy.[18] Many of these leftists and secularists saw the rise of more visible Salafi tendencies (both violent and nonviolent) in Tunisia immediately following the revolution as reflections of "Islamism" writ large—a movement they felt Ennahda was leading. They made few distinctions between Ennahda's brand of center-right politically participatory Islamism and violent jihadism. The Belaid assassination, therefore, merely confirmed their assumptions. After Belaid's death, thousands massed to accompany his coffin to the Djellaz Cemetary in Tunis, and the UGTT declared a general strike.[19]

The second assassination, on July 25, 2013, was of a lesser-known Arab nationalist member of parliament, Mohamed Brahmi. This killing ground Tunisia's already dragging transition to a standstill.[20] It also set the stage for a dramatic three-way power struggle pitting Nidaa, sometimes in criticism of but often in agreement with the UGTT, against Ennahda. This power struggle birthed the political crisis of summer 2013. Sometimes referred to as the Bardo Crisis (named for the Bardo neighborhood of Tunis in which protesters massed before the Tunisian parliament) it was this upheaval that seriously threatened to topple Tunisia's transition. The Bardo Crisis was not inevitable, but was to a large extent manufactured, inflamed, and exploited by the opportunism and self-interested positioning of competing political elites, including the UGTT.

Old Elites and the Crisis at Bardo

Nidaa, an anti-Islamist party founded in June 2012, was especially well poised to exploit political tensions that, though brewing in 2012, boiled over following the two assassinations. The party was founded by Beji Caid Essebsi, its charismatic, octogenarian founder, who has strong ties to the former regimes. While Tunisia's two best-organized political forces, the UGTT and Ennahda, contributed to the development of these tensions, it was Nidaa that capitalized on them the most.

Though Nidaa enjoyed the support of many Tunisian secularists, leftists and trade unionists, its political machine was, as we have seen, fueled at its core by ex-RCD money and manpower. Members of UTICA, which joined the UGTT-led Quartet in August 2013, represented Tunisia's traditional economic elite, and many had a heavily vested interest in maintaining the status quo ante. Together, these groups represented large segments of Tunisia's old political and economic elite—an elite that felt cheated by the victory of three largely nonestablishment parties in 2011.

For months prior to Brahmi's assassination, Nidaa's leadership had been calling for not just the resignation of the government but also the dissolution of Tunisia's core transitional body: the elected National Constituent Assembly. Essebsi appeared on Tunisian television on February 7, 2013—one day after Belaid's assassination—to demand the Assembly's resignation.[21] Essebsi and other opponents of Ennahda claimed that replacing the elected Constituent Assembly with an unelected group of supposedly apolitical "technocrats" was necessary because the Assembly had overstayed its mandate and was therefore illegitimate. (Incidentally, the Assembly's one-year mandate, which international experts labeled unrealistically short, was created by Tunisia's 2011 transitional government, which Essebsi headed.)

In demanding swift closure of the Constituent Assembly, Nidaa enjoyed the support of its broad anti-Islamist coalition, which included many Tunisian secularists, leftists and trade unionists. Prominent members of the UGTT sat on its executive and political bureaus, and supported Essebsi's push to dissolve the Assembly. Nidaa's demands were also strongly supported by the Popular Front, a coalition of leftist-communist and Arab nationalist parties in which both Belaid and Brahmi had been members. The Popular Front, which also had strong ties to the UGTT, was close to Nidaa Tounes in 2012 and 2013. It held Ennahda responsible for the assassinations, along with former president Moncef Marzouki, a member of CPR. The Popular Front also forcefully supported Nidaa's push to shutter the Assembly.

Despite the importance of support from leftists and some trade unionist quarters, the primary push to shut the Constituent Assembly came from elites within Nidaa Tounes itself—elites often linked to the former regimes of Bourguiba and Ben Ali by profits made and political careers built. Many felt entitled to rule, and were hungry for a chance to take back power.

The July 3, 2013 coup against Egyptian president Mohamed Morsi, a Muslim Brotherhood member, had injected Ennahda's critics with a boost of confidence. Essebsi, who dubbed the coup Egypt's "second revolution," was especially energized. Following the coup, he and other opponents of the Troika government redoubled their calls for Ennahda and its coalition partners to swiftly cede power to an unelected group of supposedly apolitical technocrats.[22]

It was Brahmi's assassination some three weeks later, on July 25, however, that really inflamed public anger. Boosted by opportunistic calls from Essebsi and other political elites, the assassination begat a summer of massive protests and counter-protests that almost succeeded not only in toppling the Ennahda government but also in putting a stop to the transition itself. For weeks in August, anti-Ennahda protesters who supported Essebsi's demands to dissolve the Constituent Assembly met nightly in Bardo Square, just outside the Assembly building, chanting for the government to resign.

Ennahda balked, unwilling to cede its democratically attained power to a nebulous group of Nidaa-friendly technocrats who it feared might reverse Tunisia's democratic transition and possibly reintroduce a Ben Ali-style crackdown that primarily targeted Islamists. Old elites leading Nidaa's attempt at ousting the Constituent Assembly, for their part, claimed that the large numbers of protesters in Bardo Square—who were opposed to Ennahda and broadly supportive of Nidaa—granted them a sort of supra-electoral "street legitimacy" (shar'aiya al-shary'a) that validated a restoration of their power. The competition quickly moved onto nonelectoral turf, with both Ennahda and Nidaa vying to see which party could gather larger groups. The Bardo Crisis drew the entire transition to a halt and threatened to reverse it completely—ousting not only Tunisia's first democratically elected legislative and governmental bodies, but also scrapping its nearly completed constitution and nascent democratic institutions before they had a chance to take root.

The 2013 National Dialogue Quartet Emerges

Against protesters' demands, the UGTT cast itself as a neutral mediator between Nidaa and Ennahda, determined to negotiate a peaceful solution to the Bardo standoff. In August 2013, the UGTT made the surprising decision to invite UTICA, a group whose lobbying on behalf of Tunisia's ownership class had traditionally placed it at loggerheads with the labor union, to form a three-plus-one mediation Quartet leading the Dialogue. Flanked by two of Tunisia's most formidable power centers—the labor union and the employers' association—the Quartet became impossible to ignore.

In September 2013, the Quartet presented Ennahda and Nidaa with a roadmap to resolve their differences. The roadmap rested on a two-way compromise: Ennahda and its Troika partners would leave government completely within the space of just three weeks, while the Constituent Assembly would stay on to complete the constitution and pave the way for Tunisia's 2014 elections.[23]

The UGTT and UTICA, the Quartet's other heavyweight, were not neutral actors. Both overlapped politically and ideologically with Nidaa, and both shared Nidaa's goal of booting Ennahda from power. Yet crucially, under the UGTT's leadership, the Quartet opposed Nidaa's demand of dissolving the Constituent Assembly. Had it decided otherwise, Tunisia's transition would likely be in tatters.

The 2013 political crisis presented the UGTT with an important opportunity to regain status as a national savior, recouping lost credibility after decades of regime persecution and manipulation. The UGTT burnished its reputation both locally and internationally through its successful mediation efforts. The Bardo Crisis also presented the UGTT with a platform on which to display its political and ideological weight. Indeed, though Ennahda ultimately succeeded in negotiating the terms of its exit, the UGTT's chief negotiator Houcine Abassi did not shy from using union power to cajole desired concessions.[24]

Ultimately, the National Dialogue managed to quell the highly politicized three-way struggle that produced Tunisia's 2013 political standoff. The Quartet resolved this impasse without dissolving the Constituent Assembly—a critical decision that helped keep Tunisia's transition afloat. The National Dialogue also forged a fragile consensus among Tunisia's major power players: the UGTT, Ennahda, and Tunisia's traditional political and economic elites, represented jointly by Nidaa and the Employers' Association. Throughout the 2013 Dialogue and the crisis that catalyzed it, each of these groups asserted themselves as powerful forces on Tunisia's post-revolutionary stage, demanding to be integrated—or, in the case of the old elites, reintegrated—into Tunisian politics.

Each point in Tunisia's post-revolutionary power triangle—the trade unionists, the center-right Islamists, and the old regime-linked incumbents—represented a constituency that wanted to secure increased influence on Tunisia's shifting political stage. Trade unionists affiliated with the UGTT counted on their leaders to realize Tunisians' revolutionary demands for economic dignity. Their leaders supported these demands, but also sought to restore the trade union's autonomy and political clout after decades of co-optation at the hands of Ben Ali.

Nidaa and UTICA spoke for Tunisia's traditional political and economic elites—a class that, as we have noted, felt disenfranchised and directly threatened by the results of Tunisia's first democratic nationwide elections in 2011. These incumbents sought a return to portions of the prerevolutionary status quo that preserved their social and economic advantages. They aspired to return Tunisia to the model of autocracy represented by Bourguiba's presidency, which they viewed as classier and less thuggish than Ben Ali's, while still preserving a beneficial ordering of the same oligarchs.

Lastly, Ennahda's leaders spoke for a more conservative, traditionally marginalized lower middle class that played second fiddle, both politically and economically, to the secularized upper middle class that Nidaa represented. Ennahda's constituents, excluded from participation in Tunisian politics for decades under both Bourguiba and Ben Ali, suffered political imprisonment, rape, widespread torture, blacklisting from employment and educational opportunities, and other human rights abuses during the 1990s and the first decade of the twenty-first century. For Ennahda's leaders and supporters, the revolution opened an unprecedented opportunity to secure a seat at Tunisia's political table. Ennahda's constituency therefore saw this post-revolutionary power jockeying as a matter of existential importance. Democracy, they had come to believe, was in their own self-interest. But even as Ennahda made great gains through democratic elections, they feared that old regime incumbents and ideologically opposed leftist unionists would seize any chance to snatch those gains away. The 2013 political crisis and National Dialogue therefore represented a tricky balancing act for Ennahda. But the party's leaders were savvy enough to pursue hard-nosed yet flexibly minimalist positions, opening space for a negotiated settlement. This prevented Tunisia's transition from unraveling in a scenario like Egypt's, and helped maintain the democratic character of Tunisia's transition—something that Ennahda felt served its present and future political self-interest.[25]

The Importance of Reading Forward:
Drawing Lessons from the Dialogue

The lessons of Tunisia's 2013 National Dialogue, like the lessons of its transition as a whole up to this point, are subtler and more contextually specific than popularly acknowledged. International attention, by turning to Tunisia only long enough to register the faint contours of major events like the Quartet's Nobel win or the terrorist attacks of summer 2015, has neglected the full story. Understanding the historicized arc of events is a crucial first step in formulating take-away lessons of Tunisia's transition.

The case of the 2013 National Dialogue process emphasizes the crucial importance of reading key chapters in transitional outcomes not backward, according to the poorly informed narratives of faraway analysts, but starting from the beginning, according to a historically informed consideration of events as they unfolded, and as they were lived by the participants in those events. Reading transitional processes and outcomes in this way reveals the complexities of events: the contingency and reversibility of near-misses, where different outcomes could have been achieved; the competing and sometimes counterintuitive motivations of powerful actors; and the extent to which facts on the ground confirm or contest popular narratives of events.

A Unique Counterbalance

Even at the most propitious periods in their failed uprisings, Egypt, Libya, Syria, Yemen, and Bahrain lacked the institutions, political capacity and structural factors that enabled Tunisia's transition away from outright dictatorship. In Tunisia, a unique triangle of key power players has, throughout the post-revolutionary period so far, managed to negotiate through its differences in a manner that keeps Tunisia's transition afloat.

These negotiations transpired between a delicately counterbalanced set of actors that simply does not exist in any other Arab country. The UGTT, for instance, has no parallel elsewhere in the Arab world, where civil society groups cannot meaningfully contest the power of regime incumbents. In Tunisia, the UGTT has wielded great power as an organization that represents nearly every public-sector worker in the country and can bring the economy to a standstill by calling general strikes.

Likewise, Tunisia's Islamists are without easy analogue elsewhere in the region. Though Morocco's Justice and Development Party likely comes closest, it is kept tightly under the thumb of a savvy monarchy that has curbed powers of parliament through various strategies of co-optation. Egypt's Muslim Brotherhood lacked the foresight and flexibility of Ennahda, and has not, since the coup against Morsi in 2013, demonstrated a desire to learn from the pragmatic minimalism of Ennahda's experience. Ennahda is a party with a large constituency, relatively long history (it was founded in the early 1980s), and strong internal organizational structures that were, perhaps ironically, more democratically representational than most of its secular competitor parties. It possessed the heft, organization, and leadership to serve as a crucial counterweight to old-regime-linked incumbents during the first phase of Tunisia's transition. Its size, organization, and leadership capacity made it another unique actor in Tunisia's transition, one without easy parallel among Islamist or secular parties elsewhere in the region.

Tunisia's transition does tell us much about the country's politics, and offers a fascinating example of a negotiated power transfer—one in which elements of a deposed dictatorship and leaders of long-exiled political movements, across a deep ideological divide, found a way to govern together after a crisis. Though these negotiations did, crucially, succeed in keeping Tunisia's transition afloat, the entire process underscored the fragility and reversibility of the country's political progress, and distracted principal actors from grappling with core revolutionary demands.

Political gains of the National Dialogue patterned a so-called "consensus-driven" model of engagement between Nidaa and Ennahda, in particular, which scaled up political cooperation in 2015. In the spring of that year, Ennahda joined a unity government with Nidaa—the victor in Tunisia's fall 2014 elections—and two smaller parties. A form of that unity government endured as this chapter went to press. Nidaa needed the support of Ennahda, parliament's largest and best-organized voting bloc, to pass core pieces of legislation and head off socioeconomic unrest in the face of periodic protests. It also found itself under international pressure to take an inclusive approach from Western governments who had, after Ennahda's succession of political compromises and gracious response to its defeat in the 2014 elections, begun to view the party as a more positive force in Tunisia's transition.

Ennahda, for its part, viewed the unity government as a chance to secure its newly won seat at Tunisia's political table and avoid the exclusionary politics of old, in which center-right Ennahda Islamists were sweepingly branded as terrorists and forced into prison and exile. To consolidate and expand its gains, Ennahda strategically rebranded itself as a party of "Muslim democrats," eased membership requirements, and formally separated its political and religious activities in a much-publicized national conference in May 2016. Formally abandoning the Islamist label made it a more viable partner for Nidaa and helped reinforce positive impressions of Ennahda in Western capitals. Beji Caid Essebsi, Nidaa's founder and the current president of Tunisia, even gave the keynote address at Ennahda's historic conference—a landmark signal of Islamist integration and mutual toleration between the leaders of Tunisia's main Islamist party and Essebsi, the scion of its anti-Islamist elite.

Preserving the Transition but Stalling Reform

Nidaa's willingness to offer Ennahda a symbolic if tokenistic seat at the table of government in 2015—and Ennahda leaders' willingness to cooperate in accepting that participation—reflected the extent to which Tunisian Islamists had surpassed their cousin parties in Egypt and elsewhere to achieve political normalization and integration. More importantly, cooperation between Islamists and old-regime-linked elites on the political level helped sustain Tunisia's transition toward more pluralistic and inclusive forms of governance. However, it bears noting that most Tunisians agreed that those changes had failed to translate beyond the level of elite coalition building. There has been no real progress in battling corruption, reforming inefficient bureaucracy, or stimulating job growth and infrastructure investments.

Thus, despite overcoming a major political hurdle, the National Dialogue did little to concretely advance Tunisia's pursuit of revolutionary goals, including socioeconomic dignity, institutional reform, and transitional justice. Rather than collaborating to address these critical issues, the Dialogue's protagonists spent much of 2012 and 2013 aggravating, exploiting, and eventually resolving a diversionary political crisis. That crisis sapped political and civil society leaders' energies at a critical transitional moment during which far-reaching changes might have been possible.

As a result, while polling has indicated that most Tunisians remain supportive of the revolution and a transition toward democracy, nostalgia for the supposedly more prosperous authoritarian days of yesteryear remains a potent force. While support for democracy as the best system of governance remains hearteningly high in Tunisia, this nostalgia could blunt support for more aggressive reforms.[26] In October 2016, Tunisia overcame a major political challenge as organizing by civil society groups and large public protests thwarted a so-called "reconciliation law." This law would have granted amnesty to corrupt businessmen who stole state money during the Ben Ali era. Positive polling for democracy, combined with activism like this, indicates that Tunisians have not, in general, turned their backs on the revolution's aspirations for dignity and justice. Yet frustrations over unmitigated corruption and widespread unemployment run deep. These have periodically bubbled over in major demonstrations, such as a series of unemployment protests that erupted in March 2016 and a spate of public suicides by unemployed youths that took place in October of that year.

With the Nobel Peace Prize, Tunisia's National Dialogue Quartet has been rightly applauded for helping Tunisia overcome a major political crisis. History should record that story in detail, and learn from their efforts. But history should also remember that the Dialogue's principal protagonists resolved a conflict that, to varying degrees, each one helped create, and that political power players were the primary winners in the saga. For average citizens to taste the fruits of Tunisia's revolution, their leaders must transcend the opportunistic infighting that characterized 2012 and 2013 to enact far-reaching economic and institutional reforms. Long after global applause for the Quartet has faded, Tunisians will keep asking what dividends, if any, their revolution has delivered.

Lessons Learned

Tunisia's gradual shifts toward pluralism and more inclusive governance since the toppling of Ben Ali in January 2011 have stemmed from locally contingent factors. These included the advantageous set of starting conditions, which this chapter has described, along with a core group of political parties and civil society organizations. These groups include the UGTT and other groups, like the Tunisian League of Human Rights; secular pro-revolutionary parties like CPR and Ettakatol, Ennahda's Troika coalition partners; and a highly pragmatic Islamist party, Ennahda. Together, these groups were able to counterbalance old-regime-linked incumbents as well as one another's more maximalist demands. The vibrancy and multipolarity of Tunisia's transition is difficult to replicate, but do offer a key takeaway for other transitions: the more centers of competitive power that have built up to oppose a regime, the more difficult it may be for regime-linked incumbents, as well as any other single domineering group, to capture a transition.

Another lesson of Tunisia's National Dialogue, and its transition more broadly, is the importance of learning from one's own history as well as the example of other countries' experiences. Ennahda, for instance, took such a different and more pragmatically influenced approach to power in part because its leaders had seriously reflected on the dangers of maximalism. They bore in mind the lessons of their own experience in Tunisia during 1989, and the experience of Algeria's Islamist party, the Islamic Salvation Front (better known by its French acronm, FIS) from 1990 to 1992. In both instances Islamist gains at the ballot box spooked regimes into initiating a broad-based crackdown on Islamist parties and their members. Internalizing lessons of strategic minimalism gleaned from these experiences, Ennahda's leaders adopted a careful approach oriented toward gradually securing long-term gains. This contrasted sharply with the comparatively inflexible, maximalist approach of Egypt's Muslim Brotherhood.[27] Following the 2011 revolution, Ennahda's pragmatic flexibility helped it build political influence, contributing to the survival and relative inclusivity of Tunisia's political transition.[28]

Opposition talks that crossed ideology during the first decade of the century—between Ennahda, secular political parties, and some Tunisian human rights groups—also helped build up a pattern of incremental learning, cooperation, and trust-building amongst members of the Tunisian opposition. Together, parties to talks held in Tunisia, Italy, and France throughout the decade signed documents laying out minimum conditions for a Tunisian democracy, should the Ben Ali regime ever fall. In 2005, they even joined together to create a cross-ideological opposition movement, dubbed the October Collective, or October Movement, which brought together leftists, Islamists, human rights groups, and secular parties. The October Collective resulted in the production of more oppositional platform documents, along with a lengthy series of dialogues and letters that debated key oppositional positions and jointly critiqued the Ben Ali regime.

This legacy of learning—a legacy of diverse parts of the opposition joining together to assert shared solidarity against an oppressive regime—proved crucial following Tunisia's revolution. Instead of descending into pitched infighting, Tunisians of various political and ideological persuasions who supported the revolution managed to work inclusively to lay the building blocks for Tunisia's transition. The good will built up through these efforts enabled CPR and Ettaka-tol to accept Ennahda's invitation, after the Islamist party's 2011 election win, to join the governing Troika. In contrast, anti-Islamist incumbent elites who had not been part of those trust-building talks denounced Ennahda as terroristic.[29]

Both Islamists and secularist civil society activists in Tunisia therefore did a great deal of historical learning from their own experiences, and also learned from the failures of would-be revolutionaries and Islamists elsewhere in the Arab world. Failed post-uprising transitions in Egypt, Libya, and Syria were arguably less attuned to history. To be fair, starting conditions, with military powerbrokers, weak states, sectarian cleavages, and regional interference may well have stymied these countries' attempted transitions even if more learning had taken place. Structures and starting compositions may obstruct future attempted transitions elsewhere, as well. Crucial factors include domestic hard power arrangements, and whether regional powers and global superpowers interfere in a country's transition. Disadvantageous starting conditions may hinder countries' progress toward democratic transition and consolidation, even if they perfectly follow the lessons of Tunisia's transition, including the importance of dialogue, civil society input, cross-ideological oppositional talks, and historical learning. The case study of Tunisia's transition—specifically the 2013 political crisis and the National Dialogue that resolved it—emphasizes the importance of contextually grounded power struggles in stewarding or stymying democratic transition.

Notes

1. I initially explored the role of the Quartet in my article, "What Did Tunisia's Nobel Laureates Actually Achieve?" *Washington Post*, October 27, 2015, https://www.washingtonpost.com/news/monkey-cage/wp/2015/10/27/what-did-tunisias-nobel-laureates-actually-achieve/. Portions of this chapter are drawn from that earlier piece.

2. See, for example, Sarah Chayes, "How a Leftist Labor Union Helped Force Tunisia's Political Settlement," Carnegie Endowment, March 27, 2014, http://carnegieendowment.org/2014/03/27/how-leftist-labor-union-helped-force-tunisia-s-political-settlement-pub-55143.

3. See Laryssa Chomiak, "The Making of a Revolution in Tunisia," *Middle East Law and Governance*, 3(2011):1–2.

4. See Hèla Yousfi, *L'UGTT: Une Passion Tunisienne* (Tunis: IRMC-Cérès Editions, 2015), 100–101.

5. Mongi Ammami, interview with the author, Tunis, August 2014.

6. Ibid.

7. Kacem Afaya, interview with the author. Tunis, December 2012.

8. See "À Tunis, des Milliers de Manifestants Réclament le Départ du Gouvernement," *Le Monde*, February 25, 2012, http://www.lemonde.fr/afrique/article/2012/02/25/a-tunis-des-milliers-de-manifestants-reclament-le-depart-du-gouvernement_1648506_3212.html; Hèla Yousfi, "Quand l'UGTT Brûle, C'est la Tunisie qui Brûle!" *Nawaat*, February 22, 2012, http://nawaat.org/portail/2012/02/22/quand-lugtt-brule-cest-la-tunisie-qui-brule/; Thierry Bresillon, "Le Bras de Fer entre Ennahdha et l'UGTT Dégénère Place Mohamed Ali," *Rue89*, December 5, 2012, http://rue89.nouvelobs.com/blog/tunisie-libre/2012/12/05/le-bras-de-fer-entre-

ennahdha-et-lugtt-degenere-place-mohamed-ali-229122; "Tunisia: Riot Police Fire Birdshot at Protesters," Human Rights Watch, December 1, 2015, https://www.hrw.org/news/2012/12/01/tunisia-riot-police-fire-birdshot-protesters.

9. See Ian Patel and Safa Belghith, "Leagues for the Protection of the Tunisian Revolution, *Open Democracy*, June 25, 2013, https://www.opendemocracy.net/ian-patel-safa-belghith/leagues-for-protection-of-tunisian-revolution.

10. Ibid. See also Yousfi, *L'UGTT: Une Passion Tunisienne*, Chapter 5.

11. Amel Boubekour, "The Politics of Protest in Tunisia," German Institute for International and Security Affairs, March 2015, https://www.swp-berlin.org/fileadmin/contents/products/comments/2015C13_boubekeur.pdf.

12. Lilia Weslaty, "Nominations dans le Secteur Public: 87% Pour la Troïka dont 93% en Faveur des Partisans d'Ennahdha," *Nawaat*, March 22, 2013, https://nawaat.org/portail/2013/03/22/93-des-nominations-dans-le-secteur-public-ont-beneficie-a-des-partisans-dennahdha/. These figures constitute the principle source of claims that Ennadha stacked Tunisia's public administration after coming to power in late 2011.

13. Labbaoui voiced these accusations in Tunisian media throughout 2013. See for example "Abdelkader Labbaoui: "86% des Nouvelles Nominations Appartiennent à Ennahdha," *Mosaique FM*, July 7, 2013, http://archivev2.mosaiquefm.net/fr/index/a/ActuDetail/Element/23759-abdelkader-labbaoui-86-des-nouvelles-nominations-appartiennent-a-ennahdha; "Tunisie: Abdelkader Labbaoui: 90% des Nouveaux Nommés Récemment à l'Administration Appartiennent à Ennahdha," *Tunisie Numerique*, March 20, 2013, http://www.tunisienumerique.com/tunisie-abdelkader-labbaoui-90-des-nouveaux-nommes-recemment-a-ladministration-appartiennent-a-ennahdha/170059.

14. According to a Nidaa Tounes communique, November 26, 2013. A copy is in the author's possession.

15. See Monica Marks, "Convince, Coerce, or Compromise? Ennahda's Approach to Tunisia's Constitution," Brookings Institute, February 10, 2014, https://www.brookings.edu/research/convince-coerce-or-compromise-ennahdas-approach-to-tunisias-constitution/.

16. Rory McCarthy, "Protecting the Sacred: Tunisia's Islamist Movement Ennahdha and the Challenge of Free Speech," *British Journal of Middle Eastern Studies* 42(2015): 4.

17. This insight is based on hundreds of interviews the author conducted with members of Ennahda and of CPR between 2012 and 2014.

18. See Imen Blioua, "Alleged ISIS Video: Militants Claim Responsibility for Belaid and Brahmi Assassinations," *Tunisia Live*, December 18, 2014, http://www.tunisia-live.net/2014/12/18/alleged-isis-video-militants-claim-responsibility-for-belaid-and-brahmi-assassinations/.

19. Monica Marks and Kareem Fahim, "Tunisia Moves to Contain Fallout after Opposition Figure Is Assassinated," *New York Times*, February 6, 2013, http://www.nytimes.com/2013/02/07/world/africa/chokri-belaid-tunisian-opposition-figure-is-killed.html; "Le Principal Syndicat Tunisien Appelle à la Grève Générale Vendredi," *Le Monde*, February 7, 2013, http://www.lemonde.fr/tunisie/article/2013/02/07/les-islamistes-d-ennahda-refusent-la-dissolution-du-gouvernement_1828487_1466522.html.

20. See Monica Marks, "Tunisia in Turmoil," *Foreign Policy*, July 26, 2013, http://foreignpolicy.com/2013/07/26/tunisia-in-turmoil/. See also Monica Marks, "Tunisia's Transition Continues," *Foreign Policy*, December 16, 2013, http://foreignpolicy.com/2013/12/16/tunisias-transition-continues/.

21. See "Béji Caïd Essebsi Revendique la Dissolution de l'ANC," *Business News*, February 7, 2013, available at https://www.youtube.com/watch?v=1IV-iLJtYHM.

22. For more on the impact of Egypt's 2013 coup on Tunisia, and particularly on Ennahda, see Monica Marks, "Tunisia," in *Rethinking Political Islam*, ed. Shadi Hamid and William McCants, (New York and Oxford: Oxford University Press, forthcoming in 2017), chapter 2.

23. "Le Document Officiel de l'Initiative UGTT, UTICA, LTDH et Ordre des Avocats," *Leaders*, September 18, 2013, http://www.leaders.com.tn/article/12262-le-document-officiel-de-l-initiative-ugtt-utica-ltdh-et-ordre-des-avocats.

24. See Hatem M'rad, *National Dialogue in Tunisia* (Tunis: Tunisian Association of Political Science—ATEP, 2015).

25. See Marks, "Tunisia."

26. See Michael Robbins, "Five Years after the Revolution, More and More Tunisians Support Democracy," *The Washington Post*, May 20, 2016, https://www.washingtonpost.com/news/monkey-cage/wp/2016/05/20/are-tunisians-more-optimistic-about-democracy-after-5-years-living-under-it/.

27. For more on the lessons Ennahda learned from their own experience and the experience of Algerian Islamists in the early 1990s versus that of the Egyptian Muslim Brotherhood, see Monica Marks, "Did Egypt's Coup Teach Tunisia's Islamists to Cede Power?" *Project on Middle East Political Science*, June 2016, http://pomeps.org/2016/07/22/did-egypts-coup-teach-ennahda-to-cede-power/.

28. Ibid. See also Marks, "Tunisia."

29. For more on the cross-oppositional talks and their importance, see Monica Marks, "Purists vs. Pluralists: Cross-Ideological Coalition Building in Tunisia," in *Islam and Democracy in Comparative Perspective*, ed. Alfred Stepan, (New York: Columbia University Press, forthcoming in 2017).

5

The Arab Cold War Redux

The Foreign Policy of the Gulf Cooperation Council States since 2011

MICHAEL STEPHENS

The Arab uprisings and their aftermath have precipitated the reshuffling of alliances, assertions of force, and a great deal of anxiety among the countries of the Gulf Cooperation Council, which was once somewhat placid. The rise of Iran's influence, the demise of old allies such as Hosni Mubarak in Egypt, the United States' retrenchment from the region, and the spread of sectarian conflict in many of the eastern countries of the Arab world have all shaken the Gulf monarchies. Vying for influence and backing different factions in proxy conflicts, they have begun to assert themselves on the regional stage in unprecedented ways. But while conflict rages and regimes fall around them, the Gulf countries appear, for now, to be facing futures that are internally stable—even if they will exist in an increasingly fractious, unhappy, and hostile neighborhood.

The Arab uprisings of 2011 marked a watershed moment for the Middle East, and not just for those Arab states that underwent dramatic changes in their politics, but also for the states of the Gulf Cooperation Council (GCC). Vastly wealthy, with powerful western allies, the GCC states appeared as paragons of stability in comparison to many of their fellow Arab nations. But despite their relatively comfortable positions, Arab rulers of Gulf countries have struggled to fully come to terms with the monumental changes wrought by the Arab uprisings. Fearing for their own internal stability, the GCC as a block has resisted any external pressure to liberalize politically, with all states passing laws restricting freedom of speech and detaining vocal opposition.[1] Even Kuwait, so famed for its freedom of speech, has restricted behavior on social media platforms.[2] Although officials in the Gulf states[3] talked extensively about the meaning of representative change that swept across the region in 2011, it appeared that it only applied outside of their borders.[4]

As the Arab uprisings unfolded into a series of protracted civil wars, the Gulf states were drawn even further out of their comfort zones. Long known for preferring stability—or more precisely, the absence of rapid political change—and exercising caution in regional affairs, the GCC was awoken from its slumber by the collapse of the regional order that had existed for decades. In the five years since, the GCC has moved from being a relatively passive group of states, seeking to preserve the regional status quo and working quietly through financial donations to preferred partners, into an aggressive, hawkish group that has actively engineered social and political change (or prevented it) across a number of Middle Eastern nations.

The Gulf states played a pivotal role in the way that the Arab uprisings unfolded, manipulating their direction for seemingly altruistic, but ultimately self-interested goals. It is not the first time in modern history that the wealthy Gulf states have used their political, religious, and economic influence to shape and at times dominate other Arab governments. The Kingdom of Saudi Arabia in particular has long sought to project power in the region, directly intervening in Yemen in 1934, and using its money and patronage to support military groups in Yemen against Gamal Abdel Nasser's Egypt in the 1960s, and against the Soviet Union in the 1980s. The maneuvers of Saudi Arabia and its rivals in Egypt and Syria featured prominently in Malcolm Kerr's famous account of Arab politics, *The Arab Cold War,* which rightly located political agency in Arab capitals. Kerr provided a rare counterpoint to Western analysts who tended to exaggerate the impact of outside powers on Arab regional developments, like many policy makers and analysts today. The Gulf states could hardly have been described as passive observers in the three Gulf wars involving Iraq, in which they acted in close concert with American policy—first, backing Saddam Hussein against Iran, and then forcefully opposing him in 1990 and 2003. But the period since the Arab uprisings began in 2010–11 marks a turn to a more muscular and overt role for Gulf states in regional affairs. The Gulf's backseat influence has morphed into direct political interference, and even military action and expeditionary warfare in the case of Libya and Yemen. This newfound role is often underestimated by analysts and policymakers, and is likely to remain a prominent feature of regional politics in the coming years.

Importantly, the reaction of the Gulf states to the uprisings was not uniform. Hyperactive Qatar excitedly pushing for change across the region contrasted strongly with the more conservative, and status-quo-favoring Saudi Arabia and United Arab Emirates, who mobilized to actively blunt Qatar's enthusiasm. The impact of the three most influential Gulf states playing their diametrically opposed agendas was hugely damaging for Arab democracy movements across the region. Revolutions in Syria, Egypt, and Libya turned sour as scores between Doha and Riyadh and Doha and Abu Dhabi were settled via weapons shipments, funds to proxy groups, and overt political interference. As each revolution began to break down, the Gulf troika became stuck in a cycle, playing out internal political divisions on the regional stage. The more the GCC's internal cracks grew, the more each country was drawn into activity at the regional level to blunt the interest of the others. Only by finally silencing Qatar through a concerted policy of threats and isolation could the Emirates and Saudi Arabia feel more at ease. And having solved internal GCC issues, Riyadh was free to focus on a threat that mattered far more than tiny Qatar—that posed by the Islamic Republic of Iran.

The retrenchment of the United States from the Middle East, the external security guarantor of the Gulf in the post-1945 world, has fundamentally and perhaps permanently changed the attitude of the Gulf states to become more active in pursuing their own security interests. Worn down by the failure of the state-building project in Iraq that began in 2003, and the continued instability and conflict that have plagued the region, the administration of Barack Obama pursued the dual goals of resolving the nuclear question with Iran and maintaining an increasingly strained set of alliances forged in the Cold War. Relations with Turkey, Israel, Egypt, and the Gulf—so long the pillars of U.S. containment of Soviet interests in the region—have begun to seem outdated and increasingly transactional, rather than a reflection of shared values and strategic interests. The deteriorating relationship between Washington and Riyadh in particular has had a serious impact on the course of regional events. There is little doubt that a divergence has opened up between the United States and its most important regional ally,[5] most notably around the choice to engage with Iran, rather than aggressively contain it with continued sanctions and escalatory rhetoric.

Saudi Arabia's traditional allies have been unable to check Iranian regional activity in Lebanon, Syria, and Iraq—Tehran has even been empowered by Western engagement with the country over its nuclear program.[6] As a result, the belief in Saudi Arabia, Bahrain, and the Emirates is that the price paid for Iran's signature to the Joint Comprehensive Plan of Action is too high. Riyadh has reacted, with the rest of its GCC allies in tow, by seeking its own interests in the region, using a combination of military force and indirect military action through rebel groups. Only the Sultanate of Oman stands outside this consensus, maintaining a policy of neutrality and largely preferring not to be drawn into any undue tension with Tehran.

The long-term consequences of this aggressive, militaristic foreign policy for the region are yet to be seen, but there is little doubt that it has proven costly in both lives and finances. A war in Yemen involving a Saudi-led multinational coalition fighting against Houthi militias, now dragging toward the end of its second year, has resulted in the deaths of more than ten thousand Yemenis, according to latest United Nations estimates.[7] Although no official figure of GCC casualties has been released, Saudi Arabia has admitted that more than five hundred of its own citizens have been killed as well.[8] Riyadh has upped the ante in Syria, taking the leading role in sponsoring the opposition groups fighting the Iran-backed regime of Bashar al-Assad, thereby ensuring that that war has dragged on well through its fifth year. As Tehran and Riyadh lock horns in Yemen and across the Mashreq,[9] it appears that only escalation and increasing proxy battles lie on the horizon.

At a time of depressed oil prices, the hydrocarbon-exporting GCC nations are feeling the pinch, cutting government spending, removing fuel subsidies, and increasing the price of services to citizens.[10] This fiscal restraint may slightly temper Saudi Arabia's aggressive pursuit of regional security, but it is unlikely to be overly constraining. Regional instability comes at a cost, both in blood and treasure, and for the moment it appears one that Riyadh is willing to pay if it means Iran does not get its way.

Master Strategy or Opportunism? The Rise of Qatar

Although Riyadh now holds sway over the direction of GCC foreign policy, it was not always so clear in the immediate aftermath of the Arab Spring. The turmoil and insecurity of the region in 2011 made an environment that was perfect for a small state like Qatar to operate. Too small to invade or occupy other regional states, it presented no existential threat to any, and Qatar's wealth meant that its finances could change the fortunes of any government with whom it did business. The previous decade had seen Qatar pursue a policy of mediation and balance, turning Doha into the "Geneva of the Mashreq."[11] All were welcome, from Hezbollah and Iran to Western think tanks and the Taliban, arriving in pursuit of Doha's riches and political backing. To top it all off, Qatar cemented its place on the world stage by winning the rights to host the 2022 FIFA World Cup.

Having removed his father in a bloodless coup in 1995, Sheikh Hamad bin Khalifa Al Thani—along with his cousin, Prime Minister Hamad bin Jassim Al Thani—set about constructing a grand vision to make Qatar a center of global activity, which would ensure its survival both politically and economically. Saddam Hussein's invasion of Kuwait in 1990 had taught Sheikh Hamad a lesson: being rich did not guarantee security in an unstable region. But being influential in the world might. In 1996 Qatar established the *Al Jazeera* television station. The station gave Qatar enormous influence across the Arab world, giving it the space to test the manipulation of public opinion against political rivals. In 2000, Gulf scholar Simon Henderson wrote that "the station gives special attention to criticisms of Saudi Arabia and Egypt, two governments that opposed the current emir of Qatar's seizure of power from his father in 1995 and that have subsequently tried to destabilize his regime."[12] *Al Jazeera* had landed the Qataris in hot water with Saudi Arabia and Egypt. The Kingdom withdrew its ambassador from Doha in 2002, in protest of critical comments made on the channel, and Egypt temporarily shut the station's facilities in Cairo in 2000. Qatar had also irritated the Saudis in 2008–2009 by muscling in to negotiations in Lebanon, thereby usurping Saudi's traditional influence over affairs there.[13] Long before the Arab uprisings, Qatar had built increasing numbers of friends across the region, showed a penchant for showy diplomatic initiatives, and displayed a taste for regional meddling, particularly with its television station. And so by December 2010 Qatar was well-positioned to take advantage of the chaos that would soon spread across the region.

Furthermore, the three hundred thousand or so Qatari citizens living lives of affluence, and secure in their employment at state-owned companies (often known as "Q" companies), posed no threat to the ruling house. Qatar's business elites, too—tied into the ruling house through an intricate system of familial bonds and business relationships—posed little in the way of opposition to the decisions of the executive. This domestic comfort afforded Sheikh Hamad the freedom to think about foreign policy questions and pursue regional objectives that took his fancy. His GCC brothers, by contrast, were deeply concerned by the changing order of the region. The GCC as a collective was unable to make a calculation as to how to proceed, as regional allies fell one by one, and GCC member Bahrain began to tear itself apart under the weight of popular protest. Fearing the spread of the Arab uprisings into its own borders, Saudi Arabia instigated massive social spending programs, releasing tens of billions of dollars into the economy to alleviate housing shortages for younger Saudis, and pumping up its social welfare programmes.[14] Additionally, Riyadh deployed GCC Peninsula Shield forces into Bahrain to ensure stability in the beleaguered monarchy. At the same time, Oman and Kuwait saw protests and domestic instability, which caused them to be embroiled in their own domestic problems, albeit to a lesser extent than Bahrain.

Unbridled by such concerns, Qatar ventured off into the region to begin refashioning regional politics. Qatar threw itself energetically into the politics of Tunisia, Libya, Egypt, Syria, and Palestine, all of which possessed broken political systems that offered opportunities for Qatari money and influence to operate. Qatar also made the most of its long-standing connections to political Islamists who for decades had sought refuge in Doha—and spiritual counseling from religious scholar Yusuf al-Qaradawi, the exiled clerical guide of Egypt's Muslim Brotherhood, who had moved to Doha in 1961. Qatar funneled cash, and in the case of Libya and Syria, weapons, to an assortment of political actors who broadly held a deeply Islamist view of participatory politics in the Middle East. These figures included Rachid al-Ghannouchi and his Ennahda party in Tunisia, Khalid Meshaal and Hamas in Palestine, Ali al-Sallabi and Abdelhakim Belhadj (the Commander of the Tripoli Military Council) in Libya, the government of Mohamed Morsi in Egypt, and prominent figures in the National Coalition for Syrian Revolutionary and Opposition Forces (the NCSROF) such as Mustafa Sabbagh and Moaz al-Khatib.[15]

Neither Qatar nor any of the other Gulf states created the regional conditions that triggered the Arab uprisings. But there is little doubt that the Gulf states and Qatar in particular strongly affected the course of the uprisings as they broke out across the region. Doha played a vital role during the frenetic opening months, particularly as it shaped the emerging narratives of protest through the *Al Jazeera* network.[16] As protests in Tunisia spread to Egypt and gathered strength in January 2011, *Al Jazeera* coverage fanned the flames, constantly stressing the message of change, through the use of emotive language stressing youthfulness and the use of social media as a force for good in the region.[17] Presenting itself as the voice of the voiceless, *Al Jazeera* built a wider narrative of popular mobilization around the protests in Tunisia,[18] catalyzing street protests elsewhere. Doubtless the region was already a tinderbox ready to combust, but *Al Jazeera*'s coverage only made the speed of change more dramatic and more acute.

Qatar read the signs quickly, and further sought to become increasingly active in the diplomatic arena, capitalizing on the moment to morph social change into political change. The easiest way to achieve this was through the use of money, of which Qatar had plenty. As protests in both Tunisia and Egypt gave way to elections, Qatar boosted its support for its regional allies, the Tunisian Ennahda party and the Egyptian Muslim Brotherhood. Drawing on huge troves of Qatari financial support and favorable television coverage, both were brought to power, Ennahda in October 2011, with the Muslim Brotherhood candidate Mohammed Morsi narrowly winning the Egyptian Presidential election in June 2012. Gulf money poured in from Kuwait, the Emirates, and Qatar to support Tunisia, but it was most obviously Qatar that moved to support Ennahda, funding multimillion-dollar social projects, and bankrolling the party to the tune of nearly one billion dollars.[19] Although always careful to repeat the line that Qatar was supporting the will of the people, Doha was really making politically calculated choices. Just three months after Morsi was elected, Qatar once again moved in with its money. Sheikh Hamad bin Jassim promised that his country would invest a total of eighteen billion dollars in Egypt over five years, adding that there would be "no limits" to Qatar's support.[20] It was an offer that had never been made to Hosni Mubarak. Qatar had not bought off the Arab street in either Tunis or Cairo, but it had empowered its friends in both countries to manipulate sentiments and successfully push forward political programs that Doha favored. The fact that there were willing and receptive audiences in both countries only served to convince the Al Thani that they were on the right side of history.

In Libya, Qatar went a step further, actively forcing the outcome of the revolutions that took place. It is highly unlikely that the diplomatic momentum required to authorize force against Muammar Qaddafi as he battled unrest within his country would have been possible without Qatari diplomatic activity.[21] With Saudi Arabia concerned with quelling unrest in Bahrain, Qatar and the Emirates stepped forward to push through an Arab League initiative on March 12, 2011 that supported a no-fly zone in Libya, and called on the UN Security Council to "establish safe areas" in the country.[22] Five days later the French put forward Security Council Resolution 1973, establishing a no-fly zone over Libya, and authorizing all necessary means to protect civilians and civilian-populated areas. It was unanimously passed, with only Russia and China abstaining. The resolution explicitly recognized "the important role of the League of Arab States in matters relating to the maintenance of international peace and security in the region," and requested that the League cooperate in the protection of civilians.[23]

True to the spirit of Resolution 1973, the Emirates and Qatar extended vital logistical and material support to the Libyan rebels. In 2011, the Emirates hosted meetings of Libyan provincial and tribal representatives, and both countries hosted meetings of the International Contact Group for Libya, which convened dozens of countries who wished to assist with Qaddafi's overthrow. Qatar provided some $400 million worth of nonmilitary assistance to the rebels.[24] Qatar was also one of the first countries to recognize the National Transitional Council (NTC) as the legitimate representative of the Libyan people. NTC chairman Mahmoud Jibril was largely based in Doha throughout the revolution, coordinating policy from its glitzy hotels rather than from inside the rebel stronghold of Benghazi.[25] But Qatar went further than just providing aid and political support to the uprising. Qatari special forces reportedly provided basic infantry training to Libyan rebel fighters in the Nafusa Mountains, to the west of Tripoli. And in eastern Libya, Qatari fighters were also in the thick of the fight to take Qaddafi's Bab al-Azizia compound on August 24, 2011, placing a Qatari flag on top of the building after its capture.[26] To top it off, Qatari and Emirati aircraft took to the skies alongside NATO aircraft. Qaddafi, Libya's indomitable strongman for forty-two years, was on the run; rebels caught and killed him on October 20, 2011.

Buoyed by the success of Libya, the Qataris grew in confidence and Sheikh Hamad sought to keep up the momentum.[27] Qatar believed that it could also change Syria for the better and force Assad to either reform, or step down. Doha largely focused on forming strategies to engineer political change through external pressure. But understanding that it could not act without international support, Qatar intensified its pressure on the Assad regime through the international community, and with Saudi backing pushed through support for an Arab League monitoring mission in December 2011. The mission ended in failure just one month later, but both Qatar and Saudi Arabia had already begun to seek military alternatives. However, it was the international community's inability to act to stop Assad that really began to trigger Gulf pressure. Doha openly declared its support for regime change in February 2012, urging the international community to arm the Syrian opposition and to help them to overthrow Assad "by all means."[28] While both Saudi Arabia and Qatar were visibly angered at the continuing violence in Syria, and felt a sense of moral duty to act, they were equally concerned with appearing to be leaders. Both countries held high hopes for remolding Arab politics, and were eager for the Arab League to take up a larger role in security.[29] Despite the lack of action in the UN Security Council to stop Assad, by mid-2013 there had been some limited successes. By November 2012 thirty-one countries and the EU had extended full diplomatic recognition to the NCSROF (the Syrian National Coalition) as the "sole legitimate representative of the Syrian people." Moaz al-Khatib was installed as the representative of the Syrian Arab Republic in place of Bashar al-Assad at an Arab League summit in Doha in March 2013. Meanwhile, Qatar ally and Egyptian president Mohamed Morsi became Egypt's representative. At the same time, Qatar inaugurated the first Syrian Arab Republic Embassy in Doha, which flew the flag of the revolutionary forces, in an attempt to firmly cement the future of a new Syria without Assad.[30] Qatari Prime Minister Hamad bin Jassim Al Thani highlighted the involvement in Syria and Libya as "examples of Arab League reform."[31]

Qatar's Fall from Grace, a GCC Divided

But Qatar's support for governments that had benefitted from the Arab uprisings was not backed up with a long-term strategy. Doha had assembled influence across a swathe of Middle Eastern states, ranging from Tunisia to Turkey, but no sooner had this regional belt of influence been assembled then the cracks began to appear. While Morsi basked in the grand surroundings of his Qatari friends at the Arab League Summit, the public mood at home was railing against him. Increasing numbers of Egyptians expressed their rage at both his floundering government and also at Qatar, some going so far as to burn Qatari flags in the streets.[32] Egyptian television satirist Bassem Youssef mocked Qatar's increasing influence in his country, to widespread popular support. Similar scenes occurred in Tunisia and Libya, as angry protesters decried what they saw as Qatari interference in their affairs.[33] Qatar, for its part, seemed almost oblivious of the troubles, maintaining its steadfast and rather tired line that it supported "the will of the people" across the region.[34] But Qatar's investment in Egypt was beginning to look like a big mistake. For all the money that had been invested in propping up the Morsi government (an estimated eight billion dollars in loans and deposits into the Central Bank of Egypt),[35] Qatar appeared to be getting only problems in return. Morsi's repeated failures to quell growing dissent in his own country were beginning to tar Qatar's legacy as well.

Saudi Arabia and the Emirates for their part had never supported the removal of Mubarak in 2011. As Qatar's television station was whipping up anti-Mubarak sentiment, both countries had sent messages of support to the beleaguered dictator, urging him to stay in power by all means necessary.[36] Riyadh and Abu Dhabi were deeply resistant to the idea of a Muslim Brotherhood government in Egypt, and in particular were resentful that Qatar had been such a major force in orchestrating the change. The Emirati anger was based on the competing visions of regional order and stability held by Sheikh Hamad, whose preference for dealing with Islamist actors ran contrary to that of Mohammed bin Zayed Al Nahyan, Crown Prince of Abu Dhabi. Mohammed bin Zayed and, by extension, most of the government believe that an Islamist model of government in the Emirates would upset the delicate balance of running a conservative Muslim society with a large non-Muslim expatriate population who enjoy widespread social liberties. Fiercely opposed to any internal opposition to its rule (especially from those who espouse Islamist alternatives to the current ruling bargain or had connections to the Muslim Brotherhood-affiliated Islah party),[37] Abu Dhabi chafed at the idea that rival ideological platforms that could influence its own polity were being given succor in a country less than forty minutes drive from its borders. In contrast, Qatar saw nothing wrong with the housing and support of such actors, believing that the popular will of the region's peoples would surely be expressed through an Islamic representative politics in some form. Thus, to support those actors who actively sought such reform was necessary for long-term regional stability.

In July 2013, the Emirates and Saudi Arabia backed a military coup in Egypt that swiftly removed Morsi, Qatar's strongest regional ally.[38] Qatar was helpless to stop the unfolding drama, and with no friends inside the Egyptian military they had only their money and their Muslim Brotherhood contacts to make desperate pleas on *Al Jazeera* to stop the change.[39] When forces loyal to then-Defense Minister Abdel Fattah el-Sisi killed hundreds of Morsi-supporting protesters in Rabaa Square on August 14, 2013, both the Emiratis and Saudis blamed the protesters, and doubled down on their support for Sisi.[40] The Gulf's internal disputes about regional change were becoming far more than petty ideological squabbles between rich princes: they were now costing lives.

As the hopeful protests in Libya and Syria mutated into grinding civil war, Qatar became more embroiled in military matters, arming and funding proxy militias, while futilely pursuing increasingly distorted utopian political goals. In Libya, Qatar's choice of Islamist friends was beginning to backfire badly. Libya descended into a chaotic mess of fractious militias.[41] The lack of security led to a number of serious incidents, as brigands attacked aid convoys, diplomatic missions, and even the parliament building, forcing the resignation of five ministers. On September 11, 2012 militant Islamists allegedly connected to Ansar al-Sharia attacked the United States mission in Benghazi, killing the American ambassador, Christopher Stevens, and three contractors working for the Central Intelligence Agency. Ansar al-Sharia possessed close operational links to the Libyan Islamic Fighting Group (designated a terrorist organization by the United States in 2004), whose former leader, Abdelhakim Belhadj—who had become the commander of the Tripoli Military Council—was a long-term favorite of Doha. While Qatar cannot be said to have known about the attack, it raised troubling questions about the company the country chose to keep.

Libya's increasingly fractured politics exposed Doha's paucity of understanding of the country's tribal politics and lack of institutions. By continually backing Islamists at the expense of more moderate groups, Doha spurred a series of counter-movements against it, pulling apart what little consensus existed after Qaddafi's ouster, and leading to the eventual split in administrations between Tripoli and Benghazi. That the Emirates felt increasingly frustrated and worked directly against Qatari goals served only to entrench preexisting divisions. It was this friction that complicated the task of unifying the anti-Qaddafi movement from its earliest phases and contributed to the subsequent splintering of the movement after it came to power in October 2011.[42] Qatar had also become increasingly unpopular among ordinary Libyans, who resented that external actors had taken their revolution from them.[43] As if to seal Qatar's sinking popularity, Doha favorite Belhadj lost his election for the General National Congress in July 2012. There was little doubt that his association with Qatar was a hindrance.

Syria further helped to undo Qatar, as it butted heads with another GCC partner, Saudi Arabia. As Chair of the Arab League for 2011–12, Qatar had failed to produce a consensus for an armed intervention in Syria, as it had done for Libya.[44] Doha's frustration at the lack of progress boiled over into a policy of arming Syrian rebel groups that appeared highly dubious to both Arab and Western nations alike.[45] The policy was shoddy and poorly coordinated, and knowing that funds and weapons were available, "an expanding pool of middlemen" began to appear in Doha looking for money and guns to run into Syria.[46] To complicate matters, Qatar and Saudi Arabia held strong differences over how the rebellion should be managed and "prioritized their own agendas ahead of forging a united and effective opposition grouping."[47] Both Doha and Riyadh largely agreed that Assad should step down, but their motivations for doing so were quite different. Qatar by and large supported actors with close connections to the Syrian Muslim Brotherhood, with whom it tried to populate the main opposition Syrian National Council (SNC). Rather than favor one group, Riyadh was more focused on building a coalition of Syrians that would push growing Iranian influence out of the country.[48] The Saudis were also deeply suspicious of Qatar's relationship with the Brotherhood and objected to the SNC being populated with Qatar-backed Brotherhood members. By 2013, as the war moved well into its second year, Saudi and Qatari differences over the composition and leadership of the opposition—by then represented by the NCSROF, which the SNC joined—began to pull apart the already fractured movement.

The culmination of Doha and Riyadh's interference was the resignation of Moaz al-Khatib, the one man among a series of little-known opposition leaders who held credibility among the general Syrian population.[49] In an interview in May 2013, Khatib did not pull his punches, blaming "two regional countries that sponsored their own candidates, and pulled apart the opposition."[50] As for the much-feted opposition embassy in Doha, it became merely a house with a flag, from which the remaining pro-Qatar NCSROF members increasingly struggled to exert any political authority. By mid-2013 Saudi Arabia had effectively pushed Qatar aside, with the Doha-backed Mustafa Sabbagh losing out to the Riyadh-favored Ahmad Jarba in an opposition leadership contest.[51]

The cases of Egypt, Syria, and Libya show that Riyadh and the United Arab Emirates had become deeply angered at Qatar's regional meddling; believing that Doha's alliance with militant Islamist actors, especially the Brotherhood, was detrimental to the security not only of the region, but more specifically the monarchies of the GCC.[52] This internecine bickering colored the revolutions in both Libya and Syria, and while revolutionaries in both nations benefitted from Gulf weapons and finances, allowing them to continue their fight against the regimes of Assad and Qaddafi, these gifts were not agenda-free. Meanwhile, Gulf games over Syria's opposition became a sideshow in comparison to the Russian and Iranian military interventions to keep Assad in power. The period of Qatari-Saudi infighting in 2012–13 dealt a crucial blow to the effectiveness of the opposition during the Syrian conflict's earlier years, undermining its image and credibility as government in waiting. It is not possible to know whether a more united opposition, composed of fewer Sunni Islamists and less colored by Gulf interests, would have been more palatable to either Russia or Iran, thereby causing them to drop Assad. But the opposition's weakness provided Assad and his backers with all the ammunition they would ever need to reject negotiations with a motley crew of misfits that had no unified agenda or support inside Syria.

As for Egypt, the revolution that swept the streets in January 2011 was stolen from the people. Morsi was not the enlightened reformer Qatar had painted him to be, but neither was he the villain portrayed by Saudi Arabia and the Emirates. Qatar's rush to artificially prop up the Morsi government at a time in which it was failing blinded the Brotherhood to its troubles, and caused it to cling to power when a compromise might have proven wiser. Regardless of Morsi's mistakes, what followed was nothing less than a brutal destruction of the last vestiges of the Egyptian revolution. That the coup received the immediate blessing of both Riyadh and Abu Dhabi only strengthens the argument that the Gulf had a substantial hand in ending the Egyptian revolution.

At this point it is also important to remember that for all their regional meddling, Doha, Abu Dhabi, and Riyadh were united in their positions on the unrest in the Kingdom of Bahrain. Bahrain's protests were notably absent from *Al Jazeera*'s Arabic-language coverage, and the little coverage that did exist placed the blame for civil unrest squarely at the feet of Iran.[53] The notion that legitimate domestic unrest might have arisen in one of their own was too much to champion, even for change-loving Qatar.[54]

Bringing Qatar to Heel, the GCC Acts

In 2014, the Emirates took their disagreements with Qatar to a new level by orchestrating a smear campaign against Doha in order to break its image in Western capitals.[55] Doha's name began to sink deeper and deeper into the mud, saddled with continued allegations in the press of appalling human rights records, and dirty financial dealings connected to its right to host the 2022 FIFA World Cup,[56] alongside numerous accusations from media and politicians alike that Qatar was deeply connected to global terrorist networks.[57] Qatar had once been on the ascendancy, the subject of numerous articles about "punching above its weight,"[58] and its enormous wealth. Now, the country found itself in desperate trouble. Crucially, Qatar's shining jewel in the crown, *Al Jazeera*, was haemorrhaging viewers. As conflicts across the region worsened, the station's coverage became increasingly one-sided, giving Sunni Islamists more and more preferential treatment, and pushing overtly political agendas that seemed to mirror Qatar's foreign policy objectives. Even *Al Jazeera*'s historically more balanced English language channel punished journalists who did not tow the line.[59] Elsewhere in the region the media company was banned from operating—as occurred in Egypt and Iraq—and its journalists faced harassment and unlawful imprisonment.[60] The once dynamic, nimble state and friend to all, with its television channel that espoused hope and change across the region, began to look more like an international pariah, with an overtly sectarian agenda, and troublesome penchant for military interventions.[61]

Not only did Qatar find itself rapidly declining in regional influence, but it also became the victim of a concerted attempt by Bahrain, the Emirates, and Saudi Arabia to ostracize it. The young Qatari emir Tamim bin Hamad rebuffed repeated attempts by Saudi Arabia to convince him to roll back his country's regional influence, and to quiet Brotherhood activists based in Doha who openly criticized Sisi. But Saudi patience broke on March 5, 2014 and, alongside the Emirates and Bahrain, it pulled its ambassador from Doha, alleging "interference" in internal affairs, thereby triggering the most serious internal crisis in the GCC since its formation in 1981. To further turn the screw on Doha, two days later Saudi Arabia declared the Muslim Brotherhood a terrorist organization.[62] The attempt by Riyadh, Abu Dhabi, and Manama to quash Qatari ambitions revealed the disunity of the GCC's six states on regional policy issues, ranging from the role of political Islam in the politics of the region, to the solidarity of a united front against Iran. Additionally, the lengths to which both Abu Dhabi and Riyadh went to force the renegade Qatar to heel show their level of discomfort for rival political ideologies in the Sunni world that they themselves could not control. Riyadh's ruling bargain with the clerical establishment, which forms the backbone of the family's legitimacy to rule, requires that no Islamic political movement challenge that status quo. Accordingly, the Saudi Arabia of King Abdullah moved ruthlessly in step with Abu Dhabi to snuff out the threat of rival Islamist political actors, by breaking Qatar's adventurism before any such activity could take root across the Gulf.

It has taken time, but the strength of Saudi resolve effectively forced Qatar's rulers to bend to Riyadh's will. Qatar slowly ratcheted down its regional activity, and prevented Brotherhood blowhards from making overt statements contrary to Saudi interests. Going even further to placate the Saudis, in September 2014 a number of Egyptian Muslim Brotherhood activists left Doha in order "to avoid causing any embarrassment for the State of Qatar."[63] Under King Salman, Saudi Arabia has lessened its hardline stance on the Brotherhood,[64] and restarted full diplomatic relations with Qatar, finalized by Salman's visit to Doha in December 2016, which serves as the most overt signal from Saudi Arabia that Qatar was once again back in Riyadh's good books.[65] Indeed, Riyadh's boisterous return to regional ascendancy has by and large forced the Emirates and Qatar to acknowledge its leadership on all regional, political, and security challenges. Following the change of administration in Riyadh following the death of King Abdullah in January 2015, and the accordant Saudi focus on Iran and the Islamic State as the main sources of regional insecurity, any remaining Qatari-Emirati squabbles over the Muslim Brotherhood have been relegated to tertiary status in Riyadh.

But pictures of Gulf monarchs sword-dancing in Doha do not mean the damage has fully healed. The significance of the Qatari-Emirati split, and the resulting withdrawal of ambassadors, will have ramifications for many years and its impacts across the region are still being felt. In direct defiance of Emirati anger, Qatar has never quite given up its myriad of Islamist friendships across the region, although it has certainly been much less visible in how it maintains them. The result is that the two countries still hold diametrically opposed views on a number of regional files. This is most notable in the case of Libya, where Qatar's backing of Misrata militias, with connections to militants in Benghazi, is completely divergent to the Emirates' backing of General Khalifa Haftar. And so despite both countries nominally supporting the Government of National Accord, they have both abetted the fragmentation of the Libyan state and remained very clear obstacles to the restoration of a unified government in the country. Qatari officials still privately mumble about the illegality of Sisi's rule in Egypt. Lastly, the status and power of Turkey in the region under President Recep Tayyip Erdogan—whose nation was staunchly against the 2013 coup in Egypt—has still built a strong alliance with Qatar cemented by the deployment of Turkish troops in Doha in January 2016, to serve on Turkey's first military base in the Gulf. Qatar's alliance with Turkey is one that appears uniquely strong in the Gulf, described by one Turkish scholar as a "special bond."[66] Even though Riyadh has also begun to warm its ties with Ankara, and has "sought to develop a set of close defense and security relationships,"[67] the relationship appears pragmatic and highly transactional, lacking in the warmth that the Doha-Ankara axis displays. Abu Dhabi, meanwhile, took some months to adjust to this new reality, finally ending a three-year feud with Ankara in late April 2016.[68] On the issue of Ankara's hostility to Sisi, Abu Dhabi's Al Nahyan family has understood it is better to not undermine Saudi Arabia's strategic relationship with the Turks, and calculated that it is an irritant they will have to accept for the time being.

Saudi Arabia's Bid for Primacy and the Struggle against Iran

Quite apart from being browbeaten into submission by its neighbors, Qatar's rise to the top would always be dependent on regional conditions. As regional stability and security plummeted following the Islamic State offensive across Syria and Iraq in June 2014, Iranian, Turkish, and Western military forces were dragged in. Six months later Yemen too began to destabilize following the collapse of the GCC-backed government of Abdu Rabbu Mansour Hadi, and Qatar's inability to project hard power meant that it increasingly took a back seat to those actors who possessed hard power in abundance, and had the willingness to deploy it extraterritorially. Thus the stage was set for Saudi Arabia to mobilize its vast wealth and military resources to take on the challenge of restabilizing the region, and as Qatar's influence waned Riyadh began to find its voice. Saudi foreign policy had for decades been cautious and risk averse. From King Faisal to King Abdullah, the kingdom avoided conflict if possible and preferred covert action to high-profile military intervention.[69] But the signs that Saudi Arabia was awaking from its slumber had been long in coming, far preceding Doha's attempts at regional leadership.

Alarmed by the potential for its most potent regional rival, Iran, to capitalize on the instability sweeping the Arab world, the Kingdom had looked to its closest partner, the United States, for reassurance. But Riyadh found the Obama administration largely unwilling to secure Saudi interests with bold and assertive moves. Indeed, as Riyadh looked around at a collapsing regional order, Washington appeared to be doing nothing. Rather than support Saudi ally and regional lynchpin Mubarak in Egypt in January 2011, the Obama administration effectively removed all support for him. At the same time, lukewarm American support for Bahrain as it struggled under the weight of mass protests also piqued the House of Saud, alongside what appeared American unwillingness to take the fight to Assad, as had been done against Qaddafi. Even more concerning was the increasing realization that the United States would likely seek to negotiate with Iran over its nuclear program.

Saudi cages were rattled, and in mid-2011 in a speech at RAF Molesworth, Prince Turki al-Faisal, Riyadh's unofficial official, clearly spelled out that the Kingdom was losing patience with its Western allies on a number of regional security issues. Included in the speech was the veiled threat that, as a report of the off-the-record remarks put it, "Iran [developing] a nuclear weapon would compel Saudi Arabia . . . to pursue policies which could lead to untold and possibly dramatic consequences."[70] Prince Turki again spelled out Saudi frustrations before a vote to recognize a Palestinian state at the UN General Assembly, in which he noted that by failing to recognize Palestine's importance "the United States would further undermine its relations with the Muslim world, empower Iran and threaten regional stability" meaning that "Saudi Arabia would be forced to adopt a far more independent and assertive foreign policy."[71] It was an ominous sign of things to come, and a warning that was largely ignored by Kingdom watchers and Western policy analysts.

This build-up of Saudi frustrations over several years is important to understand within the context of Saudi Arabia's currently aggressive regional role. Riyadh's regional activism is often attributed to the death of King Abdullah, and the rise to power of his half-brother King Salman, whose son, Prince Mohammed bin Salman, has accrued power across a swathe of the Kingdom's domestic and foreign policy files. Although the rise of Prince Mohammed, at just twenty-nine years of age, is indeed remarkable in a cultural milieu that values age and experience, there is a tendency to overestimate the impact of Prince Mohammed on foreign policy, attributing almost all Riyadh's adventurism to him.[72] While this may be a suitable argument for the Kingdom's enemies to tout—particularly in Iran where Prince Mohammed is seen as a dangerous and reckless youth[73]—it is both inaccurate, and misunderstands that Saudi calculations were being recalibrated far in advance of the young prince's rise.

Many thinkers across the Gulf—and not just Prince Mohammed—view Iran's regional activities as blatant interference in Arab lands by an external non-Arab power that has no business being there.[74] Indeed, with the exception of Oman, Iran has been seen by all the Gulf states as a geostrategic threat and regional competitor for decades. Relations between the Arab and the Persian side of the Gulf have waxed and waned since the coming to power of Ayatollah Ruhollah Khomeini in 1979. But for the most part the Arab countries of the Gulf could count on a combination of regional allies (or competitors in the case of Iraq's Saddam Hussein) and the United States to contain Iran. The environment after the Arab uprisings shook both pillars of this understanding, leaving Saudi Arabia feeling increasingly alone as it faced down what it perceived to be an aggressive expansionist foe. Furthermore, Iran's commitment to Shia Arab movements is seen as having foisted sectarianism upon the region, triggering the rise of extremist groups such as the Islamic State who are able to recruit from Sunni populations who seek to defend themselves.[75] Of particular concern to Riyadh is the way Iran empowers nonstate actors—such as Hezbollah, the Houthis in Yemen, or the Shia militias in Iraq—to do its regional bidding.[76] The belief is that these Iranian allies actively seek to monopolize political power; and that Iran encourages its proxies to feed off the instability and dysfunction of the states within which they operate, in order to solidify Tehran's control of security. Under this paradigm, some Sunnis in the region see the emergence of a radically violent anti-Shia group like the Islamic State as a natural reaction to attempted Iranian subversion.[77]

Thus the Saudi government feels duty-bound to step in to prevent Iran from pushing its weight around, because it does not believe the Americans or Europeans are willing to do so. For Riyadh, that means both getting its own house in order by dampening down intra-GCC disputes, and secondly, following a more aggressive policy of containing and confronting Iran using every means short of a direct confrontation. That Riyadh experienced a change of monarch in the middle of pursuing these joint goals does not necessarily mean that it would have followed a different path without that succession.

Combatting the Dual Threat of the Islamic State and Iran

The war in Syria in many ways typifies the problem that Riyadh and the rest of the Gulf face. Deeply hostile to the regime of Bashar al-Assad and its Iranian allies, the Gulf states—in particular Qatar and now predominantly Saudi Arabia—tried (albeit unsuccessfully) to build a credible alternative opposition coalition that would replace the regime, and usher in a new system of government, thereby rolling back any Iranian presence in the country. Support for the opposition has stretched into trying to directly influence the military course of the war, and Saudi Arabia, alongside Qatar, has been deeply involved in the supply of arms and logistical support to Syria. The de facto division of labor that pulled the opposition apart also existed in relation to armaments. Turkey and Qatar ran weapons shipments in through the northern border, while Saudi Arabia and Jordan took responsibility for rebels in the south. The creation of the Army of Conquest in early 2015—a conglomeration of Islamist groups, including al-Qaeda affiliate the Nusra Front (which renamed itself Fateh al-Sham in July 2016, and claims to have cut ties with al-Qaeda)—was supposed to bring a more joined approach between Riyadh, Doha, and Ankara. But to this day Riyadh has remained uncomfortable with being too close to the hardline groups that are supported by Qatar such as Ahrar al-Sham, whose links to al-Qaeda are a source of great concern to Saudi Arabia's Western allies.[78] Nevertheless, with the oversight of the United States, Riyadh has continued to funnel finances and arms toward vetted rebel groups, in an attempt to keep the fight against the regime alive, and push back against both the Islamic State and the Kurdish militia YPG (People's Protection Units) operating in the countryside surrounding Aleppo.[79]

Saudi Arabia and the other Gulf states view Assad as a staunch ally of Iran and promoter of sectarian Shia interests. But this was not the general view held by the Gulf in the first stages of the conflict.[80] On the contrary, the Gulf states were extremely cautious in their approach to Damascus, and it was not until August 2011, when the death toll in the Syrian uprising passed two thousand, that opinions in the Gulf began to harden significantly against the Syrian regime, and the GCC states recalled their ambassadors from the country.[81] Attempts from both Qatar and the Emirates to reason with Assad were rebuffed and by the end of that year, the Gulf states had firmly taken the position that Assad had to leave power. However, the sectarian lens through which the Gulf viewed the conflict was still largely absent until the entry of Hezbollah into the war during the battle for al-Qusayr in 2013.

The Iran-backed group's intervention sparked outrage in the Gulf states, and had a dramatic impact on the political rhetoric surrounding the conflict. Prominent Sunni clerics in the Gulf began to use more overtly sectarian language to describe the war, with Yusuf al-Qaradawi calling Hezbollah (which means "the Party of God"), "Hezb al-Shaytan," the party of Satan. "The leader of the party of Satan comes to fight the Sunnis," Qaradawi said in June 2013. "Every Muslim trained to fight and capable of doing that [must] make himself available."[82] This position was strongly endorsed by the grand mufti of Saudi Arabia, Abdulaziz al-Sheikh and other leading Sunni clerics.[83] Prominent Arab media outlets from the Gulf also responded, blocking the speeches of Hassan Nasrallah, Hezbollah's general secretary, from being published or broadcast. Regional media—along with Western media, to a lesser degree—increasingly framed the conflict in sectarian and anti-Iranian terms.[84] This heavily sectarianized rhetoric continues to pervade news coverage and commentary in the Gulf.

But sectarianism is often overstated, and it should not be forgotten that the issue of Iranian interference in Arab affairs is still the primary lens through which the Arab states of the Gulf view Iran's alliance with Assad. The notion that Iran with its proxy groups blunts the power of the Arabs to control their own affairs is a far more important component of Gulf frustrations than is the belief that the entire region will become dominated by Twelver Shia Islam. Saudi Arabia and Qatar in particular will accept nothing less than the complete removal of Iranian proxies from Syria, although they now concede that some form of the Assad state apparatus must remain.[85]

The reluctance of the Obama administration to take on Assad regime forces after the use of chemical weapons in August 2013 proved a watershed moment. For the Arab countries of the Gulf, this permanently solidified the view that the United States could no longer be relied upon to lead on regional security matters. If the Gulf wanted to see the end of Assad they would have to do it themselves.[86] Additionally, the entry of Russia into the conflict in the fall of 2015 has made Assad impervious to Gulf attempts to remove him (through either diplomacy or by force). The result is that the Gulf states have been reduced to being influential but not decisive in the Syrian war. The United States' choice not to confront Russia over its ironclad support for Assad has left the Gulf frustrated and angry at the current situation, but largely powerless to do anything about it.[87] This frustration was most clearly demonstrated during the rapid collapse of Gulf-sponsored militias inside Eastern Aleppo in December 2016. The rebels were powerless to fight back against the relentless onslaught of Assad's forces, backed in turn by overwhelming Russian airpower. Gulf interests, particularly in the north of the country, have become limited to protecting dwindling proxy groups that have been largely co-opted by hardline Islamist factions, such as Fateh al-Sham.[88]

In Iraq the situation is even bleaker. Unlike Syria where the Gulf states possess links to opposition groups fighting Assad, and thereby hold some sway over the future of the country, they hold little to no influence over the Iraqi state, which has gradually moved closer to Iran's orbit over the past decade. Relations between Iraq and the Gulf states are poor,[89] and recent Saudi attempts to fix diplomatic ties have gone badly. The first Saudi Ambassador to Iraq in twenty-six years was given his marching orders by Baghdad just seven months into his posting, after making highly critical comments about the role of Iraqi paramilitary organizations linked to Iran inside the country.[90] The Gulf rued the day Prime Minister Nouri al-Maliki and his State of Law Coalition strengthened their grip on power in Iraq's 2010 elections. With the help of some behind-the-scenes power brokering from Qasem Soleimani, the commander of Iran's Quds Force, differing Shia factions were persuaded to coalesce around the prime minister, thereby maintaining Shia dominance in the country.[91] The factions accomplished this despite Maliki securing fewer seats than the Gulf-backed secularist Ayad Allawi. The late King Abdullah's hatred for Maliki and his behavior has been well-documented,[92] and Qatar and the Emirates had no affection for the man either.[93] However, there was little they could do to swing the balance: Maliki's ever-strengthening grip on the state and its security services was backed by Iranian support—and of course, by the United States as well, which sought to maintain the illusion that, despite Maliki's increasing authoritarianism, democracy was alive and well.

Therefore, the uprising of Iraq's Sunnis in Fallujah in late 2013 and then the rapid emergence of the Islamic State (known as ISIS at the time) in June 2014, which shook the Iraqi state to its core, met with a degree of sympathy from the Gulf states. The messaging emerging from the Gulf after the Islamic State swept across Iraq reflected a sense that there was real disenfranchisement and anger among Iraq's Sunnis that needed to be addressed.[94] However, the way in which the Islamic State united a fractious coalition of tribes, ex-Ba'athists, and disgruntled Sunnis into a nihilistic killing machine bent on exterminating anybody who did not align with its narrow vision of Islam and politics caused the Gulf states to rapidly temper their views on the group. Additionally, the Islamic State's leadership rapidly expanded its ambitions to the entirety of the Middle East, clearly indicating that the Gulf states could be its next target. In November 2014, Abu Bakr al-Baghdadi, the Islamic State's self-appointed caliph, declared: "O sons of al-Haramayn . . . the serpent's head and the stronghold of the disease are there . . . draw your swords and divorce life, because there should be no security for the Saloul."[95] Al-Baghdadi's choice of words was designed to provoke; his sneering use of the word "Saloul" (the family who guarded the shrine of the Kaaba in pagan pre-Islamic times) to describe the House of Saud was deliberately insulting, his reference to Saudi Arabia as the "Haramayn" (two holy Mosques) noted a complete disregard for the king's status as "Custodian of the Two Holy Mosques," implying that the House of Saud had no legitimacy to rule. Almost overnight the Islamic State turned from being a serious problem for the Gulf into an enemy of all Gulf regimes—and it needed to be destroyed.

In 2014, Saudi Arabia and the Emirates, possessing by far the best-equipped and numerically strongest air forces in the region, launched strikes in the earliest days of the Syrian chapter of the United States-led campaign against the Islamic State, Operation Inherent Resolve, while Bahrain, Qatar, and Kuwait largely limited their role to logistical and basing support. Results were initially positive, most notably during the Islamic State's siege of Kobane, Syria in the autumn and winter of 2014, in which both Saudi and Emirati planes struck frequently, providing the Syrian Kurds on the ground with much-needed air support. However, the level of Riyadh's and Abu Dhabi's activity against the Islamic State dropped drastically after the opening two months of Operation Inherent Resolve. To the south a crisis far more pressing and closer to home was brewing in Yemen, which would quickly swallow up the lion's share of Saudi Arabia's military and diplomatic resources.

Distracted by Yemen, the Fight against the Islamic State Takes a Back Seat

Saudi Arabia looked on in alarm as the Houthi rebels took over the capital of Sanaa in September 2014 before driving the GCC-backed government of President Abdu Rabbu Mansour Hadi into exile in the southern city of Aden in February 2015. To make matters worse, a swift push south into Aden by Houthi militias forced Hadi to flee to Riyadh, affording Iran's allies all but total control over the country.[96] In the face of this development, Riyadh reassessed its threat perception. Although the Islamic State posed an imminent danger to the countries of the GCC, particularly ideologically, it did not present a direct military threat in the way that the Iran-supported Houthis in Yemen did. Iran would not be allowed to destabilize Saudi Arabia on its southern flank by entering Riyadh's historic back yard. The level of Iranian support for the Houthis, a Shia group that emerged in the 1990s, has long been a topic of debate. Former Yemeni president Ali Abdullah Saleh often exaggerated the extent of Iranian influence on the Houthis as he sought Saudi support for military operations against them. Nevertheless, some links did exist between patriarch Hussein Badreddin al-Houthi and the Iranians, and key individuals of the Houthi movement were in contact with Iranian state.[97] But for Saudi Arabia, there was little distinction to be made, and the defeat of the Houthis and their Iranian backers became the immediate priority for military action, a must-win for the new King Salman and his recently promoted son Prince Mohammed.[98] Saudi thinkers expressed confidence that once Yemen had been secured, all attention could be turned to Syria and Assad, shutting Iran out of the region once and for all.[99]

And so the bulk of Gulf military power was moved to Saudi Arabia's southern borders. The Saudis and Emiratis conducted tens of sorties a day, with strikes peaking as high as 126 a day.[100] As with Operation Inherent Resolve, the Emirates and Saudi Arabia became the most heavily involved in pushing back the Houthis. The two countries have provided not only air power but also training to Yemeni forces, as well as deploying troops and armored vehicles in a fierce attempt to turn the tide against the rebels,[101] although Bahrain, Qatar, and Kuwait have also become increasingly involved, and sent substantial numbers of troops as the war escalated in the latter half of 2015.[102] Once again Oman did not support military action in Yemen, preferring to stand outside of the GCC consensus on the matter. Long valuing its relationship with Tehran, Muscat refused to be drawn into a conflict that had the potential to bring its GCC partners and the Iranians into a direct confrontation. For the West's part, the United States and the United Kingdom, with their long-standing security and defense relationships with Saudi Arabia, felt a sense of obligation to support the adventure. Along with the French they pushed through UN Security Council Resolution 2216 (managing to secure a Russian abstention) to back Hadi's government, and ordering the Houthis to demobilize. This support translated into military and technical assistance, with both nations providing advisers and trainers to the joint operations center in Riyadh, and delivering emergency supplies of cruise missiles and air-to-ground missiles for the Royal Saudi Air Force.[103]

Despite international support at the war's outset, the Yemen campaign has become a real headache for the Gulf states. Although the Houthis remain out of Aden, and Iran's interference has been forcefully checked, the end to Yemen's bloody quagmire appears nowhere in sight. The Houthis remain a competent fighting force, backed by Saleh, the former president and Riyadh's one-time ally. Saudi Arabia's insistence on using airpower to back a myriad of poorly trained forces on the ground has led to a virtual stalemate with no clear winner likely to emerge in the near future.[104] Instead, accusations of Saudi Arabia's disregard for international humanitarian law, poor targeting, and rules of engagement that have led to large numbers of civilian casualties have proven highly damaging for Riyadh and its Gulf partners.[105] In London and Washington, some lawmakers, concerned that Saudi-purchased weapons are being used in civilian areas without requisite oversight, are advocating a total reconsideration of the future defense sales relationship with the Gulf, and especially Saudi Arabia.[106] So far this has not happened, and both the United Kingdom and the United States are likely to maintain their relationships with the Gulf countries well into the coming years.[107] But the scale of the human tragedy in Yemen and the inability of the Saudi-led coalition to bring the war to a conclusion has been embarrassing for Western governments,[108] and has further pulled apart the rift between Western nations and Saudi Arabia. Without a clear political track in sight, the war in Yemen is a bleeding sore the Gulf states simply do not know how to treat. While both the Yemen war and the 2011 intervention in Bahrain were largely successful in deterring any full scale military deployment by Iran, they have greatly undermined Saudi power projection in the wider region, and left Riyadh with little in the way of good options to expand its influence at Iran's expense. An end to the war that leaves Houthi militias roaming the country would be an ignominious defeat for Riyadh, but to continue an increasingly futile military operation risks alienating world opinion and draining Saudi resources at a time when money is tight, and Syria still requires Saudi attention and leadership.

Furthermore, the shift of attention away from fighting the Islamic State in early 2015, at a time in which Western powers viewed it as the key threat in the region, has left a bad taste in the mouth both in the West and in the Gulf. In February 2016, Riyadh offered to send ground troops to fight the Islamic State, but this was never taken up by the anti-Islamic State coalition, with American special envoy Brett McGurk reiterating that the "focus on empowering local actors to liberate their own territory [is] the most sustainable strategy for defeating ISIL, and will remain our fundamental approach."[109] The Gulf states have contributed to the fight against the Islamic State in other ways: the Emirates and Qatar have coordinated closely with the West on counter-extremist narratives in the region,[110] while Bahrain and Qatar have also sent advisers to work in the Global Communications Cell of the Counter-ISIL Task Force in Great Britain. Domestically, Saudi Arabia has shown little mercy for those who profess support for the group. In July 2015, the Saudis rounded up 431 of their own nationals in a series of anti-terror sweeps,[111] following Islamic State attacks on Shia mosques in the Eastern Province, and in Kuwait. But the core problem largely remains: Gulf States view the continued demands by the West to divert resources to the battle against the Islamic State as futile while the threat of Iran and its proxy groups is not dealt with. For Riyadh and its Gulf partners, to ignore Iran is to ignore the root cause of Sunni disaffection across the region, and thereby maintain the conditions necessary for groups like the Islamic State and al-Qaeda to exist. To this end it appears there is little room for accommodation between the position of Western states and their Gulf partners. Attempts by the United Kingdom to address the issue of Iran's regional activity have been welcomed by the Gulf states,[112] who now look toward the administration of the new American president, Donald Trump, for similar reassurance that Iran's regional meddling will be contained. But Western rhetoric, if not matched with action, will do little to assuage the fears that have been building over the past decade. At the time of writing it does not appear that either the United Kingdom or the United States possess the necessary resources or political will to contain Iranian influence in the way the Gulf states would like.

Security without the West

Mindful of this, Saudi Arabia has tried, albeit with limited success, to isolate Iran in other ways. In December 2015, Prince Mohammed bin Salman announced the formation of the so-called Islamic Military Alliance to Fight Terrorism, a coalition of thirty-four states stretching from sub-Saharan Africa to Malaysia. Iran and Iraq were conspicuous in their absence, and it was clear from the outset the project sought to form a global alliance to contain Iran's regional and global ambitions, particularly in the Islamic world. It appears an unwieldy grouping of states, hastily cobbled together with no genuine nexus for joint security thinking. But rather than building an Islamic NATO, Saudi Arabia wanted to signal to Iran its intent. As one Saudi diplomat put it, "the goal is not to invade Iran, or produce some sort of military alliance, but to build a framework over time that works to constrain Iran's ambitions across the globe."[113] Similarly, Saudi Arabia has also sought to more closely integrate its security needs with its Gulf brethren. Following stalled attempts at forming a Gulf Union in 2012, the idea is once again being floated by Gulf thinkers, and Riyadh has expended considerable political capital to press the Emirates, Bahrain, Qatar, and Kuwait into forging a closer bond. Such a union's possible power and reach remain uncertain, but it is clear that Saudi Arabia is seeking political assurances from its closest neighbors as the perceived Iranian threat and its associated tensions continue to build. Again, it is notable that Oman has been omitted from Riyadh's plans, and although the Sultanate has decided to join the Islamic Military Alliance to Fight Terrorism, it has still largely refrained from seeking closer political integration with Saudi Arabia. To add substance to the political agreements, the Saudis have engaged in a series of large-scale military exercises.[114] Such exercises are deliberate shows of force from Riyadh designed to impress upon Iran's leadership that Saudi Arabia can and will use force to defend its interests. But while Saudi bicep-flexing might be able to contain Iranian activity in the Gulf, it has not translated into any form of strategy to roll back Iranian influence from the Mashreq at large, and it is here that Riyadh is still largely short on answers.

Conclusion

The Arab uprisings were never going to produce a world that the Gulf states were comfortable with. Fearful of change to the status quo, and terrified that this change might mean the end for the dynastic monarchies in the Gulf, these states have played a bizarrely disjointed role in attempting to secure their interests over the past five years. That tiny Qatar quickly and forcibly mobilized its wealth to speed up change across the region was remarkably uncharacteristic of the behavior of Gulf states. Quite apart from overplaying its hand and spiking the anger of Arab populations in the countries in which it tried to assert its interests, Qatar's activism sparked the ire of the Emirates and in many ways accelerated the awakening of the Saudi juggernaut to squash the potential for instability—in the form of rival regional ideologies—from taking root in the Gulf. Unsure of anybody or anything that upset the regional status quo, Saudi Arabia was all but destined to have problems with a neighbor who set about trying to engineer regional change—especially without first consulting Saudi Arabia, which considers itself the first among equals in the GCC. King Abdullah's desire for a united GCC ended Qatar's rise almost as quickly as it had begun, but really should be seen as Saudi Arabia first getting its own house in order before setting out to engineer regional politics in its favor. Indeed, the aggressive posture of Saudi Arabia to which the region has now become accustomed required three factors to bring it to life. First, the widespread unrest of the Arab uprisings; second, the hyperactivity of Qatar; and last (and most importantly), the United States and its general policy of de-escalation with Iran.

It is this last point that has been most galling for the Gulf. Entrenched distrust and fear of Iran and its expansionist proselytizing was always tempered by the presence of overwhelming American power in the Middle East, combined with a willingness to use that power to contain Iran if necessary. The combined factors of regional destabilization, and the weakening of states—particularly those with significant or majority Shia populations such as Iraq, Lebanon, Syria, and Yemen—presented a headache to which the Gulf states possessed no answer outside of looking to external powers for assistance. But, chastened by a failure of military intervention in Libya, the Gulf's traditional allies have only hesitantly aligned with Gulf interests, preferring instead to reduce military remits to fighting al-Qaeda and the Islamic State, and playing only a supporting role to the Gulf states in containing Iranian activities, particularly at the subnational level. The simple truth is that the forces aligned to Iran's interests—the Shia militias in Iraq and Syria fighting the Islamic State and rebel groups, and the presence of Russian forces in Syria backing Assad—have expended more resources and manpower to shape the region in a manner that suits Tehran, than those aligned toward Saudi Arabia and the Gulf have spent on their allies and benefactors. Riyadh's frustration at this dynamic has triggered its activism, and has accelerated its rise to hegemony in the GCC on regional security matters.

But Riyadh's aggression has produced little of worth. A costly war in Yemen has diverted dwindling Gulf resources to a conflict that is crucial to Saudi stability, but almost no one else's. Saudi activism has not pulled Iraq away from Tehran's orbit, nor has it been able to comprehensively produce a result in Syria that prevents Iran from having a permanent foothold in the country. And in Lebanon, Hezbollah's power is now largely unchecked. Additionally, rifts with traditional partners in the West have widened even further over competing regional priorities, and the relatively poor performance of coalition airpower in Yemen.

As a result, the Middle East remains a threatening environment for the Gulf and there is no obvious way that Iran's influence can be rolled back.

With unrest in Bahrain having been largely contained, there is little that can internally threaten the Gulf, aside from Islamic State sympathizers committing isolated acts of violence. And so the Gulf states can feel relatively happy that their ruling systems have remained largely intact since the Arab uprisings. Indeed, the long-term security of the Gulf is more or less assured: the United States, the United Kingdom, and France will not leave any time soon, and Iran's ambitions across the Gulf are largely contained. But the Gulf's rulers will have to come to terms with the fact that they are but one of a series of players involved in Middle Eastern affairs, a result of American retrenchment from the region, Russian assertiveness, and Iran's reentry into the world. It is an uncomfortable reality, but ultimately not an existential threat. The decades ahead are likely to be unhappy but safe.

Notes

1. See, for example, "Qatari Poet Freed after Three Years in Jail for Reciting Poem Allegedly Insulting Emir," *The Guardian*, March 17, 2016, https://www.theguardian.com/world/2016/mar/17/qatari-poet-freed-after-three-years-in-jail-for-reciting-poem-allegedly-insulting-emir; "Bahrain: Jailing Opposition Leader Ali Salman Is Shocking," Amnesty International, June 16, 2015, https://www.amnesty.org.uk/press-releases/bahrain-jailing-opposition-leader-ali-salman-shocking; and Raissa Kasolowsky and Rania Gamal, "Leading Lawyer Arrested in UAE Clampdown on Dissidents," *Reuters*, July 17, 2012, http://www.reuters.com/article/us-uae-arrests-idUSBRE86G0CQ20120717.

2. "Kuwait: Electronic Crimes Law threatens to further stifle freedom of expression," Amnesty International, January 11, 2016, https://www.amnesty.org/en/latest/news/2016/01/kuwait-electronic-crimes-law-threatens-to-further-stifle-freedom-of-expression/.

3. Throughout this chapter, "Gulf states" refers to the Arab states of the Gulf.

4. See, for example, the speech of Prime Minister Sheikh Hamad bin Jassim Bin Jabr Al Thani at the Doha Forum 2012, available at http://www.dailymotion.com/video/x30hyot.

5. Michael Stephens and Thomas Juneau, "Saudi Arabia: Why We Need This Flawed Ally," *Lawfare*, September 26, 2016, https://www.lawfareblog.com/saudi-arabia-why-we-need-flawed-ally. For a public example of the rift see comments made in Jeffrey Goldberg, "The Obama Doctrine," *The Atlantic*, April 2016, http://www.theatlantic.com/magazine/archive/2016/04/the-obama-doctrine/471525/; and Prince Turki al-Faisal al-Saud, "No Mr. Obama We Are Not Free Riders," *Arab News*, March 14, 2016, http://www.arabnews.com/columns/news/894826.

6. Mohammed Khalid al-Yahya, "The Iran Deal Is Iran's Nuclear Bomb," *Al-Arabiya*, November 4, 2015, https://english.alarabiya.net/en/views/news/middle-east/2015/11/04/The-Iran-deal-is-Iran-s-nuclear-bomb.html.

7. "UN Says Ten Thousand Killed in Yemen War, Far More Than Other Estimates," *Reuters*, August 30, 2016, http://www.reuters.com/article/us-yemen-security-toll-idUSKCN11516W.

8. "Saudi UN Envoy Decries Houthi Attacks," *Al Arabiya*, August 3, 2016, https://english.alarabiya.net/en/News/middle-east/2016/08/03/Saudi-UN-envoy-decries-Houthi-border-attacks.html.

9. The "Mashreq" usually refers to the area of the Middle East comprising Arab lands East of Egypt, sometimes excluding the Arabian Peninsula. In this report, I take it to comprise the Arab countries of the Gulf, as well.

10. Simeon Kerr, "Saudi Arabia Cuts Public Sector Bonuses in Oil Slump Fallout," *Financial Times*, September 27, 2016, https://www.ft.com/content/765898e0-8482-11e6-8897-2359a58ac7a5; "Bahrain Says Austerity Plans in Line with IMF," *Reuters*, January 30, 2016, http://www.reuters.com/article/bahrain-economy-austerity-idUSL8N15E0FC.

11. Jamal Abdullah, "Qatar's Foreign Policy: the Old and New," *Al Jazeera*, November 21, 2014, http://www.aljazeera.com/indepth/opinion/2014/11/analysis-qatar-foreign-policy--2014111811274147727.html.

12. Simon Henderson, "The Al Jazeera Effect," Policy Watch 507, Washington Institute for Near East Policy, December 8, 2000, http://www.washingtoninstitute.org/policy-analysis/view/the-al-jazeera-effect-arab-satellite-television-and-public-opinion.

13. Sultan Sooud Al Qassemi, "How Saudi Arabia and Qatar Became Friends Again," *Foreign Policy*, July 21, 2011, http://foreignpolicy.com/2011/07/21/how-saudi-arabia-and-qatar-became-friends-again/.

14. Simeon Kerr, "Saudi Arabia Sets Lavish Spending Figure," *Financial Times*, December 27, 2011, https://www.ft.com/content/582e70d2-30a5-11e1-b96f-00144feabdc0.

15. See David Roberts, "Qatar and the Muslim Brotherhood: Pragmatism or Preference?," *Middle East Policy Council Journal* XXI, no. 3 (2014): 84-94; and Lina Khatib, "Qatar's Foreign Policy: The Limits of Pragmatism," *International Affairs* 89, no. 2, (2013): 423.

16. Kristian Coates Ulrichsen, "Qatar and the Arab Spring: Policy Drivers and Regional Implications," Carnegie Endowment for International Peace, Policy Paper, September 24, 2014, http://carnegieendowment.org/2014/09/24/qatar-and-arab-spring-policy-drivers-and-regional-implications-pub-56723.

17. Heidi A. Campbell and Diana Hawk, "Al Jazeera's Framing of Social Media During the Arab Spring," *CyberOrient* 6, no. 1 (2012), http://www.cyberorient.net/article.do?articleId=7758.

18. Marc Lynch, *The New Arab Wars: Uprisings and Anarchy in the Middle East* (New York: Public Affairs, 2016), 52.

19. Kristina Kausch, Foreign Funding in Post-Revolution Tunisia, FRIDE, 2013, 17.

20. Marwa Arad, "Qatar to Invest $18 billion in Egypt Economy," *Reuters*, September 6, 2012, http://www.reuters.com/article/us-egypt-qatar-investment-idUSBRE8850YK20120906.

21. David Roberts, "Behind Qatar's intervention in Libya," *Foreign Affairs,* September 28, 2011, https://www.foreignaffairs.com/articles/libya/2011-09-28/behind-qatars-intervention-libya.

22. "The Outcome of the Council of the League of Arab States Meeting at the Ministerial Level," March 12, 2011, http://www.lcil.cam.ac.uk/sites/default/files/LCIL/documents/arab-spring/libya/Libya_19_Outcome_League_of_Arab_States_Meeting.pdf.

23. United Nations Security Council Resolution 1973, March 17, 2011.

24. Kristian Coates Ulrichsen, "Arab Solutions to Arab problems? The Changing Regional Role of the Gulf States, Russia," *Global Affairs*, March 25, 2012, http://eng.globalaffairs.ru/number/Arab-Solutions-to-Arab-Problems-15499.

25. Ulrichsen, "Qatar and the Arab Spring."

26. David Roberts, "Behind Qatar's Intervention in Libya," *Foreign Affairs*, September 28, 2011, https://www.foreignaffairs.com/articles/libya/2011-09-28/behind-qatars-intervention-libya.

27. Ulrichsen, "Arab Solutions to Arab Problems."

28. Jonathan Schanzer, "Saudi Arabia Is Arming the Syrian Opposition: What Could Possibly Go Wrong?," *Foreign Policy*, February 27, 2012, http://foreignpolicy.com/2012/02/27/saudi-arabia-is-arming-the-syrian-opposition/.

29. Ulrichsen, "Arab Solutions to Arab Problems."

30. Roula Khalaf and Abigail Fielding-Smith, "How Qatar Seized Control of the Syrian Revolution," *Financial Times*, May 17, 2013, https://www.ft.com/content/f2d9bbc8-bdbc-11e2-890a-00144feab7de.

31. Michael Stephens, "The Arab League Actually Does Something," *Foreign Policy*, March 27, 2013, http://foreignpolicy.com/2013/03/27/the-arab-league-actually-does-something/.

32. "Protesters Burn Qatari Flag over Perceived Interference in Egypt's Affairs," *Ahram Online*, April 20, 2013, http://english.ahram.org.eg/NewsContent/1/64/69731/Egypt/Politics-/Protesters-burn-Qatari-flag-over-perceived-interfe.aspx.

33. "Qatar Pays Price for Its Generous Support to Muslim Brotherhood," *Middle East Online*, May 11, 2011, http://www.middle-east-online.com/english/?id=58685.

34. Michael Stephens, "Qatar's Top Diplomat Tackles the Rumours," *Open Democracy*, April 1, 2013, https://www.opendemocracy.net/michael-stephens/qatar%E2%80%99s-top-diplomat-tackles-rumours.

35. Simeon Kerr, "Fall of Egypt's Mohamed Morsi Is Blow to Qatari Leadership," *Financial Times*, July 3, 2013, https://www.ft.com/content/af5d068a-e3ef-11e2-b35b-00144feabdc0.

36. Lynch, *The New Arab Wars*, 54.

37. See for example, Camilla Hall and Simeon Kerr, "UAE Democracy Activists Sentenced to Jail," *Financial Times*, November 27, 2011, https://www.ft.com/content/4e2934fc-18d9-11e1-92d8-00144feabdc0; and "There Is No Freedom Here: Silencing Dissent in the United Arab Emirates," Amnesty International, 2014, 7.

38. David D. Kirkpatrick, "Recordings Suggest Emirates and Egyptian Military Pushed Ousting of Morsi," *New York Times*, March 1, 2015, http://www.nytimes.com/2015/03/02/world/middleeast/recordings-suggest-emirates-and-egyptian-military-pushed-ousting-of-morsi.html?_r=0.

39. See video Shiekh Yusuf al-Qaradawi calling Egyptian, world community to support democracy and denounce killings, YouTube, August 14, 2013, https://www.youtube.com/watch?v=MfLdReWWv_c.

40. "Reactions to the Developments in Egypt," *Associated Press*, August 17, 2013, https://www.yahoo.com/news/reactions-developments-egypt-113017930.html?ref=gs. Some estimates have put the number of dead at Rabaa at more than eleven hundred.

41. Judy Dempsey, "Libya Missing Out on a Happy End," Carnegie Europe, 2012. http://carnegieeurope.eu/strategiceurope/?fa=51756.

42. Ulrichsen, "Qatar and the Arab Spring."

43. Steven Sotloff, "Why the Libyans Have Fallen Out of Love with Qatar," *Time*, January 2, 2012, http://content.time.com/time/world/article/0,8599,2103409,00.html.

44. Ulrichsen, "Qatar and the Arab Spring."

45. "Qatar Steadfast in Its Support for Islamist Groups," *Gulf States Newsletter* 37, no. 946 (May 9, 2013): 3–4.

46. Elizabeth Dickinson, "The Case against Qatar," *Foreign Policy*, September 30, 2014, http://foreignpolicy.com/2014/09/30/the-case-against-qatar/.

47. Christopher Phillips, *The Battle For Syria: International Rivalry in the New Middle East* (New Haven, Conn.: Yale University Press, 2016), 124.

48. This included strong support for opposition activist Riad Seif, and his plan to enlarge the Syrian National Council into the National Coalition for Syrian Revolutionary and Opposition Forces (the NCSROF) thereby diluting Qatari influence, alongside a strong relationship to the Salafi Islam Army (Jaysh al-Islam) operating in the Eastern Ghouta, outside of Damascus, under the command of the late Zahran Alloush.

49. Phillips, *The Battle For Syria*, 116–17.

50. "Syrian Opposition Leader Spills the Beans on Saudi, Qatar, and the West on Syria," *Al Jazeera*, May 14, 2013, https://www.youtube.com/watch?v=Y2r7sctbwu4.

51. Hassan Hassan, "Saudis Overtaking Qatar in Sponsoring Syrian Rebels," *The National*, May 15, 2013, http://www.thenational.ae/thenationalconversation/comment/saudis-overtaking-qatar-in-sponsoring-syrian-rebels.

52. Mohammed Nuruzzaman, "Qatar and the Arab Spring: Down the Foreign Policy Slope," *Journal of Contemporary Arab Affairs* 8, no. 2 (2015): 235.

53. Thomas Erdbrink, "Al Jazeera TV Network Draws Criticism, Praise for Coverage of Arab Revolutions," *Washington Post*, May 14, 2011, https://www.washingtonpost.com/world/al-jazeera-tv-network-draws-criticism-praise-for-coverage-of-arab-revolutions/2011/05/08/AFoHWs2G_story.html.

54. Aryn Baker, "Bahrain's Voiceless: How Al Jazeera's Coverage of the Arab Spring Is Uneven," *Time*, May 24, 2011, http://world.time.com/2011/05/24/bahrains-voiceless-how-al-jazeeras-coverage-of-the-arab-spring-is-uneven/. See also Andrew Hammond, "Gulf Media Find Their Red Line in Uprisings: Bahrain," Reuters, April 14, 2011, http://af.reuters.com/article/worldNews/idAFTRE73D1HB20110414?sp=true.

55. James Dorsey, "Gulf Proxy War: UAE Seeks to Further Damage Qatar's Already Tarnished Image," *Huffington Post*, November 28, 2014, http://www.huffingtonpost.com/james-dorsey/gulf-proxy-war-uae-seeks_b_5898246.html.

56. See for example, Karl Vick, "Qatar Bribery Allegations Loom over the 2022 World Cup," *Time*, June 5, 2014, http://time.com/2822288/qatar-world-cup-bribery/.

57. See for example, "German Minister Accuses Qatar of Funding Islamic State Fighters," *Reuters*, August 20, 2014, http://www.reuters.com/article/us-iraq-security-germany-qatar-idUSKBN0GK1I720140820.

58. See for example, David Roberts, "Punching above Its Weight? Could Tiny Qatar Send Ground Forces to Libya?," *Foreign Policy*, April 12, 2011, http://foreignpolicy.com/2011/04/12/punching-above-its-weight-2/.

59. "Al Jazeera Employees Complain of Editorial Bias with Egypt Coverage," *Doha News*, September 5, 2013, https://dohanews.co/al-jazeera-employees-complain-of-editorial-bias-with-2/.

60. "Al Jazeera Journalists Arrested in Egypt," *Al Jazeera*, December 30, 2013, http://www.aljazeera.com/news/middleeast/2013/12/al-jazeera-journalists-arrested-egypt-20131230526144437237.html.

61. "Al Jazeera: Must Do Better," *The Economist*, January 12, 2013, http://www.economist.com/news/middle-east-and-africa/21569429-arabs-premier-television-network-bids-american-viewers-must-do-better; and Michael Stephens, "Qatar's Public Diplomacy Woes," *Open Democracy*, February 4, 2013, https://www.opendemocracy.net/michael-stephens/qatar%e2%80%99s-public-diplomacy-woes.

62. "Saudi Arabia Declares Muslim Brotherhood a Terrorist Group," *BBC*, March 7, 2014, http://www.bbc.com/news/world-middle-east-26487092.

63. Ismaeel Naar, "Q&A: What's Behind MB Leaders Leaving Qatar?," *Al Jazeera*, September 17, 2014, http://www.aljazeera.com/news/middleeast/2014/09/qa-what-behind-mb-leaders-leaving-qatar-201491685443765763.html.

64. "Saudi Arabia 'Has No Problem with the Muslim Brotherhood,'" *Middle East Eye*, February 13, 2015, http://www.middleeasteye.net/news/saudi-foreign-minister-no-problem-muslim-brotherhood-230201904.

65. "King Salman Performs Traditional Qatari Dance," *Al Arabiya*, December 5, 2016, https://english.alarabiya.net/en/media/digital/2016/12/05/Watch-Saudi-King-Salman-performs-traditional-Qatari-dance.html.

66. Soner Cagaptay and Oliver Decottignies, "Turkey's New Base in Qatar," WINEP Policy Watch 2545, January 11, 2016, http://www.washingtoninstitute.org/policy-analysis/view/turkeys-new-base-in-qatar.

67. "Saudi Royal Family Member (anonymous)," interview with the author, London, December 2, 2016.

68. Serkan Demirtas, "Turkey Steps up Ties with GCC, Ends Three-Year Row with the UAE," *Hurriyet Daily News*, April 27, 2016, http://www.hurriyetdailynews.com/turkey-steps-up-ties-with-gcc-ends-3-year-row-with-uae.aspx?pageID=449&nID=98372&NewsCatID=429.

69. Bruce Reidel, "Riyadh's Bold Gamble," *Al Monitor*, September 20, 2016, http://www.al-monitor.com/pulse/originals/2016/09/saudi-arabia-foreign-policy-king-salman-bold-gamble.html.

70. Jason Burke, "Saudi Arabia Worries about Stability, Security, and Iran," *The Guardian*, June 29, 2011, https://www.theguardian.com/world/2011/jun/29/saudi-arabia-prince-turki-arab-spring-iran.

71. Prince Turki al-Faisal al-Saud, "Veto a State, Lose an Ally," *New York Times*, September 11, 2011, http://www.nytimes.com/2011/09/12/opinion/veto-a-state-lose-an-ally.html.

72. See for example Bill Law, "The Most Dangerous Man in the World?," *The Independent*, January 8, 2016, http://www.independent.co.uk/voices/the-most-dangerous-man-in-the-world-a6803191.html; and Patrick Cockburn, "Prince Mohammed bin Salman: Naïve, Arrogant Saudi Prince Is Playing with Fire," *The Independent*, January 9, 2016, http://www.independent.co.uk/news/world/middle-east/prince-mohammed-bin-salman-naive-arrogant-saudi-prince-is-playing-with-fire-a6804481.html. See also a German BND report leaked on December 2, 2015 that explicitly states that "The previous cautious diplomatic stance of older leading members of the royal family is being replaced by an impulsive policy of intervention," adding that "Prince Mohammed risked overly straining relations with befriended and, most of all, allied states."

73. See for example the statement by Supreme Leader Ali Khamenei that in Saudi Arabia "inexperienced youths have taken over the affairs of the state and are replacing dignity with barbarity." In David D. Kirkpatrick, "Tensions between Iran and Saudi Arabia Deepen over Conflict in Yemen," *New York Times*, April 9, 2015, http://www.nytimes.com/2015/04/10/world/middleeast/yemen-fighting.html.

74. Saudi Policy Adviser to the GCC Secretary General, interview with the author, Riyadh, February 4, 2016. See also Prince Sultan bin Khalid al-Faisal al-Saud, "Clear and Present Danger," *Gulf Affairs Journal* Spring (2016): 25.

75. Saudi policy academic, interview with the author, London, November 2015.

76. Presentation, Brigadier General Ahmed al Asiri, The Royal United Services Institute, February 29, 2016.

77. Michael Stephens, "GCC Security Priorities Set It at Odds with the West," *Gulf Affairs Journal* (Spring 2016): 26.

78. Kyle Orton, interview with the author, London, March 19, 2016.

79. Mark Mazzetti and Matt Apuzzo, "US relies heavily on Saudi Money to support the Syrian rebels," *New York Times*, January 23, 2016, http://www.nytimes.com/2016/01/24/world/middleeast/us-relies-heavily-on-saudi-money-to-support-syrian-rebels.html.

80. Michael Stephens, "The View from the Gulf," in "Understanding Iran's role in the Syria conflict," eds. Aniseh Bassiri Tabrizi and Raffaello Pantucci, RUSI Occasional Paper, August 2016, 41.

81. Erika Solomon and Isabel Coles, "Gulf States Recall Envoys, Rap Syria over Crackdown," *Reuters*, August 8, 2011.

82. Sheikh Yusuf al-Qaradawi, "Yes I Defended Hezbollah, But after the War Against the Rebels in Syria, They Proved Themselves the Party of Satan" (Arabic, translation provided by author), *Al Arabiya*, June 9, 2013, https://www.youtube.com/watch?v=7ORtjgLrW1k .

83. "Saudi Grand Mufti Praises Qaradawi's Stance on Hezbollah," *Al Arabiya*, June 6, 2013, https://english.alarabiya.net/en/News/middle-east/2013/06/06/Saudi-Grand-Mufti-praises-Qaradawi-s-stance-on-Hezbollah.html.

84. Sultan Sooud Al Qassemi, "Hezbollah and Qatar: Friends No More," *Funoon Arabiya*, June 2013.

85. Elizabeth Dickinson, "Seeking Peace: GCC States on Regional Conflicts," *Newsweek Middle East*, September 28, 2016, http://newsweekme.com/seeking-peace-gcc-states-regional-conflicts/.

86. Goldberg, "The Obama Doctrine."

87. Dickinson, "Seeking Peace."

88. Emile Hokayem, "How Syria Defeated the Sunni Powers," *New York Times*, December 30, 2016, https://www.nytimes.com/2016/12/30/opinion/how-syria-defeated-the-sunni-powers.html?smid=tw-share&_r=0.

89. "Maliki: Saudi and Qatar at war against Iraq," *Al Jazeera*, September 18, 2016, http://video.aljazeera.com/channels/eng/videos/maliki%3A-saudi-and-qatar-at-war-against-iraq/3318997944001;jsessionid=FE44B70E559E547297CEC0393A924E6B.

90. "Iraq Asks Saudi Arabia to Replace Ambassador," *Al Jazeera*, August 29, 2016, http://www.aljazeera.com/news/2016/08/iraq-asks-saudi-arabia-replace-ambassador-160829041208479.html.

91. Dexter Filkins, "The Shadow Commander," *The New Yorker*, September 30, 2013, http://www.newyorker.com/magazine/2013/09/30/the-shadow-commander.

92. See Stratfor, "Re: [OS] PAKISTAN/KSA— Saudi King Called Zardari Greatest Obstacle to Pak Progress: Report," accessed via WikiLeaks, "Global Intelligence Files," 2013, https://wikileaks.org/gifiles/docs/10/1027118_re-os-pakistan-ksa-saudi-king-called-zardari-greatest.html.

93. Jay Solomon and Carol E Lee, "US Signals Iraq's Maliki Should Go," *Wall Street Journal*, June 19, 2014.

94. Peter Kovessy, "Qatar Slams Iraqi PM as Militants Make Gains," *Doha News*, June 17, 2014, https://dohanews.co/qatar-slams-iraqi-pm-sunni-islamists-make-gains/; Najmeh Bozorgmehr and Simeon Kerr, "Iran-Saudi Proxy War Heats up as ISIS Entrenches in Iraq," *Financial Times*, June 25, 2014, https://www.ft.com/content/fdff6240-fc46-11e3-98b8-00144feab7de.

95. "Islamic State Leader Urges Attacks in Saudi Arabia: Speech," *Reuters*, November 13, 2014.

96. Michael Stephens, "Yemen Is a Defining Moment for King Salman," *Al Jazeera*, March 27, 2015, http://www.aljazeera.com/indepth/opinion/2015/03/yemen-defining-moment-king-salman-150327065530744.html.

97. Gregory Johnson, *The Last Refuge: Yemen Al-Qaeda and the Battle for Arabia* (Oneworld Publications, 2013), 156.

98. Martin Reardon, "Saudi Arabia Draws the Line in Yemen," *Al Jazeera*, March 26, 2015, http://www.aljazeera.com/indepth/opinion/2015/03/saudi-arabia-draws-line-yemen-150326134045949.html; Michael Stephens, "Yemen Campaign Key Test for Saudi Arabia," *BBC News*, March 27, 2015, http://www.bbc.co.uk/news/world-middle-east-32091835.

99. Saudi Policy Academic, interview with the author, London, November 2015.

100. Ahmed Asiri, military briefing given in Riyadh, April 16, 2015.

101. Michael Knights and Alexandre Mello, "The Saudi-UAE War Effort in Yemen (Part 1): Operation Golden Arrow in Aden," Policy Watch 2464, Washington Institute for Near East Policy, August 10, 2015, http://www.washingtoninstitute.org/policy-analysis/view/the-saudi-uae-war-effort-in-yemen-part-1-operation-golden-arrow-in-aden.

102. "Yemen Crisis: Qatar Deploys One Thousand Troops," *BBC*, September 7, 2015, http://www.bbc.co.uk/news/world-middle-east-34173544; "UAE and Bahrain Say Fifty Soldiers Killed in Yemen Attack," *Reuters*, September 4, 2015, http://uk.reuters.com/article/uk-yemen-security-idUKKCN0R40V120150904; Kuwaiti military source, interview with the author, London, September 2015.

103. Andrew Chuter, "UK-Supplied Precision Weapons Prove Popular in Saudi-Led Yemen Campaign," *Defense News,* October 17, 2016, http://www.defensenews.com/articles/uk-supplied-precision-weapons-prove-popular-in-saudi-led-yemen-campaign. See also "RAF Bombs Diverted to Saudi for Yemen Strikes," *Defense News,* July 16, 2015, http://militaryedge.org/articles/raf-bombs-diverted-saudis-yemen-strikes/.

104. Peter Salisbury, "Yemen: Stemming the Rise of a Chaos State," Chatham House Research Paper, May 2016, 2.

105. See for example "Bombing Businesses: Saudi Coalition Airstrikes on Yemen's Civilian Economic Structures," Human Rights Watch, July 10, 2016.

106. "Twenty-Seven US Senators Rebel against Arming Saudi Arabia," *The Intercept,* September 21, 2016, https://theintercept.com/2016/09/21/27-u-s-senators-rebel-against-arming-saudi-arabia/; Jon Stone, "UK Government Refuses to Give MPs a Vote on Arms Sales to Saudi Arabia as US Senate Discusses Boycott," *The Independent,* September 14, 2016, http://www.independent.co.uk/news/uk/politics/saudi-arabia-arms-sales-british-us-senate-paul-caroline-lucas-a7307546.html.

107. See for example "Rt Hon Boris Johnson MP, Foreign Secretary Speech: 'Britain Is back East of Suez,'" Bahrain, December 9, 2016.

108. See for example Patrick Wintour, "Foreign Office Retracts Statements to MPs on Saudi Campaign in Yemen," *The Guardian,* July 21, 2016, https://www.theguardian.com/politics/2016/jul/21/foreign-office-retracts-statements-to-mps-on-saudi-campaign-in-yemen; Patrick Wintour, "MPs Split over UK-Saudi Arms Sales Amid Bid to Water down Report," *The Guardian,* September 8, 2016, https://www.theguardian.com/politics/2016/sep/07/mps-poised-to-call-for-suspension-of-uk-arms-sales-to-saudi-arabia.

109. Testimony of Brett McGurk, "Global Efforts to Defeat ISIS," United States Senate Committee on Foreign Relations, June 28, 2016, http://www.foreign.senate.gov/hearings/global-efforts-to-defeat-isis_062816.

110. Qatari diplomat, interview with the author, Doha, January 30, 2016.

111. "Saudi Arabia Announces Arrest of Over Four Hundred Islamic State Supporters," *Agence France-Presse,* July 18, 2015, http://www.telegraph.co.uk/news/worldnews/middleeast/saudiarabia/11748670/Saudi-Arabia-announces-arrest-of-over-400-Islamic-State-supporters.html.

112. "Theresa May 'Clear-Eyed' over Iran Threat," *BBC,* December 7, 2016, http://www.bbc.co.uk/news/uk-politics-38227680.

113. Saudi diplomat, interview with the author, London, December 16, 2015.

114. These included one called Northern Thunder in February 2016, which involved twenty nations and tens of thousands of troops, and Exercise Gulf Shield 1 in October 2016, which largely focused on naval drills in waters close to Oman. See Jeremy Binney, "Saudi 'Raad al-Shamal' Exercise Looks Smaller than Billed," *IHS Jane's Defence Weekly,* February 26, 2016, http://www.janes.com/article/58346/saudi-raad-al-shamal-exercise-looks-smaller-than-billed.

PART II
Civil Society

People Power and Its Limits

Lessons from Lebanon's Anti-Sectarian Reform Movement

THANASSIS CAMBANIS

Citizen-activists created a new type of popular movement in Lebanon in the spring of 2016, building on a history of activism to contest municipal elections. Their campaign, "Beirut Madinati," or "Beirut Is My City," captivated public opinion. It won an impressive 30 percent of the city vote, rattling the country's corrupt political establishment even though it fell short of obtaining any city council seats because of winner-takes-all election rules. The group's limited success illustrates the hunger for reform in the Arab world and the ongoing process of organizational learning taking place within and across borders. But Beirut Madinati's struggle to articulate an overtly political or ideological central animating idea has limited the group's impact. Its members chose not to compete in the 2017 Lebanese parliamentary elections, and are now trying to build an enduring political organization with roots in Beirut's neighborhoods. If the group survives and expands, it will represent a new threshold in activist, reformist politics. Its enduring struggles to resolve internal and ideological disputes, however, echo a wider regional problem among secular, anti-sectarian reform movements.

For most of its recent history, Lebanon has hosted an ongoing experiment in abusive governance. The country's tiny ruling class has grown even more dominant since the civil war, which lasted from 1975 to 1991. A few dozen dynastic families hold the reins of a weak state. Collectively, they have ruled as an oligarchic kleptocracy, preserving the state almost solely as a means to extract rents. This small circle of rulers has grown richer and richer as the quality of life in modern Lebanon has eroded beyond recognition for anyone old enough to remember even the early 1970s. This process of immiseration reached a nadir in the summer of 2015, when a dispute between the warlords who dominate the Lebanese government brought garbage collection to a halt. Suddenly, Beirut and its environs were literally awash in waste. Mass protests broke out in August 2015 in response to the garbage crisis, briefly mobilizing Lebanese from across a spectrum, including followers of rival sectarian warlords and people who normally defined themselves as apolitical.

The warlords swiftly united to stave off the popular challenge to their legitimacy, deploying security forces to crush protests and intelligence operatives to orchestrate sophisticated smear campaigns against protest leaders.[1] The people-power mobilization faded as quickly as it had appeared, like many street protest movements in the Arab world since 2010. Yet something new emerged in its wake. A core group of committed activists, technocrats, and citizens organized an overtly political movement, "Beirut Madinati," or "Beirut Is My City," which competed for the Beirut municipal council in the May 2016 elections. The organizers were determined to put into practice the lessons learned from decades of activism and from the Arab uprisings, and to seize the momentum of the garbage crisis. Beirut Madinati sought power, not as a protest movement but as a political party.

After an energetic campaign, Beirut Madinati surprised the political establishment by winning 30 percent of the vote—enough to claim a symbolic victory but not to win a single seat on the city council. The group then spent months deliberating whether to continue as a political party. Its members finally opted out of the parliamentary elections expected to take place in 2017, and decided, for the time being, to continue primarily as a watchdog group, pressuring the Beirut municipal council to do a better job.

This chapter's close narrative analysis of Beirut Madinati helps identify barriers to entry and electoral success for antiestablishment movements. Given the impossibility of prediction, narrative case studies and other qualitative ethnographic methods open a door to understanding the forces of popular dissatisfaction and the paths through which some movements blossom into high-impact groups.

The story of Beirut Madinati, in itself, illuminates at least three overararching reasons that it should command our attention. Firstly, it sought to attain power rather than protest. Few popular movements since the Arab uprisings have entered directly into politics, abandoning the civil society label to contest elections; still fewer have had staying power. Secondly, it overtly sought to learn from other movements in Lebanon, the Arab world, and other non-Arab countries.[2] Finally, it refused on principle to draw on existing ideologies—political or sectarian—or power structures like the ruling families and their heads, the "zu'ama." The normally fractious rival sectarian warlords and their parties understood the threat, and united to stave off the insurgents.[3]

These distinguishing features contributed to Beirut Madinati's initial success but might ultimately limit its impact. The movement's meteoric rise, its failure to achieve tangible power or attempt an entrée into national politics, and its long-term trajectory as a reform movement hold important lessons for would-be reformers in the Arab world and beyond. The experience of Beirut Madinati shows the benefit of organizational learning and opportunism, but also the limitations of an initiative that lacks an ideological core or animating central idea.

Taking Back the City: Origins of a Movement

Lebanon's peak in popular mobilization and protest came in 2005, when mass protests, perhaps involving half the country's total population, broke out after the assassination of former prime minister Rafik Hariri.[4] In quick succession followed a war with Israel, then an ultimately violent internal feud between Lebanon's sectarian factions over Hezbollah's rightful share of executive power. The showdown unfolded over nearly two years and climaxed in May 2008 with street battles in Ras Beirut and other flashpoints around the country, which finally prompted the country's ruling zu'ama to adjust their shares of government power. The outcome of the 2005–8 crises demonstrated that Lebanon's rulers were incapable of correctly estimating their actual relative power. More troubling, they had no mechanisms of negotiation and conflict resolution short of brinkmanship, confrontation, or violence. The cascades of protests in the end had no impact on the negotiations among the country's rulers. The system allowed no point of entry for citizens to shape policy, and ruling factions paid no price for destructive behavior.

The regional context also played a major role in shaping events in Lebanon. The constant threat of war with Israel hangs over Lebanon. Since 2011, the civil war in Syria has encroached on Lebanon's national security. The specter of communal conflict perpetually spurs anxiety among Lebanese: unique among Arab countries, Lebanon has eighteen officially recognized sects with relatively balanced population shares. These demographics fuel conflict, but also preserve a degree of pluralism and consociational decision-making rare in the region. In a regional context of crippled governance, frustrated people-power uprisings, and nascent initiatives for reform and revolution, Lebanon always faces the threat of foreign intervention and catastrophic security breakdown. For most Lebanese, day-to-day peace depends not on the state but on interpersonal neighborhood dynamics, the vagaries of competing foreign governments, self-serving political bosses, and transnational movements. As a result, Lebanon functions as a sort of showcase for the region's political experiments. Despite its official population, an estimated four to four-and-a-half million,[5] Lebanon carries outsize importance for the rest of the Arab world. Lebanon's strange governing recipe—with corrupt warlords and their militias securing the loyalty of their fiefdoms through patronage—has made for an oddly stable species of postwar recovery.

When revolts swept the Arab world in 2010 and 2011, many Lebanese were wary. On the one hand, the country had a free press, flourishing civil society, and organized political opposition. On the other, it also had fresh memories of the civil war and the 2008 clashes. The country's rulers had made their fortunes as warlords, and constantly reminded the public that a hard push for reform could easily spark a repeat of the civil war. Fear of anarchy meant that popular revolt had less appeal as a political tool in Lebanon than it did elsewhere in the early years of the Arab uprisings. The war that broke out in Syria in 2011 only exacerbated the anxiety, as Lebanese factions took opposite sides in their neighbor's strife. Fighting seeped across the border,[6] and refugees swelled to 20–25 percent of Lebanon's total population.[7] Even more so than in 2005–8, Lebanon appeared at risk of a violent collapse.

Garbage Piles Up

Inept at so many other aspects of governance, Lebanon's warlords proved resilient and resourceful at muddling through an acute security crisis from 2011 to 2013. Factional leaders who encouraged their followers to fight to the death under sectarian banners in Syria ordered them to show restraint at home in Lebanon. Their security efforts were surprisingly effective. When their interests were threatened, the zu'ama were capable of coordination and expeditious action. Meanwhile, as security was restored, traditional patronage and corruption thrived, salaries stalled, the cost of living rose, and basic services continually deteriorated. Electricity, water, and garbage collection, which had improved in the 1990s, had declined for a decade and a half. By 2015, the Lebanese infrastructure was experiencing unprecedented levels of strain, and the government refused to take even the most basic action to maintain the existing, poor quality of service. The collapse of governance highlighted an enraging reality: Lebanon's services were appalling by design, the result of a division of rackets among warlords, whose profits grew as official services declined and citizens were forced to turn to profiteering networks to provide everything from gas and power to, in some cases, neighborhood security.

The garbage crisis marked a turning point for many Lebanese who had been hitherto willing to accede to the ruling clique's paralyzing logic. Protests in August and September 2015 were the largest and most intense that Lebanon had seen in a decade. The climactic demonstrations on August 22–23 drew an estimated ten thousand protesters[8] and were attacked by security forces.[9] A week later maybe twenty thousand attended a peaceful follow-up march on downtown Beirut—a small number compared to the millions who demonstrated in 2005 but nevertheless a threat to the status quo because of their simple, radical, and popular message against government corruption, incompetence, and inaction.[10] The protests were catalyzed by an antiestablishment group called You Stink, whose name addressed the political class. A small core of activists carefully limited You Stink's message: the government needed to solve the garbage crisis, and all the existing movements and leaders were guilty. "We insist we don't want to have a leader or an ideology," explained one of the You Stink founders, an activist and advertising professional named Assad Thebian.[11] "We don't want to be kidnapped by the left, the right, or civil society. We don't believe in revolution. We believe in change. We believe all public figures are corrupt."

You Stink initially resisted calls to expand its critique to the sectarian political system, the electoral law, or other manifestations of public corruption. In keeping with wider regional trends from the 2010–11 Arab uprisings, it tried to divorce "legitimate" protest and popular anger, from the "tainted" game of politics. (Eventually You Stink officially expanded its critique to include Lebanese election laws.) The protest movement quickly balkanized.[12] Some factions did embrace an ideological critique of the government, usually from the left. Others targeted elections or corruption, or worked in sync with establishment political parties. Important political blocs took umbrage at You Stink, including the Future Movement, the Free Patriotic Movement, Hezbollah, Amal, and the Progressive Socialist Party, representing the bulk of Sunni, Shia, Druze, and the single most important Maronite faction.

Authorities quickly closed ranks. Police turned tear gas and water cannons against demonstrators. Many were arrested after clashes that appeared incited by agents provocateurs; activists claimed that state security services and political parties deployed violent infiltrators among the ranks of peaceful demonstrators to discredit the protests. Political leaders levied baseless but incendiary allegations that You Stink was destabilizing the country, creating sectarian strife, and insulting religion. Some politicians decried You Stink's methods but publicly sympathized with the protesters' demands for an end to corruption—even though they and their parties were integrally tied to the corruption. Government and political party officials released leaks, sometimes false, sometimes culled from sources such as individual Facebook pages and taken out of context, to paint You Stink leaders as atheists, hedonists, al-Qaeda sympathizers, foreign agents, or spoiled out-of-touch members of the elite.[13] Protests' leaders faced threats and were sometimes attacked. One political party, the Christian Free Patriotic Movement, mustered a demonstration of its own that dwarfed the anti-garbage protests, as a reminder that the status quo powers had massive reserves of resources and obedient loyalists. The campaign offered a glimpse of the machinery the state could deploy to shut down any popular movement that it considered a threat.

Many of the activists in You Stink, as well as those who went on to establish Beirut Madinati, believe that the establishment parties were behind the sudden proliferation of rival protest groups.[14] Competing messages from AstroTurf groups sapped the popular garbage protests of their vigor and drowned out You Stink's message. Fewer people joined each successive demonstration, and even supporters of You Stink feared that the movement—even unintentionally— created a risk of violence, even by threatening a corrupt status quo.[15] The waste crisis worsened, and when the winter rains came and washed through the proliferating illegal dump sites to which Lebanese had resorted, the country's rivers, streets, and seafront were flooded with garbage. But the political class remained secure, calculating that wider fears—the war in Syria, regional rivalries between Saudi Arabia and Iran, latent sectarian tensions, the threat of violence orchestrated by the very same warlords in order to preserve their fiefs—would suffice to mute popular anger. Nonetheless, they worked hard to demonize the protesters, and their smears found echoes even among fellow dissidents, who whispered that their rivals were paid foreign agents.[16]

Some protesters were arrested. One was threatened with blasphemy charges. Thebian for a time moved out of his house after receiving threats. "We are fighting a system with no mercy," Thebian said, assessing his movement's record after its public activities had dwindled to occasional, small, symbolic anti-corruption actions.[17] "Everyone thinks this system is fragile, but I think it's one of the strongest governing systems." Because all the major political parties and leaders benefit from corruption, any challenge to the way the system operates, like the assault on the garbage contract, threatens the entire system. You Stink, and the public protests, brought enormous public attention to one particularly egregious example of Lebanese corruption and dysfunction. Lebanon's rulers weathered the bump in public anger without making any concessions, or reaching a solution to the garbage issue that prompted it. Apparently, the profits to be had through a secret, extortionate waste management contract were worth any short-term political discomfort.

The Legacy of "You Stink"

The activists involved in the garbage campaign, along with many others who were watching sympathetically, or allied with the movement as technical advisers or casual protesters, internalized several lessons about organizing public opinion, and the simultaneous strength and insecurity of the ruling elite. You Stink performed well with a simple, targeted message, and the technocratic expertise it developed about the issue on which it focused. By avoiding direct attacks on specific politicians and on the sectarian system per se, it coined a message about corruption and fixing services that even politicians found themselves forced to agree with, at least rhetorically.[18] The movement galvanized a wide array of Lebanese, including some elites and some working class and unemployed, some critics of the system and some political activists who came from established parties. It also brought together a group of political activists, technical experts, and urban planners to propose alternatives to the government's garbage proposals, and some of them found a voice articulating policy plans rather than simply voicing opposition to the government.[19]

On the flip side, You Stink's reliance on volunteer work from young activists who had to support themselves with full-time jobs while simultaneously trying to run a movement left it vulnerable to organization fatigue. Its insistence on internal transparency and a horizontal, leaderless structure made it difficult to make decisions and act quickly. The unexpected vehemence of the official smear campaign, and the sudden spread of rival factions, swamped You Stink's public message. Finally, because its only tactic was protest and its only issue was garbage, the You Stink movement found itself with no *raison d'être* when large crowds stopped showing up for demonstrations and the government stalled on the garbage issue. It simply had nothing to do. Its core members, like Thebian, went back to their day jobs. Its main victory had been revealing just how easily spooked the country's political bosses were. "People were actually demanding a change in the pattern in which we were being governed since the 1990s,"

Thebian said.[20] "This frightened the politicians. Every political party that has been part of the system has been part of the corruption. This is not something they will sacrifice easily. It is something they took with power, and they will use their power to keep it."

During the garbage protests, a wide range of veteran activists and new entrants into the public sphere tackled the question of how best to improve Lebanon's entrenched political system. Arguments took place during street protests, on televised talk shows, and in private activist strategy meetings.[21] Competing protest groups contemplated mergers, and some discussed founding a political party. The youth movement galvanized cascades of conversation in different circles, including older activists who had been involved in a variety of campaigns going back decades, including labor organizing, and a loose community of Beirut urban planners, most of whom had some connection to the American University of Beirut (AUB).

Beirut Madinati took shape as the garbage movement lost coherence. By September 2015, a group of activist professionals and academics agreed that they wanted to harness the energy in the You Stink protests into a tangible project. Many ideas were floated: establishing a political party, promoting urban reform in Beirut, fighting corruption, contesting the upcoming municipal elections. Jad Chaaban, an AUB economist, brought in a circle of activists interested in traditional politics and elections, including former journalist Rana Khoury and human rights lawyer Nayla Geagea. Mona Fawaz, an urban planner at AUB, invited planners and architects. They were joined by journalists, engineers, advertising executives, AUB faculty members, and dozens of veterans of past campaigns on causes ranging from civil marriage to the Fouad Boutros Highway, a proposed road through an old neighborhood in Beirut. "It's not just about making change, but creating a nucleus of people who can create change," said Fawaz, recalling the early discussions in August and September 2015.[22] Chaaban drafted a political party platform, and Fawaz tried to formalize a core group at a dinner party at her home in September.

This core group of Beirut Madinati founders, candidates and volunteers could be roughly described as the secular middle and upper-middle class. Its membership was evenly divided among Lebanon's sects, but few of its founders or volunteers identified as observant or devoutly religious. Some had family or historical connections to dynastic clans or major political parties, but identified personally as secular, anti-sectarian, and/or independent. With some exceptions, the younger generation of volunteers were educated and activist. Some had been involved with the Secular Club at AUB, a student organization that tried to galvanize anti-sectarian politics and craft an alternative to the existing Lebanese political groupings. The older generation of activists, including the founders, represented, loosely put, the secular Beiruti professional class, traditionally identified with the Ras Beirut area. They were not, as the establishment would later allege, ultrarich, out-of-touch, Francophone, Christian elites; many came from humble or middle-class backgrounds and they operated within the solidly middle-class confines of urban Beirut. Many were white-collar professionals, in advertising, architecture, academia, or the arts, but none were members of the ultrawealthy circle that dominates Lebanese business and politics.

By November a group of political activists, academics and professionals coalesced with the specific goal of competing in the Beirut municipal elections. Within a month, they had created committees, and by January 2016, the program committee had researched and drafted what became the Beirut Madinati electoral campaign platform, which they summarized in a succinct ten-point plan that avoided Lebanese politics and focused on technocratic quality-of-life issues: traffic, parks, public transportation, housing, waste management, and the like.[23] Professionals, with experience in political campaigns, marketing, and advertising, contributed their expertise. All told, the dedicated activists and volunteers that drove Beirut Madinati numbered just a few hundred individuals, who raised and spent a total of $415,000 over the course of their campaign. They were arrayed against established parties with legions of paid employees, massive advertising budgets, and full-time operatives and loyalists throughout the city. The founders decided from the start not to include any established politicians, even if they shared the nascent movement's views, in order to avoid any taint by association with the existing system. They chose a sunny, apolitical name: Beirut Madinati, or Beirut Is My City. "The shift from You Stink to us is from saying, 'This political class is untenable, rotten, we can't work with it.' The next stop is to say, 'This is what we must do, and this is what the political class should be doing,'" Fawaz said.[24]

A Program to Make Life Better

The platform carefully enumerated a to-do list and touted the probity, expertise, and independence of the Beirut Madinati technocrats. The language studiously avoided sounding political. Beirut Madinati was a "campaign," not a political party, with a "program," not a platform. The city's inept leaders had refused all input and had failed in their obligations to citizens. Beirut Madinati's "primary objective is to make Beirut more livable: more affordable, more walkable, more green, more accessible, and, simply, more pleasant." Who could oppose such goals? Critics rarely disagreed with the aims, only expressing doubts that technocrats, even in control of the city council, would have enough authority to thwart the wealthy, politically-connected cabal of developers and family dynasties that had driven the city to ruin.

The program's mission statement imagines Beirut as a city where working people can raise children and grow old with a modicum of comfort and dignity, and where the city government serves the population. In the context of Beirut's daily dysfunction, such an image is almost fantastical. But the program tries to paint improvement as feasible, breaking down problems by sector and proposing solutions that include minimal, feasible workarounds and building up to bigger, more dreamy improvements. The campaign tended to focus on the most feasible reforms with the most immediate impact: traffic, public transportation, parks and public space, affordable housing in the rampant new construction around the city, waste management, and more transparent and inclusive administration. These weren't necessarily the most important problems in people's lives, like health care and education, but they were more easily addressed and fell under the prerogative of municipal authorities.

The movement's founders had long labored on urban issues, lobbying the city council, with occasional success. As a result, they were familiar with the actual powers of the city council in a system where the national government held most of the purse strings, and authorities crafted their proposals accordingly. If they won seats on the council, they wanted an agenda that was practical and achievable. At the top of the list was transportation. Although Beirut is a small city, geographically, there is no centrally planned public transportation system. Residents rely disproportionately on private cars (70 percent of all trips in the city, according to the Beirut Madinati platform), and an organic, uncoordinated system of privately operated minivans and buses. Beirut Madinati's platform sought to unify and rationalize the existing routes, and introduce rapid-transit bus routes. They also promised to improve traffic flow by deploying police or traffic monitors, which are currently almost nonexistent unless a VIP is trying to pass through a traffic jam. The urban planning tenor of the traffic proposals masked their profoundly political nature; traditional warlords' parties could not coordinate across municipal boundaries because of their competition and dysfunction, whereas a nonaligned group like Beirut Madinati could try to coordinate between, for example, minibus drivers based in a Hezbollah area and others from a Future Movement neighborhood.

The campaign promised, if elected, to increase the amount of green space per person in Beirut from one square meter to five. The city has almost no public parks, and what little open or green space exists is often closed to the public or slated for construction. The campaign's plan would mark a radical improvement in congested neighborhoods without any expensive intervention: the city could use its legal authority to open access to existing but inaccessible open spaces. Beirut Madinati promised to create a city recycling program to reduce the amount of waste sent to landfills. Municipal buildings would be renovated in keeping with ecologically sound "green" principles. In office, Beirut Madinati would aggressively oversee existing authorities that barely functioned but could improve public safety: monitoring water quality, street lights, and the placement of garbage bins. Finally, and easiest of all to implement, a city council with Beirut Madinati members would hold meetings, publish its records, and attend public hearings—all of which are practices that are already required by law yet do not occur.

The remaining proposals on the program were in a similar vein, but less easily accomplished. Beirut Madinati promised to open public access to the city's waterfront, establish new markets that encouraged small local producers, add social impact clauses to public contracts, and double the number of public libraries. Hardest of all to achieve, the campaign proposed to convince developers to include affordable housing units in new construction and address the problem of deteriorated housing stock for the poor, and to reform a rent-regulation regime that protected only a small number of tenants. The first items on the program could conceptually be implemented through city council authority without antagonizing any entrenched constituencies. On the other hand, the more ambitious proposals, relating to housing, development, and parking lots, were likely to face stiff opposition from wealthy individuals and constituencies who profit handsomely from the current dysfunction.

The founders of Beirut Madinati hailed from a diversity of professional backgrounds, and as a group they were connected to almost all the well-known reform efforts in Lebanon. This collective record of fighting the system, rather than any expectation of success, endowed the Beirut Madinati team with an aura of optimism and integrity. These were people who had consistently stood against efforts by the elite to take away public goods such as affordable housing, parks, public waterfront areas, union contracts, and a long list of other things. They had campaigned for the rights of the disadvantaged. They had challenged the zu'ama, the ruling families, and had even scored the occasional success. They had blocked a throughway favored by the government and big developers that would have destroyed one of Beirut's few surviving old-fashioned neighborhoods with an economically diverse population. After years of legwork, one Beirut Madinati candidate had successfully transformed an iconic building ravaged by the civil war into a museum. Several, working together, were fighting a pair of projects that are in the process of destroying the last two remaining natural spaces on the waterfront where Beirut residents can convene. Some had brought attention to the systemic mistreatment of refugees.

Beirut Madinati's founders repeated in public statements that they thought their movement's appeal stemmed from the content of its platform, and from the belief they exuded that change was possible. Interviews with volunteers, voters, and sympathizers—as well as the ultimate results—raise the possibility that the movement's popularity drew more heavily on the personal appeal of the candidates, and frustration with the status quo. In other words, the basket of technical issues—with which no one theoretically disagreed, even the ruling party bosses—were not what inspired volunteers to join Beirut Madinati. Instead, what volunteers and voters said they liked was the integrity of the candidates, their optimism, their refusal to concede defeat to the corrupt government, and the movement's orientation toward the concerns of regular citizens struggling to make ends meet in a city plagued by traffic and lacking the essential amenities of most cities in the developed world.

This dissonance has characterized Beirut Madinati throughout its existence. Some of its founders speak of the urban platform with genuine conviction, and believe the movement's longevity relies on achieving tangible results on traffic, development, pollution, and so on. Citizens and voters, on the other hand, seem to be seeking a rallying idea, along with a concrete, mobilizing activity, that will restore any level of accountability and check the runaway powers of an extractive and predatory government. My impression from extensive interviews with Beirut residents is that those who were attracted to Beirut Madinati liked the personalities involved and the sense of possibility and citizen agency that they fostered—much more so than the platform specifics.

Through word of mouth and personal circles, Beirut Madinati assembled a campaign team and solicited volunteers for the election. Traditional campaigns cost an enormous amount of money, much of it spent on advertising and personnel, including thousands of canvassers and election day monitors for the city's approximately 850 polling stations. Beirut Madinati intended to rely almost exclusively on volunteers and on free or cheap advertising, with the bulk of publicity coming through media coverage and social media shares.[25] "The experiment is very simple," said Chaaban, the AUB economist, during Beirut Madinati's launch period.[26] "There are no political parties in Lebanon. There is a leader, and followers. We want to test this with a focused objective."

The Election Campaign

Previous Beirut elections had witnessed declining turnout, dropping from a peak of 33 percent in 1998 to 21 percent in 2010 (the same proportion that voted in 2016).[27] Popular anger was high in the wake of the garbage protests and other serial governance failures. While the state was weak and municipal government had limited powers, the city council of Beirut had a $240 million operating budget.[28] Lebanon at the time had no president, and no parliamentary elections scheduled; the sitting parliament, stuffed with hereditary politicians, had unconstitutionally extended its own mandate by nearly three years in November 2014 on the grounds that a country with a vacant presidency could ill afford a disbanded parliament, and the caretaker government in place could not stage elections for a new one. Municipal elections were the only opportunity to have any impact at all. "People have had enough. It is not enough to have success in our NGOs," Chaaban said. "We need people like us in power. You can't just demonstrate and get teargassed."

Machine politics guaranteed that Lebanese elections, even at the local level, were not genuinely competitive. In most cases, the dominant parties came to agreements beforehand and avoided direct competition. Further complicating matters, Lebanese are forced to vote in their area of origin rather than where they live. The government does not print standardized ballots, and most voters use ballots distributed by parties and local chieftains that, through careful coding such as the font or order of names on the ballot, allow parties to keep track of how people vote. Such practices reinforce vote buying and bloc voting by families and other groupings. Beirut's electoral boundaries include a Sunni majority, dominated by Saad Hariri's Future Movement, and a sizable Christian population that supports multiple competing Christian parties. The city limits include about five hundred thousand registered voters, far fewer than the actual population, and do not include adjoining, Shia-dominated areas, which fall in different electoral districts. With the blessing of the other ruling parties in Lebanon, Hariri and his party select the municipal list for Beirut, negotiating with the Christian parties and other smaller groups for shares of the twenty-four seats. By tradition, the slate of candidates on the council is half Christian and half Muslim, in keeping with Beirut's identity as a mixed city. This precooked system can create interesting paradoxes. For instance, because Hezbollah is not directly involved in the Beirut elections or the city governance, its media outlets have a history of fair, aggressive, and investigative coverage of Beirut city politics. Similarly, the neighborhood bosses who instruct people how to vote hold less sway over Christians and middle-class Sunnis not embedded in Hariri patronage networks.

Normally, a group of activists from the secular intellectual elite would stand almost no chance against the well-oiled political machine of a "zaim" (the singular of zu'ama). But the municipal elections of 2016 offered a rare opportunity, because the city's dominant political boss had suffered numerous setbacks and was uncharacteristically vulnerable and distracted. As a result of various regional machinations, Saudi Arabia had withdrawn its patronage of Hariri after decades supporting the family dynasty.[29] Nearly bankrupt, Hariri faced challenges from other politicians eager to replace him as the nation's preeminent Sunni leader. This confluence of factors weakened the governing slate and meant that a challenger in the Beirut municipal race would benefit from a historical opening.

Beirut Madinati's founders conceived it as an organization that would be egalitarian, inclusive, and immune to bossman rule—leading by example in a country where "every party has evolved into a one-man show."[30] The group had a general assembly, which voted on major decisions. A campaign general coordinator and a steering committee oversaw daily operations during the campaign. Beirut Madinati's strategists might have overestimated their organizational prowess, and initially underestimated how much money they'd be able to raise. Like many reform movements of the era, the insistence on horizontal, consensus-driven, leaderless, transparent internal decision-making put a low ceiling on ideological appeal, flexibility, and speedy decision making.[31] The campaign officially launched on March 23 with a press conference at a seaside restaurant in Ras Beirut. A full slate of twenty-four candidates was unveiled. A month earlier Chaaban had expressed modest hopes for success, but heartened by the response they'd elicited in their call for volunteers and donations, the campaign steering committee now hoped to win a significant share, maybe even a majority, of the city council seats.

Good governance undergirded the platform. The slate intended to campaign door to door and neighborhood by neighborhood, relying on volunteer canvassers and open public events called "discussion spaces" or "open squares" (masahat niqash in Arabic) that would take place in underutilized public spaces and call attention to the city government's marginalization of neighborhoods and citizens. Meanwhile, the established parties opted not to fight each other and instead assembled a single establishment "Beirutis" list, which unsubtly marketed itself as the rightful guardians of the city's old-timers against a destabilizing, rabble-rousing group of upstart newcomers.

With less than two months to campaign and long odds, Beirut Madinati generated a fair amount of buzz. Lebanese media gave its candidates and founders extensive coverage, another result of Lebanon's open, pluralistic system, which meant that political bosses couldn't simply quash media coverage they didn't like.[32] Among educated, online networks, the campaign dominated social media streams. But many of the scheduled public assemblies were cancelled or failed to materialized; in some instances, Beirut Madinati blamed the Future Movement or conservative city notables for strong-arming neighborhood power brokers into cancelling support for Beirut Madinati's public meetings, while in other cases, cancellations seemed to result from gaps in organizational capacity. Discussion spaces in marginalized neighborhoods drew modest crowds, and often half or more of the attendees were already Beirut Madinati volunteers, rather than prospective voters drawn by a neighborhood forum. The organization couldn't absorb all the volunteers, and voter outreach was underwhelming: Beirut Madinati did not engage in systematic door-to-door canvassing.

In some cases, Beirut Madinati volunteers faced direct intimidation, especially in neighborhoods where established parties like the Future Movement or Amal routinely deployed thuggish cadres to signal their party's hold over an area. Many of these areas were also the most neglected, like the poor Sunni quarter of Tariq al-Jadideh, which consistently voted for Saad Hariri as a sort of tribal sectarian protector, and in return, received even less than neighborhoods of shifting loyalty. "We don't trust anyone, but we'll vote for Hariri in order to show that we exist," a Tariq al-Jadideh local boss named Ahmed Shara'i explained. "With the leaders we know, we're still losing. Imagine how much more we lose if they're gone." Against this zero-sum logic, Beirut Madinati struggled to make inroads. Even mistreated clientelistic voters understood the logic of the system, and they reasonably doubted that a movement like Beirut Madinati, even if victorious, would be able to offer them anything at all: services, security, or representation within the narrow circles of power where decisions are made.

The establishment alliance seemed to take seriously the threat posed by Beirut Madinati, but considered it a "friendly" challenge. Hariri later described it as a well-meaning list that "shares our ambitions and values."[33] In any case, the establishment list added some fresh faces and adopted much of the rhetoric of Beirut Madinati, speaking suddenly of green spaces and quality of life. Major figures, including the minister of the interior, who by law is supposed to be a neutral figure overseeing the integrity of elections, endorsed Hariri's list in the last weeks of the campaign, which also witnessed a sudden spree of billboards and radio ads. An orchestrated whisper campaign painted Beirut Madinati as Christian, elitist, and likely ineffectual—a rich claim coming from a list dominated by ultrawealthy clans and business interests. The establishment apparently calculated it could win without employing any harder tactics against Beirut Madinati.

For its part, Beirut Madinati campaigned politely, taking care not to provoke the establishment by frontal attacks. It did, however, raise expectations of an electoral victory among the core group of several hundred volunteers who immersed themselves nearly full-time in the effort in the month before the election, on May 8, 2016. Beirut Madinati spurred a national conversation about reform and obliquely raised the central concerns with the sectarian political system: that it had failed in even the most easily addressed practical ways. Members of Beirut Madinati's steering committee telephoned officials in the Future Movement, asking them to use their influence to discourage the intimidation tactics being deployed against Beirut Madinati. The request did not yield any result. Such is the power and mystique of the country's warlords that many Beirut Madinati activists worried that Saad Hariri would be able, if he chose, to simply shut down their campaign, or buy off critical activists with offers of lucrative consultancies or political positions. In any event, Hariri's alliance copied some of the urban reform policy messages of Beirut Madinati, and made clear that a loss of control over the city could create a serious risk of sectarian violence—but nevertheless allowed its rivals to campaign.

Despite the media buzz that preceded it, election day in Beirut was quiet. "We've opened a Pandora's Box," said Ibrahim Mneimneh, an engineer who headed the Beirut Madinati candidates list, awaiting results at Beirut Madinati's temporary headquarters.[34] "People wanted to give a slap in the face to their sectarian leaders, without taking a huge risk. It's just the right dose." When the votes were counted, though, it appeared that far fewer Beirutis were willing to give that slap in the face to their established leaders than Beirut Madinati strategists had predicted.

Initial results showed that Beirut Madinati performed impressively, and most media reports carried an assessment based on partial returns.[35] When final tallies were published, however, Beirut Madinati had won only 30 percent of the vote (not the 40 percent initially reported); still an impressive showing.[36] Under proportional representation, Beirut Madinati's votes might have given it ten of the twenty-four seats on the council. But under the existing rules, despite the group's performance, it did not win a single city council seat. Only 20 percent of registered voters actually voted, but Beirut Madinati won the city's mostly Christian parliamentary first district. According to Ramez Dagher's analysis on his blog Moulahazat, about 30 percent of the city's Sunni voters defected, despite a drumbeat of scare tactics. The numbers involved were quite small in absolute terms. After all the campaigning, the establishment's Beirutis list was able to sweep the council with just 47,465 people voting for the top finisher and 38,989 for the lowest. There was a sizable gap between the lowest-scoring winner and the top vote-getter from Beirut Madinati, the list leader Ibrahim Mneimneh, who won 31,933 votes. Compared to the campaign's original predictions, the number of election day voters was a disappointment, even if it was impressive for an upstart campaign with little financing.[37]

To Continue in Politics or Work as an Urban NGO?

In some ways, Beirut Madinati was incredibly shrewd, opportunistic, and pragmatic, but from another angle the same virtues could be viewed as overly cautious, bland, politically shortsighted, and conservative. The movement wanted to reject sectarianism, but carefully balanced its list: half Christian, half Muslim, half male, half female.[38] The caution didn't insulate Beirut Madinati from the slur that it was a pet project of hypereducated cosmopolitans more comfortable in bars than Beirut's hardscrabble streets, dominated by Francophone Christians. This stereotyping, backed by establishment media, completely misrepresented the reality of Beirut Madinati and ignored the fact that the establishment was decidedly richer, more elite, and packed with leaders who spent more time abroad than in Lebanon. Nonetheless the tactic worked, and Beirut Madinati's choice not to confront Hariri or other leaders directly, or to criticize sectarianism directly, might have cost the movement an opportunity to motivate otherwise apathetic and dejected voters.

Beirut Madinati carefully studied other movements and weighed the risks and possibilities of the current political moment in Lebanon. Its founders, candidates, and volunteers were almost uniformly vocal critics of their country's political leadership, endemic corruption, and governing system. Most were secular, anti-sectarian, and had no faith in the existing political parties. On the other hand, many of the secular anti-sectarians and technocrats had sectarian backgrounds, and affiliations to ideologies (leftism, socialism, resistance) or to specific political figures. They could set these differences aside for a short period while working on a ten-point quality-of-life improvement plan for Beirut, but when talk turned to national issues or root-and-branch reform of the system, the common ground quickly narrowed. Some had sympathies for the Future Movement, or for Hezbollah. Some considered themselves as communist or socialist, and had problems with what they saw as the neoliberal leanings of other members.

Elsewhere in Lebanon, voters had defected from the ruling parties in favor of groupings that were in some ways even more conservative and status quo than the ruling circle, representing tribes, families, or extreme populists from established political parties. The most successful were dissidents from within ruling circles who didn't challenge corruption, sectarianism, or warlordism, but simply vowed to do a better job within its constrictions. A prime example is Ashraf Rifi, a former justice minister who resigned from the Sunni Future Movement and won the local elections in Tripoli.

The founders of Beirut Madinati were determined that their movement endure and preserve its unique internal character. They also felt a responsibility to their voters. After a "victory rally" in the parking lot by the Beirut Forum, despite disappointment over their loss, the group's general assembly, consisting of about eighty members, met repeatedly over the summer to assess the election and choose a path forward. The internal debate quickly broke down into two almost evenly matched factions: one that wanted to focus on Beirut, and one that believed the movement should also address national politics. The Beirut faction believed the group should consolidate its electoral achievement, build a viable organization in the city, and spend the next six years of the city council's term pushing for better governance and fighting various toxic urban development projects. The core of this group included some activists who had already spent decades working on urban causes in Beirut. The politics faction believed that the entire purpose had always been to challenge the failing sectarian political system; the municipal elections had been the vehicle available to challenge the status quo, and the future would soon bring more important targets, like the 2017 parliamentary elections.

In keeping with a dominant activist ethos, Beirut Madinati's membership believed the process was as important as the outcome. They had run a leaderless campaign in order to show Lebanon it was possible to have a charismatic movement without a bossman. Now they wanted to take an existential decision in a deliberative, transparent, and inclusive fashion. In the event, the discussions turned acrimonious and stretched five months, from June through October of 2016. The debate—to run or not to run, to be a political party or an accountability movement—echoed the dilemma of anti-sectarian, secular, reform, and revolutionary movements almost everywhere. Opposition, protest, and citizen watchdog pressure were endowed with an air of unity, purity, and legitimacy, whereas power-seeking, election campaigning, and questions of national political allegiance or ideology were viewed as dirty, opportunistic, and dividing. "I'm afraid it will tear us apart," said one leader of the organization during the final stages of the debate. "We're stuck," said another.[39]

This debate took place with an amount of self-awareness, openness and sophistication rarely seen in the Middle East. For many Beirut Madinati members, even the label "party" provoked almost an allergic reaction. "The word 'politics' in Lebanon has a negative connotation. It is a major hurdle to how to organize effectively," Chaaban said during the early stages of the debate.[40] "Maybe we can find an alternative to the word 'hizb' [party] in Arabic."

In the end, the Beirut faction prevailed, and the group opted to proceed de facto as an NGO (although it employs the language of a "political platform") and explicitly not as a political party. It would focus for the time being on pressuring the new municipal council, which had continued in the style of its predecessor, keeping the budget secret, holding no public meetings, ignoring all requests for information and hearings, while pushing forward private luxury projects on the city's remaining waterfront and public land. Divisions had flared between left and right, sympathizers with Hezbollah and the Future Movement, outright secularists and more conservative incremental reformers, political savants, and idealistic activists.

"People hate politics. We want to reclaim the political," said Fawaz, who was ambivalent about the wisest option for the movement.[41] She believed that small victories were possible on practical urban issues, but that Lebanon was doomed without major national political reform. Ibrahim Mneimneh feared that politics would destroy the movement. People liked Beirut Madinati, he said, because it stayed away from sensitive issues. "Secularism is taboo," he said. "We have to be clearly against the sectarian system. We can show this system has led to terrible results. Our key to success at a national level is finding a way to talk about an issue like security or corruption without singling out any political movement or sect and making them feel targeted."

A further objection to politics was practical (and risk-averse). Under almost any imaginable scenario, Lebanon's parliamentary election laws would overwhelmingly favor the existing dominant parties in some version of winner-takes-all voting. Beirut Madinati would face even longer odds in parliamentary elections than they did in the Beirut city race, because the districts are even more heavily gerrymandered and, with high stakes, the establishment would be unlikely to be caught unprepared like it was during the municipal races. Any campaign they ran would have to be intended largely for public education and organizational capacity building. "I believe you should be with the people on the ground," said Mona El Hallak, an architect and founder of the Beit Beirut city museum, and one of the Beirut Madinati candidates.[42] "That's why I don't see parliamentary elections as something of value. I don't believe in the political discourse in this country." The general assembly voted on October 29, 2017, not to run for parliamentary elections, by a narrow vote: thirty-one for, thirty-six against.[43] Even ambivalent members said the movement just wasn't mature enough, organizationally, for a national election campaign and inevitable strains it would bring. Inexperienced in politics, many members didn't see any value in a campaign or, in the event of success, of serving as opposition members in the national legislature. "If we win parliamentary elections, what change would this bring to the people?" Mneimneh said.[44] "We would be in the opposition and unable to deliver anything."

As an organization, Beirut Madinati entered 2017 with a clear agenda to challenge the city municipality and focus on specific urban projects. Some of its activist members have mobilized to fight a major private development in Ramlet al-Baida, the only remaining public beach in Beirut.[45] A newly elected leadership structure is working to build the organization and institutionalize its ideas of neighborhood engagement and local government advocacy. Some members are planning a spinoff to run for parliament anyway, in the hopes that they can build on their learning experience inside Beirut Madinati but not endanger the parent organization if their bid fails.

The Implications of Beirut Madinati

On the tangible plane, Beirut Madinati's achievements remain modest, although important: it created a small but dynamic organization, it raised the profile of several urban planning issues in the Lebanese public discourse, and performed uniquely well for an independent movement in an Arab election. Its postelection triumphs lie in the intangible and less easily assessed: unlocked possibilities, a newfound sense of popular agency and power, and an organizational method that attempts to transcend the ideological divisions among Arab reform and opposition movements and chart a path to improve people's lives through sustained, opportunistic assaults on poor government policies.[46] At this early stage it is possible from Beirut Madinati's performance to discern a few positive trends around organizational learning and diagnose a sharp, persistent problem with ideology and pure political content, which continues to hamper, and limit, antigovernment activism.

Immediately after the election in May, Beirut Madinati's achievements created a sense of possibility. "Beirut Madinati also introduced a new way of doing politics," wrote Kim Ghattas, a longtime observer of Lebanese politics.[47] Headlines proliferated in the vein of the normally acerbic Dagher's blog post, which was uncharacteristically titled "The Example of Beirut Madinati: Change Is Possible." Several other bloggers and normally salty Lebanese commentators wrote analyses along the same lines, arguing that the style and content of political discourse, along with the parameters, of the possible, had changed "for good . . . we are winning the narrative war."[48] Sami Attalah, head of the Lebanese Center for Policy Studies, speculated that the 2017 parliamentary elections would be contested more spiritedly than ever, after the trail blazed by Beirut Madinati in the municipal polls.[49] The new municipal council abandoned the conciliatory rhetoric of the election period and acted, if anything, even more impetuously and secretively than before. But the impact of Beirut Madinati and You Stink echoed in the system, for instance in the adoption of a progressive platform by the Kataeb Party, a traditional Christian party with a warlord history that in 2016 refashioned itself as a champion of reform, devolution, and environmental causes.[50] Kataeb members joined garbage protests and sympathetically attended Beirut Madinati open discussion events. Whether or not they were opportunistically availing themselves of a new potential base as their support slipped as a result of an alliance between its Christian rivals, the Kataeb was following an agenda blazed by Beirut Madinati. Such emulation was among the movement's original goals.

The triumphalist postelection mood might have been overblown, or intentionally exaggerated for effect. Months later, several Beirut Madinati founders and members collaborated on a case study that soberly situated the group's electoral success in a context of failing trust in the Lebanese government and roiling regional insecurity, typified by the war in Syria.[51] The elections, they argued, had broken into the stale monopoly over power of the dominant ruling political parties, and could pave the way to the introduction of new entrants into the country's political scene. But the author-activists also sagely observe that their success could provoke the ruling warlords to "amplify their rhetoric of fear," fighting the upstarts by rallying their constituents along sectarian lines.[52] By their own assessment, even a limited success against entrenched powers created new dangers as well as opportunities.

Partisans of Beirut Madinati invest high hopes in the organization's model, approach, tactics, and strategy. They are contending with the regional stigma against politics, and developing an organizational structure that they believe can sustain them over the long term.[53] They correctly understand their movement, and public support, as products of unique and specific circumstances in Lebanon, the Arab region, and the modern world. Unlike some of their more idealistic counterparts during the Arab uprisings, they do not see themselves standing outside history or local context. They believe that political power requires small causes embedded in a grand vision. Even those members of Beirut Madinati who opposed entering national politics in time for the May 2017 parliamentary elections did not do so because they want to remain apolitical, but because they believed the most effective way to propel an anti-sectarian political agenda was to focus on a small arena—Beirut city politics—and deliver results. They might be mistaken in their specific choices, but they have moved from the politics of protest into long-term policy work and the pursuit of power and different modes of governance. They are opposing the status quo and simultaneously holding themselves responsible for proposing an alternative. This is credible, sustainable opposition political work.

The Case for Explicit, Mobilizing Ideology

Arab authoritarians and governing cliques might not truly believe the ideologies they invoke, but these ideologies are useful identifiers and for many of their followers, effective mobilizing tools. Without easily understandable, undeniably important core ideological markers, movements that oppose power structures and channel popular frustrations will struggle to cross a threshold from protest movement to sustainable political party or mass movement. Beirut Madinati exemplifies this "hollow core" problem.[54] Its members and founders often have bold and clear ideological convictions, but the movement itself seeks to be inclusive and nonideological, at the expense of a coherent, constructive unifying principle. One founder, Khoury, neatly if unintentionally summed up the problem: "We are trying to be a positive campaign, and asking voters to vote FOR something not AGAINST something. We are trying to keep positive relations with all stakeholders."[55] Of course, even the most successful politicians and movements don't appeal to everyone, and while it's possible to strive for civility while addressing fundamental civic concerns, it is impossible to engage in meaningful politics and at the same time "keep positive relations" with everybody. That fear of offense, exclusion and conflict characterizes many activist movements, and beyond a certain point paralyzes them.

Beirut Madinati eschewed the ideological debates of its time and place, even hesitating to make clear that it was an almost entirely secular movement. Its campaign was based on vague concepts of reform and accountability and transparency, which elided its internal, ideological, and political contradictions between leftists and liberals, between secular anti-sectarians and sectarian reformers, and other important cleavages. The slick name worked well during the campaign but in its aftermath carried a whiff of vagueness, marketing over substance. The overall packaging echoed Islamists around the region who, although from a different starting point, seek to downplay core ideologies and appeal to quality of life concerns, running for office with long, detail-rich policy platforms and parties whose names are comprised in mix-and-match fashion of the words justice, reform, development and freedom. Beirut Madinati, in its quest for virtue, still carried many of the vices of the society it wished to reform.

Any effective long-term mobilization will require a core committed cadre, resources, and ideological clarity—whether unity of purpose emerges in a negative project (oppose the corrupt state), a positive project (build a nonsectarian system of good governance), or a to-do list. One alternative to Beirut Madinati experimented with an ideological approach, but fared poorly in the municipal elections—perhaps because despite its message it looked like another one-man show in the model of the existing warlord parties. Charbel Nahhas in the spring of 2015 founded a national political party called "Citizens within a State," which openly campaigned for a secular, democratic system of government. It had a clear ideology, with a socialist economic platform, and overt national aspirations. It ran municipal slates throughout Lebanon. But the movement attracted very few members, funds, or voters, despite its sharp critique of the system, perhaps because of Nahhas's plodding rhetorical style, history as a minister, and continuing close ties to government figures.[56] He predicted Beirut Madinati would fail because it was afraid to attack Lebanon's corrupt leaders directly. "They had a managerial paradigm. They play a game within the logic of the system," Nahhas said.[57] "They present themselves as an effective alternative to the badly performing team. They are challenging the team, not the system." Nahhas put pithily a concern about Beirut Madinati's approach that speaks as well to a wide array of anti-sectarian, secular reform activists in the Arab world who focus on narrow platforms for fear of alienating a conservative, sectarian, or religious public: "We don't care about all your municipal bullshit, when the whole country and state is falling down. There is a possibility to change the whole system. Our objective is to build a political alternative."

Inclusive Organizing, Embedding Contradictions

Observers of Beirut Madinati and You Stink before it were far more likely to foist unrealistic expectations on the social movements than the actual activists involved. Internally, as we have seen, many of Beirut Madinati's architects were sanguine about the limitations of its approach, and the internal divisions it had papered over. The initiative's pragmatism, and lack of ideology, were among its central features. Researcher Deen Sharp aptly distinguished Beirut Madinati from other popular movements, in the Arab world and in Europe (like Podemos and Syriza). Beirut Madinati, "for better or worse" defined a limited program, marketed a message of hope rather than protest, embraced opportunistic tactics, and positioned itself as an urban campaign.[58] Sharp argues that Beirut Madinati exemplifies a new type of social movement, but questions whether it can achieve tangible social change.

The case of Beirut Madinati has great resonance for advocates of citizenship and alternative bases for building governance legitimacy and statehood in the Arab world. Beirut Madinati's performance, building on the record of other civil society and people-power political movements in Lebanon and the Arab region, suggests some necessary if insufficient preconditions for systemic change. Popular citizens' movements in the region will need a coherent and identifiable ideology in order to mobilize on a sustained basis and contest power. (Protest fatigue and a fuzzy ideological core hampered and ultimately divided revolutionaries in Egypt from 2011 to 2013, leaving them at a gross disadvantage to authoritarians from Islamist or secular military backgrounds.)[59] It is dreary, difficult, and often quixotic to seek to change the policies or composition of an authoritarian government. Echoing activists themselves, some researchers caution against overestimating the potential of civil society, or underestimating the resilience of malignant governing systems. Lebanese elections, like the trappings of democracy in Putin's Russia and other post-Communist authoritarian societies, have been engineered by an entrenched elite to maintain power, not as an exercise in accountability. "Carefully managed elections can also provide elites with a safety valve to protect themselves from wholesale change," write Stephen Deets and Jennifer Skulte-Ouaiss in an analysis that compares Beirut Madinati to the experience of Eastern Europe after the fall of the Soviet Union in 1991 and the transition away from Communism.[60] The system, they point out, possesses a powerful "combination of democratic stability and democratic dysfunction."[61]

On the level of tactics, Beirut Madinati avoided many of the mistakes or limiting choices of their immediate past peers. While it had a "horizontal" and inclusive internal structure, despite its pretension to being leaderless, it also had a clear and nimble leadership structure during the campaign period. It did not waste time with the sort of debates that hobbled Egyptian revolutionaries and the Lebanese garbage protest movements, like whether to talk to and meet with governing powers. Beirut Madinati was willing to talk to anyone, correctly understanding that with confident political management it could explain the distinction between talking to the system and being co-opted by it. The activists also attempted to extricate themselves from a circular debate about legitimacy, authenticity and revolutionary purity, framing their mission as a quest for tangible results—in their case, quality of life and governance improvements for Beirut. Shrewdly, this framing will allow Beirut Madinati to claim credit in the future for small but tangible achievements that might result from pressure, lobbying and public campaigning—new parks, an improvement in public services, or land use.

Finally, although it is a work in progress, Beirut Madinati has advanced a conceptual and tactical discussion about how best to pursue an activist agenda in the aftermath of the Arab uprisings. To the questions of "protest or politics?"

and "narrow issue-advocacy or broader electoral coalition-building?" Beirut Madinati has doubled down and answered, "both." As a movement and organization it might well fail. But its roadmap tries to follow multiple paths simultaneously. Its next step proposes to build a citywide organization with permanent staff, and liaisons to the community as well as to the government. Beirut Madinati could accomplish a major feat if, under the guise of inclusive technocratic organizing, it propagates an ideology of secular, anti-sectarian state-building. If it can successfully muster the resources and personnel to develop an organization that plays a sustained watchdog function, encapsulates the notions of constituent services and community advocacy, and embodies anti-sectarian, anti-corruption, and consultative democracy in the guise of community planning, then Beirut Madinati will have smuggled radical political alternatives into the stultified realm of Lebanese politics. If, on the contrary, it pursues a solely incremental urban reform agenda and never matures into a full-fledged anti-sectarian political party, it will perhaps make a meaningful contribution to Lebanon's already rich civic life, without producing fundamental change in its politics—joining the country's ranks of illustrious NGOs.

Narrative and Other Qualitative Methods

The case of Beirut Madinati also brings to the foreground questions of analysts' methods. A prevailing obsession with data and quantitative analysis often limits the ability of analysts, scholars, and participants to notice trends. A more narrative approach can inform analysis of political life, especially in contexts where there are few meaningful, easily measurable data points comparable to the constant churn of election results, opinion surveys, and household data available in open, democratic societies. Taken as a whole, the Arab uprisings and the continuing political efforts, like Beirut Madinati, suggest that political analysts should dispense with efforts at prediction, and should wholeheartedly embrace descriptive, narrative case studies, and other qualitative approaches. Quantitative analysis and other data-driven forms of analysis, which dominate some fields of social science and often seep into policy and political analysis, have their uses, especially when deployed with rich knowledge of historical context and local specifics. In fluid and opaque circumstances, however, it is important for researchers to embrace all effective methods. Ecumenical, descriptive case studies and contemporary narrative histories might provide the most important data available in politically stultified Arab countries, where ruling systems are spinning furiously to retain or reimpose control, where governance and quality of life have tumbled, and where popular movements and pressure groups have breached many thresholds in terms of organizing and mobilizing since the uprisings that began in 2010.

The framework and approaches that we have used over time to gauge citizens' movements, reform, and revolutionary and pressure groups have proven insufficient. The target is murky to begin with. Scholars, analysts, and participants alike are trying to assess the prospective appeal, viability, and power of initiatives challenging autocratic states, with highly capable agencies of repression and copious resources. Public opinion is difficult to gauge. So too are the system's weak points and the prospects for citizen engagement to cascade into effective challenges to power.

There are some useful frameworks that we use when we explore whether challenges to these autocratic systems are worth studying, whether as scholars or as policymakers who want to make sure we are looking carefully at spaces that might pose meaningful or enduring challenges to the status quo. That these challenges continue to surprise us is not only a testament to the failure of our imaginations but also to the poverty of our tools. Recent experience with the Arab uprisings, and I would suggest, with the rise of populist and right-wing leaders in the United States and Europe, suggest that we should more firmly embrace the tools of narrative, ethnography, social history, and narrow case study for their wealth of explanatory potential. No quasi-scientific tool can suffice to explain the unexpected emergence and appeal of a new movement or ideology, or sudden shifts in popular imagination that abruptly alter the boundaries of the possible. Descriptive tools can go a long way to remedy gaps in our understanding, especially if applied with an open acknowledgment of researcher bias. Analysts normatively in favor of political reform, or a certain basket of citizen rights, can openly state their preference to increase the likelihood that it won't blind them to the conditions and qualities of the movements they study.

Finally, when we speak of change and reform in sclerotic authoritarian systems, we are often speaking about the possibility of a violent historical rupture. We ought to honestly reckon with the fear that popular, successful reformists generate in autocrats and their supporters, who have designed their systems expressly to break rather than bend when pushed. It is a form of self-defense, a built-in self-destruct switch that wires "après moi le déluge" into the system of rule. Arab citizens are well-aware that the threat is not idle, having watched Egypt's security establishment and President Bashar al-Assad of Syria intentionally fuel violence and destruction to present any alternative to their continuing rule as toxic and untenable.

Conclusion: Further Questions

Lebanon is an important case; it is not an island. The same traits that make it a regional exception also make it relevant. It is an imperfect lab, but politics is not a pure science. Comparisons operate by analogy, and Lebanon offers a uniquely rich, and relevant, site for experimentation. Lebanon's much-emulated experiments include the rise of Hezbollah and its entry into mainstream politics; the enduring viability of the corrupt clientilistic system of patronage politics; the endlessly effective deployment of the threat of security chaos as a bulwark against even the most minute reform; and the manipulation by a small ruling elite of sectarian identity politics as a tool to stave off all demands for accountability by constituents.

Beirut Madinati, and the groundswell of activism from which it rose, might also serve as a model—either for a new way forward for reformists, or as a cautionary tale about the perils of avoiding ideology and overt politics. Among opposition reform movements, difference and conviction need to be addressed, just as surely as issues of organization and corruption. Its founders and new members will labor onwards, perhaps successfully expanding their organization or spinning off new ones, perhaps joining preexisting groups or political parties, perhaps retreating from public life. But Lebanon's political crisis is sure to continue. Its failures of governance and representation are part of a regional conundrum that at root is political and can only be addressed with a political solution that shifts the modes of governance and the distribution of power. Lebanon's predicament differs from that of its Arab neighbors in degree and detail, not in kind. Its efforts to harness popular outrage and articulate a coherent identity for politically engaged reforms mark a vivid step forward in a regional struggle.

The Arab world's experience since the most recent wave of revolts suggests that no change or reform of any sort is possible without challenging the status quo political system and administration of power. Brittle authoritarian systems around the region, including Lebanon, by design do not have feedback loops or release valves. It is nearly impossible to push for incremental change—to lobby for a new law, create different enforcement mechanisms, shift electoral processes, or change public contracting. Such shifts are the prerequisite of the actual holders of power, who are notoriously, and intenationally, opaque and unaccountable. Famously, even in relatively open systems like Lebanon's where at least the identity of major players is known, dispute resolution barely exists and even straightforward negotiations usually devolve into stalemate, paralysis, or violence.

Lebanon's most recent people-power success story enjoyed an initial burst of success, and despite its perhaps temporary stall over fundamental questions of political identity, it might well have an influential future. Beirut Madinati's early record suggests a deep yearning for new, more accountable and modern civic political movements, and at the same time, a persistent struggle to overcome existing ideological divisions. Without a clear animating central idea and identity, change movements, whether reformist or revolutionary, will have difficulty challenging entrenched status quo forces.

Notes

1. Rami G. Khouri, "Talking Trash in Lebanon," *Al Jazeera America*, Aug. 24, 2015, http://america.aljazeera.com/opinions/2015/8/talking-trash-in-lebanon.html.

2. For a discussion of the different mass protests that erupted across the Arab world in 2010–11, see Fawaz A. Gerges, ed., *Contentious Politics in the Middle East: Popular Resistance and Marginalized Activism Beyond the Arab Uprisings* (New York: Palgrave Macmillan, 2015).

3. Erica Solomon, "Lebanon's Political Elite to See Off Challengers," *Financial Times,* May 9, 2016, https://www.ft.com/content/c78708b0-15c3-11e6-9d98-00386a18e39d.

4. Hassan M. Fattah, "Pro-Syria Party in Beirut Holds Huge Protest," *New York Times*, March 9, 2005, http://www.nytimes.com/2005/03/09/world/prosyria-party-in-beirut-holds-a-huge-protest.html?_r=1.

5. If one counts all the refugees (mostly Palestinian and Syrian) residing in the country in addition to Lebanese citizens, the actual population is closer to six million. Population estimates for 2016 from UN Data, United Nations Statistics Division, "Lebanon Country Profile," http://data.un.org/CountryProfile.aspx?crName=LEBANON.

6. Sami Nader, "Beirut Bombing Brings Lebanon's Political Parties Together," *Al-Monitor*, March 10, 2016, http://www.al-monitor.com/pulse/fa/contents/articles/originals/2015/11/lebanon-terrorist-attack-fail-sow-sectarian-discord.html.

7. Sylvia Westall, "Syrian Refugees Set to Exceed a Third of Lebanon's Population," *Reuters*, July 3, 2014, http://www.reuters.com/article/us-syria-crisis-lebanon-idUSK-BN0F818T20140703. Official UNHCR statistics note one million Syrian refugees in Lebanon, but that number does not reflect the actual population because the United Nations stopped registering Syrian refugees in Lebanon in early 2015. UNHCR population statistics available at https://data.unhcr.org/syrianrefugees/country.php?id=122.

8. Nour Samaha, "Riot Police Break up Beirut Anti-Government Protests," *Al Jazeera*, August 30, 2015, http://www.aljazeera.com/news/2015/08/lebanon-anti-government-protests-150829112717978.html.

9. Hwaida Saad, "Clashes Break out during Protests over Trash Crisis in Lebanon," *New York Times*, August 23, 2015, https://www.nytimes.com/2015/08/24/world/middleeast/lebanese-protest-as-trash-piles-up-in-beirut.html.

10. "Lebanon Rubbish Crisis: Thousands Attend Anti-Government Rally," *BBC*, August 30, 2015, http://www.bbc.com/news/world-middle-east-34097555.

11. Assad Thebian comments at "Who Stinks? Social Protests and Political Change in Lebanon," panel discussion, Carnegie Middle East Center, November 10, 2015, Beirut, Lebanon, http://carnegie-mec.org/2015/11/10/who-stinks-social-protests-and-political-change-in-lebanon-event-5062.

12. For a description of the groups that emerged along with You Stink in the summer of 2015, see "Social Movement Responding to the Lebanese Garbage Crisis," Civil Society Knowledge Center, http://civilsociety-centre.org//party/social-movement-responding-lebanese-garbage-crisis. For details on the government garbage contract, landfills, and a timeline of the crisis, see "Waste Management Conflict (Starting January 25, 2014)," Civil Society Knowledge Center, http://civilsociety-centre.org/timelines/31033.

13. David Kenner, "There's Something Rotten in Lebanon," *Foreign Policy*, August 25, 2015, http://foreignpolicy.com/2015/08/25/theres-something-rotten-in-lebanon-trash-you-stink/; and Elias Muhanna, "The Death of Ideology and Beirut's #YouStink Protests," *Qifa Nabki*, September 1, 2015, https://qifanabki.com/2015/09/01/the-death-of-ideology-and-beiruts-youstink-protests/. See also the response of a Lebanese activist and blogger to the Free Patriotic Movement's bashing of YouStink's key representative, Assad Thebian: Elie Fares, "When the FPM Is in Full Blown Despair: Assaad Thebian Did Nothing Wrong," August 31, 2015, https://stateofmind13.com/2015/08/31/when-the-fpm-is-in-full-blown-despair-assaad-thebian-did-nothing-wrong/.

14. Interviews with the author, Beirut, Lebanon, September 2015.

15. Josh Wood, "Rally in Beirut Postponed Amid Fears 'Thugs' May Hijack the Protests," *The National*, August 24, 2015, http://www.thenational.ae/world/middle-east/rally-in-beirut-postponed-amid-fears-thugs-may-hijack-the-protests.

16. The unsubstantiated slur was widely circulated in Lebanese media and affected You Stink's public standing. As an example of how widespread the accusation was, even a former cabinet minister and outspoken critic of the sectarian political system, who ran his own

independent slate for municipal elections in 2016, claimed that the activists in You Stink were paid, although when asked he could offer no evidence. Charbel Nahhas, interview with the author, Beirut, Lebanon, July 20, 2016.

17. Assad Thebian, interview with the author, Beirut, Lebanon, February 24, 2016.

18. Protesters attracted ire when they carried a banner including multiple photographs of politicians including Hezbollah leader Hassan Nasrallah, and in the slogan, "All of them means all of them," a reference to the entire corrupt political class. But in its statements and actions, You Stink sought to target officials responsible for the garbage crisis over waste collection issues alone, in order to maintain a focused campaign. See Samia Nakhoul, "Lebanon's Rubbish Crisis Exposes Political Rot," *Reuters*, September 7, 2015, http://www.reuters.com/article/us-lebanon-protests-crisis-insight-idUSKCN0R70GO20150907.

19. For a mention of policy proposals by environmentalists to end the garbage crisis by environmentalists, see "Social Movement Responding to the Lebanese Garbage Crisis," Civil Society Knowledge Center; and "Interview with Paul Abi Rached: A Glimmer of Hope in Lebanon's Garbage Crisis," Tara Expeditions Foundation, 2016, http://oceans.taraexpeditions.org/en/m/environment/mankind-the-ocean-pollution/interview-with-paul-abi-rached-a-glimmer-of-hope-in-lebanons-garbage-crisis/.

20. Thebian, interview with the author.

21. Ziad Abu-Rish, "Garbage Politics," *Middle East Research and Information Project* 45, no. 277 (2015), http://www.merip.org/mer/mer277/garbage-politics.

22. Mona Fawaz, interview with the author, Beirut, Lebanon, July 22, 2016.

23. "The Program," Beirut Madinati, http://beirutmadinati.com/program/?lang=en.

24. Fawaz, interview, July 22, 2016.

25. Beirut Madinati set up an app to process and track volunteers. As a primary means of communicating with supporters and prospective voters, it relied on postings distributed on overlapping platforms: the personal WhatsApp networks of members, the official website, http://beirutmadinati.com/, a Facebook page updated daily, https://www.facebook.com/Beirut-Madinati/, and a Twitter feed, https://twitter.com/beirutmadinati.

26. Jad Chaaban, interview with the author, Beirut, Lebanon, February 29, 2016.

27. "The Text of the Press Conference After the Second Phase of the Municipal Elections," Lebanese Association of Democratic Elections, May 10, 2010, http://www.lade.org.lb/getattachment/000aaa07-e8ba-4774-bc45-78bdd795ec5a/The-text-of-the-press-conference-after-the-second.aspx.

28. Yassmine Alieh, "$240 Million Budget at the Municipality of Beirut," *Lebanon Opportunities*, January 26, 2017, http://www.businessnews.com.lb/cms/Story/StoryDetails.aspx?ItemID=5894.

29. Aurélie Daher, "Saudi Arabia Is Pissed: What Are the Risks for Lebanon?" *LobeLog*, March 11, 2016, https://lobelog.com/saudi-arabia-is-pissed-what-are-the-risks-for-lebanon; Tom Perry, "Cash Crunch at Saudi Firm Casts Shadow over Lebanon's Hariris," *Reuters*, September 5, 2016, http://www.reuters.com/article/us-lebanon-politics-idUSKCN11B1X7; and Yakir Gillis, "Why Lebanon's Power Struggle Is Fueled by a Loss of Saudi Support," *Newsweek*, October 3, 2016, http://europe.newsweek.com/lebanons-power-struggle-fueled-loss-saudi-support-505565?rm=eu.

30. Chaaban, interview with the author by telephone, Beirut, Lebanon, June 9, 2016.

31. For more on youth-led leaderless movements in the Arab world since the uprisings and their organizational challenges, see Vincent Durac, "Social Movements, Protest Movements, and Cross-Ideological Coalitions—the Arab Uprisings Re-Appraised," *Democratization* 22, no. 2 (2015): 239–58.

32. Beirut Madinati was heavily covered by national, regional, and international media outlets. For Beirut Madinati candidates hosted on political TV programs, see "Kalam Ennas

Report: The Cost of Garbage," *LBCI Lebanon*, September 8, 2016, https://www.youtube.com/watch?v=Dk-tIKbvADI&feature=youtu.be&app=desktop; "Nharkom Said, Keeping up with the Municipal Wlections in Beirut," *LBCI Lebanon*, May 6, 2016, https://www.youtube.com/watch?v=mCPxbccv6uE&feature=youtu.be&t=33m52s; "Beirut's Municipal Elections of 2016," *Al Jadeed Online*, May 2, 2016, https://www.youtube.com/watch?v=910DewShi7Q&feature=youtu.be&t=7m; "Bi Mawdouiyeh: The Municipal Elections," *MTV Lebanon News*, May 4, 2016, https://www.youtube.com/watch?v=gnLHHo1AMKg&feature=youtu.be; "Rana Khoury on Al Arabiya Speaks about Beirut Madinati Municipal List," *Al Arabiya*, May 3, 2016, https://www.youtube.com/watch?v=J6BKnmHkQ5I. For Beirut Madinati coverage on national news channels, see "Beirut Madinati continues its Tour of Beirut's Neighborhoods" (Arabic), *LBC Group*, Lebanon, April 23, 2016, http://www.lbcgroup.tv/watch/chapter/27417/47841/بيروت-مدينتي-تواصل-جولاتها-على-مناطق-بيروتية/ar; "Beirut Madinati Pledges to Defend Each and Every Beiruti" (Arabic), *LBC Group*, Lebanon, April 22 2016, http://www.lbcgroup.tv/watch/chapter/27407/47767/بيروت-مدينتي-تتعهد-بالدفاع-عن-كل-بيروتي/ar; "In Beirut Vote, Old Parties Face New Challenges," *MTV Lebanon*, May 5, 2016, http://mtv.com.lb/news/english_local/592567/in_beirut_vote,_old_parties_face_new_challenge. For coverage in national, regional and international newspapers, see Karim El Mufti, "Beirut Madinati: Change at the Tip of Your Vote," *Executive Magazine*, May 3, 2016, http://www.executive-magazine.com/opinion/beirut-madinati; "Au Liban, des Élections Municipales Test Pour la Société Civile," *France24*, May 9, 2016, http://www.france24.com/fr/20160508-liban-elections-municipales-test-societe-civile-beirut-madinati-dechets-hariri; Verina Al Amil, "Beirut Madinati: Discussions and Art and Sports Activities, Optimistic to the Highest Limits" (Arabic), *An-Nahar*, April 28, 2016, http://www.annahar.com/article/368242-بالصوربيروت-مدينتي-نقاشات-ونشاطات-فنية-ورياضية-انهم-متفائلون-لأقصى-حدود; "Beirut Madinati: Citizens Adopt Campaign that Challenges Political Class in Municipal Elections" (Arabic), *Huffington Post Arabic*, May 5, 2015, http://www.huffpostarabi.com/2016/05/05/story_n_9845592.html; Muhanad Al Hajj Ali, "Beirut Madinati: The Beginning of the Line" (Arabic), *AlModon*, May 6, 2016, http://www.almodon.com/opinion/2016/5/6/بيروت-مدينتي-أول-العنقود; Eva Al Shoufi, "Beirut Madinati: Not 'We Are The People'" (Arabic), *Al-Akhbar*, May 9, 2016, http://www.al-akhbar.com/node/257522.

33. Saad Hariri, "Speech on Ramadan Iftaar," June 9, 2016, https://www.youtube.com/watch?v=fiZ2MTyo8Ms&feature=youtu.be

34. Ibrahim Mneimneh, interview with the author, Beirut, Lebanon, May 8, 2016.

35. Thanassis Cambanis, "Beirut Upstarts Gain Traction in Lebanon's Political Quagmire," *New York Times*, May 10, 2016. https://www.nytimes.com/2016/05/11/world/middleeast/beirut-lebanon-municipal-elections.html.

36. For a discussion of the results by area and a rich technical analysis, see Ramez Dagher, "What Beirut's Election Results Tell: Lebanon Can Hope for Change," *Moulahazat*, May 11, 2016, https://moulahazat.com/2016/05/11/what-beiruts-election-results-tell-lebanon-can-hope-for-change/. Full results by district from the Lebanon's Ministry of the Interior in Arabic are available online at http://elections.gov.lb/getattachment/224cc789-848a-45f7-9c00-3479b2d4cb75/%D8%A8%D9%8A%D8%B1%D9%88%D8%AA.aspx.

37. Lebanon Ministry of the Interior, official election results (Arabic), http://elections.gov.lb/getattachment/224cc789-848a-45f7-9c00-3479b2d4cb75/%D8%A8%D9%8A%D8%B1%D9%88%D8%AA.aspx.

38. The candidate list and biographies are available on Beirut Madinati's website at http://beirutmadinati.com/candidates/?lang=en.

39. Interviews with the author, Beirut Madinati Discussion Square at Ghassan Tueni Park, Beirut, Lebanon, September 8, 2016.

40. Chaaban, interview with the author by telephone, Beirut, Lebanon, June 9, 2016.

41. Fawaz, interview with Sima Ghaddar, Beirut, Lebanon, June 9, 2016.

42. Mona El Hallak, interview with the author, Beirut, Lebanon, July 27, 2016.

43. Mona Fawaz, interview with the author by telephone, Cambridge, Mass., November, 19, 2016.

44. Mneimneh, interview with the author by telephone, Beirut, Lebanon, November 17, 2016.

45. Sally Haydan, "Barricades on the Beach: Beirut's Residents Fight for Their Waterfront," *Reuters*, December 2, 2016, http://www.reuters.com/article/us-lebanon-landrights-beach-idUSKBN13R1OT.

46. In a campaign post-mortem on his personal blog, Chaaban credited Beirut Madinati with restoring democracy and political discourse in Lebanon. Jad Chaaban, "On Beirut Madinati, Some Preliminary Thoughts and Reflections," *Development in a Polarized Society,* June 7, 2016, http://jadchaaban.com/blog/on-beirut-madinati-some-preliminary-thoughts-and-reflections/.

47. Kim Ghattas, "Beirut's Lovable Losers," *Foreign Policy*, May 26, 2016, http://foreign policy.com/2016/05/26/beiruts-loveable-losers/.

48. Joey Ayoub, Facebook post, May 9, 2016, https://www.facebook.com/joeyhayoub/posts/10157024987755347.

49. Scott Preston, "Can Coalition of Reformers Snag Lebanese Parliament Seats?" *Al-Monitor*, November 15, 2016, http://www.al-monitor.com/pulse/originals/2016/11/lebanon-elections-reformist-parties-political-forces.html.

50. Nazih Osseiran, "Kataeb Resign from Cabinet over 'Deal' Grievances," *The Daily Star,* June 15, 2016, http://www.dailystar.com.lb/News/Lebanon-News/2016/Jun-15/357046-kataeb-resign-from-cabinet-over-deal-grievances.ashx; and Ramez Dagher, "Did Ashraf Rifi's Resignation Inspire the Kataeb?" *Moulahazat,* June 19, 2016, https://moulahazat.com/2016/06/19/did-ashraf-rifis-resignation-inspire-the-kataeb.

51. Jad Chaaban, Diala Haidar, Ryaan Ismail, Rana Khoury, and Mirna Shidrawi, "Beirut's 2016 Municipal Elections: Did Beirut Madinati Permanently Change Lebanon's Electoral Scene?," Case Analysis, Arab Center for Research and Policy Studies, Doha, Qatar, September 2016, http://english.dohainstitute.org/file/Get/2d7f2d9d-702d-40df-ad80-5e58cea8fb81.

52. Jad Chaaban, Diala Haidar, Ryaan Ismail, Rana Khoury, and Mirna Shidrawi, "Beirut's 2016 Municipal Elections: Did Beirut Madinati Permanently Change Lebanon's Electoral Scene?" Case Analysis, Arab Center for Research and Policy Studies, Doha, Qatar, September 2016, p. 14, http://english.dohainstitute.org/file/Get/2d7f2d9d-702d-40df-ad80-5e58cea8fb81.

53. Thanassis Cambanis, "The Urban Mechanics of Beirut," *Boston Globe*, June 19, 2016, https://www.bostonglobe.com/ideas/2016/06/18/the-urban-mechanics-beirut/uPuYtkmAjXh zlfu6StQ7SJ/story.html.

54. For more on the concept of the hollow core structure in elite networks, *see* Edward O. Laumann et al., "Inner Circles or Hollow Cores? Elite Networks in National Policy Systems," *Journal of Politics* 52, no. 2 (1990): 356–90.

55. "Interview with Beirut Madinati Candidate, Rana Khoury," *So Beirut*, undated, https://www.sobeirut.com/features/59/meet-beirut-madinati. Emphasis in the original. After the campaign, Khoury expanded her ideas about political messaging. See Rana Khoury, "On positive political rhetoric and creating a space for love," *TEDxLAU*, November 16, 2016, http://rincon-technews.com/2016/11/15/on-positive-political-rhetoric-and-creating-a-space-for-love-rana-khoury-tedxlau/.

56. In the elections, Nahhas won 6,920 votes.

57. Nahhas, interview with the author.

58. Deen Sharp, "Beirut Madinati: Another Future Is Possible," September 27, 2016, Middle East Institute, http://www.mei.edu/content/map/beirut-madinati-another-future-possible.

59. These revolutionary fissures have been dissected at length elsewhere, and are the focus of my narrative study of the activist struggle in Egypt from 2011 to 2013. See Thanassis Cambanis, *Once Upon a Revolution: An Egyptian Story* (New York: Simon & Schuster, 2015).

60. Stephen Deets and Jennifer Skulte-Ouaiss, "Jumping Out of the 'Hobbesian Fishbowl' and into The Fire: Lebanon, Elections, and Chronic Crisis," *Demokratizatsiya: The Journal of Post-Soviet Democratization* 24, no. 4 (2016): 530.

61. Ibid., 518.

7

Second-Class Citizenship

Lebanese Women Fight to Pass Nationality to Children and Spouses

SIMA GHADDAR

Religiously diverse Lebanon prides itself on being a regional standout when it comes to the status of women. But since the 1920s, Lebanese women's citizenship has been incomplete. Unlike the country's men, Lebanese women do not have the right to pass their citizenship to their children or spouses. The law has broken apart families and denied basic services to children who have never known another country. This chapter chronicles the struggle of Lebanese women's organizations, beginning nearly two decades ago, to give Lebanese women full citizenship. Their campaign has been one of the most carefully planned of its kind, combining legislative advocacy, litigation, street protests, and awareness raising. Yet it has also been crippled by infighting, and has so far been unable to overcome the blend of sectarianism and misogyny that defines Lebanese politics. With interviews and historical analysis, the chapter illustrates both the importance of incremental gains, and how effective a state's stalling strategy can be in the face of demands for change.

"If I knew my children and I would be humiliated like this, I wouldn't have gotten married even if he was the richest man on the planet," says "Um Ali," a poor Lebanese mother of three married to an Egyptian construction worker. Her painful admission appears in *All for the Nation*, a film documenting the struggles of Lebanese women married to foreigners.

Um Ali lives under constant fear that her children could be arrested, or detained, and blames herself for denying her loved ones the security, welfare, and safety they deserve. That's because her children lack Lebanese citizenship, even though Um Ali is a citizen. Her children can't attend public schools; private schools are too expensive. In desperation, Um Ali sends her children to an orphanage.

Um Ali's heartbreaking story is hardly singular. Indeed, she is only one of thousands of Lebanese women whose families have had to struggle with numerous social, economic, and psychological obstacles that threaten the survival of their loved ones. That's because unlike their male counterparts, Lebanese women cannot pass their nationality to their children or husbands. Like any other foreigner, their husbands and children have restricted access to public services, including education and health care. They face restrictions on their rights relating to property ownership, on inheritance, and on working.[1]

Such difficulties were once widespread in the Arab world. But in the beginning of the new millennium, a regional alliance of women's advocacy nongovernmental organizations (NGOs) organized to push several Arab governments to grant equal citizenship rights for women.[2] This chapter follows the history of the Nationality Campaign in Lebanon as part of that trend. In Lebanon, the Center for Research, Training, and Development-Action (CRTD-A) led the campaign under the umbrella of a coalition known as the Lebanese Women's Network (LWN). The movement took on a novel approach to activism. Rather than completely rejecting the institutions that had thwarted their cause for years, they engaged and even cooperated with them. In contrast to other reform movements in the region, they focused less on headline gains and street mobilizations, and instead chipped away at the obstacles to their goal: changing the Lebanese citizenship law to make men and women equal. Here they lobbied with a possibly sympathetic legislator, there they would raise awareness about the effects of the citizenship law on individual women and their families. In the process, the activists managed to subvert, resist, challenge, and cooperate with the same state institutions and representatives that continuously halted their progress, along the way challenging sectarian politics and misogyny.

However, they still fell short of their main goal. The NGO world from which the movement emerged was riddled with personal rivalries due to its growing dependency on foreign funding. The wishes of donors overshadowed the impact of the gains CRTD-A made. And the movement was hamstrung by competing organizational principles and egos, and also by the near impossibility of reaching any common ground or seizing a political opportunity with a corrupt, misogynistic, and sectarian political class unashamed to exploit the movement for its own ends. Prolonged negotiations and governmental stalling were effective in slowing down citizenship advocates.

Much of this chapter is dedicated to uncovering the failings of the campaign, as well as the Lebanese government's systemic failure to show any genuine regard for women's rights when political interests and sectarian calculations are concerned. Still, it is impossible to simply dismiss the Nationality Campaign of Lebanon as ineffective.

Even though the movement has so far fallen short of its main aim, it still offers lessons and inspiration for activism in Lebanon and elsewhere. As this chapter shows, activists made significant incremental gains. Though they did not achieve a broad change to the laws that discriminate against women the networks they built are far from exhausted. In 2012 they came tantalizingly close to changing the law, but events out of their control—particularly the Syrian refugee crisis—overwhelmed their efforts. It is arguable that they are in a stronger position than when they started. Activists, in fact, do not see themselves as having been defeated—the shelving of the citizenship law is little more than a setback in a fight that they say could take decades. Meanwhile, they count several points of success. The conversation around women's citizenship has fundamentally changed in Lebanon—even elements of the state have tacitly acknowledged the gross unfairness of the current law. And there have been material improvements in the lives of Lebanese women who have had children with foreign husbands, in terms of access to services and a warmer treatment from bureaucracies. Finally, the activists believe their unique campaign offers something of an alternative form for citizens' movements. Through careful strategizing and organic mobilization, they were at least able to redefine the meaning of citizenship, political work, and protest politics.

In a country with little or no respect for the rule of law, women activist groups also turned legislation into a protest arena, actually bolstering the significance of the legal framework in the process. The Nationality Campaign was one of the first movements in Lebanon to use strategic alliances and legal activism to further a cause. They have proved, in a sense, that even the most corrupt legislative systems are vulnerable to a kind of de-corruption: the system responds, slowly, to an expectation that it should work. As a result, movements like the Nationality Campaign have beneficial spillovers to the political process in general.

To recount the journey of the Lebanese Nationality Campaign, I reflect on the interactions among advocacy organizations, both local and international, and the conditions and consequences of serious disagreements among its members. The campaign's dealings with an uninviting political environment and inept state institutions compelled parliament and powerful decision-makers to be more relevant and responsive to civil society. Members of the Nationality Campaign realized that no change would ensue unless civil society finally decided to play with the big boys—approach sectarian leaders and key party members, and deal with shady parliamentarians and bigoted community bosses—for the sake of incremental rewards.

The Legal, Political, and Social Backdrop

A Political Obsession with Sect

To truly understand how the seemingly simple subject of equal citizenship for Lebanese women has become such a difficult issue, one must review the fundamentals of political power in Lebanon.

As with so many other issues in the country, one of the most basic factor underlying the citizenship debate is Lebanon's political sectarianism and its obsession with maintaining a sectarian "demographic balance" in which no one sect can assume absolute power—no victor, no vanquished. Out of Lebanon's eighteen officially recognized confessional sects, some are awarded seats in parliament according to their approximate share of the population. The distribution of constitutional powers and administrative positions in government are also divided according to sect. Even more, sectarianism has become so deeply entrenched in Lebanese society that it has become part of the national and collective ethos of its many constituencies, the majority of which owe their loyalties first to their sectarian leaders and political bosses.

No one knows the real, exact population breakdown of every sect. The last full census was conducted in 1932.[3] In the last eighty-five years, Lebanese demographics have changed radically. Most analysts concede that the sectarian apportionment favors Christians disproportionately to their share of the population.[4] Due to a dramatic increase in Christian immigration and increase in Muslim population following the end of the civil war the number of Lebanese Christians was estimated in 2010 at 34 percent, down from 65 percent before the war.[5]

Add to this the approximately 1.1 million Syrian refugees who arrived in the last five years, and the approximately 450,000 Palestinians who left their homeland under duress following the creation of Israel, most of whom are Muslim, and the Christian "majority" faces an existential threat to its dominance. As a percentage of the total population, they are clearly now a minority.

Lebanese politicians fear the apportionment of important positions may one day be revised according to more accurate estimates. Many of those who stand to lose are in a state of chronic paranoia, obsessed with maintaining the only-on-paper demographic "balance."

It is smack in the middle of this morass that the Nationality Campaign found itself. And yet, power-hungry and fear-mongering politicians are only one of the challenges campaigners faced. To appreciate the full extent of the headwinds confronting the campaign, one must delve more deeply into the social and legal context of Lebanese citizenship.

An Antiquated Nationality Law

It is important to acknowledge that women's second-class citizenship is not an age-old custom in Lebanon. While it's true that Lebanese women face discrimination in many aspects of their lives (as Western women do), their legal status was better in Ottoman times, at least as far as citizenship goes. Ottoman law of the early 1800s made citizenship heritable from both mother and father. It prioritized the relationship of land ("jus soli"). But a Westernized Ottoman citizenship law issued in 1869 (modeled after the French statute) prioritized a patrilineal relationship of blood ("jus sanguinis").[6]

This set the stage for Lebanon's 1925 nationality law, issued under the French mandate (which lasted until 1945) and still in effect today. The law states that a person is considered Lebanese if he was "born of a Lebanese father," or "born in the Greater Lebanon territory [modern Lebanon] and did not acquire a foreign nationality upon birth by affiliation," or "born in the Greater Lebanon territory of unknown parents or parents of unknown nationality."[7]

The striking implication of the 1925 law is that not only is a Lebanese mother's citizenship immaterial to her descendants, but "illegitimate" children of Lebanese maternity and unknown paternity actually have greater claims to citizenship than children who can identify both their parents. Over the years, this has had the perverse effect of driving many women married to non-Lebanese men to claim their children were "illegitimate" just to pass on their Lebanese nationality.

In a further twist, the law gives foreign women more advantages than Lebanese women: a foreign woman can become naturalized through her marriage to a Lebanese man, and if that woman outlives her husband, she can grant Lebanese nationality to her minor children.[8]

The rule that children can only inherit citizenship from their fathers was once common in the Arab world, but since the beginning of the current century, many of the most prominent Arab states have amended their nationality laws, including Algeria, Egypt, Kuwait, Libya, Morocco, Palestine, Saudi Arabia, Tunisia, the United Arab Emirates, and Yemen.[9] Lebanon stands as a holdout, still beholden to an antiquated, ninety-year-old law.[10]

When this already troubled law is crossbred with other problematic Lebanese laws, it produces even more grotesque outcomes than those described above. An example is the treatment of the Palestinians, whose presence in the country figured prominently in the unfolding of the civil war. Lebanese law treats Palestinians harshly, restricting their ability to work, to receive social security and health care, and even to own property.[11] A Lebanese woman who marries a Palestinian man residing in Lebanon is thus effectively condemning her children to a lack of meaningful citizenship. (And let's keep in mind that the Palestinian man may not have the right to live in any other country in the world, let alone Palestine.) According to the 1989 Taif Agreement that ended the fifteen-year civil war, naturalizing Palestinians is even unconstitutional in Lebanon.[12] Politicians claim that Palestinians would abuse a reformed nationality law to gain naturalization.[13]

Such claims are a bald admission of the sectarian and ethnically discriminatory motivations behind politicians' stance on women's citizenship. But they also reveal, less intentionally, that sectarian concerns have their limits—and that limit is an encroachment on male privilege. No one is overly concerned with the demographic imbalance that might ensue when a Lebanese man gives his nationality to his Palestinian wife and children. His rights rank higher in the minds of the Lebanese patriarchs than even their obsession with demographics.

Politicians are aware of the hypocrisy and unfairness of the nationality laws. But they have also used that to their advantage, making gestures toward naturalization that are highly calculated to support their political and sectarian positions but do nothing to fundamentally change the inequity of the law. The precarious legal situation can easily be manipulated to serve political interests to create new electoral blocks.[14] So there have been, over the years, bulk naturalization decrees. For example, the government of prime minister Rafik Hariri (a Sunni, as the Lebanese prime minister always is) signed a decree in 1994 that granted Lebanese nationality to more than eighty-eight thousand people. Although the decree is currently under legal scrutiny, most of those naturalized were Muslims, mainly Syrian nationals.[15] Many accused the government of serving its own interests and favoring the Sunni community.

In 2014, before the end of his term, president Michel Suleiman (a Maronite Christian, as the Lebanese president always is) naturalized three hundred individuals, many of them Christian Palestinians. The number was not large, but still significant because it was wholly unconstitutional.[16] The decision did not comment on how these individuals were selected, or on what legal basis the Palestinians were naturalized.

And in November 2015, legislators formed an alliance between the two major representative Christian blocs in parliament (the Free Patriotic Movement and the Lebanese Forces) to pass a law that allows emigrants of Lebanese ancestry to attain citizenship. Christian politicians touted it as an opportunity to make demographic and political gains, though the official arguments for the law avoid sectarian language.[17]

Families of Lebanese women married to foreigners who have been living in Lebanon have never been the primary target of such decrees, or of any naturalization operation, for that matter.

All of this is but a superficial overview of the complex forces that have kept alive a law that clearly has no place in a modern polity where men and women supposedly have equal rights. The leaders of the Nationality Campaign were experts in all these issues, and set out to design a broad attack on the legal and social barriers to advancement. Their design was clever. But as we shall see, it has not yet been enough to surmount all of these considerable obstacles.

A Very Short History of Lebanese Women's Activism

The roots of women's involvement in modern Lebanon's civil society stretch back at least until 1952, when two charity organizations created the first women's joint committee, known today as the Lebanese Council of Women (LCW). A united campaign won them the right to vote in 1953, along with many other socioeconomic rights.[18] Today, the LCW comprises more than 170 NGOs from service-provision and charity organizations, to professional advocacy organizations, to women's associations and cooperatives.

Many activists regard the LCW as merely an umbrella that includes all forms of women's organizations, both active and passive ones. Some reflect the sectarianism of Lebanese politics, such as the Kataeb Party Women's Division or Women's Affairs of the Amal Movement, both of which are arms of sectarian political parties. Others are service based and do not contest mechanisms of exploitation against women in their communities.

Later in the twentieth century, new forms of organizations took advantage of the global trend for women's rights.[19] In 1985, attorney and celebrated women's rights champion Laure Moghaizel introduced the notion of legislative lobbying to activists. Moghaizel founded the Lebanese Association for Human Rights with the mission of committing the state to international standards for women's rights. The effort was successful when, in 1990, the prime minister agreed to include the state's commitment to the Universal Declaration of Human Rights in the Lebanese constitution and, in 1996, to sign the Convention on the Elimination of All Forms of Discrimination against Women (CEDAW)—though, crucially, he refrained from the articles on nationality and personal status.

In 1995, then-first lady Mona Hrawi created the National Commission for Lebanese Women (NCLW), which became the first governmental body responsible for the implementation of women's rights. The NCLW is today part of the Lebanese prime ministry and only works in a consultative capacity with the Lebanese government. But most activists think of the commission as nothing more than the government's window dressing—a representative of the prime minister to women's groups, but not a representative of women's interests in the prime ministry.[20] Traditionally, the first lady has been the NCLW's president, while the wives of the prime minister and the speaker of parliament sit as vice presidents.[21]

A counterpoint to the milquetoast women's representation of the NCLW and the LCW was the Lebanese Women's Network (LWN), established in 2001 by the late Wadad Chakhtoura, one-time president of the leftist women's rights organization known as the Lebanese Democratic Women's Gathering. The LWN is a coalition of a different nature, designed to be more of a think-tank than a network of passive organizations.[22] The LWN is made up of independent professional organizations that secure their resources through outside grants and dedicate all their time to the cause. These organizations use "legitimated methods of action" to influence policy and legal reform, and they do so effectively.

The activities of the LWN capped a half-century, beginning with universal suffrage in 1953, in which women had asserted their importance to the social and economic development of Lebanese society. In scholastic circles and professional fields, Lebanese women excelled and became a symbol of liberalism in the Arab world. However, such celebrated modernity did not mirror Lebanese women's true legal status.

The stage was set, and their contributions gave them the authority and confidence to demand their political rights.

The Nationality Campaign

Laying the Foundations

In the new millennium, concern with women's right to bequeath nationality grew throughout the Middle East and North Africa. CRTD-A, along with its partners in Algeria, Bahrain, Egypt, Morocco, Syria, and Tunisia, hosted a series of regional dialogue meetings with gender-based and women's advocacy NGOs on gender equality, citizenship and statelessness in each Arab state. They agreed that the nationality laws had to be addressed, once and for all. This thematic networking initiative around a common cause was unique: temporary and respectful of the independence of each organization yet leaving room for flexibility in short-term goals and campaigning strategies.[23]

It was a coming-into-consciousness moment for many gender-based and feminist organizations in the Arab world that had long been excluded from the public sphere. Leading activists decided to resist structural forms of violence in the media, in politics, the workplace, on the streets, and at home. In Lebanon, this meant finding new avenues of political expression. Formal political institutions had proved time and again that they could not accommodate women in powerful decision-making positions. In fact, women in the Lebanese parliament—who make up just 3 percent of all legislators[24]—are colloquially known as the "women in black dress" because they supposedly only succeed in politics because they are related to dead male politicians.[25] In the beginning of the new century, women activists increasingly turned to professional advocacy organizations as a legitimate site of political negotiation.

Before embarking on mass mobilization strategies, CRTD-A realized there was a large information gap. Lebanese women themselves did not always realize how the nationality law was shortchanging them. CRTD-A saw that concerned women needed to understand their own conditions of subordination, and to distinguish patriarchal structures and practices—in other words, to become agents of knowledge. They believed that narrating the story of the existing nationality law would highlight its origin in exploitative colonial practices, and its current anti-democratic role. To this end, CRTD-A commissioned a series of studies to review the historical record of the law and investigate its psychological and social implications on the families of women married to foreigners.[26] The general public, and even women married to foreigners themselves, did not know they had no right to pass on their citizenship until they had children.[27] Advocacy organizations needed the power of information before they could do anything.

In 2002, CRTD-A commissioned a study by Kamal Feghali, director of the Bureau of Statistics and Documentation, on the implications of the law on women's everyday lives, with the support of the United Nations Development Programme (UNDP). In 2003, a study by attorney Ziad Baroud reviewed the legal framework of the nationality law and proposed a new one. Baroud went on to become the an influential minister of the interior from 2008 to 2011. A longtime pillar of Lebanon's secular, reform, and activist communities, he was a surprise choice for the role. During his term, he introduced a wide array of reforms, some of which passed, and served as a stark contrast to the usual performance of cabinet appointees, especially in "sovereign" positions like the interior ministry. Baroud supported restructuring Lebanon's government, rewriting basic laws, electoral reform, police reform, civil marriage, and many other initiatives of a modernizing, secular, or civic nature. This would later prove to be central for the Nationality Campaign's progress. At the same time, CRTD-A assisted university students in their research projects on the nationality law.[28] Later research in academic circles, policy institutes, and development organizations added onto that mounting pile of knowledge.

In 2003, the regional network of nationality campaigners prepared the film *My Child the Foreigner* by Christine Garabedian, which featured the hardships of select families of Arab women married to foreigners, especially in Egypt, Lebanon, and Morocco.[29] The documentary gave the cause a human face, and is still used today as an educational tool at film festivals, universities and schools. Activists considered the placing of women's experiences at the center of such knowledge production to be of the utmost importance.

The studies and the film worked as intended, initiating a newfound interest in citizenship rights in Lebanon and the Arab world. The scholarship on the nationality law reestablished a correlation between the concept of citizenship and the right of women to pass on their nationality to family members. The topic had entered the public conversation.

It was in this context that Lina Bou Habib, executive director of CRTD-A, held meetings with members of the LWN and expressed her desire to embark on a campaign for women's full citizenship with their joint resources. CRTD-A also gave their moral and symbolic support to the LWN—showing up for the latter's protests, even when they weren't related to nationality, and carefully coordinating their efforts on other issues.[30] In 2005, under the representative leadership of CRTD-A, the LWN launched Lebanon's Nationality Campaign: "My Nationality, a Right for Me and My Family."

The network was not a traditionally hierarchal arrangement. It reconciled the need for leadership with the widespread rejection of hierarchy and authority among movement organizations. The campaign resolved to speak under the banner of the "Nationality Campaign," and never in the name of CRTD-A, though CRTD-A became the movement's de facto representative.

Awareness and enthusiasm would not carry the campaign alone, however. Both the CRTD-A and the LWN realized that to deal with Lebanon's many bickering bosses, deeply patriarchal and anxious about the sectarian balance, they would need powerful backers, a solid base of support, and organizational resources.

The Campaign Hits Its Stride

The Nationality Campaign members recognized that their fight would require them to take on multiple roles at once, sometimes in seeming contradiction. For example, CRTD-A became both a challenger to the state and a service provider for concerned women and their families, sometimes in coordination with the state. Their work was at once oriented towards political decision-makers and the daily needs of their own constituency.

The Nationality Campaign developed strategic alliances with supportive organizations, including the Lebanese media, research centers, key activists, and progressive political actors, and revived a culture of protest in the Lebanese public arena. It gave training workshops on citizenship rights and gender equality to a handful of journalists from major Lebanese newspapers; the journalists "remained very faithful to the campaign," recalled Roula El Masri, the coordinator of the Nationality Campaign for CRTD-A at the time of the trainings.

This multifaceted approach gave the activists a good deal of flexibility and ample options for contingencies if progress became blocked on one path or another. For example, when Lebanon's July 2006 war with Israel took all of the country's political attention, the Nationality Campaign put a halt to its public advocacy activities. But it retained its service-provision, which kept its mission alive. CRTD-A launched a hotline to assist women married to foreigners with their legal dealings with the Ministry of the Interior, the Ministry of Education and Higher Education, and the Ministry of Labor. It helped women with issues as simple as how to get a driver's license, a work or residency permit, or knowing what profession their husbands could occupy or which documents they needed to prepare.[31] At the time, state agencies were treating the children of Lebanese women and foreign men like any other foreigner. Women were justifiably afraid their families would be persecuted, detained, or deported for lacking the necessary documentation. They simply did not know what to do or where to go. CRTD-A became their guide.

When in 2008 the Lebanese government was finally formed, the campaign began enlisting some sectors of the political elite, including those that fought against it tooth and nail. According to El Masri, there were two roads to approach the state: either parliament would create a committee to study a draft law and then transfer it to the cabinet once approved, or a minister would propose a draft law for study directly at a cabinet meeting. CRTD-A decided to vigorously pursue both roads in anticipation of the right window of opportunity. Meanwhile, they kept a close eye on explicitly discriminatory politicians. "We would highlight those names on the board [in our office] in capitalized letters to remember their names, faces, and statements," explained El Masri. "But we also started studying the configurations of political blocs, seeing what each politician's position was within the same bloc."

CRTD-A wagered that even within sectarian blocs, not all politicians shared the same opinion on the nationality law—and they were right. For example, members of the Change and Reform bloc, led by Michel Aoun, founder of the Christian Free Patriotic Movement, have raised some of the most racist objections to the nationality law.[32] Still, Ghassan Moukheiber, a member of the same bloc, is one of the few members of parliament who have continuously called for reform of the nationality law. The campaign sustained close ties to key official figures such as the minister of state, Mona Ofeish, the minister of justice, Ibrahim Najjar, and the minister of the interior, Baroud, who had long sought to modernize legislation.

CRTD-A also worked to make their constituents' travails visible to state institutions and became women's go-to agency for questions about their legal status. This proved one of the most fruitful avenues for activism, creating marked improvements in the state's treatment of women and children. For example, two years after CRTD-A succeeded in getting a 2012 ministerial decision that granted children equal access to public education, women informed the legal unit at CRTD-A that the Ministry of Education was denying their children access to public schools. CRTD-A immediately sent a petition to the ministry and privately pressed the minister to solve the misunderstanding. The ministry relented, and the children were enrolled. CRTD-A was grabbing the state by the hand and telling it how to do its job, and state institutions now knew they'd be held accountable for their poor performance.

The activists also made gains on some of the most odious regulations that derived from the nationality law. Many of the restrictions placed on residency and work permits were lifted. In 2010, decree no. 4186 gave foreign husbands and their children three-year courtesy residency permits without any fees or proof of work. In 2011, Minister of Labor Charbel Nahhas, under the new labor regulation No.122/1, granted "work permits without the need of a sponsor to non-Lebanese spouses of Lebanese women, effectively making it easier for employers to hire non-nationals."[33] The latest 2012 ministerial committee decision granted those families an indefinite residency permit, equal access to education in public schools and state universities, and the right to public healthcare.[34]

On the legal front, the Nationality Campaign's outreach gained headway, but it depended heavily on the political will, effort, and window of opportunity that individual politicians and lawmakers presented. In 2009, the campaign persuaded Baroud to propose a draft amendment to the nationality law to the cabinet. The draft proposed two possible formulations to Article 4, which deals with the nationality of children: (1) "likewise, a Lebanese woman married to a foreign man has the right to grant her children Lebanese nationality," or (2) "cancelling all other legal texts on the matter, any [person] born of a Lebanese mother shall be considered Lebanese on the condition that the father's nationality is accredited by a recognized state and is not in conflict with constitutional rulings concerning the rejection of naturalization."[35]

Baroud intentionally avoided proposing an Amendment to Article 1, which would have affected husbands' citizenship and thus give full citizenship rights to Lebanese women. That omission was due to the fact that the issue of Palestinian naturalization was still too controversial to touch.

But here, the campaign's progress met a wall. The amendment was promptly rejected. Then-Prime Minister Fouad Siniora refused to support an approach that treated Lebanese women married to foreigners "exceptionally" just so that they could give the nationality to their children. There was irony in this reasoning: the state that had denied women full citizenship for so long was citing a concern with giving it to them piecemeal ("exceptionally") to reject an amendment that would have at least offered an incremental improvement.

"I was so naïve to think I would see change in my lifetime," El Masri said. "It was too good to be true."

But the setback only galvanized the campaign, even as it was a reality check. All women's advocacy organizations joined forces once again and staged their first batch of demonstrations.[36]

Schisms and Stumbles

The problems with changing the law occurred against a background of increasing problems within the campaign, which may have affected its efficacy.

There had been early signs of disagreements. Before the campaign even gained speed, it suffered from its first coalition fall-out in 2005 when two leftist Lebanese women's organizations, the Women's Democratic Gathering and the League of Lebanese Women's Rights, launched a separate campaign. Led by Linda Mattar (currently the president of the League), the campaign was called "My Nationality, a Right for Me and My Children." Mattar apparently also wanted to avoid the question of naturalization of husbands, which had become a touchier subject than ever in the atmosphere of nationalist hysteria sparked by the February 2005 assassination in central Beirut of Rafik Hariri and eight members of his entourage. They considered the focus on children's citizenship a more realistic, achievable demand, even if the Gathering and the League ultimately wanted women to also be able to pass citizenship to spouses, as Lebanese men were already able to do.

For its part, CRTD-A saw this minimalist approach as a recipe for ultimate failure. A piecemeal campaign would jeopardize unity among the movement's members. Women married to Palestinians, for example, had a much more urgent interest in gaining citizenship for their husbands (who had few rights in Lebanon) than women married to foreigners of other nationalities. Further, CRTD-A reasoned that Lebanese politicians would bargain back anything the activists requested, anyway. It was better to set the bar high and demand, from the outset, the right of women to give their nationality to their children and husbands, without any exceptions.

"Do you go to them with your basket half empty and make their job easier?" said Karima Chebbo, CRTD-A's campaign coordinator. It was also a matter of principle. "How can I, a champion of gender equality and human rights, advocate for yet another form of exclusion? We know that legal reform is not a miraculous process. It takes time," she said. "If [the politicians] want to exclude husbands or Palestinian husbands, let them do the exclusion. I speak of the right of a Lebanese woman. Period. A right is a right. It is indivisible. And when you insist on framing it that way, the more irrational and unjust the law becomes to the general public."[37]

The disagreement on the scope of demands, which was never meaningfully resolved, was a harbinger of troubles to come.

The campaign soon faced another organizational schism. In 2007, UNDP invited several gender-based advocacy NGOs including CRTD-A to a coordination meeting to propose a $270,000 project to reform the nationality law in Lebanon.[38] The project, drawn up by UNDP, included the following goals: to formulate a mapping study of the impact of the nationality law, to train NGOs on advocacy and networking, to launch a nationality campaign, and to introduce a proposal to parliament of a draft law to amend the current law.

CRTD-A refused to take part in the project. Bou Habib said the project was a duplication of all that CRTD-A had done in the last seven years—as though none of their local efforts mattered.[39] "As a civil society organization, we set our own criteria and project plan in a grant proposal, not the other way round," Chebbo said.[40]

The National Committee for the Follow-up on Women's Issues (CFUWI) was appointed as UNDP's local coordinating partner, with its current president, Fahmia Charafeddine, as lead researcher on the case.[41] CFUWI withdrew from the Nationality Campaign coalition and went on to launch UNDP's campaign, with the slightly different title, "My Nationality, A Right For Me and *Them*" (emphasis added). With the UNDP's intervention, there were now two almost identical advocacy groups pursuing the same goal.

Accusations of petty territoriality flew around. The UNDP governance program manager, Hassan Krayem, said CRTD-A considered the Nationality Campaign to be its territory and didn't want anyone else to step on it.[42] Chebbo, on the other hand, argued that UNDP had suddenly appeared on the Lebanese national stage, and wanted everyone to start again from ground zero. CRTD-A was offended UNDP would insinuate that the proposed project was one of a kind, when CRTD-A was the expert organization on the nationality cause.

El Masri acknowledges that CRTD-A was very rigid on matters of principle—perhaps to a fault. It did not like to be tied down with large funds and projects imposed by international organizations that had done little local coordination on the nationality issue. CRTD-A refused to attach any logos to the UNDP campaign and developed a sense of ownership and responsibility toward their own efforts. "To tell you the truth, there was also this issue with CRTD-A that 'this is my baby,'" El Masri admitted. "I have the utmost respect for these principles, but I now think we should have compromised, at least for the sake of the cause."[43]

An even larger dispute arose surrounding the methodology and discourse of a mapping study that UNDP commissioned, which was published in 2009. The household selection criteria categorized husbands according to nationality and Lebanese wives according to sect (Shia, Sunni, Druze) and religion (Muslim, Christian). The report's authors wanted "to better know the different nationalities recurrent with every religion" and "to understand the different trends resulting from religious and cultural influences on these options."[44]

From eighteen thousand marriages of Lebanese women and foreign men, the study found that in 88 percent the woman was Muslim (some 52 percent Sunni and 34 percent Shiite). Less than 13 percent of the marriages involved Christian women.[45]

In a political vacuum, this information might have simply been useful scholarship. But in the atmosphere of Lebanese sectarianism, it was easy to infer that the naturalization of foreign husbands would be a direct boon to Muslim blocs at the expense of Christians (assuming that most of the surveyed women married men from their own sect, as is most common in Lebanon). CRTD-A was angry: the data played right into politicians' phobias, and the framing of results diverted the debate away from the human rights and citizenship perspective they had been working on for so long. Many other NGOs were also disconcerted with UNDP's findings and feared they could be used to harm the Nationality Campaign. (The fact that the study also showed that relatively few Lebanese women married Palestinians and Syrians, which might have softened some of the Nationality Campaign's most reactionary opponents, failed to make much of a splash.)[46]

To top it off, UNDP allowed its own nationality project to expire after two years and did not extend it, leaving CFUWI to pick up the slack. Krayem of UNDP acknowledged in hindsight that CRTD-A might have been a better partner because they were "the number one organization, consistently, and continuously working on the nationality law."[47]

All these schisms affected the continuity of the campaign's work, and harmed its momentum. They also caused something of a boom and bust in public and organizational interest in the cause, which soured activists like El Masri and Chebbo on the usefulness of big publicity, protests, and grand campaigns. CRTD-A felt that it could have provided better continuity and complementarity with behind-the-scenes action. "National excitement doesn't scare me, but neither does it impress me," Chebbo said. "If you keep on protesting and set up tents and all, who is going to listen to you then? You become part of the façade. There is a time for everything: a time to hit the streets and billboards and a time to stay home."[48] El Masri, for her part, felt that protests continued to be overused, to the point that they watered down the campaign's effectiveness.

The Fight in the Courts: the Case of Samira Soueidan

On a parallel track to the rest of its activism, the Nationality Campaign also pursued strategic litigation, which it viewed as one of the many fronts of a tactical war. They used charged individual cases to highlight wider social conflicts. While their efforts have not yet led to the core changes in the law that they still seek, they did materially improve the lives of Lebanese women married to foreigners and their children. Activists also believe that they have pried open a way for further advances in the courts.

The most notable of these actions involved the case of Samira Soueidan, a Lebanese widow who had four children with her late Egyptian husband. In June 2009, a Lebanese First Instance Court in Jdeideh-Metn headed by Judge John Azzi issued a landmark decision in the case, granting Soueidan's children the Lebanese nationality based on the following legal principle: "If the legal rule is ambiguous or incomplete, the judge's essential mission consists in varying upon the rule or finding a new solution through legal interpretation in order to reach a just and humane solution in conformity with justice and equity to the extent possible."[49] Judge Azzi based his judgment on portions of the Lebanese constitution and of the nationality law. If the nationality law grants that same right to a naturalized woman from her deceased Lebanese husband under the guise of protecting family unity, he reasoned, then the law must also apply to the case of a Lebanese woman.

The victory was fleeting: the Lebanese Public Prosecutor's Office, presided by three female judges, overturned the judgment in 2010.[50] But it still provided an opportunity for activists to expand the social, political, and legal space for the treatment of such cases.

Right after issuing his judgment, Judge Azzi called CRTD-A to ask whether the organization could take up the case and make it a matter of public concern, according to El Masri.[51] The campaign met up with Soueidan multiple times to provide her with psychological and social support, protested outside the Mount Lebanon Appeals Court and the First Instance Court in Jdeideh-Metn, and attended the court hearing.[52] Public officials, politicians, and parliamentarians panicked over Judge Azzi's decision and expressed their discontent with him.[53] The Supreme Judicial Council, the disciplinary and administrative body of the judiciary, reprimanded Judge Azzi and transferred him to a consultancy position.[54]

The political pressure had ultimately succeeded in reversing the decision, but it also put the independence of the judiciary under scrutiny and again highlighted the human cost of the nationality law and the hypocrisy of its defenders.[55] As such, the judgment and the events that preceded it proved beneficial to the world of activism in Lebanon. And Soueidan's case allowed the women's movement to connect with the judiciary as it had with the media before that. A movement for the reform of the judiciary arose and gained allies in civil society. Cause lawyering and individual judges became alternative avenues of activism.[56]

Change to the Law Remains Elusive

In March 2012, for the first time in Lebanese political history, the government of Najib Mikati, the prime minister at the time, established a ministerial committee to review a draft law to amend the final paragraph of Article 4 of Decree 15.[57]

From March until the committee's first meeting in July, CRTD-A held local coordination meetings all over Lebanon with concerned women and their families to lay down a strategy for the coming months. The Nationality Campaign protested in the streets for the changes in the law they sought, calling on the state to fulfill its minimum responsibility to citizens. Meanwhile, the NCLW—which, we recall, is essentially a mouthpiece of the prime ministry—presented the cabinet with a draft law to recognize the right of women to pass their nationality on to their children and foreign husbands, excluding women married to Palestinians.[58]

The committee invited Nationality Campaign representatives for a closed discussion. Committee members felt they needed to include the Nationality Campaign, even if merely for the sake of showing off their good intentions.[59] Campaign representatives left feeling hopeful, and were invited to a follow-up meeting in January 2013 for further discussions.

But it all turned out to be a ruse. Halfway through December 2012, the ministerial committee secretly filed to Mikati's cabinet its final recommendation: the nationality law, they said, should not be amended in any way. The committee invoked legal precedent protecting "the higher interest of the state."[60] The prime minister approved their recommendation before the end of the year,[61] though the verdict was not leaked to CRTD-A until after their January meeting.

The Nationality Campaign was blindsided by the ministry's about-face, but the committee's reasoning was depressingly familiar. It had once again couched the issue of the law as being fundamentally about foreigners obtaining Lebanese nationality. Again, these political concerns had superseded women's right to the same citizenship as their male counterparts, which the committee didn't even mention.[62]

There was some very cold comfort in the fact that the immediate cause for the rejection of the amendment—which was shelved indefinitely—was not just the existing anxieties about Lebanese demographics, but also a new variable that had changed the equation. Syrian refugees had begun streaming into the country. They account for nearly one in three people residing on Lebanese soil, and those numbers only include those registered with the United Nations High Commissioner for Refugees (UNHCR). Even much of the public had lost their appetite for returning to the debate around the nationality law. Lawmakers who had long opposed changes to the nationality law now saw a chance to exploit the flagging public interest.

The file on the law was sealed for the time being. These facts, however, in no way invalidated the basic claims of the Nationality Campaign. It must be acknowledged that the activists fought a battle that may have been waged at the right pace and with the right tactics for Lebanon as it was before the Syrian civil war unleashed chaos on the region. It's impossible to know what might have transpired without the effects of the war, but the activists can hardly be blamed for not anticipating it.

Conclusion

The defeat that the prime minister dealt the Nationality Campaign left it in a critical condition. If the campaign is measured by the sole benchmark of fundamental legal change, it might fairly be called, thus far, a failure. Even by less specific metrics, the results of the campaign leave much to be desired. Women's advocacy organizations still have no decision-making power in key government institutions, or proportional representation in formal political circles. They remain dependent on individual politicians in the hope that, when a political opportunity arises, they will be prepared enough to seize it. Further, the results were an object lesson in how effective a state's stalling strategy can be.

But the activists don't see things in these stark terms, and in the wake of the ruling, they continued their activities, focusing on service delivery and advancing the significant gains they had made in the interpretation and application of the existing law. Women can now much more easily access state public services such as education and residency, because the Nationality Campaign made it impossible for politicians to completely ignore the unfair effects of the law. Even more noteworthy is the change in attitude of governmental agencies toward concerned women and their families. "If you need to process your papers, you are no longer treated as a 'foreigner' if your mother is Lebanese," explained Ghida

Frangieh, a lawyer at Nizar Saghieh Law Firm and writer for its *Legal Agenda*. "Even if your papers are not all in check, they will let it slide. They will not detain you, because they see you as an unfairly persecuted Lebanese who does not have the Lebanese nationality."

There have been other, less quantifiable effects from the campaign, as well. What the Nationality Campaign lost in strict legal reform, it gained in social attitude. The movement also reconfigured the relationship of the state with civil society and reestablished a formal link with state representatives that had been missing—not just when it came to the nationality law and its application, but for other issues as well. Even as the Nationality Campaign suffered a blow, other advocacy organizations that were part of the LWN scored historic legal successes.[63] Since the Nationality Campaign, women's advocacy organizations have ventured into alternative fields of activism. Youth organizations, student clubs, legal activist associations, universities, grassroots groupings, and professional syndicates all joined in on the same fight. Advocacy organizations concerned with domestic violence, marital rape, and other personal status law matters expanded their reform efforts to include state security apparatuses, religious and sectarian institutions, and the NGO sector as a whole.

It may also, through its insistence in working with the state, have dealt a hard-to-measure blow against corruption. Civil society can be both a challenger and auditor of the state. In a country where politics is only possible if you know the right people, are owed the right favors, and sell the right principles, the Nationality Campaign decided to do everything by the book and go through all the right channels. The campaigners' professionalism and respect for the rule of law allowed many to empathize with their struggle—even cynical representatives of the state itself.

And finally, activists simply refuse to accept that the 2012 amendment rejection represented a definitive defeat. Like civil rights strugglers the world over, they are in it for the long haul, and imagine that change will come, even if it takes a decade or more. They measure their success as much in steps moved forward as they do in goals achieved. Some activists worry that the moderate gains they have made so far make the fundamental legal change less likely—the can might be forever kicked down the road. But most cannot help but view setbacks as taken-for-granted, and as opportunities for further mobilization. There may be things they would have done differently in the last decade and a half—less infighting, for sure—but they hardly see their efforts as wasted. They are moving forward, and the UNDP-induced schism is water under the bridge. No doubt, the obstacles in their path are considerable, not least the rising xenophobia in the country directed at Syrians.

The women's Nationality Campaign has also taught us a broader lesson: social and political change does not have one universal scale. The transformative potential of advocacy organizations travels well beyond their immediate sphere of work, all the more so when that work is well-organized and energized—even when its headline goals remain out of reach.

Notes

1. Maya W. Mansour and Sarah G. Abou Aad, *Women's Citizenship Rights in Lebanon* (Beirut: Issam Fares Institute for Public Policy and International Affairs, 2012), http://www.aub.edu.lb/ifi/public_policy/rapp/documents/working_paper_series/20120504ifi_rapp_hrp_wps08_womens_citizenship_rights_in_lebanon_english.pdf.

2. See Pernille Arenfeldt and Nawar Al-Hassan, eds. *Mapping Arab Women's Movements: A Century of Transformations from Within* (Cairo: American University in Cairo Press, 2012); and Diane Singermann, "Rewriting Divorce in Egypt: Reclaiming Islam, Legal Activism, and Coalition Politics," in *Remaking Muslim Politics: Pluralism, Contestation, Democratization*, ed. Robert W. Hefner (Princeton, N.J.: Princeton University Press, 2005), 161–88.

3. *The Lebanese Demographic Reality* (Beirut: Lebanese Information Center, 2013), http://www.lstatic.org/PDF/demographenglish.pdf.

4. Todd M. Johnson and Gina A. Zurlo, "Ongoing Exodus: Tracking the Emigration of Christians from the Middle East," *Harvard Journal of Middle Eastern Politics and Policy* 3 (2013–2014): 39–49.

5. Elie Fares, "Christians Are Disappearing from Lebanon," *A Separate State of Mind*, March 4, 2015, https://stateofmind13.com/2015/03/04/christians-are-disappearing-from-lebanon/.

6. See Mansour and Abou Aad, *Women's Citizenship Rights in Lebanon*, 9-10; and Karen M. Kern, *Imperial Citizen: Marriage and Citizenship in the Ottoman Frontier Provinces of Iraq* (Syracuse, NY: Syracuse University Press, 2011), 90–93.

7. Decree no. 15 on Lebanese Nationality including Amendments [Lebanon], January 19, 1925, http://www.refworld.org/docid/44a24c6c4.html.

8. Ibid.

9. See Freedom House, "Gender and Citizenship in the Arab World," *Al-Raida Journal* 129–130 (Spring/Summer 2010): 64–73, http://iwsaw.lau.edu.lb/publications/al-raida/citizenship-and-gender-in-the.php.

10. According to Decree no. 15 issued January 19, 1925, by the high commissioner of the Republic of France to the countries of Syria, Greater Lebanon, the Alawites, and the Djebel Druze, Lebanese women cannot pass their nationality on to their children or foreign husbands. Law of January 11, 1960, Amending and Supplementing Decree no. 15 of January 19, 1925 [Lebanon], January 11, 1960, http://www.refworld.org/docid/51120f8b2.html .

11. See "Lebanon: Seize Opportunity to End Discrimination Against Palestinians," Human Rights Watch, 2010, https://www.hrw.org/news/2010/06/18/lebanon-seize-opportunity-end-discrimination-against-palestinians.

12. Taif Agreement, 1989 Section I H, https://www.un.int/lebanon/sites/www.un.int/files/Lebanon/the_taif_agreement_english_version_.pdf.

13. See Nizar Saghieh, "Trespassing on the Nationality of Lebanese Women: Renewing the Guise of Male Privilege," *The Legal Agenda*, January 20, 2016, http://legal-agenda.com/en/article.php?id=3119.

14. Ghida Frangieh, "Manufacturing Precarious Nationality in Lebanon: The Naturalization Decree of 1994," *The Legal Agenda*, February 8, 2016, http://english.legal-agenda.com/article.php?id=750&lang=en.

15. Guita Hourani, *The 1994 Naturalization Decree* (Beirut: Lebanese Emigration Research Center of Notre Dame University, 2011).

16. See "Michel Suleiman Secretly Naturalized 644 Individuals as Lebanese Citizens," *Al-Akhbar*, June 13, 2014, http://english.al-akhbar.com/node/20166. CRTD-A breaks down the list of people who benefitted from the 2014 naturalization decree to show that the majority were Christian, naturalized Palestinians, and Europeans. See also Center for Training Resources, and Development-Action (CRTD-A), *Manshour Jinsiyati* (2014).

17. Nizar Saghieh, "Restoring Citizenship Law in Lebanon: Renaturalization Without Return," *The Legal Agenda*, July 1, 2016, http://legal-agenda.com/en/article.php?id=773&folder=articles&lang=en.

18. Pernille Arenfeldt and Nawar Al-Hassan Golley, eds., *Mapping Arab Women's Movements: A Century of Transformations from Within* (Cairo: American University of Cairo, 2012), 116.

19. See Rita Stephan, "Four Waves of Lebanese Feminism," *E-International Relations*, November 7, 2014, http://www.e-ir.info/2014/11/07/four-waves-of-lebanese-feminism/.

20. Fahmia Charafeddine (president of CFUWI), interview with the author, August 18, 2016.

21. Joumana Moufarrege (administrative director at NCLW), interview with the author, August 3, 2016.

22. Roula El Masri, interview with the author, August 17, 2016; Charafeddine, interview.

23. El Masri, interview.

24. World Bank, "Proportion of seats held by women in national parliaments (%)," http://data.worldbank.org/indicator/SG.GEN.PARL.ZS.

25. On Lebanese women in parliament, See Dalila Mahdawi, "Lebanon's Crawl to Equality," *The Daily Star*, January 15, 2009, http://www.dailystar.com.lb/News/Lebanon-News/2009/Jun-15/53324-lebanons-crawl-to-equality.ashx.

26. See Ziad Baroud, "Denial of Nationality and Arab Women: Legal Research on the Lebanese Case," CRTD-A, 2003, http://www.crtda.org.lb/node/14503; and Kamal Feghali, "Denial of Nationality and Arab Women: Social Research on the Lebanese Case," CRTD-A and UNDP, 2002, http://www.crtda.org.lb/node/14504.

27. Karima Chebbo (coordinator of the Nationality Campaign at CRTD-A), interview with the author, August 23, 2016.

28. CRTD-A, *Qitaf Jinsiyati News Forecast Issue* 5 (2015).

29. In 2012, CRTD-A did another documentary with filmmaker and activist Carole Mansour, called *All for the Nation*, discussed in the beginning of this chapter.

30. El Masri, interview.

31. Chebbo, interview with the author, August 4, 2016.

32. See CRTD-A, *Qitaf Jinsiyati News Forecast Issue* 6 (2015).

33. Mansour and Abou Aad, *Women's Citizenship Rights in Lebanon*, 10.

34. Copy of the original ministerial committee decision provided to the author by CRTD-A.

35. Joumana Moufarrege and Fadi Karam, "What Is This 'Higher Interest' that Prevents a Mother Passing Her Nationality to Her Children?," *An-Nahar*, April 13, 2013, http://newspaper.annahar.com/article.php?t=kada ya&p=1&d=25047.

36. See Dalila Mahdawi, "Hundreds of Lebanese Women Demand Equal Rights to Pass on Nationality," *The Daily Star*, April 10, 2009, http://www.dailystar.com.lb/News/Lebanon-News/2009/Apr-10/52078-hundreds-of-lebanese-women-demand-equal-right-to-pass-on-nationality.ashx; and Dalila Mahdawi, "Women Demonstrations Demand Reform of Nationality Legislation," *The Daily Star,* April 28, 2009, http://www.dailystar.com.lb/News/Lebanon-News/2009/Apr-28/53024-women-demonstrators-demand-reform-of-nationality-legislation.ashx.

37. Chebbo, interview.

38. Hassan Krayem (UNDP governance program), interview with the author, August 16, 2016; El Masri, Chebbo, and Charafeddine, interviews.

39. Bassam Al Quntar, "$270,000 from the United Nations to Implement Implemented Projects," *Al-Akhbar*, October 10, 2008, http://www.al-akhbar.com/node/105566.

40. Chebbo, interview.

41. This project was also done in coordination with the Council of Reconstruction and Development (CDR).

42. Krayem, interview.

43. El Masri, interview.

44. Fahmia Charafeddine, *The Predicament of Lebanese Women Married to Non-Lebanese* (Beirut: UNDP, 2009), 16–17, http://www.undp.org.lb/communication/publications/downloads/mujaz_en.pdf.

45. Ibid., 17–19. http://www.undp.org.lb/communication/publications/downloads/mujaz_en.pdf.

46. Ibid., 19

47. Krayem, interview.

48. Chebbo, interview.

49. For more on the legal interpretation behind Judge Azzi's judgment, see Mansour and Abou Aad, *Women's Citizenship Rights in Lebanon*, 16–17.

50. "Landmark Decision Granting Citizenship to Children of Lebanese Mother Overturned," *The Daily Star,* May 19, 2010, http://www.dailystar.com.lb/News/Lebanon-News/2010/May-19/57545-landmark-ruling-granting-citizenship-to-children-of-lebanese-mother-overturned.ashx.

51. El Masri, interview.

52. Bassam Quntar, "April 13: Samira Soueidan Is Not Alone" (Arabic), *Al-Akhbar*, April 9, 2010, http://alakhbar.spiru.la/node/53124.

53. Nizar Saghieh, "When a Judge Rules" (Arabic), *Al-Akhbar,* June 20, 2009, http://www.al-akhbar.com/node/77056.

54. Radwan Mourtada, "John Al Azzi: A Judge Falls Victim to the Higher Judicial Council" (Arabic), *Al-Akhbar,* October 12, 2010, http://www.al-akhbar.com/node/38811.

55. Nizar Saghieh, "The Independence of the Judiciary and the Right of Women to Complete Equality Are Part of the Same Fight: When the Dignity of the Judiciary Is Related to Its Independence," *The Legal Agenda*, April 5, 2012, http://legal-agenda.com/article.php?id=88&folder=articles&lang=ar.

56. Carlos Daoud, "Suggestion to Organize the Relationship of the Lawyer with Media Outlets: Where Does the Cause Lawyer Stand?" (Arabic), *The Legal Agenda*, June/July 27, 2011, http://legal-agenda.com/article.php?id=6&folder=articles&lang=ar.

57. See Moufarrege and Karam, "Higher Interest."

58. Ibid.

59. All information on the series of events of this period was provided by CRTD-A documents and multiple interviews with Karima Chebbo, the campaign coordinator at the time, who was present at those meetings.

60. Specifically, it invoked ruling 2/2001 of the Constitutional Council.

61. Original Copy of the ministerial committee, provided by CRTD-A.

62. Moufarrege and Karam, "Higher Interest."

63. In 2014, a local advocacy group, KAFA (Enough) Violence and Exploitation, succeeded in amending the domestic violence law in Lebanon, after nine years of work. See "Annual Report," KAFA, 2014, http://www.kafa.org.lb/StudiesPublicationPDF/PRpdf-82-635689245975040950.pdf.

8

Egypt's Human Rights Movement

Repression, Resistance, and Co-optation

KHALED MANSOUR

Since the mid-1980s, the number of Egyptian nongovernmental organizations (NGOs) focusing on human rights has grown rapidly. But despite the proliferation of organizations, the human rights movement in Egypt has never been very effective, and is now especially unmoored. This chapter traces the sources of these problems in the history of human rights activism in Egypt. The author shows that even as the government has at times allowed NGOs a modicum of independence, it has mostly regarded them with contempt and suspicion. Additionally, Egyptian human rights organizations never formed strong bonds with trade unions and other parts of civil society. They have thus been especially vulnerable to failure. Now, the security-dominated regime of President Abdel Fattah el-Sisi is leading a fresh crackdown on human rights NGOs. For Egypt, mired in political dysfunction and economic malaise, this is a practical as well as a moral blunder. The inclusion of human rights in policy and politics, the author argues, is essential to the country's advancement.

In the last few months of 2016, the Egyptian government and security agencies worked together to freeze the assets of at least six prominent human rights defenders and three human rights organizations. In the same year at least fifteen human rights activists were banned from leaving the country, and several were summoned for interrogation. These organizations and individuals face possible charges of undermining state institutions and receiving foreign funds to harm national security. These charges could lead to lengthy prison terms and hefty fines if the ruling regime in Egypt continues to escalate its unprecedented crackdown on the freedom of civil and political action in general, and on the human rights movement in particular.

A new bill that the parliament passed in November 2016 could effectively paralyze both services- and advocacy-oriented civil society organizations (CSOs) in Egypt to an extent that, as a UN expert warned, would "devastate the country's civil society for generations to come and turn it into a government puppet."[1]

This crackdown is but the latest chapter in Egypt's troubled history with human rights. Rule-of-law and citizenship in modern Egypt have most often been unstable institutions and concepts, co-opted to serve largely authoritarian regimes ranging from the nationalist to the kleptocratic and from the state social-ist to the crony capitalist.

Though the human rights movement of Egypt has often been restricted to a tight corner of operations due to government laws and policies and judicial and security harassment, it has traveled far since it emerged in the mid-1980s. In its three-and-a-half decade lifespan, it has had varying degrees of success in the issues and causes it championed. Human rights activists contributed, even if in small ways and from the tight corner to which they were constrained, to the uprising of 2011 and the removal of former president Hosni Mubarak. They pro-ceeded to have an unprecedented impact during Egypt's short-lived democratic experiment (2011–13).

But this period of relative freedom, during which many new human rights organizations were established, now looks like little more than a detour from Egypt's main highway of authoritarianism. Security institutions, state bureaucra-cies, and their regional and business allies regained full control after the removal in 2013 of Mohamed Morsi's government—which itself was not ultimately a big supporter of the human rights movement.

Now, as a suffocating new regime has taken over, independent and credible human rights organizations are still numerous. But like ships tossed from port by a storm, they float unmoored, damaged and directionless, notwithstanding the bravery and integrity of the remaining crews and captains. The "movement" now seems barely deserving of the title. This is not just a tragedy for human rights in Egypt, I argue, but a dangerous situation for the development of the country in general. The weak situation of human rights is both a cause and a symptom of a country's broader crisis: despite appearances of relative stability in a tumultuous region, Egypt is on the verge of losing its way economically, politically, and socially in a more severe sense than it has in a very long time. It is becoming ever clearer that its authoritarianism leads nowhere.

The fact that the human rights movement in Egypt has ended up in such a weakened state is not an accident, but rather the result of a specific history in a country whose governments have long treated it with suspicion and even contempt. Successive Egyptian regimes have viewed the human rights move-ment—and civil society more broadly—in crude terms. At best it was a social pressure releaser, at worst, an annoyance that needed to be carefully constrained to keep from growing into a destabilizing danger. The Egyptian state has never recognized the movement, or had a respect for the goals it seeks, as being an integral part of becoming a better-developed society.

Movements with similar goals have fared relatively better in Morocco and Tunisia. In Morocco, a gradual political reform from the top, beginning in the mid 1990s, helped strengthen human rights organizations to varying degrees.

And in Tunisia, a more robust trade union and women's movements from the late 1950s accomplished the same, allowing human rights-oriented civil society to acquire a front-row seat in the political transition drama that ensued after the December 2010 uprising—even after decades of ceaseless security, legal, and political siege. In both Morocco and Tunisia, organic relations grew between the human rights movements on the one hand and the rest of civil and political societies on the other hand. This did not take place in Egypt, where the human rights movement existed within a restrictive political space and had no influential segments of the civil society to coordinate with, while trade unions and political parties had been eviscerated for decades and co-opted by the state.[2]

Briefly comparing these countries' experiences shows that the ability to form a robust human rights movement relies on much more complicated variables than the status of human rights in a country at any given moment. More so, it depends on the strengths of a country's social and political connective tissue—those bonds that preserve some relationship between the state, communities, religious institutions, the private sector, and most of all, civil society.[3] Examining Egyptian history shows how these bonds were systematically weakened, all but ensuring that the country's human rights movement would face almost insurmountable obstacles, even as organizations proliferated in the brief period of openness following the 2011 revolution.

This destruction of the foundations of civil society matters quite a lot for the future of the country. The difficulties of even narrowly focused rights-based campaigns, like that for expanding better health care (which I discuss later in this chapter) show how much ground Egypt must cover, based on current trends, to achieve modest improvements in well-being for most of its citizens. It is clear that without a meaningful reform in social and economic policies, the gap will widen between the poor and disenfranchised majority, who are banished from the realm of the political (except when called upon to cast their votes), and the dominant rich minority, which controls resources, wealth, power, and the management of networks of cronyism. Such reform is impossible without civil society and a respect for human rights.

The Historical and Political Context

The heart of the continuing political crisis in Egypt is the state's ceaseless emaciation and co-optation of the political and civil societies: political parties, trade unions, religious institutions, philanthropic activities, charities, and advocacy organizations. The state bureaucracy, led by the army and other security agencies, has played a pivotal role in this premeditated gutting of competing entities. Its efforts began in 1952 when army officers deposed King Farouk, ended the monarchy, and then shut down or co-opted almost all forms of peaceful protest and organization, swallowing the society into a state-led hodgepodge project of Arab nationalism and Egyptian-style state socialism.

Gamal Abdul Nasser's regime cracked after the 1967 defeat in Egypt's war with Israel, and only ended with his death in 1970, at which point Anwar Sadat assumed the presidency. Sadat and his successor Hosni Mubarak (president 1981–2011) gradually abrogated the unwritten contract under which the people had been guaranteed a minimum of social and economic rights (free education and health care, subsidized housing, controlled rents, and guaranteed state employment for graduates, to name a few) in exchange for giving up most of their civil and political rights. CSOs stepped up their networks of services and care to stem the widening gaps between social needs and dwindling government services. These organizations included the long-established, like Ansarul Sunna Society or Caritas, and foreign organizations like CARE—not to mention the politically motivated affiliates of the Muslim Brotherhood.

As the state started a slow—and disorderly and opaque—transition to a market economy in the mid-1970s, social and economic services started to deteriorate and they were no longer portrayed by the state as rights. Government officials started to complain about a population explosion problem rather than an economic production or a resource distribution challenge. By the early 1980s, Egyptians had clearly lost their access to quality social and economic services from the state—which came on top of the continued denial of their political and civil rights. Many of these services became the domain of CSOs, some religiously motivated, some politically motivated, and others focused on geographical or ethnic groups. But as Egyptians took over roles that the state used to play, they still could not freely organize into trade unions or nongovernmental associations, they lacked free media, and they had a very short and frequently interrupted experience of relatively free multiparty democracy in the late 1970s and early 1980s (though this never extended to the presidency).

It was under these circumstances in the mid-1980s that the first human rights organization was born. The Egyptian Organization for Human Rights (EOHR) was led by leftists, Nasserists, and Arab nationalists who started to think that a new social contract should be brokered with the state that did not forfeit civil and political rights for the sake of social and economic rights—the latter of which the state no longer guaranteed anyway. It was a difficult birth and a tough evolution on a zigzagging road, as I will explain in later sections.

Egyptians became increasingly disgruntled in the late 1980s, but the state was able to meet some of the economic demands in the early 1990s thanks to economic windfalls and cancelled loan payments that the government gained from its political position against the Iraqi invasion of Kuwait, and its subsequent joining of the international coalition in the war against Saddam Hussein in 1991.

Those windfalls didn't last, and by the turn of the new century, Mubarak and his aging ministers had been regurgitating promises of greater political and economic dividends for more than twenty years—and they never came through. Egyptians had already taken to the streets in 2000 in support of the Palestinian Second Intifada, and in 2003, to protest against the United States' invasion of

Iraq. But their anger at domestic conditions took longer to crystalize into public actions as their discontent deepened. Political scientist Eberhard Kienle argues that neoliberal transformations in poorer Arab countries like Egypt in the 1990s and the first decade of this century helped create

> "ingredients for unrest . . . for quite some time as rulers were less and less able to meet the expectations and indeed demands of their populations. For more than two decades, globalization and related economic reforms tended to increase the income and wealth of some constituencies while leaving behind, impoverishing or locking into lasting destitution others. . . . Public-sector workers and civil servants, as well as employers in the noncompetitive parts of the private sector, increasingly fell behind. . . . Restrictions on the freedom of expression and political participation incarnated in government-dependent media, censorship, rigged elections (or their complete absence) and the repression of strikes and other forms of collective action left the losers with little hope of making their voices heard and influencing policies."[4]

Egypt's macroeconomic indicators were encouraging from 2005 to 2010—especially the GDP growth rate, which averaged about 6 percent annually during the period.[5] But other indicators such as inequality, youth unemployment, high malnutrition rates, and deteriorating health and educational services caused grave concerns. These developments could be largely attributed to a declining public investment in social and infrastructure projects. Neoliberal policies cut down subsidies, increased inflation, and affected basic social services. Social safety nets to mitigate the harmful impact of this economic transformation were never adequately installed.

Similar developments took place in other Arab countries resulting in rampant poverty and corruption, like Syria, Tunisia, and Yemen. Various Arab republics, under domestic and international economic pressures, had shyly and slowly shifted toward ostensibly open market policies (for Egypt, beginning in the late 1970s) and then at a faster pace later on, especially in the decade preceding the Arab uprisings. Networks of corruption and cronyism acquired more control. In the absence of organized political action and with the co-optation of trade unions in most of these countries (Tunisia being a marked exception), only Islamists were able to persist as political threats to regimes, partly due to state permissiveness and partly due to their tenacity and good organization.

The Arab uprisings were surprising to many, but not necessarily for close watchers of the region who were observing how social and economic inequalities were rising dramatically. The authors Rabab El-Mahdi and Bahgat Korany argue that it was possible to predict an upheaval in Egypt if one used the right theoretical lenses.[6]

Despite all of this, Mubarak stayed in power for three decades. The late political economist Samer Soliman argues in his seminal work, *The Strong Regime and the Weak State*, that the repressive regime had just enough agility to keep the frail state alive through changing conditions.[7] He claims that Mubarak was able to placate certain important sectors (state bureaucracy, judiciary, the police, etc.) through special funds and benefits as long as the state had surplus resources (through cutting down budget lines for social services or through loans). Soliman attributes Mubarak's downfall to the decreasing surplus he could use to placate his allies, because although GDP was growing well, the state revenues were rapidly decreasing, especially since the taxation system was fraying and corruption was rampant.

By the end of 2010 in Egypt, a new parliament that completely excluded any form of opposition (and shut out the Brotherhood who had won eighty-eight seats a few years earlier) nailed shut the last opening for political mediation and expression by large sectors of those affected by the fast-paced and badly concocted neoliberal policies. The regime asserted control of most media outfits, banned protests and strikes, besieged trade unions, and emaciated political parties and independent CSOs. For Egyptians, the last straw was the 2010 parliamentary elections in which the ruling National Democratic Party (NDP) and its supporters won 97 percent of the votes. Illegally organized public protests became a daily occurrence but lacked wide popular support and political leadership.

The angry crowds that filled the streets of Cairo in January 2011, the burning down of police stations, and the amazingly fast apparent collapse of the policing apparatus were part of an unprecedented mass movement against the Mubarak regime, its repressive strategies, and its deepening failure in social and economic policies. But they were also the culmination of simmering anger at the huge and widening gap between the haves and the have-nots.

After Mubarak stepped down on February 11, 2011, the military took over the country for eighteen months. An Islamist-dominated parliament was inaugurated in early 2012. Newly established secular parties won a few seats, while the Brotherhood and the Salafis ended up with nearly 70 percent of the seats. The first truly democratically elected parliament in Egypt in nearly sixty years was disbanded a few months later when a high court ruled the election law unconstitutional. The Muslim Brotherhood's Mohamed Morsi was narrowly elected president in a June 2012 runoff, and his ascension to the presidency saw the transfer of executive authority from the military. The twelve-month presidency of Morsi was a rollercoaster ride in which he tried to placate and work with security agencies and the army, but excluded the younger generation of the Brotherhood. He also antagonized the so-called revolutionary youth groups of the left, themselves a weak and disorganized political force. After the military deposed Morsi following massive public protests, an interim president assumed power for a year until, in May 2014, Minister of Defense Abdel Fattah el-Sisi won a landslide victory in elections that followed some of the worst and bloodiest political violence in Egypt's modern history.[8]

In the years since Morsi's ouster, the military and security agencies have dominated politics. The gains made in 2011–13 by civil society and the human rights movement (which I describe more in the next section) shrank rapidly. Sisi's regime promulgated, by decree, one repressive law after another, politicized the judiciary, established effective impunity for police forces, and led a massive media demonization campaign against any form of opposition. The latter primarily focused on the Brotherhood but later extended to repress the April 6 Youth Movement—a revolutionary body that formed in 2008—and then the human rights movement. This came at a time of violations of human rights that were unprecedented in scope and intensity, including alleged extrajudicial killings by security forces, systematic and horrific torture in places of detention, lengthy and illegal "preventive detention" of thousands of people, forced disappearance, and abuse in prisons.[9]

To fully appreciate the scope of what has been lost in these years of authoritarian regression, it is necessary to review the evolution of civil society in Egypt, especially that of the human rights movement, how the state interacted with it, and how the movement dealt with its challenging environment.

The Evolution of Egypt's Civil Society and State Control

The Egyptian military led by Nasser in the 1950s had succeeded in changing the state structure, ending feudalism, initiating ambitious state-run development plans (at least until 1965), and spreading educational and health services to large sectors of the population that had been deprived of it. But in the meantime, the regime shut down public participation (after a short failed experiment with the Muslim Brotherhood as allies in 1952–54). This is why it was easy for Sadat in the 1970s and Mubarak in the 1980s and 1990s to quickly wipe out the gains achieved under Nasser in terms of social and economic opportunities for the lower classes.

Gradually one of the most important state strategies for social control became figuring out how to besiege and domesticate—or even corrupt—CSOs, political parties, and trade and professional unions. The state feared that they could challenge the burgeoning networks of power and wealth. Fewer and fewer social forces were organized enough to defend the interests of the more disenfranchised sectors and to advocate for different social and economic policies.

The first serious legal framework to regulate civil society in modern Egypt was Law 384 of 1956, which was tightened in Law 32 of 1964. The law allowed the government to intervene in the granular details of CSOs' work, and confirmed the determination of Nasser's regime to subjugate civil society to full state control. The current Law 84 of 2002 is similar.[10] These laws gave the government (as represented by the ministry of social affairs) the right to supervise CSOs, and in certain cases request that a court dissolve them. They forced organizations to maintain all records and photos of their members on file in their offices, gave the concerned cabinet minister the right to dissolve and reappoint members of CSOs' boards, and barred CSOs from working on "religious" and "political" issues without clearly defining either field.

Most CSOs were focused on social services until the early 1980s, when human rights organizations started to appear. By 2016, Egypt had more than forty-six thousand registered CSOs under Law 84, most of them very small in geographic or functional scope and many dormant. A majority of these organizations were service providers or charities (largely in the fields of healthcare and education, or care targeted to certain population sectors such as the elderly, the youth, and children). A very small number of these organizations focused on advocacy and human rights; less than fifty according to my own tally. And still the majority of the independent and influential amongst them—a number that I would put at around ten based on regular participation in the Egyptian Forum of Independent Human Rights Organizations that the Cairo Institute for Human Rights Studies hosted—declined to register under the restrictive law, preferring to work as law firms or nonprofit (or even for-profit) companies.

Almost a third of the forty-six thousand registered CSOs appeared after 2011 due to increasing governmental tolerance in the tumultuous quasi-democratic detour of 2011–13:

Year	Number of CSOs
1925	300
1950	2,000
1970	7,000
1980	8,402
1990	12,832
2000	16,000
2011	31,000
2014	46,200
2016	46,845[11]

Egyptian human rights organizations multiplied in the first decade of the twenty-first century and started to pay more attention to social and economic rights instead of their earlier, almost exclusive focus on civil and political rights. They started to link impoverishment and inequality as well as repression of minorities to repressive social policies and neoliberal economic policies. However, the many critical reports[12] and analyses produced by these organizations in that decade were never translated into a political force for change, nor did they markedly affect state policies because the political space in Egypt (and also in Tunisia and other Arab republics) stayed torn between statist forces and Islamists or sectarian factions.

There are various actors in the human rights movement (professional non-governmental organizations, research and advocacy organizations, loose networks, and individuals) that did not play a leading role in the 2011 uprising. Nevertheless, they had spent years providing a space for training and jobs for activists. The movement helped frame activists' demands, influenced their discourse, and represented their causes domestically and internationally. Activists who led confrontations with security forces on the ground and entered politics in the following months belonged, in many instances, to networks that overlapped and intersected with the human rights movement. But most of them acquired their political skills and networks from direct action on the ground through sit-ins, strikes, and workers' struggles.[13]

After the uprising, and especially in 2011–13, several nongovernmental human rights organizations engaged in serious negotiations and advocacy together with social movements and other components of the civil society on security sector reform, transitional justice, health insurance legislation, and housing policies, to name a few examples. Other organizations continued to document violations, support labor struggles, critique economic policies, work on budget transparency, and oppose legislation on settling corruption cases with Mubarak-era businessmen.[14] This participation reached a zenith in late 2013 and early 2014. But by then the military-dominated government had gradually begun to close down the public space, until street actions and public dissent almost ceased (or became limited to social media platforms). Rights-based approaches to policy and politics have become increasingly silenced by war-cries of counterterrorism and a hypernationalist discourse, especially by a media that has become, since 2013, largely controlled by the regime. The ease by which the military-dominated government cornered the human rights movement also revealed the structural weakness of all such organizations under authoritarian regimes. In the absence of genuine membership organizations and the lack of other social forces that are autonomous from the state and willing to support human rights organizations and integrate rights-based approaches, human rights defenders become easy to silence. Their only means of resistance are their courage, their perseverance, and the unshakeable commitment of many longtime defenders.

Negotiating Legal Regulation

In early 2012, almost halfway through the thirty months of hope and open channels between the human rights movement and state institutions in 2011–13, several organizations presented a draft bill on associations to the parliament. But the Islamist-dominated legislative assembly itself was dissolved in 2012 by a constitutional court whose members were appointed by the old regime. That the honeymoon lasted even this long was due to the facts that most members of parliament were outside the control of security agencies, and that even some actors within these agencies saw CSOs as a possible ally in the agencies' smoldering conflict with the Muslim Brotherhood.

During the deliberations on the association law, parliament welcomed civil society to debate with them for the first time in decades. Representatives from civil society exchanged arguments with Fayza Abou el-Naga, minister of international cooperation and a staunch opponent of CSOs. Human rights activists including renowned figures such as Bahey Eldin Hassan and Hossam Bahgat presented a bill supported by thirty-nine organizations and tabled by two members of parliament, Ziad El Aleemi and Amr Hamzawy.[15] The Supreme Council of the Armed Forces (SCAF), which exercised executive power, countered with a different bill in April 2012.[16] Human rights activists alleged that former Mubarak officials prepared the government draft, led by former prime minister Kamal Ganzouri, who continued to be close to the military, Abou el-Naga (who became Sisi's national security adviser after he became president in 2014), and former minister of social solidarity Ali Mosailhi (who became a member of parliament in 2016). Several nongovernmental organizations (NGOs) said the government bill was identical to a draft that Mosailhi presented to parliament in 2010.[17]

The government bill was yet another attempt by Egypt's patriarchal elite to control civil society rather than regulate the field and bring about more transparency. It viewed NGO board members and staff as public servants and their funds as public funds—a view that violated established Egyptian jurisprudence. It gave the government the right to intervene in the formation of an NGO's general assembly, how it called for a meeting, when it met, how members could join and leave, and how the board was elected and functions assigned. It went so far as allowing the government to freeze an NGO and seek a judicial order of dissolution if it deemed the NGO in violation of the law, or considered it no longer capable of performing its duties. The bill banned the receipt of foreign funds without prior government approval and retained the same prison penalties from Law 84 of 2002, while hiking the fines. It also brought unspecified state institutions (largely understood to refer to security agencies) into a coordination committee to decide on foreign funding.

The government bill was totally hostile to the basic concepts of how any regulated civil society could freely function while complying with reasonable requirements for transparency and accountability. The bill ensured full control by the Ministry of Social Solidarity (MoSS) and security agencies of the functioning of civil society associations and treated CSOs as if they were extensions of the state bureaucracy, accountable to the state, which could outline the vision and strategy of the CSOs at will.[18] This restrictive bill never materialized into a law, probably as a result of the critical campaign led by human rights organizations, which came four months after security forces stormed five national and foreign CSOs on December 29, 2011, arresting forty-three staff members, and later indicting them. A media smear campaign ensued, accusing human rights defenders in particular and advocacy NGOs in general of being foreign agents and conspiring to undermine the stability of the state. Reportedly following pressure from the United States, the Egyptian military allowed the foreign suspects (mostly Americans) to leave the country on bail. In June 2013, all forty-three suspects were sentenced to spend one to five years in prison (eleven of the sentences were suspended).[19]

The legal tussle between the regime and the independent human rights organizations[20] did not change much during Morsi's year in power. The Muslim Brotherhood was more welcoming of dialogue and open to compromise than the old regime, but their ethos was authoritarian and they probably did not want to risk some hard-gained political capital they thought they had accumulated with security agencies, for the sake of those predominantly secular organizations. The

Freedom and Justice party, the Brotherhood's political arm, drafted a new NGO bill that was not radically different from the one the Mubarak acolytes had put together. Like previous attempts at drafting and legislating a new bill, this one also never turned into a law due to differences between the anti-Brotherhood state bureaucracy, which pushed for a different version, and the NGOs, which criticized both iterations.[21]

For almost a year after the Muslim Brotherhood was removed from power in July 2013, the whole issue of reforming legal regulations governing CSOs apparently became a secondary concern for the state. The state's repressive machinery was almost totally focused on the Brotherhood and its supporters following the Rabaa Massacre of August 2013, when the army killed upwards of eight hundred pro-Morsi demonstrators (the precise number of deaths is disputed). The so-called democratic faction in the military-dominated government of interim president Adly Mansour attempted to introduce a new CSO bill in late 2013 but it was quickly derailed. The faction, made up of liberals, leftists, and Nasserists, was fast removed from power, and the regime went ahead to regain a new form of unchecked authoritarianism. Just several months later the new minister for social solidarity, Ghada Wali, warned all "entities" engaged in NGO-like work to register under Law 84 within forty-five days or face legal sanctions. In one of his last-ditch attempts to mend bridges with the regime before he himself had to go into exile, Bahey Eldin Hassan, the most experienced and one of the longest-serving human rights defenders in Egypt, met with Prime Minister Ibrahim Mahlab. Hassan did so on behalf of organizations that rejected the ministerial decision and a new draft bill prepared by Wali's advisers that was similar to the existing law, but went even further,[22] denying many of the NGOs from registering as law firms or companies—a tactic they had deployed against the restrictive association law for many years. Wali's threats did not lead to much. At least one prominent NGO did try to register under the law, but its repeated requests were not accepted by the government.

In September 2016, the council of ministers approved a new bill to be tabled at the parliament. Its overall philosophy was summarized in October 2016 by the United Nations Special Rapporteur on freedom of peaceful assembly and of association, Maina Kiai: The draft law "limits NGO work to 'development and social objectives,' and imposes a high level of minimum capital required to set up an NGO. Other new elements introduced by the draft law include the establishment of a specific tax for foreign funding, the banning of activists who have received a prison sentence for forming their own NGOs, and requiring the NGOs to conduct work that meets social needs."[23]

Wali had long made her position on the law clear. "We support active organizations that work for the public interest voluntarily to serve and develop the community," she said in a newspaper interview. The newspaper, *Al-Shorouk*, reported the minister's insistence that just forty-four human rights NGOs had been asked to register, arguing that they should do so because they received foreign funding, were unaccountable, and did not pay taxes.[24]

Foreign Funding

During the period from 2014 to 2016, the regime entered a war of attrition with human rights defenders and NGOs since it felt more empowered as it mended relations with Western backers such as Germany, France and the United States. In this war, foreign funding for human rights organizations was a central weapon in the hands of the regime. Pro-state media platforms used it to vilify human rights organizations as foreign agents, while the judiciary pursued organizations for allegations of breaking the law and using foreign funding to undermine state institutions and harm national security.

The case that led to the indictments of forty-three people in 2013 was reopened and before the end of 2016 about fifteen human rights defenders were banned from leaving the country, while three independent human rights defenders and five organizations had their assets frozen.[25] NGOs that were suspected of being affiliated with or sympathetic to the Muslim Brotherhood—mostly working on development and social services—had already suffered a harsh crackdown in 2014, when the government froze the assets of more than one thousand societies and branches. Some of these associations had been providing health and educational services for millions of peoples for years. They included two that were in fact founded before the Muslim Brotherhood, al-Jam'iya al-Shar'iya (the Sharia Society) established in 1912, and the Jama'iat Ansar al-Sunnah al-Mohammediyah (The Association of Supporters of the Practice of Prophet Mohammad) established in 1926. These organizations played a vital role as the state had withdrawn for many years from social services in health, education, support for the poor and the unemployed, childcare, and services for the elderly.[26]

One could argue that states should maintain a regime of oversight over transaction of funds and relations between local actors and foreign powers, this being a foundational part of international law and the rights of sovereign states to ensure that only domestic forces directly shape the political developments in the country. But this argument has been extensively abused by authoritarian states that make it difficult to raise local funds and almost impossible to raise foreign funds.[27] Several human rights organizations registered as companies to avoid the associations law and its various restrictions, especially on foreign funding, but this in turn raised issues about transparency and accountability.

The source of funding is critical for the credibility of human rights organizations "in the eyes of those whom they are supposed to be supporting, especially where most of the funding was foreign, hence a source of political (and possibly legal) liability," as political economist Amr Adly has written.[28] Foreign funding carries a risk of clientelism that could undermine what should be the genuinely domestic nature of a CSO, its priorities, and its accountability. As Adly warned: "Dependency on foreign funding would make these NGOs develop structures, agendas and programs that fit the interests of their patrons, be they foreign governments or private foundations, rather than addressing real problems in their proper contexts."

However, as far as the independent human rights organizations that were studied for this chapter, these concerns did not largely seem to apply. As a matter of fact, in addition to my personal experience and affiliation with this movement for several years, Adly has shown that the exact opposite could be said of several organizations. The foreign-funded Egyptian NGOs, some of which draw some funding from mainstream northern foundations, adopted a strong anti-neoliberal stance in clear opposition to the policies of successive Egyptian governments and international financial institutions such as the International Monetary Fund and the World Bank.[29]

The Human Rights Movement: A "Head without a Body"?

Even though the human rights movement has succeeded in defending the rights of thousands of people through legal aid, won some social and economic benefits through strategic or constitutional litigation, and built some ties with various social movements, it has remained like a "head without a body"[30] because it could not establish an organic relationship with a large social base.

However, the root of this failure to build a social and political base for the human rights movement should not be blamed on the constituent parts of this movement alone. The root cause has been the persistent policies and positions of successive Egyptian regimes, which have impoverished and almost eviscerated social and political participation.

Moreover, the human rights movement, though it emerged in the mid-1980s, did not really mature until the late 1990s and the first decade of the twenty-first century. The movement also suffered from some of the side effects of professionalization, and the transformation from groups of activists into NGOs with all the attendant political and institutional implications, including the evolution of barriers between its leading and well-established organizations and the weak but extant broader civil society and social movements. There was, as Adly has written, a lack of "common identity among the components of the two movements and hence the potential or actual divergence in interests, goals, outlooks, and rhetoric in a way that undermines or at least limits their interaction as components of a single movement aiming at social and economic change."[31] This lack of a common identity and the divergence in goals also blocked the evolution of an organic relationship between the human rights movement and the rest of civil society.

The tightly controlled space allocated to civil society under Mubarak has almost disappeared under the regime that took control in late 2013, with the thirty months after the 2011 revolution now looking—at least to many within the security agencies—more like a detour.

Human Rights Movement in Practice: Advocating for a New Health Insurance System

The grim history of human rights in Egypt is not without a few successes on the part of activists. Over the years, human rights activists have succeeded in affecting the public discourse with their regular reports, advocacy, and campaigns on violations of civil and political rights. They have also succeeded in popularizing certain concepts and terminology, especially for social and economic rights, such as empowerment, transparency, social safety networks, and participatory policymaking. Still though, these activists were unable to markedly affect actual economic and social policies. Neither could they decrease the persistently egregious civil and rights violations such as torture, religious persecution, and the impunity of security forces.

The Egyptian uprising did not, after all, succeed in changing the dominant economic and social institutions nor genuinely undermine the unaccountable control of security agencies over civil and political life. On the contrary, and especially after the military takeover in 2013, revolutionary leaders—especially among the young members of CSOs, activist workers, senior members of protest movements (such as April 6)—ended up in jail or faced constant legal harassment. Ultimately, the short-lived transition of 2011–13 brought no real reform of security agencies, the judiciary, the state-owned media, most of the established business networks and monopolies, religious institutions, state-sponsored cultural organizations, or—above all—the military establishment.

The human rights movement's attempt at fixing the crumbling national health care system is one example of a moderately successful effort to intervene in the arena of socioeconomic policy. The movement has long intervened in defense of social and economic rights using various mobilizations, litigation, and advocacy mechanisms. These efforts include a case that raised the minimum wages, and reports and analyses that supported the labor movement, and detailed policy recommendations for fixing some of the state social services. But the outcomes of all these efforts were ambiguous because recommendations were rarely translated into policies and laws. The campaign for health care is a relative exception, where rights advocates made something of an impact. As such, the campaign illustrates how important the human rights movement can be to achieving basic advancements in well-being for all Egyptians—even in cases that may not involve the most headline-grabbing topics that one might associate with human rights.

The government's share of total spending on health care in Egypt was about 38 percent in 2014, compared to nearly 57 percent in Tunisia, 77 percent in Turkey and nearly 61 percent on average for the Middle East and North Africa region.[32] This means Egyptians' out-of-pocket health expenditures exceeded 61 percent of the total national bill, a huge burden that is largely attributed to the low health insurance coverage of only 45 percent of the population. Even those Egyptians who have insurance may pay for health care, considering the low quality and shortage of government health services. The government claimed that health insurance coverage rose to 58 percent in 2012 because the coverage was expanded to cover almost fifteen million preschool children, six million female heads of households, and an unknown number of farmers.[33] But it is very doubtful that the stressed state health care system can indeed expand to cover these twenty-one million or more individuals while it is facing difficulties in covering its current caseload. Egyptian health care experts fear that this expansion (effected in large part through presidential decrees) is part of the regime's political propaganda more than a meaningful policy transformation that would make real human and financial resources available to the supposed beneficiaries. Just forty hospitals are supposed to provide health care to nearly sixty million people. And even then, the facilities are not well distributed geographically in the country.[34]

Egypt's state health insurance budget for the fiscal year 2013–14 was about 5.6 billion Egyptian pounds increasing to 7.8 billion pounds in the 2015–16 budget. Setting aside the dramatically fluctuating exchange rates (the pound has declined by more than 100 percent against the dollar in these two years) it is doubtful that this increase is based on solid calculations since the rate of actual paid subscriptions is very low (about 14 percent among the newly born and 56 percent for school children) despite the low annual premium of eight Egyptian pounds. Even if the state makes the new budget available it will not be sufficient to finance the planned expansions in health care coverage and improve the quality of the existing service. The chairman of the Health Insurance Authority (HIA) complained in late 2015 that subscriptions do not exceed 3.7 billion pounds and the balance of the budget is covered through revenues accrued from medical services offered at higher rates by the authority's hospitals and medical facilities (about 2.8 billion pounds) and another five hundred million pounds from tobacco tax.[35]

Several CSOs, led by the Egyptian Initiative for Personal Rights (EIPR), which I personally ran in 2014, have been advocating with the state and even working hand in hand with the government for years to reform this collapsing health care system. EIPR helped draft a comprehensive health insurance bill, under which the chronic shortage of funds and debilitated infrastructure could be addressed by separating the funding mechanisms from the service provision. Private health care providers could help service the insured by the state under contracts with the HIA. A new subscription and funding system is to be established with contributions from individuals, employers, and pensioners, in addition to special taxes on tobacco, alcohol, cement, steel, and car and other factories (usually polluting industries or products that saddle the state and society with additional health costs). A separate agency would supervise the contracting and service quality of all providers (public and private).

EIPR was an active member in a high-level ministerial committee that has been working on this reform for years. The regime does not mind using the free expertise of CSO experts (and bragging about it sometimes), but it would not allow the same CSOs to hold the government to account or to help revive and support patients' rights associations. The regime knows that fixing the financing and structural problems of the health care system would not work without effective governance and accountability. Such governance requires civil society oversight through free media and ensuring the rights of patients to organize as consumers or for CSOs to raise their concerns, together with decentralizing the system and enabling local councils and municipalities to have a say. Social media campaigns indicate public interest in mobilizing around these issues and standing up to a pervasive decline in services.[36] The portal for social evaluations of Egyptian hospitals—a CSO initiative to channel pressure from consumers of public and private health care services—is a good step, but does not go far enough.[37]

The issue here is that a functioning strategic social service like health care in a country like Egypt (and similar countries in the region) where democratic channels are lacking or manipulated (Lebanon is a good example of an ostensible democracy that does not pay much attention to social services) requires accountability by a vibrant civil society where CSOs can mobilize patients for their rights. Without such an active role, the planned health insurance premiums will turn into compulsory fees similar to those paid by members of state-dominated trade unions, or garbage collection fees paid to the state as part of electricity bills—neither trade union protection nor effective street garbage removal is received in return.

Conclusion

Since the mid-1950s, Egypt's successive authoritarian ruling regimes worked hard to either co-opt or vilify civil society as part of a general anti-politics strategy. The current regime wants to limit civil society to philanthropic activities and provision of services and to have state agencies closely watch CSOs.

The 2011 uprising in Egypt, unlike Tunisia, did not end a regime but simply helped reorder the ruling block. In less than three years, the army and security services came into full control of the government, much more so than they ever were during the Mubarak era. But even if Egypt has moved from controlled authoritarianism with small margins of freedom of action under Mubarak to a very repressive version of authoritarianism under Sisi, the national, regional, and global economic and political conditions could prove very challenging for such a regime and would continue to provide an opportunity for civil society actors.

There is little doubt that the regime crackdown on human rights organizations, which reached unprecedented levels by the end of 2016, will continue and even escalate to silence some of the few remaining critical voices in the public domain. In a region where several states and countries are melting down into civil war with regional and international interventions, and with a global shift toward right-wing populism and protectionism, it is unlikely that the regime will face any meaningful external pressure to improve its deteriorating human rights record or stop harassing the beleaguered human rights movement.

In any case, the regime will more likely than not have to become increasingly more repressive to face opposition to its policies, such as its speedy removal of subsidies and implementation of neoliberal policies. But even with higher levels of policing and a pliable judiciary, it will still have to buy the allegiance of certain social sectors and state institutions—a measure that is becoming increasingly difficult in light of the deteriorating economic conditions (problems include lower state revenues, lower foreign investments, and lower remittances).

The current populist and neoliberal policies of the Egyptian regime, along with its shrinking of the space for civil society, assume that economic and social problems can be handled in an apolitical environment where technocrats work undisturbed under the iron hand of the leader. Such an approach ignores the indispensable role of free civil society and open politics, which are necessary to allow citizens with less access to official power to associate freely, organize openly, strike, and protest for more equitable policies.

The promotion of human rights is not a marginal issue—it is a fundamental element of progress in all its dimensions. Though we can only guess at the thought processes of the leaders of the current regime, their actions suggest that, at a basic level, they fail to see this truth. The Egyptian people will be the first but not the only ones to pay the cost for this blindness. It will be extremely difficult, if not impossible, for the regime to make any breakthrough out of its economic and political malaise without an active and effective civil society that pumps fresh blood into the political system, and challenges the regime regularly.

Notes

1. See "Egypt NGO Bill Threatens to 'Devastate' Civil Society, UN Expert Warns," UN Office of the High Commissioner for Human Rights, November 23, 2016, http://www.ohchr. org/en/NewsEvents/Pages/DisplayNews.aspx?NewsID=20920&LangID=E.

2. The exception is Egypt's Muslim Brotherhood, whose relationship with the human rights discourse is rather problematic, to say the least.

3. The term "civil society" has a somewhat controversial origin and is sometimes bandied about without a clear sense of its specific meaning. In this paper, I use it to refer to organizations, associations, networks, and even, in certain cases, individuals that serve various social or indirectly political functions through the provision of services or advocacy, with the objective of changing socioeconomic conditions, policies, norms, and/or behavior. Such a definition would then apply to educational and health charities, human rights organizations, and trade unions.

4. Eberhard Kienle, "Egypt without Mubarak, Tunisia after Ben Ali: Theory, History and the Arab Spring," *Economy and Society* 41, no. 4 (2012): 541–42.

5. "GDP Growth (annual %), Egypt," World Bank, 2016, http://data.worldbank.org/ indicator/NY.GDP.MKTP.KD.ZG?end=2010&locations=EG&start=2005.

6. Rabab El-Mahdi and Bahgat Korany, *Arab Spring in Egypt,* (Cairo: AUC Press, 2012), 2.

7. Samer Soliman, *The Strong Regime and the Weak State* (Arabic; Cairo: The General Authority for Cultural Palaces, 2013).

8. The only credible and detailed local report was issued by the Egyptian Initiative for Personal Rights: "The Weeks of Killing: State Violence, Communal Fighting and Sectarian Attacks in the Summer of 2013," Egyptian Initiative for Personal Rights, June 18, 2014, http://www. eipr.org/en/report/2014/06/18/2124. Also see "All According to Plan: The Rab'a Massacre and Mass Killing of Protesters in Egypt," Human Rights Watch, August 2014, https://www.hrw. org/report/2014/08/12/all-according-plan/raba-massacre-and-mass-killings-protesters-egypt.

9. There is a wealth of reports by human rights organizations on the deteriorating situation in Egypt in this period. I relied on my own work, which draws on many of these reports and

interviews I conducted, to write about how rule-of-law institutions were crumbling in Egypt. For example, see "Behind the Sun: Is This the End of Rule of Law in Egypt?," *Mada Masr*, February 14, 2016, http://www.madamasr.com/en/2016/02/14/opinion/u/behind-the-sun-is-this-the-end-of-the-rule-of-law-in-egypt/.

10. For a detailed review of legal regulations see Khaled Mansour, "History Shows that Egypt Would Likely Fail to Abolish the Human Rights Movement," *Mada Masr,* September 14, 2016, http://www.madamasr.com/en/2016/09/14/opinion/u/history-shows-egypt-will-likely-fail-to-abolish-the-human-rights-movement/.

11. The source for figures until 2014 is Amany Kandil, "Changes in Structure and Function: Civil Society after the Revolution in Egypt" (Arabic), The Arab Center for Research and Studies, http://www.acrseg.org/32498. The number in early 2016 is based on an interview with Minister of Social Solidarity Ghada Wali on Egyptian television channel CBC, available on YouTube at https://www.youtube.com/watch?v=xhL36QqI-b0.

12. Reports on religious freedom, violations against sexual minorities, right to health, labor rights, freedom of expression, housing rights, etc., have been regularly issued from organizations such as the Egyptian Initiative for Personal Rights, Al Nadeem Center for the Rehabilitation of Victims of Violence, the Arab Network for Human Rights Information, and the Cairo Institute for Human Rights Studies. EIPR led a campaign from 2004 to 2009 for Baha'i rights that led to legal gains, and the issuance of birth certificates and identification cards. The same organization was able through litigation to stop the government in 2008 from privatizing the state health insurance system.

13. Kienle, "Egypt without Mubarak," 549.

14. See regular reports by Al Nadeem Center (http://www.alnadeem.org/en, in Arabic) on cases of torture and Cairo Institute for Human Rights Studies' annual reports (http://www.cihrs.org/?cat=28&lang=en) for an example of efforts of documentation. See Egypt Center for Economic and Social Rights' legal efforts to support labour rights including strategic litigation that led to the State High Administrative Court forcing the government to establish minimum wages (see samples of these legal efforts at http://ecesr.org/en/category/legalwork/page/4/).

15. "MPs Reject a Government Bill and Table a New Associations Law" (Arabic), joint statement by Egyptian human rights organizations, February 8, 2012, http://www.cihrs.org/?p=1178.

16. "Mubarak Regime Ministers Lead the MCC into More Confrontations with the People and Democratic Forces" (Arabic), joint statement by Egyptian human rights organizations, January 18, 2012, http://eipr.org/pressrelease/2012/01/18/1346.

17. "A New Bill to Nationalize Civil Society and Integrate It into the State Bureaucracy" (Arabic), joint statement by Egyptian human rights organizations, April 12, 2012, http://www.eipr.org/pressrelease/2012/04/12/1403.

18. Ibid.

19. "Egyptian Court Convicts Forty-Three NGO Employees," *BBC News*, June 4, 2013, http://www.bbc.com/news/world-africa-22765161.

20. Most of the independent human rights organizations are members of the Independent Egyptian Human Rights Organizations Forum, which brings together about sixteen organizations.

21. "The MB Lay the Cornerstone for a New Police State, Develop Mubarak Mechanisms to Repress Civil Society" (Arabic), joint statement by Egyptian human rights organizations, May 31, 2013, http://eipr.org/pressrelease/2013/05/31/1721.

22. "In a Meeting between the Prime Minister and Bahey Eldine Hassan: 23 Rights Organizations Demand that the Government Stop Fighting Civil Society and Review Its Policy towards NGOs," joint statement by Egyptian human rights organizations, July 24, 2014, http://eipr.org/pressrelease/2014/07/24/2181.

23. Maina Kiai, "UN Rights Expert Warns about Growing Restrictions on Civil Society in Egypt," UN Office of the High Commissioner for Human Rights, October 11, 2016, http://www.un.org/apps/news/story.asp?NewsID=55269#.WCHIP-F9634.

24. "Ghada Wali: I have Not Dissolved any NGO since I Assumed Office . . . The State Will Not Allow Foreign Funding without Oversight" (Arabic), *Al-Shorouk*, February 2, 2106, http://www.shorouknews.com/news/view.aspx?cdate=02022016&id=d9281f56-a4ec-4c62-8178-f124f1de4959.

25. "Egypt: Lift Abusive and Arbitrary Travel Bans," Amnesty International, November 2, 2016, https://www.amnesty.org/en/latest/news/2016/11/egypt-lift-abusive-arbitrary-travel-bans/. For asset freezing, see "Egypt: Asset Freeze Is a Shameless Ploy to Silence Human Rights Activism," Amnesty International, https://www.amnesty.org/en/latest/news/2016/09/egypt-asset-freeze-is-a-shameless-ploy-to-silence-human-rights-activism/.

26. "The Freezing of the Funds of 1055 CSOs: a Resolution Exposing the Arbitrariness of the Authorities in Dealing with Civil Society and Creates Social Problems" (Arabic,) January 20, 2014, Egyptian Initiative for Personal Rights, http://eipr.org/pressrelease/2014/01/20/1935.

27. For a reasoned argument on the rights of states to control foreign funding see Annika Poppe and Jonas Wolff, "Foreign Funding Restrictions: Far More than Just an 'Illegitimate Excuse'," *Open Democracy*, April 20, 2016, https://www.opendemocracy.net/openglobalrights/annika-e-poppe-jonas-wolff/foreign-funding-restrictions-far-more-than-just-illegiti. For an opposing view, see Hussein Baoumi, "Local Funding Is Not Always the Answer," *Open Democracy*, June 27, 2016, https://www.opendemocracy.net/openglobalrights/hussein-baoumi/local-funding-is-not-always-answer.

28. Amr Adly, "The Human Rights Movement and Contentious Politics in Egypt (2004–2014)," Arab Reform Initiative, forthcoming.

29. Adly, "The Human Rights Movement."

30. I owe this expression to political economist Amr Adly who employed it in an as yet unpublished paper. See previous note.

31. Adly, "The Human Rights Movement."

32. "Health expenditure, public (% of total health expenditure)," World Bank, 2016, http://data.worldbank.org/indicator/SH.XPD.PUBL.

33. Figures derived from an interview by the HIA chairman in *Al-Ahram*, November 28, 2015, http://www.ahram.org.eg/NewsQ/456530.aspx.

34. Ibid.

35. Ibid.

36. "'Not to Surprise Him if He Showed Up': A Campaign to Expose Negligence in Egyptian Hospitals" (Arabic), *BBC News*, June 19, 2015, http://www.bbc.com/arabic/blogs/2015/06/150610_egypt_hospitals_grim_conditions.

37. "Community Evaluation of Egyptian Hospitals" portal, run by a private company called Shamseya for Innovative Community Healthcare Solutions, can be found at http://eghospitals.com.

9

The Ultras Ahlawy

Football, Violence, and the Quest for Justice

KARIM MEDHAT ENNARAH

The "Ultra" fans of Egyptian football emerged from the world of football stands in 2011 to play an important role in street politics during the years of the revolution. Their impressive coordinated visual displays, organizing capacity, and reputed street-fighting skills inspired so many that any young person dressed in their style was identified as an Ultra. Then, in Port Said in February 2012, tragedy struck: seventy-two football fans were killed in fan violence and an ensuing stampede. The flawed quest for justice that followed resulted in a mass death sentence and more unrest. With a story that parallels the rising hopes and dashed dreams of the Egyptian revolution, this chapter traces the history of the Ultras from their creation until the present and their quest for justice in Port Said. It also considers how to achieve justice and healing after communal violence.

"For to lose a game of football is hardly a tragedy. Worse things happen in life, a lot worse." —Chris Oakley

In the 1980s, the football stands in Egypt—typically packed beyond their official capacity—were much less hostile than those in European stadiums. A style of over-the-top football fandom that had originated in Italy was starting to spread in Southern and Western Europe, and would eventually captivate Egypt, as well.[1] These so-called "Ultra" groups that had emerged in Torino and Sampdoria and other Italian cities in the 1960s and 1970s could not have imagined the influence they would have on the political life of Egypt more than three decades later. Nor could they have possibly imagined the tragedy that would occur in the stadium of Port Said in 2012, when rioting fans and inadequate policing left seventy-two football fans dead and hundreds injured.

Before the tragedy, there was revolution. What became known as the Port Said Massacre occurred on February 1, 2012, a little less than a year after President Hosni Mubarak resigned in the face of mass protests. The Port Said game was scheduled during a week of marches and demonstrations marking the first anniversary of the revolution. It was not a festive time, though the ruling Supreme Council of the Armed Forces (SCAF) and the freshly elected, Islamist-dominated parliament struggled to emphasize the celebration. They talked about a "completed" revolution that no longer required street mobilization but, rather, strong and stable institutions. But protesters, angry at undelivered promises and the precariousness of the political transition, shut down the streets of Cairo, Alexandria, and other big cities between January 25 and January 28, 2012.

Among the Canal cities, Port Said always stood out for never having been swept up in revolutionary mobilization, unlike its sisters to the south, Ismailia and Suez—the latter being one of the first cities, one year before, where riots broke out on January 25, 2011, the first day of the revolution. (This dynamic would soon change in Port Said.)

Many Egyptian Ultras, including the Ahly SC Ultras who were to visit Port Said on that day in February 2012, had been part of the revolution, and became known in street protests for their infectious chants and colorful coordinated displays. It might seem like a stretch to call them a social movement: the Ultras would always speak of their diverse political opinions and emphasize that taking part in the revolution was an individual decision. A social movement, however, does not have to be centered or created around a political objective.[2] Their relationship with the revolution was reciprocal—for the dominant discourse against police violence and brutality provided further validity to the Ultras' claims, which they had maintained since their inception many years before the revolution, that the police were the instigators of violence in the notorious clashes with football fans. The revolution thus gave the Ultras legitimacy.[3]

The Port Said match occurred at a time when tensions within the revolutionary movements were palpable. Revolutionary narratives and ideals were starting to diverge. The spreading sense of entropy had soured swaths of the populace on continued mass action. This was especially true for most of the political youth movements, which continued to engage in street politics, and for the youths organized in forms of association like the Ultras groups, or those who were not organized at all. Viewed in Egypt's specific context, where the mere act of gathering in public constituted a political act, the Ultras' energy has always been political. It is amorphous and possesses no more inherent objective than a river trundling downwards—it is even capable of turning back on itself—but it is political nonetheless. The 2011 revolution marked their birth as an overtly political subject.[4]

The confrontation between the Ultras and the state was one of many subtexts of the revolution.

From Organized Fandom to Street Politics

When did these groups made up predominantly of teenagers develop any sense of shared identity, football-centered or otherwise? And how did something so organized and capable of mobilizing youths in the hundreds come to life in the

Egypt of the 1990s and the first decade of the new millennium, when almost all forms of mass mobilization were easily reined in?

Before the revolution, during the years of Mubarak's rule, it was a commonly held opinion that football was the opiate of the masses in Egypt, an anti-mobilizer. (This is a popular view of football outside of Egypt, as well.) But if that were true—if this passion, this nearly religious devotion toward a football team, was harmless to the state, or a useful cathartic—then the government should have welcomed the phenomenon. Instead, it did quite the opposite. The state understood that the organizational capacities of any group—football fanatics or cookery fanatics, political or not—could not be allowed to grow to the extent that hundreds or more could be mobilized within a day.

The Ultras Ahlawy, or UA07, was the first of the Egyptian groups, founded in the eponymous year of 2007, and it seems that most of the other Egyptian groups were officially founded around the same time. This includes splinter Al Ahly fan group Ultras Red Devils; the Ultras White Knights (UwK) of Zamalek SC; the Blue Dragons of Ismaily SC; and the Green Eagles of Port Said, among many others.

The Ultras arose from fan groups that date back a few years earlier. In his study of the radicalization of football fandom in Egypt, Shawki El-Zatmah writes about the transformation of Egyptian football fans from the "Terso" culture to the Ultra culture. The name Terso came from Italian "terzo," or third, because for a long time they dominated the third-class ticketed stands.[5] Compared to the Hooligans and Ultras of Europe in the 1980s and 1990s, the Egyptian Tersos were definitely more spontaneous in their displays of support—and much less prone to physical violence. Terso fans predominantly belonged to the lower classes, but their presence in the third-class stands gradually gave way to domination by lower-middle class Ultras, who were a mostly younger (teenage) and more homogenous fan group.[6]

In a sense, what the Ultras became famous for—their "tifos" (an Italian word for choreographed fan displays), their street fights, and the taunting of the police—was in essence an extravagant display of youth. For them, football is no trivial matter. It is "the only viable religion of the third millennium," as Manuel Vazquez Montalban, Barcelona fan, sports journalist, and political prisoner under Franco once said about football.[7] "The cause that binds together being no more than the success of a particular side, standing in the place of seemingly loftier concerns of a political or spiritual nature . . . [is] shallow but interestingly shallow, importantly shallow even."[8] Football also forges a shared, cross-boundary community in which group solidarity is experienced.[9]

And in Italy and Spain, where the Ultra movement was born, there was already an implicit politics to the fans' activities, if one looked for it. They seemingly pitted themselves against the neoliberalization of the political order. They spoke of being "anti-media," "anti-police," and "against modern football,"[10] hinting that fan groups were partly replacing traditional forms of political association.[11] With globalization came a sudden hike in the monetary and psychic costs of being loyal to one's team: expensive tickets, star players who frequently changed teams, shareholders passing their debt onto clubs. In response, a culture of "love football, hate business" emerged across Europe.[12] But the phenomenon thrived on globalization even as it seemed to stand against it. Wherever new Ultra groups appeared, they did not just adopt a similar organizational model. Egyptian youths copied the aesthetics and even the Italian and English nomenclature and mottos.[13]

In Egypt, too, the sway of neoliberal economics and the erosion of social contracts had contributed to the emergence of politicized, liberal youth groups, as well as these new football identities.[14] All came to meet in the street movements that dominated the public sphere in Egypt from 2011 to 2013, and an interesting dialectic emerged between the different youth movements.[15] But until 2011, the Ultras had nothing to do with the politics of left and right, aside from occasional expressions of nationalist fervor or solidarity with Palestine. Most of these youth movements developed a discourse that was still, to a large extent, anti-political. While nationalist, it was almost hostile to any political ideology or political project.

Much of this energy went into gratuitous scuffles with rival Ultras. An example that stands out, and that is relevant for this story in particular, is when supporters of Al Ahly visited cities on the Suez Canal to support their side in away games with teams such as Al-Masry SC of Port Said, and Ismaily SC of Ismailia. Before such games, sports media reports constantly raised alarms about fan violence—though nothing in those days compared to what happened in 2011 and 2012. The roots of these rivalries went back decades before the emergence of the Ultras. The rivalries were stoked by the fact that the capital club had far more resources and visibility than the regional teams. The intensity of the rivalries may have been more easily felt in the home cities of regional teams than in the capital. In one famous example of how much more the bitterness was felt outside of the capital, in 1962 a star player moved from Ismaily to Al Ahly, and under immense pressure from the fan communities in the city of Ismailia (whose protests went as far as setting fire to the player's family house), shortly returned to the Canal city club—personally chauffeured by the president of Al Ahly as a sign of goodwill.[16]

Frequently, these watershed incidents were infused with the politics of the time. Popular Cairene perceptions of Port Said and Ismailia residents were strongly influenced by the displacement that occurred during the war of attrition with Israel in 1967–70,[17] which led to a mass exodus from the Canal to Cairo. Many people from the Canal cities lived transitory lives of impoverishment and unemployment in Cairo until 1975. A very popular myth that persists until today is that Al Ahly refused to host Ismaily trainings and home games after the forced displacement from Ismailia. While even some hardcore Ismaily fans acknowledge the legend is inaccurate, it is still able to fuel fan anger.[18]

The Ultras may have not been bothered with politics or with the State, but the police of Mubarak's Egypt eventually clashed with the fans. Before the revolution, there was hardly any notable violence, except for some scuffles between groups. But the police were wary of their organizational capacity, which even if apolitical was unmatched, at least until the advent of the April 6 Youth Movement of 2008 (which still could not match the numbers of the Ultras). Even if they thought of them as mere football hooligans who posed no threat to the regime, the police still had to keep the Ultras in check through measured violence. As one Ultra put it: "They tried to control the unions, they tried to control the student unions in the universities, and they tried to control the political life. Suddenly they found in front of them a bunch of young people organizing themselves in football. . . . They just weren't happy with the fact that you have twenty, twenty-five guys who have gathered five hundred people in two hours."[19] Security forces intimidated the Ultras and arrested their leaders from their homes in the early hours of the morning, just as they did with political opposition viewed as a threat to the state.[20]

Such confrontations at football matches became increasingly violent. This preemptive state violence may have backfired. Some observers claim that the clashes with the police were "boot camp" for the Ultras, providing them with useful practice for their subsequent role in larger demonstrations during the years of the revolution. Whatever the state's disposition may have been, the politicization of the Ultras was an inevitable byproduct of the revolution.[21]

The first serious clash between the police and the UA07 in the stands took place in Kafr El Sheikh Stadium in 2010.[22] Before Kafr El Sheikh , incidents were mostly confined to the Ultras lighting flares and the police harassing them. After Kafr El Sheikh, direct confrontations became more common. Police violence against Ultras, whether they were thought of as a genuine threat or not, may be best described as performative violence, intended to bolster a self-constructed image of an all-powerful agency that is firmly in control of public space. It hardly ever served any peacekeeping or crowd-control purpose.[23]

A culture of pride in resistance to police grew among the Ultras. "Fans took pride in being able to beat up the police," researcher Dalia Abdelhameed Ibraheem writes in her study on the Ultras. "Showing bravery in fights is central in the construction of Ultras' masculinity."[24] In my conversations with Hicham El Fekky, a founding member of UA07, he maintained that Ultras were not violent and that confrontations were usually provoked by the police, but conceded that "at certain junctures, the Ultras became a bit of a burden on the club when they fought back," referring to sanctions that the club received.[25] He cited the Kafr El Sheikh incident as a turning point.

Revolution

It is safe to say that most Egyptians encountered the Ultras for the first time during the revolution, in the mass demonstrations of January and February 2011. But they gained even more prominence in the year that followed. Following the ouster of Mubarak and his minister of the interior, Habib el-Adly—the Ultras' arch-nemesis—Ultra graffiti started proliferating, and became more revolutionary in its subject matter. It must have been in April 2011 when graffiti celebrating the fallen of the Ultras first appeared, to commemorate Hussein Taha, a member of the Ultra group UwK, who was killed in clashes with the police on January 28, 2011. The Ultras, who are well-embedded in their local communities, frequently organized marches to the homes of families of their fallen, where they paid tribute and waved flags commemorating the faces of their martyrs.[26] It was the Ultras who introduced in protest marches the concept of a silhouetted martyr's face that would become an important part of the revolutionary visual repertoire.[27]

With this new visibility, the Ultras suddenly became immensely popular. Enthusiasm surged for their newly energized displays in the football stadiums, now that they were unchallenged by the police. When the football league resumed after a brief lull during the first weeks of the revolt, the fans, abused by the police for so long, could finally vent, chanting against the infamous Central Security Forces (CSF). In the first such appearance, in a league game taking place on May 20, 2011, UA07 sang a song that became popular among revolutionaries, taunting the proverbial policemen who "bribed his way through education." This song and others made for some extremely catchy, bold, and occasionally profane protest chants. The Ultras introduced the protest movement to carnivalesque resistance performances and techniques, including using trumpets, whistling in unison, and brandishing huge flags.[28]

Still, many aspects of the Ultras' participation in the events of the revolution are shrouded in myth: their finances, their true numbers, and their organizational and fighting capabilities. Their numbers have always been difficult to estimate, and the Ultras clearly have an interest in maintaining some of this mystery—it can seem they are larger than they are. It helps that the number of active members, which can be in the hundreds or a few thousand in the case of the two biggest groups in Egypt (UA07 and UwK), if multiplied by the time and resources they invest in the organization of other fans, maximizes their potential beyond any other type of fandom. Thus, their impact on the revolution as part of a wider mobilization was very real, even if they did not numerically constitute a huge proportion of the protesters.

Financing of some of the Ultras' most impressive tifos, such as their pyrotechnic shows, has been a constant subject of debate. Self-financing is reported as their main mechanism for funding, but it has been contested by others who point to the impressive pyrotechnic shows they have mustered in some of the big games.

And then there is their fighting prowess. "The fighting techniques learned in hard-fought street battles" is a phrase that appeared again and again in writing and in conversations about the Ultras. Local and foreign press repeated the mantra that, because so few Egyptians had had any "fighting experience," the Ultras had to shoulder the responsibility of being on the frontlines of protests.

The Ultras' style in both dress and protesting spread like wildfire among the younger groups involved in revolutionary mobilization, so that it was not always clear who was actually an Ultra and who was simply emulating them. Indeed, the term "Ultra" began to be used for anyone who protested and dressed like football fans. After the biggest Ultras groups (UA07 and UwK) officially marched in a protest under the groups' banners on September 9, 2011 (the event is commonly referred to as the Friday of Correcting the Paths, one of many cumbersome nicknames revolutionary activists used to mobilize for big protests), anyone who was between the age of fifteen and twenty-five, donned a hoodie, and carried a huge flag was casually referred to as an Ultra and hailed at protests with the often repeated welcome cry, "The Ultras have finally arrived!" However, in my memory, the September 9 protest was the last time the different Ultras groups marched under their banners for a protest. Crowds of Ultra-lookalikes stormed the streets and participated in the Mansour Street protests outside the Ministry of Interior that lasted for four days in February 2012. As the protest surged in numbers, it was assumed that the ones leading the demonstrations were the Ultras, because of their daring, their youth, and the banners they carried. But it is doubtful that the pole that carried both the flags of Zamalek and Ahly, an iconic image of the demonstrations, was carried by a member of either team's Ultras—they are bitter rivals and attach considerable significance to these symbols. UA07 themselves denied participating as a group in a Facebook statement.

The alluring notion of a population of highly motivated, fight-hardened youths who had transferred their passion from football to revolution was at that point more myth than fact. What happened next, after Port Said, would complicate the picture even further.

Football Violence in the Wake of the Revolution

When it happened, the tragedy of Port Said seemed so sudden, so out of context. Nothing like it had occurred in the history of Egyptian football. But football during that time was not isolated from what was happening in the larger society. The relationship between the different fan groups, as well as between the police and fans, had radically changed. Higher levels of violence were becoming increasingly normalized—especially state violence, but also within society. There were precursors to the tragedy in the football stadium that went unnoticed by many.

The first visible event of such rowdiness in the stands was on April 2, 2011, a few weeks before the constitutional referendum. In an African Champions League qualifying-round game between Zamalek and their Tunisian rivals "Le Club Africain," after the referee cancelled a goal for Zamalek, Zamalek fans stormed the pitch, firing flares. (It should be noted that the UwK, Zamalek's Ultras, did not seem to be present.)[29] Le Africain's players reported being physically assaulted by some of the pitch invaders.[30] The public reaction was one of great shock, and the lazy narrative that the instigators of the chaos were "felool"—remnants of the old regime trying to undermine the post-revolutionary order—again emerged to explain away the incident. That idea was so powerful and the social landscape was changing so much faster than anyone's ability to comprehend it all that it was easy to believe that this must have been staged.

A July 2011 incident at a game in Port Said between Al Ahly and Al-Masry (the Port Said club) is frequently cited as the forerunner to the February 2012 stadium disaster. A video made by the UA07 shows that Al Ahly's Ultras were on the defensive, after clashes initiated by Al-Masry Ultras evolved into a melee with Egypt's riot police, the CSF.[31] The video is edited and is clearly biased, but it is still obvious that the tactics deployed by the CSF created violent tension and set the fans on the offensive: While the Ultras are doing nothing more than singing in unison, they are set upon by the CSF, who beat them with batons. Clashes and rock throwing ensue, along with some vandalism. In the video, UA07 members claim that "thugs" associated with Mubarak's National Democratic Party were responsible for instigating the violence and particularly for the vandalism. Al-Masry fans make the same claim in recorded testimonies.[32] It was a fantastical account that, again, had a lot of traction in the tumultuous days of 2011.

It is difficult to lay the blame for this violence on any party. And the rivalry between the fans of the capital and the Canal teams is an old tradition. Ahmed Magdy, a veteran stadium-goer, thinks that Port Said was the most violent, and the place where the hatred of Al Ahly was the most acute. "Once the buses are in the city, we would start singing and waving Ahly flags from the windows. Then things start flying into the bus—glass, rocks. Occasionally we'd have to squeeze into the middle of the bus and duck, and shortly the glass from the windows would be on the chairs."[33]

Similar incidents followed in the local league. The UA07 clashed with the CSF in a game against Kima Aswan SC on September 6, 2011, leaving many UA07 members injured and dozens arrested. The police seemed intent in that game on putting an end to the Ultras' playful, anti-police chants. UwK had their fair share of scuffles as well. The last of these events to take place before the Port Said Massacre was the match between Al Ahly and Ghazl El Mahallah SC in Mahalla on December 31, 2011, when an equalizing goal by Al Ahly elicited a riotous reaction from the Mahalla supporters, who invaded the pitch with flares. Videos of the event show the referees and stadium staff fleeing the pitch after calling off the game.[34] Al-Masry fans invaded the pitch several times in 2011— and assaulted the Alexandrian team's fans in their stadium in January 2012.

In at least some of these incidents, the police showed that they did have the capacity to effectively intervene, if they wanted to. In the Mahalla game, they simply lined up on the pitch and created a buffer between the two fan groups. A similar action in Port Said in February 2012 might have saved many lives. They probably could not have imagined the cost of their inaction.

Port Said: The Eastern Stands

Tension had been high for weeks in Port Said in anticipation of the February 1, 2012 match between Al Ahly and Al-Masry, and violence was expected. Early signs were all over the place. Throughout the game, precursors of violence by some of the Al-Masry fans were visible. One displayed by the visiting fans during the game is constantly referred to as a trigger: it questioned "the virility of Port Said fans" and led to mid-game scuffles.[35] The banner referred to Port Said as the city of "El Balla"—a reference to its famous used goods market—which is considered derogatory by some people in Egypt. Prior to the game, the Al-Masry Ultras' banners carried "death threats" for the Ahly fans who dared to come to Port Said. But all of this was not out of the ordinary for the Ultras and was commonplace in their social media battles, and such threats had never been literally executed.

The police were aware of the rising tensions—the whole country was—but no precautions were taken. In fact, most accounts stress the extremely lax security at the gates, where home fans went through defunct metal detectors visibly carrying sticks and flares. The assaults in the stands started in the first half. In a video that documents two different moments during the game, one during the halftime, an on-the-ground reporter is heard relaying the point of view that the fans of Al-Masry were acting responsibly and that hired thugs were responsible for some of the commotion. At the same moment a green-clad fan can be seen running down the pitch with a flare in hand. (Green is the color of Al-Masry's kit, and of the Ultras Green Eagles, who support Al-Masry.) A police officer half-heartedly tries to stop him from running toward the stands by reaching out with one hand, and then gives up; the man is then stopped by a fellow fan from running toward the Al Ahly supporters' stands.[36] The reluctance of the police force to act is plainly obvious. The video shows the end of the match, when almost everyone in the stands invades the pitch. It's an incredible sight that looks like ants descending on some candy. It took a while for television viewers to realize that fans were actually getting killed—and the numbers, as we watched on TV, were making great sudden leaps, from ten to somewhere above thirty to more than seventy.

Ahmed Sabry, a football writer and a former member of UA07 who survived Port Said, had a very clear view of the events. Sabry, until Port Said, was a perpetual stadium-goer. Through some connections, he and some friends managed to get executive box seats just underneath the home fans' terrace, typically reserved for the club administration.[37] From his vantage point he could see several smaller incidents of violence break out during the game. "I'd never seen such lax security and I'd seen football clashes before," he later recounted in a detailed story published in the Egyptian daily *El Watan*.[38] Sabry told me that he had left the stadium after Al-Masry scored its third goal (they won the match 3–1), but managed to make his way back. From the ground, he could see the home fans running amok around him, converging on the victims in the eastern stands. Some of his friends from UA07 died on that day, either from the human crush or the fall. "I had a couple of friends who were a bit heavy-set," he said. "I think they estimated that they could not outrun the Masry fans, so they went up to the higher levels of the eastern stands. They did not expect to be followed. They died from the blows dealt to them when they were cornered."[39] An account of the events by one of the capos (leaders) of UA07 in Ibraheem's ethnographic study describes police apathy and reluctance to stop the Al-Masry Ultras from climbing the eastern stands:

> A very important thing about us is that in the terrace we act as ONE person, the capos tell us when to move and when to stop and we act collectively. But, when the people of Port Said started to head towards us, we dispersed, we ran out of flares and we had nothing to defend ourselves with. People from our side went to the front seats to collect the banners of the group and the trumpets. Those who had something to defend themselves with remained standing in the front seats of the terrace. While they were on their way to us, the middle gate, the only one that was open, now was closed. We were surprised as they were passing through the security cordon without being stopped by the police and now they were in the running track just in front of our seats.[40]

The questions on everyone's mind were why the police had not done more to stop the Al-Masry fans, and why the gates had been locked.[41] The media narrative in the first few days of the aftermath strongly favored the theory that the massacre was orchestrated rather than tolerated. This view was initially espoused by both the supporters of the UA07 and Al-Masry's Ultras, and their sympathizers in Port Said.[42] Commentators claimed that it was all part of an organized-chaos plan to undermine the political process, a theory echoed by politicians in the newly elected parliament, who were just beginning their term at the time of the disaster.[43] It was said that UA07 was targeted because of its participation in Tahrir. Little evidence ever emerged for the conspiracy theory. The police indeed used any lapse in security to expand their powers and justify encroaching upon political life, and they did not miss an opportunity to tell people that they were paying the price for challenging their mechanisms of control. But there is no convincing evidence to support the theory that police deliberately neglected their duties for several years, orchestrated incidents of mass violence, and only resumed their work once they felt their legitimacy had been reestablished.[44]

Mobilizing for Justice

The justice process began with an investigation run by the prosecution and a parliamentary fact-finding commission that was on the ground in Port Said after a few days. Two weeks after the tragedy, several senior police officers were detained: Abdel Aziz Fahmy of the CSF; General Essam Samak, the chief of the Port Said Security Directorate; his two assistants; General Abu Hashem and General Kamal Gad El Rab; and Brigadier General Mohammed Saad, the head of the maritime police in Port Said who was put in charge of security in the eastern stands, where away fans are seated. The prosecution referred seventy-two defendants to criminal trial, more than forty of whom were thought to be members of the Green Eagles and the different Masry Ultras, and including the above-mentioned policemen, Al-Masry club officials, the club's security directors, and others thought to be "hired thugs" and petty criminals. Many of the accused were arrested weeks after the investigation, and not at the crime scene. On April 8, 2012, the minister of justice issued a decree relocating the trial to the police academy in Cairo.[45]

The police had to rush to find a perpetrator who was not the police, amid growing accusations of police complicity. It would be difficult to argue that the police had no responsibility for what happened, but now the common belief went further: the SCAF and the police orchestrated the event. Fans were killed with knives and machetes, not the stampede and the fall.[46] The image of people falling to their deaths from the higher stands was scary, all the more so if they had been deliberately thrown.

These new theories about what caused the violence were appealing because they made for a kind of facile explanation of a horrific and unprecedented incident. But football stadiums are complex environments, and the least spark of violence, from fans or from the police, can lead to stampedes and a very high number of casualties.[47] Some people claimed that Al-Masry fan violence was unlikely since the team had won. The escalation of violence, however, is often irrational, and seldom has a correlation with the outcome of the game itself. It may not have been a satisfying answer, but incompetence was probably a bigger contributing factor than sinister plotting.

"As clashes broke out towards the end of the match, the police did not intervene," one account claimed. "Instead, they withdrew from the stadium, welded the doors, and turned off the stadium lights."[48] There really were doors that were welded shut, which confused people in the stadium. But according to multiple accounts, corroborated by the inquiry of the fact-finding committee, the gates had been welded weeks before this game, after a clash between Al-Masry and Al Ittihad fans when suspended Al-Masry fans stormed the stadium.[49] But the eastern stands, typically reserved for visiting fans, had three exits, and only two of them had been welded. The third, known as the Social Club entrance, was locked by Saad, the security officer in charge, before the game's end. The tunnel leading to this last gate is where most of the deaths occurred.[50] One UA07 member who had briefly left the stadium and tried to walk back in found that the gate he used was now locked. He forced it open with a brick and the huge crowd that was forming behind the gate crushed and killed him.

The parliamentary fact-finding committee was hastily formed. It had very little expertise, since it was composed mostly of members of parliament who had little experience in politics or law to begin with. It also had a weak mandate. In light of the poor quality of the work of most quasi-official fact-finding committees in Egypt after the revolution, no one expected anything very substantial. The committee published its preliminary report about ten days after the event.[51] It was not exhaustive, but it was important nonetheless. It notes, for instance, that security measures outlined by FIFA for local football governing bodies and stadium management, such as ease of access/exit, were not followed.[52] The main gate where the crush happened opened to the inside, which violates rules of ease of access and safety guidelines issued by FIFA. The police's welding of two other gates as a "security precaution" clearly backfired.

A criminal investigation officer from Port Said, Khaled Nemnem, was put in charge of the investigation. Nemnem proved to be an extremely controversial character. Many insisted that he should have been one of the accused—since he was part of the security force responsible for the eastern stands. During the trial, Saad's legal defense called on the court to charge Nemnem, since he was just as much responsible for the security at the eastern gate as Saad was.[53] This was echoed by the colorful lawyer Ashraf El Ezzabi, who headed the criminal defense team of several other defendants.[54] Another defense lawyer in the case, Niazzi Youssef, repeated the claim in 2013, referring to the questionable position of Nemnem as a witness and aide to the investigation instead of as a defendant, and spoke of his long enmity with Al-Masry fan groups, which may or may not have been accurate.[55] But the truth is elusive, and even desperate families and friends changed their opinions of what the facts were, shifting between conspiracy theories involving SCAF and police saboteurs, to an admission of football rowdiness by the boys that was not intended to kill, to wilder fantasies involving professional murderers wearing balaclavas. One absurd hypothesis that emerged later, peddled by one of the defense lawyers in the courtroom, was that the Ahlawy Ultras killed themselves.[56] There was an abiding sense that whoever the real culprit or culprits were, they would not be easily convictable, but that charging General Mohammed Saad while putting Khaled Nemnem in charge of the investigation was inexplicable.

The first trial began in April 2012 and lasted less than a year. During that time, the Ultras mobilized their members and staged huge protests in many cities, around trial sessions and especially in the lead-up to the verdict announcement. The days between January 26, 2013 and March 9, 2013 saw the highest escalation in protest and counter-protest in Cairo and the cities of the Delta and the Canal.[57] When twenty-one provisional death sentences were announced on January 26, 2013, families of the defendants protesting outside the Port Said prison clashed with prison guards. In the ensuing violence, two prison guards were shot and more than fifty residents of Port Said were killed by the police.[58] The verdict did not stop the UA07 from protesting, and they organized during the wait for the actual sentencing day. The most confrontational of these protests was outside the Giza Security Directorate in Cairo, with thousands of protesters chanting insults directed at the minister of the interior. Protesters set a police car on fire, making it clear that they still thought the police were culpable.[59] On March 4, 2013, the UA07 staged a major street blockade on Cairo's main highway, Salah Salem, causing massive congestion. At that point the UA07 were the only movement in Egypt that was still capable of staging protests in such numbers with such consistency. In some of the protests the UA07 clashed with political activists who joined them in solidarity, over political differences: some Ultras, it was reported, wanted to suppress the activists' chants against the

Muslim Brotherhood and Mohamed Morsi, the president at the time, and focus it on the Supreme Council of the Armed Forces.[60]

On March 9, 2013, when the twenty-one death sentences were confirmed, the Ultras and their sympathizers gathered to cheer them.[61] It was a bizarre sight: a group that some considered to be a vanguard force of the revolution cheering what was then the biggest number of death sentences issued in Egypt's recent history. (That number would be surpassed when the first-instance courts started issuing deaths sentences at unprecedented rates in 2014.)

The decision issued by the criminal court in March 2013 describes in over-wrought language the murderous intentions of three different Al-Masry Ultras groups, and sketches a plan that involved three successive assaults, at the train station, outside the stadium, and in the eastern stands after the game's end. The court's verdict was that the killings amounted to murder. The most important question was how the deaths of seventy-two people happened. Was it in the stampede, or in violence that created the stampede? Or was it from more lethal, malicious use of force, involving machetes and knives, choking victims, and throwing them off the stands? Some of the victims fell from the higher levels; that much is supported by the evidence. One fall survivor testified that he was carried and thrown off by the assaulting fans.[62] On the other hand, forty or so forensic examinations referenced in the verdict suggest that most deaths happened because of asphyxiation, often caused by compression. Some other deaths were the result of blunt force trauma caused by either being struck by a firm object (sticks and bars), or falling from heights. The forensic report thus left open the question of *how* the falling from the eastern stands happened. I also found nothing in the forensic authority's statement on death caused from penetrative or sharp force injuries, or caused by strangulation.[63] But the strangulation scenario was very popular in the media in 2012, and the court still confirmed it in the verdict, as one of many other means by which the murders occurred. Most of these reports were based on preliminary forensic examinations—only four full-body autopsies were performed—another major flaw in the investigative process.

On February 7, 2014, the Egyptian Court of Cassation ordered the retrial of every one of the defendants in the case and annulled all the sentences.[64] Another criminal court circuit presided over the retrial, and on June 9, 2015 the Port Said Criminal Court sentenced eleven defendants to death.[65] The court's narrative did not change significantly, but ten people were spared the gallows and the policemen's sentences were reduced from fifteen to five years. In October 2016, the Court of Cassation's prosecutorial office recommended a retrial, again, and found procedural flaws in the previous court's decision. A new decision had not been released at the time of writing.

Conclusion

"Qasas," the Arabic word usually translated simply as "punishment," or "retribution," incorporates the seemingly irreconcilable concepts of retaliation in kind, revenge, and restorative justice.[66] It does not receive any mention in the Egyptian criminal code, but it is definitely known in Egyptian jurisprudence and scholarly legal work. It also became part of the revolutionary repertoire right after Mubarak stepped down. It was this concept, somewhere in between justice and revenge, that was frequently referred to in UA07's statements and tifos after the Port Said tragedy. Did the UA07 achieve qasas, or any other form of justice?

By some measures, things worked as they were supposed to. The Ultras, who so often are perceived to show an affinity for street justice, decidedly pursued qasas through formal channels. Suspects were tried and convicted.[67] But the investigation was deeply flawed, and the sentencing might present a miscarriage of justice. (This could be partially explained by a rising trend in which criminal courts in Egypt are becoming increasingly politicized and more vengeful.) The verdict has led to more tension between the Port Said community and the fans of the capital club (who enjoy greater nation-wide support).

In March 2013, while the ramifications of the court decision were still unfolding, James Dorsey wrote in his blog *The Turbulent World of Middle East Soccer*, reminding us of one accountability measure that was overlooked: The sanctions of the Egyptian Football Association (EFA) against the two teams were woefully inadequate. They banned Al-Masry from Egypt's premier league for two seasons, and closed the Port Said stadium for three. Fans were barred from four of Al-Ahly's games, while the team's Portuguese coach, Manuel Jose, and a midfielder, Hossam Ghaly, were suspended. "The decision was made in close coordination with Egypt's military rulers, failed to address the underlying causes of the soccer violence, and satisfied no one," Dorsey wrote.[68]

As superficial as it seems, a strict punishment by the national and regional football federations against Al-Masry could have gone a long way toward establishing accountability and introducing a sense of justice. Indeed, harsher bans would be justified considering the magnitude of loss of life, and the facts that the violence unfolded over a period of more than an hour and the stadium management failed to intervene.

Recognition of wrongdoing by the club would have also helped toward reconciliation. But the Port Said youth staged protests in the city against the relatively mild EFA decision, clashing with the military police while the protests were ongoing in Cairo. At least one protester died in these clashes when the military police attempted to disperse them. These were the days of Egyptian radicalism. Even policemen protested on a semiregular basis, and an EFA decision that was probably meant to appease Al-Masry ended up angering the team's fans.

Ashraf El Sherif, a political scientist, football fanatic, and one of the most hardcore Ahly fans I know—as well as an author of one of the first articles celebrating the Ultras' "politics of fun"—explained to me that the EFA has a complex and time-honored clientelist relationship with the football clubs, which ensures that the provincial representatives have guaranteed places in top-tier football. This relationship prevented it from imposing more serious sanctions on the clubs.

I asked him, as we waited for the latest court decision on the eleven death sentences, if he saw a way out of the mess. "Justice, if it's going to be fair to everyone, requires fundamental reform, huge political concessions, prices that no one is going to pay," he said. "The Port Said case is not going to be resolved independently of the general political context. Signs of conciliation in the near future are grim. Hate legacies between communities have multiplied. The [Ahlawy] Ultras are increasingly more apocalyptic in their discourse. Their sense of injustice is not waning. On the other hand, Al-Masry fans refuse to take responsibility and their animosity toward the capital and the centrality of conspiracy theories to their narrative is exacerbating tensions."[69]

The trends that El Sherif described are happening against a backdrop of increasing balkanization of the political space in Egypt—different institutions, communities, and identity-groups are looking ever more inward. The prospects of near-future resolution, through criminal accountability or otherwise, are grim indeed.

On December 6, 2014, Al Ahly fans were allowed to fill a stadium for the first time in around a year, to watch their team play Séwé Sport, an Ivorian club, in the final of the African Confederation Cup. Since this was a championship game and a trophy would help release some tension, the authorities allowed the whole stadium (albeit a small one) to be filled. UA07 were present in big numbers, but the message they displayed was less aggressive than in the past: "Football for Fans," written in seven different languages.[70]

The Ultras' mobilization today has shifted to the battle to return to normality in the football stadium—although justice for their fallen is still a mainstay of their tifos and chants. This is a good place to start the process of healing. Football, after all, is a public activity that can only thrive in a society where public, collective activity is tolerated to some level, where fans in the tens of thousands are allowed to assemble.

The Ultras are as plausible a candidate as any for playing a role in returning Egypt's society and politics back to some sort of balance—or at least in mobilizing against the State's attempt to turn football into a strictly televised event that only takes place behind closed doors. They face obstacles that are bigger than simply burying the hatchet between Cairo and Port Said. The Egyptian state is uninterested in allowing any kind of public assembly, peaceful or not, political or not. It in fact seems allergic to the very idea of returning to normality, for it thrives on a false state of exception. The memory of Port Said's violence is still fresh, and the inadequacy of the justice process means that many wounds are yet unhealed. It's just conceivable, though, that organized passion for football could be a path around some of these restrictions.

George Orwell famously wrote that sport was "war minus the shooting."[71] Three years after the tragedy at Port Said and all the other violence and failures and crackdowns that followed the Egyptian revolution, that does not necessarily seem to be a bad thing.

Notes

1. Rocco De Biasi, "The Policing of Hooliganism in Italy," in *Policing Protest*, ed. Donatella Della Porta and Herbert Reiter (Minneapolis, Minn.: University of Minnesota, 1998), 188–213.

2. The Ultras, even when they forayed into the politics of the revolution, seemed to be a movement centered around "collective being"— collective presence rather than protest—in the words of Asef Bayat. See Bayat, *Life as Politics* (Cairo: American University in Cairo Press, 2013).

3. It was an opportunity, in Dalia Abdelhameed Ibraheem's words, for "immortal intensity as opposed to insignificant survival," in which political, national, and football identities mixed. See Dalia Abdelhameed Ibraheem, "The Ultras Ahlawy and the Spectacle" (PhD diss., American University in Cairo, 2015), 73.

4. Davide Tarizzo, "What Is a Political Subject?" *Política Común* 1 (2012), http://dx.doi.org/10.3998/pc.12322227.0001.001.

5. The term was also used in the totally different context of cheaper Egyptian cinema houses. In these theaters, hackneyed action movies glorifying "lower-class virility" and machismo often played back-to-back. Poorer cinemagoers acted like football fans, cheering protagonists and shouting abuse at villains. See Viola Shafik, *Popular Egyptian Cinema: Gender, Class and Nation* (Cairo: American University in Cairo Press, 2007), 333.

6. Shawki El-Zatmah suggests that this shift happened in the 1990s, though I personally do not remember younger, lower-middle class fans dominating the stands at the time. Shawki El-Zatmah, "From Terso into Ultras: The 2011 Egyptian Revolution and the Radicalization of the Soccer's Ultra-Fans," *Soccer & Society* 13, no. 5–6 (2012): 801–13.

7. Manuel Vázquez Montalbán, cited in Chris Oakley, *Football Delirium* (London: Karnac Books, 2007).

8. Oakley, *Football Delirium*, 153.

9. Oakley, *Football Delirium*.

10. El-Zatmah, "From Terso into Ultras."

11. Ibid.

12. David Kennedy, "A Contextual Analysis of Europe's Ultra Football Supporters Movement," *Soccer & Society* 14, no. 2 (2013): 132–53.

13. Ibid. In Egypt and the rest of North Africa one frequently sees Ultras' banners in the stands announcing their stance "against modern football." Ultras in Egypt, for instance, always talk about the "Ultras' mentality," and they slip that exact English phrase into their Arabic conversations.

14. El-Zatmah, "From Terso into Ultras."

15. Some of the historians of the nationalist movement in early twentieth-century Egypt make the link between the origins of Al Ahly and the Ultras' involvement in politics today. Al Ahly is the "national" club (the literal meaning of its name) whose core supporters included members of nationalist student unions active in the anticolonial struggle; it was created to counter the rival expatriate club that was later to become known as Zamalek. See Dag Tuastad, "From Football Riot to Revolution: The Political Role of Football in the Arab World," *Soccer & Society* 15, no. 3 (2013): 376–88.

16. Mohamed Mostafa, "The Relationship of Ismaily and Ahly . . . the Facts and the Lies" (Arabic), *Kooora.Com Forums*, May 24, 2007, http://forum.kooora.com/?t=4455630.

17. Karen A. Rasler, William R. Thompson, and Sumit Ganguly, *How Rivalries End* (Philadelphia: University of Pennsylvania Press, 2013), 48.

18. "Facts about Hosting during the Displacement Years," Ismaily SC, September 25, 2009, http://www.ismaily-sc.com/home/index.php/history/1698.html.

19. James M. Dorsey, "Egyptian Soccer Riots Set to Spread from Port Said to Cairo," *The Turbulent World of Middle East Soccer*, March 25, 2012, http://mideastsoccer.blogspot.co.uk/2012/03/egyptian-soccer-riots-set-to-spread.html.

20. James Montague, "Egypt's Revolutionary Soccer Ultras: How Football Fans Toppled Mubarak," *CNN*, June 29, 2011, http://edition.cnn.com/2011/SPORT/football/06/29/football.ultras.zamalek.ahly/.

21. Ibraheem, "The Ultras Ahlawy and the Spectacle," 37.

22. "Al 'Ashira Masa'an," *Dream TV*, July 14, 2010.

23. Indeed, a lot of police action that falls short of actual violence may be considered posturing. Such performative acts are central to policing in the modern state.

24. Ibraheem, "The Ultras Ahlawy and the Spectacle," 39.

25. Hicham El-Fekky, interview with the author, September 5, 2016. I would be remiss not to mention that Ultras did have many interactions with rival fans that, if not actually violent, made use of aggressive language and shows of force.

26. See video of UwK march on the anniversary of the death of Hussein Taha in Alexandria, YouTube, January 29, 2013, https://www.youtube.com/watch?v=IHvRAepKe78.

27. Ibraheem, "The Ultras Ahlawy and the Spectacle."

28. Ibid., 75.

29. Korabia.com, "Zamalek Fans Storm Cairo Stadium Pitch After the End of Game with Le Club Africain," YouTube, April 2, 2011, https://www.youtube.com/watch?v=3rLncmW5yjI.

30. "Zamalek Fans Invade Pitch and Assault Tunisian L'Africain's Players," *DP News*, April 3, 2011, http://www.dp-news.com/pages/detail.aspx?articleid=79713.

31. "UA07 Video Documenting Clashes Before Ahly–Al Masry Game in July 2011," YouTube, July 20, 2011, https://www.youtube.com/watch?v=YQTQvsSL1v0.

32. Ibid.

33. Ahmed Magdy, interview with the author, October 4, 2016.

34. EgyptianAhly1, "Violence Ensues after Al Ahly Scored a Second in Ghazl Al Mahallah" (Arabic), YouTube, January 28, 2012, https://www.youtube.com/watch?v=U1vR-IRqfn4.

35. David K. Kirkpatrick, "Egyptian Soccer Riot Kills More Than 70," *New York Times*, February 2, 2012, http://www.nytimes.com/2012/02/02/world/middleeast/scores-killed-in-egyptian-soccer-mayhem.html.

36. AlMasry AlYoum, "Al-Masry Fans Storm Pitch in Game Against Al Ahly" (Arabic), YouTube, February 1, 2012, https://www.youtube.com/watch?v=RvNli-Y0oLg.

37. Ahmed Sabry, interview with the author, September 6, 2016.

38. Ahmed El-Laithy, "Stories from the Night of Death on the Green Carpet" (Arabic), *El Watan*, February 1, 2013, http://www.elwatannews.com/news/details/124027#.VXa7rAQ2tQI.facebook.

39. Ahmed Sabry, interview with the author, September 6, 2016.

40. Ibraheem, "The Ultras Ahlawy and the Spectacle," 80.

41. James Montague, "How Egypt's Revolution Descended into Tragedy on Night of Violence in Port Said," *The Daily Telegraph*, February 3, 2012, http://www.telegraph.co.uk/sport/football/news/9058104/How-Egypts-revolution-descended-into-tragedy-on-night-of-violence-in-Port-Said.html.

42. Jamie Doward, "Egyptian Police Incited Massacre at Stadium, Say Angry Footballers," *The Observer*, February 5, 2012, https://www.theguardian.com/world/2012/feb/05/egypt-football-massacre-police-arab-spring.

43. Kirkpatrick, "Egyptian Soccer Riot Kills More Than 70."

44. Karim Medhat Ennarah, "The End of Reciprocity: The Muslim Brotherhood and The Security Sector," *South Atlantic Quarterly* 113, no. 2 (2014): 407–18.

45. Ministry of Justice Decree 3001 of 2012, no. 82, April 8, 2012.

46. Tuastad, "From Football Riot to Revolution."

47. Karim Medhat Ennarah, "Policing Football in Times of Exception," The Tahrir Institute For Middle East Policy, February 24, 2015, https://timep.org/special-reports/policing-football-in-times-of-exception/.

48. Jonathan Rashad, "The Port Said Massacre: A Photo Essay," Atlantic Council, January 31, 2014, http://www.atlanticcouncil.org/blogs/menasource/the-port-said-massacre-a-photo-essay.

49. SotelSha3b, "Preliminary Report of Parliamentary Fact-Finding Committee on Port Said, Presented by Head of Committee to Parliament," YouTube, February 12, 2012, https://www.youtube.com/watch?v=DtJ0r53WpxE.

50. Ibid.

51. The report was officially posted online in 2012 but no longer seems to be available. Text of the report is available at http://www.stadelahly.net/pages.php?option=browse&id=16304.

52. SotelSha3b, "Preliminary Report of Parliamentary Fact-Finding Committee on Port Said."

53. Tarek Abbas, "Police Officer's Counsel in Port Said Massacre Trial: The Fans of Ahly Have Killed Themselves!" (Arabic), *El Watan,* November 27, 2012, http://www.elwatannews.com/news/details/85171.

54. Ibrahim Qura'a, "Criminal Defense in Port Said Massacre Case: The Criminal Investigations Officer Is Responsible and Has to Be Added to the Accused in the Case" (Arabic), *Al-Masry Al-Youm*, November 6, 2012, http://www.almasryalyoum.com/news/details/236259.

55. Niazzi Youssef, interview with the author, March 7, 2013.

56. Tarek Abbas, "Police Officer's Counsel."

57. "Five Killed and More than Four Hundred Injured in Port Said Clashes," *AlHurra*, March 4, 2013, http://www.alhurra.com/a/egypt-porsaid-clashes/219466.html.

58. "Egypt: Officials Turn Blind Eye to Port Said Police Abuses," Human Rights Watch, March 2, 2013, https://www.hrw.org/news/2013/03/02/egypt-officials-turn-blind-eye-port-said-police-abuses.

59. Jesus Givara, "Ultras UA07 Demonstrations outside the Giza Security Directorate," YouTube, March 7, 2013, https://www.youtube.com/watch?v=TT7hVDtD1AQ.

60. Wael Eskandar, "Clashing with the Ultras: A Firsthand Account," *Jadaliyya*, February 15, 2013, http://www.jadaliyya.com/pages/index/10204/clashing-with-the-ultras_a-firsthand-account.

61. Fakra WeSorah, "Abdinio, Ahlawy Capo after Port Said Verdict Pronouncement," YouTube, March 9, 2013, https://www.youtube.com/watch?v=MqN7TkTrLCA.

62. Ibid.

63. "Verdict in Port Said Stadium Massacre, Case no. 437," Criminal Court of El Mannakh, 2012, 76–85.

64. Ahmed Bagato, "Anger at Court Ordering of Trial in Port Said Massacre Case," *Al Arabiya*, February 7, 2014, http://www.alarabiya.net/ar/arab-and-world/egypt/2014/02/07/-غضب-شعبي-من-إعادة-محاكمة-المتهمين-في-مجزرة-بورسعيد.html.

65 Ihab Abdallah, "Egypt Court Sentences Eleven to Death in Port Said Massacre Case," *Al Arabiya*, 2015, http://www.alarabiya.net/ar/arab-and-world/egypt/2015/06/09/-مصر-الحكم-اليوم-في-قضية-مذبحة-بورسعيد.html.

66. Susan C. Hascall, "Restorative Justice in Islam: Should Qisas Be Considered a Form of Restorative Justice," *Berkeley Journal of Middle Eastern and Islamic Law* 4, no. 1 (2011): 35–78.

67. Ibraheem, "The Ultras Ahlawy and the Spectacle."

68. Dorsey, "Egyptian Soccer Riots Set to Spread."

69. Ashraf El Sherif, email communication with author, October 8, 2016.

70. "Top Twenty-Five TIFO Actions In 2014," *Ultras-Tifo*, January 5, 2015, http://www.ultras-tifo.net/news/3110-top-25-tifo-actions-in-2014.html.

71. George Orwell, "The Sporting Spirit," in *Shooting an Elephant and Other Essays*, George Orwell, (London: Secker and Warburg, 1950), 152.

PART III

Culture and Media

10

Culture Is the Solution

As Political Reform Stalls, Moroccan Activists Engage Citizens through Art

URSULA LINDSEY

The cultural field in Morocco today contains the most vivid expression of the energies and aspirations of the country's 2011 protest movement, which demanded greater freedom, pluralism, and equality. While the media remains tightly controlled, and the political scene is dominated by the monarchy, many activists have focused on cultural projects as a means to advance their values. They argue that all citizens should have access to the arts, and that the state should invest in education and public facilities that support the arts. Activists and artists believe culture produces more open-minded, aware, and engaged citizens. They contend that restoring this missing element of Moroccan civic life holds a key to the country's development and eventual democratization, and see themselves as working against Islamists' takeover of public space and discourse. But it is unclear how much the activists can accomplish within the current conservative, security-minded context, without the support of a broader social movement or political project.

In early November 2016, the grounds of a derelict industrial complex on the outskirts of Casablanca were transformed. The city's old municipal slaughterhouse, known as Les Abattoirs, is a vast, surprisingly attractive Art Deco building that sits unused and crumbling. For years now artists and activists have lobbied the municipal authorities, to no avail, to be allowed to turn it into a cultural space. Even without official permission, they routinely use the complex to hold events, and have slowly covered its walls with murals and graffiti.

This is where the Moroccan nongovernmental organization Racines ("Roots") staged the second edition of the États Généraux de la Culture au Maroc, a three-day "general assembly" dedicated to discussing the role of culture in Morocco, presenting data on the cultural practices of Moroccans and recommending policies that promote access to the arts for all. Racines' definition of culture, and the one that I use in this chapter, is expansive. It encompasses all fields of creative expression (such as music, theater, visual arts, cinema, literature) both amateur and professional. It includes the dissemination and consumption of creative work as much as its production. To many activists, as we will see, "culture" also connotes the values that they believe engagement with the arts can foster: freedom of thought and expression, tolerance of diversity, critical thinking and openness to debate, secularism, and pluralism.

The event in Casablanca featured concerts and art installations; workshops in graphic art and parkour; and a space in which associations connected to culture manned stalls explaining their work to the public. In the evenings, a crowd filed into a large circus tent to watch a performance by the itinerant troupe Théâtre Nomade that included traditional storytelling, giant puppets, and acrobats. Some of the most enthusiastic members of the audience were children from the neighborhood who had participated in theater classes.

The following week, the capital Rabat hosted Visa for Music, a three-year-old festival dedicated to showcasing music from Africa and the Middle East. Later that month, Rabat also hosted the sixth edition of the festival Migrant'scene, which features music, theater, and cinema on the theme of migration, and is a meeting point for migrant artists in Morocco. Meanwhile, L'Uzine, a new cultural space in the industrial town of Ain Sebaa—between Rabat and Casablanca—founded by the private Fondation Tazi, opened several exhibitions dedicated to the area: an archival show on Ain Sebaa's history; an exhibition of young photographers' takes on the neighborhood; and a "citizens' museum" of the area including artifacts and recorded testimonies.

In Morocco today, the number of associations, gatherings, spaces, and initiatives dedicated to promoting culture are hard to keep up with. In recent years the country has witnessed a sustained wave of cultural activity that includes graffiti; street theater; dance and music festivals; open-air cinema nights; mobile libraries; private galleries and museums; and new cultural centers and spaces.

Yet according to a report by the Economic, Social and Environmental Council of Morocco—an advisory body that conducts research and recommends policies—"Moroccan society is witnessing a gap between the modernization of its infrastructure and institutions and a persistent deficiency in matters of culture."[1] It is common to hear laments over the number of cinemas that have closed in Morocco in recent decades; the very limited audience for literature; or the lack of facilities for young artists and musicians to train, rehearse, and produce their work.

"There is a general feeling that the cultural question is important, but this feeling is not translated politically,"[2] said Driss Ksikes, a prominent Moroccan playwright, novelist and public intellectual.

The many cultural initiatives being launched by individuals and by civil society in Morocco are in fact the symptom of a great sense of lack and urgency. Cultural activists are working to fill a void left by the state. Most share a common vision of culture as a missing and vital element in Moroccan civic life and argue that it is key to the country's economic development and democratization.

What I call cultural activism includes efforts to make the production and consumption of culture as widely accessible as possible, founded on the argument that access to art is each citizen's right. It also includes cultural outreach undertaken to push particular agendas: to carry out voter education campaigns; to fight discrimination against migrants and refugees; to carve out a greater place for the arts in urban development; to counter the influence of Islamism among marginalized youth. Finally, cultural activism involves lobbying the Moroccan state. In most Arab countries as well as in France, which is a significant model for Morocco, the state is an important patron of the arts. Cultural activists call on their government not so much to fund the arts (although they demand that too) as to implement policies that will facilitate a vibrant local culture for all Moroccans—including its production, its dissemination, and access to it.

Cultural activism in Morocco is the most visible prolongation of the country's 2011 protest movement. Culture, more than politics or the media, is the field in which that movement's aspirations—to greater freedom, pluralism, and equality—are most clearly expressed today. It is a space from which activists feel they can push back against Islamism, social conservatism, and authoritarianism, from which to articulate new forms of citizenship.

Racines may be the most articulate proponent of this vision. An umbrella organization that partners with and brings together many others, Racines focuses on infrastructure that regulates artistic production and consumption. Its main mission is to lobby the Moroccan government to adopt public policies—be they cultural, educational, urban, or legal—that promote the daily production and consumption of art. Its ultimate goal, however, is to empower citizens by encouraging creativity and debate.

"We work with culture to have children and adults who are free in their heads; who can't be manipulated,"[3] said Aadel Essaadani, one of Racines' founders.

Cultural activism has taken place despite—or perhaps because of—the closure of most avenues for significant political engagement, especially on the part of progressives. Five years after the Arab uprisings brought prodemocracy protests and a new constitution to Morocco, its political scene remains dominated by the monarchy. Its newly elected parliament is weak, fragmented, and deadlocked between Islamists, who have gained new prominence within the political system, and opponents allied with the Palace and bent on limiting the Islamist newcomers' influence. The authorities have cracked down on human rights groups and the independent press. Public space and public discourse remain closely monitored and governed by a conservative consensus.

Yet while there is censorship in Morocco—particularly of cultural productions with the potential to reach large audiences, such as movies and rap music in the Moroccan Arabic dialect—state repression here is not as heavy-handed as in many other Arab countries. The government remains committed— rhetorically if not in practice—to a vision of progress and gradual democratization. The authorities are concerned with projecting a moderate, modernist image and sometimes find liberal cultural milieus useful in countering the influence of ascendant political Islam. This means cultural activities, if they are not too subversive and if they avoid taboo areas such as religion, the monarchy, and national "unity," have a significant margin of autonomy.

But there is an ongoing debate between those working in the cultural field on whether their activities can catalyze social and political change or whether, unaccompanied by political support or a broader social movement, their efforts can only create vibrant but vulnerable islands of openness. The cultural field may appear dynamic in Morocco largely because the energies concentrated there have nowhere else to go. The question is how much can be achieved through cultural activism and to what extent, under a system in which demands for political reform and greater economic justice have been successfully contained, culture can replace or circumvent politics as a vector for change.

Morocco's Short Spring

In February 2011, protesters took to the streets in Morocco just as they already had in Tunisia, Egypt, Yemen, Libya, and Bahrain. The February 20 movement—named after the date of the first demonstration—called for greater equality and democracy and an end to pervasive corruption.

King Mohamed VI responded quickly. In a speech on March 9, 2011,[4] he promised a new constitution that would devolve more powers to regional authorities and to parliament; recognize the indigenous Amazigh, or Berber, identity and language (which is spoken by at least a third of the country); strengthen human rights and enlarge personal freedoms; make the judiciary more independent; and hold public officials more accountable. He also raised the salaries of public officials.

By taking the initiative, and rallying political parties (including the Islamist Party of Justice and Development, or PJD) in support of a referendum to approve the new constitution, the Moroccan monarchy successfully undercut the protest movement. Although activists called for a boycott of the vote on the constitution, arguing that it did not deliver true reform, it was approved in July 2011 by an overwhelming majority. In the following parliamentary elections, the PJD, allowed for the first time to run unimpeded across the country, won the highest number of seats. Abdelilah Benkirane, the party's head, became Morocco's prime minister, according to a stipulation in the new constitution. In the elections held in fall 2016, the PJD came in first again. Although the PJD is a moderate Islamist party committed to working within the political system, its rise has troubled artists and liberals who worry about a further "Islamization" of society.

Looking back on the February 20 movement, activists have asked themselves why, as Dounia Benslimane, another Racines founder, said: "The people didn't really follow."[5] Driss Ksikes says the collapse of the protest movement led some of its supporters to conclude that "there isn't enough culture for political awareness." Ksikes laments that Moroccan society remains conformist, very religious, afraid of novelty, and unused to questioning authority.[6]

Since 2011, the balance of power in Morocco has not significantly changed. The king, Mohamed VI, is the country's preeminent political, economic, and religious authority (he holds the title of "Commander of the Faithful"). He heads the judiciary and the army and appoints the heads of "strategic" ministries and public companies. According to the constitution, he is the guarantor of the "continuity of the state" and "supreme arbiter between institutions."[7] He is the country's largest landowner and was ranked by *Forbes* as the fifth richest man in Africa in 2015. It is a crime to speak disrespectfully of him. His advisers wield significantly more influence than elected officials.

Moroccans are reluctant to criticize the king, who is seen as a source of unity and stability; very few of them would suggest curtailing his powers. However, there are frequent complaints about the "makhzen"—a key term in Moroccan politics that means "warehouse" in Arabic.[8] In precolonial times, the sultan's army would set out from "bled al-makhzen" (the land of the warehouse, where the sultan stored treasure and wheat), to collect tribute from tribes in "bled al-siba" (the land of dissent). In today's usage, the makhzen isn't the monarchy itself. Rather, it's the network of patronage and influence in public administration and business that revolves around the king and that monopolizes opportunities and resources.

It was against the makhzen that crowds chanted in the 2011 protests and in ones that have broken out since, such as in November 2016. The latter were triggered by the death of a fish vendor named Mohcen Fikri, who had a load of swordfish—a protected species—confiscated by port officials and police in the northern town of Al Hoceima. Fikri stepped into the garbage compacting truck in which his fish was being disposed of to try to retrieve it, and was crushed to death. An average citizen arbitrarily targeted by the authorities and disposed of as garbage: Fikri's death could not have been more apt to represent citizens' "hogra" (humiliation) at the hands of the state. Images of his grisly death immediately circulated online, igniting demonstrations.

Yet given the breakdowns and civil wars that have followed uprisings in other Arab countries, many Moroccans are relieved that their country did not slip into chaos and is a regional exception today. In the current context, there is little appetite for confrontation or risking a radical change.

"When people saw authoritarian regimes falling with hardly a drop of blood, it was tempting," said Fouad Abdelmoumni, who served time in jail for his student activism in the 1970s and is a pillar of Moroccan civil society today. But, he added, "when we saw what happened in Bahrain, Yemen, Libya, and Syria, we started saying, 'OK, we want change, but not at any price.'"[9]

In fact Morocco has never experienced a socialist revolution or a rupture with colonial powers, as other countries such as Egypt or Algeria did. Instead, it is the forces of conservatism that have prevailed here, more than once, and the Moroccan monarchy has played a key role in this.

Sultan Mohamed V (1909–61) supported calls for the country's independence and was exiled by the French. This only increased his popularity when he returned to the country in 1956, to negotiate the French withdrawal and rule as Morocco's king.

His son Hassan II (1929–99) took power in 1961. Faced with contestation and demands for change from leftist movements and nationalist parties, the new king revealed himself to be wily, ruthless, and dedicated to not just preserving but expanding the monarchy's powers. He survived two attempted military coups and during the infamous "years of lead"—through the 1970s and 1980s—decimated his opponents, who were kidnapped, tortured, disappeared, and exiled.

These included some of the country's preeminent artists and writers—such as poet Abdellatif Laabi—who in the late 1960s founded a groundbreaking leftist cultural magazine called *Souffles*. Kenza Sefrioui has written a book about the magazine and its "hopes of a cultural revolution." The avant-garde artists involved with the magazine thought there should be no separation of culture and politics, and that culture could be both a tool of decolonization and of contestation against local authoritarianism, a way to unite citizens. In 1972 the magazine was banned and several of its editors tortured and put on trial for trying to overthrow the state.[10]

In Hassan II's Morocco, elections were rigged; the press was censored; the security services acted with impunity. The entire political class was left, Abdelmoumni said, "emasculated" to this day.

Upon Hassan II's death in 1999, Mohamed VI (1963–) ascended the throne. The thirty-six-year-old king made a break with the country's repressive past. He fired his father's infamous minister of the interior and created a truth and reconciliation committee, which heard testimony from the victims of Hassan II's repression but did not identify their torturers. The political system and the press were partly liberalized.

It was at this time that Morocco saw the beginning of a new cultural vibrancy, as musicians, writers, artists, and filmmakers took advantage of the breath of freedom, and hope swept the country. Dubbed "nayda" (it moves)[11] by commentators at the time, an emerging underground scene—largely based in Casablanca and centered around music—was over-optimistically compared to the Spanish "movida," the cultural flowering that accompanied that country's transition from Francisco Franco's regime to democracy.

In 2004, Mohamed VI called for a reform of family law that significantly strengthened women's rights. Dubbed "the king of the poor" in the early years of his reign, he oversaw a vast expansion of roads, electricity and water services to the country's cut-off rural communities. Yet Morocco remains poor compared to its North African neighbors, with deep social inequalities. Illiteracy and poverty are concentrated in the rural hinterland and in urban slums. Corruption and the poor quality of public services are a constant complaint. While Moroccans do not demand radical change, they do have higher expectations today, and are more likely to voice them.

Five years after the Arab uprisings, the reform process in Morocco has, if not stalled, slowed to a crawl. The country's democratic transition is "an eternal transition," according to Nabila Mounib, the head of an alliance of small leftist parties, which calls for a "true parliamentary monarchy."[12]

Mounib's party won just two seats in the 2016 parliamentary elections. The leading party is the Islamist PJD, followed by the Party of Authenticity and Modernity (PAM), an anti-Islamist party created in 2009 by a childhood friend and close confidante of the king. Otherwise, the parliament is fragmented between a large number of parties that are in decline or riddled with clientelism; leftist movements and parties, weakened by decades of repression and then compromised by their entry into government in the final years of Hassan II's reign, have seen their influence erode. It is little surprise that Moroccans take a dim view of political parties and, in surveys, express very low levels of trust in public institutions.[13]

Activists are also dismissive of formal politics, where the only real change in the last five years has been the integration of Islamists. According to Essaadani, "politics doesn't work to express oneself: it's gangrened, rotten."[14]

Meanwhile, in the current regional and international context, the Moroccan authorities have had little trouble reverting to a more security-oriented discourse. They have persecuted members of the February 20 movements and other critics, muzzled the press, and harassed human rights activists. The Moroccan Association of Human Rights, the country's preeminent human rights group, has been prevented from holding gatherings and events.

"Artists expressing criticism of authorities, especially of the police, face the risk of harassment and even imprisonment on trumped up charges," notes a stakeholder submission from Racines and another Moroccan cultural association to the United Nations' 2016 *Periodic Review*.[15] This has particularly been the case for rappers. The reach of their music—which is sung in Moroccan Arabic dialect and is widely available to lower-income youth—as well as their unvarnished depiction of daily life and subversive attitude to authority have made them prime targets of censorship. The rapper Mouad Belghouat, known as Lhaqed ("The Hateful"), left Morocco in 2015 after being arrested more than once on seemingly spurious charges and prevented from performing his songs. Lhaqed became famous during the February 20 movement and is probably best known for his anticorruption and antipolice song "Kilab al-Dawla" ("Dogs of the State"). Several other young rappers have been accused of "insulting a state institution," "incitement to consume drugs," and producing and displaying content that is "harmful to public morality" for performing songs that criticize the police.

The report goes on to argue that self-censorship among artists is common and that the three main red lines are the monarchy, Islam, and territorial integrity— meaning Morocco's claim to the territory of Western Sahara, which is disputed by the Polisario independence movement.

Racines: Our Aim Is the Public

Yet despite this closure of political space and public dialogue, Morocco has witnessed a sustained series of cultural initiatives and activities. As in other Arab countries, the protest movements of 2011 triggered a renewed interest in graffiti and street art. Artists have organized public dances, festivals, and theater performances. In a country in which illiteracy still stands at about 30 percent and in which a study showed that Moroccans read, on average, two minutes a day,[16] there have been many initiatives to encourage reading, such as organizing itinerant libraries to visit marginalized neighborhoods and slums, or making books available on public transportation. New art galleries and publishing ventures have sprung forth in Morocco's major cities. Cultural centers that offer rehearsal and exhibition spaces, community outreach, and art classes have been set up in lower-income neighborhoods, either by wealthy patrons or by artists who have known how to fundraise and lobby public officials.

"If there's one thing that's interesting to observe, it's all the cultural transformation that came out of February 20," Ksikes said. He noted that this cultural dynamism intensified during the 2011 protests but that it also predated them. "February 20 was built on cultural and not only political networks," he said.[17]

Racines has been busy strengthening many of those networks. The association, founded in 2010, is an influential and dynamic force in Moroccan civil society.

While some of Racine's activism is overtly concerned with politics—such as a campaign it ran in 2016, ahead of parliamentary elections, to emphasize the value of the vote—it mostly focuses on gathering data to argue for particular cultural policies that could help artists and increase audiences. The organization lobbies on behalf of artists and cultural professionals and calls for incorporating the arts into the educational curriculum and into public spaces.

Benslimane and Essaadani, two of Racines' founders, were already members of the association Casamemoire, which is dedicated to preserving Casablanca's urban heritage. Essaadani is a scenographer and associate director of an institute that trains in technical and administrative jobs in the performing arts.

"We said to ourselves, either we go on complaining or we work on changing the framework, to place culture at the center of urban, social economic development," said Essaadani,[18] who argues that the process of producing and enjoying art is key to the development of an open-minded, thoughtful, engaged citizenry.

"We need a cultural policy that encompasses everything, that goes from the school to the marketplace," Benslimane said. "It's a chain. We wanted to focus on the chain."[19]

She continued: "Our ultimate aim is the public, how to put in place things that will benefit the public—the citizen, the Moroccan man and woman. How can we inculcate values of citizenship, of human rights, of freedom, of respect, of tolerance? That's our priority. We argue this isn't possible unless culture is at the heart of all reform plans."

"We think the political solutions haven't worked, the economic solutions haven't worked, Essaadani said. Hence the slogan of this year's États Généraux: "Culture is the solution"—which is also a rebuttal of the Islamist slogan "Islam is the solution.""

Racines' work contains a critique of Morocco's cultural policies, which tend to favor large events and landmark venues, meant to attract international attention, good press, and tourists. Many cities in Morocco host an annual music festival: a jazz festival in Tangier, a festival of sacred music in Fez, a festival of Gnawa music in Essaouira, etc. While in some cases they have successfully popularized forms of Moroccan music (particularly Gnawa, a West African genre linked to healing rituals), in others they have been criticized as expensive extravaganzas that burnish Morocco's image while doing little to promote local musicians. Casablanca's music festival L'Boulevard, which features rap and hip-hop music, is independent; it has always struggled financially, having to cancel several editions.

Morocco has also been building a number of ambitious new cultural venues. The country's first contemporary art museum opened in Rabat in 2014; in Marrakech, museums of photography and of African arts are in the works. A new opera house, designed by Zaha Hadid, is being erected in the valley between the cities of Rabat and Sale. Morocco is also increasingly a destination for international film crews—some of the movies filmed here in recent years include *The Bourne Ultimatum*, *Mission Impossible: Rogue Nation,* and *007: Spectre.*

Yet the country lacks smaller spaces where artists and amateurs can practice and perform. There are few institutes dedicated to training cultural professionals in fields such as restoration, sound and video editing, cultural management and administration, curatorial and library arts, set design, etc. Hundreds of "maisons de jeunesse" (youth houses) run by the Ministry of Youth and Sport sit largely unused, because the administrators in charge of them have neither a budget to put on cultural programming nor any training in how to do so. Only officially registered youth associations are allowed access to the *maisons.*

"The government has a policy of infrastructure, not of culture," argued Essaadani. "They built a 1,500-seat theater in Oujda," he said, referring to a town on the Moroccan-Algerian border. The theater that was opened there in 2014 is the largest in the country, although Oujda is only its tenth most populous city. According to media reports, a year after its inauguration, the theater was plagued by water leakages, poor acoustics, poor visibility from its balconies, and untrained personnel.[20] "They just want to inaugurate it and say to the world: Look, Morocco has theater," said Essaadani. "The state uses culture for its international image. No thought is given to how spaces will be used."

An important part of Racines' activism has simply been to document the presence and operations of cultural spaces. The group has created an online interactive map, featuring individuals and institutions associated with eighteen artistic disciplines (the map had more than three thousand data points in the fall of 2016). This allows users to find out what cultural venues, rehearsal spaces or arts institutes are nearby, as well as to see what parts of the country are lacking particular services.

Racines spent 2016 holding public meetings in fourteen far-flung and medium-sized Moroccan cities, documenting the kinds of cultural activities, spaces, and demands there. In some cities, it found that there were no public cultural facilities at all; or that existing ones had been closed for over a decade.

In 2016 the organization also conducted a survey on the cultural practices of Moroccans, whose results have been published online.[21] The survey found that 85 percent of Moroccans did not have library cards and 64 percent had not bought a book in the previous year. About 80 percent of respondents said they never go to the movies or to art galleries; 73 percent said they never attend the theater. On the other hand, about 70 percent of respondents said they practice some sort of artistic activity (many of them regularly). Singing was the number-one activity, followed by writing poetry and novels, dancing, drawing, and playing music.

Promoting a More Inclusive Identity

Many of the different regional cultural associations that were present at the gathering in Casablanca in November are simply focused on making the arts more accessible, giving Moroccans the chance to learn to draw, to acquire a taste for reading, or to have a space to rehearse with a band.

The association Minority Globe has a more specific focus: it is dedicated to promoting cultural expression by Morocco's migrant communities and to encouraging exchanges between them and Moroccans. The kingdom has long been a country of passage for migrants from sub-Saharan African countries hoping to reach Spain and Europe. But in recent years the migration routes have been ever more tightly policed. Meanwhile, the Moroccan authorities, with encouragement and funding from the European Union, have begun granting residency permits to migrants, encouraging some to stay and envisage a life in the country.

Ghanaian musician Reuben Odoi founded Minority Globe in 2009, as a music and theater production company (thanks to Morocco's new migration laws, Odoi has now been able to register Minority Globe as a nongovernmental organization). A self-taught guitarist, singer-songwriter, and actor, Odoi arrived in Casablanca after living in Mali and taking a circuitous and dangerous route through Algeria. He volunteered with aid groups, formed a band with Moroccan musicians, and joined activists calling for greater recognition and rights for migrants in Morocco. He became known within the migrant community, where he said he found many other musical talents who often asked him for advice on launching a career in Morocco. "Before everyone wanted to go emigrate, now everyone wants to record," Odoi said. "Migrants are performing at clubs, festivals, private parties."[22]

Minority Globe's 2016 project Mix City recruited migrants and refugees interested in workshopping their stories with Moroccan playwrights and performing them in the street. These narratives tended to be about everyday life in Morocco, and the forms of discrimination migrants face there, such as "being refused by a taxi driver, being insulted, having trouble accessing health care or education," said Odoi. The group's methods are based on "the theater of the oppressed" elaborated by Brazilian director Augusto Boal, who championed accessible, relevant, improvised theatrical forms as a way to engage audiences.

"The spectators are encouraged to become actors," Odoi said. "In the audience, some were shocked at what refugees' life is like. Some were in denial."

Minority Globe is just one of several initiatives dedicated to either supporting artistic expression by migrants or to advocating on their behalf through cultural events. Expressing solidarity with migrants and refugees who are living in Morocco is not just a way for cultural actors to spread the values of tolerance and human rights; it is also a way to question a certain conception of Moroccan identity.

Racines, for example, explicitly positions itself as part of an African rather than an Arab cultural scene. This makes sense because Morocco shares a common Francophone culture and postcolonial heritage with many African countries. But it is also a critique of the traditional Arab and Islamic identity celebrated and imposed by nationalist and Islamist forces here since independence. In the name of "unity" and of a supposedly immutable national identity, this vision of Morocco marginalized the country's indigenous Berber language and heritage. Focusing on Morocco's connections to Africa is a way to emphasize the pluralism of its culture. And as Essaadani said, "we have more to learn from Mali right now than from Egypt."

"The goal of street theater isn't just to come and go," Odoi said, "but to encourage others to advocate in similar ways as well." Yet the Mix City project was seriously hampered by the attitude of Moroccan authorities toward public performances and gatherings. Of the five cities in which they planned to perform, Minority Globe was only able to put on shows in Casablanca and—after asking government officials in the capital to intervene—the northern city of Nador.

The strong interest in street art and public performances on the part of Moroccan cultural actors is clearly linked to the protests of 2011 and the way they allowed citizens to reimagine public space as more open to all. "Demonstrating is a theatrical act," Ksikes noted. In fact, Moroccan authorities often do not make a distinction between public art performances and political demonstrations, and take a dim view of both. They are regulated by the same law and most often prevented from taking place by police in much the same way. Partly in response to these interdictions, Racines has launched a petition calling for new legislation recognizing that "cultural performances and expressions must not be forbidden without a valid reason, peaceful public debate must not be discouraged, women and minorities must have a place in public spaces." The organization is using a new petition mechanism enshrined in the 2011 constitution, which states that the government must consider any petition with more than five thousand signatures.

Claiming Public Space

Another recently launched Moroccan cultural project, Think Tanger, is also concerned with public space. The young Moroccan photographer and curator Hicham Bouzid established the organization in 2015. Bouzid had already helped found an art gallery in Marrakech and an electronic music festival in Tangier.

Think Tanger's goal, as stated on its Facebook page, is to "understand the mutation of the city today, to imagine a better future for the city of tomorrow." Tangier, after being neglected for decades by the authorities, has been experiencing massive development in the last ten to fifteen years—both in terms of ambitious urban renewal and infrastructure projects and in terms of massive unregulated housing construction on the city's peripheries.

Bouzid said the plans for the city's development fail to account for its denizens' voices and needs. "They just consider the city's residents as consumers," he said, pointing out that two of the biggest gathering spaces in the 2017 Tanger Metropole development plan are malls.[23] Meanwhile, some of the city's architectural heritage is being quickly lost. Critics of the city's development also question its allocation of resources, for example in the construction of the malls, and of a high-speed train connecting Tangier to the south of the country. Bouzid noted the shocking disparity between the new hotels and shopping centers and the expanding shantytowns just a stone's throw away.

Nor is this is unique to Tangier: rural-to-urban migration and real estate speculation is common in Morocco today, leaving citizens of rapidly growing urban centers feeling alienated. In a 2016 study on public spaces and culture, the Economic, Social and Environmental Council of Morocco deplored "the cultural void" from which most Moroccan neighborhoods suffer, the result of "policies that do not value creativity and initiative."[24]

Think Tanger has offered workshops on implementing cultural projects and held public meetings with government officials, urbanists and artists. In the Fall of 2016, eight artists did residencies with Think Tanger and developed works that commented or interacted in some way with the changes the city is undergoing. Some immortalized Tangier's vanishing landmarks; others displayed their works on the blank walls of the apartment blocks that appear almost overnight in the fields on the city's edges.

Think Tanger's goal is not to halt the city's transformation but to encourage artists and citizens to be actively involved in the city's mutation, Bouzid said. "It's another way to make your voice heard: to make art and to make social connections."

"We are trying to create a network of cultural actors so when we go to the city we will be stronger," he said. Bouzid's own proposals include using empty public buildings for cultural activities, commissioning art projects in every neighborhood of the city, and placing cultural centers within mosques—an idea he ascribes to the late Tunisian intellectual Abdelwahab Meddeb.

Artists versus Islamists

That proposal to put cultural centers in mosques is all the more striking because artists and cultural activists are almost always skeptical of the influence of religion, which they view as a tool of fundamentalists or political Islamists.

Some cultural activists take a pragmatic approach. The team at Racines said it is open to working with government officials from any ideological background, as long as they do not try to dictate the content of cultural activity. "When our interests converge, we work together," said Essaadani.

But it is clear, Driss Ksikes said, that most artists and cultural activists in Morocco see themselves as "combating the Islamization of society."

For Ksikes, it's hardly surprising that artist and religious conservatives should find themselves at loggerheads. "Islamist ideology doesn't take pleasure into account," he said, and doesn't countenance diversity and pluralism. Ksikes has been on the front lines of such culture wars himself. As editor of a liberal magazine he was taken to court in 2007 over an article he published on Moroccan humor, which featured jokes on sex and religion.[25] Threatened with jail time, he emerged with a fine and a two-month ban on his magazine.

In 2011, after the PJD won the highest number of seats in Morocco's parliament, its minister of communications, Mustapha El Khalfi, suggested the television and radio air the five calls to prayer, as well as more religious programming. Another minister, Najib Boulif, invoked the need for "art propre" (clean art),[26] raising concerns about censorship among artists. One actress responded by having her portrait taken while lying on a pile of trash.

Islamists have inveighed against some of the foreign musicians who come to play at festivals in Morocco—particularly scantily clad female pop stars. And in the media they control, they have stirred controversies surrounding hit Moroccan films, such as the 2005 movie *Marock*, which showed a teenage romance between a Muslim girl and a Jewish boy; or the 2015 film *Casanegra*, a violent noir featuring petty criminals, which was accused of encouraging debauchery.

Ksikes argued that the absence of substantive debate has led to a constant struggle over and policing of public space and discussion—a "hypermoralization." Culture is almost only perceived as a "pretext for an argument, for confrontation." Benslimane made a similar point: "We don't have a real public debate of issues, we have the illusion of debate. Issues are only raised when there is a scandal or a court case and then the buzz dies down quickly."

The latest such "buzz" surrounded the movie *Much Loved* (2015), written and directed by Nabil Ayouch. The drama chronicles, in graphic detail, the lives of prostitutes in Marrakech. The film was immediately banned in Morocco. El Khalfi, the minister of communications, said that the film was pornographic and represented "a grave insult to moral values and to the Moroccan woman, and a flagrant attack on the image of the kingdom."[27] Public opinion in Morocco was largely supportive of the Islamist minister's stance. Snippets of the film, which was shown at the Cannes Film Festival, had leaked online; they were widely viewed in Morocco, causing an uproar. The lead actress, Loubna Abidar, was excoriated online and assaulted in the street, finally going into exile in France.

During the furor over Ayouch's film, Islamists organized a sit-in outside a cultural center in the lower-class Casablanca neighborhood of Sidi Moumen. The center had been founded a few years before by Ayouch and his friend and collaborator, the novelist Mahi Binebine. The picketers warned residents not to send their children there to fall under corrupting influences.[28] The irony was that the center had been created in large part to keep local children from falling under the influence of Islamists.

The Stars of Sidi Moumen

The neighborhood of Sidi Moumen acquired notoriety in 2003, when it was discovered that twelve of the fourteen young suicide bombers who had just carried out the worst terrorist attack in the country's history hailed from the slum. The attacks targeted a hotel, a Jewish cemetery, a Jewish community center (which was empty), and a Spanish cultural center, and killed forty-one people. They shocked a country that prides itself on espousing a moderate vision of Islam.

Binebine visited the area in the aftermath of the attack and was stunned by what he saw there. Hundreds of thousands lived in poverty in this *bidonville*, tucked away behind walls along the Casablanca-Rabat freeway. Binebine saw a group of boys playing soccer in the middle of a garbage dump. "I thought, there are the heroes of my next book," he told me.[29] His 2010 novel *Les Etoiles de Sidi Moumen* (translated into English as *Horses of God*) is an imaginative and empathetic reconstruction of the lives of the young men who carried out the Casablanca attacks, describing how a life of violence and humiliation and a total lack of prospects lead the boys to religious radicalism.

After Ayouch turned Binebine's book into a successful movie, the two decided they should establish a cultural center for the children and young people of Sidi Moumen. They fundraised by auctioning donated artworks (Binebine is also a painter) and persuaded the municipal authorities in Sidi Moumen to lease them a building.

The Etoiles de Sidi Moumen ("Stars of Sidi Moumen") cultural center opened in 2014, in an already changed neighborhood. In the years since the attacks, the authorities have "cleaned up" the district, clearing away almost all the area's shacks and replacing them with functional apartment blocks. The Casablanca tramline connects Sidi Moumen to downtown.

On an afternoon in October 2016, the center was abuzz with preparations for a concert to be held in its outdoor courtyard, featuring its music teachers and some of their star pupils. Art produced by students hung in the lobby. A breakdancing practice was ongoing in one of the studios. The venue boasts a theater stage, a library, a café, classrooms, and rehearsal spaces, in which musical instruments are available. Membership costs fifty dirhams a month (less than five dollars); renting rehearsal rooms and attending classes costs an additional thirty dirhams per hour. The center offers popular information technology and foreign language classes.

Houda Boucha is a young woman from the neighborhood who has been hired to manage the center's library. The 2003 terrorist attacks "left a negative impression of the children and the neighborhood," she said. "We wanted to offer another view, to let people know that there are artists here, people who do good things."[30]

The center, like a number of cultural initiatives, has another vocation: to counter the influence of Islamists by offering youth in the area alternative outlets.

The Moroccan security services carried out a massive crackdown in the aftermath of the Casablanca attacks (a crackdown that human rights groups criticized as arbitrary and abusive). They have been on high alert again in recent years, regularly announcing the dismantling of Moroccan terrorist cells that are often alleged to have links to the Islamic State. The country is also home to the banned Al Adl wa Al Ihsane ("Justice and Spirituality") Sufi movement (which does not recognize the monarchy's religious authority) and to Salafi movements that espouse a fundamentalist view of Islam but do not advocate violence and are politically quietist. And then there is the ascendant PJD party, which views itself as representing mainstream moderate Islam and which is pragmatic rather than radical. Its positions limiting personal freedom in the name of public order and morality are in line with a social conservatism espoused by many Moroccan political parties.

Many artists, activists, and liberals mistrust all Islamists, militant or not— they view them as part of one continuous spectrum, and resent their attempts to monopolize authority through religion.

"Islamists have a lot of money, and people like them because they help them," said Binebine, describing Sidi Moumen and similar neighborhoods. "They are close to people. They are populist and know how to talk to people. We engage on the same terrain—but we have to beg for money and we teach kids the culture of life: You will read a book, you will watch a film, you will dance. We fight with our weapons." It was the mothers of neighborhood children enrolled in classes and activities at the center, Binebine said, who broke though and put an end to the Islamist protest over Ayouch's film.

It's worth noting that the outrage over Ayouch's film was not limited to Islamist circles. Although cultural activists call on the state to intervene and to protect artistic freedoms and some overtly align themselves with the state against Islamism and radicalism (often amalgamated), artists who present unflattering depictions or critiques of the status quo and treat "out-of-bounds" subjects often face state repression as well as Islamist attacks.

Binebine blames authoritarianism and the country's poor educational system for the rise of Islamism. In the 1970s, some of the fiercest opposition to King Hassan II came from high school and university students. Many observers claim that in retaliation, the government purposely hindered development of the public education system, and strengthened religious studies. "There is no greater threat to the state than a so-called intellectual," the king famously said in a 1965 speech. "It would have been better if you were all illiterate."[31]

Today, Morocco's educational system is routinely ranked as one of the worst in the region. "It was a choice," Binebine said. "They manufactured a generation of idiots."

The view that the Moroccan regime purposely promoted conservatism over enlightenment is common. "We haven't chosen a society based on culture, knowledge, intellectual debate, and creation," Ksikes said. These are not the priorities of mosques, schools, and the media—"the institutions that format minds."

The Etoiles de Sidi Moumen cultural center is financed by grants and gifts. A sponsorship system allows supporters to pay the membership fees of a child from the neighborhood; the center has close to five hundred registered members, which is its maximum capacity. The project has been so successful that with the help of private patrons there are now plans to open more venues, in the old city of Marrakech, in Fez, and in the Tangier slum of Beni Makada.

"We are two people with nothing and we are able to open four cultural centers," Binebine said. "We ask ourselves: The state, with all its means, can't do something similar? It's not that complicated."

Will the State Step In?

Racines also argues that the Moroccan state has both the resources and the responsibility to make culture available to all citizens. So far Racines has acted as a sort of shadow ministry of culture, modeling the kind of data collection, public forums, and policy elaboration it would like to see officials carry out. It relies on press coverage as a means of leverage with authorities who are concerned with their image at home and abroad. And it makes use of faits accomplis, such as when it plans a big event at Les Abattoirs without a permit, counting on the fact that since government and foreign officials and journalists are invited, the authorities will not intervene to shut it down. Yet Racines does not aim to position itself only in opposition to the authorities, nor to indefinitely perform work that should be the government's responsibility.

Their dream is for the Ministry of Culture to take over, Benslimane and Essaadani said. While it is encouraging to see so many cultural initiatives by civil society and private patrons, Essaadani said, philanthropy can only meet a small percentage of the overall need. There is a risk that by relying on private initiatives "you don't force the state to do its job."

"Our objective was to start a debate," said Benslimane, who feels they have succeeded. In her view, the États Généraux have been "a turning point." Racines has had some success in opening a dialogue with and influencing the discourse of government officials. Morocco's minister of culture, Mohamed Amin Sbihi, attended and spoke at the event, detailing how his ministry had opened more than fifty new cultural centers since 2012 and subsidized the publication of about five hundred books in 2016. The minister agreed with the members of

Racines on the need for the government to play a "structuring" role in the cultural field and to put in place a "national strategy for culture." He spoke about the need to increase his ministry's budget and about his inability so far to pass a law that would allow for cultural centers to be managed differently, and to obtain greater cooperation from other ministries.[32]

Racines and other cultural actors have also put forward a number of specific recommendations. Some of these emphasize the role of education. "We must insist on the connection between educational and cultural policies," said Raymond Benhaim, the president of Racines.[33] Without more Moroccans learning at an early age to enjoy the arts, it's hard to see how the audience and market for cultural production could increase. Racines proposes both that arts education occupy a much more significant place in the public school curriculum and that the state invest in institutes to train young people in cultural professions (restorers, set designers, audio and video editors, curators, librarians) as well as in the management of cultural institutions. Another key suggestion is to allow cultural centers that are currently inactive to be operated by private-public partnerships, in which a private association receives state subsidies to run the space according to criteria set by the Ministry of Culture. The ministry has actually drafted a law that would allow for this, but has not yet been able to persuade the government to refer it to parliament.

Cultural activists in Morocco have elaborated and pushed into the sphere of public debate a series of policy proposals that seem feasible, sensible, and promising. But their implementation depends on the will of the authorities—not just of the Ministry of Culture but of those of the Interior, Education, Youth and Sport, and Communications, which control municipal and cultural spaces, educational facilities and curricula, and distribution channels. Convincing the state to embrace a genuine, ambitious cultural agenda—one that focuses on the daily cultural exchanges, awakenings and experiences of average citizens rather than on grand public-relations-friendly projects—remains a huge hurdle.

Culture before Politics

The fundamental question remains how much cultural activists can succeed, on their own, in pressuring a political system that has proven quite adept at negotiating and resisting recent demands for change. Some view culture as refuge in which, at the current unpromising juncture, they can keep alive liberal values and democratic practices. Others, more sanguine, view it as the foundation on which to build future social movements and political aspirations.

The Moroccan authorities and the political elite simply do not view culture as a priority, Ksikes said. He argued that the country's cultural dynamism will remain fragile and marginal as long as there is not a strong will to democratize on the part of Morocco's elites and an independent rather than a rentier middle class, whose privileges largely depend on proximity to the makhzen and the state apparatus. He doesn't view this as a reason not to engage in the cultural field, however; quite the contrary. He is himself involved in the launch of a new cultural platform, an online and print publication that will also host events and public debates around the country. "People know we are in a historic phase where everything is blocked, where security is the priority," he said. "They say: At least let's make life in the commons livable."

But Essaadani argued, on the contrary, that it is culture that can jump-start both social and political transformation. "If we don't raise the level of consciousness and of demands, politics doesn't work," he said.

In very repressive regimes, such as the one Morocco once was, artists and activists have a stark choice between dissidence and capitulation. Although under the reign of Mohamed VI freedoms in Morocco are still limited, the opening that has taken place has allowed an ebullient cultural scene to emerge, one in which it is possible to negotiate with and to lobby the authorities and even to make some allies within official circles. The broad consensus around the institution of the monarchy; the general relief that Morocco has not faced the kind of polarization and chaos as other Arab countries; and the official discourse of gradual democratization all provide some common ground around which state and civil society actors can argue what reform should entail. Associations and artistic collectives have been able to pursue a variety of different agendas, to raise awareness of issues like discrimination or urban development, and to try to reach young people in areas where no artistic pursuits are on offer. Cultural life has paralleled political events in the country, waxing and waning alongside the hopes of reformers and the demands of protesters. What has been missing so far is widespread access for most Moroccan citizens to creativity and to the reflection that culture can inspire.

Today's cultural activists have been affected by the effervescence of the Arab uprisings and their disappointing aftermath. Their projects are the most visible expression of the energy and the aspirations of the February 20 movement; they are also aware of the closure that has taken place since then and of the enormity of the transformations they called for. They must confront a society that is simultaneously deeply frustrated with some aspects of the status quo and fearful of instability and change, deferential to the traditional patriarchal authority of the monarchy, and receptive to the rhetoric of a populist Islamist party. The focus in Morocco today on cultural outreach and activities is partly caused by the lack of credible progressive political projects. It is also the result of a vision of culture as a truly significant field through which to bring about change, one individual at a time.

The Moroccan state and its elites have shown little interest or commitment to promoting culture for all. They may very well view an emancipated, engaged citizenry as a threat to their interests rather than an asset. So it is likely that progress on the agenda proposed by Racines will be limited and very incremental. The Moroccan political system has proven remarkably adept at containing demands for change, adopting reform-minded discourses while setting a very slow timetable for their implementation. The current context is favorable to such foot-dragging, with the political sphere deeply divided between Islamists and those who mistrust them, and a region-wide focus on security and stability. The state of Les Abattoirs in Casablanca seems emblematic. Activists have been asking for years to be allowed to fully use the abandoned space, and have found many creative ways to stake a claim to it. But their presence there remains fragile, tolerated yet not officially acknowledged, as the authorities neither fully reject nor accept the idea of ceding control to cultural associations. They seem more comfortable with this potential public space remaining empty and unused than with it coming to life with forces out of their control.

In the meantime, culture is a way of interacting with society and spreading civic values of tolerance, open-mindedness, and equality—outside of largely discredited political channels and ideologies (or in opposition to the quite influential Islamist ones). It is also a productive vantage point from which activists can unite and diagnose what ails the country, study policies and institutions, and propose practical solutions.

Racines' goals are as specific and practical in the short term as they are broad and ambitious in the long run.

"Cultural dynamism is not an end in and of itself," Essaadani argued. "It's a tool. We're trying to make citizens, not artists." The art, he said, will come on its own.

Notes

1. "Inclusion des Jeunes par la Culture," Avis du Conseil Economique et Social, 2012, 6 http://www.ces.ma/Documents/PDF/Avis-Inclusion_des_jeunes_par_la_culture-VF.pdf. ("La société marocaine connaît un écart entre la modernisation de ses infrastructures et de ses institutions et la carence persistante en matière de culture.")

2. Driss Ksikes, interview with the author, Rabat, September 14, 2016.

3. Aadel Essaadani, interview with the author via telephone, Rabat, November 18, 2016.

4. "Discours du Roi Mohamned VI du Maroc: le Texte Intégral," *Le Nouvel Obs*, March 10, 2011, http://rue89.nouvelobs.com/2011/03/10/discours-du-roi-mohammed-vi-du-maroc-le-texte-integral-194270.

5. Dounia Benslimane, interview with the author, Rabat, September 1, 2016.

6. Ksikes, interview.

7. See Morocco's 2011 constitution, http://www.amb-maroc.fr/constitution/Nouvelle_Constitution_%20Maroc2011.pdf.

8. Mohamed Kably,"Le Makhzen Revisité," *Zamane*, September 6, 2016, http://zamane.ma/fr/le-makhzen-revisite/.

9. Fouad Abdelmoumni, interview with the author, Rabat, October 3, 2016.

10. Kenza Sefrioui, *La Revue Souffles: Espoirs de Revolution Culturelle Au Maroc* (Casablanca: Editions du Sirocco, 2012).

11. "Le Petite Histoire de la Nayda," interview with sociologist Dominique Caubet, director of the 2007 documentary "Casanayda," *Made in Casablana*, January 26, 2011, https://casablanca.madeinmedina.com/fr/article-la-petite-histoire-de-la-nayda-87.html.

12. Nabila Mounib, interview with the author, Casablanca, October 7, 2016.

13. Mohamed M. Cherkaoui, "L'Ordre Sociopolitique et la Confiance dans les Institutions au Maroc," Institut Royal des Etudes Strategiques, January 2010, http://www.ires.ma/

wp-content/uploads/2015/11/lordre_sociopolitique_et_la_confiance_dans_les_institutions_au_maroc.pdf.

14. Essaadani, interview, November 18, 2016.

15. "Universal Periodic Review, Morocco 2016," FreeMuse and Racines, 5, http://artsfreedom.org/wp-content/uploads/2016/10/UPR_Morocco_2016_Freemuse_Racines.pdf.

16. "HCP: Les Marocains Consacrent 2 Minutes par Jour à la Lecture et au Sport," *Aujourd'hui Le Maroc*, October 29, 2014, http://aujourdhui.ma/societe/hcp-les-marocains-consacrent-2-minutes-par-jour-a-la-lecture-et-au-sport-113968.

17. Ksikes, interview.

18. Essaadani, interview with the author, Rabat, September 1, 2016.

19. Benslimane, interview.

20. Ali Kharroubi, "Oujda: Le Scandale du Nouveau Théatre," *L'Economiste*, May 18, 2015, http://www.leconomiste.com/article/971555-oujda-le-scandale-du-nouveau-theatre.

21. See the website http://pratiquesculturelles.ma.

22 Reuben Y. Odoi, interview with the author, Casablanca, September 28, 2016.

23. Hicham Bouzid, interview with the author, Casablanca, November 11, 2016.

24. Conseil Economique, Social et Environnemental, Royaume du Maroc, *Lieux de Vie et Action Culturelle* (Rabat, Morocco: Conseil Economique, Sociale et Environnemental, 2013), 16, http://www.ces.ma/Documents/PDF/Rapport-AS10_2013-VF.pdf. ("Le vide culturel dont souffent les différents lieux de vie, résultat de l'absence d'un projet culturel national et d'une politique qui valorise la créativité et l'initiative.")

25. "Morocco's Serious Humor Gap," *Los Angeles Times,* January 15, 2007, http://articles.latimes.com/2007/jan/15/opinion/oe-benaich15.

26. "Maroc: l'Art et la Maniere Forte," *Jeune Afrique*, June 28, 2012, http://www.jeuneafrique.com/140890/culture/maroc-l-art-et-la-mani-re-forte/.

27. "Maroc: Le Film Polémique Raconté par son Equipe," *Courrier International*, September 16, 2011 http://www.courrierinternational.com/article/maroc-much-loved-le-film-polemique-raconte-par-son-equipe.

28. Mahi Binebine, interview with the author by telephone, October 7, 2016.

29. Ibid.

30. Houda Boucha, interview with the author, Casablanca, September 30, 2016.

31. "De la Siba à la Revolution," *Zamane*, November 9, 2012 http://zamane.ma/fr/de-la-siba-a-la-revolution/. ("Il n'y a pas de danger aussi grave pour l'Etat que celui représenté par un prétendu intellectuel. Il aurait mieux valu que vous soyez des illettrés.")

32. Mohamed Amin Sbihi, speech at the second edition of the États Généraux de la Culture au Maroc, Casablanca, November 11, 2016.

33. Raymond Benhaim, speech at the second edition of the États Généraux de la Culture au Maroc, Casablanca, November 11, 2016.

11

Speech Bubbles

Comics and Political Cartoons in Sisi's Egypt

JONATHAN GUYER

In print and online, Egyptian cartoonists have created sites of political dissent in defiance of a state-sponsored crackdown on opposition movements, public protest, and free speech. Based on analyses of cartoons and interviews with the artists, this chapter argues that cartoonists have expanded the red lines of acceptable discourse by forging workarounds and challenging official censorship. In the absence of traditional spaces for free speech and political dissent, cartoonists serve as a vanguard for pushing the envelope, opening opportunities to criticize authoritarianism and abuses of power by the state.

What does it mean to draw edgy cartoons when the edge is constantly shifting? The past five years have brought considerable political change to the Middle East and North Africa, and each new regime or policy affects the considerations of caricaturists and comic artists. Navigating these moving edges is a difficult but fundamental part of the independent cartoonist's daily work. The red lines are regularly redrawn by a variety of political forces as well as the cartoonists' personal considerations and political preferences. For cartoonists who push the limits, there always exist the risks of lawsuits, intimidation, and in rare cases violent attacks. But these limits, counterintuitively, animate creative dissent.

Since the 2011 uprisings, a new generation of Arab comic artists has built their careers on confronting boundaries and eviscerating establishment views. Underground, avant-garde, and outrageous, these artists have started horizontal comic collectives that persistently flout taboos. They are producing publications that reflect the ethos of insurrection in spite of political stagnation.

Such a task is difficult in the political void that has transpired in contemporary Egypt, as the vast majority of columnists and commentators have played along to the government's sheet music. Nevertheless, a cohort of independent cartoonists has created a vibrant political discourse within their daily contributions to broadsheets and in newly established alternative comic publications. With a rich tradition that stretches back more than a century, the form of the political cartoon itself is significant in Egypt. It figures prominently into the local press, with caricatures often appearing on the front page of newspapers and magazines; some publications run more than half a dozen per issue. In this way, cartoonists in Egypt reach a larger audience than their American counterparts. Furthermore, new comic zines have been influential. Even though such alternative comics are published in limited print runs, they have effectively convened critically minded audiences at public events and, in turn, spawned other like-minded publications in print and online.

Egyptian cartoonists' work is all the more poignant set against the backdrop of Abdel Fattah el-Sisi's reign, which has advanced an autocratic state so extreme in its suppression that prisons are overcrowded and military courts have convicted thousands of civilians.[1] At least twenty-three journalists are incarcerated for charges including "disseminating false news" or "insulting" various state institutions.[2] Public demonstrations are effectively illegal according to an October 2013 law, and many leading activists and journalists have been barred from leaving the country. Nongovernmental organizations of all stripes have been shuttered. The authorities' occasional dragnets of downtown cafés known as activist hangouts and seemingly arbitrary raids of apartments cast a shadow over all participants in the public sphere. The expression of oppositional perspectives bears serious risks, and yet cartoonists have scarcely been deterred. Whether in newspapers or in alternative zines, cartoonists have emerged as adroit critics of politics and society, vocal oppositional voices within a spectrum of conformity. The question thus becomes how cartoonists have managed to exercise a much wider range of critical speech than other media actors.

Given their power to agitate authorities, cartoons and comics also act as an informal compass for tracing the constantly shifting red lines of permissible expression. But the relationship between red lines and humor is not necessarily straightforward. It is no coincidence that the funniest cartoons rub up against the laws and rules that restrict speech. Humor has a symbiotic relationship with censorship. When cartoonists break the rules, or come close to it, the result is a laugh line. When they embrace the rules and the powers that be, the punch line is propaganda.

Upon close examination of contemporary comics and conversations with their creators in Egypt, two significant trends stand out in the past decade. The first is the state's tacit tolerance of symbolic and satirical attacks on authority, notably through caricature. While Egyptian satirists have always seemed to crack jokes about presidents, starting in 2005 in the independent Egyptian newspaper *Al-Dustour*, cartoonists began directly caricaturing Hosni Mubarak (president from 1981–2011). Since then, the red lines of acceptable speech have shifted along with the regimes that emerged in the subsequent revolution and coup. But the cartoonists who first caricatured Mubarak left an indelible mark on the public sphere. Since Sisi's 2013 coup against Mohamed Morsi (elected president in 2012), authorities have attempted to suppress dissent, especially in the form of criticisms of Sisi, who became president in June 2014. Nevertheless, the volume and barb of pokes at the president have endured the clampdown. Online dissemination has helped, but crucially the fear barrier has been shattered by creative experiments advanced a decade ago.

The second fundamental change is the rise of comic publications for adults, first in 2008 with the critically acclaimed and quickly banned graphic novel *Metro*, and then in 2011 with the emergence of the alternative comics magazine *Tok Tok*. To distinguish this new generation across the Middle East and North Africa (MENA), I will informally call them the Mad Cartoonists. They are "mad" in many senses: influenced by *Mad*-magazine-style comics; angry at the status quo; and madly defiant of laws and norms. This chapter will focus on the works of Egyptian cartoonists, as there are simply too many alternative comic artists working in the MENA region to explore them all in this limited space. Yet it is important to note that Egyptian artists are part of a wider trend of alternative comics throughout the region, with links that continue to deepen through international gatherings and publications. Though they are friends and supporters of each other, the Mad Cartoonists are by no means a political movement. Indeed, much of their work lacks overt political messaging, affinity to any party or movement, or policy prescriptions. But in today's tyrannical political climate, radicalism—or even mere dissent or political opposition—comes in many forms, including shared aesthetics or a commitment to independence.

A Metaphor for Expression

Traces of a new visual culture are developing from within Egyptian media and society. New technologies and social media have also affected the world of comics, reinforcing these two trends. Importantly, caricature of the president and the emergence of comics for adults are related, their causes and effects intertwined.

Though readers—millennials in particular—eagerly consume the new comics in print and online, the dominant perspective of graphic narratives in the country is that of conservatism, regime protection and maintenance, and the repressive status quo. To understand the extent to which the Mad Cartoonists are outliers, it is useful to analyze them alongside the country's conservative cartoonists.

One point to consider while reading comics is whether they obscure autocratic politics by providing a semblance of creative freedom in undemocratic contexts. The imagery of the safety valve has oft been used to describe this sort of pressure drop.[3] The safety valve implies stark power relations, in which the regime tolerates a limited amount of dissent in order to reduce the likelihood of a larger insurrection. In this model, the regime's omnipotent hand holds the power to twist on and off the spigot of critical speech, allowing a drip but never a deluge. That is because, from the state's perspective, types of dissent that are only mildly oppositional and have limited distribution are mostly harmless and allow for the illusion of speech. I argue that the dynamics of political speech pertain more to the risks taken by individuals and, especially in the case of

Egypt, the state's ambiguous power in suppressing speech. A more nuanced way to portray this phenomenon, then, is to think of it as a speech bubble. While the notion of the safety valve has the potential of obfuscating the role that satirists play in building communities, the speech bubble suggests communication among personalities and a shared language, either visual or written. In this way, the speech bubble—whether an expression of dissent or support—can have an impact on discourse in or out of the frame. There is the potential for individuality, as each comic artist draws speech bubbles in a unique style. Speech bubbles can expand the frame of dialogue, creating more room for debate; they can be packed with information or they can be hollow. Obviously, "bubble" also suggests a vulnerable sphere susceptible to state intervention, a space that can be popped or float away like a helium balloon. But there is one thing in common between the state's occasional suppression of cartoonists and independent artists' clarion call of opposition through their ephemeral works: small-bore modes of opposition and dissent can be the start of much larger societal movements.

The speech bubble was glaringly apparent at the 2015 Festival International de la Bande Dessinée d'Alger. There, I met dissident Algerian cartoonists who published criticism of the despotic president, Abdelaziz Bouteflika, in privately owned newspapers. They were invited to participate in the international comics festival hosted by the Algerian Ministry of Culture, and one of them was even leading a workshop on free expression. At the time, it seemed convincing evidence that cartoons were incapable of affecting society. Although the cartoonists' monographs were on sale in the bookstore, freedom of expression was nil outside of the festival.[4] Cultural events or publications can become a sanctioned space where dissent and criticism are permissible under state control, to a small, politically powerless audience—and even then criticism is allowed only up to a point.

Comics and cartoons in Egypt are indicative of a "speech bubble," at once a political force with democratizing potential in a suffocated country and a forum for ideas in a realm separate from the highly regulated sphere of journalism. As for whether the speech bubble in comics will have a broader effect on politics and speech in the country, the best way to start such an inquiry is by looking at the newspapers.

How to Draw the President

President Sisi, humble and plain-faced, walks past his predecessors Gamal Abdel Nasser and Anwar Sadat. A corncob pipe dangling from his mouth, Sadat chuckles, "I wonder if he is *really* capable of lifting subsidies."[5] A brooding Nasser replies, "I wonder if he is *really* capable of achieving social justice." In this cartoon, the once untouchable Sisi faces disapproval from the right and the left—and not from just any critics but from the two most symbolically weighty faces in the country.

Figure 1. Amro Selim, *Al-Masry Al-Youm* (September 6, 2016).

Veteran cartoonist Amro Selim, in his typically sloppy hand, drew this for the September 6, 2016 edition of the privately owned Egyptian newspaper *Al-Masry Al-Youm*. On the surface, it is a stinging critique of Sisi's cutting of subsidies and his disinterest in the common man. Yet there are deeper meanings at play. To grasp the significance of two presidents laughing at the current leader, we first need to review Selim's career and portfolio.

Selim, 54, is among the country's most influential cartoonists. While heading up the caricature department of Ibrahim Eissa's weekly newspaper *Al-Dustour* in the middle of this century's first decade, Amro Selim was among the first cartoonists in Egypt to directly attack then-president Mubarak.[6] A penal code regulation banned "insulting" the president, and at that time satirists tended to obey the regulation in their daily output. (Technically, "insults" to the president, as well as judiciary, military, and other state authorities, remain illegal, though the vagueness of the law—what constitutes an "insult"?—and the audacity of opposition illustrators means that the red line has always been blurry.) It took a clever humorist like Selim to work around the rule and play a trick on Mubarak. "For *Al-Dustour,* I started by drawing [Mubarak] from his back until people recognized it was him," Selim recalled, sitting at his desk of sketches and cartoon books. "Then, I started [directly] drawing his face and his sons."[7] He galvanized his colleagues to also take the risk. In 2006, for instance, Walid

Figure 2. "Is Hosni Mubarak a Dictator?" Walid Taher, *Al-Dostour* (August 2006).

Taher caricatured a particularly pugnacious and portly president accompanying an article headlined, "Is Hosni Mubarak a Dictator?"

This rabble-rousing approach to Mubarak created a dynamic space for experimental comic commentary. The format of *Al-Dustour* lent itself to creativity because cartoons played a central role in its layout and design. Up to eighty cartoons or comics appeared in each weekly edition. "Ibrahim Eissa wanted to make cartoons a main element of the newspaper, not just a column or corner," Taher recalled.[8] So Selim brought on board a stable of young illustrators, most of whom were virtually unknown at the time, to contribute to the broadsheet.[9] "We were trying to create a new generation of cartoonists," Selim explained. It is in this newsroom that the seeds of the current comic renaissance were planted. Key names in Egyptian cartooning arose from this moment at *Al-Dustour*, a group of artists who still affectionately call Selim "The General" for his role as mentor-in-chief.[10]

Selim was a bold watchdog during Mubarak's twilight. But since the 2011 uprising, the cartoonist's political outlook veered toward the mainstream. From 2012 to 2013, during the presidency of Muslim Brotherhood-affiliated Morsi, Selim never pulled a punch in attacking the bungling Islamist in the privately owned daily *Al-Shorouk*. These visual assaults resulted in a barrage of death threats and lawsuits from Morsi supporters. Predictably, Selim celebrated Morsi's ouster in July 2013, and given the intimidation he had faced during that difficult year, his initial enthusiasm was understandable. But virtually overnight after the coup that ended Egypt's brief experiment with elected civilian rule, the great dissident Selim transformed, for a time, into a conformist—uncritically supporting the military, unleashing invective against the severely weakened Brotherhood, and cheering on the state's indiscriminate crackdown. For more than two years, he never drew Sisi at all. When Selim did represent Sisi, he would insert a photograph of the former general, a suggestion that Sisi was unassailable and unsuitable for caricature. Selim's unreflective deference for the new military regime was emblematic of the country's tragic trajectory in the post-2013 period.

When I met with Selim in January 2015, the cartoonist asserted his affinity for Sisi. "The difference between the days of Mubarak or Mohamed Morsi and now is that we now have something we have never had before, at least since Nasser: a ruler that is loved by the people," he told me.[11]

At that time, Selim expressed openness to other perspectives. As the new head of *Al-Masry Al-Youm*'s vibrant caricature department, he was proud to say that he had never rejected his colleagues' cartoons, even when they featured the president's mug or clashed with his political preferences. Selim's colleagues agreed. "At the end, [Selim] is a cartoonist and he knows the value of free speech and he knows the value of publishing a cartoon even if it was holding or carrying counter political views, political views that he is against," said Anwar,[12] who draws a daily cartoon for the third page of *Al-Masry Al-Youm*. "Maybe we have

Figure 3. Amro Selim, *Al-Masry Al-Youm* (November 4, 2015).

different political views, but at the end, all of us are cartoonists."[13] And each of the five cartoonists on the *Al-Masry Al-Youm* team had a different approach to the ongoing political and economic imbroglio.

Only in November 2015 did Selim publish his first caricature of President Sisi, and it was rather critical. In the cartoon, a journalist sits at his desk and tries to write as Sisi sits cross-legged on his head. The president glumly frowns as he wobbles.[14] This cartoon was indicative of a shift in Selim's perspective. Occasionally, from 2013 to 2015, Selim had drawn silly gags about the pro-Sisi hysteria sweeping the country, but they were not as harsh as the image of Sisi literally weighing down on a newsman's head.

This was a milestone for Selim, but that didn't mean that he had taken to regularly lampooning the president. It is therefore notable that the next time he would caricature Sisi he would also draw Nasser and Sadat dressing him down.

When illustrated portraits of Nasser and Sadat appear in the Egyptian press, whether privately or publicly owned, they tend to be unquestionably laudatory, replete with self-evident messages of grandeur. Historically, both presidents had appeared on the cover of children's magazines, such as the Arabic version of the Disney comic *Miki* (Mickey) and *Samir*, during their reigns—comics that serve as a sort of nationalist training ground for kids. Nasser and Sadat's mugs occasionally appear in political caricature in the daily press, typically on national holidays, praising Sisi, or participating in other forms of hagiography. When Nasser has appeared in cartoons alongside Sisi, such as in the summer or fall of 2013, the Arab nationalist hero has praised his underling, saluting him or employing a nationalist slogan like "Bless your hands."[15] What a contrast to see the great Nasser questioning Sisi's efficacy.

It is also important to consider *how* Selim rendered Sisi in his caricature. Though superficially respectful—as is often the case in radical web comics about the president that emphasize his baldness or stubbiness—there is also nothing exceptional or positive about Sisi. His suit, face, and hair are all simple. He is shorter than Nasser and Sadat, whereas in the nationalist iconography they are all depicted as being of similar heights with Nasser inching slightly above the others. In Selim's illustration, Sisi also lacks the liveliness of Sadat or the masculine prowess of Nasser.

Selim's cartoon is especially plucky in comparison to the glorious representations of Sisi as military victor, sex object, patriarch, and fearless leader—images that peaked in the 2013–14 period but continue to appear in the cartoons of the state-run newspapers like *Al-Ahram* and *Al-Akhbar*, and on the covers of establishment magazines. The president is markedly different in this world of unmitigated nationalism, deified in posters and postcards of aviator-donning Sisi beside a ravenous lion, or on women's underwear, or the infamous Sisi truffles (sweets that comedian Bassem Youssef famously sent up in an episode of his show, *The Program*). In Amro Selim's pen, we see a humbler Sisi, the ghosts of the past questioning whether he is suited for the job. Furthermore, Mubarak and Morsi are missing. These ejected leaders, whom Selim frequently draws alongside one another behind bars, have been relegated to the dustbin of history.

In the decade since he first drew Mubarak, Selim has edged toward the establishment, becoming a bellwether of mainstream Egyptian politics. And even his two caricatures of Sisi seem conservative when compared to the young gang of cartoonists he cultivated a decade earlier at *Al-Dustour*.

The Mad Cartoonists of Cairo

"I must be right . . . right?!" a pensive Sisi asks himself, facing a dust-brushed Cairo.

This cartoon, "Existential President," is among the myriad disparagements of Sisi drawn by the Egyptian cartoonist Andeel.[16] In another cartoon, a juvenile Sisi plays with a superman action figure and a toy bus. ("We love you Mr. President, seriously Mr. President, don't be afraid Mr. President, beep, beep, vrrr-rooom, vrrrrooom," he babbles to himself.) In yet another, an oversized, smiling Sisi sits at a chaotic table of food and drink, a waterpipe strewn on the floor. ("Excuse me young man, who's going to pay for all this mess?" the waiter whispers to another customer.) Other cartoons by Andeel employ symbolic violence against the president—showing him as a vengeful murderer gunning down a demonstrator or an aloof autocrat seeking admiration from his staffers, wholly

Figure 4. Andeel, "Existential President," *Mada Masr* (September 9, 2016).

ignorant of just how wrongheaded his policies are and how much citizens have come to dislike him.

To be sure, Andeel's expressions of dissent are risky considering the multitude of forms that state-sponsored censorship has taken. To name but a few of the innumerable examples: in fall 2015, Andeel's colleague from the news site *Mada Masr*, the investigative journalist Hossam Bahgat, was detained and interrogated; in May 2016, the five members of the satirical musical troupe Street Children were arrested for "insulting the president" in their web videos; in June 2016, authorities kidnapped and deported a Lebanese newscaster for being critical of the state. In addition to the banning of the Muslim Brotherhood, the secular April 6 Youth Movement and the hardcore soccer fan groups known as the Ultras have also been outlawed. In the meantime, the top editors of seventeen newspapers have pledged allegiance to Sisi.

In this stifled climate, Andeel has gone on to establish himself as an audacious critic of the regime. An apprentice of Amro Selim during the busy days of *Al-Dustour*, the thirty-year-old Andeel credits Selim with teaching him "how to have a political opinion at *Al-Dustour*."[17] Andeel's work is defined by independence. Since the day of Morsi's ouster in July 2013, he has drawn scathing criticisms of the military's ascendency and impunity. Part of Andeel's brashness relates to the possibility afforded by the medium in which he works: he publishes his cartoons online on the independent news outlet *Mada Masr*.

This cult of personality around Sisi—the fact that the former general was able to garner the full support of Amro Selim for two years—is one of the primary lines of inquiry in Andeel's work. He is especially concerned with the reasons that citizens trust authority and how authority engages in indoctrination. "All these ideas that, for me, are a lot more important than saying Sisi is shit," Andeel said. "I'm interested in why Sisi is shit, why do people not know or not realize that Sisi is shit . . . And to analyze all of that you have to go into much deeper human attributes to the story."[18] For that reason, his cartoons are as critical of the citizenry as they are of the boss.

His caricatures of Sisi, as a simply drawn weakling or as an angry monster, are only powerful in relation to the cultish caricatures of the president that appear in the mainstream and official media. Andeel's jokes are funny because they swipe up against the unspeakable, like a GIF of Sisi wrecking a young boy's sandcastle. Does Andeel's graphic assault on authority suggest that cartoons are treated differently than other forms of media? Or is it that government haphazardly enforces the already vague red lines of society? Those are questions for political scientists. Andeel would rather discuss satire and aesthetics; he warns that readers shouldn't exclusively see his work through the lens of censorship. "It's true that censorship exists here," he said. "I don't think that's the most important thing about my work." He sees the most important aspects of his work to be the development of his aesthetic style, approach, and ongoing critiques of Egyptian society.

It should come as no surprise that Andeel is part of a core collective of artists who have provoked the development of comic art in Egypt. Together with

Figure 5. Andeel, "When Sisi Goes to Alexandria," *Mada Masr* (May 6, 2016).

political cartoonists and graphic artists, several of whom previously worked together as cartoonists for *Al-Dustour*, Andeel founded the zine *Tok Tok* on the eve of the 2011 uprising. Since its inception in early January of that year, *Tok Tok* has produced fourteen periodical issues and organized many events, each packed with a diversity of comic narratives and other illustrated forms (caricature, poetry, short stories with drawings) that capture aspects of Cairo often absent from the mainstream media.

Tok Tok is part of a new wave of comics across the Middle East, among them *Samandal* in Lebanon, *Skef-Kef* in Morocco, and *Lab619* in Tunisia (new publications elsewhere continue to sprout up).[19] Rather than collaborate with officialdom, these publications are finding ways to self-publish and have in turn created die-hard cult followings.[20]

Most of the tales in *Tok Tok* do not address high politics or policies, yet they rumble with political messages. Some examples include the depiction of poverty, questions about how technology envelops the quotidian, and the retelling of subversive narratives from the historical record. Sometimes straightforward editorial cartoons do figure in, like a classic centerfold by Andeel in which the president is dismissive of a yes man. ("Sir! Sir! What are we going to do with the trash, the traffic, electricity, hospitals, security, wages, judiciary, and the future? What will we do with all the ignorance?!" The president replies, "Increase ignorance.")[21]

There are also experimentations in graphic narrative. In the fourth issue, Andeel illustrated the opening scene of *Beer in the Snooker Club*, Waguih Ghali's 1964 novel that condemns the Free Officers' Movement and Nasser's widely revered nationalization project. Originally written in English, *Snooker Club* is a bildungsroman in which the beleaguered protagonist engages in antigovernment communist organizing in defiance of the authorities, though mostly he just drinks with his buddies, as the title suggests. Political cartoonist Makhlouf, 34, did something similar in a sixteen-page narrative for *Tok Tok*'s eighth issue by illustrating the Denshawai Incident from an Egyptian perspective. (In 1906, British officers on a pigeon-hunting escapade shot the wife of a local leader in the Egyptian village of Denshawai, and later fired on a mob of villagers, stirring an insurgency. Denshawai, having been recast by painters and poets over the century since it occurred, has become an emblem of revolutionary and anticolonial Egyptians.) Both Andeel and Makhlouf have unearthed overlooked antiestablishment narratives and packaged them in a form that millennials want to consume.

Another recurring theme in *Tok Tok*'s varied stories is that Cairo's hidden underbelly is brought to the foreground. Within its issues, the burgeoning city is traversed by foot—its alleys are opened up, its stairwells climbed, its characters given space to discuss their anxieties. It's fundamentally different from the traditional political cartooning in the Egyptian press, where the capital is represented by a structurally incorrect composite landscape of the pyramids, the Cairo Tower, a mosque, and a church all beside one another. Mohamed Shennawy, 38, a cofounder of *Tok Tok* and its art director, describes his personal

Figure 6. An example of "drawing the street," a page from *Tok Tok*. Shennawy, *Tok Tok* No. 6 (Cairo: n.p., May 2012).

style as "drawing the street," an approach that permeates much of the narratives in the alternative zine.[22] Even the publication's namesake—*Tok Tok*—the Egyptian version of the three-wheeled motorized rickshaw, common in Cairo's more impoverished districts, is an attempt to refocus attention on the marginal.

This recognition of Cairo's blemishes is a distinctive part of the alternative comic artists' approach to Cairo and is as significant of a development as satirical attacks on the president. In a sense, the two go hand in hand. *Tok Tok* might never have emerged if not for another comic with a vehicular name that irked the authorities, published in 2008: *Metro* by Magdy El-Shafee. Considered the first graphic novel published in Egypt, El-Shafee's tale of a marginalized computer programmer driven to commit a bank robbery captured the desperation of youth in the middle of the century's first decade. Each chapter focuses on a different Metro station, taking the reader to the city's popular neighborhoods as well as dark corners of downtown. Authorities quickly banned this Cairo noir, and the prosecutor attempted to indict El-Shafee for "violating public morality." A second edition of the Arabic comic only appeared again in Cairo in 2012, amid Morsi's very incompetent year-long tenure. It has since been republished again and is more widely available in its third edition. That *Metro* was banned under Mubarak and has been reprinted under Sisi is indicative of the red lines' fluidity. Generally speaking, Egyptian authorities haphazardly enforce the rules, if at all.

"In comics, you have to have a vision, a point of view, a perspective on life," said El-Shafee, now 55.[23] Having contributed to the newspaper *Al-Dustour* in the mid-aughts, he went on to produce three issues of the comic zine *El Doshma* from 2011 to 2012. *El Doshma* was a publication inspired by the visual culture of the revolution. It should come as no surprise that it was edited by the novelist and journalist Ahmed Naji, who was convicted in February 2016 of "harming public morality" for a fictional text in which he matter-of-factly describes sex acts and drug use (an appeals court issued an injunction for his release in December 2016, after serving ten months of the sentence in Tora Prison).[24] Many political cartoonists addressed Naji's sentencing in their cartoons, invoking punch lines that acknowledge the risks of contributing to the arts while ambiguous laws remain on the books.[25]

El-Shafee and Shennawy are the co-organizers of the Cairo Comix Festival, which convenes graphic innovators from across the Arab region for four days of seminars, panels, and trading of wares. In 2016, for Cairo Comix's second edition, El-Shafee is particularly concerned with imparting storytelling skills to young cartoonists, many of whom, he notes, are already talented artists. "What we need now is to master graphic narration," he said, explaining why he has invited top comic scholars from Europe and artists from across the Middle East and North Africa.[26] El-Shafee is taking on the role of mentor to the emerging generation of comic artists.

By all accounts, *Tok Tok* has been a success. It won the first annual Comics Guardian Award from the newly established Mu'taz and Rada Sawwaf Arabic Comics Initiative at the American University of Beirut, and its cofounders have received invitations to key cultural gatherings in Europe. Comics scholars and top publications have cited their contributions to the art form on an international level.[27] More crucially, even with its print run of five hundred to fifteen hundred copies per issue, *Tok Tok* has been influential *in* Cairo. New comic publications, like *Garage* and others, have emulated its form, as have several one-off comic projects in Cairo and Alexandria. A new foundation called Mazg has hosted comic workshops and events in its Tahrir Square office. Local publishers are increasingly interested in printing graphic novels in Arabic (although there are still relatively few on the market). And with hundreds of young fans showing up to each *Tok Tok* issue launch, soon the next generation of comic artists will be up to no good.

Cartooning the Party Line

A smug Sisi looks on, as a beaming Sadat rests a hand on his shoulder. Nasser smiles broadly and asks for a group photo. Khedive Ismail congratulates Sisi on the New Suez Canal. A white-bearded Father Time opens a door labeled "history."

This July 26, 2015 cartoon from *Al-Akhbar* is typical of how the state-run newspapers depict presidents past and present. The cartoon has a transparent message, though the illustration itself ensures its own clarity by adding (unnecessary) labels for Ismail, Nasser, and Sadat. Labeling is an example of rhetorical saturation in pro-state advocacy, attempts to ensure clarity for the reader.

Figure 7. Amro Fahmy, *Al-Akhbar* (July 27, 2015).

The illustrator, Amro Fahmy, draws social-realist caricature in service of the state. Fahmy has published more than ten books of milquetoast caricature, where he tends to take aim at characters like George W. Bush or more recently Barack Obama, while sparing leaders like Mubarak or Sisi of criticism. That his 2000 book *1/2 Dihka*—which translates into English as "Half a Laugh"—was part of a book series promoted by former first lady Suzanne Mubarak, with her smiling photograph appearing on the back cover, is fitting. Fahmy's oeuvre is the borderland where caricature becomes propaganda.

Although the cartoons of independent cartoonists sometimes contain straightforward political messages, the cartoons are distinguished by their whimsy and wit, the interplay between the written and visual. This means that the cartoons themselves are in dialogue with the reader, leaving blanks for the reader to fill in and thus to be a participant in the joke. Not so in the preponderance of cartoons in Egypt's state-run media, which convey an uncritical earnestness about the state of affairs.

The dominant discourse surrounding the president, to this day, is that of support, if not oozing nationalism and love of patriarchy. In a full-page spread on *Al-Akhbar*'s front page, Sisi grasps a giant steering wheel. He is a full head taller than the smattering of smiling adults and children who wave Egyptian flags behind him. A dove with an olive branch flies by and a crane operates in the distance, which taken together signal a glowing endorsement of the president's 2015 expansion of the Suez Canal. Sisi is rendered quite realistically, more of a portrait than a caricature. (A similarly stoic Sisi has graced the cover of the children's comic magazine *Samir* on several occasions.)

The cartoonist old guard continues to lionize the autocratic regime in their output for semiofficial newspapers as well as in salons and gallery openings cohosted by the Ministry of Culture. Any observer of contemporary Egypt recognizes that, for all the enthusiasm about street art and new experiments in visual culture, the central trend of the past five years has been a sycophantic status quo in which many media actors assert that the army and the police can do no wrong. In the realm of cartoons, this includes the persistent and uncritical support for state policies as well as tired tropes of a conspiratorial nature, namely anti-Americanism and anti-Zionism. (There are occasional bouts of anti-Semitism in the semiofficial press, although anecdotally this trend seems to have decreased since 2011.)

Xenophobia and conspiracy theories are commonplace in state-run broadsheets. For the flagship state newspaper *Al-Ahram*, Galal Omran drew Barack Obama as a Salafi with a long scraggly beard, short pants, and sandals. Obama, with derogatory features such as extra large ears and a toothy grin, holds up a four-finger salute—a Brotherhood sign of solidarity—though the grossly rendered president has long, claw-like fingernails. He stands beside a new American flag: two swords and a Quran, the Brotherhood's symbol, have taken the place of Old Glory's fifty stars.[28] Of course the assertions made in these cartoons are false. But Egypt's state newspapers have rarely critically engaged with difficult

Figure 8. Amro Fahmy, *Al-Akhbar* (August 5, 2015).

events, let alone addressed them with nuance. There are scores of other outland-ish examples. In December 2015, *Al-Ahram* published a cartoon, by Farag Hassan, in which the Statue of Liberty has sprouted a similar beard. The grotesque statue holds a bomb instead of a torch, and grips a book that says, "Renaissance," an allusion to Morsi's national project. In this fantasyland, Washington is the patron of the Muslim Brotherhood and more recently, the Islamic State.[29]

Such bizarre tropes are remarkable because they appear so infrequently in the cartoons of independent artists. The cartoonists of *Al-Masry Al-Youm* or other private outlets are censorious of the policies of Israel or the United States in their panels. However, they engage in satirical disparagement of Tel Aviv or Washington without reverting to bigoted stereotypes or ridiculous conspiracies.

In fact, these critical cartoonists sometimes make fun of the media for its trafficking in conspiracies. For instance, when the Egyptian military accidentally massacred a group of Mexican tourists in the Western Desert in September 2015, the cartoonist Anwar mocked the Egyptian media in his third-page frame for *Al-Masry Al-Youm*. In it, a newscaster exclaims, "In this episode we reveal—were the Mexican tourists part of a Zionist-Mason-American conspiracy against Egypt?!" One imagines that the cartoonists drawing for the state-run Egyptian media might answer in the affirmative.

Memes of Dissent

The smiling photograph of Sisi is crowned with Mickey Mouse ears.

That simple image packs a satirical punch, a broadside at a Mickey Mouse leader of a Mickey Mouse state. Amr Nohan, a twenty-two-year-old law graduate undergoing his compulsory military service, posted this Photoshopped gag on Facebook. He was indicted for "insulting" a national figure in August 2016 and sentenced that December to three years in prison. In his indictment, the military prosecutor claimed that Nohan possessed "thoughts inside of him that run contrary to that of the ruling regime."[30] Caricaturists and journalists have always faced this type of looming threat. Now citizens who share their political opinions online are also subject to state scrutiny.

Although the constitution adopted in 2014 protects freedom of speech, new regulations have come in the way of those rights.[31] The government has tightened control of public spaces and platforms like Facebook and Twitter through a variety of legal tactics. A counterterrorism law, in particular its Article 33, contains language that stifles journalistic practice, notably in outlawing the dissemination of reportage that is at odds with the Defense Ministry's official story. The government has also hired Western companies and software to surveil the Egyptian internet.[32] A draft cybercrime bill, approved by the parliament in September and awaiting approval from the cabinet (the prime minister and the cabinet ministers), includes a number of worrying

Figure 9. Unknown, Meme of Sisi as Mickey Mouse (n.d.).

provisions. Chief among them is a three- to fifteen-year prison charge for "Setting up, administering or using a website, private account or information system with the aim of illegitimately trading ideas, drugs, arms, and human organs, or the facilitation or advocacy of any of these forms of trade." Surely cartoonists trade in ideas (less so the latter items) and the ambiguousness of an "illegitimate" idea is a cause for serious concern.[33] There are a number of other technicalities of the bill under which online dissenters might be charged, even if their participation in such illegal behavior is unbeknownst to them (such as unwittingly visiting an illegal website).[34] Of course, with so many penal code regulations that outlaw "insults" to various state institutions, the government scarcely needs more ammunition in its potential to crackdown on dissenters.

All of these pose risks to the country's estimated forty-four million Facebook users and four million Twitter users who have come to see both spaces as relatively free compared to public forums and local media. Indeed, the state has aggressively gone after people for Facebook posts and tweets, making clear that in practice it's just as risky to officially publish as it is to "say" anything in any public platform. Even as Facebook, Twitter, and other platforms have provided new opportunities for the spread of ideas, they are also dangerous spheres. Interest groups and state actors closely monitor these seemingly open spaces.

Online dissemination has blurred the line between consumers of satire and the satirists, which poses problems for just about everyone in the current repressive environment. In 2011, during the freewheeling revolutionary period after Mubarak's ouster, business magnate Naguib Sawiris also had a Mickey Mouse problem. Sawiris tweeted an image of a bearded Mickey and a niqab-wearing Minnie, a jab about religion's increasing invasion of public discourse.[35] A group of Salafi lawyers sued Sawiris for blasphemy. The court later threw out that and another case against Sawiris for the tweet, but the thorny issues surrounding satire in the age of social media endure.[36] (It should be noted that neither Facebook nor Twitter have instituted any protections for dissidents in Egypt, even while the Egyptian state continues to target online malcontents.) In the meantime, prosecution of so-called "blasphemers" and other forms of religiously inspired repression have continued full-bore under Sisi.

The five years since the uprising have, coincidentally, seen both comic production and dissemination shift toward digital. Today, most cartoonists draw on tablets, and social media has become the primary site of distribution. For veteran illustrators, digital production allows for new artistic styles, approaches, and complexities. It also lowers the barrier of entry for the untrained, which means that cartoonists now have to compete with meme-creators. The meme, it might be argued, is the political cartoon of the early twenty-first century.

In photoshopped images or comics, GIFs, or short videos, Egyptians are mashing up the day's news with famous actors and iconic scenes from cinema, much in the same way that cartoonists do. Scholars recognize that memes represent an important cultural currency and a forum of satirical ingenuity.[37] The most popular of these meme-sharing pages, the Asa7be Sarcasm Society, has more than thirteen million followers on Facebook (by contrast, *Al-Ahram* has about three million and *Al-Masry Al-Youm* about nine million). Memes have in fact become so popular that some cartoonists are creating meme-style cartoons, notably Osama Hajjaj of Jordan.

Meme culture means that Sisi's visual gaffes—his looking up at the ceiling aloofly during a meeting at the 2016 UN General Assembly or staring out the window of an airplane knowingly as the Suez Canal is expanded below—result in a deluge of Photoshop jabs. Even if the mainstream Egyptian media is tempering its criticism of Sisi on that given day, there is always a barb online.

Sharing cartoons and other visual commentary online creates new forums for discussion. Dozens of Egyptian and Arab cartoonists have embraced the opportunities of social media. This move to social media is beneficial not only for users, but also for cartoonists, who can directly connect with their readers. Andeel has described Facebook as a platform for a meeting of the minds, where he can get into the heads of his critics and of readers he might not necessarily relate to or meet in daily life. "When I'm making cartoons, when I'm expressing my opinions on Facebook or whatever, I'm always more concerned about people who totally disagree with me," he said. "How can I talk with them rather than talking to people who already agree with me or already think I'm right?"[38] Andeel's take is an optimistic one. Expression online, however, is a space that is under risk.

Consider the case of Islam Gawish, 29, a producer of viral web comics on his page *el-Waraka*, or "The Paper." His jokes and jabs are of note not only because of their following of two million and counting; Gawish, through his experimentation with stick figures and use of acutely Egyptian satirical techniques (particularly burlesque and gallows humor), has innovated the web cartoon, always penned on notebook paper with simple doodles, along with punch lines in heavy slang.

On January 31, 2016, Gawish was due at the Cairo International Book Fair. At midday, police investigators burst into Gawish's office and hauled him off to the station for questioning. Authorities released him the next day amid a torrent of international protest, and the president himself offered a testament to the provocative power of comics. "My God," Sisi said on live TV, "I am not upset with Gawish or anyone else." Sisi continued: "Every day, the ninety million people in Egypt find many things which make them uncomfortable, like the case of Gawish . . . Such things happen, and this is natural in a country which was in a revolutionary state for four years."[39]

The most curious element of the case is that police detained Gawish overnight allegedly for "operating a Facebook page without a license." He was released the next day without charge, but this seemed to be an unprecedented accusation because no web publisher in the country has acquired a license for a social media page. It is a worrying indicator of the security state's toolkit of repressive tactics.

Figure 10. In the first frame, the man on the right asks, "Who here is from the generation of the eighties and the nineties?" "All of us," they respond. In the next frame, the older man says, "You are in need of an embrace. Come on." "Come here, come here," he repeats as he hugs them. Islam Gawish, *El-Waraka* (November 10, 2015).

On February 2, Gawish wrote a long account of his arrest and release on Facebook, concluding on a note of defiance:

> I will not stop drawing. And I will continue doing what I like and continue working in this direction. I am neither beating the drum for anyone, nor cursing anyone. And I have no biases toward anyone. I have my own opinions, whether intellectual or political. I am not extremist in my ideas and don't claim to be a hero and a role model. Thank you all.[40]

The post received thirty-seven thousand likes, more than three thousand shares, and nearly two thousand comments. Sure, that's a drop in the bucket in the broader internet ecosystem, but it is significant that a Facebook page founded in 2013 has swelled to over two million fans and remains active.

When I met Gawish, he didn't want to get into the details of his arrest and preferred to discuss the incarceration of the novelist Ahmed Naji and the satirical troupe the Street Children. I asked Gawish about why cartoons are so powerful, and his answer was as simple as his stick figures: "People want to laugh."[41]

Gawish has never caricatured the president himself, not because he quivers at authority but rather because he prefers to craft jokes that deal with social issues. He addresses politics on his own, sardonic terms. In a cartoon from November 10, 2015, a bald grownup speaks to four crudely drawn youths: "Who here is from the generation of the eighties and the nineties?" "All of us," they respond. In the next frame, the older man says, "You are in need of an embrace. Come on." "Come here, come here," he repeats as he hugs them. In the final frame, the four youngsters find themselves in a cage, and the bald man smiles. This sort of black humor is typical of Gawish. The cartoon is also a reminder that Nohan, the conscript who posted the photo of Sisi with mouse ears, remains in prison—as do countless others.

Speech Bubbles

Dissent endures in Egypt's independent broadsheets and online, in spite of the staying power of Sisi's cult and the new and pending surveillance techniques employed by the state on social media. All the while, state newspapers and the Ministry of Culture sustain proregime cartoonists. The Mad Cartoonists of Cairo are using their pens to redraw the red lines of acceptable speech, and they often face resistance.

Looking at this spectrum, it is tempting to think that cartoons in the Egyptian media—and broadly in the Arab world—represent a microcosm of perspectives about public affairs. But even this claim would be a stretch, given the absence of an entire strand of perspectives, namely that of an Islamist persuasion. The Muslim Brotherhood did print amateurish cartoons in its newspaper, *Hurriyya wa-'Adalla*, which was published daily until it abruptly ended in the aftermath of the 2013 coup. Its cartoons mirrored the qualities of earnestness and propaganda of cartoons in *Al-Ahram* and *Al-Akhbar*. Rather than critically engage the reader or question taboos, these status-quo cartoonists tend to offer steadfast support for policies or straightforward condemnation of out-groups. (In that sense, and unsurprisingly, the Islamist cartoons weren't very funny.) So what then do cartoons and comics in Egypt represent? Are they simply a badly drawn caricature of a complex society?

Comics hold out subversive potential and are best suited for transmitting progressive perspectives through tales with hidden meanings or stories of marginalized characters. And because authorities or cultural figures have rarely taken comics seriously (as an artistic, literary, or political medium), they further hold the potential to carry radical politics. But at the end of the day, the field of cartooning is all about individuals—and individuals' political preferences evolve over time. It is difficult to speak of movements, as cartooning is a solitary craft. And the hybrid art can just as easily convey conservative or revolutionary messages.

It is worth considering an idea put forward by George Khoury Jad, of Lebanon. In his column for *An-Nahar* about the 2015 Cairo Comix Festival, Jad explains that in the past few years Cairo had seized the comic mantle from Beirut. He is cautiously optimistic, expressing concern that state censorship might thwart the ongoing comic renaissance. Jad, himself a comic artist who innovated the form during the Lebanese Civil War, concludes with a hopeful question, "Aren't comics by definition dreams that provoke reality?"[42] Although comics exist in the fantastical realm of the fictionalized and exaggerated, he suggests that comics can agitate and affect reality.

Indeed, comic strips are among the most vibrant realms of speech in Egypt today. The necessarily coded language of political satire—a realm of mixed metaphors and local jokes articulated in deep slang—provides a cover for overt criticisms of the government. The dearth of other critical voices in the media makes the difficult work of Cairo's cartoonists even more potent. And in spite of imminent and frightening legislation that will further limit the sphere of social media, cartoons are eminently shareable online; the classic medium of the one-frame comic continues to gain new currency in the era of social sharing.

Perhaps this entire story boils down to one small event—that as editor of *Al-Dustour*, Ibrahim Eissa sought to fill the pages of the broadsheet with cartoons. Yet that platform brought together a group of artists who, experimenting with content and form, have left an enduring mark on the public sphere. Today, the cartoonists themselves deserve full credit for proceeding with wit and originality in forging forward through the murk of surveillance and clampdown.

In Egypt and across the Arab region, cartoonists have created new spaces for expression, speech bubbles that continue to expand and spread. There is certainly a risk that as these bubbles grow larger, the artists themselves become so emboldened that they will garner the undue attention of authorities, resulting in their repression or suppression. But as we read the works of Cairo's Mad Cartoonists, a different scenario seems more likely. The community of artists that gathered at *Al-Dustour* during Mubarak's reign has gone on to publish radical drawings against all odds. Their perseverance in the face of repression is a bold illustration of dissent, one that might boil over and erupt into other politically contested realms.

Notes

1. See, for instance, "Egypt: 7,400 Civilians Tried In Military Courts," Human Rights Watch, April 13, 2016, https://www.hrw.org/news/2016/04/13/egypt-7400-civilians-tried-military-courts; and "'We Are in Tombs': Abuses in Egypt's Scorpion Prison," Human Rights Watch, September 27, 2016, https://www.hrw.org/report/2016/09/27/we-are-tombs/abuses-egypts-scorpion-prison.

2. "China, Egypt Imprison Record Numbers of Journalists," Committee to Protect Journalists, December 15, 2015, https://cpj.org/reports/2015/12/china-egypt-imprison-record-numbers-of-journalists-jail.php.

3. Scholars are increasingly articulating the problems of the "hydraulic model" of humor, better known as the safety valve. See Anny Gaul, "Egypt, Laughter, and the History of Emotions," *The History of Emotions Blog,* March 7, 2016, https://emotionsblog.history.qmul.ac.uk/2016/03/egypt-laughter-and-the-history-of-emotions/.

4. Jonathan Guyer, "Speech Bubble: A Comic Festival in Algiers," Institute of Current World Affairs, November 12, 2015, http://www.icwa.org/speech-bubble-a-comic-festival-in-algiers/.

5. Sadat's comment in the cartoon is a jab at the fact that during his presidency he attempted to severely cut subsidies but was forced to reverse course following significant popular protests.

6. Eissa went on to establish *Al-Tahrir* newspaper in 2011 and then *Al-Maqal* in 2015. He is a complicated and controversial character in the Egyptian media, though there is not space for further scrutiny of him here. See for example Heba Afify, "Ibrahim Eissa Is 'The Boss,' but at What Cost?," *Mada Masr,* April 28, 2014, http://www.madamasr.com/sections/politics/ibrahim-eissa-%E2%80%9C-boss%E2%80%9D-what-cost.

7. Amro Selim, interview with the author, Cairo, April 3, 2013.

8. Walid Taher, interview with the author, Cairo, May 28, 2013.

9. Among that cohort are cartoonists who have gone on to be hugely successful in Egypt, namely: Andeel, Abdallah, Doaa el-Adl, Makhlouf, and Hany Shams. Other now well-known artists, like Magdy El-Shafee and Walid Taher, were also contributors.

10. Selim, interview.

11. Jonathan Guyer, "Four Years after Tahrir, Egyptian Cartoonists Face New Challenges," *The National,* February 28, 2015, http://www.thenational.ae/opinion/comment/four-years-after-tahrir-egypts-comics-face-new-challenges.

12. Following a tradition in Egyptian editorial cartooning and like many of the cartoonists in this story, Anwar uses just one name professionally.

13. Anwar, interview with the author, Cairo, February 24, 2016.

14. Jonathan Guyer, "A Headstrong Caricature," *Oum Cartoon,* November 5, 2016, http://oumcartoon.tumblr.com/post/132596864826/headstrong-caricature-selim-cartoons-sisi-egypt.

15. See for example Jonathan Guyer, "Gallows Humor: Political Satire in Sisi's Egypt," *Guernica,* May 15, 2014, https://www.guernicamag.com/features/gallows-humor-political-satire-in-sisis-egypt/.

16. For Andeel's cartoons and writing on *Mada Masr,* see: http://www.madamasr.com/en/contributor/andeel/. Also see Laura C. Dean's chapter in this volume, which discusses the history of *Mada Masr* in depth.

17. Andeel, interview with the author, Cairo, June 21, 2015.

18. Andeel, interview with the author, Cairo, Sept 29, 2015.

19. Each of these publications boasts social media pages, but their primary product is old-fashioned: a print periodical that is usually on sale at booksellers and art spaces.

20. Through their own ingenuity and limited grants from international bodies, such as foreign cultural institutes or the European Union, comic artists have been able to establish and

print independent publications, and in turn have secured a semblance of autonomy—until the funding runs out.

21. Jonathan Guyer, "Mad Magazines: Underground Comics Come to Egypt," *Harper's Magazine*, 332, Iss. 1990 (2016): 46–47.

22. Jonathan Guyer, "Shennawy's True Colors," *Oum Cartoon*, June 1, 2016, http://oum cartoon.tumblr.com/post/145264113006/shennawys-true-colors-a-recent-trend-among.

23. Magdy El-Shafee, interview with the author, Cairo, September 5, 2016.

24. Ahmed Naji, interview with the author, Cairo, December 21, 2015.

25. I gathered some of these in my blog post on A Day of Blogging for Ahmed Naji. See "Cartoons for Ahmed Naji," *Oum Cartoon*, May 16, 2016, http://oumcartoon.tumblr.com/post/144456483286/cartoons-for-ahmed-naji-i-first-met-the-novelist.

26. El-Shafee, interview.

27. See for example Paul Gravett, *Comics Art* (New Haven: Yale University Press, 2013), 73–74.

28. Jonathan Guyer, "Cartoons as Black Mirror," *Oum Cartoon*, February 28, 2015, http://oumcartoon.tumblr.com/post/112302716146/cartoons-as-black-mirror-in-todays-the-national.

29. Michael Wahid Hanna and Daniel Benaim, "How Do Trump's Conspiracy Theories Go Over in the Middle East? Dangerously," *New York Times*, August 16, 2016, http://www.nytimes.com/2016/08/17/opinion/how-do-trumps-conspiracy-theories-go-over-in-the-middle-east-dangerously.html.

30. Farid Y. Farid, "A Pair of Mickey Mouse Ears Helped Earn This Man Three Years in Jail," *BuzzFeed*, December 19, 2015, https://www.buzzfeed.com/faridyfarid/a-pair-of-mickey-mouse-ears-helped-earn-this-man-three-years.

31. Article 65 of the 2014 Constitution reads: "All individuals have the right to express their opinion through speech, writing, imagery, or any other means of expression and publication." Translation from: Gamal Eid, Karim Abdelrady, Mohammed Al-Taher, and Abdou Abdelaziz, "#Turn_around_and_Go_back: Internet in the Arab World," Arab Network for Human Rights Information, May 2015, 77. Available online at: http://anhri.net/wp-content/uploads/2015/05/turnaround_and_gobackfinal-1-Autosaved.pdf.

32. Sam Kimball. "After Arab Spring, Surveillance in Egypt Intensifies," *The Intercept*, March 9, 2015, https://theintercept.com/2015/03/09/arab-spring-surveillance-egypt-intensifies/.

33. Mohamed Hamama, "Egypt's New Cybercrime Bill Could Send You to Prison," *Mada Masr*, trans. Aida Seif al-Dawla, October 12, 2016, http://www.madamasr.com/sections/politics/how-new-cyber-crime-law-can-send-you-prison.

34. For an in-depth reading of the controversial law, see: Mohamed Abdelaal, "Egypt's New Cybercrime Law: Another Legislative Failure," *The Jurist*, July 9, 2016, http://www.jurist.org/forum/2016/07/mohamed-abdelaal-egypt-cybercrime.php.

35. Gus Lubin, "Telecom Mogul Naguib Sawiris Faces Death Threats after Tweeting This Picture of Mickey and Minnie Mouse," *Business Insider*, June 28, 2011, http://www.business insider.com/bearded-mickey-and-minnie-mouse-2011-6.

36. Associated Press, "Egypt Court Rejects Second Bearded Mickey Cartoon Lawsuit," *USA Today*, March 3, 2012, http://usatoday30.usatoday.com/news/story/2012-03-03/Egypt-Bearded-Mickey/53348284/1.

37. See for example Adel Iskander, "The Meme-ing of Revolution: Creativity, Folklore, and the Dislocation of Power in Egypt," *Jadaliyya*, September 5, 2014, http://www.jadaliyya.com/pages/index/19122/the-meme-ing-of-revolution_creativity-folklore-and.

38. Andeel, interview with the author, Cairo, January 13, 2015.

39. Jonathan Guyer, "The Pen, the Paper, and the President," Institute of Current World Affairs, March 7, 2016, http://www.icwa.org/the-paper-the-pen-and-the-president/.

40. Post on the Facebook page of Islam Gawish, February 2, 2016, https://www.facebook.com/Gawish.Elwarka/posts/1499538566736499.

41. Islam Gawish, interview with the author, Cairo, July 28, 2016.

42. George Khoury Jad, "In Focus: "Cairo Comix" Reclaims Its Role from Beirut and Launches a Movement of Change" (Arabic, title translated by the author), *An-Nahar*, October 17, 2015. http://newspaper.annahar.com/article/276214-تحت-الضوء-- كايرو- كوميكس -يستعيد-الدور-- من-القاهرة-إلى-بيروت-ويطلق-حر كة-التغيير. Title translated by the author.

12

The Politics of Egyptian Fine Art

Giving a Voice to the People

SULTAN SOOUD AL QASSEMI

Egyptian artists have a long history of political engagement. Even in the mid-twentieth century, when they mostly relied on state funding, they made critiques of the ruling regimes, and created one of the few spaces where independent political thought could brew. Egyptian artists—like their counterparts in many other countries in the region—have long been in closer touch with the mood of average people than the repressive governments have been, and they have served as both bellwethers and instigators of change. When the revolution broke out in 2011, Egyptian artists were thus well positioned to take on a much more direct, activist role, and many did. Art changed as well, becoming more accessible and purpose-driven. Now, as the tide again has turned to authoritarianism, the unbridled hope of the uprising has waned, negatively affecting art as much as any other part of the revolution. Yet there are glimmers of dissent in the art that lives on, and many reasons to think that Egyptian artists will be part of the vanguard of the next wave of social and political change, whatever it may be.

Just after 3:00 A.M. on the morning of Friday, June 15, 2012, four young Egyptians, armed with spray cans and stencils, crept through the Cairo night. It was ten days before Egypt's historic post-revolution election, the first free one in history. Their leader, underground artist El Zeft (a word that translates into "asphalt" but in colloquial Arabic is used to denote rubbish), took them to the former headquarters of the National Democratic Party (NDP), not too far from Tahrir Square, the site of the Egyptian uprising of 2011. The NDP was the political party associated with the corrupt three-decade rule of Hosni Mubarak, and the building was slated for demolition after the party was disbanded by court order and had its assets seized. The four men, all in their early twenties, were careful not to alert the officers guarding the building.

The activists silently approached the wall next to the main gate and quickly spray-painted two words, "Opening Soon," using a stencil designed by El Zeft. Photojournalist Jonathan Rashad had, within seconds of its completion, snapped a picture of the graffiti that went viral on social media even before the Friday noon prayers later that day. The message: Egypt may be about to vote, but too many signs pointed to a reemergence of the repression and authoritarianism of the *ancien régime*. The army immediately dispatched a team to paint over the graffiti, but it was too late. It was the talk of the town that week in Cairo.

It was also prescient. The freely elected if inept and divisive government of Mohamed Morsi would last little more than a year before being unseated by a coup, which in turn would lead to the installation of the current president, Abdel Fattah el-Sisi. And Sisi's regime would soon prove to be even more suffocating than the NDP's.

El Zeft's graffiti bombing was, in a way, the zenith of a period of activist popular art in Egypt, when artists and revolutionaries worked hand in hand, and were often one and the same. For decades, Egyptian fine arts had been supported and managed by state patronage. During that time, Egyptian artists accomplished much, including making works of beauty that often contained subtle critiques of the social and political status quo. The artists created a community with their salons and expositions that became one of the few fonts of independent political expression of any kind. For many years, state repression circumscribed the community's broader impact. But when the uprising of 2011 began, Egyptian artists were well positioned to play an important role in responding to the unrest and creating iconic imagery. Their passion for social justice and political change was evident in their work and activism.

The occupation of Tahrir Square, and the revolution that followed, broke open bold new spaces for Egyptian artists. They in turn broke open new spaces for political discourse. Some of the older generations of artists never got much involved with the revolution, but others happily forsook the comfort of galleries and the competition for state support in favor of the street. For a time, the lines between high- and lowbrow were blurred, and Egyptian art experienced a dynamism and immediacy unseen in recent history, as it engaged directly in political tumult. Creators like El Zeft, who had little or no professional training, were all of a sudden propelled into the limelight as major voices calling out for change on the streets of Egypt.

The pattern of melting boundaries and the flourishing of art as activism repeated itself throughout much of the Arab world during the years of the uprisings. But in Egypt as elsewhere, it didn't last. As the uprisings faltered, cynicism spread in the art world, as it did in other sectors of society. Activist street art, quick to flare in importance during the first two years of the revolution, very quickly receded to its margins under the repressive control of Sisi's rule. The pool of active artists has shrunk. Yet many have continued to create, express, and comment, and remain a highly relevant cultural force—one of the few alternatives to the stultifying mainstream political dialogue.

To trace the history of Arab art from the mid-twentieth century through the uprisings and to the present reveals a great churning of ideas, social awareness, and activism that are not evident in the study of official politics. Arab art has tapped into alternative, popular histories, within boundaries that contract in times of authoritarianism and expanded during the uprisings to unprecedented levels. The creative fire of these artists has never been extinguished. Egypt's fine arts community—even during the regimes of Gamal Abdel Nasser, Anwar Sadat, and Mubarak—grappled in meaningful ways with fundamental political questions, though artists' direct involvement with political struggles was minimal until the uprisings. The surge of politicized artists who occupied Tahrir from 2011 to 2013 was exceptional in Egypt's history, but also echoed the political activism and engagement of earlier generations of Egyptian artists.

In this chapter, I attempt to follow that story in broad strokes, focusing on the visual arts in Egypt but with an eye toward other countries in the region as well.[1] I am especially interested in the interaction of art and politics—cases like El Zeft's where the raw need to express dovetails with a movement for political change. However, I do not view art solely as an accessory to politics. Political scientists might try to gauge whether art is a valve, releasing pressure created by authoritarianism, or a force that foments change. But for me this question is only a small dimension of art's importance. Art in the Arab world has been, and continues to be, almost divinatory. As such, I follow the history of contemporary art to highlight the moods and ingenuity of the artists and their societies, and also to get a sense of where they come from and where they may be heading next.

In that vein, Egyptian art points us to a future of continued political engagement and an intense desire for social progress that the new authoritarians are quite unlikely to deliver on their own. Artists are mobile, vocal, and ever more clever with pushing boundaries. The fervor and optimism of the revolutionary days of only a few years ago may have subsided and organized political blocs may have fractured, but the new strongmen of Egypt are unlikely to succeed at completely boxing in expression.

Figure 1. Aya Tarek, *Smoke Face*, 2012. (Image courtesy of Barjeel Art Foundation and From Here to Fame.)

Egyptian Art in the Postcolonial Era

The twentieth century was tumultuous for Egypt, but a period in which the country's creators of fine art—al-fanoun al-jamila—found their footing and even flourished. Ironically, successive Egyptian regimes' repression managed to give a boost to fine art, even as they caused other forms of expression to wilt. Nasser (president 1956–70) and his successors had a respect for fine art, and considered its achievements a point of national pride. At the same time, they believed it to be mostly appreciated by elites, and therefore not dangerous. Thus, they gave artists grants and wide latitude to create what they liked, even if it subtly critiqued the state or the status quo. As long as what they created wasn't consumed or obvious enough to be appreciated by the masses, fine artists were mostly allowed to paint and sculpt as they pleased. As a result, a great deal of creative energy was channeled into the fine arts.

Yet despite their state patronage, Egyptian artists were engaged from the beginning in politics. Their postcolonial political engagement has roots in the struggle against the British and the monarchy they supported.[2] Some later evolved into propagandists, but many did not, and kept their independence.

The Monarchy under British Occupation, 1922–52

As early as the mid-1930s, a group of Egyptian intellectuals and artists influenced by surrealism and headed by author Georges Henein (1914–73) came together and launched the Art and Liberty Group. The movement was socially liberal, and favored anti-capitalist economics and Freudian psychological ideas. But it also extended deeper into attacking the British occupation of Egypt, Egyptian monarchists, exploitation of women and workers, and Islamic nationalism.[3] The movement lasted for just a decade, from 1938 to 1948, eventually disbanded by the Egyptian police and British Occupation Forces at the beginning of the Cold War. However, its impact was long-lasting and it has enjoyed a revival in 2016–17 with a series of exhibitions at the Centre Georges Pompidou in Paris and the Sharjah Art Foundation in the United Arab Emirates (U.A.E.).[4]

During this period, one of the most noted incidents of artist political activism within a work of art was that of Abdul Hadi al-Gazzar (1925–66), the son of an Alexandrian religious scholar. In 1951, when Gazzar was twenty-six years old, he submitted a painting to an exhibition at the invitation of his teacher, Contemporary Art Group founder Hussein Youssef Amin (1904–84). The work, which goes by several names but is most commonly known as *Hunger*, is now one of the most famous paintings in Egypt. It depicts a group of eight barefooted women and a child, standing side by side with empty plates in front of them, signifying poverty. *Hunger* was regarded as a clear criticism of the monarchy and the ruling elite, and resulted in Gazzar being briefly detained along with Amin.[5] Both men were released following an intervention by the renowned Egyptian lawyer-artists Mohammed Nagi and Mahmoud Said.[6] Following his release,

Gazzar painted a second version of *Hunger*, after the original was sequestered, according to an interview conducted by researcher Fatenn Mostafa Kanafani with the late artist's wife, Laila Effat.[7]

There was also artistic activism directed externally. Henein, of the Art and Liberty Group, coordinated with French surrealists to defend artistic freedom and speak out against Hitler's destruction of "degenerate" art. The Group, which included artists such as Ramsès Younan, Fouad Kamel, and Kamel El Telmisany, announced their "Long Live Degenerate Art" manifesto in 1938.[8] (Henein would later break with French surrealist friends over their support for the state of Israel, whose creation and treatment of Palestinians would be a major focus of Egyptian artists for years to come.)

The period of the monarchy was thus marked by significant antagonism between artists and the Egyptian state. In subsequent decades, the government's relationship with artists was not always adversarial. In fact, the artists under Egyptian government patronage produced much work that advanced government policies and ideas. But whatever the character of their advocacy and relation to the state, by the middle of the century it was well established that Egyptian artists were, by nature, political.

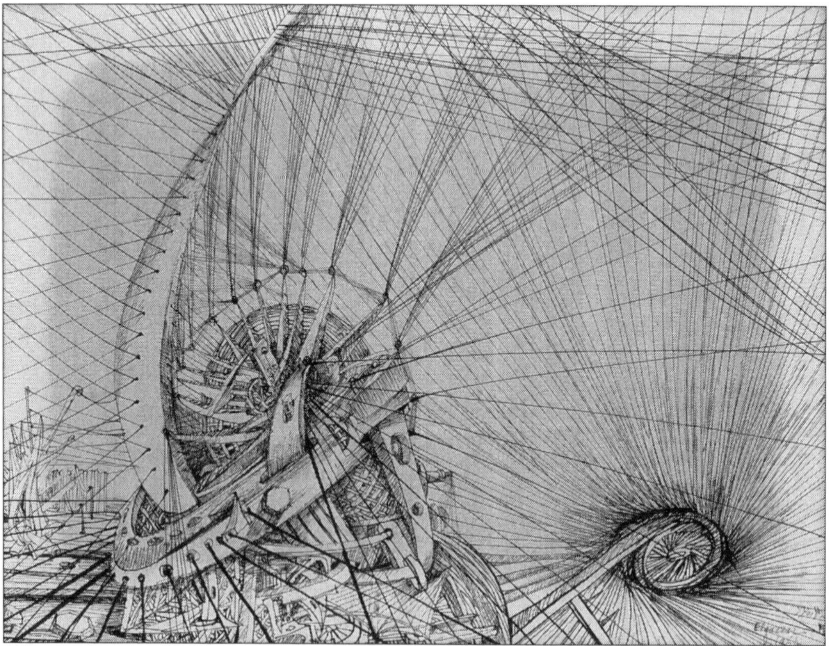

Figure 2. Abdul Hadi el-Gazzar, *Untitled*, 1964. (Image courtesy of Barjeel Art Foundation and Capital D Studio.)

From Nasser to Sadat: 1952–1981

After the revolution of 1952, Egypt, like Ba'athist Syria and Iraq, reserved a part of its budget for culture and viewed state-sponsored art as a significant arm of government information or propaganda policy. State-supported and independent artists didn't necessarily disagree at all times. Common causes such as the rejection of colonial rule and, later, anti-Zionism brought together governments and artists from opposite ends of the political spectrum across the Arab world. For instance, painter Hamed Ewais (1919–2011) repeatedly created works commissioned by Nasser's government during the nationalization of the Suez Canal[9] and even after Egypt's defeat in the war of 1967.[10]

The early years of Nasser's rule were a time of great pride in many national endeavors, and for some, significant hope about the future. In their enthusiasm, some artists who had staunchly opposed the monarchy became near-propagandists for the government. For example, Gazzar, the painter of *Hunger,* embraced the new republican regime. One of his most famous paintings, *The Charter* (1961), depicts a woman wearing a crown, holding Nasser's manifesto. The piece, which is now exhibited in the Egyptian Modern Art Museum, instantly became an icon of the 1952 revolution.[11]

Alternatively, artists who received government grants to travel to the Aswan High Dam construction site, like the painters Tahia Halim (1919–2003), Ragheb Ayad (1892–1982), and Effat Naghi (1905–94), offered critical insights into the precarious nature of the massive project. Halim, who documented Nubian villages in her paintings before the construction of the dam flooded them, showed how potentially destructive the government project could be by offering a glimpse into the lives of villagers who were forced to permanently resettle. Ayad and Naghi were similarly commissioned by the state to document the building of the dam in the 1960s. In both artists' work, we see different approaches that depict a less glorified image of the project than what the government usually promoted. In Ayad's 1964 painting *Aswan,* his waif-like characters seem to be laboring endlessly upon various heights of rocky terrain. His composition is arranged in such a way that each worker loses his individuality and appears like one of many hieroglyphic slaves constructing the Pyramids of Giza. Naghi's documentation focuses on the scaffolding that appears like a teetering edifice of wood and metal, and eliminates the presence of laborers altogether. Naghi's approach takes the loss of humanity in Ayad's work further and highlights the precarious nature of the ambitious dam project.

Implicitly critical as they were of projects like the High Dam that were usually cornerstones of patriotic propaganda, these artists' work had limited popular and certainly minimal political impact. The works appeared in museums, and though beautiful and affecting, did not reach the masses. Nor did they spur any elite revolt against the country's leadership. It would be decades until satellites and the Internet could convey images to broader audiences, but in any case the style of mid-century art was removed from the tastes of the vast majority of

Figure 3.
Ragheb Ayad,
Aswan, 1964.
(Image courtesy
of Barjeel Art
Foundation
and Capital D
Studio.)

Figure 4. Effat Naghi, *The High Dam*, 1966. (Image courtesy of Barjeel Art Foundation and Capital D Studio.)

Egyptians, and its critiques were delivered with too much subtlety to have had a direct impact on politics. Nevertheless, the artists managed to continue their community's tradition of dissent.

But artistic freedom stopped at the edge of the canvas, as Inji Efflatoun (1924–89) found out. Born to a well-to-do French speaking family, Efflatoun studied under Telmisany, who introduced her to his Art and Liberty Group during her studies at Cairo University in the early 1940s. Efflatoun also joined the Egyptian Communist organization Iskra and a number of feminist organizations. Operating under Nasser's regime, Efflatoun's staunch Marxist political leanings and active participation in demonstrations were punished when the government issued a decree that authorized the detention of women taking part in political activism. Along with twenty-five other female political activists, Efflatoun was incarcerated from 1959 to 1963. During her time in prison, Efflatoun continued championing the cause of the working class, painting peasants, laborers and her celebrated series of women prisoners.[12]

Figure 5. Inji Efflatoun, *Ta'mol* (*Contemplation*), c. 1940's. (Image courtesy of Barjeel Art Foundation and Capital D Studio.)

Figure 6. Inji Efflatoun, *Tarqab* (*Expectation*), c. 1940's. (Image courtesy of Barjeel Art Foundation and Capital D Studio.)

Figure 7. Inji Efflatoun, *Mathbahat Dinshawy* (*The Dinshawy Massacre*), c. 1950's. (Image courtesy of Barjeel Art Foundation and Capital D Studio.)

Anwar Sadat (president 1970–81), like his predecessor Nasser, tried to silence his critics, including intellectuals and artists. He became even more notorious than Nasser, however, for his blanket blacklisting of artists such as painter and sculptor George Bahgoury (1932–) who was exiled from Egypt and spent many years in Paris. Following the signing of the Camp David accords, Bahgoury published *Banned Artworks*, his famous book of caricatures mocking Sadat.

Sadat did, however, support art when it aligned with his agenda. In a move that Sadat may have organized, and certainly tolerated, the works of Egyptian modern master Mahmoud Said (1897–1964) were exhibited under the patronage of the newly inaugurated Egyptian Embassy in Israel at the Habimah National Theatre in Tel Aviv, in February 1982. The following May, Israeli artists were invited to showcase their work at Cairo's Le Méridien hotel. However, no other exhibitions took place in the following years, probably partly due to significant objections from Egypt's intellectual elite and artist community, which almost unanimously rejected—and continue to reject—normalization with Israel. For instance, Ali Salem (1936–2015), a famous Egyptian playwright, was expelled from Egypt's Writers Syndicate following his numerous visits to Israel, which began in 1994, and his open calls for normalization.[13]

Throughout this time, artists continued their expression about international political and social issues. They commemorated the Nakba (or "Catastrophe," as the events surrounding the 1948 founding of the state of Israel on historic Palestine are known in the Arab world), and the defeat of the Arab armies in 1967, known as the Naksa. They mourned the massacre of Sabra and Shatila in Lebanon in 1982, and celebrated the independence of their countries from colonial powers. All of these events were of earnest importance to broad swaths of the region's societies.

Regional Patterns of Repression and Expression

There was a similar pattern in other parts of the Arab world. In the Ba'athist states of Iraq and Syria, the governments embarked on programs to train and fund artists in the hopes of instilling a sense of national identity through art. Similarly, Algeria and Morocco were trying to shake off the decades of French cultural influence by supporting or tolerating artists such as M'hamed Issiakhem (Algerian, 1928–85), and Farid Belkahia (Moroccan, 1934–2014) and Mohammed Melehi (Moroccan, 1936–) of the Casablanca Group. Kuwait, Tunisia, and Sudan also witnessed a burgeoning art scene with the founding of galleries and art societies in the 1950s and 1960s.

In fact, from the mid-twentieth century onward and across the Arab world, art societies formed in cities such as Baghdad, Kuwait City, Khartoum, Tunis, Casablanca, and elsewhere. These societies were registered by the state and sometimes received subsidies and support, and as such they were not directed against the state. However, they contributed to the production of original works with political relevance.

Figure 8. Hamed Ewais, *The Protector of Life*, 1967–68. (Image courtesy of Barjeel Art Foundation and Capital D Studio.)

For instance, in the 1970s Algerian authorities commissioned the French-trained Issiakhem (who, as researcher Amina Menia notes, was an anti-colonial freedom fighter before becoming a recognized sculptor) to create a sculpture to replace the famous *Monument to the Dead*, which Paul Landowski made in 1928 to commemorate the fallen French and Arab soldiers of World War I. By the 1970s, the French-commissioned monument was considered an offensive relic of colonialism. Issiakhem used a large sarcophagus to enclose the sculpture as a sort of tomb, perhaps as a metaphor for the death of colonialism in Algeria.[14]

In Iraq, master artist Jewad Selim (1919–61) erected a massive government-commissioned frieze in central Baghdad titled *Monument of Liberty* in 1961. The Iraqi government commissioned the giant work to commemorate the July 14 Revolution of 1958 that led to the overthrow of the British-backed Hashemite monarchy. The bronze work comprised twenty-five human figures spread across more than two-dozen panels along with depictions of a horse and a bull, in what could be considered a nod to Picasso's *Guernica*.

Both the Algerian and Iraqi works were far from being critiques of the governments that commissioned them, yet they were hardly propaganda. Instead, they reflected popular sentiment and contributed to a vibrant mid-twentieth century arts scene that still resonates today, long after the regimes that paid for them have disappeared. As in Egypt, despite state patronage, artists' communities became petri dishes for other kinds of political change, over which the governments that sponsored them had little ultimate control.

Mubarak and the Dissolution of State Control: 1981–2011

Although Nasser and Sadat both pandered to intellectuals, Mubarak took things a step further by appointing abstract painter Farouk Hosny as his minister of culture, where he remained for twenty-four years. This maximized Mubarak's ability to control the arts, by directing funding and overseeing state-run exhibition spaces. The co-option was far from complete, however. As calculating as Mubarak's art patronage was, there were bigger forces at play that undermined his efforts—namely, the global information revolution, and the rise of a private regional art market that was closely linked to it, loosened the binds of state patronage.

In the twentieth century heyday of state-sponsored art in the Arab world, there was no art market to speak of and few, if any, galleries. Most artists were teachers who sold works on the side, and were not dependent on buyers. By the turn of the twenty-first century, this had begun to change. By the second decade of the new century, it was all but upended: satellite television, streaming video, and social media sites enabled young artists who had emerged since the late 1980s to see events that touched others' lives in immediate terms. Contemporary artists became more dynamic and able to react more spontaneously, and with wider reach. Also, far greater access to private funding became available to the young artist, thanks to a proliferation of galleries across the region. Direct criticism of government might be hazardous to an artist's physical safety, but it was no longer a direct threat to his pocket book.

Collectors in the wealthy Arab states of the Gulf were a major force in the creation of this private market. Dubai emerged as the Middle East's most important market for art. Scores of galleries opened in its industrial and financial centers, and Christie's and local galleries such as Ayyam conducted auctions.

In some cases, these museums and galleries specifically sought out politically relevant works from Arab artists.[15] Part of the impetus for such collections was historical; after a tumultuous few decades, institutions saw collecting art that documented and commented on these events as being part of their public duty. Also, with a diversified economy and large expatriate populations taking advantage of the region's wealth and growing engagement in global commerce, public opinion began to demand an arena in which to view such artworks. In the Gulf, several museums were established, including Doha's Mathaf: Arab Museum of Modern Art (established 2010), Abu Dhabi's Guggenheim (established 2006), and several others. A painting that might have been censored in Egypt—or which an Egyptian artist might have been reluctant to even create at home—found a warm reception in Abu Dhabi, Doha, or Dubai.

By the first few years of the twenty-first century, independent cultural venues had also started appearing in cities in other parts of the Arab world, and especially in Cairo. Sakia El Sawy (Sawy Culture Wheel), which opened in 2003, became one of the most popular. The Sakia, as it is commonly known, was perhaps the first non-government-affiliated cultural center in the country. It was founded by Mohamed Abdel-Moneim El Sawy, whose father is an acclaimed novelist and a former minister of culture. Within a short period of time the Sakia was hosting daily events, including concerts, puppet shows, and art performances, drawing 20,000 monthly visitors by 2009.[16]

Another milestone was the establishment in 1998 of the Townhouse Gallery by a Canadian expatriate in Cairo named William Wells. The gallery hosted groundbreaking and socially engaging exhibitions. Writing for the Middle East Institute in 2015, Maria Golia noted that the gallery "opened its doors at a time when the state exercised mind-numbing control over cultural venues and artistic output so that its establishment was tantamount to a political act."[17] Having been labeled a Zionist enterprise in the Arabic press, the gallery was repeatedly raided in its early years; in time, though, the proliferation of art galleries meant that it was no longer the sole target of negative attention.

The Rise of the New Media

In Egypt in particular, there was another factor that, perhaps coincidentally, undermined Mubarak's strategies for managing expression even more. Through the 1980s and 1990s, modern art gave way to contemporary practices, and a new generation of artists emerged whose media were harder to control through government funding and state promotion. Photography and video became more widely used, conceptual approaches made their debut, digital devices and media became available, and the dwindling cost of transport meant that complex works could be created or assembled abroad, and could be shipped internationally to be loaned for exhibitions. These developments gradually loosened the government's control over the arts industry. Cutting-edge, vibrant forms of expression were now being created outside the patronage of the state.

Among this new generation of contemporary artists is the sculptor Moataz Nasr (1961–) who has, since the early years of the twenty-first century, created socially conscious works, including *An Ear of Mud, Another of Dough*. Made of clay and dough ears, it symbolizes the deafness of the ruling class's ears to the plight of most Egyptians. Nasr also established the group Darb 1718 in 2008, dedicated to promoting social change through art.

The degree of freedom that artists had obtained around the turn of the century may not have seemed like a threat to Mubarak at the time. But the astute connoisseur could have read something of the future in the works that were emerging from Egypt toward the end of the first decade of the twenty-first century.

Indeed, many of the region's artists had an uncanny ability to capture the mood of their country and even foresee its problems. Cairo-born painter Walid Ebeid's (1970–) 2005 work *Outside Prisoners* depicts men, women and children, money in hand, clamoring to buy bread, where there clearly isn't enough for all of them. The perspective is from within a stall with prison-like bars, stopping them from making the payment. Little do those in the back know that there are just six or seven loaves of bread left. Another of Ebeid's works, the 2007 painting *Under Investigation,* depicts a young man, possibly in his twenties, sitting on a stool with his back to the viewer. The man's white t-shirt is lifted, unveiling bruises and others signs of torture and beating. In Ebeid's work we see a much more contemporary strain of Arab art that directly antagonizes the state: claims of torture, especially in the last years of Mubarak's reign, contributed to the outburst of anger that occurred in January 2011. Huda Lutfi, Professor Emerita of Arab Cultural History at the American University in Cairo, created a work in 2008 titled *Democracy Is Coming*. The work features the familiar face of Egyptian diva Umm Kulthum with a halo over her head and an inscription that reads "democracy is coming," as military planes fly above.

The quickening pace of change of communications technology during this period further undermined Mubarak's methods at control. Social media gave artists vastly greater and more immediate visibility, and it also allowed them to market their works directly, rather than going through a gallery. In some instances galleries might shun politically sensitive works, but artists could sell such pieces directly to collectors from their studios. This was the case for the Barjeel Art Foundation, which I founded in 2010 in the United Arab Emirates, when it acquired Jeffar Khaldi's *Good Stamp* (2009), which depicts Gulf Arab officials seated in a meeting hall with images of women that look like Lebanese crooner and sex symbol Haifa Wehbe, or American actress Pamela Anderson,

Figure 9. Jeffar Khaldi, *Good Stamp,* 2009. (Image courtesy of Barjeel Art Foundation and Capital D Studio.)

loitering in their minds and bodies. Further, in addition to the established Cairo galleries, a number of underground pop-up shows started appearing in the city.[18] These pop-up shows were hosted in artists' apartments and other common spaces, where they could be free of any state-imposed restrictions.

The later Mubarak years witnessed a further marginalization of the creative community in Egypt, affecting writers, journalists, and artists. But marginalization, in this new era of private art markets and amplifying technology, was far from neutralization. Sometimes, it was the opposite. The Mubarak regime might have heeded the hints of popular discontent about food prices, for example, and made incremental reforms that could have headed off a wider crisis of government legitimacy. Instead, Mubarak and his ministry of culture ignored signals from the fine art sphere, and overshadowed the work of socially conscious artists like Ebeid with inoffensive abstract works, ever widening the gulf between the government and the people.

In the years leading to the 2011 uprising, there was a final, significant change in the Egyptian art world: graffiti art became legitimized. It was a development spurred in large part by artists under 30, who did not always conform to more traditional expectations of what art should be. For them, Cairo itself became a canvas, and new media meant that their imagination was no longer limited by the physical constraints of older forms. It was this development that more than anything else heralded a new era for Egyptian artists, who were beginning to engage directly with the broad swaths of the public through art that was overtly political.

The Uprisings

It's impossible to know exactly to what degree art contributed to the actual outbreak of the Egyptian revolution, but it certainly anticipated the anger that propelled it. And when the uprisings of 2011 erupted, artists were primed as never before to take part in the turmoil.

Take the case of Nasr, the Egyptian multimedia artist. Where his creations had tackled social and political issues in oblique and symbolic (though still provocative) ways in the middle of the first decade of the twenty-first century, they now became explicit commentaries on the revolution. In 2012, he created *El Shaab* (The People)—twenty-five ceramic figures representing characters from the 2011 uprising. It is part of this sculpture, depicting a dark event that happened on the streets, which sets the work apart. On a separate shelf, but part of the same work, Nasr placed figures representing three police officers tugging at a young woman and dragging her along the street so that her bra was exposed. This was the famous "Girl in the Blue Bra," whose violent beating at the hands and feet of the police, in Cairo in December 2011, was captured by *Al-Masry Al-Youm* photographer Ahmed al-Masry. In 2012, thousands of Egyptians still treated this horrific scene as a rallying point for their continued protests calling for revolutionary demands to be met, and for the Supreme Council of Armed

Figure 10. Moataz Nasr, *El Shaab* (*The People*), 2012. (Image courtesy of Barjeel Art Foundation and the Singapore Art Museum.)

Forces—the military body that was then running Egypt—to hand over power to a civilian head of state through democratic elections.

The same image of the Girl in the Blue Bra was used by Egyptian artist Nermine Hammam (1967–) in a photo series that juxtaposes iconic images from the revolution with serene images drawn from Japanese landscape painting. Morocco's Zakaria Ramhani (1983–) also references this scene in his piece *You Were My Only Love* (2012); Palestine's Shadi Alzaqzouq featured women's underwear and protest, perhaps inspired by the same moment, in his painting *After Washing* (2012).[19]

In 2012, at the height of the presidential election season, Egypt-born Australian artist Raafat Ishak (1967–) created *Nomination for the Presidency of the New Egypt*. The artwork is a fictional manifesto by a presidential candidate created on a series of fiberboard panels that unfold like a scroll. Some Egyptians laid the blame for the deterioration of the economy on decisions taken under the country's socialist president, Nasser. In that regard, the manifesto by the candidate comes with a radical promise to dismantle the Aswan High Dam in order to reintroduce the annual flooding of the Nile, alluding "to a metaphoric deconstruction of Egypt's turbulent history and a political rebirth of the country."[20]

Some artists, especially graffiti artists, also had an even more direct role in the Egyptian revolution. Savvy with digital media and deeply invested in revolutionary goals, they were able to articulate the people's demands, or the chance to realize them, into a symbol. Ganzeer's *Mask of Freedom* (2011)—depicting a figure with a ball gag and blindfold—was a potent message about the lack of freedom of expression, which was prominently circulated in the beginning of that year. In a Cairo protest in which I participated in 2012, activists handed out spray cans and a stencil created by El Zeft. Hundreds of people used them to paint phrases like "We won't forget you" and "Glory to the martyrs."

And in the first three years following the 2011 uprising, Mohamed Mahmoud Street, which is adjacent to the old campus of the American University in Cairo, served as a shrine to the fallen icons of the uprising. It featured images of Khalid Said, whose death in 2010 was one of the sparks for revolt. A mural of Coptic icon Mina Danial reaching out to Muslim cleric Sheikh Emad Effat (both shot and killed in 2011 protests) was interlaced with politically charged phrases. Writing in 2012, critic and blogger Soraya Morayef noted that "the Mohamed Mahmoud wall remains the most powerful tribute to the revolution."[21] These works resonated with passersby who would stop and take photos, recognizing some figures, and the street came close to becoming a tourist attraction in its own right. It was a site for protests, as well. In November 2011, it erupted in clashes as security forces attempted to violently disperse a crowd of two hundred protesting family members of those who had been killed in earlier demonstrations. Similarly, following the death of seventy-two football fans in Port Said in February 2012, Mohamed Mahmoud once again became a rallying point with paintings depicting the fallen fans. Perhaps eager to turn a page, at three o'clock on a September 2012 morning, the Egyptian government dispatched workers to paint over the graffiti on Mohamed Mahmoud street.[22]

Figure 11. Ganzeer, *DIE WAHRHEIT IS KONKRET*, 2012. (Image courtesy of Barjeel Art Foundation and From Here to Fame.)

Regional Reverberations

The Arab uprisings featured in works of artists outside Egypt and across the region and in the diaspora. Beirut-born Ali Cherri (1976–) lived through Lebanon's devastating civil war and is considered to be a promising artist of his generation. His 2014–16 aerial maps print series *Paysages Tremblants* (Trembling Landscapes) is an attempt to capture the underlying tensions in Middle Eastern and North African cities, including Beirut, Damascus, and Algiers (an entire set has been acquired by the Guggenheim Museum in New York). Perhaps Cherri's work that most obviously references the Arab uprisings is *I Carry My Flame* (2011). It was created mere months after Tunisian street vendor Mohamed Bouazizi set himself alight, thereby kick-starting a series of convulsions that have since rocked the Arab world. In that artwork, eight stills are taken from a YouTube video of an unknown individual (not Bouazizi) who embarked on an act of self-immolation. Even the process of creating these works using serigraphy or silkscreen printing, where ink is forced through a fine screen onto the paper beneath, reflects the violence and duress that an individual set on fire experiences. Finally, *Le Grand Vide/Statue Assad* features a 2011 photograph of the remains of a sculpture of Syria's Hafez al-Assad that was pulled down in the early days of the Syrian uprising. The name of the work is also remarkable, denoting the void that was created following the collapse of the regime in some parts of Syria, a void that extremist groups were all too willing to fill.

The politically minded artists of the mid-twentieth century produced fine, powerful works of social commentary, but they had never so directly attacked a ruling regime. Even works that antagonized the government had nothing like the immediacy and relevance of those that commented on and contributed to the Arab uprisings. The artists of the uprisings also engaged a completely different demographic, those who would generally not be included in the political discourse of the past.

The brief free political space created following the Egyptian uprising also allowed for more politically engaging works to be shown in public. After years of making underground art, many artists came to the forefront following the revolution. Art exhibitions were more daring and thought-provoking, and attracted a more diverse crowd. In fact, art openings became places for nonartist activists to meet each other and discuss the latest political developments. The space was so vibrant that some artists in Cairo used their apartments to host semi-underground pop-up exhibitions that lasted for the evening.

In the wake of the uprisings, the Sakia also became a venue for political engagement, such as when it hosted Alaa al-Aswany, the novelist, in February 2012, drawing hundreds of men and women. Aswany began that talk with a moment of silence for Egypt's martyrs and railed against the "unconstitutional and illegal" rule of the military council.

But the fact that such art existed and played a role in the uprisings should not be confused with the idea that the artists now enjoyed more safety, any more than any of the other revolutionaries did.

Figure 12. Ali Cherri, *I Carry My Flame*, 2011. (Image courtesy of Barjeel Art Foundation and Capital D Studio.)

Figure 13. Reda Abdelrahman, *Revolution*, 2012. (Image courtesy of Barjeel Art Foundation.)

A famously tragic example is that of Ahmed Basiony (1978–2011), a thirty-three-year-old Egyptian avant-garde visual artist who was shot dead by sniper fire on January 28, 2011, three days after the start of the Tahrir Square protests.

Basiony's artistic career—which was not, for the most part, expressly political—was cut short by the revolution, which he deeply believed in. On January 26, two days prior to his death, he posted what became his last public statement on his Facebook page. "Please, O Father, O Mother, O Youth, O Student, O Citizen, O Senior, and O more," Basiony wrote, "You know this is our last chance for our dignity, the last chance to change the regime that has lasted the past thirty years. Go down to the streets, and revolt, bring your food, your clothes, your water, masks and tissues, and a vinegar bottle, and believe me, there is but one very small step left. . . . If they want war, we want peace, and I will practice proper restraint until the end, to regain my nation's dignity."[23]

Following his killing, Basiony "quickly became a potent symbol to protestors of the sacrifices they had to endure in the course of their struggle."[24] *Al-Masry Al-Youm*, a popular newspaper, included Basiony's photo on the front page of its now historic post-uprising edition under the headline, "The Flowers that Bloomed in Egypt's Garden."[25]

Basiony was shot for protesting, not for his art. Posthumously, however, it becomes more difficult to draw a line between the two. He was an artist who fully committed himself to his beliefs. Those who appreciated his art evidently recognized this: four months after his death, following the removal of the Mubarak regime, Basiony's video installation *Thirty Days of Running in Place* became Egypt's official entry to the fifty-fourth Venice Biennale, in 2011. The installation was produced in 2010 and included a series of videos that depicted a man (the artist) wrapped in a sealed suit, jogging in place for an hour every day for a month, collecting and visually projecting information about the movements of his body onto a screen. Although Basiony's work wasn't initially received as political, in Venice it was shown alongside video footage of him participating in the revolution, thereby adding a political overtone.

Art and the Faltering Uprisings

As the uprisings soured, the dangers artists faced from any number of adversaries overtook the other factors that contributed to their newfound boldness. As early as 2012, as the high hopes of the Egyptian revolution began to get more complicated—if not actually fade—the art scene began to lose some of its verve and focus. Artists became more calculated in their risks. In despair or disillusionment or fear, some turned away from direct action in politics completely.

An early example of the casualties of this changing mood is the effort of the Barjeel Art Foundation to acquire a revolution-themed neon work by Moataz Nasr, *The People Want the Fall of the Regime.* This phrase was made popular during the Egyptian uprising earlier in 2011, as people took to the streets demanding the downfall of the Mubarak government. In fact, this work was so controversial that no Egyptian shipping firm would agree to ship it to the Gulf. On June 6, 2012 we received the following email. I have removed references to the sender to protect the person's identity.

> *Dear _____*
>
> *I would like to update you on the status of Moataz Nasr Neon Light work.*
>
> *I have deliberately halted the shipping of this long overdue artwork for a serious strategic reason—my safety.*
>
> *The piece is very controversial at this time in Egypt to be shipped out through such channel to the Emirates. Our people at the airport have checked the water and advised us to either wait or to have someone take it as luggage while travelling. The statement written on it "El Shaab Yourid Iskat el Nezam" could be seen as me (name removed), an Egyptian citizen, as trying to incite revolt in the UAE. As you may know, the UAE are very important for Egypt—politically and economically.*
>
> *So bear with us. If you do come in the near future, best you or Sultan take it on your flight.*

After several tries, the work finally arrived in the Emirates in November 2013. In order to avoid customs officials discerning the content of the Arabic words that make up the phrase, they were put into four separate packages. The label on the packaging from Egypt read "LIGHTING PEICE" (sic).

The episode was a harbinger. Egyptian authorities still deeply feared free expression, though at this stage and in this instance they were more concerned about the artist's effect on foreign relations. The shipper understood that the Egyptian government might find the content of the artwork objectionable in its own right, or they might desire to censor it in order to erase any implication of Egyptians exporting revolutionary ideas around the region. By 2016, Sisi's Egypt was experiencing a wintry freeze of political artistic expression. In the post-2011 period, successive, short-lived Egyptian administrations caught in the maelstrom and consumed with crisis management paid no heed to artists, initially allowing for an unprecedented degree of openness and artistic expression. However, since the authorities largely control the levers of media in Egypt, they were able to filter or promote any artists depending on whether they considered them to be antagonistic or friendly to the government, such as denying them the opportunities to be featured on local television or newspapers. The state had lost a lot of ground with all the changes of the last two decades, in terms of technology, markets for art, and boldness on the part of the artists. But it still had some tricks up its sleeve, and with its involvement in media, its promotion of fear, and its intimidation of artists, it had quite a bit of power, perhaps more than artists at the time realized.

Figure 14. Kader Attia, *DemoNcracy*, 2009. (Image courtesy of Barjeel Art Foundation and Galerie Krinzinger.)

The State Tightens Its Vise

With the rise of Sisi, this trend has taken firmer hold day by day, to the point that some of the sheen has been lost from overtly revolutionary art. The romance of the so-called Arab Spring—a name that was hardly used in the countries where it supposedly occurred—means that revolutionary Egyptian artists could make a living selling their works abroad. The idea has proved noxious, however, and many revolutionary artists avoided any obvious commercial benefit from revolutionary themes. As the political tide turned, many artists abandoned the themes of 2011–12, some turning to more personal, abstract, or subtle subjects.

There have still been isolated instances of state criticism, and certain genres that have remained freer than others, such as editorial cartoons.[26] *JOKE*, a 2013 poster mocking Sisi, by Egyptian graffiti artist Nazeer, was modeled on Shepard Fairey's "HOPE" poster of Barack Obama. However, making fun of leaders can carry hefty fines or even a jail term. In 2015, twenty-two-year-old Amr Nohan was sentenced to three years in jail for sharing a photo of Sisi with Mickey Mouse ears on Facebook.

Sisi's regime has attacked other art movements head-on. In December 2015, it shut Townhouse for two months along with the adjacent theatre and barred Aswany, the author, from public speaking.[27]

The revolutionary fervor of artists, like other activists, has certainly been stifled. Some left art altogether. El Zeft, the artist who led the guerrilla muralists who painted the NDP headquarters, is himself an exemplary case. Five years after his daring graffiti assault, he has been drafted into the army, and is no longer active as an artist. Indeed, Sisi has made it very dangerous for anyone to attempt anything remotely resembling El Zeft's 2012 feat. The NDP headquarters have been torn down, along with the graffiti, and the piece—which had a national impact at the time—is lost, and is now hardly mentioned in Egypt.

Other artists chose self-exile, such as Ganzeer, who now lives in Los Angeles. Ganzeer, the artist who made the famous poster *Mask of Freedom* (2011), has continued his provocations with *Who's Afraid of Art?* (2014), which depicts Sisi in uniform, his face replaced by a rabbit staring from a television screen. The image was heavily shared on social media.

There is an inescapable feeling that something essential has been lost from the art world because of Sisi's repression. The raucous, pure energy of 2011–13 is gone. Speaking to artists who still practice, one feels their disillusionment, and their creeping sense of guilt when they benefit from art that references a revolution that has all but failed.

And yet, many continue to create. This fact gets to the paradox at the heart of Arab art in the wake of the uprisings. Artists' moods are as dismal as anyone's. But as a critic who watches art closely and communicates with artists all the time, it's impossible not to feel that something in Egyptian art went through an irreversible transformation during the uprisings, in terms of connecting directly with the masses. In those days of tumult artists got a vision of their power and

Figure 15. Nazeer, *Joke*, 2013. (Image courtesy of Barjeel Art Foundation and From Here to Fame.)

possibilities. I believe that Sisi's ham-handed suffocation of the art world is temporary. The government is less adept at propaganda than ever before, and artists have more tools than ever to spread dissenting messages. When the time is right, we will again see artists at the forefront of the next wave of change, whatever that may be. Their role has been diminished, but they continue to give a voice to civil society, despite the challenges of being blocked and silenced by state media.

Conclusion

Artists, far from being solely associated with the elite or even the ruling authorities in the Arab world, have shown that they identify with popular causes and even challenge elites. They have a long tradition of providing critiques of Arab regimes—with subtlety in times of great repression, with unabashed directness in times of tumult. With the symbols their media afford them, they have often been able to express the political desires of their societies' peoples in a way that has been almost impossible through any other channels.

With the uprisings of 2011, Egyptian and Arab artists became far more deeply involved in politics—both in their art and by participating as demonstrators—and the lines between elite and popular art became blurry. But there was also continuity with the role that artists have filled since at least the early part of the twentieth century: then as now, they gave voice to the people when other means failed.

Even as the vise of authoritarian control is once more closing on artists, their role remains extremely important. Political art is one of the few outlets available, along with protesting, which is increasingly untenable. One could argue that, since art is far less disruptive than protesting in the streets, it is more of a pressure-releasing valve than a fomenter of change. As the examples in this essay have shown, however, the distinction between those two functions is oftentimes remarkably murky. Pondering which is the "real" role of art is more useful as an evaluation of a state policy than in understanding art's actual significance.

Even when it is state-sponsored, art has been successful in reflecting popular sentiments ignored or repressed by Arab governments. Artists, often reflecting the pulse of general society, act as a bridge between the common man and the ears of those who will listen. As such, Arab governments such as Egypt's, even if they were unwilling to become dramatically more democratic, might have treated art not only as a cultural asset but also as a measure of popular sentiment. Instead, most reacted to art with fear. And in the last two to three years, this fear has become more and more reactionary and stifling, especially in Egypt.

But artists keep the flame of independent thought alive in dark times. As the Arab uprisings seem to have faltered and lost their way, art still has potential and value—not just for its aesthetics but also for its relevance to material developments. Whether as a catalyst for change, a space for dreaming about possibilities, or a mirror of the fears and violence that have afflicted the region, art continues to serve as a space where Arabs rehearse and explore their political aspirations.

Notes

1. In this essay, I've limited my discussion to painting and sculpture, and especially fine arts, except in the cases during the uprisings when the border between fine and popular arts became more blurred. Film and music, of course, account for an enormous proportion of Arab artistic output, but they deserve a different and longer treatment than is possible in this limited space. Though some of the themes related to the visual arts that I explore in this essay are also relevant to film and music, the history of the latter genres has been far more complicated and censored.

2. The history of political engagement by artists in Egypt and across the Arab world is well-documented by scholars such as Patrick Kane in his book *The Politics of Art in Modern Egypt: Aesthetics, Ideology and Nation-Building* (London: I.B. Tauris, 2013).

3. The Egyptian monarchs of the twentieth century were Kings Fuad I (1922–36), Farouk (1936–52), and Fuad II (1952–53); the Art and Liberty Group was active during the reign of King Farouk.

4. Much of the information in this paragraph is drawn from Don LaCoss, "Art And Liberty: Surrealism in Egypt," *Communicating Vessels* 21 (2009–10): 28–33.

5. This passage and several other portions of this chapter draw heavily from my previously published essay, "Egypt's Long History of Activist Artists," Tahrir Institute for Middle East Policy, October 13, 2014, https://timep.org/egypts-political-art-history/.

6. Kane, *The Politics of Art in Modern Egypt*, 49.

7. Fatenn Mostafa Kanafani, "The Permanent Revolution: From Cairo to Paris with the Egyptian Surrealists," *Mada Masr,* November 11, 2016, http://www.madamasr.com/en/2016/11/11/feature/culture/the-permanent-revolution-from-cairo-to-paris-with-the-egyptian-surrealists/.

8. Mona L. Russell, ed., *Egypt,* (Santa Barbara, Calif.: ABC-CLIO, 2013), 256.

9. See Hamed Ewais, *Nasser and the Nationalisation of the Canal* (1957). In the collection of Mathaf: Arab Museum of Modern Art, Doha, Qatar.

10. See Hamed Ewais, *Protector of Life* (1967–68). In the collection of the Barjeel Art Foundation, Sharjah, United Arab Emirates.

11. Jessica Winegar, *Creative Reckonings: The Politics of Art and Culture in Contemporary Egypt* (Stanford, Calif.: Stanford University Press, 2006), 270.

12. Menna Taher, "The Life of Inji Aflatoun, an Artist and a Rebel," *Ahram Online*, September 18, 2011, http://english.ahram.org.eg/NewsContent/5/25/21577/Arts--Culture/Visual-Art/The-life-of-Inji-Aflatoun,-an-artist-and-a-rebel-.aspx; and Sara Elkamel, "Between Art and Activism: Inji Efflatoun's Life Revisited," *Ahram Online*, January 6, 2013, http://english.ahram.org.eg/NewsContent/5/25/61853/Arts--Culture/Visual-Art/Between-art-and-activism-Inji-Efflatoun%E2%80%99s-life-rev.aspx.

13. Associated Press, "Writer Shunned for His Views on Israel," *New York Times*, November 10, 2002, http://www.nytimes.com/2002/11/10/international/middleeast/egyptian-writer-shunned-for-his-views-on-israel.html.

14. Amina Menia, "Enclosed," personal website, http://www.aminamenia.com/?browse=Enclosed, accessed November 23, 2016.

15. However, it must be mentioned that such collections generally avoided presenting works that addressed taboo subjects in the local political scene. In March 2012, two artworks were removed from Art Dubai, the Middle East's most prominent art fair, which was established in 2007. One of the works, *After Washing* by Paris-based Palestinian artist Shadi Alzaqzouq depicted a female protester holding male underwear daubed with the word "irhal," meaning "leave" in Arabic, which was chanted during the Arab uprisings. The other artwork that was taken down was *You Were My Only Love* by Moroccan artist Zakaria Ramhani, which depicted an Egyptian woman who was beaten by the police. (These works are discussed later in this chapter.) Colin Simpson, "Two Works Removed from Art Dubai Fair," *The National*, March 23, 2012, www.thenational.ae/news/uae-news/two-works-removed-from-art-dubai-fair.

16. "El Sawy Culture Wheel," *Majalla*, May 25, 2009, http://eng.majalla.com/2009/05/article554243.

17. Maria Golia, "Cairo's Townhouse Gallery: Social Transformation through Art," Middle East Institute, April 27, 2015, http://www.mei.edu/content/at/cairo's-townhouse-gallery-social-transformation-through-art.

18. An example of the pop up art spaces was the Nile Sunset Annex in Cairo that was started in 2012. Elisabeth Jaquette, "Nile Sunset Annex: An Artist-Run Gallery Space in Cairo," *Ibraaz,* February 28, 2013, http://www.ibraaz.org/news/54.

19. In another example of the limits on free expression in the new regional art scene, both Ramhani and Alzaqzouq were censored for their pieces at the 2012 edition of Art Dubai, as described in an earlier footnote.

20. Suheyla Takesh, description of the "Al-Seef" exhibit on the website of the Contemporary Art Platform, 2015, http://capkuwait.com/2015/al-seef/.

21. Soraya Morayef, "Return to Tahrir: Two Years and Graffiti of the Martyrs," *Suzeeinthecity*, December 29, 2012, https://suzeeinthecity.wordpress.com/2012/12/29/return-to-tahrir-two-years-and-graffiti-of-the-martyrs/. Egyptian graffiti has received significant coverage in high-profile international media outlets, one reason why I do not go into greater detail describing it here. Morayef's blog, *Suzeeinthecity*, has featured some of the best reporting on graffiti that I have seen.

22. Soraya Morayef, "The Mohamed Mahmoud Mural: Whitewashing Cairo's Memory of the Past," Atlantic Council, September 21, 2012, http://www.atlanticcouncil.org/blogs/mena source/the-mohamed-mahmoud-mural-whitewashing-cairos-memory-of-the-past.

23. Translation courtesy of Universes in Universe. Translation differs slightly on Basiony's website, http://www.ahmedbasiony.com/about.html.

24. Ahram Online, "54th International Venice Biennale Pays Tribute to Ahmed Basiouny, Egyptian Artist and Revolutionary Martyr," *Ahram* Online, May 15, 2011, http://english.ahram. org.eg/NewsContent/5/0/12164/Arts--Culture/0/th-International-Venice-Biennale-pays-tribute-to-A.aspx.

25. Mohsn Hosni, "The Flowers that Bloomed in Egypt's Garden" (Arabic), *Al-Masry Al-Youm*, April 26, 2011, http://www.almasryalyoum.com/news/details/127909.

26. See Jonathan Guyer's chapter in this book.

27. Marcia Lynx Qualey, "Egypt Shuts Down Novelist Alaa al-Aswany's Public Event and Media Work," *The Guardian*, December 11, 2015, https://www.theguardian.com/books/2015/dec/11/egypt-shuts-down-novelist-alaa-al-aswanys-public-event-and-media-work.

13

All Truth Is Worth Publishing

Mada Masr and the Fight for Free Speech in Egypt

LAURA C. DEAN

As an authoritarian cold front settles over Egypt, a newsroom full of left-leaning journalists provides one of the last redoubts for the revolutionary ideals of 2011. The online newspaper *Mada Masr* was founded in 2013 by veterans of several envelope-pushing publications. Since then, it has distinguished itself not only for its bold reporting and experimental style, but also for management based on consensus, and the pioneering of a business model that relies on revenue sources beyond advertising. The newspaper has proved exceptionally resilient to efforts to silence it, weathering the arrest and imprisonment of some of its editors and contributors. And with a fast-growing Arabic section, *Mada* is more popular than ever. A new law that would drastically restrain digital media may yet prove to be *Mada*'s undoing. Yet the paper remains fully committed to continuing its truth-telling, and has resolved to resist the ongoing crackdown on speech. The story of *Mada Masr* provides a rare case study of a grassroots institution almost wholly sprung from Egypt's uprising.

It is almost difficult to recall now, but following the uprisings of 2011, people in Egypt began to divide historical time into two periods: before the revolution and after the revolution. In the latter, all manner of things seemed possible. It was at the tail end of this euphoric time, in the early summer of 2013, that a group of young Egyptian journalists set out to build an online news site. They called it *Mada Masr*—"mada" means "scope" in Arabic and "Masr" is the Arabic word for Egypt. Since then, protests have been outlawed and many of the architects of the 2011 uprisings and of *Mada* itself have been thrown in jail or left the country. Yet the principles that drove people into the streets in 2011 survive in *Mada*'s newsroom. Its staff represent a hodgepodge of left-leaning views, but the guiding principle is one of equality: providing a voice for those who don't have one in Egypt's classist, Cairo-centric society, and highlighting injustices, no matter who perpetrates them.

As platforms for free expression and dissent have dropped away, *Mada*'s website has become one of the only places where those still brave enough to publicly express ideas can do so. The publication's English articles have served as a window on Egypt for many foreign journalists and analysts, and its Arabic coverage is expanding. But in a country of ninety million people, it is a difficult and unfolding proposition to assess the impact of a small group of idealistic journalists.

Mada is the leading representative of a post-2011 Egyptian movement to invent new types of organizing and political expression following the ouster of Hosni Mubarak. It remains one of the sole surviving public manifestations of what was once a large revolutionary wave of establishments. Most have folded due to new legal restrictions, state pressure, budget cuts, or despair. From its inception, *Mada*'s creators sought to invent a new kind of media institution, steeped in the values of the 2011 uprising—to embody those values in its coverage, as well as in its corporate ethos, making editorial as well as business decisions based on consensus. The paper attempted to lead socially as well as journalistically, by example of its work and by its day-to-day behavior as an independent collective. It often published its newsroom discussions, showing that its commitment to transparency extended to itself, as well. As a media organization, rather than, say, a political party or an artists' collective, *Mada* was unique in waging its struggle to create new media forms and collectively organize almost entirely in public.

At first, *Mada*'s readership was limited to those who spoke English—an educated, left-leaning audience that was sympathetic to the ideals of Egypt's 2011 revolution. But since its Arabic section came online in 2013 and as independent outlets and dissident voices in Egypt's mainstream media have gone silent, that community has grown. Its readership and contributors represent the broad coalition of the secular revolutionaries—Islamist-leaning Egyptians have their own outlets.[1] What began as a community geared specifically toward a generation of revolutionary youth has expanded since 2013 to include anyone looking for an independent account of what has transpired in Egypt over the three years since *Mada*'s founding.

At first, in part because it was an English language publication, *Mada* was largely ignored by officialdom. However, its recent proliferation of Arabic copy and the hiring of prominent human-rights-defender-turned-investigative-journalist Hossam Bahgat have catapulted it onto the government's radar, and scrutiny has only increased since Bahgat was detained for two days and interrogated in November 2015. Since much of the rest of the media is either under direct state control or is run by businessmen who fear falling afoul of the state or support its policies, when *Mada* does feature in mainstream Egyptian news outlets, it is often, though not always, with a negative cast.

The purpose of this research is to offer an oral history of the first three years of *Mada*'s trajectory. Researchers and policymakers interested in collective media, new media, Egyptian freedom of expression, and political speech will find much grist for further study in *Mada* and its deep online archive, which is full of attempts at self-documentation in addition to its news coverage and opinion pieces. Going forward, *Mada* may serve as a bellwether—or a casualty—of Egyptian President Abdel Fattah el-Sisi's unprecedented level of oppression.

Egyptian Media: From State Control to a Smokescreen of Semi-Freedom

Until the mid-1990s, every newspaper on the newsstand was owned and published by the government. The same was true of television channels. But in what was the twilight of the Mubarak era (though the world did not know it yet), the aging dictator began to loosen some of the laws governing freedom of the press. Adel Iskandar, an assistant professor at Simon Fraser University who has written extensively about Egypt's media, has called this "the freedom-of-the-press smokescreen" whereby the regime sought to demonstrate to international governments and human rights groups that it had a free press, while maintaining heavy censorship and clear red lines that extended to the president's family and the military, among other topics.[2] For instance, in 2007 Ibrahim Eissa, cofounder of *Al-Dustour*, one of Egypt's leading independent papers prior to 2011, was sentenced to a year in prison for writing about Mubarak's failing health. The sentence was suspended but the incident served as a reminder to Egypt's media that its freedom was conditional.

Nevertheless, private newspapers and satellite channels mushroomed. One unforeseen consequence of this loosening was that it attracted enterprising journalists who saw space in which to critique the government. The regime chose to ignore most of them, determining that they, and their readership, were small fry. "There is a sense that there isn't really a reading public, or a perception that Egypt doesn't read, referring to the non-elites and nonbourgeois society," explained Iskandar. "One could fairly convincingly make the case that Mubarak didn't see *Al-Masry Al-Youm* and *Al-Dustour* [two of Egypt's most widely-read privately owned newspapers] as threatening—even though they were critical, they represent a small constituency."[3] Ignored by the regime, these papers grew in reach and influence and began to take greater risks. The first decade of the century was fraught with labor strikes and more overt non-Islamist opposition to the regime than the country had seen in the preceding decades. In 2005, the Kefaya movement, led by a broad-based coalition, protested the corruption of the Mubarak regime and the expected succession of the president's son, Gamal. Nobel Prize winner Mohamed ElBaradei returned to Egypt in 2010 calling for political change. It was an environment of growing political boldness.

In 2009, Fatemah Farag, a sharp and idealistic journalist, was asked by *Al-Masry Al-Youm*'s leadership to establish an English section for the paper. Until then it had published an English page consisting of poor translations of selected Arabic articles. Farag proposed an independent English section that offered high-quality original journalism in addition to drawing on the Arabic content. She hoped this would also influence the journalistic standards of the Arabic edition, which could be partisan or sensationalist at times, and bring a sense of balance and objectivity to a wider audience of Egyptian readers.

But such ambition, particularly one that contained an implicit critique, did not go down easily with others at the paper. The head editor of the Arabic paper felt that Farag should report to him and was dismayed at the autonomy the English section enjoyed. Meanwhile, the paper's owners also felt entitled to weigh in on editorial decisions. "The owners of the paper were used to intervening," Farag said, explaining that it was standard practice at the Arabic paper, but she saw things differently: "We had set up quarterly targets. My argument was, you can change that, that's your right, and then you can see if I'm still the person you want for this, but you cannot pick up the phone and ask me to do something every day. That is outside the scope of what we've agreed on."[4]

Many former *Al-Masry Al-Youm* staff members recall the conflict that flared over the coverage of the Egypt-Algeria soccer match in Khartoum in November 2009. Clashes broke out between fans, after which some Algerians reportedly threw stones at a bus full of Egyptians. The Egyptian press went wild. Rumors skimmed up the Nile—none of them true—of Egyptian fans, forced to leave their bus, undertaking a harrowing march on foot, guarded by the Sudanese army. Instead of contributing to what she and her staff saw as "war mongering" and "hate speech," Farag chose to wait a day or two, and then wrote what she considered a balanced account of the events. The paper's owners accused her of "not reporting the Egyptian people's struggles" and denounced her in an op-ed in the Arabic section. Farag fired back with an editorial calling their war cries "unethical journalism." The matter was eventually dropped but left a residue of resentment with both parties.

At the time, there were no online media outlets in Egypt covering current affairs in English, and Farag's was the first English-language website started by a privately owned media company. This gave Egyptian journalists looking to write for a larger audience, and potentially one beyond Egypt, a wider platform. "It allowed Egyptian journalists to tell Egypt's story to the world not as fixers through foreign correspondents"—the glass ceiling for many of them—"but as storytellers themselves" said Sharif Abdel Kouddous, an Egyptian journalist who wrote a biweekly column for *Al-Masry Al-Youm* when he was in the United States in 2010.[5]

Despite her many successes, Farag and several other staff members left *Al-Masry Al-Youm* in 2010, after disagreements following the owners' repeated attempts to interfere in editorial decisions.[6] One of Farag's early hires, a young journalist named Lina Attalah, who had started out at the *Cairo Times*—a publication founded by compatriots of Ayman Nour, an independent liberal politician who ran against Mubarak for president in 2005—was assigned the management and rebranding of the English section, along with Saif Nasrawi, who had been the Arab affairs editor.[7] The team—about fifteen reporters—renamed the English edition *Egypt Independent*, because "the core value of the kind of journalism we were presenting was independence, the ability to write stories without being influenced," Attalah said.[8]

Some have contended that spaces like these where there were relatively free exchanges of ideas laid the groundwork for what would become the January 25,

2011 uprisings. "People coalesced around these spaces of independent media and they became revolutionaries," Iskandar added. The current regime has learned from the mistakes of its predecessor, he said: "Mubarak's approach of 'let them be and nothing will happen' is what the security apparatus has learned never to do again."[9]

After the Revolution

In the early days of 2011, young men began to light themselves on fire around Egypt to protest the stagnant economic and political conditions. They were imitating Tunisian fruit seller Mohamed Bouazizi, whose self-immolation had precipitated the revolution that knocked longtime dictator Zine El Abidine Ben Ali from power in Tunis. In Egypt, ElBaradei warned darkly of a "Tunisian-style explosion" if the government did not implement political reforms, and there were growing calls on- and offline for people to take to the streets.[10] Meanwhile, Egyptian officialdom was in a state of anxiety and denial. Eyeing the unfolding events in Tunis, they were adamant that Egypt would not be next. Yet despite the mounting pressure, in the months leading up to January 25, 2011, *Egypt Independent* didn't read like a radical revolutionary sheet. It published articles on ElBaradei's return and the labor strikes, but as 2011 began, its editors had little inkling of what was about to happen. "We did publish some articles saying that Tunisia is not Egypt," Nasrawi admitted.[11] One well-known Cairo-based journalist, Issandr El Amrani, broke ranks, writing a piece that argued Egypt would follow where Tunisia had led. But the paper's leadership, Attalah included, still fully expected that security forces would shut down the protest scheduled for January 25, 2011, as they had done for decades, and she made no special plan to cover the event. Still, she went down to the streets herself to report. She was beaten and nearly arrested. The following morning, she came into the office with a new understanding: The rules had changed, she realized, and anything could happen.

Nasrawi put together a plan to cover the unfolding events. But three days after the protests began, on January 28, Egypt went silent. The government had shut off the internet, isolating the country (including the journalists) from the rest of the world. The *Egypt Independent* team sent the website's passwords to friends abroad so that they could update it in case the journalists couldn't find a way around the internet blackout. In the meantime, they heard a rumor that the Semiramis, a luxury hotel just off Tahrir Square, still had a working internet connection. "We moved the entire newsroom to the Semiramis," Attalah remembered. "It became the unofficial broadcasting center for the revolution." The hotel, fearing a raid by government forces, tried hard to fight their presence, and indeed that of much of the international press corps.[12] One day the hotel staff emptied the restaurants of food in an attempt to starve out guests. But the journalists persevered, and the hotel, for unknown reasons, didn't close down. *Egypt Independent* was one of the few local outlets that managed to keep reporting despite the internet blackout. Most other local online news sources stopped updating until they were reconnected to the internet five days later.

Thus began what Iskandar has referred to as "the golden age of Egyptian journalism."[13] The media environment—along with everything from politics to art to traffic patterns—opened up wildly: small publications cropped up along with artists' collectives and new political parties and movements. There was new trust and interest in social media platforms and independent voices that had broadcast from Tahrir, and skepticism of state channels that had pedaled pro-Mubarak propaganda. Indeed, everything associated with Mubarak was now tainted.[14] People who had learned never to speak about politics in public were suddenly discussing political parties and complaining about leaders to anyone who would listen.

Yet despite a loosening of tongues at all levels of society, mainstream media outlets remained somewhat wary of too stark a critique of those in power. Decades of red lines were difficult to erase overnight. And though its figure-head had changed, the hand of the government was far from absent from the media space, and Egypt's public was still subject to massive propaganda from state-manipulated media. When state newspaper *Al-Ahram* declared that "The People Have Brought down the Regime" in February 2011, a newspaper vendor remarked to *Guardian* reporter Jack Shenker that "state-controlled media's own revolution had begun."[15] But soon thereafter it became clear that they had simply found new masters. Many journalists at state media outlets continued to trumpet state propaganda. And while within state news outlets there were some efforts to break away from the political interests that had long controlled them—videos circulated of state television bosses being chased from their offices—none was particularly successful.[16]

The events that have come to be known as the "Maspero Massacre" high-lighted the fact that little in state media outlets had changed. On October 9, 2011, a crowd of mostly Coptic demonstrators were protesting the demolition of a church in Upper Egypt when military personnel began attacking them, eventually running down unarmed protesters with an armored vehicle. As this was unfolding, state television and radio misreported the incident, relaying a false official claim that three members of the military had been killed by armed Coptic demonstrators and calling on "honorable citizens" to "defend the army against attack."[17] Mobs flocked to Maspero, joining a melee orchestrated by security officials. Twenty-eight protesters were killed and 212 injured. The following day, Dina Rasmy, a newscaster for the state-run Channel 2 news, told *Ahram Online* she was "ashamed" of working for state media that had "proven itself to be a slave for whoever rules Egypt."[18] The coverage of the Maspero Massacre showed how effectively the state could still manipulate the narrative to present itself as keeper of the peace in the face of rabble-rousers. Nor had there been a revision to the sectarian narrative in which the Coptic minority was portrayed as less than Egyptian, and even as traitors. Many commentators on private channels continued to parrot the state line. Much of the press made an easy mark for state propaganda.

As is true for many things in Egypt, one's class largely determines which media sources are accessible. Poor Egyptians rely on television for news, and many of them do not have satellites, so domestic channels with content from the Ministry of Information are their only source of information.[19] Satellite channels meanwhile indirectly rely on the state because their licenses are state-issued. Even in the days immediately following the uprisings, this often resulted in private channels advocating for the government or, as in the case of influential television host Yousri Fouda, being slow at first to report on abuses of state power, which were ongoing throughout the "revolutionary" period. Under the Muslim Brotherhood government of Mohamed Morsi, many of the businessmen who owned private channels aligned with the military in their hatred of the Islamists, and embarked on a campaign to demonize them. Even *Al-Dustour* founder Eissa, who had been persecuted by the Mubarak regime, threw his lot in with the military and used the publication he founded in 2011, *Tahrir*, to advocate for the military takeover and Sisi.

As for *Egypt Independent*, it had gone from struggling to extract news in a stagnant political environment to being unable to keep up with the volume of stories and interest. The newsroom was abuzz with a sense of purpose and excitement. "It was just a really special place," said Max Strasser, a former news editor who is now an opinion editor at the *New York Times*. "It's unlike any other newsroom I've ever experienced. The political commitment of people there was unlike anything I've ever seen, the enthusiasm and ambition."[20]

In Cairo, distance grew between *Al-Masry Al-Youm* and *Egypt Independent* following Mubarak's overthrow. At times the Arabic leadership would push the English editors to translate and publish stories they didn't agree with. Sometimes the differences were public, management's critiques appearing in the pages of the Arabic-language paper.

Then on December 1, 2011, pressure from the Arabic management came to a head. *Egypt Independent's* second print issue—up to that point it had been exclusively an online platform—never made it to the newsstands. It was the chief editor, not the government, who forbade its distribution. The paper contained an article by American academic Robert Springborg that discussed divisions in the military, which had been in power since the revolution. The *Egypt Independent* staff published the article and the entire issue, with an explanation, online. As is often the case with banned material, the online issue was very widely read. In response, Magdy El Galad, the editor-in-chief of the Arabic edition, published a column calling his English-language counterparts "immature" and "unpatriotic."

But there were also perks to being attached to one of the most widely read newspapers in Egypt. *Egypt Independent* had its pick of local reporting to translate from *Al-Masry Al-Youm*, which allowed it to cover far more news than otherwise would have been possible given the small size of its staff. A quarter to half of the publication's content on any given day was translated from the Arabic, according to Ahmad Shokr, a former opinion editor. "I'd solicit opinions but I'd also try to translate Arabic pieces and give a sense of what debates were happening in the

Arabic media," he said.[21] It also helped *Egypt Independent*'s reporters: "It was nice to be able to say "*Al-Masry Al-Youm*" when I was reporting and to get the name recognition. People would talk to you when you'd say it was the English edition," said Jahd Khalil, a *Mada* cofounder and former reporter with the paper.[22] As an English-language publication, it also got away with reporting on topics that Arabic papers couldn't, since it was seen as less likely to influence a large audience, and therefore, less of a threat to whoever was in power.[23]

The fractious relationship between the English and Arabic sides of the paper continued until early 2013, when *Al-Masry Al-Youm* ran into financial problems. Attalah, a leftist who seeks to live her principles, suggested that the trouble was in part too heavy a reliance on advertising revenue. So management gave her a deadline to prove what she could do with a new reader-supported model. She and her team embarked on a business plan of their creation, offering new services, including translations and news alerts, for a small fee. "Everyone brought what they knew: anyone with a bit of business experience pitched in, and all outside of the newsroom," Attalah said. Their efforts culminated in a large "save *Egypt Independent* from closing" party at a Cairo arts space, which generated $10,000—not a small sum by Egyptian standards. This they proudly handed over to the paper's accountant, only to be told a few days later that they were to be shut down anyway. "It was clear the decision was taken before we even tried to generate any money," Attalah said.[24]

"The mother has to be saved by letting go of the daughter," the paper's chairman, Abdel Moneim Said, told her—the daughter being *Egypt Independent*. "I had to tell him, I don't think *Al-Masry Al-Youm* is my mother, so I don't think the analogy makes sense," Attalah said. At the time, she and her colleagues viewed the setback as temporary. In the new media climate, the staff felt sure that *Egypt Independent* would be reincarnated. So they focused on negotiating severance packages and putting together a final issue in which they announced to readers they were closing. "We used that edition to raise questions about the state of independent media in Egypt, saying what happened to *Egypt Independent* is a microcosm," Attalah said. But someone from the Arabic paper saw the edition at the printing house and deemed it too critical. It never made it to the newsstands. Once again, the *Egypt Independent* editors published a banned print edition online. And once again, it went viral.

After the Coup

A week after *Egypt Independent* disbanded (though *Al-Masry Al-Youm*'s management kept the rights to the name and at the time of writing still publishes some English content) the newly unemployed staff began to meet to discuss what kind of publication they wanted to start, and what the name of a new platform should be. They were moving slowly, a little depressed at their unceremonious ousting from their jobs despite their unorthodox efforts to save them. Still, they had enough energy to come up with and agree on the idea of *Mada Masr*. Meanwhile, a campaign called "Tamarrod," Arabic for "rebellion," had gained huge traction across the country, with increasingly apparent support from the military. Young people had appeared at every metro stop and public building asking passersby to sign their petition calling on the newly elected Muslim Brotherhood president to step down and hold early elections. Sensing the gravity of the moment, the future staff of *Mada* decided at the last minute to peg their launch to Tamarrod's mass demonstration planned for June 30, 2013. On June 17, they met in an empty room. There was no money for furniture—at first there was no money at all—and Attalah and other staff members used part of their severance packages to get things off the ground, at times working for free or very little. On the door a sign read, "The Artists Formerly Known as *Egypt Independent*."[25] Alaa Abdel Fattah, one of the most prominent activists in Egypt and *Mada*'s web designer, stayed up into the wee hours of the morning on June 30 to finish the site. Defying expectations, *Mada* launched on schedule.

Three days after the protest, the Egyptian army arrested Egypt's first elected president, Morsi, who is still behind bars. A six-week sit-in led by his supporters followed, which preceded, as Human Rights Watch described it, "one of the world's largest killings of demonstrators in a single day in recent history," on August 14, 2013: the Rabaa Massacre.[26] In the course of clearing the sit-ins in Rabaa Square, Egyptian security forces left, by their own admission, more than eight hundred people dead. Human Rights Watch puts the number of people killed that day at more than eleven hundred.[27]

From that moment, simply reporting the news became a contentious act. "When June 30 happened we didn't have time to do the things we said we would do, we were just doing the basics of journalism: objective reporting, both sides of the story," said Amira Ahmed, a *Mada* cofounder, who led its business-development team and served as managing editor and general manager. With no one else doing such reporting, *Mada* became a sort of de facto opposition organization, which was not its editors' plan. "There was one narrative and presenting other sides of the story was considered in opposition to the state," Ahmed said. "But it was just ethical journalism—[opposition] was not our intention."[28]

Over the years since *Mada*'s founding, reporting independent accounts of events has become an increasingly dangerous task. While at first the military government focused its crackdown on the Muslim Brotherhood, soon its sweeps extended to human rights and media organizations, particularly those that espoused the principles of the January 25 uprising. On November 28, 2013, twenty men broke down Alaa Abdel Fattah's door. They beat him, slapped his wife Manal across the face and took him away.[29] After a subsequent trial on charges of violating a protest law that had just been issued, Abdel Fattah was sentenced to five years in prison. But despite the state's tactics of intimidation, his colleagues at *Mada* pressed on with their work. They decided early on that they would not be cowed. "If you decide to focus so much on red lines, you will end up not doing journalism at all," Attalah said. "We try never to ask the question, 'Is it worth it to publish?' All truth is worth publishing."[30] While sometimes they might try to minimize the sensationalism of their headlines, the most important thing, *Mada Masr*'s editors agreed, is to ensure that all assertions are supported by ironclad evidence.

A New Journalism for a New Egypt

Even in a hostile environment, *Mada*'s staff had ambitious plans. At *Egypt Independent*, there had been a sense of collective decision-making, but it was more the feel of the place rather than a stated ethos bolstered by collective procedures. Cut loose from all ties to Egypt's mainstream media machine, the young journalists set out to see if they could run their new enterprise under the egalitarian principles of their revolution both editorially and on the corporate side, while still making it financially viable. Like many of the political groups that formed after the uprising, their vision was one of collective management and ownership, as well as consensus-driven editorial practices.

The choice to make it an online publication as opposed to print, as *Egypt Independent* had been, was a deliberate one. It was in part about finances. "The reason online publications can be independent is that they can be run so cheaply," Ursula Lindsey, who worked as Mada's special projects editor from 2013 to 2014, pointed out.[31] They sought to maintain editorial independence by experimenting with new funding models. "*Mada Masr* has been a pioneer of reader-sponsored media, breaking away from state-run newspapers or those run by big businessmen," the two paradigms that constitute the norm in Egypt, Abdel Kouddous said. But the decision also had to do with Attalah's understanding of the potential of the internet. At a virtual roundtable in 2015 hosted by the Arab Council for the Social Sciences (ACSS), which was republished on *Mada*'s website, Attalah explained that she considered the internet "a laboratory for dissident politics" and uniquely suited to an organization that sought to operate horizontally, as a collective, and value individual voices equally.[32] She encouraged individual initiatives at *Mada,* as well as experimentation with nontraditional modes of expression that the internet enabled.

The staff aspired to make their newsroom different from any they had ever worked in. "It was like a student hostel. It was more than a paper," said Sarah Carr, a British-Egyptian journalist and cofounder, offering a reenactment of the scene: "You! Roll your sleeves up. You! Wash up! You! Paint a wall. You! Put up some cling film and write about Tahrir. And you! Get your dog off my leg! There was always someone's dog in there, someone's animal. It was nice, very informal. Lina's good at that." Other journalists and friends of the paper would sometimes come and work in *Mada*'s office in Garden City. It was "a little bubble inside the very regimented, conservative, and tradition-obsessed vibe of Egypt," Carr said. "Women were smoking and wearing tank tops in there and all sorts of crazy things. It was like a hippie hipster sort of atmosphere."[33] There was even talk of setting up a commune.

Mada's initial site announced itself as a repository for "independent" and "progressive" journalism. The focus of its coverage was unique in Egypt's media landscape. The priorities of its journalists were "holding those in power account-able and offering a platform for the most marginalized voices," said Abdel Koud-dous, who spent eight years working in independent media in the United States, and saw *Mada* as operating on similar principles.[34] *Mada*'s driving political belief was a commitment to a human rights-based approach. "In an ideal situation, this tendency should be filled in by a political party," said Khaled Fahmy, a professor of Middle Eastern history at the American University in Cairo and Harvard University, and a *Mada* contributor. "But as we know it's very difficult to politically organize in Egypt, and the result is what we see in human rights organizations and online publications that are professional and complex and way ahead of mainstream politics in terms of ideas."[35] With regard to journalistic standards *Mada* journalists were unique as well, trying to produce work that was unbiased and deeply sourced in a media environment where many publications were beholden to the editorial dictates of their financial backers, and opinion masquerading as reporting was widespread.

Without access to the resources *Al-Masry Al-Youm* Arabic provided in terms of day-to-day news coverage, the journalists shifted away from breaking news. Instead they focused on features and analysis, experimental writing forms, more avant-garde cultural pieces, transcripts of their meetings, and investiga-tive pieces they would likely never have been allowed to publish if they were still affiliated with a mainstream newspaper. For instance, Fahmy published a column in Egyptian colloquial Arabic.[36] Once almost exclusively a spoken language, the dialect's written form has become more standardized over the last few years through communications on social media and internet platforms. Editors frequently narrated their editorial process, and why they made certain choices. In an editor's note accompanying a piece to mark the third anniversary of the 2011 revolution, Attalah and Mark Levine explained: "We found it hard to solicit pieces commemorating the January 25 revolution, mainly because we seem to have hit a certain boundary in revolutionary prose. A moment of deep ambiguity accompanies three years of thinking, doing and rethinking. But in the spirit of resisting this submission to boundaries, we went back to what colum-nists and friends wrote during the eighteen days of the revolution and we asked them to revisit their writings. Some wrote reaction pieces, others edited them, adding reflections from today, and others rewrote them."[37] What followed was a collectively written, unattributed collection of memories and reflections on the eighteen days.

More recently, as international publications have largely turned away from Egypt, *Mada* has continued to cover the minutiae of the ongoing crackdown. Its articles often offer greater detail than those in Western publications and the fact that the reporters themselves come from the place they're writing about means they often have a deeper understanding of the history and significance of events than foreign reporters do. While their coverage of breaking news is not necessarily the most dramatic, it is their consistency and insistence on writ-ing about the everyday experience of Egyptians that makes them unique. *Mada* has time and again drawn attention to the state's opaque war in Sinai,[38] some-times sending reporters to cover it when foreign reporters have deemed it too dangerous or been denied permits. Despite the fact that the bar for what is shocking in Egypt in terms of the deaths, abuse, or disappearance of detainees has grown impossibly high, *Mada* continues to report incident after incident of torture[39] at the hands of the state. *Mada*'s reporting on Egypt's failing economy[40] has also been extensive and detailed, as well as its coverage of Mubarak era officials' corruption.[41]

Unlike most other news outlets, since its inception *Mada* has had a strong connection to the arts, placing as much emphasis on its culture section as on its news reporting. Part of this is due to Attalah's sensibilities and those of some staff members who have strong connections to Egypt's contemporary art world. They firmly believe it is of a piece with the rest of their coverage. "We are believers in how art has a prime function in intervening in reality and is not usually available in spaces of politics and basic journalism," Attalah explained.[42] *Mada*'s culture editor J.R. Evans is an artist herself.

There is a self-consciousness in *Mada*'s conception of itself as an archive of the events and ideas that defined the years since it began. The very publishing of an interview like the one Attalah participated in with ACSS indicates a desire to be transparent about its processes and its staff's thinking, though such reflections can at times have a navel-gazing quality. In that interview Attalah referred to an impulse from the days immediately following the revolution to take control of the narrative. "It was in the moments of revolutionary hope that we as activists began to be anxious about archiving our own practices. We thought we owned the present moment and wanted to extend this to the past and future."[43]

Much of *Mada*'s experimentation and growth has happened in the necessarily public space it occupies. Its sense of itself and the community it has formed extends to its readership as well,[44] and it has built a community life beyond that of simply publishing articles. For a time, the paper hosted prominent writers, thinkers, politicians, and artists at an informal Thursday morning staff breakfast. Among those who came to speak were comedian Bassem Youssef, and media figures Belal Fadl and Reem Maged. Sometimes the minutes of these meetings would be published on the website. Meanwhile, events such as its anniversary party, or the Mada Market—where the paper brought together local vendors and music and charged an entry fee—connected *Mada*'s staff directly with its readers.

This collectivist, community-based ethos was an integral part of *Mada*'s business model. But setting up a collectively owned and run business in Egypt proved challenging, and took months of talking to business experts and lawyers. Ultimately *Mada*'s staff concluded that Egypt's business climate just wasn't hospitable to the enterprise they wanted to establish. "It's an aging regulatory framework," Ahmed explained. "You don't have that flexibility in different ownership models."[45] The paper is still trying to register as an offshore company in a country such as the Netherlands, the United Kingdom, or even the United

Arab Emirates, with a legal framework built to accommodate collectively owned enterprises. Under their status as a limited liability company (LLC), if a shareholder owns 20 percent of the company, he or she can make unilateral decisions. *Mada*'s business development team is looking for a model that officially functions on more of a consensus basis—a standard practice in media startups around the world. Such structural protections are particularly important for editorial independence, especially in Egypt.

But members of the business development team were journalists first, with a smattering of business experience between them. Much of their expertise was acquired on the job.[46] Those in editorial sometimes seemed uninterested in the business side's struggles. And then there was the fundamental incompatibility at times of business and politics: "It was hard to draw the line," Ahmed said. "Where does the collective end? Where does the need for a clear structure that's a bit hierarchical come in? And should we accept it or should we fight it because we are trying to build a progressive institution?"

Attalah had long hoped that she might be able to move away from an entirely ad-based revenue structure. She saw in *Mada* "a capitalization of this imagination I always had . . . that good journalists can be supported by a base of loyal supporters who want to keep an independent newspaper running."[47] Today *Mada*'s revenue streams are diverse and include subscription-based services and events. The ads it runs are "progressive" in that they promote small businesses and creative industries whose work and mission the paper supports.

But while setting up a progressive company with multiple revenue streams consumed considerable energy, a more crucial aspect of the organization's structure was its legal status. Because of the sensitive nature of some of its reporting, an unimpeachable legal status was paramount from the start. "We are not producing something that is easy to swallow by the government and we have to protect ourselves," Attalah said. "We have to do basic things like operating legally and paying our taxes. It would be stupid not to, given our precarious position."[48] *Mada* therefore immediately established itself as an LLC while searching for a more appropriate business model for collective ownership and decision-making.

What the revolutionaries soon realized was that though the most powerful symbol of the state—Mubarak—was now gone, the bureaucracy and patronage systems that undergirded his ossified regime were still firmly in place. Many new political parties, such as those founded by the revolutionary youth, lost out to older systems of patronage and familiar personalities from the past—both members of the Brotherhood and the old guard. Many new organizations struggled to sustain themselves in the face of prohibitions on foreign funding, which cut them off from international foundation money. Increasingly draconian laws requiring nongovernmental organizations (NGOs) to register with and be approved by the state sent several of them to Tunisia, including the Cairo Institute for Human Rights—there was no guarantee of safety in Egypt.[49] As many of its contemporaries fled or folded, *Mada* struggled on, trying to live by the principles it had established.

But there were downsides to nonhierarchical management. The lack of a more traditional structure could lead to hours of meetings, and sometimes, conflict in the newsroom. "It's one of the things that makes *Mada* special, and one of the things that makes it a very challenging place to make things happen quickly and efficiently," Ahmed said.[50]

"[Lina] likes to keep it all sort of no-management, one level, grassroots and all that. So we were all in endless meetings. Like, a meeting every hour. Endless, interminable meetings!" Carr said. The system is "clunky," she added, "because someone has to take a decision at the end of the day. Eventually someone is going to say, 'it's going to be like this, piss off.'"[51] While she and others appreciated the collective decision-making up to a point, some said that at moments of disagreement, they would have preferred to have had some sort of arbiter, which might in the end have led to less conflict.[52]

One challenge was that the closeness of the team sometimes made rules difficult to enforce. "Management structure is obviously something that *Mada* is still struggling with," said Dalia Rabie, one of the cofounders and a longtime reporter at *Mada*. "This is, I guess, one of the downsides of founding something with your friends." She went on: "It's difficult to have an established hierarchy and assert your authority when you are an organic team."[53] It was also difficult to hold people to deadlines, because a lack of hierarchical structure meant it was hard to implement penalties for late work.[54]

Despite the collective decision-making, Attalah's leadership was integral to the project. "Lina has a gift for rallying the troops and getting people together," Carr said, echoing a sentiment shared by many former staff.[55] Attalah's notion of what a publication should be was an expansive one, in which not only writers and editors, but also readers and like-minded people in society at large played a role. "Lina has this wonderful convivial way of having this incredible network of people she helps and talks to," said Lindsey.[56] "She commands such respect and is trying to keep things as horizontal as possible," Abdel Kouddous said. "They seem to give a lot of space and breadth for people to do what they want and to experiment."[57] Still, some people were sometimes frustrated with what they saw as Attalah's micromanagement, though they agreed that her vision was invaluable.

New Reach and Attention with Expansion into Arabic

In October 2013, Mohamed Adam, a *Mada* cofounder, spearheaded the launch of *Mada*'s Arabic website. Everyone at the newspaper was excited at the prospect of an Arabic-language site and reaching a wider, more diverse audience inside Egypt. These days, when the world, and consequently the foreign media, has turned away from Egypt, the Arabic site often goes into more detail than the English, calibrating its stories for a local audience that already has a background in the issues and is more interested in details. Similarly, due to waning international interest, *Mada* does not translate every Arabic story it publishes into

English. The Arabic has outstripped the English in terms of readership. "The Arabic section is much more popular than the English, which is a testament to the hunger for this sort of journalism and these dissenting voices," Kouddous said.[58] Khaled Fahmy said he had noticed the influence of *Mada*'s journalistic standards on other independent online publications.[59]

The hiring in 2014 of Hossam Bahgat, one of Egypt's most influential human rights activists, had a profound effect on the Arabic side of the paper. "When he started writing the investigative pieces in Arabic, our traffic depended on him for a long time," Dalia Rabie said.[60] This in part drove the shift in the leadership's focus toward the Arabic side of the paper. "They started to feel the need to hire more Arabic writers and copy editors," she said. The combination of more content in Arabic, and the fact that part of that content was comprised of long investigative pieces—some of them about the military—by one of the most prominent human rights campaigners in Egypt, has meant greater scrutiny by the state security apparatus. *Mada*, with its expanding Arabic platform, began to have a greater capacity for influence—and thus became seen as a bigger threat.

After years of working as a human rights advocate, Bahgat had a deep and developed network of sources and an attention to detail and accuracy. Moreover, his organization had defended everyone from LGBTQ Egyptians to women to religious minorities, and he was accustomed to taking on the state. His pieces for *Mada* covered some of Egypt's most taboo topics, from tax evasion by the Mubarak family to some of the more embarrassing elements of Egypt's relationship with its largest financial backer, Saudi Arabia, to an alleged aborted coup within the military. For this third piece Bahgat was detained by military intelligence and accused of "publishing false news that could harm the nation."[61] He was later released but is currently under scrutiny (and has had his assets frozen and travel banned) in connection with a reopened case from 2011 regarding foreign funding to Egyptian NGOs.[62] In the meantime, however, Bahgat is back at work.

Adam saw the Arabic site as a place where people could write controversial pieces that no one else would publish. *Mada* became the main outlet that published letters from prominent imprisoned activists, including Alaa Abdel Fattah. It published an open letter[63] from Abdel Fattah to his sisters, and a joint letter[64] from prison that he and Ahmed Douma wrote by shouting between their prison cells. The activists described conditions in the prison, as well as the political state of affairs, and sometimes offered breaking news, as when Abdel Fattah announced the beginning of his hunger strike via another open letter published by *Mada*.[65] "It really makes me happy when Alaa Abdel Fatah writes in Arabic on [*Mada*]," Adam said in October 2016. "Imagine if *Mada* was only in English. It wouldn't make sense that Alaa is in jail and speaking only in English. Who are we talking to? It would just be confirming all the conspiracies about him," Adam added.[66]

Mada Masr was not the only outlet that started publishing after the revolution. There were several websites devoted to independent journalism and commentary that sprang up after the uprising. Each has a slightly different focus—*El Badil* prioritizes breaking news, but does little investigative work, *Al Manassa* focuses on blog and opinion pieces, *Ultra-Sout* publishes news and analysis, and respected journalist Belal Fadl contributes to *Al-Araby Al-Jadeed*. But in addition to its content, it is *Mada's* commitment to balance and accuracy that has set it apart. "I don't think there's anyone who quite has the same fairness and accuracy," said Abdel Kouddous, who is an occasional contributor. "That's what they have nailed over these other places. They rarely get the facts wrong and when they do, they correct themselves very openly and they don't publish rumor. The others have the correct spirit but are a lot less reliable."[67] *Mada* is also the only one of these independent publications that has an extensive English website, making it, and the issues it covers, accessible to a foreign as well as a local audience. Some suggest that the friendship of *Mada's* staff with funders also allows them to access grants that others cannot.

Surviving Growing Pressure under Sisi—for Now

Independent publications that criticize the state are far harder to quash than they once were. While the plotters of Egypt's 1919 revolution against the British required a printing press, which they hid in the basement of Café Riche downtown, today's dissenters need no such infrastructure. "Functionally speaking they could arrest every single person in the country and *Mada* could keep existing," Iskandar said. Even with sources of funding cut off, publications like *Mada* can operate from other countries, as many in Egypt's human rights community now do.[68]

Still, the government has a monopoly on printing in Egypt—state-owned *Al-Ahram* and *Al-Gomhuria* publish several of the independent newspapers, meaning that their content must pass under the eyes of the government employees at the printing house. And while the web has historically been less subject to these traditional forms of censorship, all this may change if proposed laws to regulate new media are passed. In December 2016, parliament passed the first of several planned media laws that created the Supreme Council for the Administration of the Media, the chairman of which is to be chosen by Sisi. He will appoint additional members on the basis of nominations from other government bodies including the judiciary and parliament. The new council is tasked with creating a list of penalties and will have the power to sue and fine media organizations that violate its rules. It will also be able to revoke or suspend the right to publish and broadcast, and extend or rescind licenses to foreign media. Regulations governing media practice—formation, ownership, and management of media outlets, media freedoms, and the relationship between journalism and national security—are to be part of a separate piece of legislation. According to the original draft of the unified media bill completed in November 2015 by the National Authority of Media and Journalism Legislation, these measures may include a requirement that any new online news site would require a permit from the council and any new media companies would require startup capital of at least half a million Egyptian pounds (more than $27,000), half of which would have to be deposited in an Egyptian bank. These financial constraints would strangle small independent outlets like *Mada* and would make the media space inaccessible to anyone but wealthy businessmen—in other words, things would go back to how they used to be, at least for publications that were actually based in Egypt.[69]

This, in addition to the fate of other journalists around them in recent years, has alarmed many members of *Mada*'s staff. Three *Al Jazeera English* journalists were imprisoned for more than a year and a half and tried for reporting false news and alleged connections with the Muslim Brotherhood. They were released in September 2015 following a pardon from Sisi. In some ways, they were lucky. Many others have been waiting in prison for years without trial. At the time of writing, there are twenty-five journalists in jail in Egypt, according to the Committee to Protect Journalists. Baher Mohamed, the only journalist of the three in the *Al Jazeera* trial who held only Egyptian nationality, was seen as being far more vulnerable to targeting by the state and for much of the trial many feared his foreign passport-holding colleagues would be rescued by their governments while he would be left to languish in prison. And he wouldn't be alone. According to the Arabic Network for Human Rights Information there are more than sixty thousand political prisoners in Egypt and 1,250 missing people.[70] Some among them were arrested at peaceful protests that have been outlawed since 2013, and hundreds of people have been sentenced to death in mass trials. "There's been a chilling effect," Attalah said. "When the *Al Jazeera* [English] trial happened I recall how my colleagues . . . kept saying they identified a lot with Baher, the local journalist."[71]

As public space grows vanishingly small in Egypt, social media—particularly Facebook but also Skype and WhatsApp—has taken on a new role and has become a very important channel for independent voices, to share news as well as generate ideas. "Silence is the only way to be safe, to not talk about politics . . . is the safest way—but online it's a different story," Iskandar said.[72] It has even affected *Mada*'s coverage. People are sharing Facebook posts that "you could easily consider an op-ed in a newspaper. A lot of very important political discussion happens on Facebook," said Ahmad Shokr, *Mada*'s former opinion editor, who joined the social networking site in 2011 because he felt he was missing out on important political discussions. As editor, he would often use it to generate content, inviting people to transform their posts into op-eds.[73] As the crackdown intensifies, many of those who once expressed their dissent in the street have shifted their critiques to Facebook.

In frightening times, *Mada* staff say their most important resource is each other. Their decisions, they explained, were often braver together. "There is comfort in having thirty other people come together and say you are going to stay the course," Ahmed said. "Thirty people who feel they have ownership in this place and can't make decisions out of fear."[74] Their perseverance provides inspiration to other journalists working in a dangerous time. Andeel, a provocative *Mada* political cartoonist, "keeps drawing Sisi and it gives me courage to continue on, it's very inspiring," Abdel Kouddous said. "If I ever have pause about any coverage, I look at [*Mada*] and say, no, if they are doing it, I'm wala haga," he added, using a phrase that means "I'm nothing" in Egyptian Arabic.[75] *Mada* also provided a sense of purpose in a time of great disappointment. "If it weren't for *Mada*, what else would we have done in this state of things?" Attalah sighed. "A lot of us have close friends in prison . . . there's a sense of fatigue and despair."[76]

Yet despite everything, *Mada* is growing. It is approaching a million views a month. Attalah is taking a backseat and was succeeded in the late summer of 2016 as editor by longtime journalist Wael Gamal, reflecting a commitment at *Mada* to transfer power internally, as a democratically run institution. Coverage is increasingly weighted toward the faster-growing Arabic section and many of *Mada*'s cofounders are moving on.

Change is hard for some. "It was still our own passion project in the beginning and a lot of the newcomers, they don't think of the project in the same way," said Amira Ahmed, who recently left the paper, though she acknowledges it's healthy to have new blood.[77] *Mada* "kind of outgrew its staff" as it expanded and its Arabic site received increasing attention, said Dalia Rabie, another one of the cofounders who recently moved on. "It needs a bigger newsroom and a bigger staff, and the kind of organic newsroom that we had was not working anymore."[78]

The website also recently underwent a redesign. In a characteristic move, *Mada* published an interview between Attalah and the new site's designer, Phil Gribbon, to explain to readers the thinking behind the new design. *Mada* "couldn't have the look of the generic-looking professional news website," Gribbon explained in the interview. "It needed to be more personal, more obviously made by real people involved in the world they're reporting on." Gribbon ultimately chose a particularly human motif to frame the site: the cartoons of Andeel—*Mada*'s and perhaps Egypt's most daring cartoonist.[79] The investment in a redesign suggests that for now, *Mada* is digging in despite growing pressures.

For years, many people, including *Mada* staff members, have been asking how *Mada* has survived in a climate that has crushed so many other outlets and organizations. No one seems to know. When new laws restricting media have been promulgated, when other civil society groups were raided, and when Hossam Bahgat was arrested, many thought it was the beginning of the end. When the paper was publishing largely in English, it was likely less of a concern to the state, but as its reach in Arabic has expanded, this is no longer true. "Especially after Hossam's arrest last year for his piece on the army prosecution of military officers, they've been put under a microscope," Abdel Kouddous said.[80] And yet *Mada*'s doors remain open. The arbitrariness of who gets caught up in the state's nets and who is left to agonize over whether they're next seems to be part of a government strategy to foster self-censorship and a compliant media. However, it's also possible that the government has been waiting to target *Mada* under the new online media law, which would provide an explicit legal justification for such an action. Whatever the case, *Mada*'s friends and former staff are very worried about the site and its employees.

Since Sisi's crackdown, many other journalists have either left Egypt, gone to work for international news organizations, or reverted to their prerevolutionary mode of operation, where they made their critiques only indirectly, to avoid the ire of the state. But at *Mada*, fundamental changes are off the table: "It's either published and we do it with the level of liberty we have right now, or we don't do it at all," Attalah said. The only reason *Mada* would shut down of its own accord would be "if the price became too high," she said—if, for example, staff members were under direct threat of arrest.

With so many people being jailed and organizations shut down, Attalah sees no reason why *Mada* will not eventually meet a similar fate. "We have to expect this to happen, we shouldn't feel comfortable to be protected from what everyone who is saying the truth is facing." But whether the paper is shut down or not, "the fact that we managed to survive these years to bear witness is an achievement," she said.[81]

Even as *Mada*'s journalists are realistic about the risks, they are buoyed by the belief that Egyptian speech has evolved in ways that cannot quickly be undone. *Mada* might be forced to shut down, its reporters might be silenced or imprisoned, but the internet continues to provide a platform that the government can never fully control. Even more significantly, the revolution changed the way that many Egyptians think about the possibilities of expression and political change. While the authoritarian crackdown has caused many people to watch what they say and scale back their public statements and activities, *Mada*'s large and growing readership is testament to the enduring interest in alternative viewpoints, and the survival of a revolutionary spirit among significant parts of the population. That many people are keeping their heads down is evidence that the battlefield has become exceedingly dangerous, not that the fight is over. If *Mada*'s particular incarnation of the revolution is dismantled, in the view of the paper's staff and supporters a new incarnation will emerge elsewhere. The revolution that animates these journalists will not so easily be extinguished. "The most difficult thing is to prevent these ideas from being thought in the first place," Khaled Fahmy said of *Mada*'s content. "And if they are thought, with these technologies and this energy, it doesn't take a genius to expect they will be expressed."

In a piece written from jail on June 12, 2014, Alaa Abdel Fattah compared his generation to his father's era of human rights activists: "I write of a generation that fought without despair and without hope, that won only small victories and wasn't shaken by major defeats because they were the natural order of things. A generation whose ambitions were lower than the ambitions of those who came before, but whose dream was larger."[82] The let-down and despair of today's revolutionaries is great. But unlike the generation of Abdel Fattah's father, they have also experienced a sense of infinite possibility, which *Mada Masr*'s endeavors have kept alive in at least one space.

Notes

1. A note on the use of the word "secular" in an Egyptian context: in other North African countries, especially Tunisia, the term "secular" is often posited in sharp opposition to "religious" or "Islamist," a dichotomy analogous to the one that exists in France. In Egypt there is no such bright line between Islamist and secular, or rather, there wasn't prior to 2013.

2. Adel Iskandar, interview with the author by telephone, September 20, 2016.

3. Ibid.

4. Fatemeh Farag, interview with the author by telephone, September 27, 2016.

5. Sharif Abdel Kouddous, interview with the author by telephone, September 15, 2016.

6. Farag now runs a news network called "Welad el-Balad," an independent community news organization that works in twenty Egyptian governorates and has ten newsrooms across the country, focusing on stories outside of the capital, a rarity in Egypt. Not everyone agreed with her decision to resign from *Al-Masry Al-Youm*. "My thinking was, we have to stay and fight," Nasrawi remembered.

7. Saif Nasrawi, interview with the author by telephone, September 29, 2016.

8. Lina Attalah, interview with the author by telephone, September 11, 2016.

9. Iskandar, interview.

10. Jack Shenker, "Mohamd ElBaradei Warns of Tunisia-Style Explosion in Egypt," *The Guardian,* January 18, 2011, https://www.theguardian.com/world/2011/jan/18/mohamed-elbaradei-tunisia-egypt.

11. Nasrawi, interview.

12. Attalah, interview.

13. Iskandar, interview.

14. As Middle East-based journalist Ursula Lindsey wrote in 2011, "The triumph of the revolution—at least in its primary demand, Mubarak's resignation—was accompanied by a discrediting of government-controlled news, a flourishing of 'homemade' media of all sorts, and a validation of outlets such as *Al Jazeera* and other pugnacious satellite channels, some privately owned." Ursula Lindsey, "Revolution and Counter-Revolution in the Egyptian Media," *Middle East Research and Information Project*, February 15, 2011, http://www.merip.org/mero/mero021511.

15. Jack Shenker, "Egypt's Media Undergo their own Revolution," *The Guardian*, February 21, 2011, https://www.theguardian.com/media/2011/feb/21/egypt-media-revolution.

16. Ibid.

17. "Egypt: Don't Cover Up Military Killing of Copt Protesters," Human Rights Watch, October 25, 2011, https://www.hrw.org/news/2011/10/25/egypt-dont-cover-military-killing-copt-protesters.

18. Zeinab el-Gundy, "Outrage over State TV's Misinformation and Anti-Coptic Incitement," *Ahram Online*, October 10, 2011, http://english.ahram.org.eg/NewsContent/1/64/23813/Egypt/Politics-/Outrage-over-state-TVs-misinformation-and-antiCopt.aspx.

19. As Ursula Lindsey pointed out in 2011," the government has kept tight control over terrestrial broadcasting, which depends directly upon the Ministry of Information for its content" and is well aware of where its largest audience base lies: "As the regime knows very well, the eight state TV channels are the only source of visual information for the many poor Egyptians who do not have satellite channels or internet connections in their houses." Lindsey, "Revolution and Counter-Revolution."

20. Max Strasser, interview with the author by telephone, September 13, 2016.

21. Ahmad Shokr, interview with the author by telephone, September 26, 2016.

22. Jahd Khalil, interview with the author by telephone, September 4, 2016.

23. Farag, interview.

24. Attalah, interview.

25. Leslie. T. Chang, "The News Website That's Keeping Press Freedom Alive in Egypt," *The Guardian*, January 27, 2015, https://www.theguardian.com/news/2015/jan/27/-sp-online-newspaper-keeping-press-freedom-alive-egypt.

26. "Egypt: Rab'a Killings Likely Crimes against Humanity," Human Rights Watch, August 12, 2014, https://www.hrw.org/news/2014/08/12/egypt-raba-killings-likely-crimes-against-humanity.

27. "All According to Plan: The Rab'a Massacre and Mass Killing of Protesters in Egypt," Human Rights Watch, August 12, 2014, https://www.hrw.org/report/2014/08/12/all-according-plan/raba-massacre-and-mass-killings-protesters-egypt#4ab8e3.

28. Amira Ahmed, interview with the author by telephone, September 18, 2016.

29. "Update: Alaa Abdel Fattah Being Held at CSF Barracks," *Mada Masr*, November 28, 2013.

30. Attalah, interview.

31. Ursula Lindsey, interview with the author by telephone, October 29, 2016.

32. Lina Attalah et al., "Who Are 'the People'?," *Arab Council for the Social Sciences*, February 11, 2015. http://www.madamasr.com/en/2015/02/11/feature/politics/who-are-the-people/.

33. Sarah Carr, interview with the author by telephone, September 18, 2016.

34. Abdel Kouddous, interview.

35. Khaled Fahmy, interview with the author by telephone, October 16, 2016.

36. Khaled Fahmy's writings in colloquial Arabic can be found at http://www.madamasr.com/ar/contributor/%D8%AE%D8%A7%D9%84%D8%AF-%D9%81%D9%87%D9%85%D9%8A/.

37. Lina Attalah and Mark Levine, "Another 48 Hours," *Mada Masr*, February 9, 2014, http://www.madamasr.com/en/2014/02/09/opinion/u/another-48-hours/.

38. See Omar Ryad, "Living under Curfew: Arish Transforms into a Ghost Town," *Mada Masr*, November 1, 2014, http://www.madamasr.com/en/2014/11/01/feature/politics/living-under-curfew-arish-transforms-into-a-ghost-town/.

39. See Heba Afify, "Disappeared, Detained and Tortured for No Reason: Islam Khalil Recounts His Story," *Mada Masr*, October 19, 2016, http://www.madamasr.com/en/2016/10/19/feature/politics/disappeared-detained-and-tortured-for-no-reason-islam-khalil-recounts-his-story/.

40. See Mohamed Hamama, "Your Guide to Understanding the Pound Devaluation," *Mada Masr*, November 3, 2016, http://www.madamasr.com/en/2016/11/03/feature/economy/q-and-a-on-pound-devaluation/.

41. See Osama Diab, "How Every Dollar Became Twelve Thousand Dollars in Less than a Decade for Gamal Mubarak," October 20, 2016, *Mada Masr*, http://www.madamasr.com/en/2016/10/20/feature/economy/how-every-dollar-became-12000-in-less-than-a-decade-for-gamal-mubarak/.

42. Attalah, interview.

43. Attalah et al., "Who Are 'the People'?"

44. For example, in its current "About Us" section it states that a part of its mandate is "reexamining the role of media in relation to its public."

45. Ibid.

46. Ibid.

47. Attalah, interview.

48. Ibid.

49. For more on the crackdown on NGOs, see Khaled Mansour's chapter in this volume, "Egypt's Human Rights Movement: Repression, Resistance, and Co-optation."

50. Ahmed, interview.

51. Carr, interview.

52. The management structure sometimes led to more serious disputes. Mohamed Adam, one of *Mada*'s cofounders, was promoted to editor when the Arabic website was launched. But after differences with management over how he was running the site, he took a leave of absence in the fall of 2014. When he wanted to come back a month later, Attalah decided against it. She said she personally supported his return but that others at *Mada* did not agree.

53. Dalia Rabie, interview with the author by telephone, October 10, 2016.

54. "I remember having a meeting with writers about meeting deadlines, about how we can encourage ourselves to meet deadlines," Sarah Carr said. "But cracking the whip wasn't part of the culture. In any other institution you meet deadlines or you'll get your pay docked." Carr, interview.

55. Ibid.

56. Lindsey, interview.

57. Abdel Kouddous, interview.

58. Ibid.

59. Fahmy, interview.

60. Rabie, interview.

61. Leila Fadel, "Egyptian Journalist Hossam Bahgat Detained over Investigative Story," *NPR*, November 8, 2015, http://www.npr.org/sections/thetwo-way/2015/11/08/455247165/egyptian-journalist-hossam-bahgat-detained-over-investigative-story.

62. Lin Noueihad and Ahmed Aboulenein, "Human Rights on Trial in Egypt as NGO Funding Case Revived," *Reuters*, March 25, 2016, http://www.reuters.com/article/us-egypt-rights-idUSKCN0WQ20X.

63. See "A Letter from Alaa Abd El Fattah to His Sisters," *Mada Masr,* January 23, 2014, http://www.madamasr.com/en/2014/01/23/feature/politics/a-letter-from-alaa-abd-el-fattah-to-his-sisters/.

64. See Alaa Abd El Fattah, "Graffiti for Two . . . Alaa and Douma," *Mada Masr,* January 25, 2014, http://www.madamasr.com/en/2014/01/25/feature/politics/graffiti-for-two-alaa-and-douma/.

65. Alaa Abdel Fattah, "An Open Letter," Mada Masr, August 26, 2014, http://www.madamasr.com/en/2014/08/26/opinion/u/an-open-letter/.

66. Mohamed Adam, interview with the author by telephone, October 8, 2016. After leaving *Mada* late in 2014 following disagreements about the management structure, Adam went on to work for *The Economist* and to do a fellowship at the Tahrir Institute for Middle East Policy. He is currently pursuing a master's degree in London, though he has remained a friend and proponent of *Mada*.

67. Abdel Kouddous, interview.

68. Iskandar, interview.

69. Mohamed Hamama, "New Plans to Regulate Digital Media," *Mada Masr,* November 4, 2015, http://www.madamasr.com/en/2015/11/04/feature/politics/new-plans-to-regulate-digital-media/.

70. Zvi Bar'el, "60,000 Political Prisoners and 1,250 Missing: Welcome to the New Egypt," *Haaretz*, September 11, 2016, http://www.haaretz.com/middle-east-news/.premium-1.741178.

71. Attalah, interview.

72. Iskandar, interview.

73. Shokr, interview.

74. Ahmed, interview.

75. Abdel Kouddous, interview.

76. Attalah, interview.

77. Ahmed, interview.

78. Rabie, interview.

79. For more on Egypt's cartoonists, see Jonathan Guyer's chapter in this volume, "Speech Bubbles: Comics and Political Cartoons in Sisi's Egypt."

80. Abdel Kouddous, interview.

81. Attalah, interview.

82. Abdel Fattah, "Graffiti for Two."

14

Mobilizing through Online Media

Why the Internet Still Matters for Change in the Middle East

MARC LYNCH

Social media had a starring role in the Arab uprisings of 2011. But since then, authoritarians have cracked down on online activists, and even on casual dissent on platforms such as Facebook and Twitter. Meanwhile, numerous reactionaries have shown they can use the web just as effectively as the liberals who were its first adopters in the region. Together, these events have unraveled the once-popular narrative that the Internet has an inherent bent toward democracy. Still, state control of communications has been forever disrupted, and online platforms continue to provide the region's most resilient sites for political and social engagement. Usually, they do not directly lead to mass action. However, such a metric underestimates social media's significance. The Internet's churn often occurs beneath the surface: ideas ferment, identities evolve, and coordination happens across geographical and social divides. Authorities may infiltrate and imprison, but online media will certainly be central to the next wave of change, whatever form it takes.

A s autocratic regimes have regained their grip on power following the extraordinary moments of early 2011, many politically engaged Arabs have retreated into online spaces to rethink, reshape, and recreate forms of contentious political action. The severe increase in state surveillance and repression of the Internet over the last five years has shaped the way online media is used in Arab countries. But such repressive measures cannot erase the generational impact of the massive increase in the availability and use of social media. Understanding how social media affects politics in this post-uprisings environment requires moving away from narrower questions of political protest. Opportunities for regime-threatening protest may be scarce over the next few years, but political engagement continues to evolve within a rapidly changing information and communications environment.

This is not to deny the role social media played in protest mobilization in the Arab world and beyond.[1] But the shocking surge of protesters into the streets in early 2011 was only one form of political action, and as is often the case, the outcome of a long process of change. It is social media's role in that pre-uprising period of political engagement, experimentation, and mobilization that is most relevant to understanding the current situation.[2] Then, as now, the power of repressive states posed a daunting obstacle to political mobilization. But during those seemingly stagnant years, activists developed new ways to communicate, to challenge state domination over the flow of information, and to organize. They are still doing so today—and in far greater numbers, across a far wider cross section of society, than in the previous decade.

Social media is only one part of the array of political, economic, social, and institutional factors shaping regional politics. Their unique causal role should not be exaggerated. But nor should it be minimized. Few other areas of social or political life have witnessed such dramatic and rapid change over the last decade. The Internet and social media have created an ever-evolving but quite resilient new informational ecosystem that shapes every aspect of the political environment.

Online media takes many forms, each of which can have different social and political implications. However, there seem to be some political and social effects that all social media platforms share in common.[3] Self-selection into communication networks seems to accelerate and intensify the flow of information, but also to direct it through communities of the like-minded. Individual Facebook pages may become centers for deliberation. Individual or group blogs may serve as a primary source of news and opinion within a particular community. Larger, more formal online newspapers and websites may become authoritative sources of alternative news and opinion. Twitter may allow a small group of local activists to transmit their message to a large international audience by connecting with influential journalists or public figures.

The effects of social media may have once been limited to a small group of young urban activists, given the relatively low levels of Internet penetration and the predominance of the English language online just after the turn of the century. Today, that is no longer the case. Consider the penetration of just one social media platform, Facebook. As of June 2016, Bahrain had eight hundred thousand registered Facebook accounts, an effective penetration rate of 58 percent. Iraq had 14 million accounts (37 percent); Jordan, 5 million (62 percent); Kuwait, 2.3 million (57 percent); Lebanon, 3.1 million (52 percent); Qatar, 2.2 million (97 percent); Saudi Arabia, 14 million (44 percent); and the United Arab Emirates, 7.7 million (83 percent).[4] Survey research suggests that most of those users engage in some forms of political communication or news consumption on social media. In one recent survey, roughly half of Algerians, Jordanians, and Tunisians regularly received news through Facebook, as did 30 percent of Egyptians, 44 percent of Moroccans, and nearly 60 percent of Palestinians.

This does not mean that traditional media has lost its significance. On the contrary, traditional media and social media have evolved together into a complex, interdependent ecosystem. Today, with much greater levels of social media use and significant social media presence by broadcast media platforms, there is even tighter integration with the reporting and discussions on broadcast media.[5] For most of the decade leading up to the Arab uprisings, the Qatar-based television station *Al Jazeera* served as a sort of common public sphere for Arabs across the region. Virtually everyone watched, or at least was aware, of its news coverage and major talk show programs, creating a sort of common ground even as most Arabs also consumed media from many other sources.[6] Today, by contrast, the Arab media has become highly polarized and fragmented, with audiences distributed along sectarian, political, and ideological lines, sharing few common sources of information or ideas. Social media reinforces this fragmentation.

The Overlooked Lessons of Social Media before 2011

In the decade before the uprisings, online media offered distinctly new public-sphere sites for organization, identity construction, formation of new solidarities, and internal argumentation—which however did not seem capable of producing mass mobilization or meaningful political change.

The experience of Egypt's Kefaya, which rose out of the anti-war protests of 2003, represents a critical example of this sort of movement. If judged by its ability to mobilize mass protest or to force meaningful political change, its political experience was one of repeated failure. But Kefaya succeeded in transforming its own members, changing the terms of Egyptian political discourse, introducing new political ideas and solidarities into the public sphere, and inspiring new movements and tactics that would in later years prove central to the revolution. The relationships forged between leftist and liberal activists with young Muslim Brotherhood members during those seemingly useless protests proved vital in the decisive early days of the January 25 uprising. Those young Islamists were themselves manifestly changed by their own participation in these social media and protest networks. As they grew dissatisfied with the Brotherhood's rigid hierarchies and cautious politics, and built friendships outside the group, many ultimately left the Brotherhood. Some did so in response to an internal crackdown toward the end of this century's first decade, and others in response to their experience of the revolution itself.[7]

We should assess the current slate of social media activities and opportunities by those longer-term standards, not by the unrealistic standard of the exceptional revolutionary moment of early 2011. There are now many small, resilient Kefaya-style networks and movements operating on the margins of politics across the Middle East. While they seem weak today, their latent potential should not be underplayed. Today's online activity resembles that in the years before the uprisings, but within a political environment profoundly changed by the aftermath of those uprisings and the reconsolidation of autocratic rule.

The social media of 2016 has a much greater potential reach than did the social media of 2006. It includes far more and far more diverse users across a much wider range of platforms. It tends to be far more organically integrated with print and broadcast media outlets, almost all of which now have robust websites and social media presences of their own. A wide variety of activists and identity groups have developed resilient communities and networks united by shared identities and interests. The extent of social media usage and the experience Arab citizens now have with its potential mean that these experiments will involve a much wider range of engagement and thus a great latent potential for sudden mobilization when a crisis hits or opportunity arises.

A decade ago, blogs and Internet discussion forums were still a novelty, used primarily by a small elite of urban, educated youth. This was both a strength and a weakness. Being early adopters gave young activists the opportunity to innovate and explore the potential of the new technologies without a great deal of competition or official pushback. The effects of social media were thus felt primarily, and disproportionately, within a distinctive slice of political society. Many studies of social media in the Arab world tended to concentrate on that small group of activists who adopted the Internet early, used it for political and social mobilization, and internalized blogging into their identity.[8] Such research offered keen insights into their role in political mobilization, but risked neglecting how the Internet was being adopted and used by the much larger nonactivist sector of ordinary citizens.

The situation today is quite different. For one, blogs have been largely overtaken by social media and by larger websites featuring collections of opinion and journalistic voices. More broadly, social media has become ubiquitous rather than exceptional. The high profile of platforms such as Facebook and Twitter during the revolutions of early 2011 brought many more users to those platforms. Social media has now become part of the regular texture of daily life rather than an exotic novelty. As such, this ubiquity makes it less of an independent causal variable and more of an environmental or structural factor for social and political outcomes. Citizens access information, talk politics, and organize for political action in an environment thoroughly structured by social media. The Internet now is less a new ingredient added to a recipe than it is the oxygen in the atmosphere.

The effects of this new media environment are felt widely across a range of political environments in and beyond the Middle East.[9] Digital media played a key role in Iranian protests against the fraudulent 2009 election of Mahmoud Ahmadinejad, and served as a vital virtual infrastructure for the organization of an alternative civil society in the years that followed.[10] In Saudi Arabia, Twitter emerged after 2011 as perhaps the single most important site for political discourse and activity.[11] Youth activists across the Gulf found creative ways to use social media to overcome state obstacles and repression, breaking taboos and connecting across social and sectarian divides in new ways.[12]

Social media platforms such as Twitter, Facebook, and YouTube played a critical role during the early days of the Arab uprisings.[13] There is no need to exaggerate their causal role, given the plethora of motivations and structural forces which went into those mass explosions of popular anger. But social media clearly mattered at the margins. It helped to accelerate and intensify protest movements, through the rapid sharing of information that galvanized protesters and helped them organize. It also helped to link together disparate local and national protests into a unified narrative, and brought that narrative out to a broad global media audience. The global phenomenon of sudden, unexpected mobilizations around focal-point issues seems difficult to disentangle from the worldwide transformation of information.[14]

But mobilization to protest was only one dimension of the transformative impact of the new media. Radical change in the structure of political communications has both observable and unobservable effects across a wide range of dimensions.[15] Political communication theorists have argued that social media changes the nature, speed, and content of information to which different individuals are exposed.[16] People suddenly experiencing a surge of photos, videos, and outraged commentary from within a trusted social movement might be more likely to take action in response. People accustomed to the free access of information experienced in social media might bridle under new censorship provisions. Social media networks might allow individuals who share interests or identities to connect with each other across physical and social distance.

Youth activists are not the only users able to exploit the opportunities of new media, of course. By far the most popular social media users in the Gulf are religious figures such as Mohamad al-Arefe, Salman al-Awdah, Nabil al-Awadhy, and Aid al-Qarni, who use their online platforms to spread religious messages, raise money for charitable causes, and to promote their political views. This diversity highlights a critical point: there is no reason to believe that this new information environment necessarily favors one ideological trend over another. The opportunities created by social media can be seized or squandered by any group. Islamists and secularists have each demonstrated the ability to use social media effectively to engage in semipublic internal discussions, to organize protests, to challenge state narratives and to influence mass media coverage. Indeed, social media likely favors populist movements, which can mobilize nationalist or other in-group identities and biases.

The State Strikes Back

Resurgent authoritarian regimes are not blind to these new developments, of course. They have taken increasingly stringent efforts to surveil, repress and censor Internet content and to intimidate or imprison influential users.[17] These efforts, while deeply damaging to the public sphere and to the individuals affected, are somewhat quixotic. Their efforts to deal with particular symptoms will do little to reverse a deep structural change in the nature of political communication. To the extent that they calculate that online activities that do not directly lead to offline mobilization are not immediately threatening—and thus can be tolerated—they may allow these new spaces to survive.

States retain considerable ability to broadcast their political messages and to mobilize their supporters, and have proven remarkably effective at adapting to the new information environment. But states have not been able to reproduce the sort of total dominance over information that characterized Arab autocracy before the new millennium. Repression now entails observing, managing, and shaping massive online flows of opinion and information rather than suppressing it.

The power of social media to affect politics was in many ways an artifact of its seeming unimportance. The regime of Zine El Abidine Ben Ali in Tunisia, like many autocratic regimes, allowed Facebook to operate in part because it seemed a nonpolitical platform for families and friends to connect. As the potency of online activism became clear, Arab regimes began to view social media as a threat, and took more seriously the need to surveil, control, and curb its use. Bahrain pioneered the deployment of online trolls to swamp opposition Twitter hashtags and pollute political discourse. Kuwait, Qatar, and the United Arab Emirates have repeatedly arrested Twitter and Facebook users for postings deemed offensive to the ruling family, imposing harsh sentences to deter others from engaging in even minor forms of subversive speech.[18] Many regimes have used social media profiles to track down and imprison activists, and have regularly infiltrated online groups to manipulate their political and organizational discussions.

State scrutiny and repression is the most obvious challenge. There has always been something of a self-limiting quality to the political power of online media. In the first decade of this century, activists could mobilize the potential of online media in large part because states did not yet recognize it as a threat. The more that their protests threatened regimes, the more that states would turn their considerable resources toward either shutting down online activism or exploiting its potential on their own terms. During that decade, some regimes cracked down at the first sign of mobilization while others viewed online activism as a useful way to allow small groups of malcontent elites to vent while surveilling their activities. After the attention devoted to social media during the 2011 uprisings, no Arab state will again overlook their potential for activism.

As social media grew in power, states cracked down by jailing prominent users for critical tweets, and expanded their surveillance over online communications. The discussion forum Bahrain Online has been blocked in the country since its founding, and its administrator, Ali Abdulemam, was repeatedly jailed and threatened as the forum became more influential.[19] The Saudi writer Raif Badawi was also arrested over his postings on a liberal forum. The Emirates, Kuwait, Qatar, Saudi Arabia, and other Arab states have arrested citizens for tweeting jokes or insults directed at ruling families. The repression can extend across borders: in Jordan, a prominent journalist was even arrested for tweeting criticism of the Emirates. Meanwhile, prominent Saudi leaders have also joined Twitter and engaged with other social media platforms in order to shape influential sites of discourse.

This overt state repression of social media both attests to its political significance and changes the nature of its use. Few Facebook or Twitter users now expect social media to provide a safe, unobserved space for organization or semi-private conversation. Social media must now be understood as, in part, public performance, and as a riskier form of talk than it seemed a decade ago. Indeed, some Arab activists suspect that online groups and platforms that are allowed to remain open are partly tolerated to allow repressive regimes to observe the participants and their possible activities. The effects of such regime interference have been to reduce the operational contributions of social media to political protest and to force online discourse into new directions.

In response to state repression and surveillance, some communities go "dark," cultivating private discussion forums open only to members, while others retreat from the most explicitly political topics to refocus on cultural or local issues.

Resilient Sites of Social Media Engagement

The most obvious site of ongoing online engagement is social media itself. There is no single site or platform today that encapsulates Arab social media. WhatsApp is increasingly central to youth communication and social interaction. YouTube has been an indispensable tool for the circulation of videos, often through embedding in other social media sites. Instagram, Snapchat, PalTalk, and many other platforms either have or will take their turn as sites for youth to creatively explore opportunities for collective action, information sharing, and online connections.

Blogs and Internet forums were the critical platforms during the first iteration of social media activism in the first few years of the century. Egyptian activist blogs formed the critical infrastructure of the Kefaya movement, playing a key role in disseminating information about police brutality and organizing protests. Bahrain Online brought thousands of Bahrainis into unprecedented open, anonymous political debate, and broke the news of several damaging royal scandals.[20] These have become less central to the emergent Arab public sphere. While some famous first-generation blogs have been abandoned, as their authors moved on to other endeavors or suffered political repression, others have taken on fascinating new forms. Arabic language sites rapidly overtook the first generation of primarily English language blogs written by young, urban elites.

Facebook has been perhaps the most important single platform for Arab online engagement. In some countries, it has almost become synonymous with civil society and the public sphere, as the principle site for ongoing, focused dialogue. Facebook does not simply exist as an enclosed universe, of course. Articles on the mainstream media are posted, circulated and discussed on Facebook pages. As Jordanian social media activist Naseem Tarawnah puts it, "Facebook manages to keep conversations alive long after they've died in mainstream media—widening the ripple effect, like throwing a stone into pond."[21] The course that those discussions take can be unpredictable, allowing for seemingly unconnected issues to suddenly resonate with each other and create new political configurations and points of agreement.

Facebook offers many opportunities for community building and the construction of networks of the likeminded. Public pages become sites for active, ongoing discussions of these issues, with far more opportunity for real engagement than in blog or YouTube comment sections or on Twitter. One of the most critical issues for Facebook is its real name policy, in sharp contrast to Twitter where anonymous accounts are common and, increasingly, bots roam freely. Egypt has been a central location for digital politics, both before and after the uprisings.[22] Innovations such as the "We are all Khaled Said" Facebook page set the standard for the political uses of social media.[23] This real name policy also creates vulnerabilities, of course, as state intelligence agencies can observe the membership and activities of public pages—and typically can gain access to private and personal pages as well.

Twitter typically has far lower penetration and usage rates than Facebook, especially in Egypt, North Africa, and the Levant. Twitter tends to be used by more politically engaged users, and especially by journalists. This gives it the ability to have a disproportionate impact by shaping mass media narratives, disseminating images and events well beyond relatively small networks. Twitter-based social networks themselves tend to be more episodic, transient, and superficial than Facebook's. At the same time, it has remarkable power to spread images and ideas extremely quickly, providing a public focal point during moments of crisis.

The primacy of Facebook over Twitter depends on context. In Saudi Arabia, Twitter emerged as one of the most influential and critical public sphere sites in the Kingdom.[24] In 2014, a study found that it had the highest per capita Twitter penetration in the world, with more than four million regularly updated accounts.[25] Social media has helped to overcome the state's restrictions over public space, including gender segregation and the physical barriers to public assembly and protest. Manal Sharif's campaign to promote the right of women to drive is probably the best known of the social media hashtag campaigns. But beyond specific activist campaigns, Twitter simply became the location where Saudi public arguments took place and where young Saudis learned how to engage with public politics.[26]

Citizen Journalism Brings Bold New Voices, and Some Rumor Mongering

Beyond these core social media platforms, dedicated citizen journalism portals have been an important node in the broader network of online engagement. Egypt's *Mada Masr* is an especially well-developed initiative allowing activists and investigative journalists to challenge the state-dominated media.[27] Iraq's *Niqash* has provided outstanding reporting from the local level across that war-torn country. Investigative journalism remains difficult in the Arab world, but the civil society organization Arab Reporters for Investigative Journalism has trained nearly two thousand journalists who have produced hundreds of local and national investigative reports over the last decade.[28]

Few of these platforms have broken out to reach a mass audience. But this limited reach can also be a strength. Regimes may be more willing to tolerate platforms that have only a small elite constituency. What is more, building the capabilities and connections of a core constituency can have long-term payoffs for democratic politics and the consolidation of civil society.

Several experiments with citizen journalism portals are particularly instructive, both for their strengths and their failings. Tunisia has a long history of creative Internet activism.[29] Several online news aggregators and political platforms, such as *TuneZine* and *Tunis News* emerged in the first decade of the century, evolving not only into sources of information but also into sites of oppositional identity formation for a small set of Tunisians inside the country and abroad. Nawaat, one of the most iconic of the citizen journalism platforms, grew out of this ecosystem.[30] Nawaat began in 2004 as a platform connecting Tunisian youth and dissident voices in France and inside Tunisia. Its founders and editorial collective had a highly political mission, often clashing with the more apolitical blogging community, which preferred to avoid political issues and repression. Its best-known achievement prior to the revolution was publishing the Wikileaks State Department documents on the corruption of Ben Ali's family.

Within a few months of the revolution, Nawaat registered as an official nongovernmental organization (NGO), in part to allow it to legally take foundation grants. It expanded its staff and professionalized its operations, focusing more on investigative journalism and multimedia. Along with its own journalism, Nawaat also maintained an "open" page where contributors could directly publish. Hundreds of people have contributed to this section, from well-known politicians such as Moncef Marzouki (who later became president) to student activists and citizen journalists. Nawaat did not replace the mass media or reach a broad Tunisian audience, even if it managed to survive and even prosper as an online platform. It cultivates a small but influential elite audience of civil society activists and educated youth, which allows it to punch above its weight in terms of agenda setting.[31]

The transition from oppositional collective to professionalized NGO has not been entirely smooth. In the fall of 2011, Nawaat's leadership infuriated many activists by censoring stories and then refusing to honor a journalists' strike, leading to an exodus of some of its founding staff.[32] Nawaat's growing prominence also opened it up to exploitation by various political factions or by individuals seeking to discredit their rivals. Leaks to its investigative journalists or posts on its open page could be used to anonymously attack political rivals or spread malicious rumors. Once published on Nawaat, these rumors and leaks would become legitimate fodder for television and newspaper coverage. This became especially problematic as Tunisian politics polarized between Ennahda and anti-Islamist groups in 2013. For instance, a stream of inflammatory leaks alleging Ennahda's penetration of state institutions likely originated with intelligence agencies seeking to fuel popular hostility to the Islamist party.

Jordan, like Tunisia, has a long history of online activism and media that belies its seemingly static political system and suggests the importance of looking beyond formal politics when examining sources of dynamism within authoritarian regimes. In the first decade of the century, a remarkable number of Jordanians developed blogs, new media companies, and online platforms. The government, while concerned about the potential political implications, viewed the emergence of a tech sector and the cultivation of entrepreneurial youth as critically important to its economic future. The leading Arabic-language web portal, Maktoob, was created in Jordan before being sold to Yahoo in 2009. King Abdullah II famously reached out to leading bloggers, even posting comments on critical blog posts and inviting them to the royal palace—a savvy public relations move that also pointedly warned bloggers that the Palace was watching them.[33]

7iber, the citizen journalism hub launched in the spring of 2007 by a group of these young Jordanian bloggers, set out to be a platform for engaging a wide range of voices in a distributed framework that would enable political conversation, investigative journalism, and community building. It relied less on diaspora-based leaders than Nawaat, reflecting the different levels of political openness in the two countries. For the first few years, 7iber attempted to focus on local issues rather than national politics. In the heat of the Arab uprisings of 2011, however, 7iber made a significant advance into the political public sphere by hosting the "hashtag debates." These monthly events combined physical salons with a robust online component. In one of the best known of these events, the former deputy prime minister, Marwan Muasher, engaged in a frank discussion about the limits of the Jordanian regime's liberalism and the need for deeper political reforms. Other hashtag debates explored questions such as the forms of constitutional monarchy. Those hashtagged moments of collective discourse faded as the protest movement lost steam, but have been reproduced at the local level in a number of dynamic ways.[34] Like Nawaat, 7iber chose to make a transition from a freewheeling collective to a media startup company attracting international grants. This transition to a more formal structure caused problems among the founders and an evolution of the platform's mission and content.[35]

A number of other widely read online news platforms have become fixtures of the Jordanian media scene, largely filling the space once occupied by weekly print tabloids. *Ammon News*, for instance, speaks to a broad audience of primarily young Jordanian nationalists who are far less dependable regime supporters than their elders.[36] *Khaberni* speaks to young liberal Jordanians, connecting out to broader Arab issues in an effort to build robust transnational solidarities without sacrificing local specificity. *AmmanNet*, run by the journalist Daoud Kuttab, became one of the first successful Internet-only community radio stations.

As in Tunisia, these online platforms were often abused to spread rumors against political or personal enemies. Indeed, the Jordanian government defended the introduction of a new online publications law in part by pointing to instances of blackmail, in which individuals were warned that failure to pay would mean the dissemination of defamatory information on these unregulated platforms.[37] While this problem was real, the draconian new Internet publications laws ranged far more broadly in cracking down on independent online platforms. The new regulations—including a requirement to register with the government—and high profile prosecutions of platforms that crossed some political line forced more restrained coverage, or drove many online platforms offline.

Ongoing Mobilization after the Uprisings

The difficulty of mobilizing large-scale protests in the wake of the uprisings does not mean that activists have stopped using social media to organize politically. Smaller-scale campaigns coordinated through social media continue to appear, offering some evidence of the ongoing discontent and latent potential for organization. Tunisia and Jordan again offer useful examples of such ongoing mobilization linked to social media.

The Tunisian campaign against the Economic Reconciliation Law offers a good example of how social media intersects with traditional civil society and political forces.[38] The Economic Reconciliation Law proposed in July 2015 by Nidaa Tounes, the ruling party, aimed to separate economic crimes such as corruption from the transitional justice process in a way that many Tunisians believed would grant impunity to the corrupt elite of the old regime. Resistance to the bill emerged quickly from a network of twenty-four different civil society organizations and a diverse group of activists.[39] The "Manich Msamah" (we do not forgive) campaign, organized through Facebook pages and Internet sites, managed to launch major protests and sustained smaller protests over the course of more than a year.[40] It used its own social media pages alongside platforms such as Nawaat, combining text and video to publicize the campaign, its protests, and its demands.[41] This campaign demonstrated how these social media platforms allowed demoralized and marginalized activists to break through and reach a broad public despite general political apathy and an indifferent mainstream media.[42]

Young Jordanians also continued to find ways to convert online possibility into political action. After the dissolution of the early 2011 protests in Amman, the Herak movement took root, connecting activists across the south of Jordan through Facebook and other social media. The movement proved able to sustain itself for years against significant odds.[43] Protests were only the most visible dimension of Herak's activism.[44] Its members argued that the dialogues and connections promoted by Herak's online presence and real-world meetings were the critical contribution. Herak participants attested to how such participation had changed their understandings of the nature of politics and the possibilities of social change.

In the summer of 2016, another interesting group of young Jordanian activists, primarily from outside Amman, came together under the name Shaghaf.[45] As Sean Yom and Wael al-Khatib observed, the Shaghaf activists adapted to draconian regime pressures not by abandoning political challenge but by moving it away from street protests into new domains. More than a dozen local chapters coordinate online through Facebook groups, Twitter, and WhatsApp on initiatives such as an accountability project for parliamentary candidates and local-level political debates. Like the Herak movement, Shaghaf brought new types of citizens into politics, experimented with new forms of online-offline interaction, and worked to advance particular ideas within a relatively closed political environment.

Such Jordanian and Tunisian political campaigns do not amount to an Arab uprising-style protest wave. They should be understood more as ongoing experiments in organization, network-building, and mobilization. They succeed by existing, developing new tactics, spreading ideas, and bringing in new members, not by overthrowing regimes.

How Social Media Really Matters for the Region's Future

Those expecting social media to produce another "Arab Spring"-style tsunami of protest are concentrating on the wrong things. Instead, the focus should be on how the complex interplay between traditional media and social media is transforming the substance and texture of politics across the region. Online news and social media networks have become a fully normalized, core element of the political space, used by all social and political actors in a variety of ways.

Those activities do not have to be directly political in order to have important effects on social mobilization, the ability of regimes to control information, and the relationship between citizens and the state. As with Egypt's Kefaya movement or other phenomena in the middle of the century's first decade, such forms of political engagement will not lead to major change any time soon. But that is not the correct metric for evaluating their significance. Some of the most dynamic experiments with social media—including both the building of new communities and experimentation with new platforms and methods—take place when formal politics is blocked. Young Arabs, including not only self-conscious activists but a wider circle of engaged citizens, continue to experiment with new ways to communicate and to organize. Such activity may seem apolitical, but this needs to be understood as an adaptive strategy in order to remain under the radar of suspicious states. The political importance of the new relationships, competencies, and networks forged through online engagement will likely only be revealed when sudden new political openings appear.

To be positioned to take advantage of such openings, however, such online platforms face steep challenges. Many online organizations and movements have already succumbed to the extreme polarization and sectarianism that has infected the broader Arab public.[46] Social media narrowcasting has both benefits and problems in this regard. The distancing of these groupings from the mainstream of society can cost them the ability to speak to a broader public and reduce their generalizable appeal. It can also drive polarization, as clusters of the like-minded value ideological purity and expressive action over moderation and pragmatism. The attractions of in-group insularity can be depoliticizing as well, as users move away from political issues of broad public concern toward issues with symbolic or material significance only to their own smaller groups.

These characteristics of social media are likely to particularly encourage populist and illiberal groupings. And the political change enabled by this online media could as easily be in populist, ethnonationalist, or hypernationalist directions. Every political trend now uses the same online platforms, minimizing any advantage that activists once gained from them. The near universality of online media virtually ensures that political and identity trends that dominate societies will also dominate online spaces.

It is a sobering reality that social media tends to promote the formation of clusters of like-minded users, where more extreme and intolerant views often flourish.[47] The very properties that give social media its mobilizing power also make it especially well-adapted to sectarian and militant groups. Social media tends to reinforce in-group identities and to encourage extremist views within those like-minded communities. It facilitates the dehumanization of targeted groups, and ratchets up emotional and angry responses to their perceived outrages. Islamists across the region have developed online platforms as robust as anything produced by liberals. So too did supporters of Egypt's military coup, ethnic nationalists in Jordan, jihadists recruiting for the Islamic State, Shia militias, and hardline sectarians across the Gulf.

The broader media ecosystem has changed significantly as well. Independent sites must compete for attention within a far more crowded media ecosystem than existed in the period before the uprisings. Online media is increasingly difficult to disentangle from broadcast or print media. Virtually every Arab television station or newspaper has a web presence today, and their stories and content typically drive online discussions. That includes the vast array of media platforms supportive of, and generally funded by, resurgent authoritarian regimes. Nationalist, mobilizing websites use the same mix of online engagement techniques as do the independent platforms, but with the overt or covert support of the state, they typically have far greater resources to amplify their message.

Still, social media has enduring real benefits, as well. Platforms dedicated to a specific political or social constituency can afford to specialize, covering stories of interest to that sector in greater depth and bringing out otherwise neglected issues. Within such specific sectors, focused media platforms can become sites for the formation of stronger and more self-conscious collective identities. They can also become useful sites for the negotiation of political strategies and the articulation of shared interests. In short, new media sites today serve many of the functions once found in offline civil society—but do so across a greater distance and with greater immediacy.

New media spaces are one key reason why, despite surface appearances, there is no going back to the old days of resilient Arab autocracy. This does not mean that the Internet can, on its own, create democracy, or even that the balance of power inexorably tilts away from states toward society. The broader significance of these new online platforms is generational. Today's Arab youth are digital natives, and will continue to use social media to explore new identities, information, and ideas. The effects of this engagement will be nonlinear, introducing new sources of turbulence and creativity into the political sphere. This will complicate the efforts of resurgent authoritarian regimes to dominate the flow of information, or to restore stability and a sense of normality. Politics will be more turbulent, as new social and political movements will come together suddenly and seize sudden opportunities to challenge authority.

This perspective offers both more and less hope about the transformative power of the Internet than has been common. Social media has degraded some aspects of state power but reinforced others. States and anti-liberal trends have learned to navigate the new informational environment, even if youth activists typically stay a step or two ahead. Social media has encouraged the emergence of new political movements, but not necessarily normatively attractive ones. Ultimately, the most important near-term effect is likely to be the evolution of new networks, identities, and strategies whose importance will only be revealed when the unexpected becomes reality.

Notes

1. Philip Howard and Muzammil Hussain, *Democracy's Fourth Wave: Digital Media and the Arab Spring* (Oxford: Oxford University Press, 2013); Zeynap Tufekci and Christopher Wilson, "Social Media and the Decision to Participate in Political Protest: Observations from Tahrir Square," *Journal of Communication* 6, no. 2 (2012): 363–79.

2. Merlyna Lim, "Clicks, Cabs and Coffee Houses: Social Media and Oppositional Movements in Egypt, 2004–2011," *Journal of Communication* 62, no. 2 (2012): 231–48.

3. For an overview of the academic literature on these effects, see Henry Farrell, "The Consequences of the Internet for Politics," *Annual Review of Political Science* 15, no. 1 (2012): 35–52; and Sean Aday, et al., *Blogs and Bullets: New Media and Contentious Politics* (Washington, DC: United States Institute of Peace, 2010).

4. Data from Internet World Stats, http://www.internetworldstats.com/middle.htm.

5. Naomi Sakr, "Social Media, Television Talk Shows, and Political Change in Egypt," *Television & New Media* 14, no. 4 (2012): 322–37; Maximillian Hänska Ahy, "Networked Communication and the Arab Spring: Linking Broadcast and Social Media," *New Media & Society* 18, no. 1 (2016): 99–116.

6. Marc Lynch, *Voices of the New Arab Public: Iraq, Al-Jazeera, and Middle East Politics Today* (New York: Columbia University Press, 2006).

7. Marc Lynch, "Young Muslim Brothers in Cyberspace," *Middle East Report* 37, no. 245 (2007): 26–33; David M. Faris, *Dissent and Revolution in a Digital Age: Social Media, Blogging and Activism in Egypt* (London: I.B. Tauris, 2013).

8. Faris, *Dissent and Revolution in a Digital Age.*

9. Marc Lynch, "Political Science and the New Arab Public Sphere," Social Science Research Council, June 12, 2012, http://publicsphere.ssrc.org/lynch-political-science-and-the-new-arab-public-sphere/.

10. Negar Mottahedeh, *#iranelection: Hashtag Solidarity and the Transformation of Iranian Politics* (Stanford: Stanford University Press, 2015).

11. Irfan Chaudhry, "#Hashtags for Change: Can Twitter Promote Social Progress in Saudi Arabia?," *International Journal of Communication* 8 (2014): 943–61.

12. Kristin Diwan, "Breaking Taboos: Youth Activism in the Gulf States," Atlantic Council Issue Brief, April 2014.

13. Gilad Lotan, et al., "The Arab Spring: The Revolutions Were Tweeted: Information Flows during the 2011 Tunisian and Egyptian Revolutions," *International Journal of Communication* 5 (2011): 1375–406; Mohamed Nanabhay and Roxane Farmanfarmaian, "From Spectacle to Spectacular: How Physical Space, Social Media and Mainstream Broadcast Media Amplified the Public Sphere in Egypt's Revolution," *The Journal of North African Studies* 16, no. 4 (2011): 573–605; and Robert Brym, et al., "Social Media in the 2011 Egyptian Uprising," *The British Journal of Sociology* 65, no. 2 (2014): 266–92.

14. Key recent theoretical interventions include: Helen Margetts, et al., *Political Turbulence: How Social Media Shape Collective Action* (Princeton, N.J.: Princeton University Press, 2016); W. Lance Bennett and Alexandra Segerberg, *The Logic of Connective Action: Digital Media and the Personalization of Contentious Politics* (Cambridge: Cambridge University Press, 2014).

15. Sean Aday, et al., "Blogs and Bullets II: New Media and the Arab Uprisings," U.S. Institute of Peace, 2012, http://www.usip.org/sites/default/files/PW80.pdf; Farrell, "The Consequences of the Internet for Politics."

16. Margetts, et al., *Political Turbulence*.

17. See the annual reports by Freedom House, "Freedom on the Net," for details on the escalating repression of the Internet in the Arab world.

18. Evgeny Morozov, *The Net Delusion: The Dark Side of Internet Freedom* (New York: Public Affairs, 2012); for recent coverage of Arab states, see "Arab Gulf States: Attempts to Silence 140 Characters," Human Rights Watch, November 2, 2016, https://www.hrw.org/news/2016/11/01/arab-gulf-states-attempts-silence-140-characters.

19. "Freedom on the Net 2015," Freedom House, 2015, https://freedomhouse.org/report/freedom-net/2015/bahrain.

20. Fahed Desmoukh, "The Internet in Bahrain: Breaking the Monopoly of Information," *Foreign Policy*, September 21, 2010, http://www.bahrainrights.org/en/node/3409.

21. Naseem Tarawnah, interview with the author, Skype, September 22, 2016.

22. Sahar Khamis and Katherine Vaughn, "Cyberactivism in the Egyptian Revolution," *Arab Media and Society* 13 (2011): 1–25; Miriyam Aouragh and Anne Alexander, "The Egyptian Experience: Sense and Nonsense of the Internet Revolution," *International Journal of Communication* 5 (2011): 1344–58.

23. Sahar Khamis and Katherine Vaughn, "We Are All Khaled Said: The Potentials and Limitations of Cyberactivism in Triggering Public Mobilization and Promoting Political Change," *Journal of Arab & Muslim Media Research* 4 (2012): 145–63.

24. Marc Lynch, "America's Saudi Problem," *Foreign Policy*, January 24, 2013, http://foreignpolicy.com/2013/01/24/americas-saudi-problem/; Robert F. Worth, "Twitter Gives Saudi Arabia a Revolution of Its Own," *New York Times*, October 20, 2012, http://www.nytimes.com/2012/10/21/world/middleeast/twitter-gives-saudi-arabia-a-revolution-of-its-own.html.

25. Ahmed Al Omran, "Saudi Royal Court Breaks Its Silence on Twitter," *Wall Street Journal*, April 7, 2014, http://blogs.wsj.com/middleeast/2014/04/07/saudi-royal-court-chief-breaks-silence-on-twitter/.

26. Caryle Murphy, *Saudi Arabia's Youth and the Kingdom's Future* (Washington, D.C.: Woodrow Wilson Center, 2012); Marieke Transfeld and Isabelle Werenfelds, "#Hashtag Solidarities: Twitter Debates and Networks in the MENA Region," Stiftung Wissenschaft und Politik Research Paper 5, German Institute of Global Affairs, March 2016.

27. See Laura C. Dean's chapter in this volume, "All Truth Is Worth Publishing: Mada Masr and the Fight for Free Speech in Egypt," for an in-depth history of *Mada Masr*.

28. Rana Sabbagh, "Despite Growing Repression, Investigative Journalism Survives in the Arab World," *Al-Ghad*, December 1, 2016, http://en.arij.net/news/rana-sabbagh-despite-growing-repression-investigative-journalism-survives-in-the-arab-world/.

29. Mohammed al-Zayani, *Networked Publics and Digital Contention: The Politics of Everyday Life in Tunisia* (Oxford: Oxford University Press, 2015).

30. Sami Ben Gharbia, interview with the author, Tunis, November 2014.

31. Tunisian youth activist, interview with the author, Tunis, November 2014.

32. Tunisian media activist, interview with the author, Tunis, November 2014.

33. See the discussion on *The Black Iris*, July 5, 2008 http://black-iris.com/2008/07/05/verifying-king-abdullahs-comment-on-the-black-iris/.

34. Sean Yom and Wael al-Khatib, "How a New Youth Movement Is Emerging in Jordan Ahead of the Elections," *Washington Post*, September 14, 2016, https://www.washingtonpost.com/news/monkey-cage/wp/2016/09/14/how-a-new-youth-movement-in-jordan-is-emerging-ahead-of-elections/.

35. Nassem Tarawnah, "Retrospective: What I Learned From My Time at 7iber," *The Black Iris*, August 13, 2015, http://black-iris.com/2015/08/13/retrospective-what-i-learned-from-my-time-at-7iber/.

36. *Ammon News* editors, interview with the author, Amman, 2011.

37. Daoud Kuttab, "Freedom in Jordan Does Not Extend to Information," *Washington Post*, October 5, 2012, https://www.washingtonpost.com/opinions/freedom-in-jordan-does-not-extend-to-information/2012/10/05/220afb18-09c8-11e2-a10c-fa5a255a9258_story.html.

38. See Marc Lynch, "Tunisia May Be Lost in Transition," Carnegie Middle East Center, September 8, 2016, http://carnegie-mec.org/diwan/64510.

39. Wissen Sghair (Tunisian activist), interview with the author, Tunis, August 2016.

40. The Manich Masamah Facebook page had more than thirty-two thousand members as of November 2016. It can be found at https://www.facebook.com/manichmsame7/.

41. For an example of how the campaign used the Nawaat platform, incorporating text and video, see "Manich Masamah Campaign Announces a State of Popular Exception," July 26, 2016, http://goo.gl/itcb0S. Also see Ramzi Mhamdi, "The Course of the Transitional Justice in Tunisia" (Arabic), Nawaat, June 26, 2016 https://goo.gl/oAwvFu.

42. Mohammed Samih Beji Okkaz, "Opposition in Tunisia: Traditional Arenas, Alternative Channels" (Arabic), Nawaat, September 8, 2016, https://goo.gl/0rzY2H.

43. See Curtis Ryan, "Five Years after the Arab Uprising, Security Trumps Reforms in Jordan," *Washington Post*, March 4, 2016, https://www.washingtonpost.com/news/monkey-cage/wp/2016/03/04/five-years-after-arab-uprisings-security-trumps-reforms-in-jordan/; Sean Yom, "Tribal Politics in Contemporary Jordan: The Case of the Hirak movement," *Middle East Journal* 68, no. 2 (2014): 229–47.

44. Ned Parker, "Jordan Democracy Activists Enjoy Camaraderie, Freedom to Protest," *Los Angeles Times*, January 24, 2013, http://articles.latimes.com/2013/jan/24/world/la-fg-jordan-herak-20130125.

45. Yom and Khatib, "New Youth Movement in Jordan."

46. Marc Lynch, "After the Arab Spring: How the Media Trashed the Transitions," *Journal of Democracy* 26, no. 4 (2015): 90–94.

47. For empirical evidence and discussion of how this happened in Egypt, see Marc Lynch, Deen Freelon and Sean Aday, *Blogs and Bullets IV: How Social Media Undermines Transitions to Democracy* (Washington, D.C.: Peacetech Lab, 2016).

PART IV
Governance

15

The Economics of War and Peace in Syria

Stratification and Factionalization in the Business Community

SAMER ABBOUD

Much is made of the sectarian and ethnic factions in Syria's civil war, but far less attention has been paid to its economic dynamics, which are essential for understanding the roots of the conflict. This study goes beyond the usual extent of such analyses to argue that the economic context is also crucial for understanding the war's persistence, and the shape of an eventual peace and reconstruction. The contraction of the Syrian economy and the emergence of a war economy have profoundly affected the stratification and composition of the Syrian business community, and the elite in particular. The conflict has created a new class of elites who are actually to some degree dependent on the war for their fortunes, and implicated in violence even when they do not directly perpetrate it. As a result, business interests have become at least as important as other factors in determining political allegiances.

The Syrian conflict has produced one of the worst humanitarian catastrophes in recent memory. In this context, popular and scholarly analysis has focused extensively on the armed groups' capacity to commit violence, various forms of international military interventions, and the dramatic rise of groups such as the Islamic State and Fateh al-Sham (formerly known as the Nusra Front). Often lost in these stories is the role that economic actors, such as the business community in general and the elite in particular, play in the perpetuation of war. These omissions are consequential. Despite the invisibility of Syrian business figures in much of the analysis around the conflict, they play a fundamental role in perpetuating it. For this reason, they need to be taken seriously as major stakeholders in Syria's postconflict reconstruction process. Ignoring the role of business actors today can have implications for how we think of the postconflict reconstruction process.

The contraction of the Syrian economy and the emergence of a war economy have had a profound impact on the stratification and composition of the Syrian business community, and the elite in particular. In the short and long term, sanctions, sustained capital flight, the reduction of enterprise assets, and the dramatic reduction of production and exchange throughout the country have adversely affected the established prewar business elite. They have seen their fortunes shrink and many have even left Syria for neighboring countries.

Simultaneously, however, the new war economy has fostered the rise of a new conflict elite whose wealth is directly tethered to the continuation of violence. While these actors do not carry arms or directly perpetrate violence, they are, undeniably, beneficiaries of the strife. Many are important players in ensuring the flow of goods between different parts of Syria[1] and transactions between regime-held areas and the outside world, including borderlands between Syria, Turkey, and Iraq. Some have gained spectacular wealth and influence in a very short time. This new conflict elite will have profound impacts on Syria's future.

In this chapter, I ask how the Syrian conflict and the attendant economic dynamics have contributed to new patterns of stratification and the factionalization of the Syrian business elite. I examine the relationship between conflict and social transformation in Syria and argue that economic contraction, international sanctions, and capital flight have generated the broader contexts in which this transformation has occurred. These transformations are important to the study of conflict and peace in Syria because they provide insight into who the main actors implicated in violence are, who potential agents of peaceful change are, and how Syrian businesspeople can advocate for and pursue reconstruction projects in the postconflict stage. In focusing on these kinds of transformations, this chapter highlights the different forms of business elites' agency (such as the rise of a conflict elite) that have emerged during the war and the emergent stratification of the business elites along political (pro-/anti-regime; neutral) and economic lines. One of the more salient features of this transformation is how it occurs alongside the regime's attempts to stave off collapse during the conflict, including by finding alternative sources of revenue and looking to regional military powers for support on the battlefield[2] during which the Syrian regime has been forced to reconfigure its social, economic, and security bases in order to survive. I conclude the chapter with a reflection on the implications of the stratification and factionalization of the elite on Syria's reconstruction after the conflict, and the role that business elites can play in this process.

Business Stratification during the Ba'athist Period

The Ba'ath Party's takeover of power in 1963 fundamentally reshaped state-society relations in Syria. The increasing dominance of the public sector as the leading economic actor in Syria during the 1970s corresponded to political and economic suppression of bourgeois and landed elite interests that had hitherto dominated Syria's political arena. Despite the measures taken by the Ba'ath to break up the propertied and commercial interests (in many cases monopolies) of the business elite, the Syrian private sector as a whole persisted as a social force but one whose political agency was neutralized and subservient to Ba'athist interests.[3] As a result, access to wealth and accumulation opportunities was shaped by the dependence of private-sector entities on the regime. Accumulation could not occur without regime sanction.

By the 1980s the stratification of the business community under the Ba'ath party had begun to take root. Joseph Bahout identifies four distinct strata of the business community:[4] (1) remnants of the old bourgeoisie that had dominated economic and political life in Syria during the late Ottoman and Mandate periods and who were negatively affected by Ba'athist policies; (2) medium-sized enterprises that had exchanged limited economic benefits for political quietism; (3) a rentier class whose members were the direct beneficiaries of the 1970s and 1980s oil booms and who were deeply connected to the military, political, and bureaucratic tentacles of the state; and, (4) finally, the state bourgeoisie that controlled the issuing and distribution of government contracts. This stratification more or less persisted throughout the 1980s and 1990s, even in the face of economic stagnation and fiscal crisis. It was not until 2000, however, after the assumption of power by Bashar al-Assad, that this stratification would be significantly reshaped by an attempt by the regime to restructure the economy and the role that the private sector played in it.

In the early years of the new century a process of marketization was set in motion and captured in the framework of the "social market economy," an economic strategy that was supposed to achieve social gains through the increasing privatization of economic activity.[5] Space considerations restrict a more thorough analysis of the policies associated with the social market economy. Suffice to say, the political goal of these policies was to preserve authoritarian rule while expanding the basis of accumulation and wealth creation. The state was to assume a more interventionist role to ensure that marketization would not induce negative social effects and that the state could protect vulnerable groups from the ills of the market. This was, of course, wishful thinking: all major Syrian social indicators stagnated or declined during the period of marketization.[6]

In addition to the disastrous social impacts of marketization, the period after Bashar al-Assad came to power brought about major changes in the business community's stratification. These changes were largely tethered to and produced by processes of privatization that shifted economic responsibility from the state to the private sector. Rather than undertaking large-scale privatization of state assets, as occurred during the breakup of the Soviet Union, the state delegated policy to the private sector through the procurement system, thus ensuring the continued dependence of the private sector elites on the state bourgeoisie.[7] The Syrian economy was liberalized to allow for limited foreign investment, with laws ensuring that Syrians would hold any projects jointly, such as banks, insurance companies, and large-scale infrastructural projects. These privatization policies opened up new opportunities for the elites to accumulate wealth while increasing their dependence on the state.

The marketization period thus significantly strengthened the economic power of the elites while expanding their social base and composition. Other economic actors similarly benefitted from, or were transformed by, this period. For example, the "religio-merchant complex,"[8] a network of wealthy merchants and urban ulama' (religious scholars) who ran charitable organizations, emerged in the context of marketization. Other, perhaps less economically powerful actors also emerged, who represented a new entrepreneurial class. These entities benefitted from direct and indirect access to the political and security arms of the regime and were loosely described as "awlad al-sultah" (children of the authority)[9] or the "new neoliberal elite."[10] Mostly urban and liberal in their political outlook, this stratum began to reap some economic benefits during marketization but lacked the access or wealth of the traditional economic elite. Finally, the largest stratum of the Syrian business community comprised the small and medium-sized enterprises that made up more than 99 percent of all businesses in Syria. This stratum was mostly negatively affected by marketization.

The transformations in the stratification of the Syrian business community that occurred in the decade preceding the uprising were brought about by changing patterns of authoritarian rule and attendant shifts in the regime's modes of economic governance. In the context of authoritarian restructuring, the market and private actors were given increased agency in the production and distribution of goods and services within the economy. At the same time, the state's retreat from a robust socially distributive role subjected millions of Syrians to the dictates of market fluctuations without any corresponding increase in salaries and wages. Thus, while the first decade of the twenty-first century was in part defined by the increased accumulation of wealth by new (and old) economic actors, it was also defined by the negative social impacts wrought by a decade of marketization, such as decreased living standards, increased unemployment and labor precarity, stagnating wages, and the like.

These negative patterns were the outcome of policies pursued during this period under the framework of the social market economy. At the same time, the government's budgetary pressures forced it to roll back spending in key areas (such as subsidies) and services (such as education and health care), thus increasing citizen exposure to price fluctuations. Public sector employment shrank and private sector employment was stagnant, thus accelerating the social problems produced by a growing, educated population. Despite these societal pressures, many indicators suggested that the economy was growing. This was deceiving, however, as the growth occurred in a very unequal way, without a redistribution of wealth. Instead, many different business actors connected to the regime in various ways were the main beneficiaries of this period.

One of the consistent features of state-business relations was mutual dependence. Businesspeople needed access to the regime to reap the benefits of these new economic policies and the regime needed businesses to generate economic growth and development. In contrast, most Syrian businesses were small and had very few opportunities in the new economic framework. They did not have the capital, political access, or collective potential to reap benefits of liberalized economic policies. These lower strata were thus economically significant insofar as they represented the largest stratum of business enterprises, but politically insignificant because they could not organize to make demands against the regime or reap the benefits of economic policies. Thus, on the eve of the Syrian uprising, the business community was not only stratified along economic lines but along political ones as well, with many in the upper echelons of the community enjoying close access to the regime while the majority of smaller enterprises remained on the peripheries of economic gains and political power.

Economic Transformation during the Conflict

Economic contraction, international sanctions, and capital flight: these are the three broad economic transformations that have contributed to new patterns of stratification and the factionalization of the Syrian business community. Pressures created by these transformations have induced new patterns of elite recruitment and elite agency, produced new entrepreneurs whose wealth and power is tethered to the conflict, contributed to the displacement of businesspeople, and led to the dramatic loss of billions of dollars in Syrian capital. Over the long-term, these transformations will fundamentally reshape the social and political composition of the business community.

Economic Contraction

The most salient and largest-scale impact of the conflict has been in overall levels of economic contraction experienced during the war. Every single economic sector in Syria has contracted since 2011. The Syrian Center for Political Research (SCPR) has provided rough estimates of cumulative annual real gross domestic product (GDP) loss by sector from 2010 to 2014 as a percentage of 2010 GDP for each sector.[11] These figures indicate severe, rapid decline in every sector, with total economic activity contracting more than 60 percent from its level before the conflict. In addition to the contraction of all productive sectors of the economy, there has been a depletion of household income and assets, hyperinflation, rampant unemployment, and an increasing reliance on armed groups and economies of violence for both employment and the procurement of basic goods. The SCPR has estimated that Syria's Human Development Index rating decreased by some 33 percent from 2010 to 2015, plunging the country from 113 in the world to 173 (out of 187 countries).[12] Poverty has increased exponentially throughout the country, especially in the areas experiencing the worst violence. There, armed groups have maintained control of local goods, driving up prices and challenging the resiliency of the Syrian population.

Fueling such dramatic levels of contraction is the de facto division of the country into four distinct geographic areas.[13] This division of the country has severely disrupted internal and external trade patterns, isolated areas and communities from one another, and reduced the mobility of people and goods, as well as produced conditions of scarcity that are often extreme. The first section of the country is what is generally referred to as the "regime-held" areas in Syria, and roughly corresponds to the western parts of the country stretching from the Damascus-Aleppo highway, covering the southern and western parts of Aleppo to the Mediterranean coast. The second region corresponds to territories held by the Islamic State in the eastern parts of the country along the Euphrates, with the major population centers of Raqqa and Deir al-Zour. The third area roughly corresponds to the Rojava areas under the control of the Syrian Kurdish authorities, which are dominated by the Kurdistan Workers' Party (the PKK). This area is not contiguous and also includes the parts of Aleppo and its northern peripheries that are under the control of the Kurdish groups. Finally, the noncontiguous areas under the control of various armed groups constitute a fourth distinct region, despite the fluidity of territorial control and the fragmentation into competing areas of control.

The geography of the Syrian conflict is both a cause and consequence of the economic contraction experienced throughout the course of the last five years. Capital flight (discussed below) from areas outside of regime control has meant that there is little capital for productive activity. The remaining Syrian capital has mostly concentrated in the coastal areas where businesspeople have found relative stability and opportunities. The borderlands of neighboring countries, especially Turkey, have also played an important role in the Syrian war economy. Many Syrian enterprises relocated to southern Turkey and continue to conduct business inside of Syria. Armed groups' control of major trade routes has meant that many of these businesspeople are implicated directly in the economies of violence that have emerged in the country. Nevertheless, the relocation of thousands of Syrian businesspeople and hundreds of millions or billions of dollars of Syrian capital is one of the primary features of economic contraction.

International Sanctions

Syria's economic contraction is not at all divorced from the catastrophic humanitarian and economic impacts of sanctions against the country. In addition to the negative impacts of sanctions, many of the new conflict elites have found opportunities in trying to circumvent sanctions. This pattern is not altogether different from what occurred in Iraq during the sanctions regime (1990–2003). In that country, many businesspeople connected to Saddam Hussein's regime engaged in very profitable sanctions busting. Since 2011, Syria has been subjected to the most comprehensive sanctions imposed outside of the United Nations framework. The initial sanctions imposed by Turkey, the European Union, and the Arab states of the Gulf were comprehensive ones and were considered very broad, focusing on certain products or national economies as a whole. As the conflict dragged on, the sanctions became more focused on individuals and state entities.[14]

The European Union's sanctions on Syria initially targeted key regime individuals and state institutions. Since 2011, the European Union has placed sanctions on more than two hundred Syrians and close to seventy state and private institutions. Targeted sanctions paralleled increasingly deep and far-reaching comprehensive sanctions, including a total arms embargo, restrictions on all imports of Syrian oil, bans on all forms of public and private financial support to Syria, bans of telecommunications equipment exports to Syria, prohibitions of financial transactions with Syrian financial institutions, and the control of exports to Syria of any goods or material that might be used for internal repression. These sanctions more or less paralleled those taken by other countries against Syria. From the outset, sanctions were intended to induce high-level defections and place pressure on the regime to end the violence and engage in a political transition process. To date, the sanctions have failed in both regards, as anyone who has observed the impact of sanctions on Iraq and Iran could have predicted. Where they have been effectual is in contributing to the humanitarian crisis, depleting the government's sources of budgetary revenue, and circumscribing the inner circles of the regime.[15]

More importantly, however, is the fact that sanctions have set in motion a series of shifts within the regime and wider business community that are contributing to new patterns of stratification and factionalization. As many people fled the country, the regime was forced to rely on a select number of loyalist businesspeople that could be counted on to secure the delivery of goods to regime-held areas.[16] Here, the regime has been forced to cultivate a new stratum of the business community that is politically loyal and economically capable of addressing many of the economic needs of the conflict, especially as capital flight (discussed below) has been so rampant. This new stratum has been empowered by the conflict and has acquired wealth in direct relation to the regime's economic needs that grew out of both the sanctions and capital flight. Paradoxically, then, the sanctions incentivized some businesspeople to become more integrated with the regime as economic opportunities arose during the conflict. Some businesspeople were driven out by economic contraction and sanctions, and some were cultivated to support the regime's economic needs.

There is considerable evidence from inside Syria of such patterns of elite recruitment and turnover occurring. Many of the elites who left the country have been relieved of their responsibilities on the boards of various chambers and executive boards of enterprises or holding companies. This has been especially pronounced at the Damascus Chamber of Commerce and the Damascus Chamber of Industry, which now have boards that consist of businesspeople who exercised very little economic power prior to the conflict. Many of the individuals who had dominated these boards for years are now gone, having been removed for technicalities such as not being present for votes. The elite turnover at places such as the chambers, in executive board positions, and on the boards of holding companies such as Cham and Souria portends a substantial shift in the composition of the economic elite, since these positions reflect a proximity to political power and an ability to secure access to the government procurement system.

Much of this turnover is being driven by the regime's need to circumvent sanctions. As such, the new elites that have emerged during the conflict have acted largely as intermediaries. They are not involved in substantial productive activity per se (although some are), but have taken on greater roles in facilitating trade and payments. For example, in 2013, the public sector company Mahrukat, which stores and distributes petroleum products, was under sanction and thus unable to import goods from Europe. Syrian laws were quickly changed to allow for private-sector imports and distribution of goods and a number of Syrian businesspeople not under sanctions quickly began importing materials. These individuals were simply fronts for Mahrukat, which remained responsible for the infrastructure of the imports and their transportation within Syria. Similarly, new barter deals have been signed between Syrian and largely Russian and some Latin American companies, especially in oil products and their derivatives. These deals are almost exclusively facilitated by companies operated by these new intermediaries, as most Syrian elites and private companies affiliated with the regime are under sanction. The reliance of the regime on these sorts of barter deals, facilitated by hitherto nonexistent or economically insignificant private-sector enterprises, is a direct consequence of the restrictions imposed by the sanctions.

Capital Flight

Quantifying capital flight from Syria is an impossible task given that so much of Syrian capital existed outside of the formal banking system even before the war began. Moreover, sanctions have discouraged many banks, especially those in Lebanon, from taking Syrian deposits, forcing many businesspeople to embed or move their assets in novel ways. This is nothing new in Syria. Capital flight had been a consistent feature of the country's political economy for decades as the threat of seizure by the government, a weak property rights regime, and the lack of investment opportunities contributed to the sheltering of Syrian capital in neighboring countries. In addition to the movement of Syrian capital outside of the country during the conflict, billions of dollars of assets, such as factories, machinery, vehicles, and supplies, have been destroyed during the fighting.

Despite the presence of hundreds of thousands of Syrians in Lebanon, there are very few noticeable trends in foreign currency deposits, since many Lebanese banks are rejecting all Syrian accounts, even those from individuals who are not businesspeople. Syrians have thus been forced to deposit money in joint accounts with Lebanese family, friends, or business partners, or simply invest immediately in order to shelter their capital. In contrast, figures from Turkey suggest that Syrian businesspeople have been extremely active with foreign currency deposits, especially in banks along the Syrian-Turkish border, reporting yearly increases from 2011 through 2016. In addition to increasing deposits, Syrian investors are the primary source of new registered enterprises in Turkey. In 2014, more than 26 percent of all new foreign companies in Turkey were established by Syrian investors.[17]

The movement of Syrian capital and the establishment of businesses in Turkey is not surprising given the extensive economic relations between the two countries prior to the war. It is also unsurprising given that Turkey was an ideal location from which Syrian enterprises could be re-established and trade with the Syrian market. Although many Syrian enterprises have been established in Istanbul, the majority of enterprises are in the geographic borderlands of Gaziantep, Mersin, and Kilis.

The mass movement of Syrian capital to Turkey and the wider region will have dramatic impacts on the business community and elite stratification. First, many Syrian businesspeople have foregone their relationships with the regime and have thus sacrificed their proximity to political power. Second, the embedding of Syrian capital outside of the country reduces its mobility, and the ability of Syrian businesspeople to repatriate assets and capital and to participate in the reconstruction of the country. Finally, the productivity of Syrian capital is increasingly untethered from the Syrian market, leaving a productivity gap that the remaining business community is unable to fill during the conflict. It will be even more unable to fill this gap after the conflict is resolved, as the demands of reconstruction will significantly outweigh domestic capacities.

Elite Factionalization

The majority of research into elite factionalization during violent conflict suggests that it occurs in the context of competing political allegiances in which various business actors choose political sides to support in a conflict. Such factionalization is understood as both a cause and consequence of conflict[18] and as a driver of violence in conflicts. But that type of factionalization does not explain much in the Syrian conflict, in which the rupture of elite cohesion, loyalty, and consensus did not occur prior to the uprising. As a result, when we speak of elite factionalization in Syria we should understand this as a process produced not solely by political alignment and the formal or informal pledging of allegiance to one faction or another, but as one produced by the underlying economic strategies of business actors who lack any natural political party or preexisting common social or economic institutions from which to articulate and advance elite interests during the conflict. Thus, political alignment and economic strategy, both driven by the economic transformations of the war, shape factionalization. I identify four categories of elites who have been differentially affected by the conflict: the integrated elite, the expatriate elite, the dependent elite, and the conflict elite.

The *integrated elite* are inseparable from the regime. They are loyalists and have not divested of their assets or moved much of their wealth outside of the country. In fact, they have been major contributors to the regime's economic efforts to stabilize the economy. Prior to the uprising, these formed the top stratum active in all major sectors of the economy, and they were the first to reap the benefits of marketization in the first decade of this century. Today, many of these elites are subject to Western and Arab sanctions because of their deep connections to the regime, and as such have interests that are indistinguishable from those of the political and security arms of the regime.

In obvious contrast to the integrated elite is the *expatriate elite*. While the expatriate elite are not beholden to the regime, they are not automatically supportive of the opposition. They nevertheless have a political and economic stake in the conflict's trajectory. Elites of this stratum had accumulated and held much of their wealth in nearby countries, mainly in the Gulf, and are thus not entwined in interdependent relationships with the regime, as the integrated elite are. As a result, they have been able to freely engage in political activity aligned with the opposition without fearing any economic reprisals in the short or long term. The most obvious example of the institutionalized role of this elite is in the Syrian Business Forum, a group of wealthy Syrian businesspeople openly aligned with the opposition. To date, they have supported efforts on relief and humanitarian aid while playing a political role within larger opposition politics.

The third category is the *dependent elite*. This group comprises elites who were not linked to the regime through social or familial ties and who have remained mobile throughout the conflict. In most cases, they represent the core of Syrian capital that fled the country during the course of the conflict. While many of them had strong business ties to the regime and the security apparatus, and were thus able to secure access to wealth prior to 2011, these ties did not bind them to the continuity of the regime as such. Moreover, during the period of marketization in the first decade of this century, this stratum grew and became composed of people from mixed social and political backgrounds, including traders and industrialists, urban merchants, and the nouveau riche and neoliberal elite. Despite their growing economic strength this stratum never functioned coherently or cohesively and thus never exerted collective pressure on the regime.

The precarious relationship between this stratum and the regime meant that they, along with the majority of the smaller private enterprises, were wont to move their wealth outside of the country. In doing so, many analysts assumed that these elites were natural allies of the political opposition. However, the current relationship between the business elite and the political opposition is tenuous at best. Some have openly worked with opposition figures, while others in exile remain publically committed to supporting the regime. Most have adopted a politically neutral position.[19] Their neutrality is strategic, since they would like to secure access to the Syrian market once the conflict ends. By playing both sides, so to speak, this stratum has tried to ensure that any political solution will not lead to its economic marginalization in Syria. As such, these elites are the most likely to be courted by any transitional and future Syrian governments.

The final stratum is an entirely new group of elites who had very little presence before the conflict. These *conflict elites* saw their privilege and wealth grow during the course of the war. Generally speaking, these are elites who operate in regime areas and who have been central to the regime's shifting modes of economic governance during the conflict, especially concerning attempts to evade sanctions. These elites are not linked to the regime through familial or social linkages but instead through a system of mutual benefit and interdependency in which the regime has been forced to rely on them to stimulate economic activity. They have taken up leadership positions in various chambers (such as the Damascus Chamber of Commerce and the Damascus Chamber of Industry) and other bodies. Unlike the dependent elites who are primarily involved in production and trade, the conflict elites function as intermediaries and facilitators to ensure that goods can be brought to regime areas. (Though in some cases, they also have some involvement in production.) This role is a function both of the conflict elites' lack of investment capital and of the specific opportunities afforded them during the conflict. And while they may lack the wealth and investment capacity of other elites, their presence in the country and their access to the political and security apparatus will make them important players in any reconstruction program.

It is worth reflecting more on the conflict elites and the potential role that they may play in shaping the trajectory of the Syrian war. They are generally of varied social and economic backgrounds and have not displayed any tendencies toward collective representation. In other words, they remain fragmented and lack the cohesion to act in a unified way. Generally speaking, they tend to have emerged from two different situations: first, those who owned small or medium-sized enterprises prior to the conflict and chose not to divest of their assets and leave the country, and second, private- or public-sector managers who established enterprises during the conflict. One of the key factors driving their formation is their relationship with regime officials, especially from within the security apparatus, and to bureaucrats. Their central role is one of intermediation. As examples from other countries' cases such as Bosnia's demonstrate, such classes have the ability to endure and maintain an economic and political foothold even after peace.

In this sense, the best way to describe the conflict elite is as a group shaped by its ability to provide conflict services. These elites' activities are dependent on the continuation of strife and the specific context of sustained economic contraction. They are implicated in all types of activity: smuggling, weapons trafficking, service provision, and human movement. One of the central roles that these conflict elites play is in facilitating transactions to ensure the supply of goods and material from outside so-called regime-held areas. The case of George Haswani, an apparent "middleman" between the regime and the Islamic State, is an excellent example of this intermediary role that many conflict elites have begun to play. Prior to the conflict, Haswani operated a very small engineering firm inside of Syria. When his business collapsed after the war began, he was brought into the regime fold as an intermediary to facilitate oil trade with the Islamic State and financial transactions with other groups. While he is now under sanctions for his role, this trajectory is exemplary of that of others within the conflict elite.[20] Other examples abound, including cases where conflict elites cooperated with public sector enterprises under sanctions to ensure imports[21] or when Syrian nationals were implicated in the Russian bank Tempbank's efforts to intermediate financial transactions for the Syrian regime. Although evidence is difficult to trace, we can also conclude with confidence that the conflict elites are contributing to the movement of weapons into Syria.

This brief categorization of the different factions of the economic elites should put to rest any assumptions about the continuity of the social composition of the elite or its homogeneity. This categorization should also encourage us to think about factionalization as a phenomenon driven as much by the individual economic interests of the elites as it is by any political allegiances. In recent research on the political loyalties and collective capacities of Syrian businesspeople during the conflict, Ching-an Chang[22] confirms some of the earlier findings[23] that Syrian business actors have failed to coalesce into any strong, representative bodies. Chang argues that in the Turkish borderland areas where so many Syrian businesspeople have reestablished themselves, competition and mistrust continue to define relations among businesspeople.[24] In many cases, Syrians will only conduct business with other Syrians who share their political allegiances—whether neutral, pro- or anti-regime—purposely avoiding and boycotting others. In earlier periods, regime repression fragmented the business community. The specific geography of the conflict and the political polarization of Syrians have ensured that this fragmentation will only continue, albeit along some new lines.

Business Elites and Conflict

The Syrian business community is implicated in the process of political and social transformation engulfing Syria today. Business actors, like other social groups, exercise distinct forms of agency during the conflict. For example, the conflict elites ensure the possibility of transactions and payments that maintain some flow of goods and materials into regime areas, while businesspeople in the Turkish borderlands secure the flow of goods to rebel groups. In many ways, business elites, while not directly controlling militias or armed groups, are deeply implicated in the violence in Syria. The movement of goods between and within areas of Syria can only occur through the guarantee of armed groups who ensure the successful delivery of products. In this way, business elites are deeply implicated in the ongoing violence in the country and need to be considered as agents who fuel Syria's violence.

Taking seriously the role of business actors in the Syrian conflict requires rejecting liberal assumptions about how to end conflicts. The liberal peace model is largely premised on the idea that factions engage in violence in order to capture the state. As such, peace agreements focus almost exclusively on the distribution of political power in the form of ministerial appointments, institutional representation quotas, and so on. Such formulas for peace motivated postconflict arrangements in countries such as Lebanon and Iraq. What these formulas completely ignored is the political economy of conflict and how different conflict drivers exist.

For many years, the dominant paradigm in which academics and international agencies understood the political economy of conflict was through the "greed versus grievance" debates: Was it political grievance or economic greed that motivated actors during conflicts?[25] While these debates have been heavily criticized as too narrow,[26] they nevertheless encouraged scholars to think of the political economy of conflict. More recent innovations in the study of the political economy of conflict suggest that various "stakeholders" exist, whose interests exist at different levels of the conflict: political, social, economic, or cultural. These stakeholders represent varied identities and agencies within any conflict. While it may be tempting to see business elites in Syria as constituting a stakeholder, this is also somewhat limiting because it suggests independence and autonomy from other agentive actors.

As should be clear from the discussion above regarding factionalization, all segments of the elite remain heavily dependent on other actors for their wealth. In this way, it may be more useful to think of business elites as embedded and implicated in wider networks of violence.[27] Thinking of conflicts as occurring between wider networks allows us to overcome the greed-versus-grievance dichotomy and to see how different forms of agency interact in a given conflict. As I have argued elsewhere, one of the main drivers shaping the trajectory of the Syrian conflict is the specific political economy that has taken root, in which the interactions of various entities—business elites, armed groups, consumers— create and constitute various networks.[28]

From a postconflict perspective, then, it may be more useful to think of business elites as actors caught up in wider networks that shape the conflict and postconflict possibilities for Syria. Business elites do not exercise enough power to bring about political change on their own. The assumptions in the early stages of the conflict that economic collapse brought about by widespread business defection would collapse the regime proved false. The regime has adjusted its modes of economic governance to meet the needs of war. Factionalization has further ensured that business elites will not act collectively during the conflict.

Increasingly, peace-building organizations such as Swiss Peace have come to recognize the differential roles, identities, and interests of business actors. While not adopting a networked analysis of conflict per se, Swiss Peace nevertheless recognizes that fragmentation among business actors produces different "logics."[29] For them, "old" business actors (such as the integrated, expatriate, or dependent elites) may have a greater interest in returning to antebellumpolitical-order peace in order to maintain or return to their previous levels of wealth and economic influence. On the other hand, "new" actors (such as the conflict elites) have developed economic interests in direct relation to conflict and the war economy and may not be interested in a return to peace, lest it threaten their economic opportunities.

While this analysis yields a useful dichotomy, we should also consider how conflicts reproduce new elites as they endure. For example, people we may consider to be old elites, such as those formerly associated with the various chambers or with holding companies such as Cham or Souria, may in fact become beneficiaries of the conflict economy, thus blurring the distinction between new and old.

What role, then, do Syria's business elites play in the conflict? Labels such as "spoilers" or "stakeholders," "new" or "old" do not sufficiently capture either the factionalization of the business elites or how embedded they are in wider networks of violence. They are not purveyors of violence but are deeply implicated in it. They also lack the political weight to bring about political change, but are central to any political efforts to end the conflict. Perhaps, however, the most important area of business elites' involvement in Syria will occur once the conflict ends during the reconstruction phase. Here, business elites will be thrust into a situation in which their capital and expertise will be called upon by local and international authorities to support Syria's reconstruction. It is perhaps for this reason that so many business elites have lurked in the political shadows, hedging their bets at the outcome of Syria's conflict and hoping to capture some of the long-term economic benefits that will come with reconstruction.

Business Elites and Postwar Reconstruction

On all sides of the conflict there are now constituencies that are newly rich and powerful—from checkpoint theft, smuggling, and the illicit petrochemical trade—and who rightly believe their heyday will quickly expire when and if the conflict ends and the state, or state-like authorities, reassert control. So despite their nominal role propping up the regime, the rebels, Fateh al-Sham, or the Islamic State, they have little material interest in the conflict ending. This might be all the more true on the regime side, where the opportunities afforded by the flight of much of the old elite opened the door for a new elite, which might be dumped the instant the state no longer needs them.

The factionalization of the Syrian business community will have profound impacts on the direction of the conflict and, when it finally ends, on Syria's reconstruction. In this sense, businesspeople have a role to play in either perpetuating or ending the war, since they are contributing to some of the main economic drivers of the conflict. The key question is how to transform their interests from those of war to those of peace. Under the current circumstances, it is unlikely that a cessation of violence will occur in the short term. In the coming years the stratification and factionalization of the business community will continue to be subject to the structural impacts of the conflict on the Syrian economy and the wider social transformations it has induced. In this section, I identify different ways in which business elites and the business community at large may participate in Syria's reconstruction given the ongoing transformations described above.

One of the central challenges of reconstruction is in generating capital for reconstruction projects. Postconflict spaces typically have a very reduced revenue base, rampant tax evasion and weak tax administration, endemic capital flight, and instability, all of which discourage investment. The first way in which business elites will exercise power in postwar Syria will be in funneling capital and resources toward reconstruction projects. Syria will be in desperate need for capital, regardless of what the ultimate political outcome of the conflict is. The most obvious source will be international lenders. However, Syrian business elites will likely want to reap the opportunities of reconstruction, regardless of their political affiliations (or neutralities) during the conflict. The postconflict political authorities are likely to actively court Syrian capital as well.

Egypt provides a useful example for comparison. In that country, many businessmen tied to the Mubarak regime were brought to trial for various reasons after the January 25, 2011 revolution. These businessmen were charged with everything from corruption to theft of public resources. Indeed, one of the hallmarks of the period following the revolution was the large number of cases against businessmen associated with the regime. However, by the time that the Muslim Brotherhood's Mohamed Morsi became president in 2012, the government began to dismiss the cases against the businesspeople—despite the Brotherhood's historic animosity toward many of them and the Mubarak regime. The reason was quite simple: the government needed some way of stimulating the moribund Egyptian economy. The Egyptian case is an instructive one, although fundamentally different from Syria, where the level of violence has been profound. Nevertheless, this suggests possible futures for state-business relations in times of political instability. While some business elites are very much indistinguishable from either the regime or the opposition, many across the political spectrum are likely to be courted by any postconflict authority to help support reconstruction efforts.

The central problem facing planners in Syria will be incentivizing capital repatriation. Prior to the war, most Syrian capital existed outside of the banking system. Efforts had been made by the regime to court and repatriate capital to support marketization policies, but this produced minimal investment. Most businesspeople inside and outside of Syria rightly pointed to the lack of property rights and the constant threat of asset seizure as obstacles to investment. It is unlikely that the postconflict situation will provide any serious property rights or satisfy the security needs of businesspeople. Regardless, this is not the only obstacle to capital repatriation. As the conflict drags on, most Syrian businesspeople have established enterprises outside of the country in which their capital is becoming increasingly embedded and, hence, immobile. In Lebanon and Turkey, for example, many Syrian businesspeople are entering into business partnerships with local capital interests. This embeds Syrian capital into regional economies and creates obstacles for repatriation, as local partners are likely to be reluctant to shift investments to Syria after the war.

There may also be a political role for Syrian business elites to play in reconstruction. In recent years, some have proposed the idea of a technocratic transition government for Syria with parallel suggestions that a Syrian businessperson could return, as a neutral figure, and lead a postconflict government. Many of these suggestions are based on the Lebanese model in which Rafik Hariri emerged as that country's consensus postconflict prime minister and as the major figure and ideologue behind Lebanon's reconstruction. Such a scenario would certainly politically strengthen the business elite and provide incentive for greater capital repatriation.

One of the common features of postconflict situations, such as those in Bosnia and Herzegovina, Afghanistan, Iraq, and others, is the continued legacy of war economies even after "peace" has been declared. In some cases, such a legacy has accomplished the cementing of the conflict elite. In Bosnia and Herzegovina, for example, the war economy successfully transformed, after the country's conflict resolved in 1995, into an underground or shadow economy in which many of the conflict elites continued to participate. The geographic fragmentation of the country into competing centers of power had created rival elites who controlled specific activities in loosely defined parts of the country. A similar situation occurred in Afghanistan, where different warlords fought over control of territory and the related economic benefits during the course of the post-Soviet conflict period. The peace process that led to the 1995 Dayton Agreement that ended the Bosnian War had a singular focus on achieving an end to hostilities, which meant that the rise of pockets of criminality and illegality throughout the country were totally ignored after the conflict. This allowed for the continuity of criminal and illegal practices that were driven by and benefitted the conflict elites. During the war, most middle and upper classes left the country, leaving a new class directly tethered to conflict and violence.[30]

Certainly, Syria is different than Bosnia and Herzegovina, Iraq, Lebanon, and other contemporary conflicts. They all have their unique and distinguishable features, especially in regards to how conflict elites emerge, what economic activities their wealth is tethered to, and what their political allegiances look like after peace—or an end to hostilities—has been achieved. In Afghanistan, for example, the war economy was such that the production and distribution of opium created some semblance of stability and a steady flow of money into the coffers of the conflict elites. This contrasts with many of the features of Syria's war economy, where predatory and intermediary activities, rather than production, define the roles of the conflict elites, warlords, and armed groups during the conflict.

The larger point here is that Syria's business elites will be differentially affected by the persistence of conflict and whether or not the process that ends the violence contains opportunities and possibilities for their participation in Syria's reconstruction. The liberal peace model's insistence on ending violence first at the expense of other arrangements, such as provisions about social policy, has negative long-term consequences on a state's reconstruction after war. In the Syrian case, given the level of destruction and humanitarian misery that has occurred, it is imperative that the country's economic future be a part of any conversation around peace efforts. As such, even though Syria's business elites remain factionalized and largely ineffectual in shaping political and military patterns on the ground, all four categories will be important players in the reconstruction period.

Conclusion

The Syrian conflict has set in motion transformations that will radically reshape social stratification in the country. The Syrian business community has undergone substantial re-patterning of its stratification in light of severe economic contraction, international sanctions, and capital flight. This has contributed to a factionalization of the business elites along various lines. While it may at first be convenient to consider these elites as either pro- or anti-regime, or pro- or anti-opposition, the political allegiances are much more complicated. Many of Syria's business actors have accrued wealth and power in the context of the conflict while others have suffered tremendous economic loss. Political allegiances are fluid and often take a backseat to pursuit of profit or loyalty to patronage (or other) networks. Economic opportunities will likely trump political affiliations. Many Syrian businesspeople are thus ultimately amenable to different outcomes that preserve their economic opportunities, rather than being inflexibly interested in any specific, ideal outcome. These networks are major drivers of the conflict and must be understood in their own right in order to properly chart Syria's war, much less plan for its resolution.

Factionalization of Syria's business elites will have profound impacts on the reconstruction period. In popular and scholarly accounts of the conflict, we tend to ignore the potential role that business elites can—and must—play in peace processes. It is unlikely that any resolution will bring about immediate peace in Syria. The conflict is likely to persist in different forms and in specific areas of the country that will remain outside of government control. Nevertheless, reconstruction will begin. Here, Syria's business elites and the wider business community will be called upon to contribute.

Many of Syria's business elites are aware that they can profit during reconstruction and are trying to position themselves outside of the regime or opposition camps in order to reap the benefits. What kind of postconflict regime emerges is anyone's guess, as well as how friendly or amenable this regime will be to business interests. If there is any international involvement in the reconstruction, there is sure to be a major push toward economic liberalization as an engine of reconstruction. Regardless of the precise form reconstruction takes, any postconflict authority will need to implement policies aimed at capital repatriation. As the conflict persists and Syrian capital becomes more embedded outside of the country, the possibilities for large-scale repatriation decrease.

More than six years on, the war in Syria has become tangled in an ever-more complex web of interests, which are not dominated by a singular force. Political ideology and political power, economics, historical grievances, sect, ethnicity, and humanitarian concerns will all factor into the ultimate resolution of the war, whatever shape that may take. Of these dimensions, however, the economic one is consistently neglected by analysts and diplomats—particularly the economics of the conflict itself and the new elites who have grown rich from it, or whose precarious fortunes are dependent on one outcome or another. The violence in Syria is staggering, but we must acknowledge that there are those who have economic incentives to keep it from ending quickly. Without addressing those incentives, peacemakers and those who are eventually charged with heading the country's reconstruction will have little success.

Notes

1. See for example Aron Lund's chapter in this volume, "Into the Tunnels," which discusses the smuggling economy of the Ghouta and suburban Damascus.

2. Steven Heydemann, "Tracking the 'Arab Spring': Syria and the Future of Authoritarianism," *Journal of Democracy* 24, No. 4 (2013): 59–73.

3. Bassam Haddad, *Business Networks in Syria: The Political Economy of Authoritarian Resilience* (Stanford: Stanford University Press, 2012).

4. Joseph Bahout, "The Syrian Business Community, its Politics and Prospects," in *Contemporary Syria: Liberalization between Cold War and Cold Peace*, ed. Eberhard Kienle (London: British Academic Press, 1994), 72–80.

5. See Samer Abboud, "Economic Transformation and Diffusion of Authoritarian Power in Syria," in *Democratic Transition in the Middle East: Unpacking Power*, eds. Larbi Sadiki, Heiko Wimmen, and Layla Al-Zubaidi (London: Routledge, 2012): 159–77; and Samer Abboud, "Locating the 'Social' in the Social Market Economy," in *Syria: From Reform to Revolt*, eds. Raymond Hinnebusch and Tina Zintl (Syracuse: Syracuse University Press, 2015), 45–65.

6. Samir Seifan, "The Social Consequences of Economic Policies in Syria," Syrian Economic Society Lectures, The Cultural Center in Mezzeh, Damascus, 2009, http://mafhoum.com/syr/articles_10/seifan.pdf.

7. Samer Abboud and Fred Lawson, "Antinomies of Economic Governance in Contemporary Syria," in *Governance in the Middle East and North Africa*, ed. Abbas Kadhim (London: Routledge, 2012), 330–41.

8. See Salwa Ismail, "Changing Social Structure, Shifting Alliances and Authoritarianism in Syria," in *Demystifying Syria*, ed. Fred. Lawson (London: Saqi, 2009), 13–28; and Thomas Pierret and Kjetil Selvik, "Limits of 'Authoritarian Upgrading' in Syria: Private Welfare, Islamic Charities, and the Rise of the Zayd Movement," *International Journal of Middle East Studies* 41, no. 4 (2009): 595–614.

9. Ismail, "Changing Social Structure."

10. Mandy Terc, *Syria's New Neoliberal Elite: English Usage, Linguistic Practices and Group Boundaries*, (PhD diss., University of Michigan, 2011).

11. Syrian Center for Policy Research (SCPR), *Alienation and Violence: Impact of Syria Crisis Report 2014* (Damascus: Syrian Center for Policy Research, 2015).

12. SCPR, *Alienation and Violence*, 44.

13. Jihad Yazigi, "Syria's Implosion: Political and Economic Impacts," in *Inside Wars: Local Dynamics of Conflicts in Syria and Libya*, eds. Luigi Narbone, Agnes Favier, and Virginie Collombier (Fiesole, Italy: European University Institute, 2016), 1–5.

14. Erica S. Moret, "Humanitarian Impacts of Economic Sanctions on Iran and Syria," *European Security* 24, no. 1 (2015): 120–40.

15. Peter Seeberg, "The EU and the Syrian Crisis: The Use of Sanctions and the Regime's Strategy for Survival" *Mediterranean Politics* 20, no. 1 (2015): 1–18.

16. Heydemann, "Tracking the 'Arab Spring.'"

17. "Economy," *The Syria Report*, First Quarter (2015): 2–23.

18. Rola el-Husseini, *Pax Syriana: Elite Politics in Postwar Lebanon* (Syracuse, N.Y.: Syracuse University Press, 2012).

19. See Ching-an Chang, "The Division and Cooperation of Syrian Businessmen in Turkey: An Investigation of the Political and Economic Behaviours of Syrian Business Migrants," paper presented at the Center for Syrian Studies Conference, Beyond the Stalemate, July 1–3, 2015; and Samer Abboud, "Syria's Business Elite: Between Political Alignment and Hedging Their Bets," *Stiftung Wissenschaft und Politiik/ German Institute for International and Security Affairs Comments* 22 (2013), http://www.swp-berlin.org/fileadmin/contents/products/comments/2013C22_abo.pdf.

20. For more on Haswani, see Lund, "Into the Tunnels."

21. Abboud, "Syria's Business Elite."

22. Chang, "Syrian Businessmen in Turkey."

23. Haddad, *Business Networks in Syria.*

24. Chang, "Syrian Businessmen in Turkey."

25. Paul Collier and Anke Hoeffler, "Greed and Grievance in Civil War," *Oxford Economic Papers* 56, no. 4 (2004): 563–95.

26. Karen Ballentine and Heiko Nitzschke, "The Political Economy of Civil War and Conflict Transformation," Berghof Research Center for Constructive Conflict Management, 2005, http://www.berghof-foundation.org/fileadmin/redaktion/Publications/Handbook/Dialogue_Chapters/dialogue3_ballentine_nitzschke.pdf.

27. Samer Abboud, *Syria* (Cambridge: Polity Press, 2015).

28. Ibid.

29. Swiss Peace, *Peace Mediation Essentials: Business Actors in Mediation Processes* (Zurich: Switzerland, 2010).

30. Jens Stilhoff Sorensen, "War as Social Transformation: Wealth, Class, Power and an Illiberal Economy in Serbia," *Civil Wars* 6, no. 4 (2003): 55–82.

16

Participatory Democracy and Micropolitics in Manbij

An Unthinkable Revolution

YASSER MUNIF

Manbij, a city in northern Syria, hosted a compelling example of successful grassroots governance during the two-year period between the Syrian regime's withdrawal from the city in 2012 and the Islamic State's takeover in 2014. Drawing on hundreds of interviews conducted in Manbij in 2013, the author shows that the city established an innovative local political system during this interregnum. The new local government faced significant challenges, and made many mistakes, which the author discusses in detail. But those mistakes were not the undoing of Manbij's revolutionaries. Instead, as in many other places in Syria, external forces derailed their efforts, buoyed by a Western narrative that seemed unable to even conceive of the kind of peaceful revolution under construction in Manbij. Still, Manbij's experience holds important lessons—and could yet be the foundation for more participatory governance in Syria over the long term.

Twenty miles south of the Turkish border, on a plateau to the west of the Euphrates, lies the Syrian city of Manbij.[1] With a population of two hundred thousand, it is located halfway between the cities of Aleppo and Raqqa, the latter of which is the de facto capital of the Islamic State. Manbij is a millennia-old city with a history, like so many urban places in Syria, of religious and ethnic diversity; it has passed through the hands of many empires, ranging from the Assyrians to the Ottomans. Today, the population is predominantly Sunni Arab but also includes several other religious and ethnic groups, including a sizable Kurdish minority.[2]

This place in the province of Aleppo was the setting for a remarkable eighteen-month period of participatory democracy, from July 2012 to January 2014, during which an entity called the Revolutionary Council (RC) controlled the city. In 2013 I was able to spend some three months in Manbij over the course of two visits, and witness firsthand its experiment in self-determined governance. I conducted around two hundred interviews with various actors in the city. My research opened a window onto a completely new perspective on Syrian revolutionaries (most refuse to describe themselves simply as members of the opposition)—one

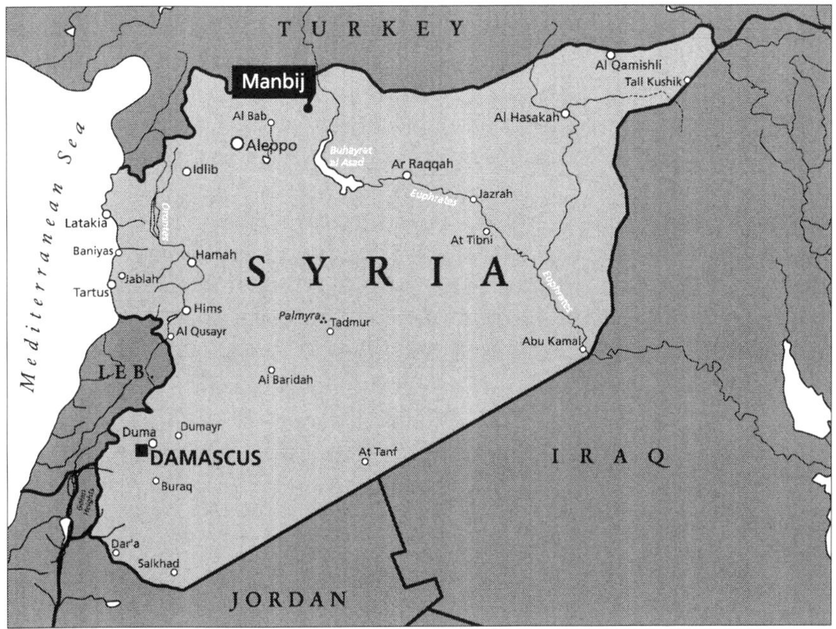

Map 1. Manbij

Source: Compiled by author.

that completely bucked the simplistic mainstream narratives of Western media.[3] Here, during an interlude of relative stability when neither the Syrian government nor foreign-backed jihadist groups had taken over the city, Syrians were deciding how to run their city for themselves. And they were excelling at it.

More than five hours from Damascus by road in peacetime, Manbij was relatively early to throw off the yoke of Syrian president Bashar al-Assad's regime, which local protesters managed to drive out in 2012. Despite the violence of the regime and military groups such as the Islamic State (which ultimately expelled the RC), and the intervention of a large number of regional and international players in the conflict, the eighteen months of locally guided government in Manbij were proof positive that Syrian society was able to produce an original democratic culture and creative alternative governance institutions that were vital to solving everyday problems.

Syrian revolutionaries like those in Manbij didn't speak the dominant academic Western language about social processes and revolutions—either because they couldn't or were unwilling to. As a result, many journalists and academics have effectively denied them any form of agency. Many Western descriptions present them as mindless fighters who are easily manipulated by the different regional and global powers. This dominant narrative is a Eurocentric one that presents the revolutionaries as voiceless victims blown hither and thither by the winds of larger political processes.

The absence of discourses about grassroots processes in the revolution, however, doesn't mean that those processes aren't there. Rather, it is a result of deficiencies in analysis. Too often, the metanarrative of "secular tyrant versus bumbling Muslim insurgents" has blinded scholars and pundits to the possibility of the uprising's piecemeal but significant achievements. A successful revolution became "unthinkable"[4] to Western experts long before external forces had actually broken its back.

This chapter is an attempt to stitch together a narrative that more adequately represents the grassroots efforts at governance that emerged between 2012 and 2014: they may have been fragmented, but they also formed an effective and constantly evolving whole. Revolutionaries actively experimented with new conceptual tools and with building alternative institutions on the ruins of the old ones. The revolutionary actions that might appear chaotic from afar acquire new meaning when scrutinized from the perspective of the population that they directly affected.

The Revolutionary Council

In the first half of 2012, a year after protests swept through Syria and many months after the protests had turned into war, Manbij was still under the control of the regime of President Bashar al-Assad. Then, in May 2012, the government and allied militias massacred more than one hundred civilians in the town of Houla in northwestern Homs province. The incident was not particularly close to Manbij, but the slaughter, which counted dozens of women and children among its victims, galvanized anti-regime protesters around the country. In response, residents of Manbij organized protests. Marginal at first, they evolved into a general strike and open defiance of the police and security forces. The activists behind these protests came from different political backgrounds. Some of them were secular and others religious, but all utilized nonviolent strategies. Activists also created a Free Syrian Army (FSA) group—the FSA had been established nearly a year before—but its main function was to fight the regime in Aleppo and other cities.[5] After the strike, which led to the shutdown of the entire city, the protests became larger and overwhelmed the security and police forces, who ultimately fled the city in July 2012.

The FSA gave pursuit, but was not the main factor in the security forces' departure. News reports said that rebels had "captured" Manbij, but the reality is that there were only a few dozen fighters in the city. The peaceful movement was the real catalyst.[6]

The RC had been founded in secret in April 2012, three months before the revolutionaries gained control of Manbij. During the initial period it mostly organized protests to expel the police and security forces, and coordinated with local and revolutionary councils in other cities. The members of the RC had diverse backgrounds, but the majority had a university education and came from middle-class families. Several were Syrian Ba'ath party members before

March 2011. Members included lawyers, engineers, doctors, and teachers, in addition to a few Muslim scholars. The RC marginalized the religious establishment because of the latter's collaboration with the regime and its refusal to take a clear stance in support of the revolution. While the person in charge of organizing the protests was the focal point of the group, others, such as the liaison between the RC and the FSA, played an important role as well. The FSA—which by now counted tens of thousands of fighters and controlled major swaths of the Syrian countryside—still had no significant presence in Manbij due to the vitality and momentum of the peaceful activists, who prevented the militarization of their activities to avoid the destruction of their city.

One of the achievements of the RC before liberation was the establishment of a network of more than fifty popular committees whose role was to protect the city and fill the vacuum on the day the security and the police would be forced to leave the city. So when the regime evacuated Manbij, the revolutionaries took over, and with the help of neighborhood committees, they prevented looting. The revolutionaries visited the different parts of the city to make sure that there were security checkpoints everywhere. The popular committees protected the entire city for three days, and not a single incident of violence or theft came to light. Revolutionaries had learned about such local organizing processes from Egyptian protesters who created their own popular committees in Alexandria, Cairo, and other cities to protect their neighborhoods from the regime's thugs and other criminals during the first stage of the 2011 uprising in Egypt.[7] The RC's tremendous success in organizing protests, forcing the police and security to leave the city, filling the political and administrative vacuum, and protecting residents during the transitional period made it very popular. Despite certain missteps, such as the marginalization of important activists and the inability to raise enough funds, the RC was able to govern for several months without much opposition because its members had symbolic capital and revolutionary legitimacy.

While the RC was able to address many urgent issues with creativity and openness, several groups challenged it because they disagreed with its politics, creating a real fracture in the city. After liberation, there were several centers of influence in Manbij. The RC had the most legitimacy because of its organizing efforts prior to liberation and the risks its members took during that period. It was composed of the representatives of the different neighborhood committees, who were active members of the community prior to the revolution and had a vast network of contacts.

But there was another center of power, revolving around Mohammed al-Bishir, an ambitious architect who felt marginalized. He didn't possess much legitimacy in the streets of Manbij, but was able to build a coalition with the individuals and families that were sidelined—intentionally or accidentally—by the RC. His coalition comprised more than twenty new groups and organizations that formed in 2012 and 2013. Some of them were active and had many members while others were ghost organizations created for the sole purpose of increasing the number of groups on Bishir's roster. Many were professional organizations: journalists, lawyers, doctors, teachers, religious clerics, and engineers. Others represented women, the youth, and the media. The coalition elected Bishir to the presidency of a new local council in December 2012, in an attempt at undermining the popularity of the RC, but failed to do so.

Besides these two major nodes of power, there were several other groupings with more or less political weight that had an influence on events after the liberation.

The Islamic religious institutions were one such grouping, but they remained marginal in 2012 due to their unwillingness to take a clear stance against the regime when the city was still controlled by the regime. Some of the young Muslim clerics were active in the protests but the religious establishment, which feared a backlash from the regime, did not support them.

Family affiliations made for another axis of power in Manbij, especially the clans. Every tribe in the Arab world is composed of several clans with uneven access to resources and power; about 15 percent of Syrians belong to a tribe. Certain clans within the same tribe sometimes had competing interests. Manbij's clans[8] were split in their allegiances, and as such didn't have much leverage on their members. Despite most clans' marginal role in the protests, some of them made more substantive contributions. For example, the al-Bou Banna clan had taken a clear position against the regime and many of their members were actively participating in the demonstrations. Most clans' sheikhs, however, were close to the regime and had left Manbij early on, fearing reprisal from the population.

The city's notables formed another cohort of consequence in the city. Local dignitaries who belonged to powerful and respected Manbij families, they had been used by the regime before 2012 as intermediaries, to control the residents. They played an important role during the protests and after liberation, as they were frequently asked to mediate between the security and the protesters. After liberation, the RC consulted them whenever it was time to make an important decision.

In addition to operating within a multipolar sociopolitical scene, the RC faced three main challenges after the liberation of the city. First, it didn't have any financial resources to run vital institutions. Second, it didn't have the necessary expertise to operate the mills or to administer the various branches of the council. Finally, the RC was unable to prevent the creation of numerous military formations. Powerful families and wealthy individuals in Manbij could form their own FSA brigade. The day of liberation, there were two FSA groups, while three weeks later their number increased to more than thirty, and by 2013 there were seventy. And the RC was losing legitimacy because of its inability to effectively protect the population from the harassment of certain FSA groups.

The presence of various military groups in the city caused old feuds to resurface, which prompted certain families and clans to establish their own military formations. While most of these formations were fighting Assad's regime, a sizable number were coercing the locals into paying tributes and taxes. One such group was led by a local thug, who called himself "the Prince" (using the

English word). He used his charisma to recruit fighters and later began looting other cities and kidnapping residents for large ransoms.[9] This enabled him to amass the necessary funds to build a large FSA faction that, at its peak, had several hundred fighters.[10] His group was affiliated with the Farouq Brigades, a large grouping of rebels within the FSA,[11] but he avoided a confrontation with the regime to focus his attention on illegal activities and increase the size of his group. Since the Prince didn't want to clash with the inhabitants of Manbij, his natal city, his kidnapping operation focused on the nearby city of Raqqa. The larger and more powerful FSA brigades disapproved of his actions but were too busy fighting the regime at the front to send fighters to Manbij to arrest or expel him. Ahrar al-Sham, one of the largest and most powerful jihadist groups, finally decided to confront the Prince and use him as an excuse to access Manbij and establish a headquarters there; they entered the city in February 2013. This strategy of coming to the rescue of the inhabitants was not unique to Manbij. Many groups used it to justify their invasion of a city and the subsequent takeover of buildings to establish their headquarters. The Nusra Front (which renamed itself the Fateh al-Sham Front in July 2016) used the same strategy to establish a presence in Manbij.

The RC was further marginalized when jihadist groups such as Ahrar al-Sham entered the city. While the RC tried to be democratic and inclusive by creating the Council of the Trustees (which we will discuss more below), the revolutionaries were unable to mobilize a large segment of the population. Their isolation allowed opposing forces to mount an effective opposition to the council.

As we have seen, the RC was very powerful immediately after the liberation of Manbij, because of the prior struggles of its members. The revolutionaries built credibility and gained symbolic capital before they took control of the city. Once they had it, they used the legitimacy they had accumulated during the previous period to build their strength. Still, the challenges we have listed stymied them, and evolved into even more complicated problems: a lack of funding; a lack of expertise to run institutions; an inability to provide the necessary resources to the internally displaced living in the city; the failure to prevent military groups' intimidation of the residents; an inability to stop the threat and violence of the regime; their unwillingness to create an inclusive space for individuals and groups critical of the revolution; the social pressure to resolve everyday problems quickly (which in turn was difficult because of their other challenges); and the inability to build a solid front against the jihadist groups. The Islamic State capitalized on each one of these weaknesses to capture the institutions one by one and later, the entire city.

Council of the Trustees of the Revolution

To regain its legitimacy after numerous setbacks, the RC decided to create a Council of the Trustees of the Revolution (CTR), a legislative formation of six hundred residents who had a reputation as revolutionaries. While women were excluded, the CTR did make efforts to be more inclusive than the RC had been thus far. Many new groups and individuals were invited to join. The council had weekly meetings to discuss issues proposed by the members. The CTR made all the important decisions, such as raising the price of bread (the RC controlled an important mill and grain silos in Manbij) or the creation of a police force in the city, while the RC implemented these resolutions.

However, the CTR's attempts at greater inclusion had limits, and the selection of members was controversial: many activists critical of the RC were not invited to join the CTR. While the RC argued that the new council should only be open to revolutionaries (those who participated in demonstrations, fought the regime forces, or supported the revolution publicly or financially), others wanted to include everyone except for those who collaborated with the regime or took a clear stance against the revolution.

The CTR's revolutionary/counter-revolutionary binary would come back to bite it. But in the beginning, tensions gave way and the CTR created a unique space where another kind of politics could be imagined. The meetings facilitated passionate debates about politics, democracy, military strategy, relief work, and various social issues. Any member of the CTR had the opportunity to discuss topics he deemed important. Unlike any other form of political consultation in recent memory in Manbij, the CTR discussed human rights with dignity, in the context of the vernacular culture's notions about respect and piety. The CTR was an experimental space par excellence where grassroots politics, experimental processes, and participatory democracy could thrive. The meetings were organized on a biweekly basis and usually started at seven o'clock in the evening, running until around midnight. They were held at the headquarters of the Revolutionaries of Manbij Battalion in the city's eastern outskirts. Since the regime had information about these meetings through its informants, it sometimes flew jets over them to intimidate participants—and impress upon them the futility of their efforts. Still, the CTR created a public sphere for debate and was very effective in preventing the FSA and other military groups from controlling the city's institutions.

The CTR gave new momentum to the RC, but it didn't last long. The RC made a serious political mistake by excluding a large section of the population. Their minimalist definition of who qualified as "revolutionary" was polarizing. Many in Manbij were insulted by their exclusion from the council, and consequently by their implicit categorization as counter-revolutionary. For its part, the RC purported to have made its classification to protect the CTR from the infiltration of counter-revolutionary forces, which were undeniably present in the city. Manbij was the target of weekly airstrikes and many informants provided vital information to the regime. In addition, a section of the population passively supported the regime for a variety of reasons. By imposing such an exclusive definition of "revolutionary," the RC prevented many neutral or passive citizens from joining the CTR. As a result, it was easy for truly counter-revolutionary forces to convince the population that a few families and notables controlled the trustees while the vast majority of common people were excluded from decision-making.

Groups such as Ahrar al-Sham and the Islamic State began questioning the legitimacy of the CTR and recruiting the residents who felt disenfranchised. Some of the excluded groups gradually built relationships with sympathizers within the CTR, but more importantly, they began organizing against the CTR from the outside. The jihadist groups and their allies used an array of tactics to undermine the legitimacy of the council. They organized lively public debates in mosques about theology and Islam. At night, they held rallies in the city center, closing streets and playing jihadist songs. In some cases, they kidnapped and assassinated members and supporters of the RC. They used intimidation and violence to take over mosques that were under the control of the Sufi[12] establishment and used them as spaces to propagate jihadist ideologies. In several instances, a preacher from the Islamic State would enter the mosque with an explosive belt and a machine gun and tell the imam to leave. In addition, the Islamic State would ask its supporters to be present to create a threatening environment if the imam refused to obey. In July 2013, the Islamic State kidnapped Sheikh Said Mohammed al-Dibo, the imam of the Grand Mosque, because of his refusal to obey their orders. A large demonstration was organized the same day and the Islamic State finally released the imam after several factions of the FSA threatened to take action. But the imam was killed one early morning a few weeks later, on his way to the mosque; the Islamic State was considered the most likely assassin. The Islamic State undermined the power of the RC by taking over vital institutions such as the mills and the bakeries. They organized protests against the RC for failing to control the prices of basic commodities or to stabilize the dollar's exchange rate. Finally, they threatened to assassinate the president and members of the RC, and succeeded in creating a climate of fear.

The Revolutionary Court

After the liberation of the city in 2012, the RC started a process of deliberation with various forces in Manbij to establish a court. The Revolutionary Court was created two months later. It was one of the first revolutionary courts in the liberated areas, but the process of setting it up was somewhat contentious. The religious establishment wanted a religious court and a legal code based on sharia. On the other side were lawyers and revolutionaries who wanted to preserve the Syrian penal code and strip it of any articles created by the Assad regime. Lawyers argued that the Syrian penal code was approved in 1949, almost twenty years before Hafez al-Assad's rise to power, and was thus still useful. In addition, article 3 of the 1973 constitution states that "Islamic jurisprudence is a primary source of legislation," which they took to mean that there was no conflict between the penal code and sharia. Lawyers also argued that only a few articles of the penal code were introduced by either Hafez or Bashar al-Assad's regime, and as such they could be easily removed. Due to these differences of opinion it took the Revolutionary Court several months before finding a suitable location to operate, and to agree on a penal code that suited both parties. In the end, a council of lawyers and clerics was formed and instead of employing the Syrian penal code, the RC decided to adopt "the Arab Unified Penal Code," which was drafted by the Arab League in 1996 and was more in step with sharia than Syria's code was. Practically speaking, however, many lawyers still followed the Syrian penal code since they were familiar with it, and with a few exceptions, Muslim clerics did not disapprove of the rulings since they had no experience with either.

The Revolutionary Court faced additional challenges, some internal and others external. Internally, the lack of funding prevented the court from having a police force to protect lawyers from retaliation and to enforce the court's rulings. The judges felt vulnerable and unable to inflict harsh rulings—which were viewed as necessary in a time of war, according to some victims. As a result many of the more serious cases were tried in the Islamic State's religious court. Also, the Revolutionary Court was unable to pay its guards adequately, which made them vulnerable to corruption; some were always seeking extra cash to complement their meager salaries. When families of prisoners began bribing the guards for favors, the power of the Revolutionary Court was undermined.

Externally, the Revolutionary Court's challenges were also severe. For example, some of the larger families and clans in Manbij argued that customary law should apply whenever one of their members was accused of wrongdoing. While clans were weakened after the liberation of Manbij because many sheikhs sided with the regime, some of them still had some influence. In addition, large military factions such as Ahrar al-Sham, the Islamic State, and before them certain FSA groups, created their own courts to evade accountability. These courts originally tried fighters accused of wrongdoing. At a later stage, the inhabitants sought them out for other types of cases because they felt that the Revolutionary Court was toothless or too secular.

The multiplicity of courts in Manbij created a conundrum. When a plaintiff or a defendant didn't agree with the rulings of the Revolutionary Court, nothing prevented him from requesting a new trial at one of the other courts in the city. An increasing number of inhabitants sought the Islamic State's court because it was much faster in issuing rulings and in implementing them. On several occasions, the Islamic State attacked the Revolutionary Court and captured prisoners. In one instance, the group executed the prisoners publicly to tarnish the reputation of the RC and terrify the population.

Due to these challenges, the RC decided to replace the Revolutionary Court with a Sharia Council in October 2013, which got the support of all the military factions present in the city except for the Islamic State. The RC also created a security brigade to protect the new council and its prison, and to improve security in the city.

But there were now, in reality, three legal systems coexisting in Manbij: the Syrian penal code, sharia, and customary law. Such a space, where several legal systems coexist, is common when the authority of a central state disappears. The experimentation with this plurality might have been productive in other circumstances, especially since previously marginal groups started having a voice. This was not exactly the case in Manbij, however. Force rather than democratic deliberation imposed certain legal discourses and marginalized others. Still, the existence of several legal systems allowed for creative experimentation, and in some instances turned law into an emancipatory rather than a coercive tool.

Conclusion

Manbij's democratic experiment was not to last. The rending forces of war proved too strong. During my first visit in June and July 2013, the RC was dominating political life in the city while the Islamic State (at the time, known as the Islamic State in Iraq and Syria, or ISIS) was marginal. By December 2013, when I went for a second visit, the Islamic State had become the dominant group and controlled most vital institutions, and the RC had almost ceased operating because the lives of its president and members were constantly threatened. As the opposition fought the Islamic State in northern Syria in 2014, Manbij fell in and out of the extremist group's hands. After being involved in some activities to resist the Islamic State, including a daring general strike, the RC was ultimately expelled and began operating in exile from Azaz, a city more than one hundred kilometers to the west, near the Turkish border. In August 2016, the Kurdish Democratic Union Party drove out the Islamic State; the RC seems to have grown much closer to Turkey since the country's military intervention in Syria that same month, and has lost its independence. It has not returned to Manbij.

Manbij's revolutionaries were marginalized by better-funded and extremely well-organized forces. But this is not a sign that Manbij's revolutionary governance was necessarily fated, from the beginning, to be short-lived. The unfortunate demise of the RC's brand of participatory politics was not due to inherent flaws—a failure of its design or implementation—but to external factors.

And one of the biggest root causes of the RC's undoing was the revolution's inability to produce a discourse that adequately represented it, in international media and elsewhere. The story has never been told well, either by analysts, pundits, or journalists.

At the international level, the Western and Arab governments have not only intervened militarily to crush the Syrian revolution; they have also produced discourses that besieged the very idea of revolution. The West has advanced its narrative either through complicit silence,[13] well-orchestrated campaigns to tarnish the image of the revolutionaries,[14] or the funding of the most reactionary military factions, such as Ahrar al-Sham and the Islam Army (Jaysh al-Islam).[15] Further, many commentators, journalists, and academics write solely about the military and geopolitical dimensions of the uprisings and ignore cultures of liberation and participatory politics that Syrians have been developing and enacting since the early days of the revolts. Even when they have good intentions, a large section of the intelligentsia has used antiquated conceptual tools and inadequate theories.[16]

It is important that the violence of the war and the hostile narratives promulgated by outsiders do not silence the stories of local practices such as those in Manbij, which were vital spaces for experimentation and the production of new cultures. The local narratives that emanated from the city stand in stark opposition to abstract global designs and regional strategies that commentators regurgitate when they write about Syria.

Local governance and participatory democracy in Manbij were not the products of ideological certainties but rather the contingent outcomes of grassroots resistance. The efforts were imperfect, but they represented the beginning of a long process of liberation—a process that has been undermined, though not necessarily aborted, by foreign interventions and the Syrian regime's politics of death and destruction. The experimental grassroots politics and micropractices in Manbij and other cities might still represent the beginning of a culture of liberation that could take several decades before reaching fruition. What's more, Manbij's revolutionaries have been aware of their experiment's potential from the beginning, even if they could not have foreseen all the obstacles that would later be thrown in front of them.

As the Syrian civil war finishes its sixth brutal year, a future without Assad is looking ever more unlikely. But there is still wisdom to be gleaned from the efforts of the Manbij revolutionaries, who stumbled not because they made any mistakes in designing their institutions, but because so much of the world turned out to be against them. Throughout the country, revolutionaries' initial experiments with governance—in Manbij, Idlib, the Eastern Ghouta, and elsewhere—will have enduring benefits for the Syrian people, whose skills and aptitude for participatory politics were expanded, however haltingly, in their interregnum of self-determination. If we are to continue to envision the possibility of a more democratic future in Syria, we would be wise to keep the lessons of places like Manbij alive, as well.

Notes

1. The research for this chapter was funded by the Arab Council for the Social Sciences (ACSS).

2. "Manbij Perishes Silently" (Arabic), *Syria Untold*, July 20, 2016, http://www.syriauntold. com/ar/event/منبج-تباد-بصمت/.

3. As I have noted, I am referring to the Manbij activists who were instrumental in setting up the RC as "revolutionaries," using the term they used to describe themselves. Similarly, I use other concepts popular among the activists throughout this chapter, such as "liberation." Although I acknowledge the risk of using normative terms such as these to describe events over which there is still a great deal of disagreement even within Syria, it would be a poor representation of my research to use excessively impartial vocabulary.

4. I borrow Haitian intellectual Michel-Rolph Trouillot's terminology for his country's "unthinkable revolution" at the turn of the nineteenth century, which was ignored in much of the world due to racism. Analogously, Western thought has ignored the accomplishments of Syrian revolutionaries and—in its ignoring of them—telegraphed the belief that a revolutionary process is inconceivable in an Arab country such as Syria.

5. The FSA was very marginal in Manbij and didn't play any notable role until after the liberation of the city. See Christoph Reuter and Abd al-Kadher Adhun, "Rebels Make a Go of Governing in Liberated City," *Der Spiegel*, October 2, 2012, http://www.spiegel.de/international/world/rebels-make-a-go-of-governing-in-liberated-city-in-syria-a-859007.html.

6. In general, the FSA in Manbij was ill-equipped and underfunded; it had less than twenty machine guns the day residents expelled the police and security from the city.

7. For more on Egypt's local popular committees, see Cilja Harders and Dina Wahba's chapter in this volume, "New Neighborhood Power: Informal Popular Committees and Changing Local Governance in Egypt;" and Aysa El-Meehy's chapter in this volume, "Governance from Below: Comparing Local Experiments in Egypt and Syria after the Uprisings."

8. For more information see Haian Dukhan, "Tribes and Tribalism in the Syrian Uprising," *Syria Studies Journal* 6, no. 2 (2014): 1–28.

9. Amjad Altinawi, "The Security Establishement Executes 'The Prince'" (Arabic), *All-4Syria*, April 21, 2015, http://www.all4syria.info/Archive/208937.

10. Zana Miso, "Faruq Brigades Leave Homs under Shelling and Head to al-Hasakeh to Fight Kurdish Forces" (Arabic), YouTube, July 23, 2013, https://www.youtube.com/watch?v=4MAOz2M6oM8.

11. Rania Abouzeid, "Syria's Up-and-Coming Rebels: Who Are the Farouq Brigades?," *Time*, October 05, 2012, http://world.time.com/2012/10/05/syrias-up-and-coming-rebels-who-are-the-farouq-brigades-2/.

12. Manbij and other regions in northern Aleppo province were dominated by the Naqshbandiyya Sufi order. Salafism had a contentious relationship with Sufism in Syria. For an in-depth discussion, see the important work of Itzchak Weismann on Salafism and Sufism in Syria.

13. Christina Zdanowicz, "Aleppo Is Being Destroyed by the Silence of the World," *CNN*, December 13, 2016, http://www.cnn.com/2016/12/13/world/aleppo-destroyed-by-worlds-silence-twitter/.

14. Idrees Ahmad, "*Russia Today* and the Post-Truth Virus," *Pulsemedia*, December 15, 2016, https://pulsemedia.org/2016/12/15/russia-today-and-the-post-truth-virus/.

15. Kim Sengupta, "Turkey and Saudi Arabia Alarm the West by Backing Islamist Extremists the Americans Had Bombed in Syria," *The Independent*, May 11, 2015, http://www.independent.co.uk/news/world/middle-east/syria-crisis-turkey-and-saudi-arabia-shock-western-countries-by-supporting-anti-assad-jihadists-10242747.html.

16. Even outlets opposed to Assad and friendly to the opposition tend to overemphasize the geopolitical aspect of the revolution. See the following articles from major outlets that have been generally critical of the Assad regime: As`ad Abukhalil, "The Left and the Syria Debate," *Jadaliyya*, December 10, 2016, http://www.jadaliyya.com/pages/index/25628/the-left-and-the-syria-debate; Max Fisher, "In Syrian War, Russia Has Yet to Fulfill Superpower Ambitions," *New York Times*, September 24, 2016, http://www.nytimes.com/2016/09/25/world/middleeast/russia-syria-ambitions.html; Nafeez Ahmed, "Syria Intervention Plan Fueled by Oil Interests, Not Chemical Weapon Concern," *The Guardian*, August 30, 2013, https://www.theguardian.com/environment/earth-insight/2013/aug/30/syria-chemical-attack-war-intervention-oil-gas-energy-pipelines; David Oualaalou, "Russia Outsmarts the U.S. in Syria: A New Geopolitical Outlook," *Huffington Post*, October 13, 2016, http://www.huffingtonpost.com/david-oualaalou/russia-outsmarts-us_b_8273562.html.

17

Into the Tunnels

The Rise and Fall of Syria's Rebel Enclave in the Eastern Ghouta

ARON LUND

Since 2011, the Eastern Ghouta has been a key front in the uprising against Syrian President Bashar al-Assad, and a threat to his control over Damascus. In 2013, regime forces managed to impose a siege on the area, creating a humanitarian crisis but also giving rise to a complex "siege economy" of clandestine trade and underground tunnels. Firebrand preacher Zahran Alloush took advantage of the conditions created by the siege to unify rebels under his control, strong-arming smaller factions into joint institutions. But what could have emerged as a viable—albeit fundamentalist and authoritarian—alternative to Assad's dictatorship soon broke down, partly due to Alloush's failure to control the tunnel economy. After his death, the enclave collapsed into infighting and Assad moved to recapture it. This chapter provides the first detailed history of the Eastern Ghouta rebellion, investigating the dynamics of a fragmented insurgency and the factors that can enable or prevent rebel unification under a central leadership.

In the sixth year of Syria's civil war, President Bashar al-Assad's government is slowly seizing ground from opposition forces. Backed by Russian and Iranian reinforcements, the government retook Eastern Aleppo in December 2016. Assad's forces also advanced against a besieged enclave closer to the capital, known as the Eastern Ghouta. The area is larger than Eastern Aleppo, possibly with as many as 450,000 inhabitants, but it has gained very little media attention.[1]

One reason is that the political situation of the Eastern Ghouta is so difficult to parse. Even as they wage war on each other, some army and rebel commanders remain connected through an informal wartime economy, muddling their political and military incentives and complicating any analysis of the situation.

The Eastern Ghouta insurgency has been led by factions indigenous to the area, such as the Islam Army, which dominated the enclave from 2013 onward. By early 2015, its leader Zahran Alloush had managed to corral most rival factions into a set of new rebel institutions under his own dominance. The disproportionate power and size of the Islam Army kept smaller factions in line and brought a modicum of stability to the enclave. Though reviled by his critics as a ruthless authoritarian, Alloush began to appear as one of the insurgency's few effective state-builders.

These attempts to establish a new political order are what makes the Eastern Ghouta so tragically relevant for the rest of Syria and, perhaps, for the study of fragmented insurgencies globally. Over six years, the anti-Assad opposition has failed to produce a sustainable model for how to govern territories abandoned by the regime. Under Alloush's heavy-handed leadership, an exception to that rule seemed to be taking shape in 2014–15 in the Eastern Ghouta. However, changes in the enclave's political economy eventually weakened the Islam Army and provoked conflicts over smuggling revenues. Alloush's death in December 2015 created a political vacuum that second-tier factions sought to fill, and, as the Islam Army's dominance faded, conflict between rebel factions resurfaced with devastating effect. A year later, the enclave had shrunk considerably and Assad was pushing for its capitulation.

Though the insurgency in the Eastern Ghouta was a product of unique circumstances, the rise of its rebellion—and now likely also its fall—remains instructive for what it tells us about the development of factionalized insurgencies, how political order may be created from the bottom up, and what conditions facilitate state-building efforts or presage their failure.

To chronicle the evolution of the Eastern Ghouta's politics since 2011 and understand the effects of the siege economy, I have relied on interviews with Syrians inside and outside the enclave, on a critical analysis of the propaganda of the various actors, and on non-Syrian news reporting and social media. While these sources have offered a wealth of information, the lack of unbiased accounts and the dearth of prior research have at times forced me to piece together information by collecting and comparing limited, unreliable, or contradictory data. I would therefore like to stress that the material should be treated with some care, and that any errors of fact or interpretation are mine alone.[2]

The Eastern Ghouta

The Ghouta is a lush agricultural region surrounding Damascus, once described by the medieval Arab historian Ibn al-Wardi as "full of water, flowering trees, and passing birds, with exquisite flowers, wrapped in branches and paradise-like greenery," indeed, as "the fairest place on earth, and the best of them."[3]

In the twentieth century, this would change. Following Syria's independence from France in 1946, urbanization and technological changes began to transform the hinterland of Damascus into a region of suburbs and satellite towns, and the ancient oasis seemed destined to disappear.[4] The outward expansion of Damascus's urban sprawl took place "without the slightest regard for environmental, aesthetic, or health concerns," creating a "belt of misery" in this conservative Sunni Muslim region.[5] After inheriting power from his father in the summer of 2000, President Bashar al-Assad ordered economic reforms that further heightened the social crisis in the Eastern Ghouta.[6]

When the Arab uprisings swept into Syria in March 2011, the comparatively affluent and carefully policed central neighborhoods of the capital hardly stirred—but the Ghouta rose fast and hard in an angry, desperate rebellion. Hundreds of demonstrators were killed or wounded by security forces in the first months of the crisis, and by summer 2011 a politicized armed insurgency was taking shape. By the end of 2011, rebel fighters had seized entire neighborhoods in eastern Damascus and Douma, the largest city in the Eastern Ghouta. In early 2013, the opposition controlled an area in the Eastern Ghouta that stretched from the Damascus suburbs in the west to the desert town of Oteiba in the east, and from Douma in the north to the outskirts of the Damascus International Airport in the south. Within these lines, Assad's government had ceased to exist.

Too weak and overstretched to defeat its opponents, the army opted to contain the Eastern Ghouta rebellion. In April 2013, the government retook the desert town of Oteiba, fending off a rebel counteroffensive the following month. "The battle of Oteiba was a tipping point between success and disaster," said a member of a rebel faction in the Damascus region, noting the town's key role as a link between the Eastern Ghouta and smuggling routes through the desert and the Qalamoun Mountains. "It was not the only such place," he said, "but it was the last one."[7]

Having failed to break the siege, the insurgents were drawn deep into the Damascus suburbs, where they were hit by repeated nerve gas attacks,

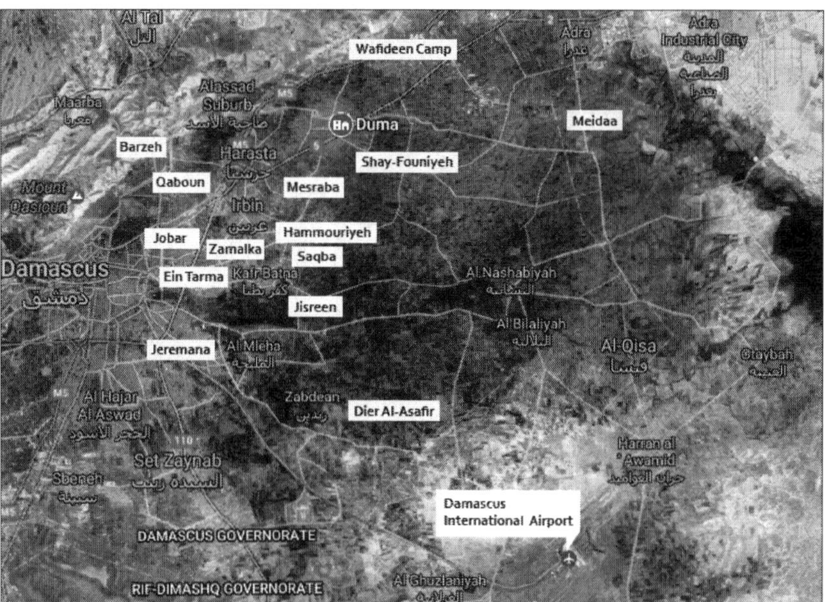

Map 1. Eastern Ghouta

Source: Compiled by author.

culminating in a gruesome massacre of civilians on August 21, 2013. As the siege hardened, the horizons of the Eastern Ghouta shrank, and its defenders were increasingly preoccupied by the question of how to rule the enclave in which they had been trapped.

2011–12: Zahran Alloush and the Early Insurgency

The most important of the armed factions to emerge in the Eastern Ghouta was the Islam Army (Jaysh al-Islam), which rose to dominance from 2013 onwards under the leadership of Zahran Alloush. Born in 1971 to a Salafi preacher in the conservative city of Douma, Alloush reportedly had his first run-in with the security apparatus as a teenager in 1987.[8] When the uprising began, he was in jail for his Salafi connections, rubbing shoulders with Iraq War veterans in Sednaya Prison, north of Damascus. Like many of his fellow inmates, Alloush was released in a presidential amnesty in June 2011, and he immediately joined the budding insurgency in Douma.[9]

Alloush initially worked with the Obeida Ibn Jarrah Battalion, an early armed group that was ostensibly part of the Free Syrian Army, a very loose militant network that was in reality more of a brand name.[10] By September 2011, he had created his own armed faction, called the Islam Company (*Sariyat al-Islam*). It recruited chiefly from the Salafi milieu in Douma, including among religious students and scholars linked to the Tawhid Mosque, where Alloush's father had officiated.[11] Alloush served as its all-powerful leader, inspiring great loyalty in his men but also evincing a centralizing, authoritarian streak that would soon make its mark on the Eastern Ghouta insurgency. The group's first documented attack seems to have been a nighttime raid against a checkpoint in Mesraba, near Douma, in September or October 2011.[12] But the Islam Company's distinguishing feature was not, at this early stage, its military capacity, but rather its overtly religious and missionary character.

Much of the early insurgency in the city was led by local toughs who, though they wrapped themselves in Sunni Islamic rhetoric, were not particularly religious or ideological. One Syrian researcher refers to them as "qabadayat," an old term for the opportunistic neighborhood strongmen who ruled the streets and played politics in Ottoman and French mandate days.[13] According to one of Zahran Alloush's early associates, Essam Boueidani, the Islam Company approached these factions as an ally and "taught them how to do the ablution and establish the prayer. Most of them didn't pray. They were kind people but they didn't pray."[14]

Although Alloush's fundamentalist rhetoric and Saudi connections caused alarm among secularists and some anti-Salafi Islamic scholars, his views were not unpopular with the conservative population in Douma, a traditional stronghold of the Hanbali school of Sunni Islam. The Islam Company's ability to portray itself as a religiously observant and uncorrupted force drew recruits from non-ideological Free Syrian Army factions, which ended up in the hands of opportunistic elements who "had no strategy and no vision."[15]

An important source of Alloush's growing influence was his connections with Salafi clerics in the Arab Gulf states, such as the Riyadh-based Syrian Salafi televangelist and fundraiser Adnan Arour.[16] Alloush also benefited from his role in a Qatar- and Turkey-backed arms smuggling trail passing through northern Syria. It had been organized under the auspices of Colonel Khaled al-Habbous, who now accuses Alloush of having diverted weapons to his own faction.[17]

In early 2012, Alloush renamed his rapidly growing group the Islam Brigade, or Liwa al-Islam. Then, in July 2012, Alloush made global headlines by claiming responsibility for the assassination of several senior Syrian officials at the National Security Office in Damascus, including Bashar al-Assad's brother-in-law, General Assef Shawkat, and the Minister of Defense, General Dawoud Rajha.[18] The incident remains murky; it is possible that this was a false claim on Alloush's part or an operation by a foreign intelligence service that credited the Islam Brigade in order to escape attention. Whatever the case, the Islam Brigade was able to use its newfound notoriety to attract additional funds and recruits.

2013–14: Rise of the Islam Army

As the conflict entered its third year, Zahran Alloush was becoming a figure of national importance. He developed a broad network in northern Syria and Turkey, where some of his former comrades from Sednaya Prison now played key roles in groups like Ahrar al-Sham and the Nusra Front. But his primary focus seems to have been Douma and the Eastern Ghouta, where the rebels still struggled to fill the governance vacuum after expelling Assad's forces.

Through much of 2013 and 2014, Alloush tangled with two local Douma commanders, Abu Ali Khibbiyeh and Abu Subhi Taha. Their Free Syrian Army factions were notorious for their involvement in organized crime, but they were able to attract some support by positioning themselves as opponents of Alloush and his Salafis.[19] For a time they seemed evenly matched, but Alloush had soon outgrown any accommodation with his rivals. One reason for the rapid rise of the Islam Brigade was a steady influx of funds from a Salafi charity in Kuwait called the Council of Supporters of the Syrian Revolution.[20] Alloush also reportedly began to receive Saudi state support "in return for loyalty and staying away from al-Qaeda."[21] Riyadh stepped up support for the insurgency after the United States declined to intervene in Syria in September 2013, which seems to have led it to clear Alloush for support despite concerns over possible ties to religious dissidents in Saudi Arabia.

Wherever the money was coming from, Alloush was now able to buy up smaller groups and expand his organization. On September 29, 2013, he declared the merger of the Islam Brigade and forty-two other factions under a new name: the Islam Army, or Jaysh al-Islam. It later claimed to have grown to sixty groups.[22] The Eastern Ghouta had by that time been firmly sealed off by the army siege, which left Alloush as the biggest fish in a shrinking pond, able to impose his own rules on rival factions.

As his power grew, Alloush made enemies among the other commanders, many of whom resented his domineering behavior. He also came under scrutiny for human rights abuses. In particular, the abduction of the human rights lawyer Razan Zeitouneh and three other activists in December 2013 left a stain on Alloush's international reputation, though he denied involvement.[23] Critics also drew attention to Alloush's opposition to democracy and his Sunni-sectarian rhetoric.[24]

Although Alloush's opinions were at odds with the idealized democratic revolution envisioned by the Western media, Western officialdom, and the democratic opposition itself, his views were at this point not outside the mainstream of the armed insurgency. Rather than shunning Alloush, other rebel leaders courted his support. On November 22, 2013, the Islam Army cofounded the Islamic Front alliance alongside some of the most powerful factions in Syria, including the Tawhid Brigade, Suqour al-Sham, and Ahrar al-Sham. Though it was of little consequence for the Eastern Ghouta, the alliance raised Alloush's profile as a national opposition leader and cemented his standing as first among equals inside the enclave.

The question of how to govern the Eastern Ghouta had by this time become a pressing problem. Each rebel faction ran its own affairs in a chaotic tangle of rival sharia courts, revolutionary councils, civilian groups, and residual state and municipal institutions. The fact that most other rebels now grudgingly recognized Alloush's dominance finally gave the enclave a clear center of gravity, paving the way for serious coalition-building.

2014: The Joint Institutions

On June 24, 2014, the Islam Army and several other local groups created the Eastern Ghouta's Unified Judicial Council, led by a panel of religious scholars.[25] It was endorsed by every major faction in the Eastern Ghouta, though the al-Qaeda-aligned Nusra Front[26] quickly broke away.

On August 27 came the creation of a Unified Military Command, intended to serve as the highest political and military authority in the Eastern Ghouta. Its most important members were the Islam Army, the non-Salafi Islamists of Ajnad al-Sham, and a Free Syrian Army-branded faction known as Failaq al-Rahman. Alloush became head of the alliance, with Ajnad al-Sham's Yasser al-Qadri as his deputy and Failaq al-Rahman's Abdel-Nasr Shmeir as field commander.[27]

One source later estimated that "close to half" of the enclave's rebels had stayed outside of the Unified Military Command, including the Nusra Front and numerous small factions.[28]

In September 2014, Zahran Alloush's old Douma rivals Abu Subhi Taha and Abu Ali Khibbiyeh gathered several holdout factions into a coalition known as the Umma Army. Alloush reacted with outrage, declaring that the Eastern Ghouta could not suffer "two heads on the same body."[29] In the ensuing power struggle, Alloush seized control over Khibbiyeh's smuggling business near Douma. The trade disruptions sparked a humanitarian crisis, and in mid-November 2014, protesters stormed Islam Army warehouses, provoking armed clashes. However, if the Umma Army leaders had thought that they could force Alloush to share power, they had badly misjudged the man. In late December 2014, the Islam Army launched a military offensive against the "corrupt filth" of the Umma Army.[30] Other members of the joint institutions criticized the Islam Army for not having sought a resolution via the Unified Judicial Council, but none intervened.[31] Alloush later claimed to have jailed thirteen hundred Umma Army members, though most were eventually released.[32] Abu Subhi Taha's fate remains unclear, but the Islam Army later released a video in which a subdued-looking Abu Ali Khibbiyeh, captured in January 2015, confessed to being a criminal, a narcotics trader, and a homosexual. According to some reports, he was executed nine months later.[33]

From summer 2014 until spring 2015, Alloush also overpowered other rivals, including local cells of the so-called Islamic State and a faction known as Failaq Omar, while the Eastern Ghouta branch of Ahrar al-Sham collapsed in a complicated split.[34] During these conflicts, the Unified Military Command decreed a ban on the creation of new groups in the Eastern Ghouta.[35] This led the insurgency to consolidate at a faster pace around the "big three" members of the Unified Military Command: the Islam Army, Ajnad al-Sham, and Failaq al-Rahman. As the factional muck drained away, only the Nusra Front remained as a strong and explicit challenger to the new system.

This exception aside, the new institutions were gaining considerable traction. By early 2015, every major faction in the Eastern Ghouta except the jihadists had endorsed them. Remaining civilian institutions and other opposition bodies were forced to play by the rules laid down by the commanders and their religious sheikhs. Society also came under pressure to conform to their values. In summer 2015, a new religious police appeared on the streets of Douma to promote Islamic morals and sharia law. Though critics complained that it was a way for the Islam Army to unilaterally impose its worldview on others, the group's leaders shrugged off the criticism, claiming to act on behalf of the Unified Judicial Council.[36]

It was one example among many of how Alloush used the new institutions to legitimize and magnify his own power, even as he refused to be constrained by them and blocked their attempts to investigate the Islam Army's own conduct.[37]

Though the joint institutions were weak and riddled with problems, the Eastern Ghouta did seem to be moving away from the violent anarchy that had plagued the area since the expulsion of the Assad regime. With Alloush now in the process of solidifying and formalizing his authority, a monopoly of force—that is, state-like authority—began to seem within reach. Apart from the areas controlled by the Islamic State's "caliphate" in the east of the country, and the northern self-ruled areas controlled by groups aligned with the Kurdistan Workers' Party (the PKK), this was virtually without precedent in Syria.

In April 2015, the world got a glimpse of what could have been, when the Islam Army released video footage of a large military display in which rows of uniformed soldiers and tanks marched past a parade stand where Zahran Alloush sat on a chair flanked by his lieutenants. The spectacle seemed designed to emulate a traditional Arab army, with Alloush in the role of the traditional Arab president.[38]

The Economy of a Siege

The siege imposed on the Eastern Ghouta in 2013 has played a major role in the evolution of its politics. Restrictions on trade and aid deliveries left rebel factions dependent on the government but also increased those factions' influence over the population. In the climate of scarcity created by the siege, a small number of semiofficial frontline crossings and tunnels became immensely valuable, engendering new forms of rent-seeking competition among the rebels. Actors on the government side also profited from the siege and acquired a vested interest in maintaining it.

Understanding the background and the functioning of this peculiar siege economy is crucial to understanding the Eastern Ghouta's rebel politics, and it provides an instructive example of how financial constraints and opportunities can shape the political and military situation in counterintuitive ways.

As previously described, the government initially laid siege to the Eastern Ghouta after its capture of Oteiba in April 2013. In the following months, the army sealed the enclave's main entry routes at Mleiha in the southwest and near the Wafideen Camp in the north. Some trade quietly continued, but the siege was tightened into a comprehensive economic blockade in early 2014, when the army captured Mleiha and took steps to close the lines near the Wafideen Camp. Later in 2014, a limited trade resumed via progovernment businessmen and their rebel intermediaries. But while this allowed food and fuel prices in the enclave to stabilize at a high level, supplies remained spotty and prices sometimes spiked due to fighting, checkpoint closures, the destruction of smuggling tunnels, or market manipulations. Civilians remained trapped inside the enclave, prevented from leaving by both government forces and local rebel groups, who feared infiltration and demanded payment to allow crossings.[39]

The blockade sent prices skyrocketing, causing severe human suffering. In March 2015, the pro-opposition Douma Coordination Group published a table comparing prices in the Eastern Ghouta and what it termed "Occupied Damascus." Units differ from product to product, while prices are listed in Syrian pounds:

Product	Eastern Ghouta	Damascus
Sugar	2,750	120
Eggs	5,100	750
Bread	750	35
Tea	8,000	1,200
Heating oil	1,100	120
Potatoes	1,300	90
Lentils	1,600	125[40]

The blockade crippled the local economy and quickly depleted necessities like fuel, pharmaceuticals, and medical equipment. The opposition-friendly Syrian American Medical Society estimated that more than two hundred civilians in the enclave died from a lack of food or access to medical care between October 2012 and January 2015,[41] and Amnesty International has concluded that the Syrian government's restrictions on food and medicine amounted to a crime against humanity.[42]

The blockade also had a profound impact on the Eastern Ghouta insurgency. On the one hand, new types of conflict emerged, as rebel commanders jockeyed for control over scarce resources, smuggling routes, and government-approved imports. On the other hand, those who managed to monopolize some facet of the siege economy immediately gained leverage over other actors. Government-connected businessmen used the siege to expand their influence both in Damascus and in the Eastern Ghouta, while army and intelligence commanders made money from checkpoints and exploited their control over trade to win concessions and destabilize the enclave.

The Million-Pound Checkpoint

Though neither side has been eager to talk about it, a deal emerged in 2014 by which select traders were allowed to bring goods through the frontline at the army-controlled Wafideen Camp, near Douma. Since then, the Wafideen Crossing has been the most important outside source of food for the enclave, and it is sometimes described as the "lung" of the Eastern Ghouta.

In June 2015, a local trader explained to Amnesty International how the Wafideen trade operated:

> To leave Douma I need to pass by a non-state armed group checkpoint then I drive for a couple of minutes passing by an area that is not controlled by anyone. Then I pass by three checkpoints controlled by the Air Force Intelligence and State Security forces. I reach al-Wafedine camp where I buy the food. I do not leave the truck. Two women with me in the car transfer the food and non-food items to the truck and pay the security forces. For every item I pay a price equivalent to eight or ten times the price in central Damascus.[43]

Commanders on both sides of the front would demand a cut to let goods pass, forcing consumers inside the Eastern Ghouta to pay enormously inflated prices.[44] The crossing became so profitable that people in Damascus nicknamed it "hajez al-milyoun," meaning "the Million Checkpoint," in reference to the earnings of the soldiers manning it.[45]

On the rebel side, the Douma–Wafideen route was initially controlled in whole or in part by Abu Ali Khibbiyeh's Free Syrian Army faction, but the Islam Army seized the checkpoints as part of Alloush's crackdown on the Umma Army in November 2014. From then on, businessmen were reportedly forced to acquire signed permits if they wished to bring food into the Eastern Ghouta, and to sell and offload foodstuffs at designated warehouses under Islam Army guard. In this way, Alloush and his businessman allies gained near-monopolistic control over food imports and the ability to influence access and prices. However, traders were allowed to bring nonfood items like cigarettes into the Eastern Ghouta and sell these privately at a higher profit.[46]

Eastern Ghouta activists accused the Islam Army of making "unimaginable" profits by taking a 30 percent cut from each shipment, but the Islam Army denied having any economic stake in the trade.[47] The Wafideen Crossing "is open only to some civilians who transport small amounts of certain goods by foot, or to humanitarian convoys, as well as to a trader who runs a barter operation through the crossing. He brings out certain products from the Ghouta and brings in some of the things it needs," said Mohammed Bayraqdar, a member of the Islam Army's political office. "The role of the Islam Army in all of this is simply to provide security, so that agents of the regime do not infiltrate via the crossing."[48]

The Cheese King

The trader that Bayraqdar referred to was Mohieddine Manfoush. Also known as Abu Ayman, this businessman from Mesraba, southwest of Douma, had since 2014 become the most important figure in the Eastern Ghouta's siege economy. He resided in government-held territory, with offices in the western suburb of Mezzeh, but still controlled the Manfoush Trading Company factory in Mesraba, which supplied the markets of Damascus with cheese, yoghurt, and other dairy products under the brand name Almarai.

According to the the Syrian researcher Youssef Sadaki, who has studied the Eastern Ghouta's siege economy, Manfoush started providing support for bakeries and bringing in wheat to the Eastern Ghouta in 2014. He later began to pay stipends to teachers in his hometown, Mesraba, and the nearby village of Medyara. Eventually, he emerged as a middleman between the rebels and the markets in Damascus, negotiating permission from regime commanders to bring in truckloads of food and other supplies through the Wafideen Crossing, while taking out his own dairy products for sale in Damascus. Sadaki claimed that Manfoush had some two thousand employees and his own armed force in Mesraba, which was apparently spared the air strikes that had devastated other Eastern Ghouta towns.[49]

The government was certainly aware of Manfoush's ties to the rebels and senior figures in the Assad regime likely benefited from his operations. Yet Manfoush has been described as "beloved by both the opposition and the regime."[50] Some rebels even expressed surprise at the notion that he could be perceived as a progovernment figure, apparently viewing him as one of their own who just happens to live and work on the other side. "No, Abu Ayman does not take part in the revolution," said Wa'el Olwan, a Failaq al-Rahman leader and spokesperson. "He has continued to work in Damascus and reached a deal between the revolutionaries and the regime. This allows him to work with both sides and, yeah, of course he makes money from it."[51]

Though the Islam Army was at pains to deny that it profited from Manfoush's operations at the Wafideen Crossing, it, too, spoke positively of him. "Manfoush does not serve the Islam Army, he serves the Ghouta in its entirety," said Bayraqdar. "Our interests are in harmony with the interests of the people and our relationship is merely that of facilitating his services. If there were another person [who performed the same function], we would provide the same services to him in return for his services to the people of the Ghouta."[52]

Whatever his motives or the nature of his relationship with the regime or its opponents, Manfoush had clearly emerged as a major powerbroker in the Eastern Ghouta. It seemed likely that he could play a significant role in future truce negotiations, perhaps also in a postconflict settlement. Yet, by 2016, he had only been mentioned in a small handful of articles in the Arabic press and hardly at all in English, demonstrating how wartime entrepreneurs may operate in the gray zones of the economy and become influential actors on the ground, without even registering in the politicized media coverage of the conflict.

The Tunnel Trade

Apart from the Wafideen Crossing, the Eastern Ghouta has also been supplied through a system of secret tunnels and informal frontline crossings. The Wafideen Crossing could handle a greater volume of trade, but the tunnels served to bring in goods that were restricted or banned by the government (such as fuel, medical supplies, weapons, and wanted people) and to challenge food prices set by the Wafideen monopolists.

Much of the tunnel trade has taken place in collaboration between two or more groups, sometimes leading to ideologically awkward alliances. In 2015 and 2016, violent skirmishes broke out over profit sharing, allegations of price dumping, and, more straightforwardly, over who should control which route. To many Eastern Ghouta activists, the tunnels emerged as an emblematic symbol of rebel corruption.[53]

The tunnel trade has been concentrated in the Damascus suburbs that line the western and northwestern side of the Eastern Ghouta enclave, and it has relied on a system of local ceasefires to work.

In early 2014, the Barzeh and Qaboun neighborhoods in eastern Damascus signed truce agreements with the Syrian army. Contiguous with each other, the Barzeh region is also adjacent to rebel-held Harasta, across the Damascus-Homs highway.[54] By the terms of the truces, opposition fighters in Barzeh and Qaboun had been allowed to retain their arms, though they were now surrounded by army checkpoints. The government also eased its ban on aid deliveries and trade, though traffic to Barzeh and Qaboun would still be filtered through checkpoints and was sometimes blocked.[55] However, once goods had entered the truce zones, some of them could be smuggled on to the Eastern Ghouta through tunnels. Both government officials and rebels profited from the trade, giving all sides some reason to preserve the status quo.

The largest crossing between Barzeh and Harasta was variously known as the Zahteh Tunnel or the Central Tunnel, and it seems to have begun to operate soon after the truce deals came into effect in 2014. The Eastern Ghouta insurgents also dug smaller smuggling tunnels to Barzeh and Qaboun, as well as to the semi-isolated frontline neighborhood of Jobar, which juts deep into Damascus. In fact, numerous tunnels were dug along the frontlines for military purposes, though only around four or five—including the Zahteh Tunnel—seemed to be in regular use for commercial smuggling.

All of these underground routes were controlled by the armed factions, either alone or in joint ventures. Failaq al-Rahman reportedly dug a tunnel from Erbeen to a Nusra-controlled location in Qaboun in spring 2014. According to some reports, the Nusra Front acquired a separate tunnel in 2015 after tension with Failaq al-Rahman over how to share their Erbeen-Qaboun route. The Islam Army also dug at least two tunnels in 2014–15, linking Zamalka and Erbeen with Jobar and with Qaboun. As for the Zahteh Tunnel and other Harasta routes, they fell under the control of a local group called the Fajr al-Umma Brigade in late 2014.

Military-purpose tunnels were blown up by the army whenever found, but the commercial smuggling appeared to face less resistance. Though the government was aware of the traffic, it seemed keen to preserve the Barzeh-Qaboun truce deals, whether for strategic purposes or because well-connected security officials profited from their control over frontline checkpoints.

Rebel leaders downplayed the importance of the trade. "There are a lot of exaggerations regarding these tunnels," said Failaq al-Rahman's Wa'el Olwan, who insisted that all tunnels combined "cannot provide for even 10 percent of the needs of the Ghouta" and that they were insignificant compared to the Wafideen Crossing.[56] Rebel officials also typically insisted that their own tunnels were only used for military purposes and to help civilians, but they were quick to blame other groups for profiteering. In practice, every major faction in the Eastern Ghouta seems to have had some stake in the commercial tunneling business.

The Zahteh Tunnel and Fajr al-Umma

The Zahteh Tunnel in Harasta has been the most important commercial smuggling route in the Eastern Ghouta since 2014. It is also the one most associated with profiteering and factional conflict. Though sources portray it differently, the physical route is most often described as a large tunnel or underpass that allows movement beneath the Damascus-Homs highway.

Initially, the Zahteh Tunnel appears to have been controlled by a local Free Syrian Army group known as the Fateh al-Sham Brigade, which pioneered its use for trade with the armed groups in Barzeh.[57] In September 2014, the Fateh al-Sham Brigade leader Fahd al-Kurdi joined in the creation of the Umma Army to challenge the Unified Military Command, banning Zahran Alloush's men from using his tunnel. Soon thereafter, Kurdi was murdered by unknown assailants and a rival Harasta faction known as the Fajr al-Umma Brigade moved in to seize the Zahteh Tunnel. The group then took control over all of Harasta.

Under Fajr al-Umma's control, the tunnel has reportedly run triple shifts to transport food, cigarettes, livestock, and even weapons. Eastern Ghouta residents who wished to leave the enclave could also use the tunnel, but only after paying a fee that could amount to hundreds of dollars. (It reportedly peaked at $1,500 in March 2016, at a point when the average monthly income in Syria was around fifty or sixty dollars.)[58] The Fajr al-Umma leader Abu Khaled al-Daqr, alias al-Zahteh, is said to have banned food imports except from selected merchants, from whom he demanded a "tunnel tax" ranging between 25 and 45 percent of the value of the shipment. The final sales price inside the Eastern Ghouta could rise by several thousand percent over the purchase price in Damascus.[59] Other factions also paid Abu Khaled to bring in ammunition, fuel, and other necessities.

Abu Khaled's tunneling business drew the ire of many in the Eastern Ghouta, but Fajr al-Umma sympathizers did not seem overly concerned by these accusations. "Regarding the tunnels, we have a right to trade in order to feed the mujahideen and our revolutionaries after people ganged up on us," retorted a Harasta-based supporter of the group.[60]

Originally created in March 2014 as a subfaction of the non-Salafi Islamist group Ajnad al-Sham,[61] Fajr al-Umma seemed far more invested in its identity as an "army of Harasta" than in any particular ideology. It drifted in and out of alliances without much regard for political consistency, largely to escape pressure from the Islam Army, which in 2015 repeatedly sought to muscle in on the Zahteh Tunnel profits. "Fajr al-Umma is a populist faction [fasil sha'abi]," said Wa'el Olwan, who, as the spokesperson of Failaq al-Rahman and formerly of Ajnad al-Sham had been allied with Fajr al-Umma in 2014 and again in 2015–16. "They have no ideology. They work in Harasta. There are some tunnels there and they control them. The tunnels are what gathers the group, not ideology."[62]

2015: Lead-Up to Conflict

Two years into the siege, the war economy had reshaped the Eastern Ghouta's politics in fundamental ways. Rebel commanders constantly struggled to ensure access to supply lines, and some were drawn to the smuggling economy for reasons that had little to do with the war effort. Infighting escalated, and, for the Islam Army, 2015 would be a difficult year; worse, it would end in disaster.

In the first few months of the year, however, Zahran Alloush seemed more powerful than ever. He had just eliminated the Umma Army and was now in sole control of the Wafideen Crossing. He had ensured the near-hegemony of the Unified Military Command, led by himself. Although the Islam Army had a weaker grasp on the Unified Judicial Council, it was powerful enough to ignore any problematic rulings. A rudimentary political system finally seemed to be coalescing around these new institutions, with the Islam Army operating as the central pillar of the new order.

Below the surface, however, the Eastern Ghouta was seething with factional unrest and resentment against Alloush. His brutal campaigns against the Umma Army and the Islamic State had poisoned the atmosphere. Some former Umma Army members seem to have found sanctuary in Ajnad al-Sham, which became the new champion of opposition to the Islam Army. Meanwhile, Abu Khaled al-Daqr's Fajr al-Umma was building an economic empire on the back of the tunneling business in Harasta, and the Nusra Front waited in the wings for any opportunity to weaken Alloush.

The Islam Army also seems to have suffered from financial and logistical problems. Alloush's tunnel operations in the Damascus suburbs were targeted by the Syrian army in spring 2015 (and, according to the Islam Army, also by Fajr al-Umma).[63] American pressure on the Gulf Arab states had led to a crackdown on private donation networks, which, although mostly aimed at the Nusra Front and the Islamic State, also had a chilling effect on Alloush-friendly donors like the Council of Supporters in Kuwait. The Islam Army's finances reportedly worsened to the point where its leader was forced to start borrowing money from local merchants.[64]

As he looked for ways to limit his dependence on the Wafideen Crossing, Alloush's gaze naturally fell on the Zahteh Tunnel. Using his near-monopoly on the Barzeh-Harasta smuggling, Abu Khaled al-Daqr demanded exorbitant prices from factions that needed to bring goods through his tunnel. Alloush began to press for better terms, but a May 2015 deal on how to share the tunnel fell apart almost immediately.[65] To dissuade the Islam Army from seizing the tunnel by force, Ajnad al-Sham resumed its lapsed alliance with Fajr al-Umma in June.[66] After sending tanks to the outskirts of Harasta in August 2015, the Islam Army was ultimately forced to back down to avoid a major conflagration.

Separately, Zahran Alloush began to look for support outside the enclave, and tried to deepen his collaboration with more moderate insurgents. The infighting with the Islamic State had shifted the politics of the rebellion, and Saudi Arabia was now about to join a U.S.-supported peace process. In May 2015, the Islam Army leader smuggled himself out of the enclave and traveled to Turkey and then to Jordan, to meet with some of his Islamist sponsors as well as foreign diplomats and intelligence services. For the first time, he gave interviews to English-language media, suddenly appearing as a "model of pragmatism" and describing his former denunciations of democracy and non-Sunnis as the unfortunate result of "psychological stress."[67]

Though violence had been avoided in the disputes over the Zahteh Tunnel, the mood in the Eastern Ghouta was getting tense. All through summer 2015, the enclave was rocked by protests against rebel corruption and abuses, as well as demonstrations by partisans of one group against another. In some instances, protesters were shot and killed by the armed groups. A report from the London

School of Economics noted that relations between the armed groups and local residents had become "highly strained:"

> Citizens told us that they are fed up with the armed groups who coerced the population by manipulating aid and food supplies in a situation of near starvation. There was widespread resentment at the armed groups who have enough to feed themselves during a siege, enriching themselves while civilians suffer. This is being expressed overtly through protests. No one participant expressed sympathy with the main armed groups of Ghouta, although all the participants were very clearly against the government and many had participated in the early days of the revolution.[68]

In this climate of tension and conflict, the Eastern Ghouta's joint institutions, so painstakingly forged a year earlier, began to come apart. Second-tier rebel factions had long ago lost faith in the institutions, viewing them, not unreasonably, as tools of the Islam Army. After unsuccessfully demanding reforms, they turned to boycotts.

In July 2015, Ajnad al-Sham's Khaled Tafour resigned from the presidency of the Unified Judicial Council.[69] In early August 2015, both Abdel-Nasr Shmeir, the head of Failaq al-Rahman, and Yasser al-Qadri, of Ajnad al-Sham, suspended their participation in the Unified Military Command.[70] Alloush was furious. At a meeting with a group of Eastern Ghouta notables, he raged against his rivals and warned that if they tried to break away, it would lead to the unraveling of the entire administrative apparatus, including courts and police.[71]

The war against Assad was also taking a turn for the worse. On September 30, 2015, the Russian Air Force had intervened against the rebels, reversing the flagging fortunes of the Syrian government. In December, the Syrian army captured the Marj al-Sultan Air Base in the southern part of the enclave. The agricultural region around Deir al-Asafir was now at risk of falling, which would spell disaster for the enclave's ability to withstand the blockade. It was no time for infighting, yet the leaders of the Eastern Ghouta seemed blind and deaf to everything except their smuggling feuds and power struggles.

Ideology and Regional Links

By 2015, mergers and takeovers had reduced the factional chaos in the Eastern Ghouta to five major groups: the Islam Army, Ajnad al-Sham, Failaq al-Rahman, the Nusra Front, and Fajr al-Umma. But ironically, as the insurgency progressed toward what seemed like greater unity, its internal polarization increased. Ideological and religious differences began to take on a new visibility, and political strategies and foreign linkages emerged as serious obstacles to cooperation.

Though many of the conflicts between the enclave's armed factions revolved around mundane matters like access to money, weapons, or fuel, political and religious differences have played a part and sometimes intensified rivalries. They are worth studying in some detail.

Religious and Political Ideology

Three of the main Eastern Ghouta factions—the Islam Army, the Nusra Front, and Ahrar al-Sham—have adhered to some variety of Salafism, a neo-fundamentalist movement that seeks to cleanse the faith of what it views as exogenous traditions. To an outsider, their politics could well seem indistinguishable, as all favored the imposition of a Sunni theocracy based on sharia, were overtly anti-democratic and hostile to Shia minorities and Sufis, and were fond of quoting the same scholars, such as Ibn Taymiyya (1263–1328) and Mohammed ibn Abdelwahhab (1703–92). But despite a considerable overlap in their religious and political thought, subtle doctrinal differences and incompatible foreign connections have divided the Eastern Ghouta's Salafi camp.

The Islam Army

Salafism is hardly a monolithic movement and its ideological dividing lines were always blurred. However, many "mainstream" Salafis tend to focus on missionary activity to promote doctrinal purity and enforce social norms. Some view political activism as suspect or even impermissible, and are suspicious of both al-Qaeda-style Salafi-jihadism and the reformist activism of the Muslim Brotherhood.

This was true for the Islam Army, whose leaders seem to have tended toward this so-called scholarly Salafism (al-salafiyya al-'ilmiyya), in the tradition of the Syrian-Albanian scholar Mohammed Nasreddine al-Albani (1914–99), under whom Alloush had studied. He had also studied under two of the foremost religious luminaries in modern Saudi Arabia, Ibn Baz (1910–99) and Ibn Othaimin (1925–2001). However, Alloush's connections seem to have ranged from quiescent Saudi establishment figures to independent-minded ideologues in the so-called Sahwa movement and probably also the politically dissident Surouri trend.[72]

Regardless of its precise affiliations, the Islam Army always resisted being labeled an exclusively Salafi organization.[73] "The Islam Brigade [as it was then called] carries the name of Islam, not the name of any particular school of thought or any particular jihadi line," noted Mohammed Alloush, a close companion and relative of Zahran who ran the group's political offices.[74] The Islam Army-friendly Salafi preacher Abu Ammar Hawwa said the group "believes in confessional pluralism within a Sunni framework" and stressed that though it is largely Salafi, the Islam Army did include non-Salafi members and even leaders, such as the locally influential Sufi sheikh Said Darwish.[75]

The Nusra Front

The Nusra Front drew on the teachings of al-Qaeda-friendly clerics in the so-called Salafi-jihadist trend, an insurrectionist reinterpretation of Salafism that focuses on global armed struggle. It is a modern revolutionary ideology shaped by radical thinkers like Abdullah Azzam (1941–89), Sayyed Imam al-Sharif

(1950–), Abu Mohammed al-Maqdisi (1959–), and Abu Qatada al-Falastini (1960–). More mainstream, nonrevolutionary Salafis tend to view Salafi-jihadism as an adventurist diversion at best and at worst a criminal attack on legitimate governments, particularly that of Saudi Arabia. The disagreement is thus at heart a political one, flowing from contradictory relationships to established governments of Muslim countries, and to the international system, even though both sides of the argument are keen to dress it up in religious scripture.

Ahrar al-Sham

Many of Ahrar al-Sham's founders came from a Salafi-jihadist background, but the group stopped short of endorsing al-Qaeda's global jihad. When war erupted with the Islamic State in 2014, some of its chief ideologues publicly renounced Salafi-jihadism and the group as a whole moved closer to the Turkish and Qatari governments. Its rhetoric evolved toward something more resembling a militant Salafi version of the Muslim Brotherhood, echoing a style of jihadism that was more prominent before al-Qaeda's rise to prominence in 2001.[76] However, Salafi-jihadist hardliners remained well implanted in its ranks—and it included a small number of non-Syrians, though not to the same extent as very foreign-fighter-heavy Nusra Front—and has suffered from severe factionalism.[77] After splintering in spring 2015, the Eastern Ghouta wing of Ahrar al-Sham had only a small membership that worked closely with the Nusra Front.

Ajnad al-Sham

In contrast to these three, Ajnad al-Sham was not a Salafi organization at all, albeit still Islamist and committed to some form of sharia-based government. The group had been created with support from a powerful cast of mainstream Damascene clerics, including Sufis and others who were hostile to Salafism on doctrinal grounds. Among them were some of Syria's most well-known Islamic leaders, like the brothers Osama and Sariya al-Refai.[78] Inside the Eastern Ghouta, Ajnad al-Sham was strongly influenced by Khaled Tafour, a Sufi preacher from Douma.[79]

Many of the clerics that supported Ajnad al-Sham had worked within state-approved Islamic institutions before drifting into overt opposition in 2011. For decades, the Assad family has used its control over political and economical life to cultivate ties to conservative but politically pliable traditionalists like Mohammed Said Ramadan al-Bouti (1929–2013) and Syria's longtime Grand Mufti, the Naqshbandi Sufi scholar Ahmed Kuftaro (1914–2004).[80]

By contrast, the Salafis had been largely shut out from state patronage, both because the government was "terrified"[81] of their influence and because of pressure from the traditionalist clergy. Hostile to Sufism and other forms of traditionalist Islam, the Salafis tended to view such clerics as religiously wayward government cronies. Indeed, a Salafi preacher in the Eastern Ghouta described Ajnad al-Sham as having been set up "by traditional sheikhs who used to be supporters of Assad as long as he and his father ruled, but who were forced to jump on the bandwagon of the revolution because they feared that people would otherwise turn away from them."[82]

Ajnad al-Sham was also accused by its enemies of serving as a front for the Muslim Brotherhood.[83] While this may have been an exaggeration, some Ajnad al-Sham subfactions had been created with Muslim Brotherhood start-up money and there were family connections and considerable ideological and social overlap between senior Ajnad al-Sham and Muslim Brotherhood leaders.[84] "Ajnad al-Sham stems from Damascus's traditional (non-Salafi) Islam, which when it politicizes is virtually indistinguishable from the Muslim Brotherhood," explained Thomas Pierret, an expert on Syrian Islamic politics at the University of Edinburgh. "In the Ghouta, Ajnad al-Sham have been frequently dubbed 'Ikh-wan' [Brotherhood] by locals because they look like Ikhwan, speak like Ikhwan, have leaders with Ikhwan background, etc."[85]

Failaq al-Rahman

In contrast to the above-mentioned four groups, all of which were overtly Islamist, Failaq al-Rahman presented itself as a faction of the Free Syrian Army and sought to emphasize nationalist and military themes, though its rhetoric was certainly infused with a sense of Sunni religious piety. The Failaq al-Rahman leader Abdel-Nasr Shmeir was neither a scholar nor a student of Islam, unlike his counterparts in the other groups, but a defected army captain (though he had married into the family of Abu Rateb Abu Diqqa, a sheikh from Douma). The group still seemed to draw on the support of local, non-Salafi clerics whenever possible, which may have created some ideological affinity with Ajnad al-Sham.[86]

The Fajr al-Umma Brigade

The Harasta-based Fajr al-Umma brigade, finally, seemed to pay little attention to ideology. One of its forerunner factions had ties to the Brotherhood, but there was no sign of a surviving connection.[87] Insofar as its members followed any religious school, they seem to have been close to local, traditionalist clerics. Interestingly, a Fajr al-Umma-friendly activist accused the Islam Army of seeking to impose a "single way of thinking, namely the Salafi-Wahhabi thinking supported by Saudi Arabia," which, he argued, "contradicts the Shami [i.e. Syrian or Damascene] Islamic thought that is spread throughout the Ghouta."[88] But although such views dovetailed with the traditionalist perspectives promoted by Ajnad al-Sham, of which Fajr al-Umma was originally a part, the group never followed a clear ideological path.

Regionalism in the Eastern Ghouta

Some of the tension in the Eastern Ghouta seemed to relate to regional and geographic loyalties, rather than to ideology. Despite being a small area, many towns in the enclave clung to a distinct identity. In particular, Douma stood out as by far the largest city in the enclave, but also for its religiousness. As a rare stronghold of the Hanbali rite of Sunni Islam, it had been a center for

Salafi missionary activities even before the war. The social climate in the Eastern Ghouta's recently urbanized or agricultural areas, or in some Damascus suburbs, could at times seem very different.

The only group to wear its geographical origin on its sleeve was Harasta's Fajr al-Umma, which did not seek influence outside its home area. But the Islam Army was also seen by some of its rivals as not merely an Islamist group, but specifically as representing the Salafi movement of Douma. By contrast, Failaq al-Rahman was best implanted in the Damascus suburbs, though this was perhaps no more than a military coincidence.

Some Syrians argued that regionalism was mainly an issue among the armed factions. "Not among the civilians. The civilians all stick together, from Erbeen to Mesraba, Douma, or Harasta," said the activist Alaa al-Ahmed, who hailed from Douma but now resides in Erbeen. "But it does exist among the military factions and they plant it in society. It is about trying to cultivate support, regardless about whether we're talking about the Islam Army, Failaq al-Rahman, or the Fustat Army. They all want to be the main power in the Ghouta."[89]

International Connections and the Role of the MOC

Religious ideology was never in itself a decisive cause of conflict among the Eastern Ghouta's rebel factions, but it influenced their regional and international affiliations. These, in turn, seem to have mattered greatly to local politics.

The Islam Army

From the start, Alloush's group received strong support from private Salafi donors in Saudi Arabia, Qatar, and Kuwait.[90] From summer or autumn 2013, the group was widely understood to receive some support directly from Saudi Arabia, but Alloush had cast his net widely and also courted Qatar- and Turkey-aligned allies. His ability to self-finance through private religious networks and the Wafideen Crossing may also have guaranteed him some level of autonomy. Descriptions of Alloush as a mere Saudi proxy therefore seemed exaggerated, but by 2016 the political alignment between the Islam Army and Riyadh had become "*very* close."[91]

Fajr al-Umma

The epitome of a self-funded faction, Fajr al-Umma's main source of support was of course the Zahteh Tunnel. The group hardly engaged in diplomacy or political outreach at all and it was unlikely to enjoy any meaningful foreign backing. However, Fajr al-Umma's quest for security inside the Eastern Ghouta repeatedly led it into alliances with larger factions that were in turn linked to foreign interests, including Ajnad al-Sham in 2014 and 2015–16 and the Nusra Front in 2016.

The Nusra Front

Like other al-Qaeda factions, the Nusra Front seems to have funded itself through donations from radical clerics in the Arab Gulf. There have also been persistent allegations of Qatari and Turkish support, whether delivered in the form of ransom payments for hostages or funneled through Ahrar al-Sham, which, unlike the Nusra Front (known as the Fateh al-Sham Front since July 2016), is not sanctioned by the United Nations. However, the Nusra Front has remained critical of the governments in Doha and Ankara, refusing, for example, to work directly alongside the Turkish army in northern Syria. The Eastern Ghouta wing of the group may have been forced to self-finance to a higher degree and it seems to have collaborated pragmatically with non-jihadist factions like Failaq al-Rahman and Fajr al-Umma to develop its tunnel infrastructure.

Ahrar al-Sham

Ahrar al-Sham initially relied on private religious fundraisers, but by late 2014, it seemed to have grown dependent on payments and arms deliveries from Qatar and Turkey. The Eastern Ghouta wing of Ahrar al-Sham never seems to have had a major stake in the tunnel economy, which may help explain its decline from 2014 onward. By summer 2015, it was reduced to a virtual appendage of the local Nusra Front.

Ajnad al-Sham

Ajnad al-Sham reportedly enjoyed good ties to Turkey and Qatar. However, the group's primary affiliation seemed to be to the Syrian Islamic Council, which included some of Syria's most influential Sunni Islamic leaders, mostly of a traditionalist and non-Salafi stripe, including members of the Muslim Brotherhood.[92]

Failaq al-Rahman

While Failaq al-Rahman also turned to the Syrian Islamic Council for religious edicts and political cues, it was strongly associated with the Free Syrian Army brand, which could suggest American funding.[93] Indeed, many sources insisted that the Central Intelligence Agency had vetted Failaq al-Rahman to allow support from the multination Military Operations Center (MOC) in Jordan.[94] (Failaq al-Rahman itself denied this.)[95] However, several sources argued that the MOC had refrained from supporting any armed group inside the Eastern Ghouta for fear of sparking a destabilizing battle in the Syrian capital. A likely explanation is that the MOC had restricted its support to Failaq al-Rahman sub-units battling the Islamic State in the Qalamoun Mountains, outside the enclave.[96]

Did Alloush Seek Support from the MOC?

Several sources have claimed that Zahran Alloush met with Western officials to seek MOC support during his trip to Jordan in summer 2015. According to these claims, the Islam Army leader was presented with such burdensome conditions that they effectively amounted to a refusal.

Different versions of this story exist, but all accounts seem to agree that Alloush was told not to upset the situation in the capital or shell targets inside Damascus. Members and supporters of the group have also claimed that Alloush was asked to release the kidnapped human rights activist Razan Zeitouneh and the Umma Army leader Abu Subhi Taha. Other rumored conditions included ridding itself of the Islam Army's religious leader Samir Kaakeh and his allies, destroying the Soviet-made 9K33 Osa surface-to-air missiles captured from the government, voicing support for democracy and minority rights, and even changing the name of the group to something less conspicuously Islamist. However, it is possible that Alloush simply faced a laundry list of American complaints rather than an actual negotiation over terms.[97]

The Islam Army's relationship to the Western-backed support structures in Jordan remained tense. When rebel infighting peaked in spring 2016, many of the group's leaders and propagandists accused the MOC of trying to undermine the Islam Army in order to weaken the resistance to Assad.

Talking Peace and Provoking the Jihadists

In autumn 2015, the Islam Army publicly endorsed the United Nations-led peace process known as Geneva III. Failaq al-Rahman and Ajnad al-Sham did the same. Islam Army representatives then participated in a major opposition meeting in Riyadh in December 2015 to prepare for the talks.

Since the Islam Army was both the most powerful rebel group and the most hardline Islamist faction to join the peace process, its participation was of major importance. However, Salafi-jihadist hardliners were bitterly opposed to the peace process, assuming, correctly, that any agreements in Geneva would come at their expense. For this reason and others, tension between the Nusra Front and the Islam Army rose in autumn 2015. When information began to trickle out in winter and spring that the Islam Army had been in touch with Russian ceasefire negotiators, the Nusra Front and the Islam Army found themselves on a direct collision course.

2016: The Breakdown

On Christmas Day 2015, a pilotless drone circled a nondescript, walled-off compound in the farming areas east of Hammouriyeh, filming a group of men who entered as a car slowly rolled past on the road outside. Without warning, a massive explosion tore through the building, sending billowing white and brown clouds of smoke into the air.

Later that day, it was confirmed that a precision air strike had killed Zahran Alloush. Early reports spoke of a Russian operation, but the Syrian military claimed credit, saying its air force had hit a meeting between Alloush and commanders from Failaq al-Rahman and Ahrar al-Sham.[98] Apparently it was a lucky shot: the government had been told by local informants that militant leaders were in the building, but not that its enemy number one in the Damascus region would be among them.

The Islam Army leader was quickly replaced by his deputy Essam Boueidani, but it seemed unlikely that anyone could truly fill the void after Alloush. "A confrontation was a foregone conclusion as soon as Zahran died," said a Syrian who

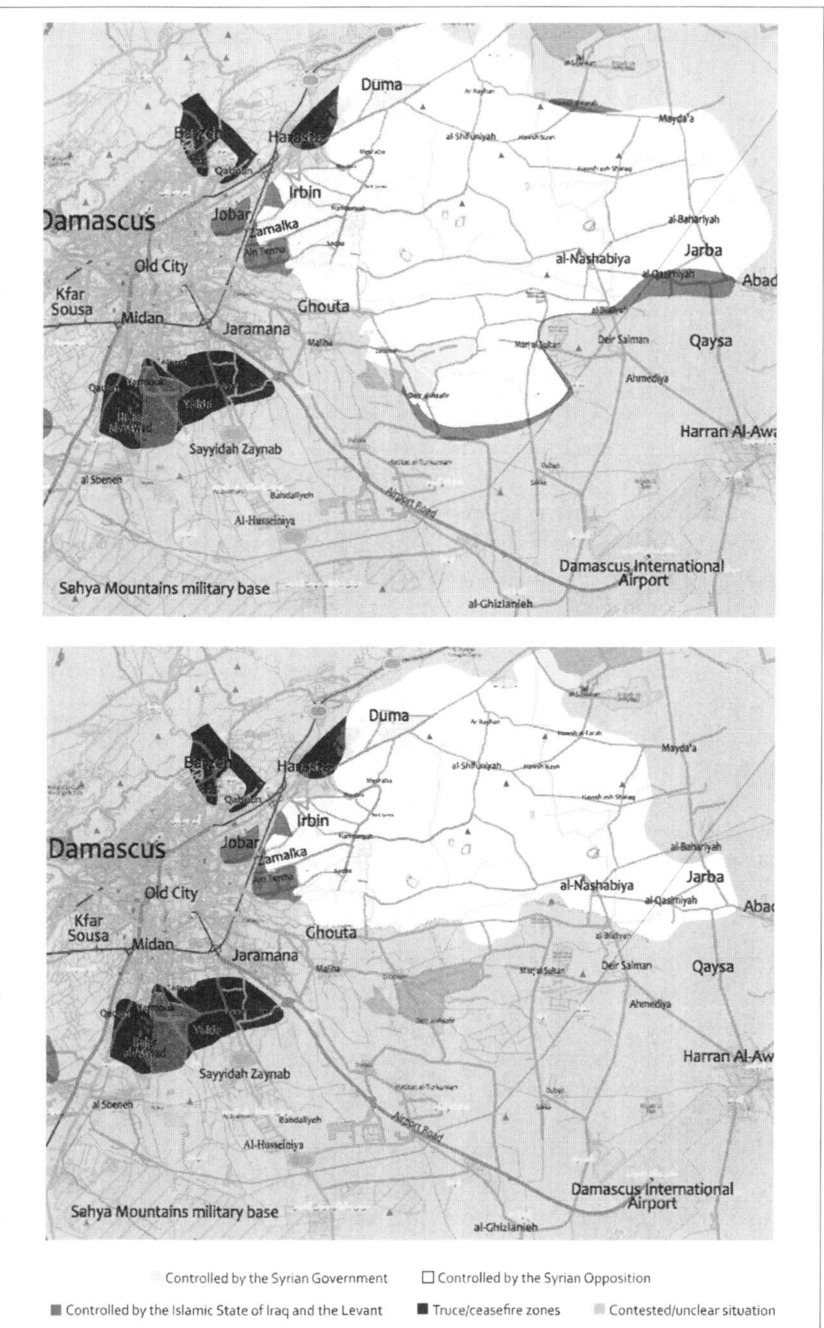

Map 2. Frontlines in the Eastern Ghouta Enclave, December 2015 (top)–June 2016 (bottom)

Source: Wikimedia Commons.

is closely involved with the politics of the armed groups. "There was a power vacuum that Failaq al-Rahman and the Nusra Front will rush to fill. It's like when a powerful mafia don gets killed and rival families move in to take advantage."[99]

In February 2016, Ajnad al-Sham announced that all its troops in the Eastern Ghouta would place themselves under the command of Failaq al-Rahman.[100] The merger of the Eastern Ghouta's second and third factions mean that for the first time since 2013 there existed a credible competitor to the Islam Army. Some sources attribute this to an intervention by the MOC to empower the Failaq al-Rahman and undermine the Islam Army,[101] though Failaq al-Rahman described this as "lies."[102]

Whatever the case, coalition-building proceeded apace. The following month, Fajr al-Umma joined with the Nusra Front in another anti-Islam Army alliance called the Fustat Army.[103]

The Islam Army handled the situation very poorly. Boueidani seemed pre-occupied with internal matters and ceded public space to the group's head of religious affairs, the hardline Salafi figure Samir Kaakeh, whose relentless verbal assaults threw fuel on the fire.[104] In late March, Failaq al-Rahman blamed the Islam Army—and specifically Kaakeh—for having made an attempt on the life of Khaled Tafour, the spiritual leader of Ajnad al-Sham who had helped orchestrate their merger a month earlier. When Tafour's supporters sought to open an investigation through the semi-defunct Unified Judicial Council, Islam Army loyalists refused to cooperate and the council broke apart.

After a few weeks of tit-for-tat violence, Failaq al-Rahman and the Fustat Army launched a surprise assault on the morning of April 28, 2016, overrunning Islam Army positions in Jisreen, Zamalka, Hammouriyeh, and Ein Terma. Deprived of important weapons caches, arms factories, and the two smuggling tunnels in Zamalka and Erbeen, the Islam Army countered by rooting out all opposition from Douma. As the Eastern Ghouta splintered into two parts, an internal frontline emerged in Mesraba.

Civil society groups and opposition leaders in other areas of Syria reacted with outrage, pointing to Assad's attacks in the south of the enclave, but the infighting continued. On May 19, the Deir al-Asafir pocket fell, handing Assad control of much of the farmland that had sustained the Eastern Ghouta during three years of siege. This finally shamed the warring groups into accepting a Qatar-mediated agreement, which came into effect on May 25.[105]

Although fighting ceased, the factions remained distrustful of each other and did not fully implement the Qatari deal. The Eastern Ghouta remained split into rival territories, with Douma and the rural east now under the exclusive control of the Islam Army, while the Damascene suburbs south of Mesraba were held by Failaq al-Rahman.[106] The Fustat Army's Fajr al-Umma remained in control of Harasta and there were Nusra Front concentrations in otherwise Failaq al-Rahman-dominated suburbs like Hammouriyeh and Jobar and on the southern frontline.

The Unified Military Command and the Unified Judicial Council were completely shredded by the infighting. "Even the humanitarian institutions and the educational institutions have been divided into two," said the independent opposition activist Alaa al-Ahmed. "We now have two military councils, one belonging to Failaq al-Rahman and one belonging to the Islam Army. We have some educational institutions belonging to Failaq al-Rahman and others that belong to the Islam Army, and the provincial authorities led by Akram Toumeh have also split into two parts."[107]

The Syrian government did not fail to exploit the infighting. Soon after seizing Deir al-Asafir, the army shifted its attention to the Islam Army-held eastern front of the enclave. Islam Army leaders complained that they could not defend themselves without the heavy arms confiscated by Failaq al-Rahman.[108] Simultaneously, for the first time in years, the Syrian government began to permit aid convoys to enter Failaq al-Rahman- and Fajr al-Umma-controlled suburbs, in what seemed like a divide-and-conquer strategy.

Though violence eventually resumed in the Damascus suburbs, the army continued to focus its firepower on the Islam Army, seizing about a third of the enclave in six months. By October-November, the government was meeting with notables from Douma and Harasta to propose terms of surrender.[109] There was little hope of a reversal of fortunes, and, for the Eastern Ghouta insurgents, there now seemed to be no light at the end of the tunnel.

Conclusion

The uprising in the Eastern Ghouta began as a chapter of the Arab revolts of 2011, drawing on and exacerbating a preexisting undercurrent of anti-government sentiment. As in other parts of Syria, numerous social and political forces responded to the call for revolution, but religious fundamentalists were powerful from the outset and became dominant with the turn to armed insurgency.

The success of the Islamists is not difficult to understand. They hit the ground running with an experienced and highly motivated cadre and a mosque-based local infrastructure. Their ideologies were perfectly suited to mobilize fighters in a sectarian civil war, and they enjoyed easy access to private funding in the crucial first months of the conflict. By contrast, the non-Islamist factions were off to a slower start, tended to be politically parochial and personality-based, and could offer little ideological guidance or spiritual comfort to their communities. Many such groups would later be supported by outside funders to boost the Free Syrian Army brand, but they lacked the characteristics necessary to shape and direct the rebellion.

The siege imposed in spring 2013 had paradoxical effects on the Eastern Ghouta's internal politics. It weakened the local insurgency as a whole, but also delineated a truncated playing field over which the Islam Army could more easily dominate. By nurturing competition for scarce resources and for a handful of high-value import routes, the siege had the dual effect of increasing internal conflict and of concentrating power in fewer hands.

This strange environment allowed Zahran Alloush to establish himself as the strongman of the Eastern Ghouta from 2013 until his death in 2015. By balancing weaker factions against each other, he secured a dominant role in the Unified Military Command and the Unified Judicial Council, which were set up to govern the enclave in summer 2014. He violently eliminated two of the three main sources of resistance to the new order, namely the Umma Army and the Islamic State, while avoiding direct conflict with the Nusra Front. These purges brought a relative internal stability that allowed for Alloush's continued entrenchment. While the new institutions were weak and deeply dysfunctional, they could potentially have evolved into a new political system through which Alloush could have made a bid for a monopoly on force and state-like authority.

However, the struggle for control over smuggling routes—in particular, the Wafideen Crossing and the Zahteh Tunnel—also engendered destructive new rivalries. Even after gaining the upper hand militarily and politically, Alloush failed to marshal enough resources through the siege economy, making him vulnerable to subversion by rival commanders who were better implanted in the tunnel trade.

By mid-2015, the institutions Alloush had used to fortify his own dominance were falling apart. The Russian intervention that September further raised pressure on the rebels. In this situation, Alloush's death in December 2015 had a catastrophic effect on the enclave's internal stability. Rival factions immediately banded together in counter-alliances to fill the void, possibly with some foreign encouragement. The emergence of almost evenly matched power blocs led straight to civil war in April 2016. Since then, the Eastern Ghouta has enjoyed no joint governance and only limited military coordination, creating a situation ripe for exploitation by the Assad government. On current trends, there is a strong likelihood that the insurgency in the Eastern Ghouta is going to be defeated, perhaps even in the first half of 2017.

The rise and fall of the rebels in the Eastern Ghouta parallel the wider war in Syria. Inside the besieged enclave, rebel politics played out with particular speed and ferocity, but the underlying mechanisms were in many ways the same as elsewhere in Syria. Hobbled by their pervasive factionalism, the rebels failed to fill the vacuum created by the destruction or withdrawal of the Syrian regime. The opposition's manifest inability to provide basic governance made both Syrian and foreign supporters of the uprising recoil from the prospect of a battlefield victory over Assad, who exploited this ambiguity to devastating effect.

To be sure, some of the fragmentation has had to do with government bombing, aid blockages, and other problems, but that is not the whole story. From the PKK and the Fuerzas Armadas Revolucionarias de Colombia (FARC) to the Afghan Taliban and the Liberation Tigers of Tamil Eelam, history shows that nonstate movements can and often have set up centralized military forces and organized legal systems (that is, they have created the primary building-blocks of government) despite extremely adverse conditions. Even in contemporary Syria, this has happened in the Kurdish north and in areas controlled by the

Islamic State—just not among the Sunni Arab opposition groups that Western governments have sought to empower.

In Syria and in similarly splintered polities, only centrally organized, highly motivated, and ruthlessly violent factions—likely motivated by strong ideology and ideally with access to reliable funding sources or outside support—seem to stand a realistic chance of imposing themselves on rivals and gaining the critical mass necessary to construct a new order from within a factionalized and competitive environment. So it was with the Kurds of Rojava, and so with the Islamic State in eastern Syria, notwithstanding their many differences.

When and where Syrian Sunni Arab factions have shown some promise as state-builders, such as Ahrar al-Sham and the Nusra Front in Idlib, or the Islam Army in the Eastern Ghouta, it is, I believe, because at least some of these elements have been present. Very likely, mere bottom-to-top organizing and foreign encouragement for negotiated mergers cannot overcome divisions on such a scale as those affecting the Syrian opposition. Evenly matched factions will rarely create functioning alliances, and if they do, they do not last long—it takes a strong centralizing force able to overpower all others and establish itself as the undisputed center of gravity. Indeed, the Syrian war seems to demonstrate what should have been obvious from the start: fragmented insurgencies do not unite without coercion.

Notes

1. Population estimates are unreliable and differ wildly. In May 2014, the World Health Organization estimated that the Eastern Ghouta had a population of almost one million inhabitants ("WHO Reaches the Besieged Town of Douma in East Ghouta with Life-Saving Medicines," World Health Organization, May 29, 2014, www.emro.who.int/syr/syria-news/douma-medicines-delivery.html). In summer 2015, the United Nations counted 163,500 people under siege inside the enclave (Report of the Secretary-General, S/2015/468, June 23, 2015), which was later revised to 176,500 (Report of the Secretary-General, S/2016/60, January 21, 2016). Siege Watch, a project of the Dutch nongovernmental organization Pax and the American think tank The Syria Institute, has noted that some areas of the enclave were "inexplicably" excluded from the United Nations' list of besieged communities ("First Quarterly Report on Besieged Areas in Syria," Siege Watch, February 2016, https://siegewatch.org/wp-content/uploads/2015/10/PAX-RAPPORT-SIEGE-WATCH-FINAL-SINGLE-PAGES-DEF.pdf), estimating the enclave's true population to be more than 435,975 ("Third Quarterly Report on Besieged Areas in Syria," Siege Watch, May–July, 2016). A non-Syrian nongovernmental source with access to aid statistics has also suggested to the author that the real figure would be closer to half a million than to the above-mentioned UN estimates (interview with the author, early 2016). In November 2016, the United Nations added several previously uncounted towns to its list of besieged communities in the enclave, which will raise its population estimate. (Statement by Under-Secretary-General for Humanitarian Affairs Stephen O'Brien to the UN Security Council, November 21, 2016.) It should be noted that UN estimates of the population in Eastern Aleppo, long listed as 250,000–275,000, turned out to be overestimated. After the fall of the enclave in December 2016, the UN produced a revised count of 144,000.

2. For a much longer version of this chapter, see Aron Lund, "Into the Tunnels: The Rise and Fall of Syria's Rebel Enclave in the Eastern Ghouta," The Century Foundation, December 21, 2013, https://tcf.org/content/report/into-the-tunnels.

3. Loose translation from an excerpt in Samir Bishri, "1,000 Dunum of Ghouta Land Are Transformed Annually to Buildings and Facilities" (Arabic), *Tishreen*, March 15, 2012, archive. tishreen.news.sy/tishreen/public/read/253435. Unless otherwise noted, all translations in this report are the author's own.

4. See Anne-Marie Bianquis and Guillaume Fantino, "La Ghouta de Damas, une Oasis en Mutation," in *La Syrie au Présent: Reflets d'une Société*, ed. Baudouin Dupret et al. (Arles, France: Actes Sud, 2007), 119–29.

5. Cha'ban Abboud, "Les Quartiers Informels de Damas: Une Ceinture de Misère," in *La Syrie au Présent: Reflets d'une Société*, Baudouin Dupret et al. (Arles, France: Actes Sud, 2007), 169–76.

6. According to one pre-war study, militant Salafism was largely a rural phenomenon and approximately 30 percent of Syrians imprisoned on charges of "Salafism, Jihadist Salafism, or affiliation to militant religious terrorist organisations" hailed from the Damascus countryside, of which the Ghouta region forms a large part. Abdulrahman Alhaj, "State and Community. The Political Aspirations of Religious Groups in Syria, 2000–2010," Strategic Research and Communication Centre, United Kingdom, 2010.

7. Member of an armed rebel faction in the Damascus region, interview with the author via Skype, September 2016.

8. Haitham Mohammed al-Kinani, "Dialogue with the Leader of the Syrian Islam Brigade Faction" (Arabic), *al-Bayan*, No. 311, May 7, 2013, www.albayan.co.uk/MGZarticle2. aspx?ID=2790.

9. Kinani, "Dialogue with the Leader of the Syrian Islam Brigade."

10. Sermon by Essam Boueidani, *Nida al-Islam*, no date given. See Saleh Abu Mohammed's May 2, 2016 YouTube upload, https://www.youtube.com/watch?v=MiSNBLcGMzQ. The Obeida Ibn Jarrah Battalion was reportedly led by Mohammed al-Sanbaki (a.k.a. Abu Mohammed), a retired Kurdish colonel from the Rukneddine area.

11. Alloush drew allies from Douma families linked to the Salafi movement, including the Boueidani, Delwan, and Sheikh Bzeineh families. See Orwa Khalifa, "On the Salafi Infrastructure in Syria: The Islam Army as an Example" (Arabic), *Al-Jumhuriya*, September 9, 2016, aljumhuriya.net/35519. For example, the Salafi preacher Sa'id Delwan (a.k.a. Abu Nouman, 1948–) had led Friday prayers in the Tawhid Mosque in the 1980s, and now lent his support to Alloush's militia. Hassan Delwan (Abu Anas), later became head of the group's Sharia Commission.

12. abo omar, "Douma—The First Operation of the Islam Company—002" (Arabic), YouTube, March 28, 2012, https://www.youtube.com/watch?v=IW7j3pTfGY8.

13. Youssef Sadaki (research assistant at the Orient Research Center), interview with the author, Skype, September 2016.

14. Sermon by Essam Boueidani.

15. Sadaki, interview.

16. "When money started rolling in to Zahran Alloush and he was able to pay his soldiers $150 or $200 a month, which is a lot inside the Ghouta, people left [the other Douma factions]." Sadaki, interview.

17. Colonel Khaled Habbous, interview with the journalist Orwa Khalifa, audio file posted in September 2016 at https://soundcloud.com/user-493689171/9syeorhbjjb6.

18. Statement No. 1 of the Islam Brigade—General Command, July 19, 2012.

19. "Abu Ali Khibbiyeh didn't have that many people with him anymore [in 2012], but by the end of 2013 and in 2014, people were drawing closer to Islamic and Salafi thoughts, and some opposed this. For them, it was not about whether Abu Ali Khibbiyeh was a bad person or not, or about whether he smuggled and stole. It was about Zahran Alloush becoming all-powerful and trying to finish off everyone else. So people gathered around Abu Ali Khibbiyeh." Sadaki, interview.

20. On Kuwaiti Salafi sponsorship of Syrian rebels, see Hamad al-Jaser, "The Kuwaitis Supported the 'Syrian Resistance' with Close to $100 Million" (Arabic), *Al-Hayat*, November 4, 2013, www.alhayat.com/Details/568664; Elizabeth Dickinson, "Playing with Fire: Why Private Gulf Financing for Syria's Extremist Rebels Risks Igniting Sectarian Conflict at Home," Brookings Institution, December 2013, https://www.brookings.edu/wp-content/uploads/2016/06/private-gulf-financing-syria-extremist-rebels-sectarian-conflict-dickinson.pdf; Zoltan Pall, "Kuwaiti Salafism and Its Growing Influence in the Levant," Carnegie Endowment for International Peace, May 2014, carnegieendowment.org/files/kuwaiti_salafists.pdf.

21. Khaled Yacoub Oweis, "Insight: Saudi Arabia Boosts Salafist Rivals to al-Qaeda in Syria," *Reuters*, October 1, 2013, www.reuters.com/article/us-syria-crisis-jihadists-insight-idUSBRE9900RO20131001.

22. rayat al - sham, "Announcing the Formation of the Islam Army with the Participation of Forty-Three Military Formations" (Arabic), YouTube, September 30, 2013, https://www.youtube.com/watch?v=_iJFxe2bpY0; "Syria: Jaysh Al-Islam Rejects Geneva II Conference," *Al-Sharq Al-Awsat*, November 12, 2013, english.aawsat.com/2013/11/article55322150.

23. Yassin al-Haj Saleh, "Why Zahran Alloush Stands Accused" (Arabic), *Al-Jumhuriya*, April 22, 2015, aljumhuriya.net/33430.

24. Joshua Landis, "Zahran Alloush: His Ideology and Beliefs," *Syria Comment*, December 15, 2013, www.joshualandis.com/blog/zahran-alloush.

25. The council was created by the Islam Army, the Nusra Front, Ajnad al-Sham, Ahrar al-Sham, and Failaq al-Rahman, with around eleven lesser factions endorsing it. Its first leadership included President Abdelaziz Uyyoun (alias Abu Ahmed, or Abu Shujaa al-Azhari), Vice President Zeinelabidine bin al-Hussein (Abu Abderrahman), and members Khaled Tafour (Abu Suleiman), Anwar al-Sheikh Bzeineh, and Bilal Khreissat (Abu Khadijah al-Urduni). In spring 2016, its had expanded to seven members: Hussein, Abu Diqqa, Tafour, Sheikh Bzeineh, Ali Dandal, Abu Adnan Erbeen, and Abu Mohammed Hammouriyeh. In practice, they represented the various armed factions. For example, Khreissat was appointed by the Nusra Front (which split from the council almost immediately), while Tafour belonged to Ajnad al-Sham, Hussein had links to the Islam Army, and Abu Diqqa to Failaq al-Rahman.

26. The Nusra Front rebranded itself as the Fateh al-Sham Front in July 2016. This chapter uses the name of the group at the time of the events described, the vast majority of which occurred before July 2016.

27. The Unified Military Command also included the Eastern Ghouta branch of Ahrar al-Sham and a local faction known as the al-Habib al-Mustafa Brigades. al-ittihad al-islami li-ajnad al-sham, "Statement Announcing the Unified Military Command in the Eastern Ghouta" (Arabic), YouTube, August 27, 2014, https://www.youtube.com/watch?v=syCxOW0uCNk.

28. Mohammed al-Youssef, "Eastern Ghouta: The Unified Military Command . . . A Project for Unification or Infighting?" (Arabic), *Al-Modon*, April 29, 2015, www.almodon.com/arabworld/2015/4/29/الغوطة-الشرقية-القيادة-العسكرية-الموحدة-مشروع-إتحاد-أم-إقتتال.

29. Khaled Atallah, "As Syrian Army Closes in, Douma Residents Turn against Rebels," *Al-Monitor*, November 24, 2014, www.al-monitor.com/pulse/originals/2014/11/syria-douma-protest-jaish-al-islam.html.

30. Heba Mohammed, "The Islam Army in Syria, Led by Zahran Alloush, Seizes the Headquarters of the Umma Army, and There Is Conflicting News about the Killing of Its Leader Ahmed Taha" (Arabic), *Al-Quds Al-Arabi*, January 5, 2015, www.alquds.co.uk/?p=274455.

31. "Statement by the Factions of the General Command of the Eastern Ghouta about Today's Events" (Arabic), *Al-Dorar Al-Shamiya*, January 4, 2015, eldorar.com/node/66925.

32. "Zahran Alloush: The Decision to Shell the Security Centers in Damascus Was a Collective Decision" (Arabic), *Rasd*, April 8, 2015, www.rasd-sy.net/-زهران-علوش-قرار-قصف-المراكز-الأمنية-ف/.

33. Dimashq Al-An, "The Gunmen of the Ghouta Admit to Homosexual Practices among the Foremost Leaders of the Armed Groups in the Damascus Countryside" (Arabic), YouTube, February 15, 2015, https://www.youtube.com/watch?v=ScxyZUKcQ3o; "The Islam Army Executes Abu Ali Khibbiyeh in the Eastern Ghouta" (Arabic), *Enab Baladi*, September 1, 2015, www.enabbaladi.net/archives/43690.

34. Most members joined Failaq al-Rahman, but a small rump faction remained under the protection of the Nusra Front. Ahmed Aba-Zeid (Syrian researcher and opposition member), interview with the author online, May 2016; member of Ahrar al-Sham in the Eastern Ghouta, interview with the author online, May 2016.

35. Haya Khitou, "Syria: the Unified Command Bans the Creation of New Factions in the Eastern Ghouta" (Arabic), *Al-Arabi Al-Jadid*, February 20, 2015, https://www.alaraby.co.uk/politics/2015/2/20/سورية-القيادة-الموحدة-تمنع-تشكيل-فصائل-جديدة-بالغوطة-الشرقية.

36. Sameh al-Youssef, "Divisions in the Damascus Ghouta over the Implementation of Hesbah" (Arabic), *Aljazeera*, August 9, 2015, www.aljazeera.net/news/reportsandinterviews/2015/8/9/انقسام-بغوطة-دمشق-حول-تطبيق-الحسبة.

37. Judiciary Council: We Can't Issue Verdicts without Jaish al-Islam Files," *Syria Direct News Update*, June 8, 2015, syriadirect.org/news/syria-direct-news-update-6-8-15.

38. Ahmir Hussain, "Jaysh al-Islam 'The Army of Islam' Military Parade" (Arabic), YouTube, July 12, 2015, https://www.youtube.com/watch?v=ZE8u1fPtMhg.

39. "'Left to Die under Siege:' War Crimes and Human Rights Abuses in Eastern Ghouta, Syria," Amnesty International, August 2015, www.amnesty.be/IMG/pdf/embargoed_eastern_ghout_report_left_to_die_under_siege_-_august_2015.pdf.

40. Douma Coordination Group, March 2015. Copy posted on the author's Twitter account on March 4, 2015, https://twitter.com/aronlund/status/573189184707547136.

41. "Slow Death: Life and Death of Syrian Communities Under Siege," Syria American Medical Society, March 2015.

42. "'Left to Die under Siege,'" Amnesty International.

43. Ibid.

44. Rim Turkmani, Ali A. K. Ali, Mary Kaldor, and Vesna Bojicic-Dzelilovic, "Countering the Logic of the War Economy in Syria: Evidence from Three Local Areas," London School of Economics, July 2015, www.securityintransition.org/wp-content/uploads/2015/08/Countering-war-economy-Syria2.pdf.

45. Salam al-Saadi, "The Million Checkpoints in Syria" (Arabic), *Al-Arabi Al-Jadid*, April 13, 2015, https://www.alaraby.co.uk/supplements/2015/4/12/حواجز-المليون-في-سورية.

46. "'Left to Die under Siege,'" Amnesty International.

47. "War over the Crossings of East Damascus between Two Opposition Currents" (Arabic), *Al-Sharq Al-Awsat*, January 5, 2015, archive.aawsat.com/details.asp?section=4&article=800771&issueno=13187#.WD6n1dyto0p.

48. Mohammed Bayraqdar (member of the Political Office of the Islam Army), interview with the author online, August 2016.

49. Sadaki, interview.

50. Salami Mohammed, "The Regime Siege on the Eastern Ghouta Revealed a 'Leading Personality' with Powers Greater than Those of the President" (Arabic), *Al-Quds Al-Arabi*, March 18, 2015, www.alquds.co.uk/?p=312250.

51. Wa'el Olwan, interview with author via Skype, May 2016.

52. Bayraqdar, interview.

53. The tunnel trade has proved difficult to research, with rebel sources generally unwilling to talk and some civilian activists avoiding the topic for fear of retribution. The following information has been pieced together from multiple sources and should be treated with some caution.

54. While most of Harasta was inside the Eastern Ghouta enclave, a western portion became subject to the Barzeh truce agreement. For simplicity's sake, I have chosen to refer to the truce zone (i.e. Barzeh and western Harasta) as "Barzeh," while references to "Harasta" should be understood to mean its rebel-held eastern areas.

55. The Syrian government refers to these deals as "reconciliations" (musalahat) and conceives of them as a three-step process: first, an end to active hostilities; then, a resumption of municipal services, traffic, and trade; and finally, a complete restoration of government control. "Sometimes we succeed 100 percent, sometimes we do less well. Barzeh is still at the second stage of the process, I would say," argued Syrian Minister of Reconciliation Ali Heidar, in response to a question posed by the author at a conference in Damascus in October 2016.

56. Olwan, interview.

57. Not to be confused with the Fateh al-Sham Front, which is the name used by the Nusra Front since it announced that it had cut ties with al-Qaeda in summer 2016.

58. Youssef Sadaki, "The Siege Economy of Eastern Ghouta," Atlantic Council, March 23, 2016, www.atlanticcouncil.org/blogs/syriasource/the-siege-economy-of-eastern-ghouta.

59. Majd al-Khateeb, "Tunnel Traders: The Cancer of the Ghouta" (Arabic), *Al-Modon*, April 10, 2016, www.almodon.com/arabworld/2016/4/10/الغوطة-سرطان-الأنفاق-تجار.

60. Fajr al-Umma-friendly activist in Harasta, interview with the author online, May 2016.

61. al-ittihad al-islami li-ajnad al-sham, "Formation of the Fajr al-Umma Brigade in Harasta City under the Banner of the Ajnad al-Sham Islamic Union" (Arabic), YouTube, March 28, 2014, https://www.youtube.com/watch?v=jDoeMYwWGFk.

62. Olwan, interview.

63. Salami Mohammed, "The Eastern Ghouta on the Brink of an Explosion, as Heated Conflicts Based on Tunnels, Power, and Doctrinal Differences Ravage the Opposition Formations" (Arabic), *Al-Quds Al-Arabi*, July 31, 2015, www.alquds.co.uk/?p=380115; "The Islam Army and Ajnad al-Sham . . . Arrests, Followed by a War of Communiqués" (Arabic), *Zaman Al-Wasl*, August 7, 2015, https://www.zamanalwsl.net/news/63161.html

64. Mohammed, "The Eastern Ghouta on the Brink of an Explosion."

65. According to the deal, the Islam Army and Fajr al-Umma would be allowed exclusive use of the Zahteh Tunnel for five days each, while the Nusra Front would have four days and Ajnad al-Sham three. The rest of the month would be shared between civilian organizations. Sabr Darwish, "Struggle over the Crossings in the Eastern Ghouta . . . May Ignite a War between the Factions" (Arabic), *Al-Modon*, July 3, 2015, www.almodon.com/print/607ac4ab-1f1e-41e5-95e1-487ce7b405af/408b8b00-6006-4d9f-b54b-feaad73da86e.

66. "The Fajr al-Umma Brigade Activates Its Membership in the Ajnad al-Sham Islamic Union" (Arabic), *Al-Dorar Al-Shamiya*, June 8, 2015, eldorar.com/node/78548.

67. Roy Gutman and Mousab Alhamadee, "Islamist Rebel Leader Walks Back Rhetoric in First Interview with US Media," *McClatchy DC*, May 20, 2015, www.mcclatchydc.com/news/nation-world/world/article24784780.html.

68. Turkmani et al., "Countering the Logic of the War Economy in Syria."

69. Amjad al-Tinawi, "Khaled Tafour Presents His Resignation from the Presidency of the Unified Judicial Council in the Eastern Ghouta" (Arabic), *Kulluna Shuraka*, July 5, 2015, all-4syria.info/Archive/229777.

70. Abdullah Suleiman Ali, "Demonstrations in the Ghouta . . . And Signs of the Disintegration of the Unified Command" (Arabic), *Al-Safir*, August 5, 2015, assafir.com/Article/435229.

71. syria2tv, "Dangerous Leak: Zahran Alloush, the Leader of the Islam Army, Scandalizes the Agents of the Noseiri Regime in the Eastern Ghouta" (Arabic), YouTube, August 8, 2015, https://www.youtube.com/watch?v=8BdO-SLJwYo.

72. After the Syrian Salafi scholar Mohammed Surour Zeinelabidine (1938–2016).

73. "Zahran is the son of a famous Salafi scholar but he got angry when we asked him," said Mohammed al-Amin, the pseudonym of a prolific online commentator active in Syrian Islamist circles. "He said, find me a single quote where I say I am Salafi . . . I am not Salafi, I am a Sunni only." Mohammed al-Amin, interview with the author online, September 2013.

74. Mohammed Alloush, interview with the author online, June 2013.

75. Abu Ammar Hawwa, interview with the author online, May 2016. Said Darwish declined to be interviewed.

76. Sam Heller, "Ahrar al-Sham's Revisionist Jihadism," *War on the Rocks*, September 30, 2015, warontherocks.com/2015/09/ahrar-al-shams-revisionist-jihadism.

77. Aron Lund, "Divided, They May Fall," Diwan, Carnegie Middle East Center, December 14, 2016, carnegie-mec.org/diwan/66413?lang=en.

78. Thomas Pierret and Kjetil Selvik, "Limits of 'Authoritarian Upgrading' in Syria: Private Welfare, Islamic Charities, and the Rise of the Zayd Movement," *International Journal for Middle East Studies* 41 (2009): 595–614.

79. Also known as Abu Suleiman, Khaled Tafour was a Naqshbandi Sufi preaching at the Hassiba Mosque in Douma. Despite a strained relationship with the Ministry of Religious Endowments, the fall from grace of the Assad-friendly Naqshbandi leader Salaheddine Ahmed Kuftaro in 2008–9 allowed Tafour to curry favor with the government. Thus empowered, he turned around to support the protests in 2011. As regime control over the Ghouta crumbled in 2012, Tafour directed his followers to join the armed insurgency, where they became the nucleus of Ajnad al-Sham. By 2014 he had emerged as one of the most powerful opposition leaders in the Damascus region.

80. Thomas Pierret, *Religion and State in Syria: The Sunni Ulama from Coup to Revolution*, (Cambridge: Cambridge Middle East Studies, 2013); Leif Stenberg, "Muslim Organizations in Bashar's Syria: The Transformation of the Shaykh Ahmad Kuftaro Foundation," in *Syria from Reform to Revolt, Volume 2: Culture, Society, and Religion*, ed. Christa Salamandra and Leif Stenberg (New York: Syracuse University Press, 2015), 147–68.

81. Stenberg, "Muslim Organizations in Bashar's Syria."

82. Hawwa, interview.

83. On the Syrian Muslim Brotherhood, see Raphaël Lefèvre, *Ashes of Hama: The Muslim Brotherhood in Syria*, (New York: Oxford University Press, 2013), and Aron Lund, "Struggling to Adapt: The Muslim Brotherhood in a New Syria," Carnegie Middle East Center, May 2013, carnegieendowment.org/files/struggling_to_adapt_mb.pdf.

84. Raphaël Lefèvre, an expert on the Syrian Muslim Brotherhood, noted that whether or not there is a direct connection between the groups, they "share indirect family links, and with it potentially common fundraising networks, and also seem to appeal to a similar constituency." As an example of family links, the influential Brotherhood leader Marwan al-Qadri (1943–) was the uncle of Ajnad al-Sham's leader. (Lefèvre, email to the author, December 2016.)

85. Pierret, email to the author, October 2016.

86. Failaq al-Rahman followed a Jobar-based scholar named Riyad al-Khiraqi (Abu Thabet), who "was clearly part of traditional religious networks, as opposed to Salafi ones." Khiraqi was assassinated in May 2015, reportedly by the Islamic State. Pierret, email.

87. Abu Khaled al-Daqr previously led the Der' al-Asima Brigade, which was backed by a Muslim Brotherhood-connected group. See Lund, "Struggling to Adapt."

88. Ahmed al-Boustani (Fajr al-Umma-linked Harasta activist) interview with the author online, May 2016.

89. Alaa al-Ahmed (independent activist in the Eastern Ghouta), interview with the author via Skype, November 2016.

90. Abdulrahman Alhaj (Syrian opposition figure and expert on Islamism), interview with the author via Skype, September 2016.

91. Charles Lister (senior fellow at the Middle East Institute), interview with the author online, September 2016.

92. Thomas Pierret, "The Syrian Islamic Council," Syria in Crisis/Diwan, Carnegie Endowment for International Peace, May 13, 2014, carnegie-mec.org/diwan/55580.

93. See Charles Lister, "The Free Syrian Army: A Decentralized Insurgent Brand," Brookings Institution, Analysis Paper No. 26, November 2016. https://www.brookings.edu/wp-content/uploads/2016/11/iwr_20161123_free_syrian_army.pdf.

94. Lister, interview; Lister, "Free Syrian Army;" Abu al-Hareth (commander of the Islam Army in northern Syria), interview with the author online, May 2016; Syrian working on rebel politics, interview with the author online, May 2016.

95. Olwan, interview.

96. Anonymous official in an international organization, interview with the author, 2016; Ahmed, interview.

97. Interview with international official, 2016; Ahmed, interview. See also the December 31, 2015, episode of "With Syria Until Victory" (Arabic) on *Shada al-Hurriya TV*.

98. "General Command: Syrian Air Force Eliminates Terrorist Zahran Alloush and Large Number of Terrorist Organizations' Leaders," *Syrian Arab News Agency*, December 25, 2015, sana.sy/en/?p=64870.

99. Anonymous Syrian who works closely with rebel politics, interview with the author online, May 2016.

100. Albin Szakola and Ullin Hope, "Damascus Rebels Merge Amid Jaysh al-Islam 'intimidation,'" *Now*, February 22, 2016, https://now.mmedia.me/lb/en/newsreports/566633-damascus-rebels-merge-amid-jaysh-al-islam-intimidation.

101. Anonymous Syrian, interview 2016.

102. Olwan, interview.

103. The Fustat Army stated that it included the small local branch of Ahrar al-Sham. However, Ahrar al-Sham's Idlib-based leaders wanted no conflict with the Islam Army and ordered their Eastern Ghouta members to withdraw. Some Ahrar al-Sham fighters seem to have continued to work with the Fustat Army in an informal capacity. Aba-Zeid, interview; member of Ahrar al-Sham, interview.

104. "We had some minor problems with Zahran Alloush when he was alive, but thanks to his charisma he was mostly able to maintain discipline in the Islam Army," recalled Failaq al-Rahman's Wa'el Olwan. "That has changed now. We didn't see this aggressive rhetoric from the religious officials of the Islam Army while he was alive, but now we do." Olwan, interview.

105. The Fustat Army had apparently delegated Failaq al-Rahman to negotiate on its behalf and immediately blessed their agreement. Fustat Army on Twitter, May 25, 2016: https://twitter.com/FustatOfficial/status/735518957084549120.

106. Mesraba itself was supposed to function as a buffer zone. Bahira al-Zarier et al., "Fearing Bombardment, East Ghouta Town Demands Armed Groups Leave," *Syria Direct*, August 1, 2016, syriadirect.org/news/fearing-bombardment-east-ghouta-town-demands-armed-groups-leave.

107. Ahmed, interview.

108. Bayraqdar, interview.

109. On Douma, see Noura Hourani and Jessica Page, "East Ghouta Negotiator: 'I Don't Think That the Regime Is Serious about a Ceasefire,'" *Syria Direct*, October 25, 2016, syriadirect.org/news/east-ghouta-negotiator-'i-don't-think-that-the-regime-is-serious-about-a-ceasefire'. On Harasta, a government-linked source in Damascus who claims personal involvement stated that meetings began in mid-November 2016 between Syrian military officials, the Ministry of Reconciliation, and representatives from Harasta. Online interview with the author, November 2016.

18

Keeping the Lights On in Rebel Idlib

Local Governance, Services, and the Competition
for Legitimacy among Islamist Armed Groups

SAM HELLER

Since the government of Bashar al-Assad lost control of Syria's Idlib province in 2015, the opposition stronghold has hosted one of the country's most comprehensive experiments in rebel governance. Local civilian administrations have posed a basic challenge to the Assad regime's legitimacy by providing municipal services. Islamist and jihadist factions also have stepped in to administer services and try to capture popular support. Intra-opposition tensions have played out as a (mostly) bloodless competition over which groups can best serve Idlibis. But all these bodies have met with mixed success. No overarching authority has replaced the state, rival families and armed factions have competed for influence, and Idlib residents have had to contend with international sponsors who hold most real authority. Building on original research and extensive interviews, this chapter examines the complex reality inside the province, as well as its lessons for Syria's future.

As the regime of Bashar al-Assad recaptured strategic sections of insurgent-controlled Syria in 2016, Syria's rebel-held Idlib province increasingly became the heart of the uprising in the north of the country, the dynamic center of the armed opposition. As the sole province almost entirely under rebel control, Idlib emerged as a key proving ground for Syria's rebels as they sought to demonstrate how they would govern Syria's "liberated" areas.

The Assad regime has staked its claim to legitimacy in large part on the continuity of its state institutions, including normal municipal services. Opposition governance and service provision in Idlib and elsewhere have thus posed a direct challenge to regime authority. Yet governance and public services in Idlib have also become another space for intra-opposition competition. Nascent civilian bodies have contended for resources and public support, but they have also been joined by major rebel factions and service institutions linked to armed groups.

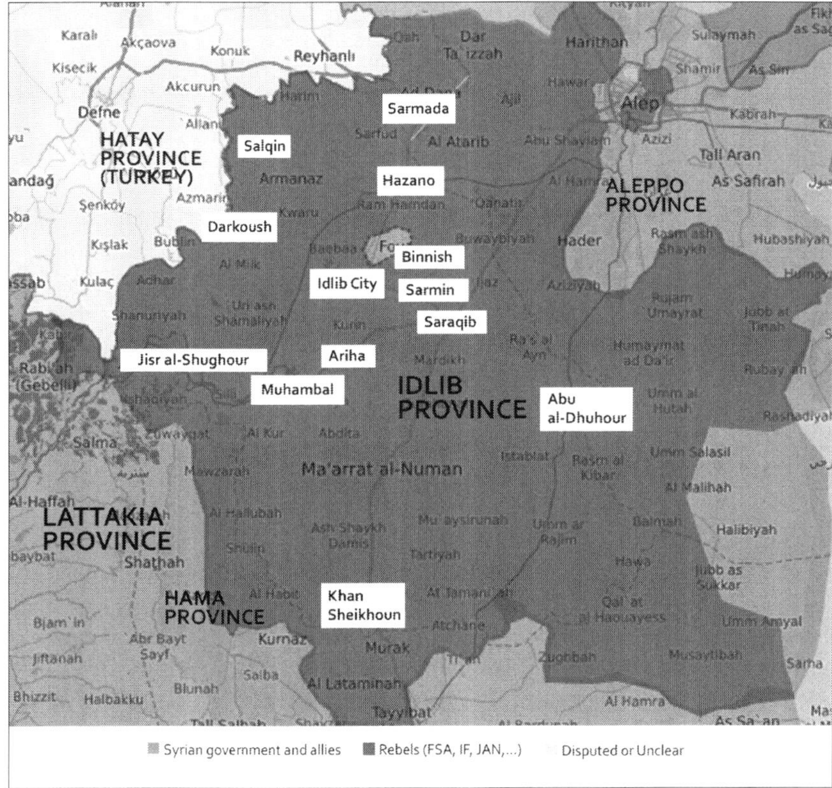

Map 1. Rebel Idlib

Source: Agathocle de Syracuse. Labels added by author.

The Syrian opposition has remained broadly united by its resistance to the Assad regime. But an examination of opposition governance in Idlib shows how civilian and military elements of the opposition, in parallel with their ongoing war against the regime, have engaged in a lower-key struggle behind the lines to secure influence and define the political order for which they're fighting.

The dislocating effects of Syria's war and a mechanism for international assistance that coordinates directly with local authorities have together produced a fragmented Idlib, administered by more than a hundred city- and town-level bodies, known as local councils. These miniature governments have provided the basic services that have maintained some minimum quality of life in Idlib's opposition communities, including utilities repairs, sanitation, sales of subsidized bread, and relief distribution. They have also served as an experiment in participatory government after decades of authoritarian control and, in theory, a center of popular legitimacy independent of both the Assad regime and armed factions.

Armed Factions Step In

The uneven performance of the local councils, their inconsistent foreign backing, and the lack of any supra-local organizing framework have provided an opening for service bodies linked to armed groups. Idlib's two main Islamist or jihadist factions, the Fateh al-Sham Front (known as Nusra Front until 2016)[1] and Ahrar al-Sham, have backed service bodies that compete with each other and with civilian bodies supported by foreign donors, like the Idlib Provincial Council.

In the city of Idlib (the capital of the province), Ahrar al-Sham and Fateh al-Sham have also jointly established an alternative to the purely civilian local council model, a civilian service administration under a council of armed factions.

According to local observers in Idlib Province, these bodies with links to armed groups have aimed at either rationalizing Idlib's governance and services sector or magnifying their respective factional backers' influence on the ground. But none have been perfectly successful, in part because of the impossibility of restoring normal civic life under periodic, indiscriminate aerial bombing, and these bodies' own limited resources and capacity.

The local councils, as the main vector for international support, have been made the focus of an assortment of Syrian parties interested in steering external assistance. Constituencies such as powerful local families have attempted to co-opt or replace local councils and thus shape civic life in their communities, as have armed groups, both through linked service bodies and as individual hometown rebels.

"If you're not a guy with a gun or backed up by someone with a gun, then your connection to power is through assistance," said one Western development worker, interviewed on condition of anonymity because he is not authorized to speak publicly.[2]

But it is often international relief organizations, charities, and development contractors based outside Syria's borders that wield ultimate control over assistance inside the country, and which armed groups and other actors have learned to operate with and around. The result is a rebel territory that is simultaneously atomized and bound up in overlapping, tangled relationships of influence and control between local service bodies, influential clans, armed groups, and international organizations.

Rebel-held Idlib is a showcase for how rebels can pursue influence in nonmilitary spaces, as they reverse-engineer international aid dynamics and, through relatively sophisticated administrative structures, compete with each other for legitimacy. It also demonstrates how, in a civil conflict, even seemingly mundane municipal services like trash disposal and road repairs can be inseparable from issues of political and military control. The civilian and military opposition in Idlib had hoped to create a revolutionary alternative to the Syrian state under the Assad regime. In important ways, they have fallen short. But the service bodies and administrations they have built have shown how insurgents can challenge an incumbent regime's claims to state legitimacy; how they can construct functioning, participatory government, even amid an ongoing civil war; and how they can invest those efforts to win local support.

This chapter is based on more than two dozen interviews conducted in person in Turkey and over WhatsApp with Syrians inside Idlib in May, July, August, September, and October 2016, as well as a review of relevant Syrian press and social media. Interviewees included Western development workers and Syrian activists, rebels, humanitarian workers, and officials involved in local governance and service provision. Restrictive border measures taken by the Turkish government and the security situation inside Idlib mean that access to Idlib is limited. Dangers include aerial bombing, but also the threat of kidnapping by entrepreneurial criminals and some of the groups referenced in this chapter. With some exceptions, independent Western researchers and journalists can no longer safely work inside Idlib province. This chapter instead relies on interviews conducted remotely, including with local council officials contacted through their councils' Facebook pages, or through in-person meetings in neighboring Turkey. This chapter aims to be transparent about its sources and methods, and its assertions should be considered in light of the limitations on qualitative research inside Idlib and the rest of northern Syria.

Revolutionary Idlib

Even before Syria's uprising, Idlib province was marginalized, rural, and poor. The mountainous northwestern province, which shares a long border with Turkey's Hatay, depended primarily on agriculture, including olive crops. Idlib's people were largely conservative Sunnis, with small Druze, Shia, and Christian minorities. Yet the province was denied the political attention and investment given to other peripheral Sunni-majority provinces. That, coupled with lingering resentment over the Syrian government's 1980s crackdown on Islamists (many of them Idlibis), helped ensure the province became a hotbed for opposition.[3]

Idlib joined nationwide protests against the Assad regime in spring 2011 and became, from summer 2011, an early bastion of the country's armed insurgency. Though the regime's security forces and paramilitary auxiliaries initially managed to suppress opposition in the province's main urban centers, including the city of Idlib, Ariha, and Jisr al-Shughour, they progressively lost their hold on the Idlib countryside. By 2014, the regime was confined to a few reinforced cities and towns and a set of fortified but mostly encircled military bases.

In December 2014, rebels overran one of the most important and stubborn of those bases, Wadi al-Deif. Then, in March 2015, the newly announced Army of Conquest coalition seized the provincial capital. The Army of Conquest, which was led by the Nusra Front and Ahrar al-Sham and included several other factions, then swept south, taking the regime's remaining bases and the towns of Ariha and Muhambal. Separately, another rebel coalition made mostly of the same factions took the crossroads city of Jisr al-Shughour in Idlib's southwest corner in April 2015. With the exception of two loyalist Shia towns stranded and besieged in northern Idlib, the province has been entirely rebel-held ever since.

As rebel-held territory in neighboring Aleppo province has been broken by a 2016 Russian-backed regime offensive, the rebel north has mostly been reduced to Idlib and contiguous sections of adjacent Lattakia, Hama, and Aleppo provinces. For all of Idlib and its environs, the only outlets to Turkey are, officially, the Bab al-Hawa crossing, run by a nominally civilian administration controlled in practice by Ahrar al-Sham; and several smaller unofficial crossings used for humanitarian purposes, including the Khirbet al-Jouz crossing. There are also unofficial smuggling routes along the length of Idlib's western border with Turkey, mostly controlled by the Fateh al-Sham Front.

In October 2014, the Nusra Front and a smaller, hyper-extreme Nusra splinter called Jund al-Aqsa led a campaign to destroy a number of nationalist Free Syrian Army (FSA) factions in Idlib and Hama.[4]

Since then, Ahrar al-Sham and the Fateh al-Sham Front have been the twin dominant factions in Idlib, although other, smaller factions have swum in their wake. They have also, according to Idlib locals, been locked in a mostly bloodless contest for control across the province.[5]

Many of the province's remaining FSA factions are seen to operate under the effective protection of Ahrar al-Sham, which has intellectual and organizational roots in al-Qaeda-style transnational jihadism but has abandoned jihadism's commitment to universal war in favor of a narrowly Syrian focus and a more populist, inclusive approach, an approach I have termed "revisionist jihadism." Ahrar al-Sham has aligned itself with the FSA rebel mainstream, while carefully cultivating a separate, more militant identity.[6]

The rise of Islamist and jihadist rebels in Idlib has been accompanied by the imposition of Islamic law (of varying degrees of harshness) and conservative social norms. Many of Idlib's religious minorities have fled. Jihadists obliged Druze towns to convert to Sunni Islam en masse, and in one instance, Druze villagers were massacred.[7] The province's two holdout Shia towns have been encircled and periodically attacked as a tool of rebel pressure on the regime and its allies. The Assad regime, for its part, has been happy to hold up Idlib as the alternative to regime control in its own messaging.

Idlib province's residents numbered roughly two million in mid-2016, according to one Syrian relief worker who agreed to speak on condition of anonymity,[8] including an estimated 700,000 internally displaced people (IDPs) from across Syria.[9] They have had to get by in a half-functional war economy sustained in large part by international relief.

Some areas enjoyed interrupted grid water and electricity. In many others, electricity has been provided by privately owned generators for which residents pay subscriptions, and water has been sold from tanker trucks. Residents worked in small businesses, construction, and smuggling. Many also worked in agriculture, including on farmlands seized by Ahrar al-Sham, Fateh al-Sham, and other factions, and leased back to tenant farmers. Some public-sector employees—teachers in particular, but also municipal workers and others—have regularly crossed into regime-controlled Hama to collect wages from the Syrian state.[10]

But many Idlibis depended on food, sanitary products, temporary housing, and other relief provided by aid organizations including the International Rescue Committee (IRC), Mercy Corps, People in Need, and GOAL. Much of that relief was, in turn, quietly sponsored by the United States and other donor governments.[11] And it largely ran through the province's local councils.

Idlib's Local Councils

City- and town-level local councils as well as subsidiary, village-level "branch councils" have filled the service and governance void left by the Assad regime across Idlib province and Syria's other rebel-held areas.

As with nearly everything in Syria's war, arrangements for local governance have varied from one area to the next and from town to town, but councils have typically amounted to a central administrative council and a set of specialized executive offices focused on areas like relief and municipal services.

As of August 2016, there were 144 local councils across Idlib, including thirty city councils, according to former Saraqib Local Council head and Idlib Provincial Council member Osama al-Hussein.[12]

Much of local councils' importance has hinged on their relationships with "munazzamat" (organizations), a catchall term that includes everything from development contractors to international NGOs. Although some donors that still recognize the Syrian state in Damascus prefer to work with local NGOs and relief associations instead of local councils that operate in defiance of Assad regime authority, most relief organizations and charities have designated the councils their go-to civilian partner at the local level.

Local councils are thus the main vehicle for external support to their community. They routinely submit lists of vulnerable relief recipients and help coordinate and oversee relief distribution, including going house to house with donor organizations' representatives to deliver food baskets and other assistance.

In addition to helping organize relief distribution, councils also provide some intermittently successful municipal services, ranging from operating bakeries[13] to street-cleaning and trash disposal,[14] repairs to the water grid,[15] and road maintenance.[16]

Many of these more resource-intensive services are supported by international donors such as the United States Agency for International Development (USAID) and the United Kingdom's Department for International Development (DfID), which have made support for civilian governance and service provision a priority. Local councils coexist and cooperate with other nascent local institutions, including Syria Civil Defence emergency first responders (the "White Helmets") and the Idlib Free Police, that are also supported by international donor governments.[17]

All these councils' work is typically broadcasted on their Facebook pages, complete with thanks to their various organizational partners and donors.

Local councils originally had their roots in early, local activist collectives ("local coordinating committees") and relief associations. Various donors later pushed to standardize the local council model across rebel-held areas and fold those councils under the then-nascent Idlib Provincial Council and Syrian Interim Government, the exiled opposition's executive body.[18]

Councils are elected or nominated in local arrangements that differ from town to town. In whatever interpolation is deemed locally workable, these processes represent a first-of-its-kind experience in participatory government for Syrians accustomed to life under an authoritarian security state.

"Before the revolution, people would be named [to municipal positions] by the security services, or there would be show elections in which the votes weren't counted," said Muhammad al-Mustafa, director of the opposition-leaning research organization Toran Center. "We used to hear about someone winning before the elections—[we'd say] 'Congrats, you won.'"[19]

Still, these first attempts at self-governance have run up against a number of challenges. A major obstacle to councils' effectiveness and professionalism, both according to council members themselves and others who work with them, has been that council members typically aren't paid a regular living wage.

Many employees of dedicated municipal service offices, such as water maintenance teams, have continued to collect wages from the Assad regime.[20] But members of the councils themselves have largely worked on a volunteer basis. Many qualified Syrians have been drawn to better-paying work for international NGOs or development contractors, and the well-intentioned dentists and lawyers who can afford to volunteer on councils often haven't been the best-equipped to handle the actual work of administering a town.

After years without real taxation, it has seemed impossible for a local council that provides only a few spotty municipal services to ask its community to start contributing more. "People would burn down the council," said Saraqib's Osama al-Hussein.[21]

Without a tax base, the continuity of service projects has depended on continued external support. Amr Tarrisi, Director of Programs with Syrian relief organization Binafsaj, said his organization had supported municipal services in some areas with dumpsters, equipment, and fuel. But after his organization's support stopped, the projects, initially successful, fell into disrepair. "There's no sustainability, because they can't fund themselves," he said. "And any project might be a target for bombing."[22]

Corruption, Nepotism, and Armed Group Interference

Local councils' work has also been marred by corruption and, more often, nepotism, favoritism, and waste in local council staffing and aid distribution.

Irregularities have often been more pronounced in rural areas and small towns than in Idlib's cities, where local councils tend to be more organized and professional. Many of these city councils have simply assimilated the Assad regime's existing municipal service offices, complete with most of their staff, who proceed with their work more or less normally. But in smaller villages and rural areas, more municipal responsibilities have been arrogated directly to a council whose seats might be divided between a handful of big families or clans.

"The mindset is that you have the headman of the family who serves as the family authority and reference point, so you put him forward as your representative on the local council," said Nour Hallak, who trained local council members for an international development contractor. "But then you end up with old men who can distribute largesse without real qualifications."[23]

Local councils have also had to contend with local rebel factions. Rebels may be formally involved in approving key local council appointments or may impose civilian members understood to be linked to a faction. Local commanders can also take it upon themselves to investigate and arbitrate in a claim of council malfeasance.

Some factions also maintain Islamic courts, but these courts seem not to normally meddle in councils' work.

In many areas, rebels have seized the property of regime supporters and divided public property as "spoils." That can sometimes mean that rebels control the local sources of revenue that could help make the area council self-sustaining.

"For example, the local council doesn't control the water," said Hallak, "so it can't collect a utility bill for water, so it can't [afford to] operate the water pump. So the local faction gets to keep selling the water in tanker trucks."

In the ideal case, a popular, well-resourced local council would reverse this power dynamic and either dictate to or establish a mutually beneficial working relationship with area factions. But no local council can operate in a hermetically sealed bubble, isolated from the wartime context and the armed groups around it.

"Part of what makes a local council successful is that it can navigate relationships with armed groups, not that it insulates itself from them," said another Western development worker who also spoke on condition of anonymity. "The challenge is to be as independent as possible while meeting as many needs as possible."[24]

Most interviewees for this chapter said they thought the majority of local councils were hardworking and honest. (Ones that weren't, they said, often saw support for their communities cut off by frustrated aid organizations.) But when irregularities have happened, there's been nobody to systematically supervise councils and hold them accountable.

The Idlib Provincial Council

In theory, Idlib's local councils exist within an official, donor-promoted superstructure of opposition institutions. These include the Idlib Provincial Council, an opposition counterpart to the regime's provincial authority; the National Coalition for Syrian Revolutionary and Opposition Forces, the opposition's deliberative body in exile; and the Syrian Interim Government, the opposition's executive authority.

At one point, these bodies were a Syrian state-in-waiting, a sort of revolutionary simulacrum of the regime's structures. Yet as Syria's war dragged on, the political rationale for an opposition shadow state has become increasingly unclear. The Coalition and the Interim Government have seen dysfunction and allegations of corruption tarnish their image. Donor support fell off.

Still, the Idlib Provincial Council has continued to work to serve the province's residents. It has been able to claim some functional relevance as a channel for important donor assistance and, amid a vacuum of legitimacy in the province, at least a partial democratic popular mandate. And, at least on paper, it should be the supervisory authority Idlib's local councils need.

The Provincial Council was established in 2013, but for several years it remained based in Turkey and only semi-functional. It took on a more active role in 2015, when it moved its headquarters to Hazano, Idlib, with another office in Gaziantep.

Yet unlike the relatively influential provincial council in neighboring Aleppo, the Idlib Provincial Council has struggled to assume a really central, authoritative role in a province where Islamist and jihadist armed groups—many with mixed feelings about institutions like the Coalition—hold sway.

"It's a tough thing to work in Idlib," said one Western development worker.[25]

Like a super-sized local council, the Provincial Council has a set of specialized offices focused on areas like education and agriculture, as well as representative offices across the province. Yet the real measure of the Provincial Council's impact is not its own programming, but its direct support for local councils and for projects implemented in conjunction with councils.

Some key support for local council service provision runs through the Provincial Council, including larger projects from USAID/Office of Transition Initiatives' (OTI) Syria Regional Program aimed at linking and strengthening the province's civilian institutions.[26] A service project might come from an OTI implementer as part of the Syria Regional Program, said Osama al-Hussein of Saraqib, but the local council would sign the contract with the Provincial Council.[27]

The Provincial Council's influence has depended on what it can provide, especially to local councils, according to current Provincial Council head Ghassan Hammou. "We need to meet these local councils' needs—for basic goods, electricity, water, food, transportation," he said. "We need to provide, so we get legitimacy and strength, so the people are with us."[28]

But the Provincial Council has otherwise had to grapple with scant resources and limited influence over local councils. In practice, the Provincial Council is closer to another organization among many furnishing support to these councils than it is to a supreme body. Many relief organizations opt to deal directly with local councils, weakening the Provincial Council's leverage.

"The Provincial Council is both the strongest and weakest link," Hussein said. "Strongest in that it is the only party that has legitimacy, inside or outside the country, as a representative, elected body. So it's the strongest, and it can affect [foreign] support. But it's the weakest in that it isn't given resources, something that could pull together the province."[29]

The Service Administration Commission

A weak Provincial Council and local councils that have been, in important ways, structurally deficient have helped invite other bodies to set themselves up as a partial alternative—in particular, the Service Administration Commission (SAC) backed by Islamist faction Ahrar al-Sham.

Ahrar al-Sham official Ammar Labib ("Abu al-Zahra"), an engineer by trade, established the SAC in September 2015 to coordinate service bodies in Syria's rebel-held north.[30] It was Labib's idea to establish an independent, civilian body, "out from under the skirts of these military organizations," said SAC external relations official Firas al-Raslan.[31]

The SAC's primary mission has been to coordinate and complement Idlib's local councils, although it has provided a broad range of its own support and service projects across Idlib and adjacent areas of Lattakia and Hama, ranging from road repairs[32] to the maintenance of civil registries[33] and relief for IDPs.[34] The SAC has typically formalized its work with "memoranda of understanding" with local councils and various relief bodies, agreements that in some cases have given the SAC oversight of councils' work and finances.[35] The SAC has also supervised the formation and restructuring of local councils in areas where they've been nonexistent or dysfunctional.[36] Among its specialized offices, it has advertised an Oversight and Follow-Up Administration meant to check corruption and misuse of public funds in local councils.[37]

SAC officials and Ahrar al-Sham have deliberately kept their relationship ambiguous. Labib, for example, has stressed in media interviews that the SAC is "civilian and independent."[38] But Idlibis interviewed for this chapter all understood the SAC to be quietly backed by Ahrar al-Sham, something Raslan himself acknowledged.

"A body that belongs to Ahrar?[39] Sounds good," Raslan said. "I don't have a problem saying that it's a body that belongs to Ahrar if Ahrar protects us."

"Our work and organization are independent," he said, "but Ahrar protects us because they see that as being in the public interest."[40]

Both Raslan and his deputy, Qutaiba al-Shiqran, had served with Ahrar al-Sham, although they said that so long as they were working for the SAC, they were outside Ahrar. They said only a handful of top SAC officials, including the two of them and Labib, had been with Ahrar al-Sham and that the SAC's other employees were civilian technocrats.[41]

But the SAC's case for its efficacy and legitimacy has hung in part on its relationship with Ahrar al-Sham. The SAC has claimed resources, technocratic expertise, and a tangible presence inside rebel-held Syria. It has also said it can credibly play the sort of oversight role these councils need. But it has been able to do that in large part because of its ties with Ahrar al-Sham, which also give it the weight it needs to keep other, more menacing armed factions out of civilian life.

The SAC's case has been a realist one: it can make things work. As for armed group influence, it's just a fact inside the country, and civilian actors need to align with a faction to protect themselves. "The councils need to build relationships with whoever's closest to them if they're going to succeed," Raslan said. "That's a reality."

But the SAC's ties to Ahrar al-Sham had complicated its outreach to donor organizations, Raslan said, exasperated. The SAC had approached some development contractors to forge partnerships and even to appeal for direct support, he said, but had been rebuffed because of concerns over armed group control. The SAC's military "cover" had proved to be a problem, he said, even though he emphasized that this cover was a practical necessity inside the country and that the SAC enjoyed popular support.

"The same way 'Abu Lahya'"—a nickname meaning "Father of the Beard," or some guy with a beard—"is considered a terrorist in America, the SAC is considered Ahrar," he said. "I don't know how to convince them we're a civilian body."

Still, Raslan said he thought the SAC had been successful so far, given its limited means, and he thought the SAC could be a service component within Syria's future, post-revolution state. "Anything we can do for people inside, we'll do," said Raslan. "But within a specific framework that we won't go beyond. We don't work for anyone."[42]

The SAC Builds Relationships

Relief workers in neighboring Turkey said they had sat with representatives from the SAC in meetings that had been, on the whole, positive.

"Their officials are engineers, doctors, educated people," said a Syrian relief worker who agreed to speak on condition of anonymity. "Whereas the Nusra Front's people are a little stubborn—it can be difficult to deal with them."[43]

Some officials involved with governance inside Idlib were more critical of the SAC. They agreed that Idlib's local councils needed some sort of supervising authority, but they said the SAC didn't serve that function.

Saraqib's Osama al-Hussein said that the SAC had deliberately brought on locally influential people from across the province who could turn around and convince their respective local councils to sign memoranda of understanding with the SAC. To appeal to local councils, he said, "They'd offer a little project, and a wage to the head of the local council—like a bribe."[44]

Other local council officials said the SAC had made some headway in winning over local councils, but that its reach was more limited than it claimed. It had mostly established itself in areas with poorly resourced local councils or councils that had been denied outside support, they said.

Ibrahim Nabhan, deputy head of the Sarmin Local Council and head of its media office, said his council had signed a memorandum of understanding with the SAC but that it was voided after the Sarmin council bristled under the SAC's oversight. "They wanted everything inside Sarmin to go back to them—what comes to us, they would take it, then it would be distributed through them," he said. The SAC's promised services weren't enough to keep the Sarmin local council on board, Nabhan said. He also said there were problems between the SAC and Sarmin's shura council (or "consultative council"), which includes a member from Ahrar al-Sham but also representatives of a number of other jihadist and Islamist rebel factions.[45]

Part of why the SAC has run into resistance from some foreign donors may be concerns that it is edging out the Idlib Provincial Council. Raslan said the SAC has coordinated and had a strong relationship with the Idlib Provincial Council.[46] But speaking about the SAC, Provincial Council head Ghassan Hammou was clearly unnerved by the body's appeals to some local councils.

"They come and say, 'We're with you,' or they offer some wages," Hammou said. The SAC and other military or military-linked actors, he said, were "frustrating the people's will."

The previous leadership of Provincial Council had signed a memorandum of understanding with the SAC, Hammou said, but only for a single project to provide flour. He said he now considered that memorandum expired.

"If we're weakened, that's a problem," he said, "It'll take years to recover the people's right to decide for themselves."[47]

The Public Service Administration

The Fateh al-Sham Front's Public Service Administration (PSA)[48] seems, like Fateh al-Sham itself, less interested in managing its image outside the country and juggling a complex, political set of relationships. The PSA is Fateh al-Sham's service administration, which is more or less how it has presented itself.

"[The SAC] shows Ahrar's sophistication in terms of its longer vision and sense of the bigger picture, with things like its mergers-and-acquisitions strategy," a Western development worker said. "It's just better at navigating these relationships and being the glue that holds things together." The PSA, he said, "is much less nuanced."

The PSA and its approach seem to have been a sort of translation of Fateh al-Sham's operating philosophy as an armed faction into the service sector. Like Fateh al-Sham itself, it has been dislocated from dynamics outside the country and cut off from foreign backing. Yet, even as it has lined up local revenues to ensure its own sustainability, it has lacked the sort of resource base that would allow it to take sole control of the service sector. Instead, it has mostly focused on a few extremely visible, high-impact services and sectors that have demonstrated its value and indispensability to the local public, not unlike how Fateh al-Sham's car bombs and shock troops have served as the tip of the spear for rebel offensives.

Also like Fateh al-Sham, the PSA has existed parallel to but clearly apart from the opposition mainstream, in this case the local councils. The result has been a sharp contrast to the bridging and coordinating role Ahrar al-Sham has played between Syria's nationalist and jihadist armed factions, as well as the SAC's own efforts to link revolutionary bodies.

The PSA was originally established in and around Aleppo city, where it focused mainly on maintaining and operating key infrastructure, including the Suleiman al-Halabi water station and sections of the electrical grid.[49] The body expanded into Idlib in summer 2015.

Like the PSA in Aleppo, the Idlib PSA maintains key electrical infrastructure, including the main electrical line that runs north from Hama to Aleppo[50] and secondary electrical connections across Idlib province.[51] The body also provides additional municipal services in areas considered Fateh al-Sham strongholds.

The PSA at the Local Level

Instead of complementing and reinforcing existing local councils, as the SAC does, Fateh al-Sham's PSA seems instead to have taken more overt control of service provision and to have filled service gaps itself through PSA offices.

The actual shape of the PSA and its executive offices seems to vary by area. In some areas, the PSA has advertised the work of an Electricity Directorate[52] and a Water Directorate.[53] In the western Idlib countryside, interviewees said the Nusra Front had moved in 2015 to change at least some local councils to "municipalities," but Nusra later retreated after its municipalities ran up against objections from relief organizations that insisted on working with local councils. (Nusra renamed itself Fateh al-Sham in 2016.) Now these areas have both local councils that handle relief and communication with outside organizations, and PSA municipalities that handle service matters like phone lines, water, and sanitation.[54]

"With respect to these names, this is just normal," said Ahmed al-Shami, an engineer and head of the PSA's media office. "Every city, town, and village has its own way of life, so this has to do with the residents of these areas."[55]

Khan Sheikhoun Local Council head Osama al-Sayyadi said Fateh al-Sham's PSA has borne much of the service burden in his city, including the operation of bakeries and water and electricity provision.[56] "Every [service] institution needs support," he said. "It needs generators, maintenance, operating costs. The council doesn't have these things. Whereas the PSA, in principle, has the resources— even if they're not much—to provide these services."

Sayyadi said his council had recently agreed with the PSA to take over sanitation services in the city.[57] He said he hoped the council could take over water provision next. "The local council, in general, is the designated, formal body for organizations to work with," Sayyadi said, "whereas only a few organizations will deal with the PSA."

Sayyadi estimated that 90 percent of the PSA's employees in Khan Sheikhoun were locals.[58] Interviewees said the PSA was mostly civilian, but that its managers were Fateh al-Sham members.[59] The PSA denied this, saying that all the PSA's employees were civilian. Critically, the PSA pays its employees a regular wage, albeit not a particularly large one.

The PSA Works (Mostly) Alone

The PSA's Shami acknowledged that many relief and development organizations would not work with the PSA. "Every organization has its own policy," Shami wrote. "Some refuse to deal with us, while others deal and coordinate with us in some way." He declined to name the organizations that coordinate with the PSA, so as not to "embarrass" them.

But he said a lack of cooperation from foreign organizations wasn't a major obstacle. The PSA has relied on resources inside the country, including revenue-generating projects, but he declined to specify what they were "for fear they might be targeted and dried up."

Fateh al-Sham and, by association, the PSA have also had real and reasonable concerns about security and the role of outside organizations, which may collect data on local demographics and atmospherics to further their programming.

By late 2016, the PSA seemed to have stopped growing, and at least its normal municipal service provision seemed confined to clear zones of Fateh al-Sham dominance. In these areas, it has likely made sense to consider the PSA part of a larger apparatus of Fateh al-Sham control, a suite of institutions that also include "Dar al-Qada" courts and the Islamic Police. Although these bodies have operated separately from the PSA, the cumulative effect has been that Fateh al-Sham had imposed order in its areas of control, including accountability for workers in the municipal service sector.

"The country needs something like [Fateh al-Sham's authority]," said one relief worker. "There are weapons everywhere. There needs to be someone whose word is carried out by everyone."[60]

The strategic objective behind the PSA has been somewhat vague. The SAC has had the relatively clear aim of becoming the connective tissue of local governance in the north, even as it has fallen somewhat short of this goal because of its limited resources and donor resistance. But beyond capturing some raw popular support and, more altruistically, serving Fateh al-Sham members' communities, it's not obvious what has justified Fateh al-Sham's investment in the PSA. Its expansion into Idlib may have been basically defensive, meant to counterbalance Ahrar al-Sham's newly established SAC and to give Fateh al-Sham some rural leverage in a contest for influence within the Army of Conquest's Idlib Administration.

The Idlib Administration

The origins of Idlib's armed-group-linked service institutions all seem to trace back, one way or another, to the Army of Conquest's string of victories in spring 2015. The capture of nearly the entire province raised the ceiling for the political ambitions of the entire Syrian opposition, civilian and military.

The capture of Idlib city was seen by many in the opposition as a second chance to govern responsibly after their failure in Raqqa city. Ahrar al-Sham, the Nusra Front, and several FSA units took the northern city of Raqqa in March 2013, making it the first provincial capital to fall to the Syrian insurgency. But then, in April 2013, most local Nusra Front fighters flipped to the newly announced Islamic State in Iraq and Syria (ISIS, since renamed the Islamic State), and the Islamic State subsequently expelled the FSA from the city. The city was divided between Islamic State and Ahrar al-Sham. Ahrar al-Sham tried to fill the service vacuum in the city and present a model for mature Islamist government but, by its own leaders' admission, mostly failed.[61] In January 2014, the Islamic State seized sole control of the city, which has since served as its de facto Syrian capital and, for the Syrian opposition, a bitter reminder of what they lost.

The capture of Idlib city was followed by confusion and looting, witnesses said,[62] and then months of debate over how the city would be run. But eventually, the Army of Conquest's member factions agreed to establish the Idlib Administration under their Shura Council, the province's first real experiment in joint governance by Idlib's Islamist factions. The Army of Conquest's joint Idlib Administration has run Idlib city, Ariha, and Muhambal since summer 2015.

The Idlib Administration has been "like a local council, but bigger," said its external relations representative Muhammad Jaffa. It comprises a set of directorates responsible for areas like education, telecommunications, health, and municipal services that all answer to a central administration. It has also operated the faculties of Idlib University, which Jaffa said had enrolled 4,500 students at nominal tuition.[63]

The Idlib Administration has been "a more advanced experiment" than Raqqa, said Uqba al-Sayyid Ali, a humanitarian worker with Binafsaj. Binafsaj has provided relief and other assistance in Idlib city.[64]

The Idlib Administration has answered to the Army of Conquest's Idlib Shura Council, made of representatives from the Army of Conquest's various factions. Order in these areas has been maintained by the Executive Force, a police unit manned by rebels from various factions.

The Administration itself has been mostly civilian and technocratic, but leadership of the Administration, the Shura Council, and the Executive Force has rotated between the Army of Conquest's factions. Of the four heads of the Administration to date, three have come from Ahrar al-Sham and one from Fateh al-Sham.[65]

Jaffa stressed that the Army of Conquest's military factions haven't intervened in civilian affairs and that the Shura Council is primarily concerned with interfactional disputes. Civilian city residents have also formed a notables' council that can receive complaints and appeal for change.[66]

The relationship between the Army of Conquest's factions themselves has occasionally been tricky. Some say that, as in the rest of the province, Ahrar al-Sham and the Fateh al-Sham Front have also vied for influence inside Idlib city, including within nominally joint institutions.

One Idlib activist who requested anonymity for his safety said members of the Executive Force from the Nusra Front and Jund al-Aqsa (which subsequently withdrew from the Army of Conquest[67] and the Idlib Administration[68]) had done an end-run around the Ahrar al-Sham head of the Executive Force to seek approval to break up revolutionary protests in the city in March 2016.[69]

After initially excluding the National Coalition and other opposition institutions from the city of Idlib, the Idlib Administration and the Army of Conquest eventually softened on cooperation with these bodies.[70] The Idlib Administration's Education Directorate, administered jointly with the Coalition, has unified the education sector across Idlib, including setting examination times and dates. As of summer 2016, Idlib's health sector was also run out of Idlib city. Jaffa said the Administration was working to unify Idlib's telecommunications and that it had achieved some cooperation on agriculture.[71]

The hope, he said, was that the Idlib Administration could administer the entirety of Idlib province and eventually be the nucleus of a minigovernment. But he also said the Administration was struggling with resistance from donors. "In Idlib, they look at the military element that's in control, and use that as a pretense [not to provide support]," he said. "Even though no military faction ever interferes in the work of the civil administration in Idlib."[72]

Some outside organizations seem to have been deterred by issues of armed group control and by mandatory licensing with the Idlib Administration's Organizations Office. This has not been the case for all, however: foreign relief organizations like Polish Humanitarian Action[73] and German relief organization arche noVa have both donated equipment to the Administration.[74]

Jaffa said that a lack of resources was a persistent problem facing the Idlib Administration and that it had so far been unable to return to the level of service provision in the city under the Assad regime.

The Administration has collected some limited fees, Jaffa said, but not much, and it received no support from the Army of Conquest's military factions. Many employees worked on a volunteer basis, he said. The Administration had appealed to donors to sponsor wages, but had been turned down.[75]

Interviewees were sharply divided on the Idlib Administration's performance. Some said it had been a success, albeit one sabotaged in part by regime bombing, while others said it had been paralyzed by factional dysfunction. Significantly, the city's notables' council has itself sharply criticized the Administration's poor performance. In a September statement, it alleged, among other complaints, that Idlib "lacks a real, civilian administration that's independent of this factional tug of war and enjoys sufficient authority."[76]

Some have argued for the establishment of civilian local councils that could work with foreign organizations and receive more expansive international support.

"The Army of Conquest's Administration has failed everywhere," said Ariha's Nour Hallak. He and others have been lobbying to reinstate a local council in Ariha, instead of a local counterpart of the Idlib Administration. A civilian Ariha local council could benefit from projects from USAID and DfID contractors, he said. "We told them [Ariha] needs a local council, because [relief] organizations will bring you food baskets, but big companies won't enter a city that's under military authority," Hallak said.[77]

Idlibis against Each Other

Even as the Syrian opposition in Idlib remains united in its resistance to the Assad regime, Idlib's service sector has opened up secondary and tertiary cleavages among Idlib's residents, splits over issues ranging from the province's civic character to super-local familial disputes.

Saraqib's Osama al-Hussein described a race for influence between the Idlib Provincial Council, the PSA, and the SAC. "The struggle is between those three axes," Hussein said, "and each one is trying to win the local councils for itself."

In one extreme example, PSA-SAC competition helped lead to actual bloodshed between Ahrar al-Sham and Fateh al-Sham in the west Idlib city of Salqin. As outlined in a subsequent judicial ruling[78] and according to knowledgeable interviewees, the PSA was already operating in the city, but, in coordination with the local council, the SAC established a service office. A scuffle between the locals responsible for each service office escalated into a deadly shootout and a larger mobilization of Ahrar al-Sham and Fateh al-Sham's fighters before calmer heads ultimately prevailed.[79]

The deadly clash was, on some level, between Ahrar al-Sham and Fateh al-Sham, and between the SAC and PSA. But interviewees also emphasized the specific, local dimension of the Salqin episode. As with so much of the big-picture, faction-on-faction tension in the province, they ascribed the Salqin episode to an essentially local contest for influence between two Salqin families who happened to fly different factional flags.

"You're from a family, and I'm from a family," said the Idlib Administration's Muhammad Jaffa. "So we bring our disputes into our work. You want to help with electricity, and so do I. You want to win over people, and so do I. So that leads to a clash."[80]

PSA spokesman Ahmed al-Shami said the province-wide competition between various service authorities had both an upside and a downside for Idlib's residents.

"It has a positive side, in that there's competition to provide better services for the civilian public," he said. "And it has a negative one, because of this division and unilateralism you see sometimes." He said he thought these service bodies had managed to mitigate this negative aspect by coordinating with each other.[81]

And it is true that, even as these service bodies attempt to edge each other out and occasionally inflame local divisions, they have sometimes collaborated and intersected in unpredictable ways.

Khan Sheikhoun and the surrounding area, for example, have also been served by the SAC in addition to the PSA and the local council, although the PSA has been the most active locally. The SAC has had a representative office in Idlib city and Ariha, although the Army of Conquest's Idlib Administration has served both cities. The SAC advertised its role in helping organize Provincial Council elections in Jisr al-Shughour,[82] as well as in Harem[83] and Ariha.[84] And in one update on a disruption to the northern electricity grid, the PSA described repairs coordinated between the PSA, the Idlib Administration, the Idlib Electricity Directorate, and maintenance teams from the Assad regime sent north from Hama.[85]

Where political or ideological imperatives have conflicted with practical needs, these bodies have often erred on the side of the functional. Jaffa, of the Idlib Administration, said that in the immediate aftermath of the capture of Idlib city, rebels were sensitive to bringing on former municipal employees seen as sympathetic to the regime. With time, though, they recognized the need to benefit from these civilians' expertise. "If they hadn't taken up arms, it's normal," he said, "If they were with the regime rhetorically, no problem."[86]

Binafsaj's Amr Tarrisi put it succinctly: "You can't have a university run by someone who's illiterate."[87]

At the Mercy of Outside Forces

Yet even as Idlib's service bodies and residents compete with each other, they have also had to grapple with forces beyond their control.

The regime's aerial bombing seems to have been the main obstacle to predictable, sustainable civic life in Idlib. "Any discussion always needs to focus on the bombing," said Fouad Sayyed Issa, a relief worker with Binafsaj.[88]

Idlib judge Ziad al-Basha described going through the work to procure, install, and operate mechanized bakeries in Idlib towns—only to have the regime's air force bomb the bakeries into fragments, and then have to start all over. "Every time we try to improve civil society," Basha said, "we run into aerial bombing that destroys these institutions' infrastructure and empties the area of its residents."[89]

These service bodies have also had to contend with the galaxy of local and international organizations on which they and their constituents depend for support.

Without some supervising or organizing authority for the province's local councils, oversight of service and relief projects has mostly been left to the sponsoring NGOs and contractors. Continuing support for these councils and the communities for which they are responsible has essentially been at the mercy of these organizations, which can, per their own assessments, build up a council or abruptly cut it off.

"The local council is integrally linked to this [external] support," Ariha's Hallak said. "If it ends, the local council ends."[90]

Donors "are creating these little cantons, where they don't accept anyone else being involved or any interference," said Provincial Council head Ghassan Hammou.[91]

In some instances, interviewees involved in governance complained, development programming had deliberately targeted specific towns and not others. Instead of highlighting model governance and spurring the other councils to reform, they said, it had only turned resentful councils against each other.[92]

And the specific focus on local councils and many organizations' refusal to work with other bodies have likely incentivized armed groups to try to coopt and infiltrate them. The SAC's Firas al-Raslan made this point himself when criticizing donors' unwillingness to work directly with the SAC.[93]

Yet those same organizations have also found themselves in a profoundly insecure position inside the country, particularly as they try to work around armed factions. Aid shipments into Idlib have regularly required three or more approvals, including from the Bab al-Hawa border crossing, the court in Sarmada backed by Fateh al-Sham, and the Ahrar al-Sham-backed court in Binnish.

"Issues in north Idlib could ruin everything," said humanitarian worker Alaa', who agreed to speak on the condition that only his first name be used. "The same people manage everything—civil life, the army, and the police."[94]

When NGOs encounter dysfunctional local partners, interviewees said, they had limited options if they want to continue to work in that area. In theory, they could do anything from giving councils polite recommendations to coordinating the formation of a new local council with civilian actors in the town.[95] But according to Alaa', "the last thing we want to do is intervene to form a local council," which he said would be "nearly impossible" for an NGO. "We're already facing challenges related to our assistance itself, our funding: 'Why are you here?' 'You're thieves,' 'you're spies.'"[96]

At least some foreign organizations have also been sensitive to the legal and ethical complications of providing material support or reputational benefit to armed factions, particularly those that the United States and United Nations have designated terrorist groups.

For Syrian civilians on the ground, the effect has been frustrating. "Suppose I'm from so-and-so Organization," said Muhammad Jaffa of the Idlib Administration. "If I provided support for the service sector in, say, Harem, and Harem is an area that Nusra controls militarily, then that means Nusra might succeed. No! You're providing for the regular citizen. He's the one who benefits. I don't know how they're figuring it, it's backwards."[97]

Khan Sheikhoun Local Council head Osama al-Sayyadi said he had appealed for support for his city, but that the city and its council had become locked in a sort of vicious cycle—he couldn't get support because Fateh al-Sham (or the Nusra Front) was providing services, and he couldn't take over service provision because no one would provide him with support.

"I told you before that the local council doesn't have any resources, that it hasn't received any operating costs to work," he said. "So who's provided most services in the area? The Nusra Front."[98]

A Microcosm of the War

Idlib's governance and service sector has been, in many ways, a microcosm of Idlib's fractious rebel scene and the Syrian war. As with the province's armed opposition, an existing tendency towards localism and disparate, uncoordinated streams of external support have resulted in a service sector that is discombobulated and fractious.

Foreign donors have propped up a nationalist, democratic model—but instead of FSA armed factions, they have backed local councils and a provincial council that, at least in theory, answer to internationally recognized opposition institutions like the Coalition. And like the FSA, these donor-approved service bodies have coexisted with less palatable actors that collaborate with and occasionally try to displace them.

The entrance of Ahrar al-Sham and the Fateh al-Sham Front into the service sector has mirrored their domination of Idlib's military scene. Fateh al-Sham's PSA, like Fateh al-Sham itself, is a blunt instrument, considered toxic by international backers. Meanwhile, the Ahrar al-Sham-linked SAC and its coordinating mission are another illustration of Ahrar al-Sham's relative sophistication. Yet even as the SAC, like Ahrar al-Sham, has been willing to engage with outsiders, those outside parties have remained unwilling to provide it with normal support—it has gotten meetings, but not money. For its part, the Army of Conquest's Idlib Administration has shown similarities to rebels' improvised factional coalitions, and it seems to have been subject to many of the same centrifugal forces.

The end result, as with conditions in Syria's rebel-held areas more generally, has been a service sector that doesn't really fit together. "To the extent I'm willing to see some signal in the noise, I think Ahrar probably has it," said a Western development worker. "In most other cases, we're probably looking at static."[99]

Governance and service provision in Idlib are another reminder that, as with the opposition's armed factions, in Syria results have been the currency of legitimacy. Fateh al-Sham (formerly the Nusra Front), apparently earned the support of opposition Syrians not because of those Syrians' ideological predisposition to al-Qaeda's worldview and mission, but because they saw Nusra fighting and sacrificing for them. In the service space, results likewise have mattered. That local councils are, to varying extents, representative and accountable appears to have earned them goodwill. But democratic experiments aside, Idlib's people have also had to worry about basic questions of service functionality just to stay alive.

"The way they have to live, their lifestyle—they're preoccupied with things you take for granted, that you don't even think of," said humanitarian worker Alaa'.[100]

Gaps and failures in service provision have been an opening for armed groups to meet civilian needs and earn popular support; to advance their specific alternative to regime order; and even, as the SAC's Firas al-Raslan suggested, to position themselves for a role in a possible postwar system.

It's not clear that any of this will be successful, of course. Projects like the SAC point to the complexity of these armed groups, as well as to their evident ambitions beyond simple warfighting, even as armed conflict is ongoing. Yet their efforts have been stunted by larger dynamics, including the prevailing mechanism for international assistance and the disruptive effect of Syrian regime airpower.

And it isn't obvious that whatever goodwill services earn these armed groups will merit the investment in terms of resources and time, or that Syrian civilians will even attribute these service bodies' work to their factional sponsors. Even many of the Syrians interviewed for this chapter, including interviewees involved in relief and service provision themselves, confused the similarly named PSA and SAC.[101]

Still, these service efforts are evidence of the continuing evolution of non-state armed actors. Ahrar al-Sham and Fateh al-Sham in particular belong to a broader continuum of Islamist militant groups that have attempted governance, and it seems likely that these factions' experiments in governance and services will inform other Islamist armed groups around the world.

Idlib's service scene and how armed groups have acted in and around it also highlights how, in a civil conflict such as Syria's, outside aid and more politicized support for governance are not dictated from without. This kind of assistance is a sort of dialogue with local actors, including armed groups that are ready to work around prevailing aid dynamics and even, in some instances, lobby donors directly for support.

And, when taken in the broader context of the Syrian war, Idlib's experience raises larger questions about the logic of a humanitarian or development intervention in a military conflict that donor states are unwilling or unable to end.

Provincial Council head Ghassan Hammou highlighted the apparent absurdity of Western civilian intervention in Syria when recounting a capacity-building exercise with a development contractor. "We got training on financial systems," he said, "but what's the point when there are planes overhead?"[102]

The scope of the violence and disorder of Syria's war has seemed magnitudes bigger than anyone's means, individually or collectively. Any project to build and re-build semi-normal, functioning governance amid Syria's war—and, most importantly, as Assad regime and Russian aircraft continue to indiscriminately bomb opposition-held cities and towns—has been, on some level, Sisyphean. Nearly every attempt at civic organization has been partially frustrated by aerial bombing and violence. The people best-equipped to help, Syrian professionals educated before the war, continue to leave the country. And none of these civilian institutions and exercises in participatory self-government have built toward a broader political transition that, nearly everyone now acknowledges, will not happen.

"I'll be honest with you," said humanitarian worker Alaa', "When I started doing this job, I always wondered, why is the U.S. paying this money? Why is the UK paying this money? Why don't they just stop the war instead of fueling the war and. . ." He left the thought unfinished.[103]

Despite this, the Syrians interviewed for this chapter all seemed genuinely concerned for the well-being of their towns and families. Even when some of them fudged issues of armed group control, or angled for donor funding, or talked down rivals, they all seemed moved by their loved ones inside Idlib.

And even when Idlib's various civilian- and militia-linked service bodies have competed with each other to repair the water pipes or replace road signs, they have been, at base, competing to make Syrians' lives marginally better.

These bodies' attempts to serve Syrians have been, on some level, about a competition for influence and legitimacy between nascent civilian institutions and armed factions. Yet the inverse also seems to hold: This contest for a role in local governance and a foothold in the service sector has been, for civilian administrators and militants, about serving Syrians.

Together, the efforts of these competing and overlapping service bodies have helped ensure that rebels have had somewhere worth fighting for; that they have been defending their home communities and an alternate political order, not simply waging a mountain insurgency. And these service projects have also given Idlibis experience organizing and governing themselves independently of the Assad regime, or really any larger political authority. The question now is how and whether these bodies survive continued war—and, if the regime manages to retake some of these areas, whether it can reinstall its control over Idlibis who have, over five years, learned to rule themselves.

Notes

1. Because research for this chapter spanned the period when the Nusra Front became the Fateh al-Sham Front, both names are used, depending on the time period being discussed. Some interviewees who spoke after the announcement of the Fateh al-Sham Front also continued to call the group the Nusra Front. But the Fateh al-Sham Front and Nusra Front are essentially the same entity, regardless of the change in name.

2. Western development worker, interview with the author, Turkey, August 2016.

3. Aron Lund, "Assad's Broken Base: The Case of Idlib," The Century Foundation, July 14, 2016, https://tcf.org/content/report/assads-broken-base-case-idlib/.

4. Sam Heller, "Al Qaeda's Screwing Up in Syria," *The Daily Beast*, April 5, 2016, http://www.thedailybeast.com/articles/2016/04/05/al-qaeda-s-screwing-up-in-syria.html.

5. Sam Heller, "The Home of Syria's Only Real Rebels," *The Daily Beast*, June 17, 2016, http://www.thedailybeast.com/articles/2016/06/17/the-home-of-syria-s-only-real-rebels.html.

6. Sam Heller, "Ahrar al-Sham's Revisionist Jihadism," *War on the Rocks*, September 30, 2015, http://warontherocks.com/2015/09/ahrar-al-shams-revisionist-jihadism/.

7. Aymenn Jawad al-Tamimi, "The Massacre of Druze Villagers in Qalb Lawza, Idlib Province," *Syria Comment*, June 15, 2015, http://www.joshualandis.com/blog/the-massacre-of-druze-villagers-in-qalb-lawza-idlib-province/.

8. Syrian worker for an international relief NGO, interview with the author, Antakya, Turkey, July 2016.

9. United Nations Office for the Coordination of Humanitarian Affairs, "2016 Humanitarian Needs Overview," October 2015, https://www.humanitarianresponse.info/en/system/files/documents/files/2016_hno_syrian_arab_republic.pdf.

10. Idlib activists, relief workers, and local governance officials; interviews with the author; Antakya, Reyhanli, and Gaziantep, Turkey, as well as remotely over WhatsApp; May, July–August, and September 2016.

11. Liz Sly, "U.S. feeds Syrians, but secretly," *Washington Post*, April 14, 2013, https://www.washingtonpost.com/world/middle_east/us-feeds-syrians-but-secretly/2013/04/14/bfbc0ba6-a3b3-11e2-bd52-614156372695_story.html.

12. Osama al-Hussein, interview with the author, Gaziantep, Turkey, August 2016.

13. Post on the Facebook page of Al-Majlis al-Mahalli li-Madinat Khan Sheikhoun (Khan Sheikhoun City Local Council), May 11, 2016, https://www.facebook.com/khanshykhoun2014/posts/1045527545538621.

14. Post on the Facebook page of Al-Majlis al-Mahalli fi Madinat Binnish (The Local Council in Binnish City), August 16, 2016, https://www.facebook.com/binnish.local.council/posts/1232959800101082.

15. Post on the Facebook page of Al-Majlis al-Mahalli fi Madinat Binnish (The Local Council in Binnish City), July 26, 2016, https://www.facebook.com/binnish.local.council/posts/1218039851593077.

16. Post on the Facebook page of Al-Majlis al-Mahalli li-Madinat Saraqib wa-Rifiha (The Local Council for Saraqib City and Its Countryside), April 28, 2015, https://www.facebook.com/MjlsAladartAlmhlyLmdyntSraqbWRyfha/posts/781039345352918?match=2KXYtdmE2KfYrQ%3D%3D.

17. On Syria Regional Program support for Syrian Civil Defense, see "Syria," USAID, last updated May 27, 2016, https://www.usaid.gov/political-transition-initiatives/syria; for one description of Free Police programming, see this job description: "Strategic Communications Advisor, Gaziantep, Turkey," UNJobs.org, accessed November 12, 2016, http://unjobs.org/vacancies/1451074922309.

18. For a narrative of the local councils' genesis and donors' role in encouraging their standardization, as well as a circa-2014 account of their functioning, see "Local Administration Structures in Opposition-Held Areas in Syria," Centre for Humanitarian Dialogue (for the Ministry of Foreign Affairs of Denmark), April 2014, http://um.dk/en/danida-en/partners/research/other//~/media/UM/English-site/Documents/Danida/Partners/Research-Org/Research-studies/Local%20Administration%20Structures%20Syria.pdf.

19. Muhammad al-Mustafa, interview with the author, Reyhanli, Turkey, May 2016.

20. The regime has continued to pay public-sector wages, even in insurgent-held areas, in an apparent effort to demonstrate the continuing viability of the Syrian state and to maintain Syrians' link to the state and its institutions. To collect public-sector wages, Syrians in opposition-held areas must cross the front lines into regime-held areas; for residents of Idlib province, that typically means traveling to regime-held Hama city. The trip is now reportedly less attractive, given the erosion of the Syrian pound's value and thus the value of Syrian pound-denominated wages, which are further reduced by bribes that must be paid at checkpoints en route.

21. Hussein, interview.

22. Amr Tarrisi, interview with the author, Reyhanli, Turkey, July 2016.

23. Nour Hallak, interview with the author on WhatsApp, September 2016.

24. Western development worker, interview with the author, Turkey, May 2016.

25. Western development worker, interview with the author, Turkey, August 2016.

26. For example, see the post on the Facebook page of Majlis Muhafazat Idlib al-Hurrah al-Safhah al-Raisiyyah (Idlib Provincial Council Main Page), June 28, 2016, https://www.facebook.com/permalink.php?story_fbid=1756204811267437&id=1658340264387226.

27. Hussein, interview.

28. Ghassan Hammou, interview with the author, Gaziantep, Turkey, August 2016.

29. Hussein, interview.

30. Post on the Facebook page of Hayat Idarat al-Khidamat (Services Administration Commission), September 13, 2015, https://www.facebook.com/service.ma.au/photos/a.1481903925439084.1073741828.1477608789201931/1481903848772425/?type=3.

31. Firas al-Raslan, interview with the author, Reyhanli, Turkey, August 2016.

32. Post on the Facebook page of Hayat Idarat al-Khidamat (Services Administration Commission), September 19, 2016, https://www.facebook.com/service.ma.au/videos/1580978985531577/.

33. Post on the Facebook page of Hayat Idarat al-Khidamat (Services Administration Commission), September 24, 2016, https://www.facebook.com/service.ma.au/posts/1582551535374322.

34. Post on the Facebook page of Hayat Idarat al-Khidamat (Services Administration Commission), August 16, 2016, https://www.facebook.com/service.ma.au/videos/1570308089932000/.

35. "SAC Head to Kulluna Shuraka: Bombing Most Important Obstacle to Work in Liberated Areas" (Arabic), *Kulluna Shuraka*, February 20, 2016, http://all4syria.info/Archive/293627.

36. For example, see the post on the Facebook page of Hayat Idarat al-Khidamat (Services Administration Commission), March 2, 2016, https://www.facebook.com/service.ma.au/posts/1520532148242928.

37. Service Administration Commission, "SAC Head Eng. Ammar Labib Explains Work of Oversight and Follow-Up Administration" (Arabic), YouTube, September 4, 2016, https://www.youtube.com/watch?v=I_dPHvE78YY.

38. "SAC Head to Kulluna Shuraka," *Kulluna Shuraka*.

39. Raslan used the term "tabi'ah li," as in a body "tabi'ah lil-Ahrar." "Tabi'ah" can be tricky to translate exactly into English, but I've opted to use "belongs to."

40. Raslan, interview.

41. Firas al-Raslan and Qutaiba al-Shiqran, interview with the author, Reyhanli, Turkey, August 2016. Shiqran has since left his position with the SAC.

42. Raslan, interview.

43. Syrian worker with an international relief NGO, interview with the author, Antakya, Turkey, July 2016.

44. Hussein, interview.

45. Ibrahim Nabhan, interview with the author on WhatsApp, September 2016.

46. Raslan, interview.

47. Hammou, interview.

48. The PSA's name is also translated, variously, as the General Services Administration (GSA); and, by Fateh al-Sham itself, the General Administration for Public Services (GAPS). In other contexts, "khidamat 'ammah" is translated as "public services," so I've opted for "PSA."

49. "Challenges Face PSA in Aleppo" (Arabic), *Al Jazeera*, March 31, 2014, http://www.aljazeera.net/news/reportsandinterviews/2014/3/31/%D8%AA%D8%AD%D8%AF%D9%8A%D8%A7%D8%AA-%D8%AA%D9%88%D8%A7%D8%AC%D9%87-%D8%A7%D9%84%D8%A5%D8%AF%D8%A7%D8%B1%D8%A9-%D8%A7%D9%84%D8%B9%D8%A7%D9%85%D8%A9-%D9%84%D9%84%D8%AE%D8%AF%D9%85%D8%A7%D8%AA-%D8%A8%D8%AD%D9%84%D8%A8; Ibrahim Hamidi, "Nusra's Tactics to Fill Void Left by Da'esh Retreat," *Al-Hayat,* republished in *Kulluna Shuraka* (Arabic), January 12, 2014, http://www.all4syria.info/Archive/124758.

50. Post on the Facebook page of Al-Idarah al-'Ammah lil-Khidamat (PSA), September 1, 2016, https://www.facebook.com/edara3amah/photos/a.1532636220332449.1073741828.1525290301067041/1729474263981976/?type=3&theater.

51. Post on the Facebook page of Al-Idarah al-'Ammah lil-Khidamat (PSA), July 16, 2016, https://www.facebook.com/edara3amah/posts/1711599289102807.

52. Post on the Facebook page of Al-Idarah al-'Ammah lil-Khidamat – Fara' Hama (PSA – Hama Branch), July 20, 2016, https://www.facebook.com/khadamat.hama/posts/989132894517516.

53. Post on the Facebook page of Al-Idarah al-'Ammah lil-Khidamat – Fara' Hama (PSA – Hama Branch), July 18, 2016, https://www.facebook.com/khadamat.hama/posts/987828964647909.

54. Syrians involved in relief and local governance, interviews with the author, Antakya, Reyhanli, and Gaziantep, Turkey, July–August 2016.

55. Shami, interview.

56. For water repairs, for example, see the post on the Facebook page of Al-Idarah al-'Ammah lil-Khidamat (PSA), July 16, 2016, https://www.facebook.com/edara3amah/posts/1711514295777973.

57. Post on the Facebook page of Al-Majlis al-Mahalli li-Madinat Khan Sheikhoun (Khan Sheikhoun City Local Council), September 22, 2016, https://www.facebook.com/khanshykhoun2014/posts/1139505549474153.

58. Osama al-Sayyadi, interview with the author on WhatsApp, September 2016.

59. Interview with local governance officials, Gaziantep, Turkey and WhatsApp, August–September 2016.

60. Syrian worker with an international relief NGO, interview with the author, Antakya, Turkey, July 2016.

61. Al Jazeera, "Film Ahrar al-Sham (Ahrar al-Sham: the Movie)," YouTube, March 3, 2016, https://www.youtube.com/watch?v=_lydv7dr6qE.

62. Idlib residents, interview with the author, Antakya and Gaziantep, Turkey, May 2016.

63. Muhammad Jaffa, interview with the author, Antakya, July 2016.

64. Post on the Facebook page of Idarat Idlib (Idlib Administration), September 21, 2016, https://www.facebook.com/Idlib.management/photos/a.703811656422844.1073741828.703177089819634/843774879093187/?type=3&theater.

65. Muhammad Jaffa, interview with the author on WhatsApp, October 2016. The first head of the Administration, Mudhar Abdussalam Hamdoun ("Abu Abdussalam al-Shami"), was fatally wounded fighting with Ahrar al-Sham against the Assad regime in south Aleppo. See "Abu Abdussalam al-Shami, One of Idlib's Most Prominent Civilian Cadres and Ahrar al-Sham Fighter, Martyred in Southern Aleppo Countryside" (Arabic), *Fresh Online*, December 17, 2015, http://www.fresh-syria.net/archives/29146.

66. Post on the Facebook page of Majlis A'yan Madinat Idlib (Idlib City Notables Council), May 4, 2016, https://www.facebook.com/permalink.php?story_fbid=1721801354771151&id=1720956944855592.

67. Sam Heller, "The End of the Army of Conquest? Syrian Rebel Alliance Shows Cracks," *World Politics Review*, November 9, 2015, http://www.worldpoliticsreview.com/articles/17163/the-end-of-the-army-of-conquest-syrian-rebel-alliance-shows-cracks.

68. "Jund al-Aqsa Objects to Execution of Assassination Cell in Idlib, Suspends Its Work within the Army of Conquest" (Arabic), *STEP News Agency*, January 8, 2016, http://stepagency-sy.net/archives/69610.

69. Osama Abu Zeid et al., "Nusra Deflects Blame for Protest Suppression; 'Mandate Flag' . . . Sows Division," *Syria Direct*, March 8, 2016, http://syriadirect.org/news/nusra-deflects-blame-for-protest-suppression-%E2%80%98mandate-flag%E2%80%A6sows-division%E2%80%99/.

70. Officials involved in local governance, interviews with the author, WhatsApp, October 2016.

71. Jaffa, interview in Antakya, Turkey.

72. Ibid.

73. Post on the Facebook page of Idarat Idlib (Idlib Administration), May 18, 2016, https://www.facebook.com/Idlib.management/posts/774517919352217.

74. Post on the Facebook page of Idarat Idlib (Idlib Administration), March 30, 2016, https://www.facebook.com/Idlib.management/posts/750658505071492.

75. Jaffa, interview in Antakya, Turkey.

76. Post on the Facebook page of Majlis A'yan Madinat Idlib (Idlib City Notables Council), September 10, 2016, https://www.facebook.com/permalink.php?story_fbid=1776347572649862&id=1720956944855592.

77. Hallak, interview.

78. "Verdict on Killing Between Nusra and Ahrar in Salqin" (Arabic), JustPaste.it, April 12, 2016, https://justpaste.it/t7qk.

79. Activists and officials involved in local governance, interviews with the author, Istanbul, Antakya, and Reyhanli, Turkey, May, July, and August 2016.

80. Jaffa, interview in Antakya, Turkey.

81. Shami, interview.

82. Post on the Facebook page of Hayat Idarat al-Khidamat (Services Administration Commission), June 25, 2016, https://www.facebook.com/service.ma.au/posts/1554701294826013.

83. Post on the Facebook page of Hayat Idarat al-Khidamat (Services Administration Commission), June 25, 2016, https://www.facebook.com/service.ma.au/posts/1554700844826058.

84. Post on the Facebook page of Hayat Idarat al-Khidamat (Services Administration Commission), June 27, 2016, https://www.facebook.com/service.ma.au/posts/1555225001440309.

85. Post on the Facebook page of Al-Idarah al-'Ammah lil-Khidamat (PSA), April 6, 2016, https://www.facebook.com/edara3amah/photos/a.1532636220332449.1073741828.1525290301067041/1677272312535505/?type=3&theater.

86. Jaffa, interview in Antakya, Turkey.

87. Tarrisi, interview.

88. Fouad Sayyed Issa, interview with the author, Reyhanli, Turkey, July 2016.

89. Ziad al-Basha, interview with the author, in Gaziantep, Turkey, August 2016.

90. Hallak, interview.

91. Hammou, interview.

92. Officials involved in local governance, interviews with the author, Gaziantep, Turkey, August 2016.

93. Raslan, interview.

94. Alaa', interview with the author, Antakya, Turkey, July 2016.

95. Humanitarian workers in Antakya and Reyhanli, interviews with the author, July-August 2016.

96. Alaa', interview.

97. Jaffa, interview in Antakya, Turkey.

98. Sayyadi, interview.

99. Western development worker, interview with the author, Turkey, May 2016.

100. Alaa', interview.

101. Tarrisi, interview.

102. Hammou, interview.

103. Alaa', interview.

19

New Neighborhood Power

Informal Popular Committees and Changing Local Governance in Egypt

CILJA HARDERS AND DINA WAHBA

After the uprising of 2011, new forms of political participation emerged, among them the popular committees (lijan sha'abiyah). Initially convened mainly to ensure security at the neighborhood level, the committees came to life after the withdrawal of police forces from the public in Cairo, Alexandria, Suez, Port Said, and many towns of the Nile Delta. After the initial eighteen days of the Egyptian revolution, the popular committees expanded their activities and, in different ways in different places, became vehicles to advocate for local needs through informal and formal channels. To a limited degree, the committees gave voice to groups and individuals that had been marginalized. Drawing on original fieldwork in several neighborhoods of Cairo and Giza, the authors argue that the committees embody a new form of political participation in Egypt, which has endured despite the country's sharp return to authoritarianism. Although the committees are varied and imperfectly democratic, they are a dividend of the revolution that will continue to be relevant in Egypt's political future.

In the night of January 28, 2011, as police forces retreated from the public after massive attacks on police stations all over Egypt, an unprecedented form of local political organization was born.[1] Residents in both poor and rich areas of Cairo and other cities drew on their neighborhood networks to form so-called "popular committees." The groups' first and foremost aim was safeguarding their lives and assets under circumstances of extreme uncertainty and the threat of repression.

Some two weeks later, at the end of the eighteen days of the Tahrir Square uprising,[2] the popular committees immediately began taking quite different paths, leading to a huge variety of local activism.[3] They changed in tune with the major developments on the national level. New committees emerged, some of the original ones continued—often in new forms and with new goals—and still others disbanded. Some embraced formal politics while others eschewed them; some were explicitly revolutionary and others service-oriented. Youth initiatives, local media outlets, and formally registered development nongovernmental organizations (NGOs) emerged from the committees. Some groups built close relationships with the security establishment, while others kept a distance.[4] Later, some of them engaged intensively in the "Tamarrod" (rebellion) campaign against Islamist president Mohamed Morsi, and turned into active supporters of the then-minister of defense, Abdel Fattah el-Sisi. Others stayed away from such activism on the national scale.

But the military takeover in summer of 2013 put a chill on the dizzying array of activities the committees had become involved in, as even local politics became increasingly difficult. These difficulties frustrated many, but also encouraged others to soldier on, using the presidential and parliamentary elections of 2014 and 2015, for example, as occasions to go public again for local grievances.

At the end of 2016, we conducted extensive interviews with people involved and affected by the popular committees, and, drawing on many years of previous research in the neighborhoods in which they are most active, sought to better understand their roots, their history since the January 25 revolution, and their current status and trajectory. What we found were committee members torn by frustration and fear in light of heavy and arbitrary repression of any civic action. Still, some continued their activities, while looking for a meaningful way to frame their circumstances.

"When we established the neighborhood committee, our aim was to take the revolution out of Tahrir Square and bring it to our neighborhood," an Egyptian activist in his fifties reflected, while sitting in a coffee shop in one of Cairo's poor-to-middle-class neighborhoods in 2016. "After 2013 everything changed, we were targeted and deconstructed," he added later, after we had talked about the political work of the past five years, its ups and downs, its victories and bitter moments. "The network we created was hit by deep divisions, arrests and a deep sense of frustration among everyone. But still there's hope. The most important result of the revolution is that people raise their voice. They speak out and they will not stop."[5]

In this chapter, rather than focusing on the national and formal level of political change, we propose to use our research to understand the state from below— from the perspectives of those who shaped local politics in mostly informal ways. Looking at the local dynamics of political participation is highly productive for policymakers and scientists alike. It allows us to understand resistance and acquiescence to the powerful political, economic, and social structures that shape ordinary people's lives. Such an analysis of the state from below understands local spaces to be contested testing grounds for changing state-society relations. Thus, the local scale is also important for policy-interventions, as target groups and their needs can be identified more easily, and the results often materialize more quickly and are more tangible. The local arena is of course not a void sphere, in which domestic or foreign policymakers and activists can easily intervene. It is, we argue, as fraught with power structures, conflicts of interest, competition, and indeed authoritarianism as it is a space of resistance and hope.

In their studies, Jennifer Bremer, Hatem Hassan, and Asya El-Meehy already hint at the ambivalent qualities of the committees. El-Meehy argues that they were neither entirely democratic nor fully inclusive.[6] Our data also indicate that the internal dynamics of popular committees have contained many contradictions, most prominently between older and younger people, between men and women, and between rich and poor. Many activists have sought to challenge class hierarchies, the disrespect of women, and the devaluation of the young. But we find that translating their criticism into new practices was daunting. This is partly the case because the groups were deeply rooted in existing social and political structures. Their members built them on the networks they already had access to, such as those provided by family, friends, neighbors, and work. By tapping into existing networks, the committees were able to quickly take on some of the responsibilities of the state as its agencies broke down. However, this also meant that they inherited some of the problems of the informal social contract that had evolved in the poisonous context of authoritarianism. But the committees are also spaces for new people testing new ways of doing politics. The sheer number of groups that came to life after the eighteen days of uprising in 2011 makes for a substantial change in the local political landscape.

Our data show that the revolutionary moments and transformative events the Egyptian people have lived through since 2011 created new political spaces. Much of this happened on the local level and in informal ways—among them, the popular committees. Rather than asking whether the revolution failed, we look at the long-term impact of the mass uprising of 2011. Our approach thus dovetails with that of other analysts and the perspectives of many of our interview partners, who see important processes of change beyond the level of landed elites and formal institutions. The fact that people protested en masse and brought down Hosni Mubarak (president from 1981 to 2011) is an important achievement. This experience of empowerment cannot be erased, and in many ways it was highly productive: it changed the perceptions and the actions of social and political actors. After years of acquiescence, they spoke out and used the committees to struggle both for a better life and to have a voice. These processes then feed into new political subjectivities, which are more inclusive, and less patriarchal and authoritarian—as many of our interview partners and academics have suggested, including Hania Sholkamy, Asef Bayat, Sari Hanafi, Mohamed Bamyeh, and Samuli Schielke.[7] At the same time, the committees should not be romanticized as spaces of popular resistance. Rather, we see them as highly ambivalent spaces, in which the old notions of appropriate gender, age, and class-relations are sometimes accommodated and sometimes challenged.

In order to substantiate our claims, we conducted qualitative fieldwork and spoke to activists in the Cairo and Giza neighborhoods of Umraneya, Boulaq Abu Eila, Boulaq Dakrour, Maspero, Dokki, Bassatin, Dar al-Salam, and Agouza. For the safety of our informants, in the following narrative, we will withhold names and any information that could compromise their anonymity. Still, a brief introduction of some more general features of the Cairene and Giza neighborhoods in which we worked can give some context. Most of them are socially diverse, but tend to be lower- to middle-class areas. Some of them are part of historical Cairo, but many others have only been built up since the 1970s due to the heavy influx of migrants from rural Egypt. Most neighborhoods have a lively and bustling market area or street, some of them old and famous, which attracts visitors from other parts of the city. Often, the communities include an old section (mostly the old village, which existed before the city expanded into the area), which is often especially poor and run-down. The neighborhoods are considered by their inhabitants and other Cairenes alike to be "sha'abi"—popular. This often means that the streets are narrow, the buildings have been erected without official permission or regard for building codes, and public services are limited or of bad quality. But on the other hand, people have a strong sense of ownership and community, neighborly networks are closely knit, and people tend to support each other. In comparison to more "modern" or wealthy parts of the city, where people move anonymously, the urban environment in these sha'abi neighborhoods enables community action.[8] The quarters are politically diverse. Some of them are known for the conservative leanings of their inhabitants, whereas others are traditional strongholds of certain political parties for various reasons, such as being the original home of a party leader.

In addition, some of the neighborhoods with desirable locations have experienced intense pressure, with threats of evictions and speculation on land. A famous example is the Maspero neighborhood surrounding the eponymous riverside building that serves as the headquarters of the Egyptian Radio and Television Union. The neighborhood was frequently the site of protests and violent clashes in 2011 and 2012. Maspero residents have long contested the constant attempts to evacuate them and sell their highly attractive plots on the banks of the Nile to investors. Moreover, most buildings in Maspero are very old and in bad shape to the point of being unsafe. But the government has not offered any reconstruction or development services, in the hopes that the inhabitants might leave due to the bad circumstances.

In this chapter, we first place some of these dynamics in the broader context of political transformation after January 25, 2011. Next, we delve into the political context of prerevolutionary Egypt's authoritarian social contract, before analyzing the popular committees in more depth, showing how they have both challenged and accommodated the authoritarian social contract. We specifically look at gender, class, age, and the interplay of formal and informal organizations. We conclude with a handful of policy recommendations that could make the most of the enduring political promise that the committees hold—even as politics at the national level may appear ever more discouraging.

Contextualizing Cairo's Neighborhood Committees

Usually, when political scientists talk about the role of the state, they assume that formal institutions and political elites determine how public services are delivered and contribute to the welfare and security of citizens.[9] We use a different approach to examine the dynamic between society and the state, which places a lot more importance on local power struggles and the social contract. This approach, known as "state analysis from below," allows us to focus on the agency of marginalized groups, and to understand how their local actions relate to broader trends and structures.[10] A perspective "from below" focuses on poor, excluded, or marginalized communities. The "local space" is a small-scale place such as a neighborhood or a community. It is not defined only in administrative ways, such as being a voting district or a city district. The meanings and boundaries of a neighborhood are also linked to how the inhabitants use the space and define its limits.

Power relations become tangible on the local scale. Abstract concepts such as "the state," "governance," or "politics" take concrete form when looked at through the eyes of ordinary citizens. The state is more than a set of formal institutions. We take it to be an arena of power struggles, which constitute "politics." Usually, political science takes voting behavior and membership in organizations to be the most relevant forms of political participation. But this often does not matter for ordinary people in Cairo. They opt for other, less visible, often informal ways of doing things. Participation then includes many activities: informal, individual, hidden, illegal, and nonpolitical actions and networks. But even the informal politics are not open to everybody in the same way. Access to resources depends on one's gender, class, ethnicity, or religious creed. Elderly middle-class men dominate many political spaces in Egypt.[11]

Politics is structured according to certain rules, which some political scientists call the social contract. This means that there is an unwritten deal between rulers and the ruled. In Egypt since the days of Gamal Abdel Nasser, this deal meant swapping independent political voice for access to welfare. This social contract was authoritarian in nature and it changed over time as the welfare state became weaker and services diminished. Under Mubarak, it turned into a "social contract of informality." Informality became a distinctive feature of state-society relations since before the turn of the twenty-first century. It first became tangible when Cairo and other cities began to grow substantially and informally and the so-called informal settlements (ashwa'iyyat) began to spread.[12] Especially in poor-to-lower-middle-class neighborhoods, informal family and neighborhood networks were constantly used to organize saving and housing. People built on these relations of trust and reciprocity for the collective or individual appropriation of public resources. For example, people dug wastewater canals in order to keep their neighborhood clean. They appropriated electricity by branching from stations, and they squatted on land or built homes without official permission. As early as 1997, Asef Bayat described these practices as a massive, visible, and informal "nonmovement," which he called the "quiet encroachment of the ordinary."[13] It is through these individual actions, that "ordinary people change the Middle East."[14] The aim of these acts of open, everyday resistance was simply the improvement of living conditions, not the direct delegitimizing of state authority. Many other dimensions of life became informal, too. School students and even university students were drawn into a system of officially illegal private tutoring in order to finish their educations. Patients needed to pay for food, medication, and doctors' attention while being officially treated in public hospitals. The formal transportation system of the city did not reach out to the growing settlements, and people established informal services, among them the infamous cheap motorized rickshaw taxis called tuk-tuks. This in turn was linked with police corruption and racketeering. For the rich, informal spaces of action often allow for individual enrichment and corruption. Even though these modes of action were not completely new to the Egyptian state-society relations, their degree and scope decisively increased during the last twenty years. In this "social contract of informality," the state offers space for informal types of agency and participation rather than citizenship rights and a functioning welfare system, and it still expects loyalty and political demobilization.[15]

But the formal and the informal, the local and the national are closely linked. Informal appropriation of resources is based on the state's tacit toleration of these practices. And state agencies turn a blind eye to such practices because they cater to pressing needs in a market-oriented way and compensate for the weaknesses of the state and its lack of services. In addition, state agencies often lack the capacity to control and prevent these activities. But at the same time, police and courts have the last word on who can use informal spaces and who cannot, using violence in order to keep people in place. Often, the poor are the most vulnerable to such actions: street vendors are raided and their goods confiscated. They need to bribe the police in order to get their property back. Police officers especially harass and intimidate young men of the sha'abi quarters.[16]

In the social contract of informality, rights and claims of citizens are replaced by hard-to-regulate possibilities of informal action within informal organizations and institutions. But even this deal is embedded in the web of citizens' expectations concerning minimal service delivery. As the Egyptian state cannot cater to these expectations in the long run, the social contract of informality also generates a long-term crisis of legitimacy, as citizens are increasingly aware of the lopsidedness of the contract. Such a crisis of legitimacy, in addition to rising activism, a deepening economic crisis, and massive state violence, were crucial in bringing about the uprising of January 25, 2011. When protesters shouted, "The people want the downfall of the system," they were quite aware that substantial change would require more than a new president. We hold that they claimed their right to renegotiate the social contract and to change their relationship with state institutions.

In and of itself, the mass mobilization of January and February 2011 represented a major shift in the framework of an authoritarian and repressive system. Rather than showing fear in the face of repression, citizens took to the street in order to fight for "bread, freedom, and social justice." This revolutionary experience politicized a previously demobilized population, and thus brought forth new political subjectivities. More than six years after the revolution, this change seems to be less tangible, because the authoritarian social contract and its main logics are back full force. After the "coup-volution"[17] that unseated Mohamed Morsi in 2013, and in the wake of the Rabaa and al-Nahda mass killings in the summer of that year, the Egyptian government declared a "war on terror" on the Muslim Brotherhood. This was followed by a massive wave of repression, a new rigid protest law, unprecedented cases of mass death sentences, widespread torture, arbitrary detention, and disappeared detainees. There have been vicious campaigns against human rights organizations and activists, raids on offices and, overall, a continuously narrowing public space. These developments on the national scale had strong repercussions on local politics. But at the same time, as our data show, neighborhood activism continues.

Committees as Security Provider

When the popular committees came to life on the night of January 28, 2011,[18] they were a mostly urban phenomenon, crossing class boundaries: neighborhood committees were set up in rich and poor areas alike. They were predominantly male. Citizens took over police functions in securing the lives and assets in the face of real and imagined insecurity. Umm Hassan of an informal settlement recounted: "When we heard about the events on Tahrir and about the burning of police stations, the men of our street went out in order to protect us. But nothing really happened. The people who were really scared were our Christian neighbors. They felt threatened. But nothing happened. And after the eighteen days, we all went back home and the committee stopped."

Enrique Klaus, in the anthropological account of his participation in the committee of his neighborhood, El Manial, tells a similar story.[19] People were afraid of thieves and "baltagiyya" (thugs), but more often than not, there were no criminal incidents. Some big supermarkets were looted in more affluent areas, which were located at the outskirts of Alexandria and Cairo. But all the lootings happened in areas with no neighborhood communities around them, whereas in other urban settings, foreign and local businesses alike were protected by the committees.[20]

The fear of thugs is a recurrent theme, which gained much prominence in local and national public discourses alike. Thugs were known as criminals who also supplemented police and state security before 2011, and were regularly deployed during election times when the open use of police would have belied the democratic façade.[21] The thugs, who operate using local networks in the places they come from, have also been integrated in various activities in the gray zone between criminality and informality. In his in-depth study of the neighborhood committees in Alexandria, Ahmed Saleh argues that, in the days after the uprisings, as fear about thugs and rumors of escaped prisoners gripped the city's neighborhoods, committees assumed a broad array of police-like behavior, including very violent treatment of alleged perpetrators. Committees checked identification and opened car trunks just like the police. Some even used untrained street dogs in order to stage searches for drugs. Others set up an umbrella under which a leader would sit and have the identification cards of suspects brought to him. At this time, criminals and police forces were the main targets of such activities. Many committees issued passes and carried badges. Their activities, argues Saleh, amounted to a curfew on the police, changing the balance of power in favor of the revolutionaries. "After the army decided not to attack Tahrir, the police remained the only force willing to do so," he writes. The police force was "forced to withdraw on January 28, and the [popular committees] prevented it from even considering regrouping or remobilizing."[22]

As for gender relations, the committees were almost exclusively male, even though women contributed in the framework of traditional gender roles—bringing food and drinks to the men in the street, helping with communication, and with encouraging "their men" to be strong and daring. In addition, women were also wary of the committees as they impeded their freedom to move, be it in the neighborhood or in the vicinity of Tahrir. Often, they did not know the men who claimed to be of the quarter and were questioning women on the move, chaperoning them into "adequate" behavior.

People in Tahrir Square also set up popular committees in order to protect themselves from attacks and infiltration by the state security apparatus. The committees also organized the daily needs of those occupying the square: they distributed food and medication, managed the division of labor, and served as communication hubs. On the square, some of the old boundaries were torn down. Committees included women as well as men, poor as well as rich. The relationship of the square with the neighborhoods around it was ambiguous, however. Thugs and other pro-regime forces who controlled some areas tried their best to prevent supporters from reaching the square. Other groups were proud of their support to the square, as this member of a neighborhood committee in the vicinity of Tahrir recounted: "Our role during the Friday of rage on January 28, 2011 was to facilitate the mission of the people who wanted to reach Tahrir Square. We are considered the center and anyone who wants to reach the square has to pass through here, and the police were hammering us. We were helping the people to get there and telling them about alleys and other streets they could go through so that they didn't get lost."[23]

Thus, the popular committees took over security functions on the local scale during critical periods of mass mobilization in January and February 2011. The experience led to closer social relationships even in neighborhoods that were not traditionally closely knit. As a result, some of these new networks served as resources for activism after the eighteen days of revolution. But as Saleh rightly points out, as much as the committees influenced the balance of power, they did not challenge the politics of the army, and except for some in Tahrir, they maintained traditional class, property, and gender relations.

Reclaiming Politics from Below

The breakdown in the winter of 2011 of the barrier of fear—or, as detained activist Alaa Abdel Fattah pointed out in a recent, very sad letter from prison, the breakdown of the "barrier of despair"[24]—encouraged many newcomers to the formal and informal political scenes, including youth, women and the urban poor.[25] Many people engaged for the first time in local activism, and thus, intentionally or not, challenged the old authoritarian social contract while claiming their right to have a voice. A youth activist recounted: "As a popular committee we had three main goals: to foster community participation, to establish popular monitoring of local government, and trying to create alternative media."[26] A resident of a different neighborhood said that activists "wanted to bring the revolution" to their quarter. "Now, finally, we can implement plans to make the neighborhood cleaner and better," a female head of a development NGO said. "We had these plans for years, but the authorities did not listen to us."[27]

The popular committees, even though they all carry the same name, represent a broad variety of people, ideas, and actions. They all share a sense of local empowerment and, at least in 2011 and 2012, all possessed a huge sense of enthusiasm. They all focus on local issues, using different strategies in reaching out to their areas' inhabitants and to the authorities. Some of them developed close affiliations with formal political organizations such as parties; others were careful to stay away from such a stand. A previous history of confrontation with the state—for example, if residents of an informal settlement had in the past been threatened with eviction—impeded some groups, while others started anew, with no legacy to carry. Overall, the sheer amount and variety of activism in the first two years after the January 25 revolution make generalizations difficult. We further wish to complicate the picture by looking into the renegotiation of the class, gender, and age structures of the authoritarian social contract. These struggles shaped dynamics within the committees and between the groups. They also affected the relationship between committees and more formalized actors such as parties or local bureaucracy.

Between Social Issues and "Real Politics"

Political dynamics on the national scale led to a surge in the foundation of new political parties, and a massive pluralizing of the political field. But local activism, especially in poorer neighborhoods, had to confront the many supply crises that deeply affected people's daily lives and that shaped the groups' work. To mention but a few: the cooking gas crisis, the rubbish-collection crisis, the constant power cuts of 2013 in the run-up to the coup, and the 2016 crisis in access to sugar and baby milk. Lack of services came with ever-rising prices of basic commodities since 2011. Thus, people got organized in order to make sure that they got the supplies they needed. Especially in the cooking gas crisis, many women were mobilized and saw this as a legitimate cause to enter the public sphere and demand their rights.

Another major issue that came up in the interviews was the lack of garbage collection even though people had paid their fees. Committees used their newly created local media outlets and social media to spread awareness and pressure the local administration to take action. With glowing pride, poor and less-poor people recounted stories of confronting corrupt and arrogant civil servants, who would normally refuse to even talk to them even though they were legally responsible for catering to the people of their district. "We went to the building of our district's administration. We confronted them with our demands," said a woman from a poor neighborhood in Cairo who talked about this new and empowering experience after the uprisings. "We were loud! And can you imagine that these people really talked to us? They never did that before. But after the revolution, they were afraid."[28]

More than one initiative in Giza mobilized inhabitants to collect their garbage and throw it on the steps of the governor's office. By mobilizing publicly, the local inhabitants gained voice and were able to exert pressure on the authorities to either finally implement projects they had approved years ago, or to react to the grievances of the inhabitants. According to our research, this included getting access to the gas network of the city, getting streets redone, having illegal garbage dumps removed, planting trees, restoring public recreation spaces, and setting up a new local library and a small youth center. However, local groups were rarely visited or supported by any of the national political leaders, members of parliament, or members of political parties on the national level, and thus felt let-down by the more formal political actors. "None of those political parties even thought of creating legal units to support the causes of certain poor neighborhoods," a party member and youth activist self-critically confirmed. "They don't engage with people's everyday lives and their problems. For example, women in these neighborhoods have issues with alimony and divorce cases and they should have gotten support with the problems that matter to them. Men have problems with pensions, arbitrary suspensions, and other issues that [the parties] should help with. And this doesn't need much resources."[29]

Still, in 2011 and 2012 other NGOs and many young middle-class activists from outside the neighborhoods tried to cater to these needs, tried to support local organizations in order to spread a new consciousness and help people voice their concerns. But they were also frustrated with the often service-oriented attitude of the poor and the way that other political forces exploited this focus on services. "They are giving the people the fish, we want to teach them how to fish," a youth activist pointed out in 2012 when discussing the difference between his committee's work and the charity work of the Muslim Brotherhood. "Our aim is to teach people their rights and help them to claim their rights rather than ask for services."[30]

The activist's attitude speaks to the very valid concept of empowerment, but at the same time, it also underestimates the pragmatism of local actors. It does not take into consideration people's capacity and need to accommodate their circumstances rather than engage in lengthy legal contestations. The young, middle-class activists with no background in the sha'abi quarters they entered to help also underestimated the social stratification within neighborhoods and the competing interests of different inhabitants, which often came to the fore when property and housing rights were concerned.

Neighborhood committees offered the urban poor a platform to prioritize their issues and needs. Party politicians do not see garbage collection, electricity, better access to local services, claims-making on the local administration, and catering to immediate supply crises as political fights, but local activists certainly do see them that way. Class relationships within the neighborhoods played out as much as class differences between activists from the outside and those within the neighborhoods. The groups were able to successfully implement a host of activities including setting up small buildings and even cafés. But after the bloody confrontations of the summer of 2013 and the authoritarian rollback, many of these initiatives became ineffective due to repression. Mass arrests in one of the districts we surveyed, as well as constant intimidation in the others, created fear and major rifts. At the same time, the authorities tried to co-opt active group members by offering small consultancy contracts or by promising jobs. Thus, groups dissolved and members dropped out, and arguments arose about how to confront these strategies of the state. Not least, some of the committees' gains were literally destroyed by security forces. For instance, one of the major achievements in one of the districts was setting up a community cultural center, which was subsequently torn down by orders from the local government, after a struggle in which local organizers occupied the building for days to attempt to stop the demolishment.

A New Space for Women?

From the early beginnings of the revolution, women were celebrated for their notable participation and there seemed to be a lot of euphoria about the egalitarian spirit of Tahrir, which at times even allowed women to transgress gender norms.[31] However, after the eighteen revolutionary days had passed, women who wanted to participate in national politics—whether in political parties, civic initiatives, or even in mobilizations and demonstrations—were again excluded. This disempowerment took several forms, ranging from old policies to harassment during protests and other forms of brutal aggression.[32] Male community leaders confronted women with an old discourse, similar to the one that youth faced, claiming that women's supposed lack of real political experience meant that their primary role should be to help mobilization efforts rather than claiming leadership positions. The situation in local initiatives wasn't any different. The fact that neighborhood committees were originally formed with a focus on security issues—traditionally a male domain in most societies, and certainly so in Egypt—relegated women to supportive roles right from the beginning. "During the eighteen days, when the committee was mainly responsible for the safety of the neighborhood women would cook for us our meals or stay awake to make us tea," remembered a young male activist in his thirties.[33] This might also have informed the committee's capacity to develop into a political space that could be used by women.

Still, women were active in the groups after the eighteen days. Often, male activists held the women's involvement to be most legitimate when it came to issues linked to traditional gender roles. "When we were protesting the price of gas cylinders, women came out in great numbers, each with their own gas cylinders," recounted a male group leader in his fifties. "We stood in front of the governorate office and chanted while banging on the cylinders."[34] Women were rarely the leaders of the committees, but they often used their networks to mobilize other women.

A female youth activist and NGO community worker recounted women's involvement in a way that illuminated some of the challenges:

> "In almost all the areas we were working in, there were very active and strong women who knew all of the problems and details of their districts and were involved in all the activities. However, once we have any for-mal meeting or press conference the women would disappear. Even if we sometimes insist that certain women join in, men would ask: why? Both men and women feel that this isn't a woman's place. It is as if there's a subtle agreement about this arrangement. This is logical; these are gender roles that kick in whenever there are moments of representation. The same level of exclusion was happening in Tahrir within the entities that were supposedly representing the revolution, so I am not surprised that this was happening in local communities within neighborhood committees."

This sobering assessment is indicative of the fact that the struggle for a different gender order is ongoing and has to confront deeply rooted values and traditions. At the same time, many of our interviewees from both local committees and domestic NGOs are convinced that subtle changes in gender relations have emerged. They say that more women speak out, that their voices are louder and that the January 25 revolution enabled young women to break important taboos, such as those regarding naming sexual harassers and in openly addressing sexual violence.

Empowerment or Exploitation of Youth in Politics

After the uprising, generational conflicts immediately came to the fore in the formal arena of newly established political parties. The passion and fresh ideas of enthusiastic newcomers met with the resistance of those who were socialized into formal politics under Mubarak, and who considered the young to be naïve. According to our data, in almost every newly founded party and coalition, the old guard perceived the young as power-hungry while lacking experience. In addition, they believed that, before running for office, youth and women should work at the grassroots level and help mobilize voters during elections or demonstrations so that they could first learn "to do politics." Women and youth activists fiercely resisted this line of thinking.

Interestingly, after the eighteen days the neighborhood committees seemed to offer more space for formally marginalized actors, including youth. Their loose structures and their focus on service delivery with empowerment attracted many young people and allowed them to play a more influential role within their local communities. In this sense, the committees were somewhat more inclusive than formal political organizations on the national scale. Our data suggest that many of the leaders and founders of those committees were young people, or considered themselves young. Activists constantly refer to themselves as the shabaab el-mante'ah ("youth of the neighborhood"), with youth often including quite a large age range, from twenty-five to forty-five. Thus, the committees offered spaces for political newcomers to practice grassroots politics while being trained to be leaders. At the same time, the new groups partially sidelined the old vested networks of power and authority, controlled as they were (and continue to be) by members of important families with access to material and symbolical resources.

In 2011 and 2012, the word "shabaab," meaning "youth," had a good sound to it. It seemed to be distant from "siyasah"—"politics"—which was understood to be a dirty game. Politics meant being co-opted and corrupted, and it was an arena for the self-interested. Thus, activists were not surprised to find their power constrained when they interacted with party politicians. Being young and from a marginalized community was a disadvantage in politics. And even the better-off youth within the parties were facing massive generational conflicts. In almost every discussion we had with politically active youth during 2011 and 2012, the general sentiment was that political leaders claimed to guide and empower youth, but in reality they were only exploiting young people to serve their political agendas. Party youth felt that the old guard was only repackaging the Mubarak regime's corrupt and opaque ways of doing politics. These feelings led to deep divisions in many parties, with mass youth resignation and the dissolution of parties' youth wings.

"The state is actually doing a better job in reaching out to youth than the opposition or newly established parties through establishing the presidential program for empowering youth," lamented a young opposition party member in 2016. His disenchantment with his own party was so deep that he welcomed youth-inclusive measures from a government he otherwise despised. He went on: "Even some of the political parties that are known for their close relations to the state are led by youth. This is something that we [the opposition] didn't do. There isn't one party in Egypt that has special programs for youth. Most of the youth coalitions in their wide range of agendas aren't supported. Most opposition parties are built around the idea of the 'strong man' [the patriarch] who doesn't give any space to youth. . . ." [35]

Class, gender, and age relations were constantly challenged and renegotiated in the political space of the popular committees. These struggles are indeed indicative of how many different people from quite different strands of life have been contesting the authoritarian and informal social contract since 2011, how they have been struggling for new spaces, trying new political languages, and new political practices—while at the same time being confronted with and limited by the powerful old ways.

Between the Formal and the Informal: Committees and Elections

The persistent influence of the old political ways, and their give-and-take with the new practices, became even more complicated during the national elections. At these times, local activists approached political parties for support—and the parties also reached out to local networks, hoping to gain new constituencies. But what could have been a mutually empowering relationship was often fraught with conflicts over priorities, what was properly addressed through politics, and a certain condescending attitude of middle-class and elite actors toward their poorer compatriots.[36]

There existed autonomy at the local level that was deeply interconnected with events on the national level. The 2012 electoral campaigns for both parliament and the presidency are cases in point. Some committee activists revived their old party affiliations, while others searched for new more promising ones in the vibrant and expanding political scene. Others completely rejected closer cooperation with formal actors because they feared co-optation and corruption. Many groups engaged in some type of awareness work, and used the elections and the votes on the constitution in order to again claim public space and discourse, and struggle for more accountability. One seasoned party and community activist recounted how his group organized a series of public meetings with more than one hundred candidates in the neighborhood and how they consulted with them and challenged their programs. As a result, they developed a proposition of whom to vote for. "Our committee was politically diverse, including many different forces, from the Left to the Brotherhood," he said. "After scrutinizing many candidates, we came up with a list of ten good candidates from different political camps in order to help people to make their choices."[37]

Political parties needed neighborhood committees for local access and grassroots mobilization, and neighborhood committees needed political parties to gain access to local and national politics. "The power and strength of local coalitions and neighborhood committees became evident in the various electoral manifestations after the revolution," a member of a committee in Giza recounted. "For instance, our district voted for Hamdeen Sabahi in the presidential elections in 2012. The only reason for his good results here is the strength of those local coalitions that supported this candidate on the ground. Unfortunately, the political parties weren't able to fully integrate those local movements and if they had been able to, they would have produced great results."[38]

Often, the prominent locals did not support the more revolutionary candidates, leaving new political forces in a weak position at the local level. In addition, the political elite and even revolutionaries were often limited by ideas of what was political and what was not. To both groups, the lack of garbage collection was not a political problem, but a constitutional amendment was. Thus, as time progressed, neighborhood committees became more and more frustrated with political parties. Even the ones that carry the banner of social justice seemed to practice exclusionary policies and dismissed the political agendas of the urban poor.

In 2012, members of the old regime's local elites were already trying to co-opt the new political actors into their networks. In the 2015 parliamentary elections, the elites' strategy paid off when they won most of the constituencies. Still, even in 2015, neighborhood committees decided to support selected candidates, which were either independent or oppositional and threw their local weight behind them and their campaign. Some of these locally supported candidates were successful: "The victory of the pro-revolution candidates in the last parliamentary elections in our district can be attributed to the work that we have done on the grassroots level in our neighborhood—this is our victory," claimed a local activist from Cairo, who leads a neighborhood group.[39] In addition, some of the few oppositional members in parliament are accountable to their local community, as this story from the same activist indicates: "We supported two candidates in the parliamentary elections and they made it, also thanks to us. After one year in office, we invited them to come and speak to us. We wanted to take account of their actions in our names in parliament. They actually agreed to do so, paid for the set-up of a decent sitting area, and then we had a long day of discussion and questions. They stayed, and they answered all the questions. We even invited people from the local administration and they came."

Other committees were less enthusiastic about the performance of "their" man in parliament, as one seasoned local activist recounted: "We supported him under the condition that he also work for our local demands. But it was a compromise from the beginning and we are not satisfied. As leftists and socialists we know that capitalist businessmen will never care about demands—the owners of factories never care about the rights of laborers. Thus, now, we decided to start a local campaign to withdraw confidence from him."[40]

Even under the difficult circumstances of 2015 and 2016, with most of the logic of the old authoritarian social contract back in force, these men, and a few women, claimed their rights as citizens and voters. They insisted on public accountability and on public debate. This is indicative of another shift in the public mood. In 2014 and 2015, the public atmosphere was dominated by discourses of a nation and a state in danger, which needed the unconditional support of all its citizens, including the opposition. A young, well-educated, male candidate of the 2015 election recounted: "It was basically impossible to speak about anything else. You always needed to first say how much danger Egypt is in, how much you care about the state and its security and then, maybe, you could challenge the authorities. There was no politics, really."[41]

In addition, several community leaders from neighborhood committees wanted to run for parliamentary elections to be able to represent their districts. They expected both financial and political support from political parties, but more often than not, they received none. Others felt abandoned by the opposition. "I made a mistake in the parliamentary elections of 2015 that I won't make again," said an unsuccessful candidate. "In this election I insisted on running with the civil front [opposition] and with the Egyptian Social Democratic Party—even though state-affiliated parties such as 'Future of the Nation' were insisting that I run on their name. Once we started the campaign, I found myself alone. Me and my campaign only. I found myself fighting a battle on my own in front of strong coalitions. I felt like I was simply neglected and left to go through the experience on my own."[42]

Given that competition on the national level is fierce and requires a lot of resources, many local leaders hope that long-awaited local elections might offer a better chance to serve their communities. (Local elections have been postponed over and over again, since the last elected local councils were dissolved in the summer of 2011.) A few initiatives, such as the Mubadara Mahiliyya (the local initiative), the Mahaliyyat Thawriya (revolutionary localities), and the Mahaliyyat lel-Shabaab (localities for youth) work in order to enhance the legal and political expertise of young men and women in order to enable them to run. Young and old leaders of neighborhood committees consider running for office, because they feel responsible and because they are encouraged by their constituencies: "You do not just decide to run for elections; the people ask you to do so and this is . . . why I am considering running for local elections," said a man who was a former candidate for the national elections.[43] The work that the neighborhood committees have done in terms of prioritizing local problems, mobilizing the people in their communities and negotiating with local authorities seemed to have given their members the local legitimacy and the self-confidence to consider such an office.

Conclusion and Policy Outlook

Neighborhood committees are new political spaces, which are used in a variety of different ways by different people. In the last six years, they took many shapes; many stopped working altogether after the traumatic summer of 2013 and the ensuing "war on terror." Others continue to claim their space, even in the face of fierce repression. Neighborhood committees can be empowering spaces, especially for young men and some women. This new type of political participation feeds into emerging new political subjectivities, which are more inclusive and less authoritarian. Thus, even as the regime stayed more or less the same by many measures, the people changed. They are transformed by the revolutionary experiences and by the new political practices they have engaged in. This is one of the most important results of the events the Egyptian people lived through since 2011. But the committees are also highly ambiguous, contentious, and power-loaded spaces. Here, actors constantly renegotiate notions of gender, age, class-relations, political orientation, and creed. They also challenge and at times accommodate the logics that stabilize the authoritarian social contract. This social contract sets limits to the contestation of conventional gender, class, or age relations.

The complex experiences of the popular committees have several implications for policy on the local level. First of all, as we showed, the local space is not a void. To the contrary, it is a power-laden, contested sphere, in which formal and informal institutions, state and nonstate actors, and the citizens struggle for access to resources and for control. And even if people are "only" interested in getting better access to services, this necessitates addressing deeply entrenched power relations and vested interests. So, supporting women, youth, or the urban poor is necessarily a political endeavor. In addition, broad labels need to be broken down, based on detailed knowledge of the social structures of a certain place. This knowledge needs to be developed in a bottom-up and participatory manner in order to avoid class, race, or age bias.

The current political situation in Egypt is imposing a heavy toll on any local political and social activism. Change agents on the ground are confronted with ongoing human rights violations, an intimidating political climate, and the soaring economic crisis. International cooperation has become increasingly difficult since 2013. Thus, the challenges to action are enormous. But as many of our interlocutors go on with their work, we offer some policy ideas, against the odds.

Holding competitive, open local elections could empower local constituencies vis-à-vis state authorities. The representation of a wide range of women and youth and their independent movements and coalitions—and not only the regime's women and youth—should be ensured. Changing the law concerning the role, budget, and set-up of local elected councils according to the many available propositions of Egyptian activists and lawyers would be another useful step.

Further, most of the interventions by international organizations thus far have been focused on training and educating grassroots activists on local governance. As useful as this might be, it seems that there has been a saturation and to some extent over-training of local leaders. More emphasis at this point should be put on working with the parliament to ensure that the law on local elections is up to the expectations and needs of grassroots activists. Attempting to apply pressure on the Egyptian government to ensure that transparent and inclusive local elections take place in 2017 is crucial so that local initiatives have a legitimate channel to participate in local and national politics. Another priority should be working with various political parties to integrate diverse local youth in the lists of national parties. Supporting local activists as candidates for local elections can be done not only through training but also by creating nationwide networks among youth candidates, ensuring that they are aware of the available legal support mechanisms and connecting them to other national NGOs working on local governance.

International and national organizations should ensure that any training opportunities are more inclusive to women and other marginalized communities, rather than over-training the same people. Awareness-raising activities in local spaces should also include gender equality and make sure that existing opportunities do not repeatedly empower certain community leaders, and thus help reproduce unequal power relations.

Finally, several local activists have been detained under the pretense of various charges since 2013. Unlike some national activists who are internationally connected and well-supported, local victims of this repression remain largely unknown. The cases of local activists who have disappeared or been imprisoned should be systematically addressed to ensure that they receive the needed legal and political support.

It goes without saying that the impact of training, empowerment, and awareness work will be limited as long as general political freedoms are heavily curtailed by repression.

Notes

1. This chapter is based on research funded by the Deutsche Forschungsgemeinschaft (DFG, German Research Foundation) in the framework of the project "Political Participation, Emotion, Affect and Transformation," SFB 1171 (collaborative research center "Affective Societies").

2. Labeling the uprisings of 2011 and their aftermath is a contentious issue, both academically and politically. In our understanding, the mass protests led to a revolutionary situation (as McAdam, Tarrow and Tilly coined it), while they did not produce revolutionary outcomes in terms of radical regime change (Doug McAdam, Sidney Tarrow, Charles Tilly, "To Map Contentious Politics," in *Mobilization: An International Journal* 1, no. 1 [1996]: 17–34). Throughout the chapter, we refer to the "January 25 revolution" or a variant, as this is the most commonly used term in Egyptian media and in our conversations alike.

3. For an excellent overview of local activism see Diane Singerman and Ibrahim Kareem, "Urban Egypt—On the Road from Revolution to the State? Governance, the Built Environment, and Social Justice," *Égypte/Monde Arabe* 3, no.11 (2014), http://ema.revues.org/3281.

4. As of yet, there are only a few systematic studies of the popular committees on which we can build. Among them are Jennifer A. Bremer, "Leadership and Collective Action in Egypt's Popular Committees: Emergence of Authentic Civic Activism in the Absence of the State," *The International Journal of Not-for-Profit Law* 13, no. 4 (2011), http://www.icnl.org/research/journal/vol13iss4/art_2.htm; Jennifer Ann Bremer, "Leadership and Collective Action in Egypt's Tahrir Revolution: Emergence of Civic Activism in Response to Repression," paper presented at the International Association of Schools and Institutes of Administration Annual Conference in Rome, Italy (2011); Asya El-Meehy, "Egypt's Popular Committees: From Moments of Madness to NGO Dilemmas," *Middle East Report* 42, no. 265 (2012), http://www.merip.org/mer/mer265/egypts-popular-committees; and Hatem Hassan, "Extraordinary Politics of Ordinary People: Explaining the Microdynamics of Popular Committees in Revolutionary Cairo," *International Sociology* 30, no. 4 (May 8, 2015).

5. The conceptual reflections of this chapters are built on qualitative research by Harders in different popular neighborhoods in Cairo (al-Waili, al-Sayyida Zainab, Bassatin, and Dar al-Salam) conducted since 1994. We conducted interviews in one poor settlement in Bassatin and in Dar al-Salam again in September 2011 (Harders) and November 2012 (Harders, Heba Amr). In April 2016 (Wahba) and October 2016 (Harders, Wahba) we conducted more than twenty in-depth semistructured interviews with local activists of neighborhood groups and related initiatives in the Cairo and Giza districts of Boulaq Dakrour, Boulaq Abu Eila, Umraneya, Agouza, and Dokki. In addition, we use field notes from informal visits and walks in the areas. We monitored the online presence of the committees and included photos, videos, and other forms of documentation of their activities. The work is supplemented by the analysis of media

reports, reports prepared by NGOs and initiatives, and content of websites, including the official pages of other relevant actors on Facebook.

6. El-Meehy, "Egypt's Popular Committees."

7. See Hania Sholkamy, "Women Are Also Part of This Revolution," in *Arab Spring in Egypt: Revolution and Beyond*, eds. Bahgat Korany and Rabab El-Mahdi (New York, Cairo: American University in Cairo Press, 2012), 153–74; Asef Bayat, "Revolution and Despair," *Mada Masr*, January 25, 2015, http://www.madamasr.com/opinion/revolution-and-despair; Sari Hanafi, "The Arab Revolutions: The Emergence of a New Political Subjectivity," *Contemporary Arab Affairs* 5, no. 2 (2012): 198–213; Mohammed A. Bamyeh, "Anarchist Method, Liberal Intention, Authoritarian Lesson: The Arab Spring Between Three Enlightenments," *Constellations* 20, no. 2 (2013): 188–202; Samuli Schielke, *You'll Be Late for the Revolution: An Anthropologist's Diary of the Egyptian Revolution and What Followed*, personal blog, http://samuliegypt.blogspot.de.

8. For an excellent account of the daily life and politics of a sha'abi neighborhood of Cairo see Diane Singerman, *Avenues of Participation: Family, Politics, and Networks in Urban Quarters of Cairo* (Princeton, N.J.: Princeton University Press, 1995).

9. This section is based on earlier work of Harders and collaborative work with Malika Bouziane and Anja Hoffmann in Cilja Harders, "'State Analysis from Below' and Political Dynamics in Egypt After 2011," *International Journal of Middle East Studies* 47, no. 1 (February 2015): 148–51; Anja Hoffmann, Malika Bouziane, and Cilja Harders, "Analyzing Politics beyond the Center in an Age of Transformation," in *Local Politics and Contemporary Transformations in the Arab World*, ed. Malika Bouziane, Anja Hoffmann, and Cilja Harders (Basingstoke: Palgrave MacMillan, 2013), 3–21.

10. This concept draws on critical, feminist, constructionist, and ethnographic works as sources of inspiration. See for example Salwa Ismail, *Political Life in Cairo's New Quarters: Encountering the Everyday State* (Minneapolis: University of Minnesota Press, 2006); Paul Amar, *Dispatches from the Arab Spring: Understanding the New Middle East* (Minneapolis: University of Minnesota Press, 2013); Michel-Rolph Trouillot, "The Anthropology of the State in the Age of Globalization: Close Encounters of the Deceptive Kind," *Current Anthropology* 42, no. 1 (2001): 125–38; Akhil Gupta, "Blurred Boundaries: The Discourse of Corruption, the Culture of Politics, and the Imagined State," *American Ethnologist* 22, no. 2 (1995): 375–402; Donna Haraway, "Situated Knowledges: The Science Question in Feminism and the Privilege of Partial Perspective," *Feminist Studies* 14, no. 3 (1988): 575–99.

11. *From Patriarchy to Empowerment: Women's Participation, Movements, and Rights in the Middle East, North Africa, and South Asia*, ed. Valentine M. Moghadam (Syracuse, N.Y.: Syracuse University Press, 2007).

12. Eric Dennis, "The Commodification of the Ashwa-iyyat: Urban Land, Housing Market Unification, and De Soto's Interventions in Egypt," in *Popular Housing and Urban Land Tenure in the Middle East: Case Studies from Egypt, Syria, Jordan, Lebanon, and Turkey*, eds. Myriam Ababsa, Baudouin Dupret, and Eric Denis (Cairo: The American University in Cairo Press, 2012), 227–58.

13. Asef Bayat, "Un-Civil Society: The Politics of the 'informal people,'" *Third World Quarterly* 18, no. 1 (March 1997): 53–72.

14. Asef Bayat, *Life as Politics: How Ordinary People Change the Middle East* (United States: Stanford University Press, 2009).

15. Cilja Harders, "The Informal Social Pact—The State and the Urban Poor in Cairo," in *Politics from Above, Politics from Below: The Middle East in the Age of Economic Reform*, ed. Eberhard Kienle (London: Saqi Books, 2003), 191–213.

16. Salwa Ismail, *Political Life in Cairo's New Quarters: Encountering the Everyday State* (Minneapolis: University of Minnesota Press, 2006).

17. Amal Hamada, "Understanding the Military Role in the Egyptian Revolution," in *Arab Revolutions and Beyond: Change and Persistence*, ed. Naoual Belakhdar et al. (Berlin: Center for Middle Eastern and North African Politics, 2014), 36–37.

18. See Bremer "Leadership and Collective Action in Egypt's Tahrir Revolution," paper presented at the International Association of Schools and Institutes of Administration Annual Conference; and Ahmed Saleh, "The Popular Committees: The Local, The Ordinary and the Violent in The Egyptian Revolution," (MA thesis, Central European University, June 2016).

19. Enrique Klaus, "Égypte : 'La Révolution du 25 Janvier' en Contrechamps: Chroniques des 'Comités Populaires' d'Al-Manyal au Caire," *Revue Marocaine des Sciences Politiques et Sociales* IV (2012): 119–45.

20. Saleh, "The Popular Committees," 57–63.

21. Mona El-Ghobashy, "The Praxis of the Egyptian Revolution," *Middle East Report* 41, no. 258 (2011), http://www.merip.org/mer/mer258/praxis-egyptian-revolution.

22. Saleh, "The Popular Committees."

23. Neighborhood committee member, interview with the authors, Cairo, April 4, 2016.

24 Alaa Abd El Fattah, "Jan 25, Five Years On: The Only Words I Can Write Are about Losing My Words," *Mada Masr,* January 2016, http://www.madamasr.com/en/2016/01/24/opinion/u/jan-25-5-years-on-the-only-words-i-can-write-are-about-losing-my-words/.

25. Of course, these labels effectively gloss over the differences among the people who they include, but we use them here for the sake of simplicity.

26. Youth activist, interview with the authors.

27. Head of a development NGO, interview with the authors, Downtown Cairo, November 6, 2016.

28. Female community leader of a poor neighbourhood, interview with Harders/Amr, Cairo, November 2012.

29. Youth and party activist from Cairo, interview with the authors, Downtown Cairo, November 3, 2016.

30. Youth activist from Cairo, interview with Harders/Amr, Cairo, November 2012.

31. Hanan Sabea, "A 'Time out of Time': Tahrir, the Political and the Imaginary in the Context of the January 25 Revolution in Egypt," *Cultural Anthropology Hot Spots*, 2012, https://culanth.org/fieldsights/211-a-time-out-of-time-tahrir-the-political-and-the-imaginary-in-the-context-of-the-january-25th-revolution-in-egypt.

32. Nadje Al-Ali, "Gendering the Arab Spring," *Middle East Journal of Culture and Communication* 5, no. 1 (2012): 26–31.

33. Young activist, interview with the authors, Downtown Cairo, November 3, 2016.

34. Political activist, interview with the authors, Giza, November 8, 2016.

35. Youth activist, interview with the authors, Downtown Cairo, November 3, 2016.

36. Youth activist, interview with the authors, Downtown Cairo, November 3, 2016.

37. Male political activist, interview with the authors, Giza, November 8, 2016.

38. Political activist, interview with the authors, Giza, November 8, 2016.

39. Political activist, interview with the authors, Giza, November 8, 2016.

40. Male neighborhood committee member, interview with the authors, Cairo, April 4, 2016.

41. Young activist, interview with the authors, Downtown Cairo, November 3, 2016.

42. Youth activist, interview with the authors, Downtown Cairo, November 3, 2016.

43. Youth activist, interview with the authors, Downtown, Cairo, June 13, 2016.

20

Governance from Below

Comparing Local Experiments in Egypt and Syria after the Uprisings

ASYA EL-MEEHY

In the wake of the uprisings in Egypt and Syria, new modes of grassroots governing emerged. In both countries, new bodies arose to perform a range of services that were formally fulfilled by central governments, or by local institutions that were organized in a top-down fashion. In Egypt, it was the Local Popular Committees (LPCs), and in Syria, the Local Administrative Councils (LACs). The LPCs and LACs both held promise as examples of bottom-up governance with democratic ambitions, in countries where such efforts had been in extremely short supply. With original empirical research, the author investigates the success of the LPCs and LACs in fulfilling their aims of building inclusive, democratic, locally led governance. She finds that by several metrics, and for different reasons that depend much on the contrasting contexts of Egypt and Syria, the bodies have so far fallen short of empowered participatory governance principles. Still, they represent a watershed moment for governance practices in the two countries, and indicate that locally driven organizing will be enduringly relevant in the years ahead.

The Arab uprisings that began in 2011 opened space for the emergence of new modes of governance-from-below in the region.[1] As regimes fell or became embroiled in civil wars, activists improvised nascent grassroots structures in spaces where state institutions no longer functioned. These structures ambitiously aimed to self-manage their communities, coordinate provision of collective goods, settle disputes, and act as the representatives of residents. In Egypt, "lijan sha'abiyah" (Local Popular Committees, or LPCs) evolved from neighborhood watch brigades aimed at protecting property to autonomous forums for debating and devising collective solutions to long-neglected local development problems. Between 2011 and mid-2013, the committees proved notably successful at extracting concrete gains from successive transitional governments. Along parallel lines, as Syria's civil war unfolded, activists turned their focus to responding to the needs of the population in opposition-held areas, where the central government no longer exercised control. Revolutionary local councils were established as bottom-up institutions aimed at stabilizing society.[2] While many councils were short-lived, or proved incapable of administering local public policies, some—like those in Idlib and Aleppo—emerged as successful experiments in local governance.

In both Egypt and Syria, the establishment of these local structures stemmed from practical needs, like restoring or improving access to public services, as well as a normative commitment among activists to inclusive democratic governance. They represented unique developments against the Arab region's backdrop of long-centralized states with hegemonic control over civil society. Their emergence carried implications for the de facto exercise of power on the ground, as well as future dynamics between localities and the central government. Thus, Egypt's LPCs were viewed as enabling citizens not just to assert their rights, but even to contest the ways that the state governed—and the ways they engaged with the state as it did so. Advocates hypothesized that such localized mobilization could potentially evolve beyond community-centered needs to build broader coalitions for decentralization of state institutions[3] and transforming "local government into capable, responsive, transparent and accountable entities."[4] Similarly, observers praised the Local Administrative Councils (LACs) in Syria as a "laboratory par excellence" for new experiments in decentralized governance, and the cornerstone of any state-building efforts in postwar Syria.[5] Yet little comparative empirical work has been done on the actual mobilization patterns, internal organization, or the evolution of these unique forms of activism. What are the characteristics of these recently emergent modes of local governance? To what extent do they plant the seeds for empowering citizens? I argue that governance-from-below experiments in Egypt and Syria share similar traits as far as their autonomous voluntary nature, lack of access to sustainable sources of financing, and the dual roles of democratic citizenship ideas and practical needs in driving their activities. The profile of their participants, decision-making, and links to the communities where they operate reveal important democratic deficiencies. In both contexts, local governance efforts actually fall short of empowered participatory governance principles. Given the larger contexts of instability in Egypt and civil war in Syria these experiments should, nonetheless, be seen as promising signs of grassroots organizing in the region.

The presence of "alternative" governance structures is not exactly a new phenomenon in the Arab region.[6] Global shrinking of economic space, since the late 1980s, has translated into the proliferation of dynamics of expulsion from core social and economic orders, a process that coincided in the region with the shift from statist models of development to market-led growth.[7] As states withdrew from their developmental responsibilities, informality grew and the process of socioeconomic expulsion increasingly affected the middle classes that traditionally constituted the state's social bases of power, resulting in a rising sense of relative deprivation among them.[8] In many cases, governments did not keep pace with rapid urbanization failing to press state authority into unregulated areas. As a result, even in the "geographic heart of the nominal state itself" the region witnessed "territories becoming effectively stateless," lacking access to state services or rule of law.[9] Far from being ungoverned or anarchic, however, these spaces saw new actors—such as gangs, militias, thugs, local men of influence, and religious political parties—assuming functions previously considered strictly the preserve of the state. Often, these actors effectively exercised local authority by providing public services and common goods, arbitrating disputes, and mediating relations between citizens and the state.[10] The emergence of Hezbollah as a contending authority in Lebanon crystallized the power of nonstate actors and the diminishing of territorial state sovereignty.

But though historical parallels exist, the new modes of governance from below that emerged after the uprisings are distinct in important ways. Not only did they emerge in the context of state vacuums and go on to exercise revolutionary authority, but they also often adopted democratic reform goals. Furthermore, these initiatives were *not* spearheaded by conventional civil society actors, such as Islamist activists. Rather, they were initially established by newly politicized youth, who strived to ensure that they were not captured by political forces or armed militias. In other words, the modes of governance under study need to be understood in the revolutionary context of the Arab uprisings. They resulted from significant ruptures in the historical trajectories of states and societies in the region, rather than merely representing continuations of earlier forms of mobilization, survival tactics, and self-organization among the marginalized.

This chapter comparatively explores two local modes of governance—the Egyptian LPCs and the Syrian LACs—that emerged after the uprisings. The trajectories of the two uprisings differed significantly as the incumbent regimes responded to early waves of protests in contrasting ways. Hosni Mubarak, the president of Egypt for thirty years, stepped down fairly quickly, which brought the army to the forefront of the transition. Syrian president Bashar al-Assad was more resilient and moved the country into civil war. This divergence reflects differences in state-building processes, the institutionalization of the coercive apparatus, and international dynamics.[11] Indeed, difference in trajectories created space for the emergence of more elaborate modes of governance from below in Syria, under the LACs, compared to forms of grassroots contestations and self-governance by the LPCs in Egypt. Nonetheless, I will argue that, after the uprisings, both the Egyptian and Syrian forms of local activism share largely similar traits. In both contexts, local efforts at governance resulted from power vacuums, and excluded certain social groups—sometimes inadvertently, and other times deliberately. They often lacked embeddedness in their local communities. These local experiments varied widely in their effectiveness, and for the most part proved unsustainable. Collectively, despite their shortcomings, they represent unprecedented forms of political empowerment in the region's postcolonial era. Rooted in autonomous local voluntary initiatives, the establishment of these nascent structures was uniquely driven by both practical needs and secular democratic ideas. Their emergence constituted a systematic grassroots challenge to the centralized authority of fragile Arab regimes—regimes that had failed to uphold the social rights of citizenship in spaces beyond their reach.

My analysis is based on fieldwork conducted with Egyptian and Syrian activists. I conducted in-depth interviews with core members of six local committees in Egypt during the period 2011–14. Additionally, I conducted focus groups and semistructured interviews to explore the views of residents across three neighborhoods in Cairo in April 2013. Findings on Syria came from a focus group of local activists held in March 2013. I complemented and updated findings through semistructured interviews with activists as well as members of the Syrian opposition. It should be kept in mind that lack of access to Syria hindered my ability to observe the working of local councils or to assess residents' attitudes toward them. Still, my research yielded enough data to identify trends and draw the limited conclusions presented here.

Origins

Police withdrawal and the resultant security vacuum in the wake of Egypt's January 25, 2011 uprising triggered unprecedented growth of civic activism in the form of neighborhood-based citizen watch brigades, called popular committees. Young men typically led the formation of popular committees by first organizing at street level, and then capitalizing on social media (particularly Facebook) to coordinate new networks at the neighborhood level during the eighteen days preceding Mubarak's resignation, on February 11. According to early analyses, most committees spontaneously emerged in urban areas, with around 34 percent operating in Greater Cairo.[12] Outside these areas, in rural contexts, there were signs that patronage networks of Mubarak's National Democratic Party (NDP) played a vital role in the top-down establishment of committees that were dominated by larger families and concerned with maintaining local stability.[13]

Many local committees disbanded after public order was gradually restored. But some reinvented themselves to engage in self-governance initiatives, particularly those in informal settlements—communities with high population density that typically had been developed on private agricultural land in contravention of building regulations. The peak of the committee movement's activity was between February 2011 and June 30, 2013. In response to the effective freezing of government institutions, the dissolution of local popular councils and the ex-ruling NDP, as well as worsening economic conditions, they extended their activities beyond self-policing and basic security. Access to medical clinics, main roads, public spaces as well as services—particularly butane cylinders for households, waste collection, and street lighting— emerged as the most prominent rallying cries for committee activists in informal settlements. Across Cairo, there were numerous examples of committees taking matters in their hands. Ard al-Lewa's committee successfully self-financed a railway crossing to minimize accidents among residents. It also mobilized around the establishment of a park, a school, and a hospital on fourteen feddans[14] of vacant land owned by the Ministry of Religious Endowments (Awqaf) in the neighborhood. Next door, the committee in Imbaba organized effective nonpayment campaigns for public services the state failed to provide, such as garbage collection, while Nahia's committee constructed an on/off ramp to connect the neighborhood to the ring road.[15] My research shows that in these instances, activists were often not just motivated by fulfilling practical needs of their communities. Many also saw themselves bringing the revolution to the grassroots level by becoming local watchdogs of the government, while others saw themselves as engaged in redefining popular understandings of citizenship, emphasizing empowerment and implanting democratic values.

As a secular revolutionary impulse, Egypt's local committees faced deep-seated suspicion among power-holders. The end of Mubarak's autocratic rule brought about greater tightening of government controls over civil society organizations, coinciding with the monopolistic presence of Islamist parties in formal political institutions. Successive transitional authorities have attempted to capitalize on the committees as a revolutionary force, in order to bestow legitimacy on their policies at the local level. Under the rule of the Supreme Council of the Armed Forces (SCAF), local committee activists were harassed as thugs, while simultaneously encouraged to join a "national council," which was created top-down to represent them. Joining would make them formally organized state-sanctioned groups bearing government-issued identifications. The majority of committees, however, declined to cooperate with these SCAF measures. A few committees collaborated with the state by signing a protocol with the Ministry of Supply by which local activists would be recruited to deliver butane cylinders to households, but the protocol was cut short by the Muslim Brotherhood's ascendance to power.[16] Indeed, the election of Mohamed Morsi as president was marked by heightened competition at the local level, as Brotherhood activists sought to claim the work of LPCs. Cooperation between the LPCs and Muslim Brothers was rare, and relations were marked by mutual suspicion. The military coup on July 3, 2013 ushered in a popular neo-authoritarian regime, and a new low for the LPCs. The new regime has attempted to recentralize authority under the army's patronage and heavily cracked down on civil society activism, particularly in informal areas, including the local committees. To a large extent, the committees' movement has waned, as the state has criticized their activity as illegal.

Similar horizontal forms of committee-centered grassroots activism initially emerged in Syria as young people began to organize meetings in neighborhoods and towns across the country. Known as tanseeayat, ad hoc local coordination committees were established to empower the revolutionary movement by coordinating nonviolent protests, and documenting them through citizen journalism. They also extended support for families of prisoners, provided emergency relief to internally displaced persons, and committed local armed groups to sign up to an ethical code of conduct for observing human rights.[17] As armed conflict escalated, however, and the regime withdrew from territories, activists gradually broadened their focus to meeting the needs of local populations and established local councils, which are relatively more formalized hierarchical structures. As a focus group respondent explained "Local coordination committees were the nuclei of the councils, for they brought the financial and logistical support. But, unlike the coordination committees, the local councils were trying to monopolize the violence. . . Of course there are political agendas connected to them and they provide services under the umbrella of these agendas."[18] As a matter of fact, the establishment of local councils was not just aimed to "support the people in managing their own lives independent of institutions and state agencies,"[19] or preserving the social fabric of communities at risk of disintegration.[20] Rather, they were also conceived by early advocates of their creation as potentially progressive "spaces for collective expression" that served to embed democratic revolutionary initiatives at the local level.[21]

Following government forces' withdrawal from areas of resistance in 2012, public services were completely or partially halted by the regime.[22] In response, the first local councils were founded that year in Aleppo and al-Zabadani. They quickly spread such that by 2014, there were more than nine hundred councils in Syria operating in Idlib, Aleppo, Hama, Homs, Dera'a and al-Hasakeh.[23] Unlike the case of Egypt's LPCs, which centered on neighborhoods, the largest shares of Syria's LACs seem to operate at the levels of municipalities (43 percent) and villages (28 percent).[24] By 2016, the number of active LACs had fallen sharply to around 395 with the majority located in opposition areas closest to the Turkish border.[25]

As civilian-led structures opposed to the regime, the councils operate like "small governments" in managing the affairs of their regions.[26] Facing arbitrary violence by armed militias, increasing lawlessness, and spikes in criminality, activists have generally strived to maintain councils' autonomy from rebel groups, including the Free Syrian Army, whose priorities sometimes clashed with those of LACs' leaders. Indeed, the trajectory of the councils' development has been influenced, overall, not just by the intensity of confrontations, or the degree of accommodation with the regime, or by fluctuations in donor priorities, but also by competition from militias.[27]

Councils have predominantly assumed coordination of civil defense, education, health, and development projects, in addition to the extension of resource-intensive services like water, electricity and waste collection. To a lesser extent, they have also been directly involved in restoring infrastructure, as well as extending relief to the local communities, which are areas where nongovernmental organizations (NGOs) and charity organizations became dominant players. According to participants in the study, LACs made themselves particularly felt in the education sector as they operated schools and amended curricula by removing Ba'athist ideology and references to the Assad regime. They struggled to protect civic and secular values in the curricula, however. In the face of pressures from militias and some donors, they also incorporated Islamist ideology.[28]

LACs faced stiff competition from armed militias that sought consent from civilians, which they attempted to achieve by devising their own governance structures and fashioning service-delivery mechanisms in territories under their control. For instance, at issue is control of the justice system, which militias affiliated with Fateh al-Sham (formerly the Nusra Front) have attempted to run as "hay'aat shari'iya," or legal commissions consisting of religious courts applying Salafi interpretation of sharia. Similarly, the councils' control over bakeries has been fiercely contested due to attempts by militias to control food supply and legitimize their political authority.[29] In some cases, like parts of rural Aleppo, members of the councils are exclusively drawn from the Harakat Nour al-Din al-Zenki brigade, which controls the day-to-day administration of the territories under its control. However, there are exceptions to this pattern. For instance, in Darayya the militants seem to operate under the control of the local council. Also, midway, there are cases like Douma, where the militants and local councils segregate their activities, and do not actually seek to dominate each other's work. In these contexts, the local council, as an activist put it, "carries a lot of moral weight, they hold meetings in mosques, have immunity from militias and civil society groups have collaborated with them."[30]

The councils' dynamic with the regime and its allies is another important factor that has shaped their evolution. At the beginning of the uprising, there were instances of accommodation with the regime. Activists from Douma, for instance, recalled striking an agreement with the governor of rural Damascus in 2013, whereby the local council would be responsible for local administration and not be met with regime interference, in exchange for ending the presence of militias, the rehabilitation of Hamdan hospital, and provision of medical supplies.[31] More recently however, the regime has sought to undermine emerging alternatives to state institutions in opposition areas. This is particularly the case since Syria's opposition in exile has tried to capitalize on the legitimacy of the councils as locally embedded grassroots structures. And the councils were indeed represented within the Syrian Opposition Coalition.[32] Later, with the establishment of the Syrian Interim Government in Gaziantep, Turkey, a Local Administration Ministry designated to coordinate donor funding to LACs was formed. The Ministry has also been instrumental in attempting to standardize the internal structures and operation procedures of LACs based on Assad's 2011 local administration law.

Comparing Local Bottom-Up Governance in Egypt and Syria

To what extent do Egypt's LPCs and Syria's LACs constitute channels of participatory empowerment? Such local mobilization is often celebrated as a sign of healthy civil societies and even regarded as the embodiment of democracy, of its promises of citizenship, and self-government. In light of growing dissatisfaction with the way democratic institutions function, since the late 1980s citizens in the West and developing countries alike have experimented with participating in decision-making through a variety of innovative locally rooted mechanisms.[33] Globally, local governance reforms have been promoted by international organizations such as the World Bank on the grounds of expanding participation, deepening accountability, and improving provision of services by bringing them more in line with local demands. The following section analyzes the democratic credentials of the two modes of alternative governance in question along three dimensions: Inclusion, decision-making, and embeddedness.

Inclusion

In Egypt the LPCs were often founded on the bases of preexisting friendships, peer networks, and previous waves of activism. Committee members often belonged to the same graduating class and shared a privileged middle-class background. Further, in many cases they had previous experiences in voluntary social service or charity work, or were relatively more politicized as members of the April 6 Youth Movement,[34] student unions, or affiliates of Kefaya (the Egyptian Movement for Change). Their involvement in the committees represented a form of voluntary activism. In Syria, however, membership of LACs was often drawn from the local social elite and affluent families. Their selection or election was made by informal so-called "lijan al-sharaf" (honor committees) consisting of local notables and dominant families. One activist succinctly explained the rationale for these committees in these terms: "Those wealthy businessmen and figures with social status who financed the councils wanted to know where the money is being spent and wanted to have some influence over who holds office."[35] Officials at the interim government's Local Administrative Councils Unit[36] attempted to bestow democratic legitimacy on these entities by referring to them as "electoral commissions" that make nominations for public office. "We formed electoral commissions consisting of eighty people drawn from civil society, civil defense, and notables. They make twenty-five to thirty nominations. Half of these become LAC executive office holders and the other half serves as watchdogs."[37] Opinions varied on the extent to which this mechanism ensured adequate representation. Some argued that it allowed competent individuals to hold office, regardless of their political weight, while others argued that it particularly served to marginalize youths. A recent survey confirms findings revealing that only a third of LACs were formed through some form of "elections" while more than half were formed by consensus.

As a result of their recruitment dynamics, bottom-up local governance remained, to a large extent, exclusionary. There are signs that the poor were not significantly included. Women, too, were poorly represented in both the Syrian and Egyptian structures. That said, variations across Egypt and Syria translated into some differences in degree of major social groups' accessibility to participation. For instance, membership profiles show that youths and minorities were included less in the Syrian bodies as compared to those in Egypt. Further, the distinction between members and nonmembers is sharper in the Syrian case.

In Egypt, activists reported that young citizens in the eighteen-to-thirty-five age group represented 80 percent of LPCs' membership base. However, my in-depth research on the committees shows that those in leading positions have tended to be in their forties and fifties. Syria's local councils, on the other hand, are less accessible to youths. Those in the eighteen-to-thirty-five age bracket represented only 30 percent of all members. Indeed, participants explained that even though youths often pioneered the establishment of LACs, they were actually more likely to be involved in relief initiatives than hold office in the councils.

With Christian membership an estimated 30 percent of the total, Egypt's LPCs broadly incorporated religious minorities—even over-representing them as compared to their proportion of the general population.[38] Activists have attributed their success at inclusion of minorities to a "deliberate effort to create and maintain trust," rather than interest among Copts for greater participation.[39] In contrast, given deepening ethnic cleavages in the context of Syria's civil war, the country's LACs tend to have more homogenous membership. My interviewees, however, stressed initial inclusion of Alawites and Christians in Douma's and Hama's LACs. They blamed the increased militarization of the uprising for their current exclusion.[40]

As for women's participation, it is significantly low in both cases, ranging in Egypt from 2 percent in rural areas to 20 percent in cities, and averaging just 2 percent in Syria. Participants in my research recognized that the low representation of women was problematic but often blamed cultural values for women's choice not to participate. In the case of Syria, they also highlighted poor security, as well as the opposition of powerful actors and militias in the areas. Activists stressed that they were aiming to increase women's representation through the establishment of specialized women's offices in the LACs.

Finally, the informal character of Egypt's committees and the density of networks they are embedded in translated into the absence of a clear distinction between members and nonmembers. Thus, it is not uncommon to find individuals from one neighborhood being actively involved in the founding and activities of popular committees in another neighborhood. This contrasts sharply with the situation in Syria, where LACs did not include individuals from outside the local community, a situation that has led to the exclusion of sizable internally displaced populations.[41]

Decision-Making

Given the participatory nature of Egypt's committees, they face dilemmas when it comes to decision-making. The decision-making process that activists described is often ambiguous and opaque. The majority of the committees rejected voting as a way of reaching decisions, which they associated with formal entities. Instead, activists described forms of collective deliberation involving consultations among core members in a decentralized fashion. They were also careful to reject any form of hierarchy guiding the internal workings of the committee. As one committee member from Imbaba explained, "The system is decentralized . . . we do not believe in hierarchy, we collectively decide."[42]

Syria's local councils were more likely to reach decisions based on majority voting. In fact, a recent study found that 69 percent of the councils relied on voting by members to reach decisions. Only 28 percent assigned decision-making to specialists within the council or relied on experts, while just 3 percent reported that decisions were taken by heads of local councils.[43] This arguably reflects activists' deliberate efforts to develop more formalized local structures, as well as the fact that the councils heavily depend on financing from donors, who emphasize transparency.

Social Embeddedness

Activists in the two cases were keenly aware of the importance of socially embedding their work by establishing effective communication channels with residents. Yet my findings show that in line with top-down governance practices of the centralized old regimes, activists' awareness did not necessarily translate into systematic efforts to broadly consult with citizens in order to identify their needs or respond to evolving demands. In Egypt, LPCs typically attempted to embed their activities in the community during the initial stages of their operation. Shortly after the establishment of the committee, meetings were held in the neighborhoods and residents were invited to identify local needs and priorities. This practice, however, was short-lived. Committee leaders did not continue to broadly consult with residents on their needs by holding such meetings. And in the course of my interviews they often dismissed the importance of local needs assessments, arguing that since they were from the areas in which they worked, they already knew the community's needs. Indeed, simple updates to Facebook pages were the focus of local committees' communication with residents. The one exception to this trend was a committee in Umraneya that formed its own news network on Facebook, as a form of citizen journalism facilitating interactive communication with residents. With more than thirty-two thousand followers, the news network allowed activists to embed their work in the community by documenting problems in the neighborhood and using professional-quality videos and interviews with residents.[44]

Respondents from Syria explained that due to war conditions they couldn't always hold large-scale meetings with the locals. "Our preference is to not communicate in secret in liberated areas," an activist said. "This is easier to do when enlightened militiamen reject theft and violence. They provide security for the local council to operate."[45] Often LACs relied on mosques to communicate with residents. "LACs' primary means of communication for anything important is through mosques," a focus group participant said. "Every Friday relief assistance is redistributed and the medical committee which monitors infectious diseases activity conducts tests."[46] With parallels to the case in Egypt, 85 percent of activists in Syria reported that they selected projects based on local needs, yet just 9 percent identified these needs through some form of public consultation.[47] Similarly, councils maintain Facebook pages, but it is not clear if these are geared toward residents or outside donors.

Sustainability

Egypt's local committees operated as loosely structured entities lacking access to sustainable sources of financing. While virtually all of the research participants identified lack of funding as the number-one weakness of the committees, they expressed concern regarding the charging of membership fees on egalitarian grounds. Instead, committees to a large extent relied on a combination of seasonal contributions by members, according to their financial means, as well as in-kind contributions from outside actors. My interviewees unanimously dismissed the option of fund-raising from the community, which they said would stigmatize their committees.

Egyptian activists I interviewed recognized that the ability of the LPCs to access sustainable sources of financing hinged on formalizing their status. Many dismissed the prospects of becoming officially registered NGOs, however, even though it would open the door to legal fundraising. Activists viewed NGOs as elitist entities disconnected from their neighborhoods. They also feared heightened state surveillance of their work, and expressed skepticism about the feasibility of receiving official licensing. Lastly, the risks of being accused of following "foreign agendas"—in the midst of widely publicized lawsuits targeting NGO workers—were among the reasons cited for avoiding formalization. As a result, only two out of the six committees actually formalized as NGOs.

Similarly, LACs in Syria were in general poorly equipped to perform their functions due to severe shortages of resources. The councils lacked the capacity to levy taxes. In some cases, they nominally charged for services, such as electricity, by introducing flat rates, but activists noted that this was not always feasible given civilians' deteriorating living standards. Only in a few cases were the councils successful in launching profit-generating projects. One was Douma's recycling initiative, which converted waste into organic fertilizers to be sold on markets in the Eastern Ghouta, the rebel-controlled enclave on the outskirts of Damascus in which Douma is located.[48] The lack of resources has rendered the LACs heavily dependent on external support to implement projects, particularly from the American, British, and German governments. Indeed, it is estimated that as many as 75 percent of the councils received donor support, which in total financed one fifth of their projects. The remaining 25 percent of LACs depended on foreign funding to finance a bigger portion of their activities, according to a survey published in 2015.[49]

Following an international meeting in Paris in October 2012, Western governments pledged to directly support local councils in opposition-held areas in Syria, thus making donor assistance available. However, many councils could not actually access this funding, which was soon channeled through the Syrian Opposition Coalition. Instead, councils relied on erratic donations from affluent residents or Syrian expatriates from the area. Direct support to the local councils seems to have been poorly coordinated, at times placing them in competition with the better-financed NGOs.[50] This has in turn affected the evolution of LACs' activities. For instance, as local NGOs became the preferred implementing partners for UN and international agencies, local councils became less involved in humanitarian assistance and field hospital management. Instead, local councils started to assume monitoring and evaluation functions for these activities. For the most part, activists viewed NGOs not as mutually empowering partners in local governance but as competitors. Lastly, activists also stressed that shifts in donor priorities toward fighting terrorism undermined their work in supporting civilians. (Though even before the rise of the Islamic State, militarization of the uprising posed risks to their autonomy vis-à-vis the increasingly much better-financed Free Syrian Army and Islamist militias.)

Conclusion

The emergence of new modes of local governance from below occurred against the backdrop of voids created by lapses in the functions of state institutions, or withdrawal by the state from spaces and territories over which it could no longer exercise control. I have argued that the drivers for the establishment of both the LPCs in Egypt and the LACs in Syria were both practical, as well as ideological. A new generation of activists attempted to plant the seeds of democratic change at the grassroots level. My close analysis of the two modes of local governance, however, reveals that these nascent structures do not meet democratic criteria.

Even though the record of Egypt's popular committees is better, both modes of governance are by and large exclusionary. This is particularly the case when it comes to the poor and women, who are not represented in their activities. Egypt's LPCs were particularly successful in incorporating Copts among their ranks. This success in inclusion was not achieved by Syria's LACs, however, where deepening ethnic and territorial cleavages impeded the incorporation of minorities and the internally displaced. Similarly, the committees in Egypt seem to have been relatively more accessible to youths. Notwithstanding these nuances, looking closely at the two modes of governance reveals that they both did not develop inclusionary recruitment processes. Membership in Egypt's local committees largely depends on activist connections through prior networks, and Syria's councils seem mostly accessible only to prominent families and social elites who constitute the honor committees (lijan al-sharaf).

As far as decision-making, Syria's councils seem for the most part to adopt majority voting, making them relatively more transparent than Egypt's committees. Nonetheless, whether or not they used voting, both modes of local governance failed to embed the voices of local communities in their decision-making processes. Egyptian and Syrian activists often did not develop mechanisms for back-and-forth consultations with the citizenry. They also shared skepticism about the work of NGOs, which were regarded as elitist or competing with their own efforts, rather than complementary or mutually empowering. Finally, the records of both the LPCs and LACs demonstrate their lack of sustainability. LPCs could not generate sustainable sources of financing, and rejected the prospects of becoming official NGOs, which contributed to the demise of the movement. The local councils in Syria are heavily dependent on external support and donors to cover the growing local needs of civilians. This has limited their autonomy, and often put them in a precarious position in relation to armed militias.

Finally, while the local governance efforts I have examined fall short of participatory empowerment ideals and may prove to be short-lived, their emergence is still a promising sign of grassroots, local organizing. These experiments demonstrate the capacity of activists to establish locally rooted autonomous structures and to effectively meet the needs of citizens, often despite the opposition of central authorities. Notwithstanding the shortcomings of these local efforts, they pioneered alternative ideas for bottom-up governance that are framed in democratic secular terms of citizenship, a development that is likely to alter the exercise of power by centralized authorities in the long run.

Notes

1. I use the term governance in reference to the various institutionalized modes of social coordination to provide collective goods, as well as to produce and implement collectively binding rules. See Tanja A. Börzel and Thomas Risse, "Governance Without A State: Can It Work?," *Regulation and Governance* 4 (2010): 114.

2. Other studies in the project explore revolutionary governance in Manbij, Idlib, and the Eastern Ghouta in Syria, and popular committees in several districts of Cairo.

3. Ibrahim Kareem and Diane Singerman, "Urban Egypt: On the Road from Revolution to the State? Governance, the Built Environment, and Social Justice," *Égypte/Monde Arabe* 11 (2014), http://ema.revues.org/3281.

4. Yazid Sayigh, "Above the State: The Officer's Republic in Egypt," *Carnegie Papers*, Carnegie Endowment for International Peace, Washington, DC, 2012, http://carnegieendowment. org/files/officers_republic1.pdf.

5. Agnes Favier, "Local Governance Dynamics in Opposition-Controlled Areas in Syria," in *Inside Wars: Local Dynamics of Conflicts in Syria and Libya,* eds. Luigi Narbone et al. (Florence: EUI, 2016), 6–15, http://cadmus.eui.eu/bitstream/handle/1814/41644/Inside%20wars_2016.pdf.

6. See discussion in Anne Marie Baylouny, "Authority Outside the State," in *Ungoverned Spaces: Alternatives to State Authority in an Era of Softened Sovereignty*, eds. Anne L. Clunan and Harold A. Trinkunas (Stanford: Stanford University Press, 2010).

7. Saskia Sassen, *Expulsions: Brutality and Complexity in the Global Economy* (Cambridge, Mass.: Harvard University Press, 2014).

8. See discussion in Asya El Meehy, "It's the Economy, Stupid! Analyzing the Uprisings in Bahrain, Egypt and Tunisia," *Critique Internationale* 61, no. 4 (2014): 55–59.

9. Baylouny, "Authority Outside the State."

10. Ibid.

11. Nadine Sika, "Arab States, Regime Change, and Social Contestation Compared: the Cases of Egypt and Syria" in *The Arab Uprisings: Transforming and Challenging State Power*, eds. Eberhard Kienle and Nadine Sika (London, I.B.Tauris, 2015), 158–76.

12. Jennifer Ann Bremer, "Leadership and Collective Action in Egypt's Popular Committees: Emergence of Authentic Civic Activism in the Absence of the State," *International Journal of Not-for-Profit Law* 13, no. 4 (December 2011): 90, http://www.icnl.org/research/journal/vol13iss4/art_2.htm.

13. Asya El-Meehy, "Egypt's Popular Committees'," *Middle East Report* 42 (2012), http://www.merip.org/mer/mer265/egypts-popular-committees.

14. A unit of land measurement that is a little more than an acre.

15. See Ibrahim Kareem and Diane Singerman, "Urban Egypt."

16. For more on this see Meehy, "Egypt's Popular Committees."

17. Kawa Hassan and Hussein Yaakoub, "Syria's Local Coordination Committees: The Dynamo of a Hijacked Revolution," Knowledge Programme Civil Society in West Asia, 2014, https://hivos.org/sites/default/files/syrias_lccs-dynamo_of_highjacked_revolution.pdf.

18. Syrian Activist, focus group conducted by the author, March 2013. Throughout this chapter, I have withheld some details on the identities, locations, and precise dates of focus groups and interviewees, to protect their anonymity.

19. The architect of the LACs is Omar Al Azizi, a Syrian intellectual and activist who pioneered the idea and was arrested in October 2012, and died under torture in jail in February 2013. See Omar Al Azizi, "A Discussion Paper on Local Councils in Syria," 2013, https://theanarchistlibrary.org/library/omar-aziz-a-discussion-paper-on-local-councils-in-syria.

20. Doreen Khoury, "Losing the Syrian Grassroots," SWP Comments, German Institute for International and Security Affairs (2013): 5, http://www.swp-berlin.org/fileadmin/contents/products/comments/2013C09_kou.pdf.

21. Ibid.

22. The central government maintained its presence in opposition-controlled areas by selectively paying salaries to teachers, public employees, and civil servants, depending on their alleged political loyalties.

23. Syrian activist, interview with the author, October 1, 2016.

24. According to a survey of 405 local councils (which were formed or reformed during the Syrian revolution and were almost all active in the first quarter of 2015). The survey was held in all Syrian districts except for Raqqa and al-Suwayda. *Local Councils of Syria Indicator Needs*, Local Administration Councils Unit, July 2015.

25. The expansion of the Army of Conquest (Jaysh al-Fateh) into Idlib in April 2016 seems to have severely lowered the number of active local councils on the ground.

26. Sabr Darwish, "Syrians Under Siege: The Role of Local Councils," *ARI Policy Alternatives*, Arab Reform Initiative, September 13, 2016.

27. Favier, "Local Governance Dynamics."

28. Ibid.

29. Syrian activist, interview with the author, October 1, 2016.

30. Syrian activist, interview with the author, October 3, 2016.

31. Syrian Activist, focus group conducted by the author, March 15, 2013.

32. The question of LACs' representation is controversial because the fourteen LAC members of the Syrian Opposition Coalition have not been changed, despite the fact that LACs inside Syria hold elections every six months. This has led some councils to form an alternative body to represent them, known as the Higher Council for the Local Councils.

33. Archon Fung and Erik Olin Wright, *Deepening Democracy: Institutional Innovations in Empowered Participatory Governance* (London: Verso, 2003); Dantella della Porta and Massimiliano Andretta, "Social Movements and Public Administration: Spontaneous Citizens' Committees in Florence," *International Journal of Urban and Regional Research* 26, no. 2 (June 2002): 244–65.

34. The April 6 Youth Movement is a worker-focused Egyptian activist group that was established in 2008.

35. Syrian activist, focus group conducted by the author, March 15, 2013.

36. The unit functions under the umbrella of the interim government's Ministry of Local Development.

37. Official at Local Administration Council Unit, interview with the author, October 2, 2016.

38. Meehy, "Egypt's Popular Committees."

39. Abu Tarek (nickname), interview with the author, April 2, 2013.

40. Syrian activist, focus group, March 15, 2013.

41. Syrian activist, interview with the author, October 3, 2016.

42. Marwan Youssef, interview with the author, Cairo, April 20, 2013.

43. Local Administration Councils Unit, *Indicator Needs*.

44. Mahmoud Allam, interview with the author, May 28, 2013.

45. Syrian activist, focus group conducted by the author, March 15, 2013.

46. Ibid.

47. Local Administration Councils Unit, *Indicator Needs*.

48. Darwish, "Syrians Under Siege," 3.

49. Local Administration Councils Unit, *Indicator Needs*.

50. Favier, "Local Governance Dynamics," 8.

Index

274–75; military quiescence under, 18, 24; political cartoons and, 214, 217–19, *218*, 221, 227, 229; Qatar and, 78, 80; resignation of, 422, 423; social contract of informality and, 404; survival of strongman regime of, 158–59; trial of, 38; U.S. failure to support, 86

Mubarak, Suzanne, 229

Much Loved (film), 205–6

Munif, Yasser, 8, 330

Musa, Salama, 16

Muslim Brotherhood: 2012 parliamentary elections, 159; Ajnad al-Sham and, 359, 361; basic services provided by, 409; compared to Tunisian Ennahda, 66, 69; economic policies, lack of, 24; Egyptian journalists aligning against, 275; electoral success of, 28; human rights movement and, 157, 162–65; judiciary and, 37; local government and, 406, 409; loss of support for, 20–21; LPC cooperation with, 424; media and, 277, 285; Mubarak's repression of, 159; Nasser's repression of, 17; in political cartoons, 229; political cartoons published by, 235; Qatar funding to, 77, 78, 82; reformist activism of, 357; Saudi Arabia's and Emirates' relations with, 80, 84; Sisi's repression of, 160, 223, 406; social media and, 294; as sole political outlet under Sadat and Mubarak, 21; Syrian, 82; as terrorist organization, 84; Ultras and, 185. *See also* Morsi, Mohamed

al-Mustafa, Muhammad, 380

My Child the Foreigner (film), 142

Nabhan, Ibrahim, 384–85

el-Naga, Fayza Abou, 162–63

Naghi, Effat, 245; *The High Dam*, 247

Nagi, Mohammed, 243

Nahhas, Charbel, 124, 144

Al Nahyan family of United Arab Emirates, 85. *See also* Mohammed bin Zayed Al Nahyan

Naji, Ahmed, 227, 235

Najjar, Ibrahim, 143

narrative histories, research use of, 126–27

Nasr, Moataz, 254; *El Shaab* (The People), 256, *256*; *The People Want the Fall of the Regime*, 262–63

Nasrallah, Hassan, 88

Nasrawi, Saif, 272–73

Nasser, Gamal Abdel: as beloved leader, 219; civil society controlled by state under, 160; economic problems blamed on, 257; fine arts community and, 242, 245, 247; human rights and, 157; Islamism and, 17; judiciary and, 36; militarization under, 18; Muslim Brotherhood and, 17; in political cartoons, 216, *217*, 220–21, 225, 228, *228*

Nasserism/Nasserites, 20–21, 23–24, 157, 164

National Authority of Media and Journalism Legislation (Egypt), 284–85

National Coalition for Syrian Revolutionary and Opposition Forces (NCSROF), 77, 79, 82, 381–82, 389

National Commission for Lebanese Women (NCLW), 140, 148

National Committee for the Follow-up on Women's Issues (CFUWI), 146, 147

National Constituent Assembly (NCA, Tunisia), 46–47, 62–64

National Democratic Institute, 27

National Democratic Party (NDP, Egypt), 38, 159, 180, 240, 241, 423

National Dialogue Quartet (Tunisia), 54–70; 2012 negotiations, 61; 2013 negotiations, 56, 57, 64–65; assassinations, effect of, 61–62; Bardo Crisis (2013) and, 62–64, 68; as consensus-driven model of engagement, 67; drivers behind formation of, 55–57; Ennahda-UGTT relationship, 59–61; lessons learned, 56, 57, 68–70; Nidaa's leadership of old elites, 62–64; Nobel Peace Prize to, 54–55, 57, 61, 66, 68; sustaining transition but stalling reform, 67–68; UGTT labor union role in, 56, 57, 57–59; unique aspects of, 66–67

national health care system in Egypt, 166–69

nationalism and nationalists, 16, 157, 176

Nationality Campaign in Lebanon. *See* Lebanese citizenship rights for women

National Transitional Council (Libya), 79

National Transitional Justice Consultation (Tunisia), 43

Nation's Future Party (Egypt), 25

About the Contributors

Samer Abboud is an associate professor of historical and political studies at Arcadia University. His most recent book, *Syria* (Hoboken, N.J.: John Wiley & Sons, 2015), analyzes the country's descent into civil war.

Nathan J. Brown is a professor of political science and international affairs at George Washington University.

Thanassis Cambanis is a senior fellow at The Century Foundation in Beirut and columnist for *The Boston Globe.* His research focuses on Arab political and social movements, and U.S. policy in the Middle East.

Laura C. Dean is a journalist who specializes in Egypt and the Middle East and North Africa region.

Asya El-Meehy is a governance and public administration officer at the United Nations-Economic and Social Commission for Western Asia. She holds a Ph.D. in comparative politics from the University of Toronto and was recently a visiting scholar at the University of California Berkeley's Center for Middle East Studies.

Karim Medhat Ennarah is a researcher on criminal justice and policing at the Egyptian Initiative for Personal Rights. He is also a member of the Law and Society Research Unit at the American University in Cairo.

Sima Ghaddar is a policy associate at The Century Foundation in Beirut. She studied political sociology for her master's at the London School of Economics.

Jonathan Guyer is a fellow at the Institute of Current World Affairs and contributing editor of the Cairo Review of Global Affairs. From 2012 to 2013, he served as a Fulbright fellow researching political cartoons in Egypt. A regular contributor to Public Radio International, he has written for *The Guardian, Guernica, Harper's, Le Monde Diplomatique, The New Yorker, The New York Review of Books, Nieman Reports,* and *The Paris Review.* He blogs about comics and caricature at Oum Cartoon, oumcartoon.tumblr.com.

Michael Wahid Hanna is a senior fellow at The Century Foundation in New York and an adjunct senior fellow at the Center on Law and Security at New York University School of Law. His research focuses on international security, international law, regional politics, and U.S. policy in the Middle East and South Asia.

Cilja Harders is the director of the Center for Middle Eastern and North African Politics at the Otto-Suhr Institute for Political Sciences at Freie Universität Berlin, where she is currently co-directing a project on emotions and political participation in Tahrir and Taksim.

Benjamin Helfand is a J.D. candidate at George Washington University Law School.

Sam Heller is a Beirut-based fellow at The Century Foundation. He has written extensively on the Syrian war for outlets including *Jane's Terrorism and Insurgency Monitor* and *War on the Rocks*. He lived in Syria, where he studied Arabic, in 2009 and 2010.

Ursula Lindsey has lived in the Middle East since 2002, reporting on culture, media, politics, and education in the Arab world. She covered the Arab uprisings from Cairo and currently lives in Rabat, Morocco. She has worked as a reporter and editor with local independent media in the region and has written for the *New York Times,* the *Financial Times, The Nation, The Economist*, and *The Chronicle of Higher Education.* She is an editor of The Arabist blog.

Marc Lynch is a professor of political science at George Washington University and director of the Project on Middle East Political Science. His most recent book is *The New Arab Wars: Uprisings and Anarchy in the Middle East* (PublicAffairs: 2016). In 2016 he was named an Andrew Carnegie Fellow.

Aron Lund is a Swedish writer on Middle Eastern affairs and a fellow at The Century Foundation who has published several books and reports on Syrian politics.

Khaled Mansour is an independent writer and consultant on issues of human rights, humanitarian aid, and development. He served for thirteen years in the United Nations including for UNICEF, peacekeeping missions, and the World Food Programme. He also led the Egyptian Initiative for Personal Rights in 2014.

Monica Marks is a researcher with the WAFAW program in Aix-en-Provence, France, and a Rhodes Scholar and Ph.D. candidate at Oxford University. She lived in Tunisia from 2012 to 2016.

Yasser Munif is an assistant professor of sociology at the Institute for Liberal Arts and Interdisciplinary Studies at Emerson College. He is currently working on a book project about participatory democracy and grassroots politics during the uprising in Syria.

Sultan Sooud Al Qassemi is a nonresident fellow at the Middle East Institute in Washington, D.C., and founder of the Barjeel Art Foundation.

Michael Stephens is a research fellow for Middle East studies and head of the Royal United Services Institute (Qatar).

Dina Wahba is a research associate at the Centre for Middle Eastern and North African Politics at the Freie Universität Berlin.